Composing the Soul

Composing the Soul

Reaches of Nietzsche's Psychology

Graham Parkes

The University of Chicago Press
Chicago and London

GRAHAM PARKES is professor of philosophy at the University of Hawaii and the editor of *Nietzsche and Asian Thought* (1991), also published by the University of Chicago Press.

The University of Chicago Press, Chicago 60637
The University of Chicago Press, Ltd., London
© 1994 by The University of Chicago
All rights reserved. Published 1994
Printed in the United States of America
03 02 01 00 99 98 97 96 95 94   5 4 3 2 1

ISBN (cloth): 0–226–64686–6

Library of Congress Cataloging-in-Publication Data

Parkes, Graham, 1949–
    Composing the soul : reaches of Nietzsche's psychology / Graham Parkes.
       p.   cm.
    Includes bibliographical references and indexes.
    ISBN 0-226-64686-6 (alk. paper)
    1. Nietzsche, Friedrich Wilhelm, 1844–1900.   2. Nietzsche, Friedrich
Wilhelm, 1844–1900—Psychology.   3. Psychology and philosophy—
Germany—History—19th century.   4. Psychology—Philosophy—Germany—
History—19th century.   5. Psychologists—Germany.   I. Title.
BF109.N54P37   1994
193—dc20   94-12479
                                                                CIP

For Setsuko

As happens in great men, he seemed, by the variety and amount of his powers, to be a composition of several persons.

Ralph Waldo Emerson, *Representative Men*

Contents

Acknowledgments

Lacking a mentor in philosophy during graduate school, I was grateful to find an encouraging guide in the person of James Hillman. Had it not been for a clap on the shoulder many years ago from that eloquent psychologist—who said, with reference to a blocked doctoral dissertation, "Just do it!"—I might have ended up as a bass player in a soulful but less than outstanding rock band. (I also learned a great deal about the workings of the psyche from Gareth Hill in Berkeley during the same period.) The neo-Freudian and post-Jungian ideas Hillman has elaborated under the name of "archetypal psychology" have informed a number of the approaches attempted in what follows. Closer to this end of the project, I was fortunate to make the acquaintance of the philosopher and sinologist Angus Graham. I was much inspired by a series of conversations by the ocean, not long before his death, and regret not being able to learn from his reactions to the completed manuscript.

A sorry indication of how long this study has taken to complete is the grateful acknowledgment of two grants that enabled travel for preliminary research in libraries: from the National Endowment for the Humanities Travel to Collections Program in 1985 and the American Council of Learned Societies in 1988. The following year I was able to learn more about Nietzsche's life thanks to a grant from the N.E.H. Programs in Media for a projected (though still to be made) film.

Work was impeded by the geographical isolation of the workplace, insofar as the book would have benefited greatly from discussion with other Nietzsche scholars during the writing. (Honolulu is not only the most remote city, farthest from anywhere, on the face of the globe, but also almost the perfect antipodes to Basel and Sils-Maria, where most of the writings the manuscript is about were written.) I should nevertheless like to thank for their encouragement from afar over the years: Ernst Behler, David Brent, Ed Casey, Werner Dannhauser, Jacques Derrida, Volker Gerhardt, James Heisig, Kathleen Higgins, Bernd Magnus, Alexander Nehamas, Jay Ogilvy,

John Richardson, Richard Schacht, Charles Scott, Hans Sluga, Robert Solomon, Joan Stambaugh, Bruce Wilshire, and John Bell Young; and in Honolulu: Roger Ames, Lee Siegel, and students in my seminars on Nietzsche (Tim Freeman especially).

Daniel Breazeale generously provided comments on chapter 7, of a manuscript by someone he has never met or spoken with. The greatest gratitude goes to Dan Conway and Laurence Lampert, who both read the entire manuscript and offered a variety of insightful comments. Danny Coyle and Marty Heitz provided good-natured assistance with the index.

My daughter Helen deserves mention for being serenely understanding about the time I have had to devote over the past several years to this other (less interesting) child.

Parts of chapter 9 appeared under the title "Ordering the Psyche Polytic: Choices of Inner Regime for Plato and Nietzsche" in the *Journal of Nietzsche Studies* 2 (1991): 53–77, and were reprinted in revised form in Daniel W. Conway and Rudolf Rehn, eds., *Nietzsche und die antike Philosophie* (Trier, 1993), 113–30. I am grateful to the editors for their permission to reproduce excerpts from those essays here.

Lastly, my thanks to the Reischauer Institute of Japanese Studies at Harvard for kind hospitality in connection with a different project—interrupted by the unexpectedly prolonged final throes of this one.

Cambridge, Massachusetts
November 1993

Abbreviations

Works by Nietzsche

AC	*The Antichrist(ian)*
AOM	*Assorted Opinions and Maxims (Human, All Too Human 2/1)*
BGE	*Beyond Good and Evil*
BT	*The Birth of Tragedy*
CW	*The Case of Wagner*
DM	*Dawn of Morning*
DS	*David Strauss, the Confessor and Writer (Untimely Meditation 1)*
EH	*Ecce Homo*
GM	*Toward the Genealogy of Morals*
HA	*Human, All Too Human*
HKA	*Werke Historisch-Kritische Ausgabe* (H. J. Mette)
HL	*On the Use and Disadvantage of History for Life (Untimely Meditation 2)*
JS	*The Joyful Science*
KSA	*Werke. Kritische Studienausgabe* (Colli and Montinari)
PG	*Philosophy in the Tragic Age of the Greeks*
PT	*Philosophy and Truth: Nietzsche's Notebooks from the Early 1870s*
S	*Werke in drei Bänden* (Karl Schlechta)
SE	*Schopenhauer as Educator (Untimely Meditation 3)*
TI	*Twilight of the Idols*
WB	*Richard Wagner in Bayreuth (Untimely Meditation 4)*

WP   *The Will to Power*

WS   *The Wanderer and His Shadow (Human, All Too Human* 2/2)

Z   *Thus Spoke Zarathustra*

References to the aphoristic works will cite the abbreviated title followed by the aphorism number (for example: *WS* 59) and to the works divided into longer sections *(The Birth of Tragedy* and the *Untimely Meditations)* the section number *(BT* 2, *HL* 5). In the cases of *Thus Spoke Zarathustra, Toward the Genealogy of Morals, Twilight of the Idols,* and *Ecce Homo,* references will be to the part and section numbers *(Z* 2.16, *TI* 4.1). The discussions of previous works in the third part of *Ecce Homo,* "Why I Write Such Good Books," will be cited simply by the appropriate abbreviaton followed by the section number *(EH,* "DM" 2). Passages in the prefaces to Nietzsche's works (in the prologue in the case of *Zarathustra)* will be referred to by "P" followed by the section number *(JS,* P2). In quoting from the *Nachlass,* references will be to the volume, notebook, and note numbers of the *Kritische Studienausgabe* in cases where the notes have been so arranged by Colli and Montinari *(KSA* 11:26[409]), so that the passage can also be located in the *Kritische Gesamtausgabe* of the *Werke;* otherwise to the volume and page number *(KSA* 1:887).

Works by Other Authors

EMS   Herder, *Vom Erkennen und Empfinden der menschlichen Seele*

SEF   *The Standard Edition of the Complete Psychological Works of Sigmund Freud*

WWR   Schopenhauer, *The World as Will and Representation*

Other frequently cited works are referred to by shortened forms of their titles: Hölderlin's *Hyperion* is cited as *Hyp.* Works by Plato are abbreviated as follows: *Euthyphro* as *Euth., Phaedo* as *Pho., Phaedrus* as *Phr., Republic* as *Rep., Statesman* as *Stat., Symposium* as *Symp., Theaetetus* as *Theae.,* and *Timaeus* as *Tim.*

Introduction

> Strange! I am dominated at every moment by the thought that my history is not only a personal one, that I am doing something for many people when I live like this and work on and write about myself this way. It is always as if I were a multiplicity, which I address in intimate, serious, and comforting terms. (Unpublished note, 1880)

Strange, too, that now, a century-and-a-half after his birth, when Nietzsche touches more people's lives than ever before, this labor on his part—his living and writing about himself for the sake of others, his work on himself as on us—should remain largely undiscussed. That his psychological acumen—the insights through which he discerned his inner multiplicity and the adroitness of his integration of psychology with philosophy and vice versa—should have gone uncelebrated for so long stems from a failure to discern the figure of the man behind the works, the person in the thoughts, the soul and life in the corpus.

If a more intriguing picture of Nietzsche should emerge from the pages that follow, it will be because the work has been approached in the context of the life—and from two other perspectives that have seldom been brought to bear: those of twentieth-century depth psychology and certain forms of East Asian thought. These foreign perspectives, which are seldom explicitly mentioned, help one avoid the compartmentalization into disciplines that vitiates so much modern scholarship, and which Nietzsche himself fought against. In the Chinese and Japanese traditions, philosophy is generally interfused with poetry and music, psychology and religion, as well as with training of the body and the task of self-cultivation. Modern depth psychology has itself been deeply influenced by Nietzsche, and many of its ideas, though arrived at by very different (and somewhat more empirical) methods, are remarkably congruent with his psychological insights. Indeed the original plan of the present work called for an articulation of these insights using terms and concepts borrowed from the theories of Freud and Jung.

But as the work progressed, it became clear that although Nietzsche does not undertake a systematic presentation of his psychological ideas, they nevertheless have a "logic" of their own, and that it would be best to proceed more phenomenologically and let the structure emerge from the topics themselves rather than impose it from outside.

"That a *psychologist* without equal speaks from my writings—this is perhaps the first insight gained by a good reader" (*EH* 3.5). Thus wrote Friedrich Nietzsche in 1888, a few months before the end of his career. "Who among the philosophers before me was in any way a *psychologist?*" he asks, rhetorically, responding with genial hyperbole: "Before me there simply was no psychology" (*EH* 4.6).

To judge from the response Nietzsche's writings have evoked in the course of the hundred years that have since elapsed, the man has hardly been blessed with a surfeit of "good readers." Perhaps what has disconcerted is the gross immodesty of his claims to psychological acumen; at any rate the secondary literature, now burgeoning more than ever, has generally ignored the psychological dimensions of Nietzsche's thought.[1] This book is a response to his claims to be a psychologist and has the modest aim of presenting his psychology—in the twofold sense of outlining the contours of his psychological ideas and imparting a sense of their force in the context of his own psychological development.

Along with his conviction that the good philosopher will also be a psychologist, the other distinctive feature of Nietzsche's thinking is his understanding of philosophy as essentially autobiographical—and thus a discipline as multifaceted as life itself. In view of his repeated assertions that it is illegitimate, if not impossible, in the case of a philosopher to separate the thought from the life, and least of all feasible in his own case, Nietzsche's ideas about psychology are most fruitfully studied in the light of the ongoing organization of his own psyche. But despite this insistence on the highly personal nature of philosophy—and of his own thinking especially—most of the secondary literature pays insufficient attention to the life, and so misses much of the vitality of his texts.

Perhaps this book's aim is not so modest after all, since the task of presenting Nietzsche's psychology in the context of his life requires a reading of most of the published works and selections from the letters and unpublished notes. Because psychology was central to his enterprise, even before he himself realized how crucial it was, the book may also serve as an introduction, from a novel perspective, to Nietzsche's thought as a whole. The psychological approach illuminates sides of his thinking and aspects of his imagination that are unfamiliar to many readers. But while some of the implications of his psychological ideas are mentioned—consequences for issues in ethics, epistemology, and politics, for instance—it is impossible in a single volume to pursue them. The primary task is to say what Nietzsche's psychology is, or is like; and to this end the best way is for the author to step aside and let the texts speak for themselves. Thanks to the selection of texts, of course, it will be the selector's Nietzsche who speaks—but a more congenial character than many of the other Nietzsches we have been presented with.

The Practice of Psychology

The moment our discourse rises above the ground line of familiar facts, and is inflamed with passion or exalted by thought, it clothes itself in images.

Emerson, "Language"

Thanks to a broad education through an enlightened curriculum at one of the best schools in Europe at the time, the illustrious Schulpforta, Nietzsche was introduced early on to literature rich in psychological insights. In addition to the writings of Plato and other ancient authors, he read widely in the works of Goethe, Schiller, and Hölderlin, and was impressed by their psychologies—as expressed in the persons as well as in the works of these authors. But he was especially inspired by two Anglophone figures: Byron and Emerson, whose poems and essays provided perfect nourishment at just the right time.[2] Again it was their personalities as much as their writings that he admired. The emphasis on such precursors in what follows is meant by no means to detract from Nietzsche's originality as a thinker, but rather to highlight the multiple origins of his ideas, to show how many streams of psychological thinking flow or are chaneled into the main current of his thought.[3]

Having started out in classics and then moved over to philosophy, Nietzsche first turned overtly to psychology at a crucial juncture in his life, at the time he was pulling away from his decade-long relationship with Wagner. He had been laying the groundwork all along, even in the writings from his youth; but it was not until the publication of the first part of *Human, All Too Human* in 1878 that he self-consciously took up the practice of "psychological observation," which he characterizes as "reflection on the human, all-too-human" (*HA* 35). A major stimulus came from his friendship with Paul Rée, a brilliant Jewish intellectual, five years Nietzsche's junior, who had audited his classes at Basel five years earlier and subsequently published a book entitled *Psychologische Beobachtungen* (Psychological observations) in 1875. The friendship with Rée, which Nietzsche had embarked on in full knowledge that it would jeopardize his relationship with Wagner (on account of the latter's rabid anti-Semitism), was crucial to his development. In Rée he found a friend who was close to being his intellectual equal, and whose quickness and lightness of wit helped Nietzsche escape from the heavy atmospheres of Wagner's thinking and Schopenhauer's metaphysics.

While at Basel in the early 1870s Nietzsche had been introduced to a variety of French authors—primarily through his acquaintance with two women who were important to him during this period: Ida Rothpletz (who would marry the man who became his firmest friend, Franz Overbeck) and Cosima von Bülow (soon to be Cosima Wagner). These ladies encouraged him to read Montaigne, Diderot, Rousseau, and Voltaire, as well as Sainte-Beuve, Fontenelle, Montesquieu, Beaumarchais, La Rochefoucauld, Vauvenargues, and La Bruyère. Montaigne above all impressed Nietzsche with his combination of "honesty and cheerfulness": "That such a human being has written, has truly augmented the joy of living on this earth" (*SE* 2). No more fitting motto could be found for the undertaking on which Nietzsche would now embark than the following observation from Montaigne (as related in a gem of an essay by Virginia Woolf):

> It is a rugged road, more so than it seems, to follow a pace so rambling and uncertain, as that of the soul; to penetrate the dark profundities of its intricate internal windings; to choose and lay hold of so many little nimble motions; 'tis a new and extraordinary undertaking, and that withdraws us from the common and most recommended employments of the world.[4]

From Montaigne Nietzsche learned a technique that would become a primary feature of his psychology—and of his philosophy in general: the *experimental* method ("experimental" in a distinctive sense that has nothing to do with rats running mazes). Montaigne's *Essais* are experimental in the sense of being "tests or trials of his judgment, his natural faculties, and indeed his life," designed to test his responses to various topics and situations.[5] Emerson was also a master of this technique, who on first reading Montaigne wrote: "It seemed to me as if I myself had written the book, in some former life, so sincerely it spoke to my thought and experience." And in considering Nietzsche's psychology it is well to keep in mind these words of Emerson's, from the essay "Circles," in which he attempts to convey the sense in which his own work is experimental:

> But lest I should mislead any when I have my own head and obey my whims, let me remind the reader that I am only an experimenter. Do not set the least value on what I do, or the least discredit on what I do not, as if I pretended to settle anything as true or false. I unsettle all things.

Why, then, read him?—or Nietzsche for that matter. Because there is a value to participating in the unsettling of things, and the process of experimenting with the self experientially (the words share a common root) enhances human existence.

The *Untimely Meditation* on history (1874) begins with a quote from Goethe that captures the sense in which Nietzsche's thinking would become "experimental": "I hate everything that merely instructs me without enhancing my activity or directly enlivening it." And from *Dawn of Morning* (1881) on, Nietzsche explicitly advocated an experimental method for philosophy—and, by extension, for his psychology.[6] This means that his texts are intended not as expositions of the truth or accounts of the way the world really is, but rather as invitations to entertain a variety of perspectives and consider what changes this effects on one's experience. His psychological insights are presented in the same spirit: not as ultimate truths about the human condition but as hypotheses to be tested in one's experience, as experiments to be conducted in the "laboratory" of the psyche. In the light of Nietzsche's frequent plays on the ambiguity of *Versuch(ung)* between "experiment" and "temptation," his role as a psychologist is also that of a tempter who would lure the reader into the labyrinths of the soul—the reader's soul and its matrix in the soul of Western culture.[7]

Nietzsche was especially taken with the dry wit and wry styles of Montaigne and the later French masters of elegant prose; but it was not until he read and discussed them with Paul Rée that he came fully to appreciate what insightful psychologists many of the *philosophes* and *moralistes* were. A few years later, he discovered the novels of Stendhal, whose psychological acuity he never tired of praising: he calls Stendhal "the last great psychologist" and "one of the most beautiful fortuities of my life . . . with his anticipatory psychologist's eye."[8]

When Nietzsche himself begins to address the topic of psychology explicitly (in *Human, All Too Human*), he writes, with only a slight tinge of irony, that psychological observation

> belongs to the means whereby one can alleviate the burden of life, that the practice of this art grants one presence of mind in difficult situations and entertainment in the midst of boring surroundings, and that one can cull maxims from the thorniest and most unpleasant stretches of one's own life and thus feel somewhat better about it. (*HA* 35)

The next aphorism, however, warns that "psychological perspicacity" may well not conduce to the *happiness* of the individual, that in fact "psychological error and general obtuseness in this domain help human progress," and that philanthropic natures (as opposed to those guided by the spirit of science) will curse the psychological art, "which seems to implant in the human soul a sense of depreciation and suspicion." "Nevertheless"—the title of the next aphorism—however unpleasant the experience may be, the time has come, in Nietzsche's opinion, when "humanity can no longer be spared the gruesome sight of the psychological dissecting table and its knives and forceps."[9] One of the major aims of this surgical procedure to be performed on the corpus of Western culture is to expose the origins of the moral sentiments—a task that Nietzsche pursues with cool precision and relentless fervor in *Human, All Too Human, Dawn of Morning,* and *The Joyful Science* (1878–82).[10] Since during this period there is little change in his understanding of psychology, there is little explicit mention of the discipline in the texts themselves.

With *Thus Spoke Zarathustra,* which was Nietzsche's own favorite book, a sea change takes place in his style, reflecting a further transformation in his thinking. This work is so rich in psychological themes that it deserves a book for itself—and has been the subject of several book-length studies.[11] With this work Nietzsche solves the problem of how to write philosophy after "the death of God" by simply depicting a particular soul, charting the development of a highly complex psyche—a soul composed of many souls—in a network of vivid images woven into a dramatic narrative. He presents a life, Zarathustra's life, without commendation or condemnation: it is left to the reader to be moved (or not) by the forces animating that depicted existence.

It is not until 1886, with the publication of *Beyond Good and Evil* and several retrospective prefaces to previous books, that Nietzsche begins to talk again about psychology and his being a psychologist—talk that is sustained through to the last works of 1888. He now makes the greatest claims for the discipline he has been practicing: psychology as "morphology and doctrine of the development of will to power" is to be recognized as "queen of the sciences," and as again "the way to the most fundamental problems" (*BGE* 23). Heralding the depth psychology that would be developed several decades later by Freud and Jung, Nietzsche deplores the way all previous psychology has "got stuck in moral prejudices and fears [and] has not dared to descend into the depths." He announces a psychology that has the courage to recognize that "the 'good' and 'bad' drives mutually condition each other" and even that "all good drives are derived from the bad ones." And if one were to engage such a discipline—which would demand that "one take the affects of hate, envy, covetousness, and lust for power as affects that condition life, as things that fundamentally and essentially must be present in the great total economy *[Gesamt-Haushalt]* of life"—one would "suffer from this kind of judgment as from a seasickness." This, then, is Nietzsche's mature conception of psychology: a discipline for adventurers willing for the sake of the quest to risk more than a little nausea, for explorers of experience, plumbers of the depths, negotiators of the most convoluted labyrinths of the soul.

Nietzsche did not discover Dostoevsky until 1887, six years after the novelist's death, and the impact occasioned a flurry of letters to friends to express his enthusiasm. In *Twilight of the Idols* (1888), which originally bore the title, *Müssiggang eines Psychologen* (Leisure hours of a psychologist), he writes of Dostoevsky as "the only psychologist from whom I have learned anything: he belongs to the most beautiful strokes of luck of my life, even more so than my discovery of Stendhal" (*TI* 9.45). Had Nietzsche been able to study Kierkegaard, as he had intended, he would surely have found that great psychologist to be another beautiful incursion into his life.[12]

Given these precursors and fellow travelers, it is natural that Nietzsche's psychology should be above all imagistic, a discipline practiced in *images* rather than in concepts. (*Zarathustra* is the epitome in this respect.) Couched as it is primarily in images, his psychology has a great deal in common with that of a precursor whom he resists acknowledging as a fore-runner—or even as a major (let alone father) figure in the field: Plato. When Plato writes of the soul in psychological terms he usually has recourse to imagery, and often to images of the most vivid kind. This remark of Socrates in the *Phaedrus,* for instance, could stand as a major maxim of Nietzsche's psychology:

> To say what [soul] really is would require a long exposition of which only a god would be capable; but it is within human power to say more briefly what it is *like*.[13]

Indeed, nothing seems to penetrate Nietzsche's "Odysseus-ears" better—however much he may try to seal them with the wax of the new—than the siren-song of Plato's psychological imagery. When Socrates says, as he so often does when about to speak of the soul, "Listen to this image" or "Come, let me tell you another image," Nietzsche's "Oedipus-eyes" open wide, glancing sidelong around the blinding mask; and when the Apollo of philosophical discourse proposes "molding an image of the soul in speech," the archenemy of Platonism turns highly impressionable in his eloquent hands. More remarkable than the striking imagery Plato employs in speaking of the soul is the number of his images Nietzsche adopts—and adapts, since he generally reverses or inverts them as he borrows. All this in spite of the major difference: that while for Plato the way of images is merely preparatory and provisional, the imagery through which Nietzsche presents his psychology is germane to his philosophical enterprise as a whole.[14]

In several of Plato's dialogues the soul is imagined, for example, to contain arable soil suitable for the sowing of seminal speeches *(logoi).* In the

Republic the individual psyche is envisioned as a chimera consisting of human, lion, and many-headed snake, and in the myth of the *Phaedrus* as having wings or consisting of two horses and a charioteer. The soul's "animal" nature is evident from the issue of its proper nutrition (whether it feeds on "the true and the divine" or else on mere opinion) and also from the passages where the soul is said to engage in sexual intercourse, be pregnant and in labor, and to give birth to live offspring. All these images Nietzsche picks up and plays on, transforming and twisting them in various ways; but none more so than Plato's richest and most extended metaphor—of the psyche as *polis,* the single soul as political community. In spite of their being poles apart with respect to metaphysics, the comparison of Nietzsche with Plato, his greatest rival, on psychological issues will sharpen our sense of what the later thinker is saying—and perhaps also shed light on an obscure aspect of the ancient master himself. More generally, to look at Nietzsche against a Platonic background will help us situate his psychology in the broader context of the Western philosophical tradition, as well as enhance our sense of that vast sweep designated by the phrase "from Plato to Nietzsche."

Philosophy as Autobiography

[Man Thinking] then learns, that in going down into the secrets of his own mind, he has descended into the secrets of all minds.
Emerson, "The American Scholar"

Nietzsche came upon the idea of philosophy as autobiography early, and it informs the rest of his career. In a posthumously published note from 1872 he emphasizes the personal element inherent in the activity of the contemplative philosopher, who "does the same as everyone does with physiological, personal drives, but transferred to an impersonal world."[15] In *Dawn of Morning* he wonders whether his entire philosophy "with all its detours" is anything more than a "translation into reason [of] the drive for mild sun, bright and vibrant air, southerly vegetation, the breath of the sea"—he mentions several more of the driving forces in his life on the coast of the Mediterranean at that time—and whether *all* philosophies are "nothing other than intellectual detours of such personal drives" (*DM* 553). Since for Nietzsche "all great problems demand *great love,*" the true thinker will stand in a fully personal relation to them, rather than merely "touch them with the antennae of cold, curious thought." And yet the personal does not in this case exclude the historical dimension: what is required is "experiments in scientific curiosity, and the discriminating and seductive imagination of the psychologist and historian" (*JS* 345).

The retrospective prefaces to *The Joyful Science* and to the second volume of *Human, All Too Human* elaborate the sense in which Nietzsche's philosophy is autobiographical, but the fullest elaboration occurs in the major work from the same year (1886), *Beyond Good and Evil*. The preface to this work criticizes "dogmatic philosophy"—the paradigm of which is Platonism—for being no more than "audacious generalization from very narrow, very personal, very human all too human facts." Traditionally the philosopher has been thought to transcend his personal situation, rising above the contingent particulars of the everyday world to the realm of the universal and totally impersonal ideas, from there to propound discourses concerning reality and truth. With Nietzsche, an enthusiast of Heraclitus and precursor of depth psychology, the philosopher goes *down* and *in* to the things of his life for the sake of deeper insight into their hearts.[16] When his writing speaks from his experience, it is not only that the *life writes itself* (enacting the parts of "auto-bio-graphy"); such writing is written also from other, earlier experiences, from layers of life deeper than the particular person's. Such depth is possible now by virtue of the philosopher's realizing himself as "heir of all the energies that have been cultivated and disciplined by the fight against the error . . . of denying the *perspectival* [as] the basic condition of life." Resistance to dogmatic philosophy has built up over time, and the accumulating strength been passed down through generations of resisters, creating "a magnificent tension" in the European spirit which will enable great things.[17]

The first section of *Beyond Good and Evil* is entitled "On the Prejudices of the Philosophers," the major prejudice under attack being the idea that philosophy is an objective enterprise having nothing to do with the personality of the thinker who is practicing it.

> It has gradually become clear to me what every great philosophy up to now has been: namely, a confession on the part of the author and a kind of involuntary and unwitting memoir. . . . I do not believe that a "drive for knowledge" is the father of philosophy, but . . . anyone who has looked at the basic human drives to see the extent to which precisely here they may have played the role of *inspiring* spirits (or demons and kobolds) will find that they have all done philosophy at some time—and that each single one of them would all too gladly present *itself* as the ultimate purpose of existence and the legitimate *master* of all the other drives. For every drive is domineering in its lust to rule, and *as such* it tries to philosophize. . . . [Contrary to popular belief] there is absolutely nothing impersonal about the philoso-

pher; and in particular his morality bears decided and decisive witness to *who he is*—that is, to the order of rank in which the innermost drives of his nature are disposed to each other. (*BGE* 6)

While he was apparently rather self-effacing in person, modesty was not among Nietzsche's virtues as a writer, and he clearly means to include his own thought among the "great" philosophies he is talking about here. The "up to now" is ambiguous: it could be taken to imply that Nietzsche's insight will allow him to develop a philosophy—the subtitle of the book announces it as a "Prelude [*Vorspiel:* foreplay] to a Philosophy of the Future"—that will not be the unwitting autobiography that previous philosophies have been. However, it is clear from his writings as a whole that he does not intend to exclude his own thought from the ranks of confessions and memoirs. Its difference from previous philosophies will consist in its being *self-consciously* autobiographical.

We can now see why Nietzsche thinks that the philosopher needs to be a psychologist as well. If philosophy is motivated unconsciously by the basic drives of human nature, the good philosopher will need to become familiar with those drives—and especially with the way they play through his own life and thought. And according to several passages in the next two sections of *Beyond Good and Evil,* the study of the workings and interplay of the drives that make up the psyche is precisely what psychology is about.[18]

Supposing one accepts Nietzsche's invitation to regard philosophy as autobiography, as a writing of the life of the self, the question arises: the life of *which* self? of the same self as is writing? Is it a question of the solitary self, who travels, as Nietzsche did, from place to place from time to time? Or, since he argues against the idea of a unitary self and advocates conceiving the soul as "a multiplicity of subjects" and "a social structure of the drives and affects" (*BGE* 12), is a plurality of persons speaking and writing? Or is it after all some impersonal self or selves who, though they may speak through the many masks *(personae)* of the personality, do so from some locus higher or deeper than the perspective of the personal and from a time more distant than the present?

One has a right to expect the answer yes, at least in some sense, to this last question; for if the philosopher engages in *mere* autobiography, simply writes the story of his or her life, the results are unlikely to be of interest to many beyond that person's circle of acquaintances. How can the thinker-autobiographer, granted that he reflects upon his experiences of life, produce anything that goes beyond the personal, all too personal? Nietzsche poses this question in a retrospective preface from 1886:

> Shall my experience—the history of an illness and recovery—have
> been only my personal experience? And only *my* "human, all too hu-
> man"? I should like today to believe the opposite; the confidence
> comes to me again and again that my travel books were not after all
> written only for myself, as sometimes they seemed to be. (*HA* 2, P6)

He goes on to recommend his "travel books" (*Wanderbücher,* chronicles of
journeys to foreign climes of the soul) to those who are afflicted with any
kind of "past"—a recommendation that remains enigmatic until we appreciate the sense in which Nietzsche regards us as heirs of a long tradition
and better understand the relations between the personal and the impersonal.

In the same preface the author expresses gratitude to his ill health for
preventing him from drifting away from his task in life (§4), with pain here
acting as a warning signal concerning the entire being rather than just the
body. Illness alienates us from our everyday existence, while recovery
allows us to return to ourselves with a completely new perspective on our
lives. Forced to act as his own physician, Nietzsche did what many physi-
cians do—prescribe a change of environment: "I compelled myself . . . to
an opposite and unexplored *clime of the soul,* and to a wandering in foreign
parts, in foreignness itself, to an inquisitiveness concerning all kinds of foreign things."[19] On recovering, we return to life not only wiser but also grateful for the enhancement that our experience has undergone, enormously
grateful for "the smallest, tenderest, most fleeting gifts" life gives us.

At the time of *Beyond Good and Evil* Nietzsche's writing takes an explicitly autobiographical turn as he goes back to several of his earlier works
(*The Birth of Tragedy,* the two volumes of *Human, All Too Human, Dawn
of Morning,* and *The Joyful Science*) and writes prefaces for them that emphasize their depth-psychological dimensions. He had concluded the first
section of *Beyond Good and Evil* with a call for psychology to dare finally
to "descend into the depths" (*BGE* 23). In the preface to *Dawn of Morning*
he refers to the author of that text as an "underground man," one who
"bores, mines, and undermines" as he undertakes "work in the depths."[20]
Anticipating similar claims by Freud and Jung, he goes on to say: "At that
time I undertook something that not everyone may undertake: I descended
into the depths, I bored into the foundations" (*DM,* P2).

The preface to *The Joyful Science* begins by doubting whether anyone
who has not lived through something similar will be able to *experience* the
book adequately. Nietzsche writes of how the work welled forth during a
convalescence from a prolonged illness, a period of utter disability and
powerlessness. Suddenly a different voice breaks in:

But let us leave Herr Nietzsche: what is it to us that Herr Nietzsche has become well again? (*JS*, P2)

The original voice continues, without commenting on the interruption, but answering the question by saying that "a psychologist knows few more fascinating questions than that concerning the relationship between health and philosophy." Herr Nietzsche's recovery is something to us because his illness will have inhibited habitual interpretations of the world and allowed a different configuration of drives to philosophize. A thinker who goes through "many healths" thereby goes through many philosophies: "He is *unable* to do anything other than translate his state every time into the most spiritual form and distance: this art of transfiguration *is* precisely philosophy" (*JS*, P3). If this sounds much like the traditional conception of philosophy as a discipline concerned with "the most spiritual form and distance," the difference must lie in the range of experiential states that are translated. Western metaphysics has tended to separate the soul from the body and assimilate soul to spirit—to that aspect of our being that is farthest from the body and the physical world. Thus when traditional philosophy has deigned to concern itself with the body and associated phenomena such as nutrition, sickness, procreation, drives, emotions, passions, and so on, it has usually been to dismiss them as unimportant.

Nietzsche's kind of philosopher, by contrast, is not free to separate soul and body in this way, much less soul and spirit.

We must constantly give birth to our thoughts out of our pain, and nurture them with everything we have in us of blood, heart, fire, pleasure, passion, agony, conscience, fate, and catastrophe. Life—to us that means constantly transforming everything we are into light and flame, as well everything that happens to us. (*JS*, P3)

The idea is Emersonian: in "The Divinity School Address" Emerson said of "the true preacher" (Nietzsche was known as "the little preacher" at one of the schools he attended) that "he deals out to the people his life—life passed through the fire of thought." For both thinkers all conditions of the human being, not just certain privileged states, are potential candidates for philosophical transformation—and especially those that have traditionally been neglected. The idea is well expressed in the quotation from Emerson that stands (in German translation) as the epigraph to the first edition of *The Joyful Science:*

To the poet and sage all things are friendly and hallowed, all experiences useful, all days holy, all human beings divine.[21]

Nietzsche finds illness philosophically valuable and psychologically enlightening insofar as pain "compels us philosophers to descend to our ultimate depths" and prevents us from taking anything for granted (*JS,* P4). The disruption of normal modes of functioning and the awareness of death that comes with severe illness makes one *question* more deeply: "The trust in life has gone; life itself has become a *problem.*" This idea, especially as formulated in a later, unpublished note—"The value of all morbid states is that they show in a magnifying glass certain states that are normal but as normal are difficult to see"—prefigures an important theme in subsequent depth-psychology.[22]

Life as constant self-transformation "into light and flame" signifies the transformation of experience into something illuminating: in the case of the philosopher, into his writings. Nietzsche addresses himself to the problem of the relation between the author and his works in an aphorism in *Human, All Too Human* entitled "The Book Become Almost a Human Being" where, in opposition to the tradition that opposes living, spoken discourse to the dead letters of writing, he asserts the vitality of the written work and its independence from the bearer of the name under which it appears: "Every author is surprised anew how the book, as soon as it has become free of him, goes on to live a life of its own. It seems to him as if a part of an insect had become separated and is now going its own way."[23] There is something uncanny—*unheimlich*—about the way separated insect parts are capable of continued animation, at least for a while, and the capacity for physical regeneration on the part of lower life-forms in general tends to disturb.[24] Something of the author's self has come away from him, as if the body of work, the corpus (as distinct from the corpse-to-be), is somehow constituted by the body of the author. Or is it part of his soul that becomes embodied in the work?

Nietzsche stands here in direct opposition to the first significant characterization of writing in the Western tradition, at the hands—or, rather, from the tongue—of Socrates in Plato's *Phaedrus.* Socrates styles writing as terribly strange in being like painting *(zōgraphia)* insofar as the creatures in paintings come across "like living beings *[zōnta]*" and yet do not respond—as living beings would—to questioning, and are impossible to engage in dialogue. Written words *(logoi)* are similarly dumb, according to Socrates: one is easily inclined to think that they are intelligent, but when questioned they "always signify only one and the same thing" (*Phr.* 275d). And once separated from their "father" (the author), they are helpless and incapable of defending themselves. These words are "bastard brothers" to what Socrates famously styles as "the living and breathing word *[logon zōnta kai empsuchon]* of one who knows, of which the written word may justly be called the image" (276a).

As a writer, Nietzsche shares none of Socrates' anxiety concerning the fate or viability of his progeny:

> [The book] seeks out readers for itself, ignites new life, delights, terrifies, engenders new works, becomes the soul of plans and actions—in short: it lives like a being endowed with spirit and soul and yet is not a human being. (*HA* 208)

No mere receptacles of dead letters Nietzsche's books—but vital presences in the world, beyond their author's demise. But how does a writer endow his progeny with such vibrant life? Through transmuting his own life "into light and flame":

> That author has drawn the happiest lot who can say as an old man that everything in him that was life-engendering, energizing, elevating, enlightening still lives on in his writings, and that he himself is now nothing more than the gray ashes, while the fire has everywhere been saved and carried forward.[25]

It was Nietzsche's fate never actually to become an old man; but happily he would experience the fortunate author's lot in the autumn of his life—as recounted on the interleaf page to *Ecce Homo*, that magnificent autobiographical flourish of his last productive months.

> Not in vain did I bury my forty-fourth year today, did I *rightfully* bury it—whatever of life was in it has been saved, is immortal. *The Revaluation of All Values [The Antichrist(ian)]*, the *Dionysus Dithyrambs*, and, as relaxation, the *Twilight of the Idols*—all gifts of this year, in fact of its last quarter! *How could I not be grateful to my entire life?* And so I recount my life to myself.[26]

It is no surprise, in view of Nietzsche's understanding of the relation between author and work, that the recounting of the life should turn out to be mainly a writing about the author's writings. It is tempting to regard *Ecce Homo*—"Behold the man!"—as the culmination of Nietzsche's career as a thinker.[27] There he is, soul bared and face masked at the same time; practicing psychology by letting *psuchē* speak its own *logos* through him; one (or more) of the prime sayers of the soul: a great psychologist who may count as a beautiful fortuity in many lives.

Methodical Overview

Let me remind the reader that I am only an experimenter. . . .
No facts are to me sacred, none profane; I simply experiment,
an endless seeker.

Emerson, "Circles"

Few issues divide Nietzsche studies more clearly than the attitude of their authors toward use of the unpublished notes from the *Nachlass*. Writers with finely developed philological sensibilities—sensitive to Nietzsche's own philological sensitivity and his often expressed desire for painstaking readers—hold that responsible interpretations will be responsive to the differences between the texts Nietzsche chose to steer into print (which was generally a difficult and laborious task) and those he did not. Some have argued—Heidegger most prominently—that the real Nietzsche is to be found in the *Nachlass* and the published texts are merely a series of masks.[28] More recently, a variety of "post"-whatever commentators have declared themselves at liberty to take everything at equal value, deconstructing all orders of rank, on the grounds that there is no author of the texts in any case. The present writer belongs with the distinguishers on this question (the "splitters" rather than the "lumpers"), with those who take account of what appear to be Nietzsche's considered decisions concerning the dissemination of what he wrote.[29] This study will thus make sparing use of the unpublished notes, presenting the ideas primarily by way of passages he chose to publish, and adducing the notes only where they serve to amplify some theme already found in the published works.

There are distinct advantages to a *chronological* examination of the unfolding of Nietzsche's ideas. A shortcoming in many commentaries, and more so in treatises that make indirect use of his ideas, stems from a failure to consider the development of his thought. While hardly more than sixteen years separate *The Birth of Tragedy* from *Ecce Homo,* Nietzsche "sloughed his skin" many times during this period, which contains works that differ enormously in content and orientation as well as style. Wherever possible, therefore, particular themes will be presented chronologically, so that the reader can appreciate the genesis and development of the ideas. Tracing the elaboration of strands of imagery though Nietzsche's texts fails to do justice to the aesthetic unity and arc of thought informing each individual text, and it is difficult, this way, always to read Nietzsche's texts as he asked that they be read—"*slowly . . . well . . .* deeply, looking carefully back- and forwards" (*DM,* P5). Nevertheless, the benefits accruing from the method will become apparent as the themes unfold; and while many passages and images will be discussed without reference to the context, they will not be given a sense that is counter to the direction of the essay or aphorism in which they occur. But since there are few major topics in Nietzsche still requiring global treatment, let more of the books written on him from now on be devoted to discussions of a single text. (*The Joyful Science* and *Beyond Good and Evil* call loudest for monographs treating each alone.)[30]

Insofar as the chronological approach runs up against the limits of what can be accomplished in a single volume, the present study places greater emphasis on Nietzsche's earlier works at the expense of the later. A twofold rationale can be offered: the early writings have not previously received the attention they deserve in the secondary literature; and the psychological themes in the later works—after *Beyond Good and Evil,* which contains the most explicit exposition of Nietzsche's psychology—are easier to follow on one's own. While the later engagements with these themes are flagged by Nietzsche himself by the use of the terms "psychology," "psychologist," and cognates, their early developments—in works prior to *Human, All Too Human*—are more difficult to discern. Limitations of space also preclude a consideration of Nietzsche's poems, even though some of them are rich in psychological insight and some rank among the best in the German language.

Then there is the question of stance and distance. An eminent British philosopher has remarked in a review of a book on Schopenhauer that the author "may leave himself open to critical nigglings of various degrees of significance by his enthusiastic resolution to stand up for Schopenhauer, and not just to expound him from a safe distance."[31] While Nietzsche no longer needs to be stood up for, the present study makes no attempt to attain a safe distance from which to palpate the ideas with what he called "the antennae of cold, curious thought." Since his psychology has been so little discussed, the primary task is simply to present it; and this is best done from a sympathetic standpoint—though one mindful of Nietzsche's ultimately recommending to his readers, and especially to those who would write on him, an attitude of "ironic resistance."[32]

> Unfortunately no one has yet been clever enough to *characterize* me ... I have never yet been characterized—either as a *psychologist,* or as an *writer* ("poet" included), or as the inventor of a *new* kind of pessimism (a Dionysian kind, born out of *strength* . . .) It is *not at all* necessary, and not even *desirable,* to side with me: on the contrary, a dose of curiosity, as if confronted with some strange plant, and an ironic resistance would seem an incomparably *more intelligent* attitude toward me.

Since, a century later, Nietzsche has still not been adequately characterized as a psychologist, a full characterization is the primary task. While there will be in what follows some discussion of extensions and implications of his psychological insights, especially in the last part of the book, the main aim is to articulate them and show their interconnections—since only when this has been done can the stance of ironic resistance be productive.

The plan of the book is as follows. The first three chapters, in acknowledgment of the benefits of the chronological method and in deference to Nietzsche's insistence that the philosopher's work is intimately intertwined with his life, proceed from the earliest writings through to the crucial point in his career, at the end of the 1870s, when he breaks with Wagner, resigns from his professorship at Basel, and embarks upon a nomadic existence and a correspondingly new style of writing. By the time one has worked from the juvenilia up through the publication of the four *Untimely Meditations* (1873–76), all the relevant psychological themes have been encountered.

In the second part, the exposition switches to a different mode, in order to distinguish and examine several "levels" in the metaphors Nietzsche employs in speaking of the soul. This approach disrupts the chronological sketch of events in his life, which are from this point on dealt with episodically where appropriate. The middle three chapters examine the development of Nietzsche's psychological imagery after the "break," beginning with the publication of the first volume of *Human, All Too Human* in 1878. Chapter 4 considers imagery of the soul drawn from the world of nature at the *elemental* level of earth, water, fire, and air. Following the schema suggested by Aristotle in his work on the soul *(De Anima),* the next chapter examines the role and function of the *vegetal* imagery in Nietzsche's texts, which likens psychological work to the practice of horticulture or agriculture. This is followed by a study of psychological metaphors drawn from the realm of *animal husbandry,* with an emphasis on images of breeding and procreation—which brings us to the fourth level, the realm of the *human.* Discussion of imagery drawn from the realm of human *community* will be reserved for part 3.

The taxonomy of the images has been carried out as exhaustively as possible (at the risk of exhausting the reader), in order to demonstrate the global—even cosmic—scope of Nietzsche's imagistic treatment of psychological themes. Acquaintance with the full catalog of images he employs to talk about the soul affords a new perspective on Aristotle's statement that "the soul is, in a sense, all existing things."[33] An attempt has been made to give a sense of the psychological significance of the strands of imagery that are traced in the second part, but restrictions of space make a full account impossible. At worst there will be areas where the text can be treated as a sourcebook, from which the interested reader can proceed with independent investigation and reflection.

It should be emphasized that the ordering of the several levels is a heuristic device for the purposes of exposition, and not something articulated by Nietzsche himself. Nor is it to be taken as representing any kind of fixed hierarchy: while Nietzsche is concerned in other areas to establish orders of rank, none of these is fixed or absolute. The levels are in a sense interpenetrating and nonobstructing: the various narratives are not mutually exclusive, insofar as the psyche can be understood to operate on all levels at once. The appropriate image would be the circle of Heraclitus, in which "beginning and end are the same," rather than the hierarchical *ordo creationis* of the Christian tradition. (Think of the ways that gods and spirits— traditionally considered as enjoying a higher mode of being than humans— are imagined in many cultures to manifest themselves as animals or plants, and to reside in inanimate entities such as rocks and streams.)

The last part of the book presents in greater detail the most revolutionary aspect of Nietzsche's psychology, his idea of the multiple soul. In view of the importance here of the idea of the *drives (Triebe),* chapter 7 interrupts the exposition to sketch some of the historical context from which this idea emerged in German thought around the turn of the eighteenth to the nineteenth century.[34] Special attention is paid to the precursors of the idea that a multiplicity of drives form a structure of power relationships within the individual psyche. The next chapter considers Nietzsche's suggestion that most of the presences in the soul have an inherently *personal* nature: that the multiple drives, each of which has its own perspective, are transformed in the medium of the imagination into autonomous *persons.* The final chapter considers the archaic nature of the drives (and hence of the persons they manifest themselves as) and the idea that the experiences of millennia continue to flow through us at every moment—through phantasy and the dream as well as the actions and passions of waking life.[35] The origins of the persons of the psyche are approached from another angle, through a consideration of Nietzsche's ideas on masks and masking in the context of life experienced as drama. From a picture of the psyche as a multiplicity of persons there arises what may be regarded as the fundamental question in Nietzsche's psychology: what disposition among the various drives or persons within the soul leads to the most fruitful life? This question is engaged in terms of the major metaphor of the psyche as *polis* (as in the *Republic* of Plato) and of the optimal inner regime for the greatest psychological health.

This variety of narrative strategies has been adopted in an attempt to be adequate to the variety of Nietzsche's styles. One consequence will be an occasional impression of circularity prompted by the reappearance of certain themes or passages from Nietzsche's writings. But the method is rather *spiral,* insofar as the same ground will sometimes be covered again from a different level, as it were, such that the same passages or ideas will not in fact be the same—thanks to their different contexts.

Because Nietzsche's psychology is couched in experimental images rather than articulated in concepts constituting a theory, a presentation in English of his psychological ideas depends on careful translation of the relevant passages in his texts. This process must be responsive to the play of his imagery and ensure that the images are not lost in the translation. Unfortunately the English editions currently available are often less than faithful to the images; indeed, the otherwise fine translations by Walter Kaufmann are sometimes so cavalier in this respect that it is hard to follow the important strands of Nietzsche's imagery in them. Because the extant translations would have required too much modification, quoted passages have been translated directly from the texts of the critical edition of Nietzsche's works by Colli and Montinari, though the citations have been made in such a way that the passages will be easily found in any edition or translation. In view of the amount of Nietzsche's texts to be quoted, the translated passages constitute an important part of the interpretation offered here.

Lastly, some readers may wonder about the word "soul" in the book's title and its ubiquity in the text. The simple response is that "soul" is the appropriate translation for *Seele,* which is the term Nietzsche uses to denote the topic of his psychology. In calling in *Beyond Good and Evil* for the abolition of the idea of the "atomistic" soul that has been promoted by the Christian tradition—"soul as something indestructible, eternal, indivisible"—he adds the following pertinent remark:

> Between ourselves, it is by no means necessary to the get rid of "the soul" itself at the same time, and thereby renounce one of the most ancient and venerable hypotheses. . . . Rather, the way is open for new conceptions and refinements of the soul-hypothesis: [for] concepts such as "mortal soul" and "soul as subject-multiplicity" and "soul as social structure of the drives and affects." (*BGE* 12)

While Nietzsche proposes and undertakes a revisioning of the Western conception of the soul, the results have something in common with—for example—the Homeric psyche, certain aspects of the Platonic soul, and the soul as understood in Renaissance and Romantic thought. In the traditional triad of body-soul-spirit, soul occupies the middle, mediating position. which suggests that the psychical is more closely interfused with the body and the physical than are the mental, intellectual, and spiritual aspects of our being. (In what follows, the terms "soul" and "psyche" will be used more or less interchangeably: as long as they are kept distinct from "mind" and "spirit," they serve as equally good translations of Nietzsche's *Seele.*)

There will be relatively little reference in what follows to the traditional Christian notion of the soul, since when Nietzsche engages this topic critically he generally conflates it with the notion of soul from the Platonic tradition.[36] He also tends to ignore two great psychologists in the Christian tradition, Saint Augustine and Descartes, whose *Confessions* and *On the Passions of the Soul* are classics in the field.[37] The notion of soul elaborated in Nietzsche's psychology is on the other hand a significant precursor of the idea of soul developed in the depth psychologies of Freud and Jung, both of whom are concerned with *Seele* rather than with the more cerebral *Geist,* or spirit.[38] But there is no need to try to say more about the idea of the soul at this point, since much of what follows is concerned precisely to articulate what Nietzsche means by *Seele.* The aim is thereby to contribute to a more comprehensive and fruitful understanding of the complexities of the psyche, and of how to engage experientially the problems involved in the undertaking of harmoniously composing the manifold soul.

Part One

In order to set the stage for what follows, the first part of the inquiry will trace the development of Nietzsche's early psychological ideas, in the context of a sketch of his life, from when he first started writing to the end of his career as a university teacher in 1878. A deep sense of kinship with the natural world, dating from his earliest childhood, was further nurtured by his readings of such nature-intoxicated geniuses as Goethe, Byron, and Hölderlin. In this context one can trace the sources of several streams of psychological imagery Nietzsche draws from the natural world, the later courses of which will be followed in part 2. His other great love as a child was music, and in his youth he turned his hand to composing numerous pieces for piano (and voice). He would gradually integrate this talent into his writing of books.

An early engagement, during his schooldays, with the ancient Greek and Roman classics provided Nietzsche with a health-promoting distance from the somewhat claustrophobic Lutheran milieu in which he had grown up. The dialogue begun at this stage with Socrates and Plato would continue to the end of his career as a thinker. His intensely personal relationship with great figures from the past instilled in him a strong sense of earlier epochs of Western culture as vital presences, as sources capable—when selectively tapped—of greatly enriching life in the present. As a youth Nietzsche was remarkable above all for the fertile multiplicity of his talents, and his early concern with how to handle such a multiplicity established a theme that would run throughout the subsequent development of his psychological ideas. The dynamics of this initial multiplicity were further intensified by the inspiration he received from a series of genial mentors: Emerson, Ritschl, Schopenhauer, Wagner, and Burckhardt. These paternal figures themselves represented a wide range of talents—with Wagner as the most vital epitome (so it seemed to Nietzsche at the time) of the genius who had succeeded, as Goethe had, in forging widely disparate tendencies into a series of great works.

From his multiply imaginative engagement with past cultures Nietzsche came to understand the powers of phantasy as drives that project the worlds of present experience, and to appreciate the constant—though mostly unconscious—contribution of the imagination to our perception of the ways things are, and can be.

By the time we reach the point in Nietzsche's biography where he abandons his professorship at the university and embarks upon a nomadic life, all the major themes of his psychology will have been introduced. A change in narrative strategy is then required in order to follow separately the development of the several strands of imagery through which these themes are elaborated in his subsequent works.

I

Seeds in Psychical Soil (1850–1870)

> *Don't you know that the beginning is the most important part of every work and that this is especially so with anything young and tender? For at that stage it's most plastic, and each thing assimilates itself to the model whose stamp anyone wishes to give it.*
>
> Socrates, in the Republic

"Youth and childhood have a value *in themselves* and by no means only as passageways and bridges" (*HA* 207). Insofar as philosophy for Nietzsche consists in a transformation of "the most comprehensive—perhaps disturbing and destructive—experiences" (*BGE* 205), the experiences of childhood and youth are not to be dismissed as insignificant—and especially in the case of a philosopher who understands philosophy this way. Attention to Nietzsche's early writings is all the more worthwhile since they have generally been ignored in the secondary literature (in part because so little is available in translation), even though they contain the seeds of most of his later thinking and in any case "have a value *in themselves*."

The first formulations of ideas are more important in Nietzsche than in most other thinkers, of greater interest than those of a Kant or a Hegel, for example, because of the unusually multiple sources of his thinking. Nietzsche's works do not advance uniformly in a certain direction or proceed from one stage to the next, building upon what has gone before or else leaving behind premature formulations. The appropriate metaphor would come instead from an art he himself practiced early on but did not pursue: namely, painting. He is less concerned with constructing a system that embodies the truth of the universe than with presenting a picture of life through painting—mainly portraits. In writing, a facility with images comes earlier than conceptual sophistication; and since Nietzsche's philosophy is ultimately a play of images rather than a work of concepts, his juvenilia are like the charcoal marks a painter initially sketches on the canvas. The major figures are there from the beginning and their interrelations more or less established, even though they remain vague and lack definition. As the thinking and writing mature, the sketch is gradually filled out, the images made clearer and more precise, becoming more vivid as layer after layer of color is added over the years, bringing body and depth to the features that compose the larger picture—just as the features composing the soul gain greater definition over time.

In this chapter, the early biographical background is provided mostly by the subject himself, with supplementation where appropriate from other sources.[1] This because the accounts of Nietzsche's childhood in the extant biographies rely heavily on his own letters and copious autobiographical writings, in the absence of much else in the way of documentation. It is true that these early essays are highly stylized, but the other major sources— his sister Elisabeth's several biographies—indulge in so much idealization (prospectively as well as retrospectively) that they are hardly more reliable. Nietzsche's autobiographical reflections appear in any case to be fairly faithful and his narratives candid, and they are corroborated by the meager outside evidence that is available.

Goethe, Byron, Hölderlin

> *The greatest genius is the most indebted man. . . . The great man finds himself in the river of the thoughts and events, forced onward by the ideas and necessities of his contemporaries.*
>
> Emerson, "Shakespeare"

Nietzsche was one of the most prolific of modern writers, his total output remarkable in view of his ever-deteriorating eyesight and the curtailment of his career at the age of forty-four. He did, however, start early: correspondence in his hand from as far back as 1850 (when he was five) has been preserved. Two letters home to his grandmother while on holiday with relatives in a nearby village indicate impressive epistolary precociousness. It may be reassuring to note that the five-year-old himself belonged to the ranks of those who misspell his name as "Nietsche" and "Nitzsche" (though after turning six he gets it consistently right).[2] Or else it could be taken as a sign of incipient multiple personality.

Accounts of this early phase of Nietzsche's life are available from his own hand, since on reaching the age of twelve he decided to begin keeping a diary, "in which everything that moves the heart, whether joyfully or sadly, is consigned to memory."[3] He went on to become a remarkably assiduous autobiographer, authoring multiple versions of essays with such titles as "My Life" and "The Course of My Life." (Indeed, his passion for writing about himself continued throughout his career, culminating in the remarkable *Ecce Homo* of 1888.) Nietzsche's first formally autobiographical piece, written when he was thirteen, is entitled "From My Life" and bears the subtitle "Part One: Youth, 1844–1858." The most striking feature of these essays is the devoutly religious character of the young author. The piety of the concluding sentence of the introduction to "From My Life" is typical: "It is in any case always instructive to contemplate the gradual formation of the understanding and the heart and thereby the omnipotent guidance of God!" (S 3:13).

After giving the place and date of his birth, the first topic the young author takes up concerns his father. Karl Ludwig Nietzsche, had been a Lutheran pastor in the small village of Röcken in Prussian Saxony. A cultured man of some intelligence, pastor Nietzsche fell painfully ill and died at the end of July 1849—a few months before his son Friedrich, with whom he had been especially close, turned five. The son describes him in retrospect as the consummate country parson, respected and loved by all who made his acquaintance. He writes of his father's love of music and considerable gifts as a pianist, especially as a free improviser. Nietzsche's own musical talent was already apparent by the time of this essay (he had written his first musical sketch at the age of eight), and in later years he would earn a reputation as a master of free improvisation on the piano. This is the major respect in which Nietzsche "became" the father he lost so early.

There are several accounts of his father's death in the early autobiographical sketches, couched in similar words and imagery. The first employs a grand meteorological style:

Up to this point happiness and joy had always shone on us, and our life had flowed by untroubled as a bright summer's day. But now dark clouds heaped up, lightning flashed and devastating blows fell from the heavens. In September of 1848 my dear father suddenly succumbed to mental illness. (S 3:15)

To the horror of the entire family the eventual diagnosis was "softening of the brain," and Nietzsche relates how his father suffered terrible pain as he gradually went blind. The version of three years later employs similar imagery: "The clear skies that had up till now smiled upon me were suddenly darkened by black clouds pregnant with doom" (S 3:92). One could well imagine Nietzsche's wanting to deny the influence of heredity in matters of health and illness after this experience, but in fact his psychology emphasizes the importance of what is inherited by the individual from his or her parents and forebears. Indeed his chronic headaches and eye trouble, which began in his mid-teens, later generated constant anxiety that the fate that befell his father would similarly befall him. It is characteristic of Nietzsche that he made no attempt in his thinking to construct defensive rationalizations against the haunting fear—real, as it would turn out—of his own mental collapse.

The thirteen-year-old autobiographer likens his bereaved family to a tree "bereft of its crown" which is deserted by the birds as it withers and becomes bare (S 3:39). This marks the beginning of an important strain of vegetal imagery in Nietzsche's psychology—though the tree will usually be a metaphor for the individual rather than the family. "But hardly had the wounds begun to heal a little," he continues, "when they were painfully torn open again." He recounts a prescient dream in which his father emerges from the grave and returns to it carrying Nietzsche's little brother Joseph. The next day Joseph fell suddenly ill and died, close to his second birthday and six months after the father's death. This second blow from the heavens struck terrifyingly close to home, prompting the understated remark later in the essay that these early experiences of mourning instilled in the young writer a somewhat melancholic disposition.

Nietzsche grew up as the only male in a household with six women: his grandmother, two neurotic maiden aunts, his mother, his sister Elisabeth, who was almost two years younger, and a maid. On the loss of its head, the family was obliged to move out of the parsonage. They settled in the nearby town of Naumburg, where Nietzsche was sent to the public elementary school, both because the family was now possessed of only very modest means and because his grandmother believed it was good for the scions of cultured stock to mix early on with children from "the lower classes." Having just lost his father and brother, however, and been removed from the idyllic environment of his childhood home, the melancholy five-year-old was not in much of a mood for mixing, tending instead to be rather solitary. He admits to a liking for solitude from early on, and to finding solace in the world of nature: "I would feel best . . . in the open temple of nature, where I would find the truest friends."[4] His love of nature still has at this stage a conventionally religious quality: "Thunderstorms would always make the most magnificent impression on me; the distant crashing of thunder and the brightly flashing lightning would only increase my reverence for God."

Through their grandmother's connections with the upper layers of Naumburg society, the two Nietzsche children came to move in circles from which young Friedrich acquired "a certain aristocratic bearing and manner which he never lost."[5] After a year of elementary school he was transferred to a private institution, and it was not long before he made two fine friends there, whose company helped him flourish again: Gustav Krug, the son of a privy councillor, and Wilhelm Pinder, whose father was a judge. The Krugs were a highly musical family, numbering Mendelssohn among their friends, while the interests of the Pinders were more literary. Goethe was a particular favorite, and Nietzsche enjoyed regular readings of his works at the Pinder residence. A passage from an account by Wilhelm Pinder of his friendship with Nietzsche at this time is noteworthy in that it accords with the highly stylized reports in the latter's own self-depictions.

> The basic trait of [Nietzsche's] character was a certain melancholy, which was expressed in his whole being. From his earliest childhood he loved being alone in order to give himself up to his own thoughts; he tended to avoid the society of other people, and sought out places endowed with sublime natural beauty. . . . Among his chief virtues were modesty and gratefulness.[6]

The early exposure to Goethe was definitive for the young Nietzsche, especially since from the age of ten he began writing poems and plays himself.[7] Like all young men of the time, he will have identified to a greater or lesser degree with Goethe's arch-Romantic hero, Werther. *The Sorrows of Young Werther* contains several ideas and images that later assume key roles in Nietzsche's thinking, especially in its nature-derived metaphors. Many passages in the juvenilia echo Werther's talk of "the full, warm feeling of my heart for living nature, which used to inundate me with so much bliss and would make all the world around me a paradise."[8]

One of *Werther*'s main psychological ideas concerns the problem of how to employ all one's powers to optimal effect. The agonized protagonist feels constrained, as the young Nietzsche clearly did, when forced to "socialize" with other people: "There are so many other powers in me that are decaying through lack of use and which I must carefully conceal [when in company]." The presence of his former beloved, however, would engender the opposite feeling:

> [Then] I felt the great soul, in whose presence I seemed to be more than I was, because I was everything that I could be. Dear God! Was there then a single power of my soul that remained unused? With her wasn't I able to develop that wonderful feeling with which my heart embraced the whole of nature?[9]

The problem of how to order and employ the multiplicity of one's powers is germane to Nietzsche's psychology from the beginning, though he does not appear—unless with Lou Salomé—ever to have enjoyed the kind of solution described here by Werther. (Indeed, it seems as if the ideal of Romantic love set up by much of his early reading may have inhibited later his ability to develop relationships with flesh-and-blood women of his own age.) In a prefiguring of Goethe's idea of systole and diastole, Werther puts the problem in another way that becomes definitive for Nietzsche's experience:

> I have pondered in various ways the desire of human beings to expand, to make new discoveries, to roam far and wide; and also the inner drive [Trieb] willingly to limit oneself, to travel the customary path and not to concern oneself with what lies to the left or right.[10]

One can see Nietzsche suspended between these two drives for most of his subsequent career and seeking productive ways to sustain the tension. Another important influence around this period, having to do in particular with the idea of drives, came from the work of Goethe's younger contemporary Friedrich Schiller (to be discussed in the next chapter).

While Nietzsche was naturally a great appreciator of Goethe's work, it was the *person* that prompted his greatest admiration—one of the few admirations to persist undiminished throughout his life. Although Goethe had died twelve years before Nietzsche was born, his person was immortalized in Johann Peter Eckermann's *Conversations with Goethe* of 1835, which Nietzsche later called "the best German book there is" (*WS* 109). Eckermann's elegant prose portrait is a remarkable work from which the reader comes away with a most vivid picture of the great poet (as well as of the book's author). Its signal virtue from the psychological standpoint is that it imparts such a vital impression of the richness of Goethe's personality. As Eckermann writes in his preface: "This extraordinary human being can be compared with a multifaceted diamond that reflects a different color from every angle." Eckermann's technique—eminently effective—is to portray his subject in many different situations and interacting with various kinds of persons, without any attempt to annul the contradictions that may thereby emerge, until the fullest possible picture of the man becomes manifest.

A salient feature of the *Conversations* is the frequency with which the talk turns to Lord Byron and his works. While Goethe is clearly aware of Byron's limitations and shortcomings, his praise for the work and appreciation of the poet's personality is impressively evident. Such enthusiasm is contagious, and the young Nietzsche was seized by a devotion to the Lord that was anything but short-lived. In 1861 he presented a lecture to the Germania student society (a discussion group founded two years earlier whose membership consisted of Gustav Krug, Wilhelm Pinder, and himself) entitled "On Byron's Dramas" and based on readings of the plays that date back to his discovery of *Manfred* some three years before. This discovery had prompted him to read widely in Byron's writings—not only the poetry and plays, but also the letters and journals—and he continued to read him, though with diminished fervor, until the end of his career.[11] Almost at the end, in *Ecce Homo,* Nietzsche writes: "I must be profoundly related to Byron's Manfred: all these abysses I found in myself; at the age of thirteen I was ripe for this work" (*EH* 2.4).

The lecture opens, significantly, with a comparison of Byron's poetry with Goethe's, and praise for the range of the Englishman's protean powers:

> The primary attraction of Byron's poetry is that it lets us engage the Lord's own world of feeling and thought, not in the calm and golden-clear composure of Goethe's poems, but in the storm-pressure of a spirit of fire, of a volcano that now spews glowing devastating lava and now, its peak hidden in wreaths of smoke, looks down upon the verdant meadows that garland its base.[12]

The mysterious charm of Byron lies in the fact that "in every character the poet draws he presents himself, yet without succumbing to boundless one-sidedness—for Byron knew how to embrace everything lofty and noble, the most tender and sublime feelings, within the magnificent universality of his spirit." The overall sense of this last comment, and the commendation for avoiding "onesidedness" in characterization, suggest that what impressed Nietzsche was Byron's ability to present radically different parts of himself in his various characters. A few pages later, however, the young critic claims that Byron was "no master of characterization": "There is basically only one character that he is able to depict fully and exhaustively, and that is his own. All the other characters are, so to speak, parts of his own character—a phenomenon we shall examine more closely" (*HKA* 1:12). What appeared at first to be a strength now seems to be grounds for disappointment; but closer examination helps resolve the ambiguity.

> If we have said that Byron could only portray his own character, this sounds more paradoxical than it is. In the four characters of Manfred, Marino Falieri, Jacopo Foscari, and Sardanapalus, we are pre-sented—in spite of the apparent diversity—with one and the same: namely, Byron himself in the multifacetedness of his comprehensive spirit.

The air of paradox dissipates if one regards the poet's self not as something unitary but as inherently multiple.

Nietzsche goes on to say which several traits of Byron's personality are to be found in each of the four characters, and concludes by remarking on something missing from the picture he has presented, namely

> [Byron's] almost feminine delicacy of sensibility and subtlety in the conception of noble women characters, gifts that are especially evi-dent in the wonderful figures of Myrrha, Angiolina, and Marina. When one considers that Byron is free of all religiosity and indeed of any belief in God, inconstant in love and partaking of an abundance of sensual pleasures, and when one considers these eternally feminine women so finely depicted by his masterful hand, one must be truly

astonished at the greatness of his genius. And it is precisely the fact that we become acquainted with the multifacetedness of his character down to the very depths of his soul that compensates for the considerable dramatic shortcomings of his works. (*HKA* 1:13–14)

In the *Conversations with Goethe* Eckermann had praised Byron's women characters during a discussion of *The Two Foscari;* Goethe had concurred, saying that female characters were now "the only vessel that remains for us moderns to pour our ideality into" (5 July 1827). This remark is in keeping with Byron's own judgment of his women characters: "My writings, indeed, tend to exalt the sex; and my imagination has always delighted in giving them a *beau idéal* likeness, but I only drew them as a painter or statuary would do—as they should be."[13] If Nietzsche was aware of this evaluation of Byron's, the excess of ideality does not appear to have diminished his admiration for the women of his imagination.

Ultimately then, while Nietzsche follows Goethe in finding Byron limited as a dramatist, he does admire his ability to portray a genuine multiplicity of characters by drawing from the depths of his own soul. The comments on the women characters suggest that Nietzsche was especially impressed by the poet's ability to give expression to the feminine aspects of his "comprehensive spirit." His admiration for Byron's godlessness shows that he was himself inclined toward moving away from the religion in which he had been brought up, and in his praise of Manfred as a "spirit-mastering *Übermensch*" and of *Manfred* as "an almost superhuman *[übermenschliches]* work" (*HKA* 1:10, 14) suggests that Byron contributes material that will in the hands of the mature Nietzsche become the basis for a new and earthier religiosity. It was also around this time that Nietzsche first began reading Shakespeare, whom he came to regard, following Goethe, as the greatest of dramatists.

Along with Shelley (of whose works the young Nietzsche was also an avid reader), Byron was the ultimate heir of the British Romantic tradition, which had in turn absorbed influences from German thought. Indeed, Byron was remarkable in being, like Goethe, a distinctly *European* phenomenon—which must have been as appealing to Nietzsche as it was salutary for him.[14] More extensively than in *Werther,* the worlds of nature and the human soul are deeply interfused in Byron's works, and this encouraged the nature-mystical tendencies engendered by Nietzsche's love for the countryside in which he had grown up. Echoes abound in much of the juvenilia of lines such as these from *Childe Harold's Pilgrimage:*

> Are not the mountains, waves, and skies, a part
> of me and of my Soul, as I of them?

> Is not the love of these deep in my heart
> With a pure passion? . . .[15]

Or these lines from an adjacent stanza, which he will have been heartened to come across, cited in the presentation of a metaphysical theory, when several years later he read Schopenhauer for the first time:

> I live not in myself, but I become
> Portion of that around me; and to me
> High mountains are a feeling, but the hum
> Of human cities torture.[16]

Nietzsche had not actually seen much in the way of high mountains at this point, but they would soon become far more than "a feeling" for him.

Although he apparently read almost all of Byron, *Manfred* remained his favorite work—understandably, when one considers that the protagonist's account of his youth reads like an extreme version of what Nietzsche himself experienced, especially concerning the tensions between relations with people and with natural phenomena.

> The thirst of their ambition was not mine,
> The aim of their existence was not mine;
> My joys—my griefs—my passions—and my powers,
> Made me a stranger . . .
>   . . . and with the thoughts of men,
> I held but slight communion; but instead,
> My joy was in the wilderness,—to breathe
> The difficult air of the iced mountain's top,
> Where the birds dare not build—nor insect's wing
> Flit o'er the herbless granite; or to plunge
> Into the torrent, and to roll along
> On the swift whirl of the new-breaking wave
> Of river-stream, or Ocean, in their flow.
> In these my early strength exulted . . .

Manfred is set in the high Alps, which Nietzsche would not actually experience until twenty years later; but the mountain landscapes established in his imagination by his reading of Byron remained vital presences throughout his life.

Though lacking the majesty of the Alps, the countryside around Naumburg had considerable charm in those days, and Nietzsche was by no means merely a passive observer of it. He was from an early age a passionate hiker—and remained so for the rest of his career, within the limitations imposed by gradually deteriorating eyesight. He became a keen swimmer and skater and enjoyed through these sports an active as well as receptive engagement with the forces of nature.

> To give oneself over to the current and glide along effortlessly on the gentle waves: can one imagine anything more delightful? And swimming is not only pleasant but also very useful in dangerous circumstances, while at the same time strengthening and refreshing for the body. . . . In winter its place is taken by skating. It is something quite unearthly, to glide with winged foot across the crystalline surface. And when in addition the moon sends down its silvery beams, such evenings on the ice become nights of enchantment. (S 3:32)

In his earliest autobiographical essay, dating from 1858, Nietzsche's account of the first event to cast a pall over the family's life after the move from Röcken is couched in typically Byronic imagery: "Until now our life in Naumburg had flowed by untroubled, like a clear stream. But suddenly the waves turned dark again, a thunderstorm raged throughout nature, a cloudburst caused the dark waters to swell and rush along" (S 3:28). The dismal event adumbrated by these words is the death of his Aunt Augusta, which was followed several months later by his grandmother's falling ill and dying. The passage is also the source of a stream of aquatic imagery (fed by Goethe and Byron) that will form a major current in the psychological reflections of the mature philosopher.

In a later report about school life at Schulpforta, Nietzsche makes the first of many notes on his extreme susceptibility to the weather: "It is true: gloomy weather evokes gloomy thoughts; a darkening sky makes the soul darken, and when the heavens weep my own eyes overflow with tears." [17] His extreme sensitivity to meteorological phenomena evinces an important respect in which the membrane between the self and the world remains in Nietzsche's case unusually permeable. It is noteworthy that the following short poem evoking the radical ephemerality of life is said to have been composed (in early August) in response to "the bitter feeling of autumn awakening in the soul" rather than to an experience of literal autumn:

> The leaves fall from the trees,
> Prey to the wild wind's lust;
> Our life with all its tears
> Dissolves into ashes and dust.
> (S 3:46)

An isolated psychological observation in these early biographical sketches deserves mention. In an account of his regimen at school in 1859, Nietzsche writes:

It is remarkable how active phantasy is while we are dreaming. I always wear elastic bands around my socks at night, and I dreamed that two snakes were entwined around my legs. I immediately grasp one of them by the neck—and wake up to find that I have a sock-band in my hand. (S 3:47)

The idea that some kind of phantasy activity occurs during sleep, and composes the minimal stimulation that impinges upon the organism during the night into a dream narrative, will some twenty years later undergo philosophical elaboration into one of Nietzsche's most fruitful insights.[18]

The lecture on Byron had ended by praising the "abundance of ideas" in his works, and especially in *Manfred,* where the "storm of his thoughts" is said to outweigh all else (*HKA* 1:14). Another figure Nietzsche refers to as his "favorite poet" around this time, and whom he similarly praises for the profundity of his thought, is Hölderlin. The earliest discussion of Hölderlin is a fictitious letter dated 19 October 1861, bearing the title "Letter to my friend, in which I recommend that he read my favorite poet."[19] Though Hölderlin had succumbed to madness in 1802, he did not die until the year before Nietzsche was born. Nevertheless his genius was still generally unappreciated when the schoolboy composed his letter of praise.

It is clear that among Hölderlin's works *Hyperion* (1797–99), that magnificent hybrid prose-poem, is the one that most affected Nietzsche in his youth. "Nor do you know," he pretends to write to a friend, "*Hyperion*":

With the euphonious movement of its prose and the beauty and sublimity of the figures that rise up from it, it makes the same impression as the wave-beat of a restless sea. In fact this prose is music, gentle dissolving sounds with intervening painful dissonances, finally expiring in strange and mournful funeral hymns. . . . Nowhere else has the yearning for Greece been manifested in purer tones; nor has the kinship of soul between Hölderlin and Schiller and Hegel, his close friend, been anywhere more evident.

Nietzsche will later characterize *Thus Spoke Zarathustra* in retrospect as "music," and there is nowhere a closer paradigm of the language and imagery of that work than in *Hyperion.*[20]

Hyperion has been called, with some justification in spite of the differences, "the Greek Werther"; and at the outset the protagonist is grappling with the Goethean problem of the proper employment of one's powers.[21] The following description gives vivid expression to the situation the young Nietzsche found himself in at the time.

I had grown up like a grapevine without a prop, with wild shoots trailing aimlessly over the ground. You know how many a noble power perishes in us if it goes unused. I wandered around like a will-o'-the-wisp, catching everything, being caught by everything, but only for the moment, and my unskilled powers wore themselves out in vain. I felt that everywhere I was lacking, and was unable to find my goal.[22]

As with Werther, focus and enhancement of powers come through a love relationship, with the divinely beautiful Diotima—but also through Hyperion's friendship with Alabanda. His account of the beginnings of this friendship employs imagery drawn from natural phenomena:

> We encountered one another like two streams rushing down from the mountains . . . making their way toward one another and breaking through to where . . . united in a single majestic river they begin their journey to the far sea. . . . Like storms that drive playfully but relentlessly through forests and over mountains, so our souls rushed forward in colossal projects. (*Hyp.* 1.1.7)

Nietzsche's conception of the love relationship was doubtless informed by the story of Hyperion's love for Diotima. With the lofty expectations and demands he tended to make on his friendships, Nietzsche was identifying with Hölderlin's protagonist—while at the same time ignoring the wisdom of Hyperion's female counterpart. Diotima (who bears deliberate similarity to the hieratic figure who instructs Socrates in the *Symposium*) advises Hyperion to try to see his friendships with a more down-to-earth and human eye:

> What you are seeking is a better age, a more beautiful world. It was this world that you embraced in your friends; with them you *were* this world. . . . It was not human beings that you wanted, believe me, you wanted a world. The loss of all golden centuries, as you felt them compressed into a single glorious moment, the spirit of all spirits of better ages, the power of all heroes' powers: those were to be replaced for you by a single, human being! (*Hyp.* 1.2.16)

There is no doubt that Nietzsche frequently felt such moments; and those readers familiar with the course of his friendships will easily see the Hyperion syndrome in them.

Once again like Werther, Hyperion strives to harmonize the natures outside him and within.

> Sacred nature! you are the same inside and outside me. It cannot be so difficult to unite what is outside me with the divine in me. If the bee succeeds in its small realm, why should I not then be able to plant and cultivate what is necessary? (*Hyp.* 1.2.19)

The reason is that he has not yet learned what he will have learned much later, after the death of Diotima:

> Must not all things suffer? And the more excellent a thing is, the more deeply! Does not sacred nature itself suffer? . . . But the bliss that does not suffer is sleep, and without death is no life. . . . Yes! yes! pain is worthy to lie in the human heart and to be your intimate, O nature! For it but leads from one bliss to another, and there is no other companion than pain. (*Hyp.* 2.2.6)

Heartening words for a sensitive youth to read who had suffered unusual extremes of joy and sorrow. And indeed this Heraclitean idea of the mutual interdependence of such opposites as pleasure and pain would remain a feature of Nietzsche's philosophical psychology throughout its development.

Hölderlin's idea of Dionysian *life* that is eternally self-renewing, which receives lyrical expression in the finale of *Hyperion,* deeply impressed Nietzsche just when he was beginning to formulate his first philosophical ideas. This passage in particular prefigures the principal imagery he will employ (especially in *Zarathustra*) in articulating the central notion of *Leben:*

> Let human beings fall from you like rotten fruit, oh let them perish *[untergehen]* that they may return to your roots; and may I too perish, o Tree of Life—so that I may become green again with you and breathe your crown about me with all your budding branches! peacefully and fervently, for we are all sprung from the same golden seed!
>
> You springs of earth! you flowers! and you woods and eagles and you, brotherly light! how ancient and new is our love! . . . How should the mode of Life not vary? yet we all love the aether, and in our innermost selves are profoundly alike. (*Hyp.* 2.2.8)

The Mentor from Concord

> *The secret of the world is the tie between person and event. Person makes event, and event person. The "times," "the age," what is that, but a few profound persons and a few active persons who epitomize the times?*
>
> Emerson, "Fate"

One of Nietzsche's first overtly philosophical pronouncements concerns a conception of life similar to that expressed by Hyperion and occurs in the initial installment of a three-version series from 1861 entitled "The Course of My Life." Against the view that an abstract, lifeless creative principle could be guiding our fates, he maintains a radical hylozoism, saying that "everything that is, is alive" (S 3:89). There is, however, an order of rank to the various life-forms:

> There are hierarchies throughout creation, which must extend even as far as invisible beings, unless the world itself is to be the Primordial Soul *[die Urseele]*. Thus we see a progression of life, beginning with stone . . . progressing to plants, animals, and human beings, and issuing in earth, air, heavenly bodies, world or space, matter, and time.

The belief in the existence of a divine "Primordial Spirit" that directs the course of the world will disappear upon the university student's disaffection with Christian monotheism, and will be replaced—under the influence of Schopenhauer—by a pagan equivalent: "the artist of the world" (*BT* 5). What will endure, however, is the related idea that all things are inextricably linked, which plays an important role in the unconditional affirmation of the world in which Nietzsche's mature thinking issues. At sixteen, he puts it like this:

> There is no such thing as chance; everything that happens has a significance, and the more that science searches out and researches, the more illuminating the thought will be that everything that is, or happens, is a link in a hidden chain. (S 3:90)

The rest of this passage is a marked antithesis to the mature Nietzsche's uncompromising refusal to seek any kind of metaphysical consolation after the collapse of his faith in divine providence.

> Just look at history: do you think that the numbers line themselves up meaninglessly? Look at the sky: do you believe that the heavenly bodies follow their paths without law or order? Whatever happens does not happen by chance; a higher being knowingly and meaningfully guides all creation.

By the time of *Thus Spoke Zarathustra* it will be precisely the nihilistic thought that there is no such thing as divine providence, and that the events of history are devoid of intrinsic meaning or purpose, that will be the terrifying yet liberating stimulant to Nietzsche's alter ego's ultimate affirmation of life.

By 1862 the last major influence on Nietzsche's youthful intellect had become operative—through his discovery of the work of Ralph Waldo Emerson.[23] In the first of two presentations on the topic of fate he gave that year to the Germania society, Nietzsche paraphrases a line of Emerson's about temperament; but the whole essay attests to the impact of a major intellectual mentor.[24] The ground of his psyche was already receptive to the American thinker's ideas, given his penchant for nature mysticism and his prior immersion in classical culture and elements of German Romantic philosophy.[25] But it was also a case of perfect timing and a harmonious blending of personalities, such that Emerson's writings were introduced into the ferment of literary influences at just the right time to provide the most fecund stimulus for the beginning thinker. (The less theistic and anthropocentric work of Henry David Thoreau would no doubt have held an even greater appeal for Nietzsche, had he had access to it; the parallels between the two—in style of life as well as writing style and imagery—are quite remarkable.)[26]

Emerson's influence on the early development of Nietzsche's thinking has been largely ignored or underestimated. Fortunately the supple power of the sage of Concord's prose translated into German successfully, and Nietzsche was granted an initial exposure to both the early Emerson of the *Essays* and the later, less theistic and idealistic author of *The Conduct of Life*. Nietzsche apparently took his copy of the *Essays* with him when traveling: in 1874 he reports with distress that "the splendid Emerson" was stolen along with his travel bag at a train station in Switzerland.[27] He went back to Emerson around the time he was writing *The Joyful Science*, and the first edition of that text carries an epigraph from the essay "History."[28] A telling note from 1881 with the heading "Emerson" reads: "I have never felt so at home in a book, and in my own house, as with—but I can't praise it; it's too close to me"; and then in a letter to Franz Overbeck Nietzsche asked him to tell his wife Ida, who had also become an Emerson enthusiast, that he felt Emerson to be a "brother-*soul*."[29] A year later, in the course of having the essay "Historic Notes of Life and Letters in New England" translated into German, he sends Overbeck the now ambivalent judgment:

> I don't know how much I would give to be able to bring it about, retroactively, that such a magnificently great nature, so rich in soul and spirit, could have undergone *strict* discipline, a really *scientific* education. As it is, in Emerson we have *lost* a philosopher![30]

Nietzsche mentions in his letter that the essay has given him some insight into Emerson's development, but it is not immediately clear which elements of it led him to denigrate the author as a philosopher. It is true that Emerson did not undergo an intellectual discipline as severe as the one Nietzsche would later arrange to have inflicted on himself, through studying philology at Bonn and Leipzig; but the last part of this remark seems distinctly uncharitable to an important mentor—or else betrays a temporarily restricted view of what constitutes a philosopher. Perhaps Nietzsche mistook Emerson's disparagement of exclusively analytical thinking ("The young men were born with knives in their brain") and the scientistic worldview for a condemnation of rigorous thought in general. He would certainly have been disconcerted by the sage's praise for Kant and Hegel's producing "the best catalogue of the human faculties and the best analysis of the mind."

If we really did lose a philosopher in Emerson, we gained a great psychologist. At any rate, seeing the sage of Concord as a worthy heir of Plato and Montaigne—with his serenely aristocratic elitism, his conceptions of power, experimentation, tyranny and order of rank in nature, and above all his vital prose and poetic imagery—one can appreciate how much his essays provided salutary nourishment for the young Nietzsche's soul.

What is striking about the opening of the first presentation to the Germania is Nietzsche's self-conscious distancing with respect to Christianity, and the suggestion that it would be salutary to "adopt a more liberal standpoint in order to be able to deliver an impartial judgment, in keeping with the times, of religion and Christianity" (*HKA* 2:54). This is for the intrepid student no mere intellectual exercise, but rather a spiritual and psychological adventure that is not without its perturbations.

> To venture out onto the sea of doubt, with neither compass nor guide, is foolishness and ruin for undeveloped souls; most are destroyed by storms, while only a few discover new lands.... From amidst the immeasurable ocean of ideas one often yearns for *terra firma*. (*HKA* 2:55)

The maritime imagery is prominent throughout this early presentation, and similar images will resurge in several of Nietzsche's later adventures in ideas. The young Nietzsche goes on, now in a distinctly Cartesian mode, to ponder the necessity for firm foundations for the construction of a philosophical edifice, and to lament the difficulty of preparing the ground by tearing down the constructs that shape our current existence.

> I have tried to deny everything: oh, tearing down is easy, but building up is hard! And even tearing down seems easier than it is: we are so conditioned in our innermost being by the impressions of our childhood, the influences of our parents, and our education that those deeply rooted prejudices are not so easily eradicated by common-sense reasons or sheer strength of will.

The vegetal imagery leads to further hylozoistic speculation concerning the continuity between human life and the inorganic realm of stone, when the author asks: "Is the human being not perhaps simply the evolution of stone through the medium of the plant and the animal? . . . Has this eternal becoming no end?" (*HKA* 2:56). There is an anticipation here of Nietzsche's later speculations that *the world* (not just life) might be understood as will to power.[31] Indeed, the essay on fate goes on to project a prefiguration of the idea of will to power as an ocean of interpretive forces.

> How could we human beings see higher planes of existence? We see only ideas forming themselves under external influences out of the same source, humanity; we see these ideas assuming life and form . . . and how the eternal productive drive uses them as material to re-work, such that they form life and direct history; we see the struggle in which they take from each other and the way new formations emerge from these fusions. A clashing and surging of the most disparate currents with ebb and flood, all into the eternal ocean. (*HKA* 2:56–57)

Some twenty years later Nietzsche set down one of his most lyrically speculative notes, which brings together the ideas of eternal recurrence and will to power. There we hear that the world is "an ocean of forces storming and flooding into themselves, eternally transforming themselves, eternally running back in monstrous years of recurrence, with an ebb and flood of its forms."[32] This "Dionysian world . . . without a goal, unless there is a goal in the happiness of the circle, without will, unless a ring has good will toward itself," is ultimately *will to power.*

In his student presentation Nietzsche follows Emerson in arguing that temperament and mood play a much larger role than external events in constituting our experience, and suggests that these internal factors also tend to obscure the influence of outside forces. "It is a painful feeling to give up one's independence in an unconscious reception of impressions from outside" (*HKA* 2:58). But the second presentation emphasizes that the range of one's activity extends far beyond individual receptivity:

> The activity of human beings does not begin simply at birth but already in the embryo, and perhaps . . . already in the parents and ancestors. . . . The Hindu says that fate is nothing but the deeds we did in an earlier condition of our being. . . . We understand fate as the principle that guides us in our unconscious activity.[33]

The idea (again found in Emerson) that the being of the individual stretches back through the parents and ancestors into the prehistory of humanity and animality is central to Nietzsche's mature psychology.[34]

By the time of the last autobiographical essay ("My Life," 1864), the author's talents have begun to flourish along many different dimensions. He attributes some of this efflorescence to the loss of his father at such an early age: "I am convinced that precisely the death of such an excellent father, in depriving me on the one hand of paternal help and guidance for later life, on the other sowed the seeds in my soul of seriousness and contemplation" (S 3:117). By the time he was twenty, Nietzsche had produced a large body of poems (which he had already divided into three periods and submitted to a written critique) and almost as many musical compositions; he had learned Greek, Latin, and Hebrew and studied the classical literatures and the Old Testament in the original languages; he had authored several plays and shown himself to be a creative architect of small-scale structures, as well as a passable draftsman and painter; and he had been drawn to the passionate study of a wide variety of subjects at one of the best schools in Europe at the time.[35] Such a multiplicity of talents imposed major stress on the mortal frame of one so young.

Perhaps the most remarkable feature of Nietzsche's character during this period was the seriousness with which he struggled to apply his several talents. Exemplary here is the case of his work on the Nordic saga of Ermanarich, warrior king of the Ostrogoths. He began in 1861 with an essay, based on thorough research, for a German class at school. Later that year he attempted to cast the material of the essay in the form of a "symphonic poem" for piano for four hands. The next year he tried the topic in three different media: a long poem entitled "The Death of Ermanarich," which he presented to the Germania; a score for a piano version, intended as an excerpt of a composition for full orchestra; and a sketch for a drama. In 1863 he tried the essay again, this time informed by more sophisticated scholarship; and in 1865 he returned to the theme for the last time with a scenario for an Ermanarich opera.[36] The teenager's perseverance in trying over a period of four years to find the appropriate medium for the expression of his emotions and ideas about the figure of the warrior king, and about the Slavic-Hungarian world he imagined him to inhabit, is clear testament to his multiple abilities.

Given that none of the works on Ermanarich had effected a fully adequate treatment of its subject, it is not surprising that toward the end of his time at Schulpforta Nietzsche was at a loss to know what subject to study at the university. But he appears to recall Emerson's advice in the essay "Power" in this regard: "The one prudence in life is concentration; the one evil is dissipation. . . . You must elect your work; you shall take what your brain can, and drop all the rest." In letters to his mother the future student anticipates being able to resolve his confusion through summoning sufficient resolve: "Perhaps I could still study any subject whatsoever if I had the strength to reject everything else that interests me." But the uncertainty is aggravated by an illness that confines him to the sickroom—the worst consequence of which is that he is unable to play the piano: "Everything seems dead to me when I can't hear any music."[37] With so many intellectual interests, the difficulty lies in finding a path that will lead to a career.

I am still in the particularly unpleasant situation of having a host of interests dispersed among the most diverse subjects, the complete satisfaction of which would make me into a learned man but hardly into one with a solid occupation. It is thus clear to me that I must strip away some of my interests, just as I must acquire some new ones. But which ones will be so unfortunate as to be thrown overboard—perhaps precisely some of my favorite children![38]

Nietzsche is becoming quite unsentimental with respect to features of his life that have to be let go of if he is to make something of it. He realizes that a certain ruthlessness toward parts of himself—as expressed in the image of psychical infanticide—may be necessary if he is to reach his goal.

Looking back on his career at Schulpforta, he sees that it was not entirely lacking in direction after all. Signs of a solution were beginning to appear on the horizon: "In opposition to this aimless wandering in all fields of the intellect I began after some time to develop a counter-will; I wanted to force myself into a constraint, so that I might penetrate a few things deeply and thoroughly to the core." From a bewilderingly seductive array of possibilities, the task would be to will *a few.* Now that the first stage of his education is coming to an end, Nietzsche lays down for himself the unbreakable law "to combat the inclination to a superficial knowledge of many things, and thereby to promote [his] tendency to lead each particular thing back to its deepest and broadest foundations" (S 3:118).

After some deliberation, he opted to go to the University of Bonn. A major attraction was the presence there of a highly distinguished faculty in classics, a field in which he had already received an excellent training at Schulpforta. But more important than training in the narrow sense had been the effect the teachers' personalities had exerted on the young student's psyche, who was fortunate to have had teachers who were not only eminent scholars but fine human beings. The following retrospective remarks are exemplary:

> Perhaps I would have been put off by the sober stiffness of philology: but Steinhart [professor of Greek and Hebrew] was of great value to me as an image of a universally animated personality who enlivened his field. . . . Our image of a profession is usually abstracted from the persons of the teachers who are closest to us. (S 3:149)

The importance of personality is emphasized in another passage written the same year.

> The most fortunate thing was that I encountered excellent philology teachers, *on the basis of whose personalities I formed my judgment of their field.* . . . There lived before my eyes philologists such as

Steinhart, Keil, Corssen, Peter: men with open views and invigorating characters, who also in part bestowed upon me their closer inclinations. (S 3:152; emphasis added)

The personal factor was decisive—and would remain so, insofar as Nietzsche would always be attracted by the human being and the sense of life mediated through the books he read, rather than by the ideas in them. This trait he inherited from Emerson, who constantly emphasized personality, in contemporaries as well as in "Representative Men" of the tradition. In the Dartmouth Oration, "Literary Ethics," Emerson extols "the power of character" and takes heart from the prolific souls of great predecessors: "I console myself in the poverty of my present thoughts . . . by seeing what the prolific soul could beget on actual nature;—seeing that Plato was, and Shakspeare, and Milton,—three irrefragable facts. Then I dare; I also will essay to be."

But there was another factor at work in the young Nietzsche; these further comments on the attraction that classical philology held for him at that time reveal a soul that considers itself in need of discipline and a separation between heart and task.

I was seeking a counterweight to the erratic and unsettling inclinations that had plagued me up to now, a science that could be pursued with cool circumspection, cold logic, and steady work, without one's having to take the results to heart. All this I believed at that time could be found in philology. (S 3:151)

The proposed separation of the work from the life, which went against his own ideas and ideals, would generate some unsalutary tensions.

Moods of the Interior

> *Our moods do not believe in each other. . . . Alas for this infirm faith, this will not strenuous, this vast ebb of a vast flow! I am God in nature; I am a weed by the wall.*
>
> Emerson, "Circles"

The concern with resolving psychological tensions and imposing order on a multiplicity of inclinations is a major theme in another essay from 1864, "On Moods" ("Über Stimmungen"), which marks a transition from writing in the autobiographical mode to a somewhat less personal style. *Stimmung* comes from *stimmen,* which means to be in tune with, to fit, to accord, to voice, to vote, to put (someone) in a mood, to be "right" in the sense of appropriate to the context. The musical associations work in English as well as in German: a mood would be an expression of one's attunement with the world, with other people—also among voices or elements within the psyche. If a person is in a bad mood, or in the wrong mode, his actions will be disharmonious with others'; just as in certain moods we find ourselves modulating into the minor, our pitch flattened or a key or two depressed, not so well tempered.

"On Moods" begins with an invitation to imagine the nineteen-year-old author, clad in a dressing gown, sitting down on an evening around Easter to write about moods. Staring at a blank sheet of paper, pen in hand, he is beset by "a turmoil of things, events, and thoughts all demanding to be written down." Some of the ideas clamoring for attention are youthfully aggressive, "effervescent like new wine," and they run into conflict with those that are more mature and established—with "many an old, ripened, clarified thought, who like an old master measures the exertions of the young world with an ambiguous eye." Our state of mind is "conditioned and attuned by the conflict between that old and young world, and we call the current state of the conflict a mood."[39]

The essay gets underway in a mode that is self-consciously reflective: the writer feels fortunate to be in the mood to write about moods. One reason for the appropriate attunement is that he has been playing the piano earlier in the day—the *Consolations* by Liszt, whose tones are still ringing within him. He recalls a recent experience that was psychologically painful and realizes that the residual emotion has fused with the strains of the *Consolations*. This prompts the insight that "the soul always seeks to draw to itself what is similar in kind," while at the same time an element of newness or difference always enters in. Nietzsche now introduces an image of the psyche as a kind of boarding house. As new experiences enter the domicile of the soul *(Seelenwohnung),* those unable to find anything related to them are obliged to "reside there alone, often to the displeasure of the older residents with whom they often run into conflict." But if the newcomer is fortunate, it will not be long before "new guests stream in from all sides into the open house, and the one who was just then standing alone finds many and noble relatives" (S 3:114).

The metaphor of the soul as a household occurs in Plato's *Republic,* in the course of a discussion of the nature of justice within the individual. The relevant passage articulates the issues with which Nietzsche was dealing at the time of "On Moods," capturing in an image a problem that will constantly recur. Socrates offers Glaucon a characterization of the just individual in terms of his "minding his business . . . with respect to what is within":

He doesn't let each part of him mind other people's business or the three classes in the soul meddle with each other, but really sets his own house *[ta oikeia]* in good order and rules himself; he arranges himself, becomes his own friend, and harmonizes the three parts, exactly like three notes in a harmonic scale.[40]

Nietzsche's use of the metaphors of the soul as domicile and of harmony (attunement, *Stimmung*) between different elements may well have been prompted by his reading of the *Republic;* these are, in any case, key images in the development of his later ideas about the psyche.[41]

The next paragraph of "On Moods" concerns the factors that govern what comes into the domicile of the soul and which thereby determine the nature of its population.

> But it is quite remarkable: it isn't that the guests come because they want to, nor that the guests come just as they are; but it's rather that those come who must, and indeed only those come who must. Anything that the soul is *unable* to reflect fails to touch it; but since it's in the power of the will to let the soul reflect or not, only that touches the soul which the soul wants to.[42]

One is reminded here of Emerson's characterization of life as "a train of moods" in the essay "Experience":

> Dream delivers us to dream, and there is no end to illusion. Life is a train of moods like a string of beads, and as we pass through them, they prove to be many-colored lenses which paint the world in their own hue, and each shows only what lies in its focus. . . . We animate what we can, and we see only what we animate.

Nietzsche realizes that his talk of the power of the will may seem paradoxical since there are certain moods and feelings we feel we have to struggle against.

> But what ultimately conditions and attunes the will? Or how often is the will asleep and only the drives *[Triebe]* and desires awake! One of the strongest desires of the soul is for what is new, an inclination toward the unaccustomed, which explains why we often allow ourselves to be put into moods that are unpleasant.

Much of Nietzsche's subsequent thinking about psychodynamics concerns the relation between the will and the drives—though instead of will *versus* the drives the issue becomes the will *as* drives.

The conception of the soul as a kind of dwelling lets Nietzsche imagine its inhabitants as alive and capable of animated interaction with each other. It will develop into the broader notion of the soul as household, *Haushalt* or *oikos,* and thereby open up the idea of the "great economy" *(grosse Öko-nomie)* of the soul and of life in general—a central notion in Nietzsche's

mature thought and another that he borrowed from Emerson.[43] It is clear
from Emerson's expansion of the notion of economy in the essay "Power"
(and indeed from this essay as a whole) that Nietzsche's later conception of
a grand, cosmic economy of will to power has a major source here: "An
economy may be applied to [this force or spirit of Nature] . . . it may be
husbanded or wasted; every man is efficient only as he is a container or
vessel of this force, and never was any signal act or achievement in history,
but by this expenditure."[44]

In "On Moods" the ability of the soul to take things in is not entirely
under the control of the will: sometimes an event will not "strike a responsive chord," with the result that the ensuing mode of attunement will lie
heavily upon the soul, oppressing and constricting its contents.

> Moods, then, come either from internal struggles or from external
> pressure on the inner world. Here a civil war between two enemy
> camps, there an oppression of the people by a particular class, a small
> minority. (S 3:114)

A *Stimmung* is then an expression of a *tension* between two forces or
realms, just as the tuning of a stringed instrument depends on the strings'
being held in a certain tension. An echo here of the passage from the *Republic* quoted above, where the condition of justice is imagined as resulting
from a harmonic attunement of the three parts of the soul.

The idea of a population within the soul is now presented in social and
political metaphors. Some of this imagery might have suggested itself to
Nietzsche from his reading of the Homeric epics, where the psyche is sometimes imagined as an inner society, though the extended political metaphor
for the soul in the *Republic* may have been a more immediate influence.[45]
The idea of warring factions within the soul is germane to much of the
argument of the *Republic,* as well as to Nietzsche's mature psychology; and
we shall later see both of them frame the question of how to live the best
life in terms of which agents or forces within the soul should be in charge
and which should be ruled.[46]

Nor are the parties in the soul that speaks of itself in "On Moods" only
political ones. The Dionysian theme hinted at earlier, with the talk of effervescent wine, is alluded to again:

> Often, when I eavesdrop on my own thoughts and feelings and si-
> lently attend to myself, it is as if I heard the hum and buzzing of wild
> parties, as if there were a rushing *[Rauschen]* though the air as when
> a thought or an eagle flies to the sun.[47]

This passage illustrates the keenness of Nietzsche's inner hearing and the
vivacity with which the auditory is translated into visual imagery. The allu-

sion to the Dionysian through the wild parties is reinforced subliminally by
the word *Rauschen:* "*Rausch*" is the physiological correlate of the Dionysian in *The Birth of Tragedy,* where it refers to the "rush," or mood of intoxication, at the heart of the Dionysian rituals.

The next paragraph begins and ends with some explicitly Heraclitean
dicta:

> Conflict is the soul's constant nourishment, and the soul well knows
> how to draw from it sufficient sweetness and beauty. She thereby
> annihilates and gives birth to new things, she fights fiercely and yet
> gently draws the opponent to her side for inner union. And the most
> wonderful thing is that she is never concerned with the outer—names,
> persons, places, fine words, handwriting—everything is of lesser
> value to her, since she treasures that which lies inside the outer cov-
> ering.

Just as important as the high regard in which Nietzsche holds *polemos* (here
his psychology is in harmony with William Blake's as well as Emerson's) is
the emphasis on nourishment, which develops into an abiding concern with
the kinds of nourishment needed by the soul at different times. Also hinted
at here is one of the methods germane to the psychological enterprise as
Nietzsche will conceive it—that of "seeing through," or unmasking, and
hinterfragen, a questioning that gets behind things or approaches them from
within or below.

The young author marvels at the seemingly endless depth of moods, in
accord with the pronouncement of Heraclitus that one can never get to the
bottom of the soul owing to its immeasurable depth. Something that may at
first appear to be the peak of good fortune or the nadir of misery can turn
out to be "only the garment of a yet deeper feeling": "And thus our moods
deepen themselves continually, no one of them is quite the same as the next,
but each is unfathomably young and the birth of the moment."[48] The idea
of endless deepening anticipates Nietzsche's later conception of will to
power as continual self-overcoming. The unceasing drive towards deeper or
more elevated moods shows how "for the spirit it is intolerable to pass
through the same stages again which it has already passed through; it wants
to expand more and more in depth and height." The concluding apostrophe
resounds with Byronic and Emersonian overtones: "dear moods, wondrous
changes of a storm-filled soul, manifold as nature is, but greater than nature,
since you eternally heighten yourselves, striving eternally upward."

With the last page the essay reverts to the autobiographical mode in
which it opened. As Nietzsche sits in the bedroom of his home in Naumburg, an early summer evening turns to twilight. The voices of children in
the streets are heard, and in the distance the noise and music of a fair. People

are dancing; wild animals growl. From outside the "eye of day" looks into the young writer's heart, who longs for it to look deeper—

> into the very core of this heart which, hotter than the light, more dusky than the evening, more excited than the voices from the distance, deep within trembles and vibrates, like a great bell being sounded for a thunderstorm.
>
> And I implore a thunderstorm; doesn't the tolling of the bell attract the lightning? Now, you approaching thunderstorm, clarify, purify, blow fragrances of rain into my dull nature; welcome, finally welcome![49]

Here is a call for a breaching of the boundaries between human physiology and physical nature, an invitation for atmospheric phenomena to suffuse the realm of the psychical. A bolt of lightning obliges by striking to the center of the entreater's heart.

> Heavy sultriness; my heart swells. Nothing moves. There—a light breath, on the ground the grass trembles—welcome, rain, soother, my savior! It is barren here, empty, dead: come plant anew.[50]

A second flash pierces the speaker's heart, splitting it asunder and exposing it to the elements. The storm comes, and the rain. And then a third bolt of lightning:

> Right through the middle of my heart. Rain and storm! Thunder and lightning! Right through the middle! And a voice rang out: "Become new!" (S 3:115–16)

One person—or divine personage—who was brought to new life out of a bolt of lightning was Dionysus, god of the sap and moisture that nourishes all life, both physical and psychical, and through whom we may participate in the deeper processes of the natural world. The speaker's heart is an earth, his soul a soil, thirsty for the rain that will penetrate and fecundate it; the mood is receptive, open to the elements, and expectant of fructification. We shall soon see such imagery proliferate and flourish.

Let us sum up what has been learned from the autobiographical musings of the young Nietzsche. We are given a picture of a sensitive soul, rendered reflective and somewhat morbid by the premature deaths of his father and other members of his immediate family. There is a consequent fascination with fate, as well as with the corresponding inner drives of the individual soul as they work outward into the world. As the distinction between inner and outer is put into question, so is the primacy of consciousness over the unconscious. There is a progressive loss of faith in the Christian God, and hints of a reversion to the powers of Greek polytheism in signs of the god

Dionysus. There is a radical hylozoism, or panpsychism, as manifested in a penchant for psychological discourse couched in metaphors drawn from natural phenomena—weather, soil, vegetation, and so on. There is the idea of the soul as household (and, on a larger scale, as *polis*), which in turn raises the issue of the various possible relationships among its inhabitants. There are also anticipations of the complex (and much misunderstood) idea of will to power.

Schopenhauer and Wagner

> *God offers to every mind its choice between truth and repose.*
> *Take which you please—you can never have both. Between*
> *these, as a pendulum, man oscillates.*
> Emerson, "Intellect"

Although Nietzsche had decided to study classical philology, pressure from his family forced him to matriculate in theology at the University of Bonn. His subsequent switch to classics caused considerable consternation at home, and his sister Elisabeth wrote at once to convey the family's displeasure. Nietzsche wrote back in June of 1865 with an expression of his disregard for faith:

> Are we searching in our explorations for peace and quiet and happiness? No, only for the truth, however terrifying and ugly it may be. . . . Here the ways of human beings divide: if you want peace of soul and happiness, then believe; if you wish to be a disciple of truth, then search.[51]

Emerson had expressed in his essay "Intellect" a similar sentiment in images (following the epigraph above) that provide the perfect motto for the subsequent direction of Nietzsche's intellectual quest:

> He in whom the love of repose dominates will accept the first creed, the first philosophy, the first political party he meets—most likely his father's. He gets rest, commodity, and reputation; but he shuts the door of truth. He in whom the love of truth predominates will keep himself aloof from all moorings, and afloat. He will abstain from dogmatism, and recognize all the opposite negations between which, as walls, his being is swung. He submits to the inconvenience of suspense and imperfect opinion, but he is a candidate for truth, as the other is not, and respects the highest law of his being.

Nietzsche was somewhat disappointed by student life in Bonn, though this was more than compensated for by the excellence of two members of the classics faculty in particular: Otto Jahn and Friedrich Ritschl. But when Ritschl announced that he was going to take up a position at the University of Leipzig, Nietzsche decided (along with several other students) to follow him there. He also had an eye to studying and playing music in the culturally richer environment of the bigger city, which was, among other things, the birthplace of Richard Wagner. Ritschl was one of the most eminent philologists of the time, eccentric, genial, and an inspiring teacher. He became especially fond of Nietzsche and was highly impressed by the young student's written work. Nietzsche in turn enjoyed a magnificently supportive relationship with his mentor, who became a beneficent father figure for him, able to criticize constructively and with warm encouragement. A passage from a letter indicates that Nietzsche's misgivings concerning the academic profession were outweighed by his admiration for his teacher as a human being: "You can't believe how personally attached I am to Ritschl: I am quite unable—and unwilling—to tear myself away from him."[52]

Shortly after his arrival in Leipzig Nietzsche happened to be browsing in an antiquarian bookstore when he came upon the masterwork of the thinker who was to become his primary philosophical mentor, Schopenhauer's *The World as Will and Representation.*

> I picked up this totally unfamiliar book and began to leaf through it. I don't know what demon whispered to me: "Take this book home with you.". . . Once home, I threw myself onto the sofa with my new-found treasure and began to let that vigorously gloomy genius work its effects on me. . . . Here I saw a mirror in which I beheld the world, life, and my own soul in terrifying magnificence. Here I was subjected to the disinterested gaze of the solar eye of art; here I saw sickness and cure, banishment and sanctuary, heaven and hell. I was seized by a powerful need for self-knowing—and even for "self-gnawing" *[Selbstzernagung].* (S 3:133)

The initial immersion in Schopenhauer does tend to have a powerful impact.[53]

Nietzsche will have been especially pleased to find in Schopenhauer's opus a philosophical theory to explain the strong feelings of identification he had always felt with natural phenomena. Since the world of multiplicity is nothing more than the phenomenal aspect of the one underlying will, our inner nature as human beings, what animates and drives us, is constituted by the same forces that govern the rest of the natural world—the animal, vegetable, and mineral realms.

Schopenhauer speaks of the will as the "innermost being *[Wesen]* of the whole of nature":

> [The reader] will recognize that same will not only in those phenomena that are quite similar to his own, in human beings and animals, as their innermost nature, but continued reflection will lead him to recognize the force that drives and vegetates in the plant, indeed the force by which the crystal is formed, the force that turns the magnet to the North Pole . . . and finally even gravitation, which acts so powerfully in all matter, pulling the stone to the earth and the earth to the sun; all these he will recognize as being different only in the phenomenon, but the same according to their inner nature . . . [and] as that which is immediately known to him . . . [as] *will.*[54]

This idea, which is elaborated at length throughout Schopenhauer's masterwork, afforded Nietzsche an understanding of an important feature of his experience and became a key element in the development of his psychology. In particular, it encouraged him to keep thinking along lines that would eventually issue in the idea that not only all life but *the entire world* is will to power.

At the time he picked up Schopenhauer's book, almost as if by chance, the twenty-year-old student was making every attempt to break with his past and especially with the influence of his family, an attempt that—characteristically—took two opposing forms. On the one hand, he was leading an urbane social life in Leipzig, and as a theater reviewer for one of the major newspapers he was much in demand at receptions and dinner parties. But it was during this period, when Nietzsche threw himself into the vortex of social life as he never had before, and was more gregarious and sociable than ever after, that he may have discovered the true nature of the father-focused disaster he feared. Shortly after his mental collapse some twenty years later, a catastrophe punctuated by fits of lucidity, Nietzsche told his doctors that he had twice been treated for a syphilitic infection while in Leipzig.[55] This would not have been an uncommon condition for a student at that time and place to have been in, since visits to brothels were customary, if not *de rigeur,* in many student circles. (Nietzsche may have paid more than one visit to a whorehouse in Köln the previous year, while a student at Bonn.) If he did undergo such medical treatment at that time, since syphilis was considered incurable, the doctors may not have revealed their diagnosis to him. Though if he did not know, he may well have suspected. At any rate, the life of social engagements and hectic cultural activities steadily lost its appeal for Nietzsche after his student days in Leipzig.

On the other hand, perhaps in reaction, the attempt "to construct [for himself] a suitably authentic life" also took the form of sporadic bursts of ascetic self-discipline in solitude—a tendency much encouraged by his contact with the gloomy genius of Schopenhauer. Again this contact was personal rather than merely intellectual, as evidenced in the *Untimely Meditation* on Schopenhauer of six years later, which maintains a discreet silence about the philosopher's ideas (which Nietzsche had by that time repudiated) while remaining grandly enthusiastic about the man's personality and life. What Nietzsche admired so much about this mentor was the way he had continued to write and elaborate his philosophical system in the absence of any acknowledgment from the academic world—and indeed in the face of its undisguised contempt. Schopenhauer had survived in intellectual solitude, remaining true to his calling, and had in effect sacrificed his life to his philosophical task. These are two of Nietzsche's own most admirable traits, and he was acutely aware from the beginning of being Schopenhauer's heir in this respect. In a retrospective account of his discovery, Nietzsche compares Schopenhauer to Montaigne on the basis of a common integrity and serenity, and goes on to speak of the almost "physiological impression" that Schopenhauer first made on him: "that magical outpouring of the innermost power from one natural creature onto another . . . [from] a whole, harmonious, well balanced, unconstrained, and uninhibited natural being" (*SE* 2). But the young student had discovered only a book rather than a natural creature:

> I thus strove all the harder to see through the book and to imagine the living human being whose great testament I had to read, and who promised to make his heirs only those who would and could be more than merely his readers: namely his sons and pupils.

Nietzsche's biographers frequently remark that the early loss of his father prompted a continual search for father figures during his subsequent youth. It is less often noticed that Nietzsche himself remarks this phenomenon in his biographical reflections from 1868.[56] Noting that as a result of his father's premature death much of his upbringing and education was left to himself, he writes: "I lacked the strict guidance of a superior male intellect. When I went to Schulpforta as a boy, I became acquainted with a mere surrogate of a fatherly upbringing, in the form of the uniform discipline of a strictly ordered school" (S 3:151). He goes on to observe that the almost military degree of compulsion to conform with the group had the welcome effect of leading him back to himself as an individual.

The desire for *Selbstzernagung* by which Nietzsche was seized on his first encounter with his philosophical mentor shows the extent to which his conscience "gnawed" at him (in German one speaks of the "bite" of conscience rather than "pangs") for not living up to its high expectations of achievement in the discipline of ascesis. It became clear to him that if dis-

turbing tendencies continued to distract him from his task they would simply have to be cut off or "gnawed away." In psychoanalytical terms, one
would say that Nietzsche had by this time developed an extremely severe
"super-ego" (*Über-Ich*, "over-I"), that agent of conscience in the psyche
which oversees all one's actions.[57] Given the early death of his father, it is
not surprising that the voice of the son's conscience and the gaze of his
"over-I" should have been especially severe.

Around the time of Nietzsche's discovery of Schopenhauer another, quite
unusual voice is mentioned in a notebook entry that has puzzled biographers
because of its peculiarity with respect to the other notes from that period.
(Its uniqueness has prompted speculation as to whether other, similar notes
may have been suppressed by Elisabeth when she had the *Nachlass* in her
possession.) It reads as follows:

> What I'm afraid of is not the terrifying figure behind my chair, but its
> voice *[Stimme]*; not even its words, but the horrifyingly inarticulate
> and inhuman tone of that figure. If only it would speak as human
> beings speak! (S 3:148)

There is nowhere a hint of what this terrifying voice had to say, and in fact
the note suggests that whatever words the voice spoke did not constitute
much in the way of what philosophers nowadays call "propositional content." If Nietzsche was accustomed to hearing the sounds of wild parties
when eavesdropping on himself around the time he wrote "Über Stimmungen," it is not so surprising that he would hear inarticulate voices four
years later. And to judge from a number of passages in his later work, the
experience of hearing quite articulate "inner" voices was far from alien
to him.

Other voices became more audible to Nietzsche at this stage in his career,
as he began to initiate himself into the community of genius described by
Schopenhauer, whose members, towering like mountain peaks above the
rest of humanity, converse with one another across the mists of the ages.
Hearing the call of such lofty figures as Goethe, Schiller, Hölderlin, Heine,
and Schopenhauer himself (the irreverent might call them the Grand Teu-
tons), he aspired at this stage to escape the confines of his historical and
geographical milieu in order to ascend to the heights and join with that
exalted company.

Nietzsche's joy at finding an intellectual guide in the form of Schopenhauer
was compounded by his encountering, not long thereafter, a more broadly
cultural mentor in the vital, flesh and blood person of Richard Wagner. Up
to this point Nietzsche's tastes in music had been remarkably conventional:
he admired the great classical composers—Bach, Haydn, Mozart, Beetho-

ven, Schubert, and Mendelssohn—and was rather dismissive of the new music of Wagner and Liszt.[58] Once in Leipzig, however, his attitude began to change, as evidenced by a report in a letter to his friend Erwin Rohde about a concert where two of Wagner's works had been performed.

> I revitalized myself with both the Introduction to *Tristan und Isolde* and also the Overture to *Die Meistersinger von Nürnberg*. I cannot bring myself to be coolly critical toward this music: every fiber, every nerve in my body tingles, and I have not experienced in ages such a prolonged feeling of rapture as with the latter overture. (27 Oct 1868)

Two weeks after this stirring epiphany, Nietzsche received an unexpected invitation to the home of an orientalist professor at the University in order to meet Richard Wagner himself. The first encounter with the Master went superbly, to judge from Nietzsche's subsequent report to Rohde.[59] The twenty-four-year-old graduate student was quite overawed by the exuberant presence of the man—exactly his father's age—who was widely regarded as one of the greatest artists on the planet. Not only was Wagner a musician, he was also a dramatist and a poet. In addition, he was one of the very few great composers to have also been an intellectual of some standing, having authored a large number of treatises on music theory, as well as numerous essays on a wide range of other subjects.

Nietzsche was especially impressed by Wagner's before- and after-dinner performances on the piano, in which he played excerpts from *Die Meistersinger,* singing with gusto all the various voices himself in a protean procession of personalities. He was overjoyed to discover, in addition, that Wagner's favorite philosopher was Schopenhauer. Wagner was in turn impressed by his young admirer, and at the end of the evening he issued Nietzsche a warm invitation to visit him at his home near Luzern in Switzerland, so that they might continue their discussions about philosophy and music.

Luzern is far enough from Leipzig, and the journey in those days sufficiently long, that Nietzsche would have had no way of accepting this invitation had it not been for the following turn of fate. Ritschl had become so impressed by Nietzsche's abilities that when the chair in classical philology became vacant at the University of Basel, Ritschl recommended his protégé for the job. Nietzsche's first reaction was ambivalent. On the one hand, to be offered the equivalent of a full professorship at the age of twenty-four was an honor almost without precedent; and in addition the salary promised to alleviate his constant financial difficulties. On the other hand, since his discovery of Schopenhauer, he had felt more and more drawn to philosophy; and while he was grateful to philology for having instilled in him the intellectual discipline he had felt lacking, he had grave doubts about committing himself to a career in that traditionally narrow field. In fact he had resolved not to even consider an academic position until after granting himself some respite from the strictly disciplined life he had subjected himself to for so long. For some time he had been nurturing plans to spend at least a year in Paris with Rohde, during which they would alternate studying in the libraries and visiting museums with strolling the boulevards and frequenting outdoor cafés—"a pair of philosophical *flaneurs*."[60] Three months before his first meeting with Wagner, he had written to Rohde:

> Nothing must prevent us from spending a year in Paris together first. Afterwards, may it be granted to each of us to be at some university where we can strew various false doctrines into various "milk-sucking" souls. But beforehand we must learn the divine power of the Cancan and practice drinking "yellow poison," so that we may later march in the vanguard of civilization. (6 Aug 68)

One wonders what effect such a Dionysian curriculum would have had on Nietzsche's later career in "dancing with the pen."[61] But what surely tipped the balance away from this sybaritic sabbatical and in favor of taking the chair was the proximity of Basel to Wagner's home at Tribschen, which was located in an idyllic lakeside setting just a few hours' journey away.

Upon his arrival in Basel in April of 1869, Nietzsche did two things to try to resolve his ambivalence: he rented a grand piano for his lodgings and played it often, and he gave his inaugural lecture at the university. The lecture was remarkable in that it proposed a vision of the inauguratee's field of research as the discipline it *could be* rather than as it actually was. Speaking on the topic "Homer and Classical Philology"—or "The Personality of Homer"[62]—Nietzsche stood on the stage of the auditorium of the University Museum and projected his own personality onto the profession into which he was being inducted.

The new professor begins by remarking the "multifragmented" *(vielspältig)* nature of philology, its lack of conceptual or organic unity, its composite character consisting of tendencies and elements from aesthetics, ethics, history, and the science of nature.[63] The rhetoric was no doubt headier than the speeches that had resounded within the walls of the Museum Aula hitherto, and the philologists in the audience must have been disconcerted to hear their discipline referred to as "a magic potion brewed from the most exotic juices, metals, and bones." At the end of his introduction, the speaker offers an ideal summation of his raison d'être and that of his chosen profession, which he refers to as a "centaur":

> The total scientific-artistic movement of this singular centaur is directed—with monstrous power but cyclopic slowness—to the bridging of the gulf between ideal antiquity . . . and the real thing. And

classical philology thereby does nothing other than strive for the consummation of its ownmost being: namely, the growing together and unifying of the initially hostile drives that had been brought together only by force. (S 3:161)

A "centaur" in the figurative sense is "an unnatural hybrid creation; an intimate union of two diverse natures"—and a name Nietzsche will give to his first (and only) major work as a philologist. As applied to philology in the inaugural lecture it is in fact a modest image, insofar as that discipline is said to aspire to the synthesis of *several* diverse drives. The task is all the more formidable since some of the drives concerned emerge from the deepest layers of the collective psyche with the force of mighty rivers. Anticipating a theme in *The Birth of Tragedy,* Nietzsche speaks, for instance, of "a mysterious streaming forth, a profound artistic *folk-drive [Volkstrieb]* that manifests itself in the individual lyrist as an almost indifferent medium," and of "the Homeric poems as the expression of that mysteriously flowing drive" (S 3:166).

Having been grappling for some time with the problem of psychical multiplicity, Nietzsche here projects a vision of philology as a discipline that would resolve it. In retrospect one can see this less as a bold exercise in public wishful thinking (which it surely is) than as an enactment of what Nietzsche would later regard as the primary task of the philosopher—namely, to *legislate* (*BGE* 211). As the philosopher he was striving so hard to become, he is proclaiming through the persona of the professional philologist: "Classical philology *shall be* this! And as a member of that discipline I *will be* such-and-such a person!"

As a way of resolving the tension between the powerful attraction of art, and especially of music, and his desire for scientific rigor, Nietzsche goes on to imagine a rebirth of classics as a *musical* discipline by emphasizing the musical strains in the Greek poetic spirit, which have been muffled by the prejudices of older, more drily academic research into antiquity.

Philology is admittedly not the creator of that world, nor the composer of this immortal music; but surely it is a service, and a great one, even to be only a virtuoso and to let that music for the first time sound forth again, that music which for so long lay in a corner undeciphered and unappreciated. (S 3:173)

If the towering presence of Wagner was inhibiting Nietzsche's development as a composer, it would never detract from his abilities as a virtuoso pianist. He will in any case proceed to practice his new profession *as* music, and also (as announced in the closing sentences of the address) as philosophy.

Toward the end of his remarks, the young professor reverts to the vegetal imagery used earlier in talking of the "growing together of the initially hostile drives." Nietzsche's penchant for imagery of plant growth reflects his faith in what one might call "the wisdom of unconscious thought processes." The previous year, during a break from his studies at Leipzig occasioned by a period of compulsory military service, he had written to Erwin Rohde that his latest philological essay finally had "a philosophical background." "Moreover," he continues, "without my intending it, but precisely on that account to my great delight, all my works are taking quite a definite direction."[64] The counterpart to Nietzsche's self-imposed task of disciplining the various drives that dissipate his energies into dilettantism is a trust that some of this inner chaos will work itself out without his conscious intervention. This is the trust of the cultivator that what goes on beneath the surface of the soil will turn out best when it is not interfered with from above. The vegetal imagery at the conclusion of the inaugural address issues in a final flourish of utopian phantasy:

> One senses everywhere that philologists have lived together for almost a century with poets, thinkers, and artists. And this is why the pile of ashes and cinders that one formerly considered classical antiquity to be has now become fruitful and even fecund farmland. (S 3:173)

Nietzsche was soon to realize that the field of philology was not nearly as fertile, nor the discipline as musical, as he hoped it could be made. But fortunately, the fact that his first forays into philosophical legislation failed did not deter him from future attempts.

After his move to Basel, Nietzsche began to lead a distinctly double life. As a professor of classics at a small but venerable university in conservative Switzerland, he enjoyed the teaching and was by all accounts a gifted and charismatic teacher, but he found the social life he was forced to lead somewhat suffocating.[65] On the other hand, Basel—a city with a rich cultural heritage, situated on the borders between Switzerland, Germany, and France—was far more cosmopolitan than anywhere he had lived so far. It turned out that Wagner was keen to enlist the young professor in his cause, which lacked academic respectability, and so he extended an open invitation to Nietzsche to visit Tribschen whenever he pleased. This enabled the young classicist to escape from Basel on long weekends and holidays and take refuge in the Wagners' house on the lake. A remark in a letter from the period gives an indication of his attitude toward the two sides of his life: "These days I have spent at Tribschen this summer are absolutely the most valuable result of my professorship at Basel."[66]

The atmosphere at Tribschen could not have been more different from the ambiance of Basel. Wagner was living "in sin" with Cosima von Bülow, a daughter of Franz Liszt (whose acquaintance Nietzsche also made around this time). Although Cosima was still married to the conductor Hans von Bülow, she had already borne Wagner two daughters; and Wagner's son by her, Siegfried, came into the world—quite auspiciously—on the first evening of Nietzsche's second visit. Nietzsche was blissfully happy at being welcomed into this Bohemian ménage, through which there flowed a steady stream of visitors—musicians and writers mainly—from all over Europe. The place was a source of intellectual as well as cultural stimulation, insofar as both Wagner and Cosima were highly intelligent, if somewhat dogmatic, minds. Wagner liked to think himself an expert on the ancient Greeks, and saw himself as the modern epigone of Aeschylus and destined to bring about the cultural rebirth of Germany—and thereby of Europe and the world. Nietzsche was overjoyed to be invited to participate in this grand artistic enterprise as its philosopher-spokesman.

It was in this rich and duplex medium that the ideas for Nietzsche's first book began to germinate. In Basel he had as colleagues two of the greatest historians of the time: J. J. Bachofen, who had been one of the first to explore the ideas of the Dionysian and to write about ancient matriarchies, and Jacob Burckhardt, a historian of art and culture, best known for his classic work on the Italian Renaissance. In Tribschen, where he was given a room on the third floor to use as his study, Nietzsche was able to witness at first hand the towering genius of Wagner as he worked on *Der Ring des Nibelungen,* and at the same time to enjoy the admiration and inspiration of Cosima, whom he was to revere until the end of his life. Although Burckhardt came rather quickly to appreciate Nietzsche's genius, there was no comparison between the receptions accorded his ideas in the two places: the public lectures Nietzsche gave in Basel on Greek tragedy were greeted with "horror and incomprehension," while his surrogate family in Tribschen constantly urged him to make his various essays on the topic into a book.[67]

The strain of living two lives was beginning to tell, insofar as Nietzsche was finding it more and more difficult to perform the social functions expected of a professor at the University of Basel. He wrote to Rohde, whose company he was sorely missing, that he (Rohde) was prudent not to take a position at a small university (like Basel) where it is not possible simply "to withdraw into one's own work."[68]

> But the most burdensome thing is that I always have to be representing myself—as a teacher, as a philologist, as a human being—and that I have to prove myself to everyone with whom I come into contact. I am so very bad at doing that, and am becoming worse and worse at it.

Even if Nietzsche had been able to withdraw from social contacts and immerse himself in his work, the tensions would hardly have been reduced—insofar as the work with which he was engaged at the time was itself profoundly duplex. His attempts to eradicate tendencies toward dilletantism by submitting to the rigorous discipline of philology had been only partially successful. One of his teachers at Bonn had been Otto Jahn, who was on the classics faculty but was better known as a musicologist and biographer of Mozart, and some of Nietzsche's motives for moving to Leipzig were clearly musical. He never ceased entertaining phantasies of music as a career, and these seem to have been encouraged (at least at first) rather than blighted by the proximity of Wagner. Some time before, Nietzsche had resolved to try to modulate his writing into a more musical mode:

> I lived for too long in stylistic innocence. . . . I sought to write well . . . Above all some cheerful spirits need to be liberated in my style, on which I can learn to play as on a piano—not only pieces learned by heart but also free improvisations *[Phantasieen]*, as free as possible, yet always logical as well as beautiful.[69]

There were now signs that this resolve was beginning to be effected, insofar as he wrote to Rohde in 1870: "Scholarship, art, and philosophy are growing together in me to such an extent that some day I shall certainly give birth to centaurs."[70]

An unexpected incursion into Nietzsche's life in Basel was the outbreak of the Franco-Prussian War. He had given up his German citizenship in order to take up the professorship; but when France declared war on Prussia in July of 1870, he felt it his duty to enlist—though the university granted him leave to do so only as a medical orderly. His service was cut short by his contracting diphtheria and dysentery after spending three days and nights in a cattle wagon tending to severely wounded soldiers.[71] While Nietzsche's physical constitution was in general strong, he had been plagued by migraine-type headaches since his schooldays at Schulpforta; this brief experience of war would deal a blow to his system from which it would never fully recover. But he was also aware that his ever-worsening health, which was beginning to render him incapable of teaching for several days at a time, had another etiology connected with the tensions being generated by his professional life.

In early 1871 the chair of philosophy at the University of Basel was about to become vacant, and Nietzsche asked to be considered a candidate. In a letter to his superior, Wilhelm Vischer-Bilfinger, he cites the tension between his desire to be a philosopher and his position as a philologist as the major cause of his worsening health.

I live here in a peculiar conflict, and it is this that is exhausting me so much and is grating on me even physically. . . . I feel that my real task [*Aufgabe*], my *philosophical* task, to which in case of emergency I would *have to sacrifice any profession,* is suffering and being reduced to a side-activity. . . . Should they recur more frequently, [the sufferings I am now undergoing] will force me physically to give up the philological profession altogether. (January 1871)

Nietzsche's application for the chair was not successful. Not only did he lack formal training in philosophy, but he had made no secret of his enthusiasm for Schopenhauer, who was not regarded by the academic establishment as a real philosopher. Thanks to his being trapped in the wrong discipline, the tensions would continue to heighten.

II

The Melodic Centaur (1870–1872)

> _The thought of genius is spontaneous; but the power of picture_
> _or expression, in the most enriched and flowing nature, implies_
> _a mixture of will, a certain control over the spontaneous states,_
> _without which no production is possible. . . . The imaginative_
> _vocabulary . . . does not flow from experience only or mainly,_
> _but from a richer source._
>
> Emerson, "Intellect"

The centaur that Nietzsche was to bring into the world in 1872 under the
title _The Birth of Tragedy_ was composed in the main of three parts conceived earlier and delivered in 1870: the public lectures "The Greek Music-
Drama" and "Socrates and Tragedy," and the essay "The Dionysian
Worldview."[1] Whereas he had formerly envisaged classical philology as a
rigorous science in the pursuit of which one would not need "to take the
results to heart," Nietzsche now found that his attitude toward the ancient
Greeks was far from "coolly scientific." In a letter to Rohde from February
1870 he writes: "I find that I am coming to love Hellenism more and more:
there is no better way of approaching it than through tireless development
of one's own person." We are thus to take what Nietzsche says about the
Greeks and their drama not only as scholarship but also on a personal level
(both his and ours).

We saw from Nietzsche's letters from this period that he was feeling
constrained by the social world of Basel to play a role that had not formerly
been required of him. But it was not only in Basel that Nietzsche felt compelled to represent himself: blissfully happy as his stays at the Wagners'
house in Tribschen were, they were not without strain. Intellectually, he had
been finding himself growing away from his old mentor Schopenhauer,
while his new mentor Wagner had lost none of his enthusiasm for the
thinker they called "our philosopher." So Nietzsche also found himself drifting away from Wagner intellectually; yet because of his love of the man's
art and his desire to contribute to the Master's cause, which was sustained

by the genuine enthusiasm Wagner and Cosima entertained for their young friend's ideas, he felt constrained to keep this drift a secret.

This circumstance accounts for some of the strangeness of *The Birth of Tragedy:* it was in part an extended application of Schopenhauer's ideas to the problem of Greek tragedy and in part a piece of propaganda for Wagner's cultural revolution; yet its author was already entertaining grave doubts about the intellectual integrity of these two influences. In view of this distance between his self and his representations of it, Nietzsche's meditations upon the dual themes of ancient Greek drama and modern opera had two separate bases, in personal as well as academic concerns. A letter to Rohde written shortly after *The Birth of Tragedy* was published shows how difficult the book was for Nietzsche to write and why.

> Nobody has any idea of the way a book like this comes into being, of the trouble and torment it takes to keep oneself this clear in the face of so many *other* ideas pressing in from all sides . . . and perhaps least of all of my enormous task vis-à-vis Wagner, which has certainly been the cause of many heavy clouds in my heart—the task of being independent even here, of adopting an alienated stance, as it were.[2]

Labor before *The Birth*

"The Greek Music-Drama" begins with an excoriation of modern opera (with an unstated qualification: up to, but not including, the work of Wagner) for its superficiality. It has developed artificially, "without the unconscious force of a natural drive [and] according to an abstract theory."[3] Indeed the development of all the modern arts has been retarded by "conscious knowledge": "all growth and becoming in the realm of art must take place in the depth of night." Nietzsche's criticisms in this period of the hypertrophy of cool, conscious rationality (soon to be associated with the figure of Socrates), as opposed to the deep, dark wellsprings of the creative unconscious, are very much in line with late Romanticist thinking about the creative process. But the more immediate influence is Schopenhauer—as embodied and enlivened in the person of Wagner—and his ideas on music in *The World as Will and Representation.*

> The invention of melody, the disclosure in it of all the deepest secrets of human willing and feeling, is the work of genius . . . far removed from all reflection and conscious intention, and might be called inspiration. Here, as everywhere in art, the concept is unfruitful. The composer reveals the innermost nature of the world, and expresses the

profoundest wisdom in a language that his reasoning faculty does not understand, just as a magnetic somnambulist gives information about things of which she has no conception when awake. (*WWR* 1:52)

Of interest is the reference to "the magnetic somnambulist" (nowadays called the hypnotized subject, or medium) and her gender, since such figures will play an important role in the development of the idea of the multiple psyche.[4]

Nietzsche goes on to argue that, as a result of conscious, eclectic experimentation on the part of modern composers of opera, "the roots of an unconscious art growing out of the life of the folk are cut off or at least badly mutilated." In Germany, "the natural root of the drama is the Fastnacht play," but this has been obscured by the fashion of taking over "ready-made models from foreign nations."[5] The roots metaphors and xenophobic tone come from Wagner, many of whose writings Nietzsche was reading at this time. A brief note from the autumn of 1869, the first year he was in Basel, had characterized "the root of drama" as "the excited, ecstatic carnival mood *[Faschingslaune]*."[6] Basel was—and still is—famous for its Fastnacht carnival at Lent, a remarkably Dionysiac affair (by contrast with the normal tenor of life there) involving frenzied drumming and masquerading in extravagant costumes. One would like to imagine Nietzsche's being inspired to think and write about the significance of Dionysiac festivals by firsthand experience of Fastnacht, but the festival would have been over by the time he first arrived in Basel in mid-April. Nor is there evidence that he was ever present at the Fastnacht carnival during his ten years there.[7] Presumably his sense of the carnival mood came from his reading, and perhaps also from hearsay—with elaboration by vivid imagination. At any rate, the locale of Basel was appropriate for entertaining thoughts of the Dionysian.

The essay on the Greek music-drama goes on to argue that because modern art lacks a sound root in the unconscious, it is subject to a quite un-Dionysian dismemberment that conduces in turn to an unwholesome fragmentation in its audience. "We are no longer able to enjoy [art] as whole human beings: it is as if we are torn into pieces by the absolute arts and so only enjoy fragmentarily, now as ear-people, now as eye-people, and so on."[8] By contrast, the constitution of the Athenian theatergoer was more robust, thanks to his soul's having in it "something of that element out of which tragedy was born"—namely, "the overpoweringly explosive spring-drive *[Frühlingstrieb]*," the "rush" of intoxicated ecstasy that characterizes the cult of Dionysus.[9] There is good reason to think that when Nietzsche speaks of this spring-drive it is from the feeling of being himself in the spring of his life. Enthusiastic encouragement from such mentors as Ritschl and Wagner, and external validation in the form of the Basel professorship combined to produce in the twenty-five-year-old scholar a vernal surge in his creative powers, the like of which he would never feel again.[10]

Nietzsche suggests that the modern "Fastnacht plays and masquerades were originally spring festivals," and posits the same Dionysian drive behind the Saint John's and Saint Vitus's dancing manias of the Middle Ages, as well as similar epidemics of spring fever festivals in ancient Greece. To take such outbreaks of collective mania as "the cradle of the drama" affords a different perspective on the nature of dramatic mimesis, on what it means to "play a part." Nietzsche denies that the drama achieves its effect through someone's disguising himself so as "to stimulate an illusion in others." Rather,

> the person is outside himself and believes himself to be transformed and enchanted. In the condition of "being-outside-oneself," of ecstasy, only one step more is necessary: we do not return to ourselves, but enter into another being, so that we behave as people under a spell. That accounts ultimately for the deep amazement on seeing the drama: the ground wavers, the belief in the indissolubility and rigidity of the individual. And just as the Dionysiac enthusiast believes in his own transfiguration . . . so the dramatic poet believes in his own figures. (*KSA* 1:521–22)

These remarks are not based on Nietzsche's attending performances of Greek tragedy; insofar as they stem from his experience of "the Greek music-drama" the drama was played out in his imagination while reading the texts in the original. His actual experience of music-drama around this time came from performances of Wagner's operas, and in particular *Die Meistersinger,* which he went to twice in 1869.

On first hearing just the overture to this opera the previous year, Nietzsche had claimed not to have "experienced in ages such a prolonged feeling of rapture." And on his first meeting with Wagner, the latter had played "all the important passages on the piano, imitating all the voices in a most exuberant manner."[11] Here was Nietzsche's hero, in person, entering into other beings as if under a spell, living counter-evidence of the indissolubility of the individual.[12] In a letter to Rohde, he calls one of the performances of *Die Meistersinger,* conducted by Hans von Bülow in Dresden, "the greatest artistic rapture this past winter has brought me":

> God knows, I must after all have a good bit of the musician in my body, for throughout the performance I had the strongest feeling of being suddenly at home and in familiar surroundings, and my former doings seemed like a far-off mist from which I was now redeemed.[13]

On the way from his home in Naumburg to take up the chair in Basel, Nietzsche had made a detour to Karlsruhe to attend another performance: "I refreshed myself that evening with a superb performance of this my favorite opera. It was my farewell to the land of Germany."[14] *Die Meistersinger* is hardly a tragedy, but one can imagine its theme of unconventional genius triumphing over ultraconservative mediocrity holding natural attraction for Nietzsche on the brink of a new career. The music's appeal to the musician in him would have contributed to the realization that he also had "a good bit of [Hans Sachs in his] body" too. For all the talk of *Tristan und Isolde* as the ultimate in Dionysian music, Nietzsche did not actually attend a full performance of that work until after the manuscript of *The Birth of Tragedy* had been sent to the printers.[15]

There is an interesting passage concerning Dionysiac enthusiasm in a longish fragment dating from the spring of 1871. After a discussion of the last, choral movement of Beethoven's Ninth Symphony, which he claims is paradigmatic of choral music insofar as "the content of the words is drowned *[untergeht]* in the general sea of sound," Nietzsche goes on to argue that the lyric artist creates without regard for an audience.

> The person subject to Dionysiac excitement no more has a *listener* to communicate something to than does the orgiastic crowd. . . . It lies rather in the essence of Dionysian art that it knows no regard for the listener: the inspired follower of Dionysus is . . . understood only by his peers. And if we imagine a listener for those endemic outbreaks of Dionysiac excitement, we would have to predict for him the fate suffered by Pentheus [in the *Bacchae*], who was discovered eaves-dropping: namely, to be torn apart by the Maenads.[16]

As evidenced by the phenomenon of Saint Vitus's dance, the Dionysiac mood is nothing if not infectious. What would hold things together in Greek drama was the original satyr chorus: "Although a multiplicity of persons, musically it does not represent a mass of people, but only an enormous individual being endowed with supernatural lungs."[17] However, as a member of the audience at a modern performance of Dionysian music one might well find oneself dis-membered by the tonality and overwhelmed by a sea of sound.

With the background set, we can turn to the centauric text Nietzsche sent to the publisher in 1872, *The Birth of Tragedy out of the Spirit of Music.*

Dionysian and Apollonian Drives

Nietzsche's first book presents itself, in spite of the preface dedicated to Richard Wagner, as a serious though innovative work in the field of classical studies—while at the same time being an act of near-insanity, professionally speaking, on the part of the young professor who published it. At that time it was unheard of for a scholarly book to be published, as *The Birth of Tragedy* was, without footnotes. Indeed this monstrous hybrid, in practicing philology as philosophy and philosophy as music and drama, subverts altogether the compartmentalization of academic studies that was becoming firmly established in the late nineteenth century. While Nietzsche remarks the specifically psychological nature of the text only in retrospect, he does so both in the "Attempt at a Self-Criticism" which he added to the new edition of 1886 and in the later commentary in *Ecce Homo*.

The retrospectively prefatory remarks of 1886 describe *The Birth of Tragedy* as "a book full of psychological innovations," and characterize the origin of tragedy in the Greeks as "a difficult psychological question" (§§2, 4). In calling the text "image-mad and image-confused" (§3) Nietzsche is being uncharacteristically modest; but the imagistic mode of presentation turns out to be distinctive and definitive of the subsequent elaboration of his psychological ideas. He goes on to ask in this preface whether madness may be something other than "a symptom of degeneration and decline" (§4)— his reference to this as "a question for psychiatrists" bespeaking a terrible irony, insofar as it was the question farthest from the minds of the psychiatrists into whose supervision he was remanded less than three years later.

In 1888, close to the brink, Nietzsche reiterates that the book offers "a psychological analysis" of the Dionysian phenomenon among the Greeks (*EH*, "BT" 1). But at the same time he allows that his comprehension of "the wonderful phenomenon of the Dionysian" grew out of his discovering "the only parable and parallel in history for [his] own inmost experience," complimenting himself (more characteristically, now) on "the sureness of [his] psychological grasp." He goes even further by saying that the entire book—just like the essay *Richard Wagner in Bayreuth,* written four years after *The Birth of Tragedy*—is about his own psychology: "In all psychologically decisive places I alone am discussed" (*EH*, "BT" 4). So when reference is made to Apollo, or Dionysus, Socrates, the actor, or the satyr chorus, Nietzsche is speaking primarily of himself. We can thus take this first book as presenting in more than one sense the psychology of its author, while masquerading as a study in classics in the guise of a philosophy of art and music.

Nietzsche begins the book by introducing the Apollonian and Dionysian as two radically opposed *drives* (*BT* 1). A significant prefiguration here is Schiller's idea that beauty is generated by the "play-drive" *(Spieltrieb)* which comes from the interaction of the two basic human drives, the "form-drive" and the "sense-drive."[18] The imagery of Nietzsche's first paragraph is predominantly sexual: in the opening sentence the interplay of the Apollonian and the Dionysian in the production of art is likened to the duality of the sexes that enables procreation, and the paragraph ends with the statement that the "coupling" of the two drives eventually generated Attic tragedy—the "birth" of the book's title. Given that Apollo and Dionysus are both male, the image of a birth's resulting from their coupling seems unnecessarily perverse. It is more comprehensible when one considers that while Apollo is the epitome of masculinity, Dionysus is somewhat feminine. Not only is the cult of Dionysus composed almost exclusively of women, but the feminine traits that are combined with his phallic nature suggest an inherent bisexuality.[19] Nietzsche would have been familiar with the relevant ancient sources—and also with the distinction made by his colleague Bachofen, who in his book on mother right *(Mutterrecht)* calls Apollo "the advocate of father right" and Dionysus "primarily the god of women [in whom] all aspects of female nature find satisfaction."[20]

It is also significant that after introducing the interplay of the two drives, Nietzsche immediately begins talking about "the separate art-worlds of the *dream* and *intoxication*" as "physiological phenomena." What started out by promising a discussion of aesthetics turns immediately into a treatment of the "art-drives of nature" *(Kunsttriebe der Natur)*—itself a very telling expression.[21] It is clear that the author is not operating with the traditional divisions between the realms of human being and of nature, insofar as the motive forces for art are understood as being basically natural (as opposed to artificial or cultural) and the dynamism of nature is understood as manifesting itself (at least in part) in "*art*-drives."

In view of Nietzsche's existential approach toward historical scholarship, the ancient Greek understanding of human being presented in *The Birth of Tragedy* will still be accessible, *mutatis mutandis,* to the modern psyche. In discussing the interplay between the Apollonian and Dionysian drives, he broaches two major topics in his psychology: the dream and productive phantasy on the one hand, and the dissolution of the individual self on the other. Nietzsche distinguishes between the Apollonian and the Dionysian in terms of their being patrons of different kinds of arts practiced by the Greeks, Apollo being associated with sculpture and Dionysus with music. The difference hinges upon the role of images *(Bilder)* in each: the German text contrasts "the art of the sculptor *[Bildner]*" with "the nonimagistic *[unbildlich]* art of music," underlying which are "the art-worlds of the dream and intoxication *[Traum und Rausch]*"—themselves products of the "art-drives of nature." While Nietzsche does not make the point explicitly here, there is an implication—important for his later psychology—that these drives not only have worlds underlying them but are also actually *productive* of worlds. His presentation of the interplay between the Apollonian and Dionysian drives naturally alternates between the two; but to look first at the way he presents the Dionysian drive (which has to do with the very boundaries of the individual self) will help us to see more clearly the duality inherent in the phenomenon, and how this duality naturally issues in a multiplicity.[22]

The Dionysian drive dissolves the boundaries of the individual self in two ways: it breaks down the barriers separating it from other human selves, leading to a feeling of oneness with the social group or—by extension—with the human race; and it also dissolves the boundaries between the individual human and the world of nature, conducing to a sense of unity with the cosmos. The discussion of the Dionysian begins with a reference to Schopenhauer and quickly establishes the duplex nature of the phenomenon. After quoting *The World as Will and Representation* (1:63) on the *principium individuationis* and relating this principle to the figure of Apollo, Nietzsche goes on to say that in the same work there is depicted

> the tremendous *terror* that grips the human being when he suddenly loses faith in the cognitive forms of phenomena as a result of the principle of sufficient reason's seeming to undergo an exception in one of its manifestations. (*BT* 1)

The argument here is not as clear as it might have been, insofar as his close paraphrase substitutes "the cognitive forms of phenomena" for Schopenhauer's "*principium individuationis*." The passage from *The World as Will and Representation* asserts that the faith in our individuality is shaken by chance occurrences of the following kind: "whenever it seems that some change has taken place without a cause, or that a deceased person has come back again, or that in any other way the past or future has become present or the far has become near."[23] Schopenhauer explains the strangeness of such experiences by saying that they give us a momentary intimation of our fundamental identity with the primordial will, that "boundless world, full of suffering everywhere, throughout an infinite past and an infinite future." For there lies concealed in the depths of the awareness of every individual "the wholly obscure presentiment that all that [boundless world of will] is not really so foreign to him after all, but rather has a connection with him from which the *principium individuationis* cannot protect him."

The counterpart to "the ineradicable terror" occasioned by the breakdown of the *principium individuationis* is the serene bliss that supervenes, according to Schopenhauer, upon the total *extinction* of the will through asceticism. While the influence of this "gloomy genius" on Nietzsche's first book is strong, the response is ambivalent and there are some important divergences. For Nietzsche the annihilation of the sense of individuality itself has a blissful aspect—but that has nothing to do with ascetic extinction of the will.

> If we add to this terror the blissful rapture that arises from the innermost ground of human being and of nature itself at the same shat-

tering of the *principium individuationis,* we are then looking into the
essence of the *Dionysian,* which is brought home to us most closely
in the analogy of intoxication.

The Dionysian *Rausch,* whether engendered by the advent of spring or by
the "narcotic draught," causes all subjectivity to fall into forgetfulness, resulting in a reunion of the previously encapsulated self with the whole of
humanity and nature. If one can transform the final movement of Beethoven's Ninth Symphony into a painting, Nietzsche suggests, one will approach the Dionysian. (We shall return to consider some further consequences of this shattering of the *principium individuationis* in chapter 8,
below.)

The ecstasy of the Dionysiac experience also produces works of art; it is
not, hower, the human being but rather "the artistic power of all nature" that
is here responsible for the production. As this natural power plays through
the human being "in song and dance," there issues "something supernatural" that makes the human medium "feel like a god." Along with the reunion
of the individual with the race and with the world of nature in the Dionysiac
experience, there goes something akin to divine possession which lifts the
experiencer beyond the natural and human realms altogether.

In the second section of the book, Nietzsche gives a historical account
of the way Dionysian forces flowed into Greece from Asia Minor but were
for a time resisted with the help of the Delphic God, Apollo. After a while,
however, "similar drives [to the Dionysian] burst forth from the deepest
roots of the Hellenic nature," forcing an accommodation between the powers of Apollo and Dionysus. This reconciliation depotentiated the "horrible
[combination of] sensuality and cruelty" characteristic of the barbarian festivals of Dionysus, but did not nullify "the strange mixture and double nature of the affects of the Dionysian revelers" even in Greece. In referring to
this double nature of the Dionysian affect as "the phenomenon that pain
gives rise to pleasure and jubilation wrings from us sounds of agony,"
Nietzsche broaches an issue that will concern him for some time to come.
By way of an initial explanation, he remarks that in the Greek festivals it is
as if nature herself "has to heave a sigh over her dismemberment *[Zerstück-
elung]* into individuals"—an allusion to the infant Dionysus, who (as Zagreus) was torn to pieces at the hands of the Titans.

The talk of dismemberment echoes Schiller's concern with a pernicious
fragmentation of individuals that he sees as characteristic of the modern
age. In the sixth letter of the *On the Aesthetic Education of Man* (1795),
Schiller compares the modern individual unfavorably with the ancient
Greek, who—in spite of having a highly developed rational intellect—was
able to remain a total human being. In the modern state, the "mechanical

life" of which is produced by the "piecing together of an infinite number of lifeless parts," the individual is "eternally chained to only a single small fragment of the whole," and thus develops himself "only as a fragment." While this fragmentation is a tragedy for the individual, however, humanity as a whole actually thrives on it: "As little as the individuals derive benefit from this dismemberment of their being, the race as a whole could not have made progress in any other way." It is Schiller's "Ode to Joy" that is the text for the final movement of the Ninth Symphony, that epitome of Dionysian music and art.

The image of dismemberment and fragmentation is deeply inherent in the *Zeitgeist* at the turn of the eighteenth to the nineteenth century, and pertains to the duplex problem of ordering the multiplicity of the self and integrating it into society. Hölderlin elaborates the image with special reference to his countrymen, when he has Hyperion say:

> I can think of no people more disintegrated than the Germans. You see craftsmen but no human beings, thinkers but no human beings, priests but no human beings, masters and slaves, young people and adults, but no human beings—is it not like a battlefield, where hands and arms and limbs lie everywhere dismembered, while the life-blood flows from them into the sand? (*Hyp.* 2.2.7)

Hölderlin is here claiming that any solution to the problem of psychical multiplicity that would simply have the person identify with the one power associated with his job or profession is necessarily impoverishing. Emerson expresses the same sentiment in a similar figure a few decades later in his address "The American Scholar":

> The state of society is one in which the members have suffered amputation from the trunk, and strut about so many walking monsters—a good finger, a neck, a stomach, an elbow, but never a man. Man is thus metamorphosed into a thing, into many things.

These two images occur together in the chapter of *Zarathustra* entitled "On Redemption," where Zarathustra speaks to a hunchback with disgust of what he calls "inverse cripples"—"human beings who are nothing more than a large eye, or a large mouth, or a large stomach, or something else large" (Z 2.20). He then turns to his disciples and says:

> Verily, my friends, I wander among men as among fragments and limbs of human beings!
> That is what is so dreadful in my eyes, that I find man in ruins and scattered as over a battlefield or butcherfield.
> And should my eye flee from the present to the past, it finds always

the same thing: fragments and limbs and terrible accidents—but no human beings!

Later in *The Birth of Tragedy* the theme of dismemberment recurs as "the genuinely Dionysian *suffering*" and "a transformation into air, water, earth, and fire" (*BT* 10). Here is a mythical image of the experience Nietzsche had known since boyhood, the philosophical ground of which he had seen Schopenhauer disclose: the dissolution of the individual self into the basic elements of nature. The Dionysian dismemberment thus operates in two directions: an original unity is dismembered into the multiplicity of phenomena, and the unity of the individual is dissolved into the multiplicity of the world of nature—yet in a move back toward original oneness.[24]

There is another kind of union that goes along with the dismemberment of Dionysus, insofar as the Titans go on to devour the infant after tearing him limb from limb. They literally "incorporate" the devoured deity. The followers of Dionysus may be regarded as reenacting this episode: not only do the Maenads in the *Bacchae* suckle young gazelles and wolves, they also manifest the wilder side of their patron deity by falling upon calves and goats, clawing them to pieces, and devouring them. The interplay of the motifs of dismemberment and reunion and dismemberment and incorporation serve to subvert in several senses the identity of the individual self.[25] The full nature of the multiplicity consequent upon the Dionysian dissolution is made apparent only after Nietzsche's text has brought the Apollonian and Dionysian drives together. After the turn of Apollo we shall revert to Dionysus and his attendant multiplicity.

In the opening section of the book, Nietzsche writes that Apollo, as patron of the plastic arts, presides over

> the beautiful sheen *[der schöne Schein]* of the dream-worlds, in the production of which every human being is an artist [and which] is the prerequisite of all plastic *[bildend]* art. . . . [In the dream] all forms speak to us, there is nothing unimportant or unnecessary.[26]

Philosophers have generally not had much to say about dreams, and what little they have said has usually been derogatory. (Emerson is an exception, as evidenced by this Apollonian comment from the essay "Intellect": "We may owe to dreams some light on the fountain of this [graphic] skill; for as soon as we let our will go and let the unconscious states ensue, see what cunning draughtsmen we are!") Nietzsche's later appreciation of the interplay between the dream-world and the day-world is prefigured in his characterization—influenced by Schopenhauer and Wagner—of the role played by dreams in the psyche of "the artistically excitable human being." Such a person "looks closely and with pleasure at [the actuality of the dream]: for he interprets his life from these images and in these processes he practices for life." In keeping with the Romanticist view of the dream as a manifestation of the soul of the world (what Freud and Jung will call the unconscious), Nietzsche observes that "our innermost being, the deep common ground of us all, experiences dreams with profound pleasure and joyous necessity."[27] The affirmation of the role played by dreams in the "great economy" of the psyche is one of the major contributions of Nietzsche's mature psychology.[28]

Emblematic of the individual's experience of this common ground in the images of the dream is the figure of Apollo, "the God of all artistic *[bildnerischen]* forces." More generally, Apollo is—as the etymology of the name Phoebus suggests—"the shining one *[der Scheinende]*, the deity of light," and as such he also presides over "the beautiful sheen of the inner world of phantasy." Behind Nietzsche's association of Phoebus with phantasy and imagination are *phōs* (light) and *phainesthai* (appearing in the sense of shining forth), which are in turn at the root of the word *phantasia*.[29] So while the world of Apollonian phantasy may be ultimately illusion *(Schein)*, a significant connotation of the German word is the radiant beauty of the images projected in phantasy.

Nietzsche goes on to adduce two further characteristics of Apollo, his being the god of prophecy *(Wahrsagen)* and measured restraint. The *wahr* of *Wahrsagen* means "true": although the world of beautiful sheen is always suffused with an air of seeming *(Scheinen)* that distinguishes it from the world of actuality, it also declares the wisdom of its patron Apollo. This explains why one might "interpret one's life from the images [of the dream]" and "practice for life" by participating in the dream process. Just as there is little substantive difference in form between a prophetic dream and a prophetic vision while awake, so the roles played by dream and phantasy in Nietzsche's psychology become more or less equivalent. The association of Apollo with measure and restraint allows Nietzsche to call him "the magnificent divine image of the *principium individuationis*," alluding to Schopenhauer's term for that which maintains the individuality of the particular human being. This feature of the Apollonian evokes its counterpart in the Dionysian, insofar as the *principium individuationis* prevents the energies that constitute the person from overflowing into the boundless.

The topic of the Apollonian is broadened when Nietzsche ponders the origin of the world of the Olympian gods and concludes that "the same drive that embodied itself in Apollo gave birth to the entire Olympian world" (*BT* 3). On the basis of the ancient myths concerning the gods' origins, Nietzsche argues that "out of the original Titanic divine order of terror the Olympian order of joy was developed over slow transitions by virtue of the Apollonian drive for beauty *[Schönheitstrieb]*." The earlier order is invoked

through the "folk wisdom" concerning life expressed by the *daimōn* Sile-
nus, companion of Dionysus: "What is best for [human beings] is utterly
unattainable: not to have been born, not to *be,* to be *nothing.* But the second
best is—to die soon."

Delivered over to a life of perpetual struggle in the midst of suffering
inflicted by the implacable powers of fate, and issuing only in the extinction
of death, the ancient Greeks—Nietzsche maintains, against the view of the
serene Hellene prevalent in European culture at the time—had ample
grounds for pessimism and despair.

> The Greek knew and felt the terror and horror of existence: in order
> to be able to live at all, he had to place against them the radiant dream-
> birth of the Olympians. . . . [The horrors of existence] were overcome
> again and again by the Greeks through that artistic *middle-world* of
> the Olympians—or were at any rate veiled and withdrawn from
> sight.[30]

With this interpretation of the Greeks Nietzsche projects an image of the
abysmal structure of human existence in general. This understanding underlies the confrontation with nihilism that informs his later works, the confrontation with the collapse in the early nineteenth century of the values
that had hitherto sustained the Western tradition. Nietzsche's remark in the
first section of *The Birth of Tragedy* that it is by virtue of the arts "that life
is made possible and worth living," though made in the context of a discussion of the Greeks, assumes a broader validity in his later search for a solution to the problem of nihilism in general.

Related to this remark is the often quoted line, which occurs twice in the
text: "It is only as *aesthetic phenomenon* that existence and the world are
eternally *justified.*"[31] To appreciate the import of this statement, which has
often been misunderstood, we need to recall that Nietzsche understands the
Apollonian drive for beautiful shining as "an *art-drive of nature.*" This
means that the projection of a world of images in dream or phantasy is not
simply an avoidance strategy on the part of a people who finds the "real"
world a vale of tears, nor an arbitrary piece of self-indulgent whimsy on the
part of an individual wishing to escape the constraints of reality: it is rather,
he claims, a process inherent in the nature of things and informing the structure of all existence.[32]

In comparing "the two halves of life . . . the waking half and the dreaming half," Nietzsche suggests that our normal preference for the former
might be replaced by a quite different valuation of the dream in relation
to "that mysterious ground of our being of which we are the phenomenon
[Erscheinung]."[33] He goes on:

For the more I become aware of those omnipotent art-drives in nature and see in them an ardent longing for *Schein* and for redemption through *Schein*, the more I feel impelled to the metaphysical assumption that the true Being and primal One *[Ur-Eine]*, as that which is eternal suffering and contradiction, at the same time needs the rapturous vision, the pleasurable *Schein*, for its own constant redemption. (*BT* 4)

It is not often that one finds Nietzsche driven to "metaphysical assumptions," and the language of this passage suggests that the immediate impulse comes from Schopenhauer. At any rate, we are compelled, Nietzsche continues, to experience this shining emanation from the primal One as the "empirical reality [of] continuous becoming in space, time, and causality," which means that we ourselves are "completely wrapped up in [this *Schein*] and composed of it." If we understand our empirical existence (and the world as a whole) as "a representation of the primal One that is generated at every moment," then the dream has to be seen as "der *Schein des Scheins*"—as sheen emanating from the sheen that emanates moment by moment from the primal One.

Now we can appreciate the force of Nietzsche's remark about the justification of existence as "aesthetic phenomenon," which appears as a parenthesis in the following passage (in which "the true creator" is a type of Schopenhauerian Will):[34]

This must above all be clear, to our humiliation *and* exaltation: that the entire comedy of art is not put on for us at all, for our improvement or education, and that we are just as little the true creators of that world of art. We must rather assume that we are simply images and artistic projections *[Projektionen]* for the true creator and have our highest dignity in our significance as works of art—for it is only as aesthetic phenomenon that existence and the world are eternally *justified*—while of course our consciousness of this significance is hardly different from that which the soldiers painted on a canvas have of the battle represented on it. (*BT* 5)

In thinking of existence as aesthetic phenomenon in this sense, it helps to remember that a phenomenon is originally something that shines forth *(phainesthai)* in the manner of the *Schein* projected by the primal One. And just as dreams are the sheen of sheen, the images and projections of the human artist will be images of images and projections of projections.[35]

The opposition between the Apollonian and the Dionysian is invoked again in the course of a discussion in which Nietzsche questions the value of the distinction between subjective and objective in the realm of aesthetics by inquiring into the status of the "I" in the cases of the epic and the lyric poet. He had earlier characterized the Homeric epics as depending on "the complete victory of Apollonian illusion" (*BT* 3), and he now goes on to discuss the more complex case of the lyric poet as a precursor of the Attic tragedian. He takes his cue explicitly from Schiller, who writes of the way artistic creation begins (in his own case) from "a *musical mood*," and asserts on this basis the "identity of the lyrist with the musician" for the ancient Greeks. (Behind this assertion stands the figure of Wagner, who will later be revealed as the modern epitome of the Dionysian artist.) Although Nietzsche is talking here about how two different types of artist relate to the art-drives of nature in order to create, the artistic experience is to be taken—as always, in this psychology—as a paradigm for creative existence in general.

As a Dionysian artist, Nietzsche argues, the lyric poet has become one with the primal One *(das Ur-Eine),* Thus when he says "I" this does not refer to his empirical personality: rather "the 'I' of the lyric poet sounds from the abyss of Being *[aus dem Abgrunde des Seins]*."[36] But he is also subject to the Apollonian dream state which produces in him a further re- flection in "a *symbolic dream-image,*" which presumably corresponds to the visual imagery expressed by the words of the lyric. One can thus distinguish between the epic and lyric poets in terms of their relation to their imagery. The former (and also the plastic artist, who is related to him), absorbs him- self in "pure contemplation of images" and is thus protected "by the mirror of *Schein*" against "becoming one with and fused with his figures." Homer, for example, is imagined to have some distance between himself and the figure of Achilles, who remains "only an image." The image-world of the lyric poet, on the other hand, grows out of "the mystical state of self- abnegation and oneness," so that

> [his] images are nothing other than *he* himself and, as it were, only
> various objectifications of himself, which is why he may say "I" as
> the moving midpoint of that world. This I-ness *[Ichheit]* is not, how-
> ever, the same as that of the waking, empirically real human being,
> but rather the one and only truly existent and eternal I-ness that rests
> in the ground of things, through whose images the lyric genius sees
> into that very ground of things. (*BT* 5)

The objectification of the lyrist's self in a multiplicity of images will have important implications for Nietzsche's later psychology, insofar as the I is no longer something stable and fixed, but is rather labile and dynamic: "a moving midpoint."

There is a danger, however, for the lyric poet—since his image-world is a direct outgrowth of the primal One—that he might become fused with his figures and collapse into the "primordial pain and reechoing" with which the Dionysian musician is said to be identified "without any image." One cannot help wondering whether Nietzsche's eventual collapse and *Umnachtung,* his enfoldment in the dark night of madness, was a function of fusion of his figures. He will, after all, report to Jacob Burckhardt that he has become "every name in history."[37]

Platonic Prefigurations

Nietzsche's description of the lyric poet parallels Plato's account of "how the soul of the lyric poet works" in the *Ion,* with the primal One (true I-ness) taking the place of the God or Muse that is considered the ultimate source of poetic inspiration.[38] The poet is said by Socrates to be inspired, *entheos,* filled with the god, in a state of enthusiasm in the original sense of the word—possessed, like the devotees of Dionysus.

> Just as those carried away by Corybantic frenzy are not in their right minds when they dance, so also the lyric poets are not in their right minds when they make these fine songs of theirs. But when they launch into melody and rhythm, they are frantic and possessed, like Bacchic dancers who draw honey and milk from rivers when they are possessed but cannot when they are in their right minds. (*Ion* 533e–534a)

And according to Nietzsche's description of the Bacchic dancer:

> Just as the animals now talk and the earth yields milk and honey, so there sounds from him something supernatural: he feels himself a God, he himself walks about ecstatic and uplifted, like the gods he saw walking in his dreams. (*BT* 1)

Furthermore, the features Nietzsche mentions as characteristic of Dionysian music, whether the dithyrambic chorus or the overtures of Wagner, are likewise melody and rhythm. However, while Socrates' saying that the lyric poet is "inspired and out of his mind" and "without intelligence" (*Ion* 534b–d) is a criticism intended to demonstrate the limitations of the poet's powers, the Nietzsche of *The Birth of Tragedy* follows Schopenhauer and Wagner in extolling unconscious inspiration and deprecating reflection and conscious intellection.

Nietzsche's opposition to Plato on this topic is best seen against the background of the famous fulminations against poetry in the *Republic.* Socrates is especially hard on the "dramatic" mode of poetry—where the poet mimics his characters by having them speak directly in the first person—as involving the most harmful form of *mimēsis*. (There is of course a heavy element of irony here, insofar as Plato is himself a great poet and master of the dramatic dialogue, and the excoriation of dramatic poetry is issuing from the character of Socrates "directly in the first person.") Whereas in third-person narrative "the poet himself speaks and doesn't attempt to turn our thought elsewhere, as though someone other than he were speaking," in the dramatic mode "he speaks as though he himself were [for example] Chryses and tries as hard as he can to make it seem to us that it's not Homer speaking, but the priest, an old man."[39] The danger is that the impersonations of the mimic will infect the persons of his audience, eliciting involuntary imitations on their parts. Socrates is concerned that the guardians of the *polis* not be exposed in their education to poetry in the dramatic mode, and to tragedy in particular, since poets are imitators of a multitude of pernicious persons and things, and on the grounds that "[such] imitations, if they are practiced continually from youth onwards, become established as habits and nature, in body and sounds and in thought."[40]

The education of the guardians in the *Republic* is aimed at having them become expert in one single activity rather than attempting to master many (*Rep.* 394e)—and thereby falling into a dilletantism of the kind Nietzsche was striving so hard to avoid. The writer and reciter of poetry in the dramatic mode, which "involves all species of changes," is dismissed by Socrates as one who "doesn't harmonize with our regime because there's no double *[diplous]* man among us, nor a manifold *[pollaplous]* one, since each man does one thing" (397d–e). An especially Apollonian stance this insistence on the unitary individual, with these apotropaic gestures against anyone who would follow Dionysus in being many-formed (*polueidēs* and *polumorphos*—both common epithets of the god of becoming), or in over-stepping ecstatically the bounds of the self and entering into other persons. A shoemaker has to be a shoemaker, insists Socrates, and not a pilot along with his shoemaking.[41] (A philologist has to be a philologist, and not a pianist or a poet or a philosopher as well.)

The attack on imitative poetry is stepped up in book 10, which begins with Socrates' saying of the works of "the tragic poets and all the other imitators" that all such things "maim the thought of those who hear them and do not have knowledge of how they really are as a remedy *[pharmakon]*" (*Rep.* 595b). Poetry is here imagined as some sort of psychical toxin so strong that it cripples the intellect and requires an antidote in the form of proper understanding; rather than nourishing the mind, imitation appeals only to the lowest part of the soul (602–3, 606). The effect of imitative poetry is to disrupt the unity of the individual, so that instead of being "of one mind" there is "faction in him" and he "does battle with himself"; and in the resulting multiplicity, "our soul teems with ten thousand such oppositions arising at the same time" (603c–d). One is reminded of the conflicting factions that give rise to poor psychical attunements in "On Moods." In terms of political psychology, the imitative poet, far from conducing to a harmonious society within the individual, "produces a bad regime in the soul of each private man" (605b; 608b).

For several years up to the writing of *The Birth of Tragedy,* Nietzsche had been doing his best to avoid being a "multifold" or a "double" man— at least in terms of his profession, which we saw him in his inaugural lecture try to remake into his own idealized image. And yet, perhaps as a result of the springlike surge of creative energy around this time, or of his current topic's having so much to do with music, the urge to compose again asserted itself. He had spent the autumn vacation of 1871 in Naumburg and Leipzig, where he had enjoyed a reunion with his two best friends, Carl von Gersdorff and Erwin Rohde. After his return to Basel, the warm afterglow of their meeting became the womb from which a new composition sprang, *Nachklang einer Sylvesternacht* (Echo of a New Year's Eve). This piece, the score of which he would present to Cosima—now Cosima Wagner—for Christmas, was the first of several substantial compositions that were to come forth over the next few years.[42] In a letter to Rohde announcing the new arrival, Nietzsche writes: "Our meeting . . . revitalized me to such an extent that I have once again, after a hiatus of six years, become a composer."[43] Although he had continued to play the piano, Nietzsche had not produced any formal compositions since the time of "On Moods"—not since he had begun writing in earnest. At one level the efforts at disciplining the multiplicity within him by applying himself to the rigorous science of philology were having some effect. Even though Nietzsche would later say of the author of *The Birth of Tragedy,* in self-deprecating retrospect, "It should have *sung,* this 'new soul'—and not spoken!" the *Birth* is a distinctly melodic creature that was written "out of the spirit of music."[44] It is truly a work of philology as philosophy as music.

To resume the theme we were following in that text: the transition from the lyric poet to the Attic tragedian is effected by a discussion of the role of the satyr chorus, which according to tradition was the origin and originally the sole constituent of tragedy (*BT* 7). The satyr, as the "primordial image of the human being, the embodiment of its highest and strongest emotions," was thereby "something sublime and divine" (*BT* 8). On the basis of the division of the stage of the Greek theater into the *orchēstra* (the "dancing-place" occupied by the chorus of satyrs) and the narrow *skēnē* behind it (where, in the later drama, the action of the play took place), Nietzsche argues that the *scene* is to be understood as a vision projected by the chorus of satyrs—who as it were sing and dance it into existence. The dithyrambic song and dance of the chorus induce a kind of trance state on the part of the spectators who, through identifying themselves with the chorus, become totally blind to the rest of the audience in the *theatron* ("seeing place") around them, and experience the projected vision of the chorus (the action of the drama) as a higher—indeed the only—reality.

Nietzsche goes on to argue that the artistry of the members of the Dionysian chorus consisted in their ability not only to project a vision of hosts of spirits onto the scene behind them, but also to induce the audience to identify with them and thus participate in the projection. Again he emphasizes the radical nature of the self-transformation undergone in the Dionysian experience by contrasting it with the phenomenon of the rhapsode who (in reciting the Homeric epics) "does not become fused with his images, but . . . with a contemplative eye sees them outside himself." In the collective Dionysian experience in the Greek theater, "we have a surrender of individuality through entering into an other nature *[in eine fremde Natur]*." It is this surrendering of individuality, together with the dramatic effect of the mask, that gives Greek tragedy its enormous power.

> The dithyrambic chorus has the task of exciting the mood *[Stimmung]* of the audience to such a Dionysian degree that, when the tragic hero appears on the stage, they see not the awkwardly masked human being but rather a visionary figure born as it were from their own rapture. . . . Involuntarily [the spectator] transferred the image of the god [Dionysus] which magically trembles before his eyes to that masked figure and, as it were, resolved its reality into a spiritlike nonactuality. (*BT* 8)

The tragic mask, through concealing the all-too-human face behind it, helps induce the collective projection of the superhuman image onto the figure of the actor.[45] One can imagine that the mask also helps the actor lose his sense of individuality and allow the image of his role—which the truly gifted actor will see "hover perceptibly before his eyes"—to play itself out through him.

Plato wanted imitative and dithyrambic poetry banned from his ideal regime because he was so keenly aware of their magical power. Socrates impresses Ion with the "divine power" of poetic inspiration through the image of the magetism exerted by a loadstone on iron rings:

> You know, then, that this spectator is the last of the rings which I said get their power from one another through the Heraclean stone? And you the rhapsode and actor *[hupokritēs]* are the middle, and the top is the poet himself, but the god through all these draws the soul of human beings wherever he wishes, transmitting the power from one to the other. (*Ion* 535e–536a)

It is probable that Plato's hostility to the dramatic style of poetry forms part of an attack on the educational system of his time, which depended almost entirely on recited poetry or performed drama to transmit moral and technical instruction.[46] The method depended on the reciter's or actors' inducing in the audience a kind of trance state in which the listeners would fully identify with the characters portrayed. The powerful erotic component to the phenomenon made Socrates even more wary of the potential charge of the imitative performance: "You know that [even the best of us] enjoy it and that we give ourselves to following the imitation; suffering along with the hero in all seriousness, we praise as a good poet the man who most puts us in this state" (*Rep.* 605d). Indeed, he admits that "we ourselves are charmed by it" and proposes—not without irony—the following remedy: "When we listen to [poetry] we'll chant this argument [*logos*] we are making to ourselves as a countercharm."[47] So seductive is the siren song of the mimetic muse that the otherwise "unmusical" Socrates is stimulated to apotropaic incantation.

We learn more about the nature of projection when Nietzsche recommends that we look away from the surface character of the Sophoclean hero who is no more than "a photographic slide [*Lichtbild*—literally, "light-image"] projected onto a dark wall" in order to penetrate "to the myth that projects itself in these bright mirrorings" (*BT* 9). Just as dark spots hover before eyes that have looked into a bright light, "as a cure, as it were," so bright spots appear before eyes that have gazed into the ultimate dark.[48] The implication is that Sophocles had looked into the abysmal dark of, say, the myth of Oedipus, so that "those bright image projections of the Sophoclean hero— the Apollonian of the mask—are necessary products of a look into the innermost terrors of nature: luminous spots to cure eyes damaged by gruesome night."

Greek tragedy is informed, then, by a complex twofold projection of the Apollonian and the Dionysian. The dithyrambic music of the chorus elicits on the part of the audience an identification with it and a collective projection of the god Dionysus onto the masked figure on the stage; while the hero is at the same time a projection from the myth behind the drama of "the Apollonian of the mask," of a luminous afterimage from a look into the abyss.

Muthos versus *Logos*

One last, dual topic needs to be touched on here: the destruction of *muthos* by *logos* in the form of dialectic. Nietzsche argues that after Aeschylus and Sophocles Attic tragedy degenerated, largely as a result of the influence of Socratic rationality on the works of Euripides. His criticism focuses on

Socrates' famous *daimonion,* the inner voice that on occasion dissuades him from following a certain course of action.

> This voice, when it comes, always *dissuades.* In this quite abnormal nature, instinctive wisdom shows itself only in order to *hinder* conscious knowledge now and then. While in all productive human beings it is instinct that is the creative-affirmative force and consciousness operates critically and dissuasively, in Socrates instinct becomes the critic and consciousness the creator—truly a monstrosity *per defectum*! (*BT* 13)

The hypertrophy of intellect in Socrates renders him, for Wagner as for Nietzsche, hopelessly inartistic and unmusical.

After quoting at length from *The World as Will and Representation* on the topic of music (*BT* 16), Nietzsche gives a close paraphrase of another passage from the same chapter (*WWR* 1:52) on the basis of which he describes the Dionysian factor in Greek tragedy and associates the latter with modern—and specifically Wagnerian—opera. In speaking of music as a direct expression of the will itself, Schopenhauer writes:

> Hence it arises that our phantasy is so easily stirred by music, and tries to shape that invisible yet vividly aroused spirit-world that speaks to us directly and to clothe it with flesh and bone. . . . This is the origin of the song with words, and finally of the opera.

Wagner's music takes the place of the dithyrambic chorus and serves a similar purpose of "arousing the spirit-world" and prompting the audience to project in phantasy onto the flesh-and-blood singer on the stage the aura of an archetypal presence. Wagner's enthusiasm for Schopenhauer is easy to understand when one considers passages such as those just quoted, which encouraged his tendency to exalt instinctive drive over clear logic in his own theoretical writings. However, Nietzsche will soon move away from this extreme anti-intellectualist position held by his two mentors.

There is another prefiguration of Nietzsche's idea of the role of the Dionysian in tragedy (and life) in a passage where Schopenhauer takes up again the topic of hypnotic trance. He writes of how an encounter with death may reveal to us that "a mere illusion has limited our existence to our person," and that such an awareness may be afforded also by states that are similar to death "through abolition of the concentration of consciousness in the brain" (*WWR* 2:47).

> Of these states magnetic sleep is the most conspicuous. When this sleep reaches the higher degrees, our existence shows itself through various symptoms, beyond our persons and in other beings, most

strikingly by direct participation in the thoughts of another individual, and ultimately even by . . . a kind of omnipresence.

Remember Schopenhauer's magnetic somnambulist. Under hypnosis, the boundaries of the self dissolve in such a way as to allow a Dionysian identification with other persons and things.[49]

It is remarkable how important a role is assigned in *The Birth of Tragedy* to myth—especially since the topic receives so little discussion in the rest of Nietzsche's works. He argues here that, for the Greeks, myth was annihilated by "the spirit of science"—faith in the explicability of nature and in knowledge as a panacea—as first embodied in the figure of Socrates (*BT* 17). Now, however, one can expect a rebirth of myth along with the rebirth of tragedy out of the spirit of German music, to be occasioned by the cultural renaissance generated by Wagnerian opera. Nietzsche sees a role for myth in modern opera analogous to its protective, Apollonian role in Attic tragedy: although secondary to the music, the words and images of the myth will protect the audience against fatal inundation by the Dionysian sea of sound (*BT* 21).

Although the extended paean to *Tristan und Isolde* into which Nietzsche now launches is based on imaginative reading rather than direct experience, his more general account of Dionysian *Rausch* stems directly from musical experiences. He prefaces his praise as follows: "I have to appeal only to those who are directly related to music, have in it their maternal womb, as it were, and are related to things almost exclusively through unconscious musical relations." No wonder Nietzsche was so concerned with *Stimmung* as a mode of attunement to the world. He asks the genuine musicians whether they can imagine a human being capable of listening to the third act of *Tristan* "without any help from word and image simply as an enormous symphonic movement . . . without expiring from a convulsive spreading of all wings of the soul." In view of the progression from the "prolonged feeling of rapture" occasioned by the Overture to *Die Meistersinger* in 1868 to the point where, four years later, the impending death of Tristan makes one feel that "one will expire from lack of breath, in a convulsive distention of all feelings, [since] so little connects [one] with this existence," it is perhaps a good thing for the history of modern thought that Nietzsche's subsequent estrangement from Wagner prevented him from ever attending a complete performance of *The Ring*.

Nietzsche goes on to discuss the necessity of myth, understood as "a concentrated image of the world," for the development of both the individual and the culture.

Without myth every culture loses its healthy, creative natural power: only a horizon defined by myths completes and unifies a whole cul-

tural movement. Myth alone saves all powers of phantasy and Apollonian dream from indiscriminate wandering. The images of myth
must be the unnoticed omnipresent daemonic guardians under whose
protection the young soul grows up, and whose signs help the man
interpret his life and his struggles. (*BT* 23)

When things are going well, myth provides bearings, directions, guidelines;
its images guardians, genuine *daimōnes,* personal protectors for the otherwise errant soul. By contrast, the modern age has espoused a mythophobic
Socratism which produces "the abstract human being, untutored by myth"
and gives rise to "a disorderly roving of artistic phantasy that is unchecked
by any native myth." In short, "the tremendous historical need of unsatisfied
modern culture" is to be understood as a symptom of "the loss of myth, the
loss of the mythical home, of the mythical maternal womb." Fears aroused
by the term "cultural movement" are realized when the tone turns nationalistic (as at the end of *Die Meistersinger*) and "German myth" in particular
is singled out for special praise. But these first are more or less the last notes
of nationalism in Nietzsche's published works, which suggests that this outburst of Germanophilia was for Wagner's benefit.[50] What is important here
is the idea that myth provides a kind of channel or container for the spontaneous outflow of phantasy.

   Given the prominent role assigned to myth in *The Birth,* it is remarkable
how seldom the topic recurs in the later works. Virtually the only other
mentions of myth appear in texts written in the next two or three years;
thereafter, though various mythemes play through Nietzsche's texts, he
forgoes any discussion of myth as such. In the second section of the unpublished essay "On Truth and Lie in the Extramoral Sense" (1873), he speaks
of the "fundamental human drive to produce images and metaphors," and
says that if this drive is suppressed by an overlay of conceptual thought it
will nevertheless find an outlet "in *myth* and *art* generally."[51] He goes on to
make a connection (central to depth psychology) between the operations of
myth and the dream.

   The waking life of a mythically inspired people such as the ancient
   Greeks, is, because of the way myth assumes the constant operation
   of miracles, in fact more similar to the dream than the waking life of
   the scientifically sobered thinker. If every tree can suddenly speak as
   a nymph, or a god in the shape of a bull can abduct young maidens
   . . . —and this is what the honest Athenian believed—then, as in a
   dream, anything is possible at every moment, and the whole of nature
   swarms around human beings as if it were only a masquerade of the
   gods.[52]

Again unnoticed but omnipresent daemonic guardians animate the cultural landscape; nature driven by personal presences all around. And by one of those strange concatenations of circumstances, there exists a perfect exemplification of this conception in the contemporaneous paintings by the Swiss artist—and fellow resident of Basel—Arnold Böcklin. In his canvases from the 1860s and 1870s depicting satyrs and fauns, nymphs and centaurs, mermaids and sea monsters, and even gods such as Apollo and Dionysus—all without the slightest trace of sentimentality—experience of the type characterized by Nietzsche in the passage quoted above is rendered palpably and uncannily present.[53]

In *Richard Wagner in Bayreuth* Nietzsche explains the phenomenon of Wagner, and his ability to effect a grand synthesis of the arts, by the fact that "he thinks in terms of visible and palpable processes, rather than in concepts, which is to say that he thinks mythically" (*WB* 9). He goes on to dispel a misconception of the nature of myth which is characteristic of the early modern period: "Myth is not based on a thought, as children of an artificial culture believe, but is itself a thinking *[ein Denken];* it imparts an idea of the world, but in a sequence of processes, actions, and sufferings." A truly depth-psychological conception of myth—not as some kind of primitive proto-science or frivolous poetry, but rather a way of thinking about the world, and the human being's place in it, that proceeds through a play of images rather than a framework of concepts.

The apparent distaste for explicit discussion of myth in Nietzsche's works after *Wagner in Bayreuth* no doubt has to do with his subsequent estrangement from the Master. Wagner's interest in mythology was encouraged by ideas he gleaned from Schopenhauer, with the result that myth came to occupy a central place in his view of the world—and especially in connection with his thinking about "the folk" *(das Volk)*. It is plausible to suppose that one way for Nietzsche to distance himself from Wagner intellectually, and from the latter's obsession with the folk in particular, was to be reticent to the point of silence on the topic of myth.

III

Struggles for Multiple Vision (1872–1877)

*It seems to be a rule of wisdom never to rely on your memory
alone, scarcely even in acts of pure memory, but to bring the
past for judgment into the thousand-eyed present, and live ever
in a new day.*

Emerson, "Self-Reliance"

The Birth of Tragedy came into the world at the beginning of January
1872 and was greeted with unqualified enthusiasm by the Wagners, by
Nietzsche's friends and fellow scholars Erwin Rohde and Franz Overbeck,
by Jacob Burckhardt and Hans von Bülow. The conductor even asked
Nietzsche if he could dedicate his recent translation of Leopardi to him as
a token of his admiration for such a fine literary debut. Cosima's father,
Franz Liszt, read the book twice immediately on receiving it, and wrote to
the author: "Surging and flaming in this book is a powerful spirit that stirred
me profoundly."[1] These accolades were important to Nietzsche since he had
been plagued by doubts about whether the proper audience existed for such
an unusual hybrid work. In a letter to Rohde the previous November he had
written of the manuscript:

> I continue to fear that the philologists won't want to read it because
> of the music in it, the musicians because of the philology, and the
> philosophers because of the music and the philology, and am thus
> feeling anxiety and sympathy for my good publisher.

The beginning of 1872 was a period of unprecedented ferment for
Nietzsche. He was asked if he would consider a professorship at the university in Greifswald on the northeast coast of Germany, but he declined—no
doubt because of the extreme remoteness of the place, especially from the
Wagners' residence in Tribschen. On hearing the news that he had rejected
an offer from another institution, the students at Basel proposed holding a
torchlight procession to express their appreciation, but Nietzsche persuaded
them to abandon the idea. When the university officials learned of the affair
they awarded him a raise in salary.[2]

Proximity to Wagner was becoming increasingly important to Nietzsche insofar as he and the Master had "formed an alliance" to bring about a cultural revolution.[3] "You have no idea how close we are now," he wrote to Rohde, "and how closely aligned our plans are." But exhilaration at the prospect of a glorious association with Wagner is countered by a premonition of impending hardship:

> A tremendous seriousness grips me whenever I hear [about the reaction to my book], because such voices presage the future of what I intend. This life will become very much more difficult. For some time I have been living in a mighty current; almost every day brings something astonishing; just as my goals and intentions become ever higher.

The book on tragedy had been an extremely difficult birth, preceded by a long and painful labor.[4] Since Nietzsche was already moving away from Schopenhauer and beginning to find himself at odds with Wagner intellectually, it was important to him that the work be well received by non-Schopenhauerians and readers outside the Master's circle; but his more pessimistic premonitions regarding its reception were fulfilled. Although *The Birth of Tragedy* has since become powerfully influential for a range of artists, musicians, writers, and even literary critics and classical scholars, the initial response from the academic world (and, by implication, from classical philology in particular) was a deafening silence—at least for the first few months.

Nietzsche was deeply hurt by the silence from one quarter in particular—the lack of response from his teacher Ritschl in Leipzig. Ritschl had read the book and written in his diary, "Clever dissoluteness."[5] Unable to bear the lack of response, Nietzsche wrote him at the end of January, saying how "astonished" and "disturbed" he was by his teacher's silence. Ritschl's entry in his diary reads: "Amazing letter from N—megalomania." The letter the senior professor wrote two weeks later was noncommittal and by no means encouraging: he was not in a position, and would continue not to be, to discuss his former student's work, being too old to countenance changing his ways of thinking. This dismissal with the consequent estrangement was a major blow to Nietzsche, since a teacher was for him—and Ritschl was a paradigm in this respect—not just a purveyor of learning but an inspiring personality and great human being. For the first time (second, to the extent that Karl Ludwig Nietzsche had been more a figure than a father) Nietzsche was failed by a father figure of whom he was inordinately fond.

In June a polemical pamphlet excoriating *The Birth of Tragedy* appeared in Berlin, from the hand of the young classical scholar Ulrich von Wilamowitz-Moellendorf, under the title *Zukunftsphilologie! (Philology of the Future!*—a deprecatory allusion to Wagner's *Zukunftsmusik).*[6] The polemic was something of a hatchet job, insofar as the author had an axe to grind that dated back to the time he had been a younger classmate of Nietzsche's at Schulpforta. Nevertheless, in spite of rapid ripostes from the pens of Wagner and Rohde, Wilamowitz's criticisms of Nietzsche's "creative" scholarship carried enough weight to guarantee that the academic community almost totally ignored the book. It was not as if the philologist in Nietzsche was the sole author of the text that had been criticized or ignored: remember the talk in his inaugural address of "philologists [living together] with poets, thinkers, and artists." Nevertheless, insofar as the thinker played a part in the creation of *The Birth of Tragedy,* the role was clearly not being well received. And the most devastating effect of Wilamowitz's attack had yet to manifest itself; it was something quite unexpected, and was to hurt Nietzsche more deeply than vilification by a conventional classical scholar.

The situation was becoming grim. The diphtheria and dysentery Nietzsche had contracted during the war had taken their toll on his health, while his migraine attacks were becoming more frequent and debilitating the more he felt trapped in the wrong field of the profession at Basel. In April of 1872 the Wagners left Tribschen to take up residence in Bayreuth, site of the future Festspielhaus and locus of the imminent cultural renaissance of European art. Wagner had often been quite imperious in his demands that Nietzsche visit them at Tribschen, so their increased distance from Basel reduced the pressure Nietzsche had been feeling from the friendship, while at the same time it must have appeared to him a metaphor for his increasing intellectual alienation from the Master. Nevertheless, the Wagners' move from Tribschen signified the end of one of the happiest periods of Nietzsche's life, as evidenced by an account of his last visit there.

> Last Saturday saw the sad and deeply moving departure from Tribschen. Now Tribschen is over. . . . We packed up manuscripts, letters, and books—it was so miserable! These past three years I have spent close to Tribschen, during which I made twenty-three visits—what they mean to me! Without them what would I be! I am fortunate to have been able to crystallize that Tribschen world for myself in my book.[7]

It was of some consolation to attend the laying of the foundation stone for the Festspielhaus in Bayreuth later in the month, where Nietzsche and Rohde—"the two Wagnerian professors"—were guests of honor. But the downward trend was to continue.

At the end of June, Nietzsche went to Munich to attend two performances, two nights apart, of *Tristan und Isolde* conducted by Hans von Bülow. As one might expect from such a rapid double exposure to that singularly overwhelming work, he was rendered more or less speechless. In a letter to Rohde a week after the second performance, all he could write was: "Ah, my dear friend! About *Tristan* it is impossible to say a thing!" After a further two weeks he had recovered enough to be able to commit some feelings to paper. To Rohde he wrote: "I wish you could hear *Tristan:* it is the most tremendous, the purest, and the most unexpected thing I know. One swims in sublimity and happiness." Five days before, he had written an admiring letter of congratulation to von Bülow.[8] He apologizes to the great conductor for having been unable to express his appreciation after the performances, ascribing this inability to "a condition of being shaken to the core, in which a person does not speak, does not thank, but hides himself away." As a token of his appreciation, Nietzsche made the mistake of enclosing the score of his latest composition for piano, the *Manfred-Meditation,* which he dedicated to the conductor.

This piece does not number among Nietzsche's more successful compositions; but the hypercandid response he received four days later was devastating. A few excerpts from von Bülow's almost sadistically extended invective:

> Your *Manfred-Meditation* is the most extreme fantastical extravagance, the most unpleasant and antimusical thing I have seen put down on music paper for a long time. Its psychological interest aside . . . your meditation has from the musical point of view the value of a crime against morals. . . . You yourself characterized your music as "frightful"—it is indeed . . . and is tantamount to a rape of the Muse of music.[9]

This kind of criticism from a musician for whom he had such great admiration must have hurt Nietzsche more deeply than Wilamowitz's polemic against *The Birth of Tragedy,* since by this time he saw classical philology as merely a profession for which he happened to have been trained, whereas music had always been something that sprang from the core of his being. It is thus with remarkable contrition that he was eventually able to write to von Bülow some months later, saying *mea culpa* and expressing gracious (and by no means ironical) gratitude for the helpful criticisms.[10] While Nietzsche the pianist would continue to play, the composer in him would from this point—for a while, at least—be suppressed. If the composer was to work at all, it would be in the medium of the written text and on the soul.

Feeling an understandable need to get away from it all, Nietzsche decided to spend the autumn holidays on his own. He had planned to go to Italy, but ill health forced him to stop in Splügen, high in the Swiss Alps. It turned out to be the perfect place, affording him the opportunity for long, solitary hikes amid magnificent scenery: he was finally coming to discover true Byron country. However, when he returned to Basel, much refreshed, at the beginning of the winter semester, he was greeted by the aftershock of Wilamowitz's polemic. Not a single student had enrolled in his classes.[11] (Fortunately, two nonclassics students expressed interest in taking courses from him, so that his teaching at Basel did continue.) After the peaks of the premature professorship and the ecstasies of exposure to the genius of Wagner and the muse of Cosima at Tribschen—experiences embodied in the text of *The Birth*—there follows the descent into the vales, into depths of gloom and pain: the tragedy begins. *Incipit tragoedia.*

Changes in Guiding Images

> *The soul is impatient of masters, and eager for change. . . . We are tendencies, or rather, symptoms, and none of us complete. We touch and go, and sip the foam of many lives.*
> Emerson, "Uses of Great Men"

Given the general lack of intelligent response to *The Birth of Tragedy,* it is understandable that Nietzsche should entitle his next publishing project *Untimely Meditations.* But before this series of essays began to appear in 1873, he wrote several other pieces that have psychological implications: the essay "On Truth and Lie in the Extramoral Sense," the longer unfinished manuscript "Philosophy in the Tragic Age of the Greeks," as well as a large number of unpublished notes. He also delivered a series of five public lectures in Basel under the title "On the Future of Our Educational Institutions."[12] Although Nietzsche decided against having the texts of these lectures published, some passages in them deserve mention here.

The lectures take the form of a first-person narrative in which the speaker and a friend come across an old philosopher and a former pupil in a rather bucolic setting. (The dramatic element is somewhat contrived, and while a scintillating delivery in the lecture hall may have enhanced the effect, it is probably a good thing that Nietzsche never reverted to this form.) A major theme of the lectures is that contemporary educational institutions fail to enforce the kind of *discipline* that is necessary if young people are to acquire culture through education. (Much of the thrust of the lectures depends on the ambiguity of the German *Bildung* between "education" and "culture"—as well its connotation of "imaging.") By so failing, they obstruct the emergence of genius from the ground of culture. The influence of Wagner as well as of Schopenhauer is evident here, insofar as the lecturer claims that "the genuine, deeper regions [of the human psyche] . . . where the *Volk* nurtures its religious instincts and furthers the poetizing of its mythical images" is in any case unreachable by teaching. The drive to promote universal education is thus pernicious, insofar as it goes against "the natural order of rank in the realm of the intellect." Worse still, it is likely to destroy

> the roots of those highest and most noble formative powers *[Bild-ungskräfte]* that break forth from the unconscious of the *Volk,* and which are the maternal condition for the birth of the genius and for his proper education and care. Only through the figure of the mother can we grasp the significance and obligation that devolves upon the true culture of a *Volk* with respect to the genius. . . . The genius can emerge only if he comes to term and is nourished in the womb of a *Volk*'s culture.[13]

The association (to be found in the ancient Greek tradition) between a ground in which roots can take hold and a womb from which something can be born underlies the later development of Nietzsche's psychological imagery.[14]

The imagery of natural processes is set in context by a remarkable passage in the fourth lecture, where the old philosopher expatiates in somewhat Schopenhauerian terms upon the role of the relationship to nature in the process of imparting culture.

> If you want to lead a young person onto the right path of education and culture, be careful not to disturb his naively trustful and personally immediate relationship with nature: forest and cliff, storm and vulture, the single flower, the butterfly, the meadow and the mountainside must speak to him in their own tongues; at the same time he must recognize himself in them as in countless dispersed reflexes and reflections and in a multicolored whirl of changing appearances; in this way he will unconsciously sympathize with the metaphysical oneness of all things in the great metaphor of nature, and at the same time calm himself with their eternal perseverance and necessity. (*KSA* 1:715–16)

The philosopher goes on to bemoan the fact that few youths are fortunate enough to enjoy such close and "almost personal" relations with the natural world, since education teaches them early on "how one subjugates nature toward one's own ends." With the imposition of the scientific stance, "the instinctive, true and unique understanding of nature" is lost, and "in its place we now have clever calculation and a cunning overcoming of nature." (A nice anticipation of the ecological problems engendered by the unmitigated technological assault upon the natural world during the ensuing century.) Here the young Nietzsche can be heard speaking clearly through the figure of the old philosopher:

> Thus one who is genuinely cultured is afforded the invaluable gift of being able to remain true without any breach to the contemplative instincts of his childhood, and thereby to arrive at a condition of peaceful oneness, a harmonious context, that cannot be even imagined by one who has been brought up for the struggle of life.

It was to be one of Nietzsche's few consolations, after attempting to moderate his participation in "the struggle of life" by breaking his ties with the academic profession and embarking on the nomadic phase of his career, not to be cut off from the intimate inhabitation of the natural world that he enjoyed throughout his childhood and youth. He would later arrive at the view that the human being needs to be "renaturalized," not by way of a simple return to a naive relationship with nature but rather through an *advance,* "a *coming up* to high, free, even terrible nature and naturalness."[15]

At the finale of the lecture series the theme of the need for discipline and subordination reverberates in an unusual constellation of images. A talented but directionless university student (a familiar figure) is caught in a dilemma: while numerous "proud and noble resolutions form themselves and grow within him, he is terrified by the prospect of sinking prematurely into the small narrowness of one particular subject."[16] The educational setting offers nothing by which he can take his bearings: "He analyzes his capabilities, but it is just like looking into empty or chaotically filled spaces." In despair he is inclined to relinquish control altogether and "let the reins fall"—all this, it turns out, "for lack of a guide *[Führer]*" in education and culture.[17] The old philosopher, who had earlier emphasized the need to impose strict *artistic* as well as intellectual discipline on university students, offers a diagnosis and prescription:

> All education begins with the complete opposite of everything that one nowadays glorifies as academic freedom [for the student]; it begins with obedience, with subordination, with discipline, with subjection. And just as great leaders *[Führer]* are in need of people to lead, so those who are to be led need a leader. Here in the order of minds there is a mutual predisposition, even a kind of preestablished harmony. (*KSA* 1:750)

Because of the chaos that results from the failure of contemporary education to impose sufficient discipline on its charges, it difficult for a student to find the appropriate master, and a follower the right leader. But when those who are destined for each other—"struggling and wounded"—finally find each other, there arises "a deep feeling of bliss, as with the sounding of eternal strings."

The suspicion that the old philosopher might be describing an experience of the young Nietzsche in relation to Wagner is confirmed by the orchestral-theatrical metaphor that ends the lecture on a note of triumphant affirmation. We are invited to think of the typical German orchestra, and especially of how its members *look* while playing. Asked to imagine that one is deaf and has never dreamed of the existence of something like music, a viewer will be fascinated by the prospect of enjoying "the orchestra's performance as a dramatic play and its members purely as plastic artists." It would come across as a comedy or farce, "a harmless parody of *homo sapiens*"; and even if one were to then open one's ears, the sounds produced under the leadership of the average pedestrian conductor would be no more inspiring.

> But now on wings of phantasy set a genius, a real genius, in the midst of this mass, and you will immediately notice something remarkable. It is as if this genius had in a lightning-fast transmigration of the soul entered into all these half-animal bodies, and as if there now looked out from them a *single* daemonic eye. . . . If you now look at the orchestra again and sense the nimble tension in every muscle and the rhythmic necessity in every gesture, you will then be able to feel the preestablished harmony between the leader and the led, and how in the intellectual order everything presses toward an organization of this kind. (*KSA* 1:751–52)

A configuration similar to the position of the satyr chorus in Greek tragedy, but with the actor become director through Dionysian dispersal. It is true that the "intellectual order," or hierarchy of minds, that the philosopher is speaking of here is meant to be understood in the context of the university, and that the leader is to be seen as a guide in the domain of culture—a role played in exemplary fashion, for Nietzsche at this time, by Wagner. But it is clear from the context in which the idea of the *Führer* is first introduced, that Nietzsche's discussion is also motivated by the need for an *internal* leader or guide: a figure to compose the various forces within the soul, or to lead one through the labyrinths of the psyche.

Turning to the notebooks from the early 1870s, one discovers a number of psychological themes—concerning the drives and their mastery, and the operations of images, memory, and phantasy.

Most of the discussion of the drives has to do with the tasks of the philosopher and artist understood as "keeping the drive for knowledge in check."[18] Nietzsche considers the "indiscriminate drive for knowledge" as manifested in the sciences (among which one can confidently count philology) to be a sign of decadence, and calls for a "selective" knowledge-drive in the form of philosophy.[19] But a look back to the pre-Socratic philosophers shows how the indiscriminate knowledge-drive can be kept in check by means of philosophical thinking and artistic powers, in such a way as to minimize abstraction and thereby enhance *life*. The reason the drive for knowledge has to be kept under control is revealed by Nietzsche's comment on "the Hellenic *will*," understood as a multiplicity of different drives: "Each of these drives tries to be the only one to exist to infinity." The drive for knowledge is typical of drives in general in its tendency to assimilate the forces of other drives: "Certain sequences of concepts can become through isolation so vehement that they attract to themselves the strength of other drives."[20] If the drive for knowledge is allowed to dominate, the soul as a whole suffers through being deprived of the felt but unknowable fullness of life.

The drives that constitute psychical life have, on Nietzsche's view, a long prehistory that stretches back far beyond the individual's existence. The beginnings of this idea can be found in the early notebooks. Under the influence of Schopenhauer and some reading in physics, Nietzsche entertains the possibility—latent in his earlier hylozoistic speculations—that memory and sensation might pertain to the nature of all things, which would then have to be regarded as possessing will.[21]

> If everything has sensation, then there is a chaos of centers of sensation from the smallest to the largest. These sensation-complexes, whether larger or smaller, would be called "will."

Through linking up sensation with the capacity for reflex movements, he concludes that some kind of memory must be comprised in sensation and so be "an original property of things." This conclusion is supported by the existence of some kind of memory in the plant world: "With the mimosa, for example, we have memory but no consciousness. With plants this is naturally a memory without *an image*." Nietzsche is talking about a memory that "has nothing to do with nerves or the brain. It is an original property, for the human being carries with him the memory of all previous generations." This is the first mention of a kind of memory at the cellular level and the beginning of an important quasi-Lamarckian strain in Nietzsche's psychological thinking; while talk of the will as a multiplicity of "sensation-complexes" continues the line of thinking begun with the dissolution of the I in the Dionysian experience.

Interspersed with the notes mentioned so far are numerous reflections concerning images and the image-creating power of *phantasy* in the constitution of human experience. When a people such as the ancient Greeks begins to develop a culture, what "masters the knowledge-drive" is phantasy.[22] Although Nietzsche stands in the tradition of German Romantic thinking about the power of the imagination, the importance he assigns to creative phantasy has been for the most part neglected by his commentators.[23] In these early notes he argues that productive phantasy is a necessary component of all thinking, referring to "the extraordinary productivity of the intellect" as "a life of images" *(Bilderleben)*.

Nietzsche posits a "twofold artistic power" at work, one element of which "produces images" and one of which "selects" them. The productive power is attested to by the "dream-world" where, by contrast with waking experience, "[one] is not led or modified by images streaming in through the eyes." (Remember Apollo as the patron of the dream-state and shining phantasy.) The idea is that in dreaming there is very little constraint from outside—if not for sock-bands around the ankles—on the images produced by the imagination. But Nietzsche goes on to emphasize that even here it is not a matter of "a totally free artistic inventing"; rather the images are conditioned by "the finest emanations from the activity of the nerves seen on a surface." He proposes an analogy between the relation of the underlying nervous activity to the images produced in the mind and the relation of the vibrating string beneath the surface in Chladni's experiments to the "sand-figures" produced on top of it.[24]

But let us digress for a little to consider some prefigurations of the themes we have just been considering, in the work of an important precursor: Johann Gottfried Herder.[25]

Flows of Phantasy

> *Souls never touch their objects. An unnavigable sea washes with silent waves between us and the things we aim at and converse with.*
>
> Emerson, "Experience"

Born exactly a hundred years before Nietzsche, Herder was an older contemporary of Goethe's (and a major influence on the poet's early development), who began as a theology student at Königsberg and became one of Kant's favorite pupils. But while Nietzsche constantly praises Goethe—sometimes as the greatest figure in Germany's history—his infrequent remarks about Herder are generally unenthusiastic.[26] It is only toward the end of his career that he associates himself with Herder, autobiographically, as if affirming an affinity after all.[27] The most relevant text is *Vom Erkennen und Empfinden der menschlichen Seele* (On the cognition and sensation of the human soul), which was published in three successive versions, in 1774, 1775, and 1778.[28]

One of Herder's primary concerns was to combat the fragmentation of human existence that was encouraged by the various "faculty psychologies" prevalent at the time (most stemming from the rationalism of Christian Wolff), which tended to divorce thinking from feeling and performed similar dichotomies between the other capabilities of the human soul. While acknowledging of a world full of *Kräfte*, forces animating the phenomena of nature as well as the activities of culture, Herder insisted upon the essential unity of the various powers of the human soul. He speaks of the nature of the soul as being "one," insofar as its powers of feeling and knowing are intimately intertwined.[29] Following Leibniz, he emphasizes the "inner force," the "*Gestalt* of the soul . . . [which] rules over outer presentations," concluding that "we live always in a world that we form and imagine for ourselves *[das wir uns selbst bilden]*" (*EMS* 565–66).

Herder places great emphasis on the role of what he calls *Reiz*—which means at once stimulation, irritation, and attraction—a force acting through the finer "fibers" of the organism and which he understands as the "seed" of sensation (*EMS* 590). Before focusing on the nervous system as the ultimate medium of *Reiz*, he offers a preliminary characterization of its operations in metaphors drawn from organic nature. "We must begin from these dark abysses and roots of sensation," he writes, in adumbrating the nature of *Reiz*, "for without roots no tree can grow, and without stimulation there is no sensation" (591). At the same time he interleaves images from the art of weaving, speaking of stimulation as "the dark *stamen*" (the warp stretched on a loom), from which the fabric of sensation is made: "Nature has woven together these small living threads into a thousandfold conflict, contact, and counter-striving." He speaks of the heart as "the inexhaustible fountain of *Reiz*," where the term means "attraction" as much as "stimulation," and of "excitability *[Reizbarkeit]*" as "this enormous sowing of the seeds of sensation," in which "ebb and flood perform their vital motions" (592).

Herder then launches into a lyrical description of the currents of life through the vegetal realm, where sap rises and nourishment is drawn from earth and water; the animal realm, where "the stings and drives of hunger and thirst" lead to more complex forms of assimilation; and the human realm, where *Reiz* finally becomes love—through which, as ultimate attraction, the "overflow" (*Überstrom*) of force generates new life (*EMS* 593–94). We shall be tracing the schema of this progression in Nietzsche's imagery, but for now let us hear Herder talk of the way nature has arranged to have the source of stimulation remain hidden in the darkest depths. Since it would be impossible for us to "grasp stimulation, as the seed of every sensation, in its inner strength . . . nature laid it in the innermost darkness."

It should and could not depend on clear or distinct consciousness: nature therefore placed it at a distance from the surface of the senses . . . If the soul were able to make vivid to itself . . . the obscure condition of the machine that is animated by stimulation, what a rushing oceanic cosmos of dark waves coming from afar she would sink into, and that would surround her with the anxiety of hell! . . . For that reason mother nature darkened the world that serves the soul and is unknown to her precisely because she is unable to know it. . . . Not to hear the modulation of the blood's circulation . . . the dissonances and sounds of death beneath which the dark rivers of hell rush toward her, but rather to live, work, and act in their entire result. The soul stands on the abyss of an infinity, which she does not see: forces drift toward her from dark bushes and roots that are covered with night for her, and from which she gathers only blossoms and fragrances. The living physiology of the human body, the subordination of stimuli and feelings in so many grades and contributions in free and open play, is an abyss of goodness and wisdom! (*EMS* 595–96)

Compare the following passage from Nietzsche's "On Truth and Lie in the Extramoral Sense" (1873), which—though never published—contains a wealth of psychological insights:

What does the human being actually know about himself? . . . Does nature not conceal most things from him, especially about the human body, in order to banish and enclose him in a proud, illusionistic consciousness, far from the windings of the intestines, the rapid flow of the bloodstream, the intricate quivering of the nerve fibers? She threw away the key: and woe to that fatal curiosity which might one day be able to peer out and down through a crack in the chamber of consciousness, and thereby have the premonition that the human being rests, in the indifference of his ignorance, upon a basis that is merciless, greedy, insatiable, and murderous—as if hanging in dreams on the back of a tiger. Given this situation, where in the world could the drive for truth have come from?[30]

While Nietzsche's emphasis on the savage nature of the forces that underlie human awareness contrasts with the more optimistic tone of Herder's musings on the topic, the resonances with his predecessor's ideas are striking. While the immediate stimulus for Nietzsche's thoughts on the matter may have come from Schopenhauer, who was equally concerned to downplay the importance of consciousness in relation to the deeper workings of the human body, the images are definite echoes of Herder's.

Herder moves his discussion explicitly to the level of physiology when he associates the phenomena of *Trieb* and *Reiz,* more or less identifying them at the level of animal life—"The drive of the animal is obviously *Reiz*" (*EMS* 600)—with the emphasis now on the "attraction" aspect of the latter phenomenon. He now links stimuli and drives directly with the network of nerves in the organism: "The marrow of the nerves is nothing more than a finer fabric of fibers, the vibrating strings *[Saitenspiel]* of a stimulus" (601). Herder employs some striking imagery to suggest the *active* aspect to perception, in language Nietzsche will later apply to the drives: "This nerve wants to enjoy: see how it *wells out* toward its object! how the ends of its outermost branches strain upward. The tongue tastes in advance: juices, life-spirits rush to welcome the new guest."[31] Herder's answer to the question of how the manifold of sensations is unified into a coherent image of the world is psychological and physiological at the same time: the power of the soul is imagination (*Einbildung,* the forming into an image), and the locus where the inner and outer worlds are unified is the nervous system (*EMS* 606–7).

Nietzsche will have found all these ideas attractive—except for Herder's introduction of the figure, albeit in striking imagery, of the divine creator of it all: "It was an act of paternal benevolence when the Creator concealed the dark abyss of organic stimulation. . . . The electric current of the nerves is the fiery script of the Creator in us for the inner human being" (*EMS* 608). Being disinclined to invoke the Creator in order to illuminate the mysterious transformation that takes place in the medium between outer and inner, Nietzsche is content to let the mysteries stand.

The mysteries are presented, if not demystified, in the essay "On Truth and Lie," in the context of a more general characterization of the abyss that yawns beneath the human receptivity to stimulation.

> Humans are deeply immersed in illusions and dream-images, their eyes merely glide over the surfaces of things and see "forms," their sensation leads nowhere to truth but is content to receive stimuli *[Reize]* and to play, as it were, a groping game on the backs of things. Moreover, humans allow themselves to be deceived every night of their lives in dreams, without their moral sense ever trying to prevent it. (*KSA* 1:876; *PT* 80)

To compound the sense of mystery, Nietzsche duplicates the abyss, introducing another unbridgeable cleft into the process: "A nerve stimulus is first translated into an image—first metaphor. The image is then imitated in a sound—second metaphor. And each time a complete overleaping of one sphere into the midst of a quite new and different sphere." At this point Nietzsche again invokes Chladni's acoustical figures, supposing that a deaf person is looking at the vibrating string and the pattern of the sand and imagines he thereby knows what "sound" is. "We believe we know something of the things themselves when we speak of [them] . . . but we have nothing other than metaphors of things, which in no way correspond to the original entities."[32]

The claim that human awareness of the world is radically metaphorical plays on the root meaning of the word, which is "carry across" or "translate." The most puzzling process is the translation of nerve stimuli into visual images, involving as it does a move from one (physiological) sphere into another (psychological), which Nietzsche characterizes as a *projection* of *forms*.[33] He thinks that this projection depends in part upon an "all-preserving memory": "Perhaps the human being can *forget* nothing. . . . all forms that have once been generated by the brain and nervous system are often repeated from then on in the same way. The same nervous activity generates the same image again."[34] The mystery is a mystery because, as philosophers of mind since Descartes have kept on rediscovering, there is no plausible *causal* relation between an object in the world and one's experience of it, between some thing and images of it in consciousness.

> Even the relationship of a nerve-stimulus to the image produced is not a necessary one; but when the same image is produced a million times and is passed down through many generations of human beings . . . it eventually acquires the same significance for them as if it were the sole necessary image. (*KSA* 1:884; *PT* 87)

As the play of images on the surface of consciousness is translated into the sounds of words, concepts are formed by abstraction from individual images and are then used to construct a framework by means of which the dynamic manifold of experience can be controlled and made secure. This construction—which Nietzsche characterizes in magnificent imagery of pyramids, Roman columbaria, spiders' webs, and bees' hives—comes to stand on a foundation of "running water," over the unstoppable flux of life.[35] Experiential stability is achieved by virtue of ignoring the flow below:

> Only by forgetting that primitive world of metaphor, only through the solidification and rigidification of a primordial mass of images streaming forth from the primal faculty of human phantasy in a fiery fluidity . . . and only through the human being's forgetting himself as an *artistically creating* subject does he live with any peace, security, and consistency. (*KSA* 1:883; *PT* 86)

This is the first full formulation of Nietzsche's radical conception of the phantastic relation of the human self to the world, which will remain at the core of his mature thought. The world of everyday experience is a construct imposed by conceptualization upon an underlying flux of imagery. Nor does the flow of images bear any logical or causal relation to any objective reality outside or beyond it:

> Between two absolutely different spheres, as between subject and object, there is no causality, no correctness, no expression, but at most an *aesthetic* relation, by which I mean an allusive transference, a stammering translation into a completely foreign language—for which there is required a freely composing and freely inventing intermediate sphere and mediating force.

The medium of the imagination is not simply the human faculty responsible for casual reverie or daydreaming, but an *Urvermögen,* a primal capability that makes for the possibility of any kind of experience whatsoever. Near the beginning of the second, unfinished section of "On Truth and Lie," Nietzsche writes of "the fundamental human drive":

> This drive to imagine metaphors *[Trieb zur Metapherbildung],* which is impossible to think away for even a moment—since to do so would be to think away human beings altogether, even though a regular and rigid new world is built over it as a fortress out of its own products evaporated into concepts, it is not truly subdued and is scarcely even mastered. It seeks a new field for its operations and another channel, which it finds in myth and in art generally. (*KSA* 1:887; *PT* 88–89)

The idea that "the fundamental human drive" is to act as an artistically creating subject in the medium of phantasy, while anathema to many modern epistemologists, is a basic tenet of much of the German Idealist tradition. It is even prefigured in the thought of as sober a thinker as Kant, in his idea of the transcendental imagination (see chapter 7, below). Perhaps Nietzsche's participation in this tradition has gone unnoticed because he rarely uses the traditional term *Einbildungskraft,* preferring the more poetic *Phantasie* and its cognates. We shall return to this theme later, in Nietzsche's elaborations of it, in the early 1880s, into a primary feature of his thinking (see chapter 8, below).

If effectively suppressed by the powers of reason, primal phantasy finds expression in myth and art. Before Socratic rationalism came to prevail, philosophical thinking was itself, in its reflections on *archai,* a product of "archetypal" phantasy. Indeed Nietzsche argues in another unpublished monograph from 1873 that the greatness of pre-Socratic philosophy came primarily from its imaginative powers.[36] There he asks what distinguishes philosophical thinking from calculative thinking (*rechnendes Denken*—a favorite term of the later Heidegger) and brings it more quickly to its goal. The answer is that philosophical thinking is sustained by "an alien, unlogical power: phantasy," by virtue of which it is able to "leap from possibility

to possibility."[37] The pre-Socratic philosopher is said to unite both Apollonian and Dionysian powers, as well as features of the saint and the scientist,
in one person—though the Dionysian seems to be dominant.

> Feeling himself swell out to the macrocosm, he nevertheless stays
> sufficiently collected to regard himself coolly as the reflection *[Wied-
> erschein]* of the world, retaining that restraint possessed by the dra-
> matic artist when he transforms himself into other bodies and speaks
> out of them—and yet can project this transformation to the outside in
> written verses.[38]

Nietzsche often wondered about the nature of the philosopher at this time—
being in the process of becoming one himself. In his writing, the tendency
of the philosopher's self to swell to excess, to cosmic proportions, is kept in
check by a moment of Apollonian contemplation, which is now assimilated
to the self-projection that presumably prevents the dramatist from dissolving into the multiplicity of his characters.

From a psychological perspective, the significance of *Philosophy in the
Tragic Age of the Greeks* lies less in its readings of the fragments of the
major pre-Socratic figures than in its basic premise concerning the importance of the *personal* element in any philosophy. The work begins with the
claim that all philosophical systems have one absolutely incontrovertible
point to them: "a personal mood *[Stimmung]*, a coloration, which can
be used to realize the image of the philosopher, just as one can deduce the
nature of the soil from the kind of vegetation it supports."[39] Nietzsche's
concern is thus "to set into relief that part of each system that is a piece of
personality," so as to bring to light "the great human being" behind the
philosophy. He characterizes the difference between us moderns and the
ancient Greeks as one concerning the personal: "Whereas for the moderns
even the most personal things are sublimated into abstractions, for [the
ancient Greeks] even the most abstract ideas kept running back into a
person."[40]

An unpublished note from 1873 sums up this theme beautifully, and is
sufficiently pregnant to merit, in spite of its brevity, being indented:

> The product of the philosopher is his *life* (primarily, before his *works*).
> That is his art-work.[41]

While he continued to believe in the priority of life over works, Nietzsche's
own life was to become more and more dominated by what he saw as his
task, his *Aufgabe*—which was to devote his life to writing. A dreadful task
for one who suffered from the kinds of eye ailments to which Nietzsche was
becoming ever more prone. Indeed his first book, *The Birth of Tragedy,* was
also the last he would write totally on his own, without assistance. While

working on the first of the *Untimely Meditations* in 1873, his eyesight dete-
riorated so far as to force him to resort to dictation—an expedient that
would be necessary for (at least parts of) all his subsequent works. In May
of that year his doctor forbade him to do any reading whatsoever, which
meant that he had to lecture for some time without notes.[42] Gradually more
frequent medical prohibitions against reading and writing would necessitate
his resignation from the university six years later.

Rootings through the Past

> *The world exists for the education of each man. There is no age
> or state of society or mode of action in history, to which there
> is not somewhat corresponding in his life. . . . He should see
> that he can live all history in his own person.*
>
> Emerson, "History"

Nietzsche at one point projected a series of a dozen or so monographs under
the title *Untimely Meditations,* but he published only four: the first in 1873,
the second two in 1874, and the fourth (though begun the same year) in
1876. The first *Meditation,* "David Strauss, the Confessor and Writer," was
instigated to a large extent by Wagner and is of minor psychological interest. Its opening section, however, is remarkable for its excoriation of German "culture"—insofar as it marked a decisive step *away* from the Master
and his cult. Wagner's racial intolerance included a pronounced contempt
for French culture, and nobody had been more delighted when the Prussian
forces defeated France in the war of 1870–71. It is thus a subtle declaration
of hostilities when Nietzsche begins his essay on Strauss by warning against
"the grave and dangerous consequences of war, and especially of one that
has ended victoriously." He goes on to say that the delusion that "German
culture too was victorious in the struggle" is pernicious, insofar as it may
lead to *"the defeat, if not the extirpation, of the German spirit for the sake
of the 'German Reich'"* (*DS* 1).

   That Wagner did not take offense at this may suggest more about the
degree of attention with which he read the essay than about his tolerance
for antipathetic ideas within his circle. The relations between the Master
and his eager disciple were beginning to become strained. In order to preserve his independence, Nietzsche would decline invitations to visit, and
this would offend the magnanimous host. And yet when they were together,
Nietzsche's demeanor would often be so self-abasing as to cause Wagner

considerable irritation. Perhaps the alienation from Ritschl intensified Nietzsche's father-complex, but in any case the grace that formerly informed his relations with Wagner was ebbing away.

In a letter to Gersdorff Nietzsche writes that he had no idea that his failure to visit the Wagners in Bayreuth for the New Year had caused such grave offense.

> God alone knows how often I manage to offend the Master: I never cease to be amazed by this, and am absolutely incapable of fathoming the reason for it. . . . I simply cannot imagine how one could be more loyal to Wagner in all major respects and more deeply devoted to him than I am. . . . But on minor, peripheral points and through a holding back from *more frequent* personal living together that is necessary for me in an almost "sanitary" sense, I must retain a certain freedom in order to be able to maintain that loyalty in the higher sense.[43]

But when he actually did take up the invitation to visit Bayreuth, Nietzsche's nervousness seems to have made the situation worse rather than better. If the abject tone of his letter of thanks after the visit is any indication of his demeanor during it, one can perhaps sympathize with Wagner's irritation.

> If you did not seem happy with me when I was with you, I understand it all too well, without being able to do anything to change it. . . . I know well, dearest Master, that such a visit can hardly be relaxing for you, and must even be unbearable. I have so often wished I could give the appearance of greater freedom and independence, but in vain. Please, I beseech you, take me as merely your pupil, if possible with pen in hand and notebook ready before me, and moreover as a pupil with a very slow and quite unversatile intelligence.[44]

The obsequiousness of this passage makes it hard to believe it was meant in all sincerity. It represents a remarkable nadir of self-obfuscation on Nietzsche's part, a desperate attempt to hide from himself the truth that another father figure was failing him—by ascribing the failing to himself instead. When we consider the third and fourth *Untimely Meditations,* on the figures of Schopenhauer and Wagner, we shall see how they enact Nietzsche's struggle to separate from these two mentors and detach himself psychologically by withdrawing his projections onto them.

The last three *Meditations* are rich and richly textured essays; in bringing out the psychological themes, the context will of necessity be neglected. The second essay, "On the Use and Disadvantage of History for Life," has a distinctly Emersonian tone to its images.[45] Its major theme is that while history—in the sense of a conscious relationship to the past—is necessary for the life of an individual or a people or culture, a surfeit of historical knowledge is detrimental to life as lived in the present. The key notion of the essay's opening is the *horizon* that every living being has to draw around itself in order to survive (*HL* 1). There is a need for a kind of membrane to separate self from other, inner from outer, the present moment from past and future; and the health of the living being will depend on the permeability of that membrane and its flexibility with respect to expansions and contractions. To be fully human we must *remember,* in ways that animals do not; and yet if we remember too much we are crushed by the burden of the past and go under. Nietzsche posits it as "a general law" that

> every living being can be healthy, strong, and fruitful only within a horizon: if it is unable to draw a horizon around itself, or is too selfish to be able to include its own view within that of another *[eines fremden],* it will waste away slowly or else hasten too quickly to its timely end *[Untergang].*

In order to thrive one must resist closing oneself off completely and be flexible enough to be able to adopt a view foreign to oneself, to participate in the perspective of another being. The point upon which the full health of the organism hinges is

> the *plastic power* of a human being, or a people, or a culture, the power to grow out of oneself in one's own way, to transform *[umbilden]* and incorporate what is past and foreign, to heal wounds, to replace what has been lost, to reform out of one's self broken forms.

Several metaphorical strands are entwined in this passage. The primary image behind the "plastic power" is artistic, having to do with "molding, forming, sculpting" (the meanings of the Greek root, *plassein*). But this image is conjoined with natural images having to do with growth, nourishment, and healing. It is difficult to preserve in English the rich linguistic ramifications of Nietzsche's discussion of these themes: the German translation of *plassein, bilden,* has the advantage of connoting the image *(Bild)* as well as the process of formation—which makes it all the more appropriate a term in the context of *Bildung,* which means both "education" and "culture."

There is in the *Untimely Meditations* an important development (of which the author may well not have been conscious) in Nietzsche's metaphorical discourse concerning the workings of the soul. In the earlier writings the natural imagery was for the most part elemental, having to do with the earth, rivers and seas, skies, storms, and lightning. The elemental level persists in the *Meditations* too: in the third essay the culmination of the educator's task is imagined cosmically as the reorganization of "the entire human being into a vitally dynamic solar and planetary system" (*SE* 2); and in the fourth, the artist's drives are said to cross in their vectors between earth and the ether, while his tempestuous will is imagined as a mountain torrent plunging through gorges and ravines (*WB* 9). But now the imagery also develops out of certain combinations of natural elements, interactions between the powers of heaven and earth, into a new realm—that of *organic life*.

The "root metaphors" in the essay on history are drawn from the realm of vegetation, with special emphasis on a primary feature of the vegetal psyche distinguished by Aristotle: the capacity to absorb nourishment.[46] This figures importantly in Nietzsche's psychology, insofar as the process of nourishment involves a crossing of the boundary between outside and inside, as something *other* is incorporated through a membrane into the self. While a being may remain healthy through avoiding such absorption, by forgetting, more powerful natures gain strength by appropriating the past through appropriate remembrance, sinking roots through to the deepest strata of history.

> The stronger the roots of a human being's innermost nature, the more one will appropriate and arrogate to oneself; and for the most power- ful and tremendous nature there would be no limit to the historical sense . . . it would draw to itself and take in the entire past, its own and the most foreign, and as it were transform it into blood. (*HL* 1)

Maximum openness by way of the appropriate kind of historical sense is something Nietzsche will continue to consider worth striving for, as we shall see. However, at the end of the essay, he offers the following diagnosis of the sickness of modern life: "An excess of history has attacked the plastic power of life, such that it no longer understands how to use the past as strong nourishment."[47] Nietzsche is dealing here again with the problem of how to order psychological multiplicity, which has been aggravated by the opening up for him of new and farther historical horizons. Questions of which field to explore, which talents to nourish, are deeply compounded by the greater influx of historical possibilities. In his encounter with the figures of Western history, Nietzsche's desire to incorporate massively is tempered by the fear of being overwhelmed, the desire to grow by assimilating the other nutritively is checked by the dangers of excessive ingestion, which could lead to breakdown or explosion.[48]

The second section of the essay distinguishes among the monumental, the antiquarian, and the critical species of history—corresponding to the human being who acts and strives, who preserves and reveres, and who suffers and seeks liberation, respectively. Nietzsche warns that each of the three species can flourish only in the proper "soil and climate": "in any other it grows into a devastating weed" (*HL* 2). The image of the *tree* in particular becomes important in the context of the antiquarian kind of history (*HL* 3). One who cultivates this strain of the discipline will be rewarded by "the sense of well-being that the tree has in its roots, the happiness of knowing that one is not completely arbitrary and accidental but grows out of a past as an heir, blossom, and fruit." But should there be excessive focus on the past, an over-concentration on the roots, and insufficient openness to the atmosphere of ongoing life in the present, "the tree dies an unnatural death, from the top gradually down to the roots—until finally the roots themselves perish too."

If one is to flourish in the present, another way of regarding the past is necessary, what Nietzsche calls the "critical" kind of history: "one must have the strength, and exercise it from time to time, to break up and dissolve parts of the past." When one sees that some strain from the past deserves to perish, "one takes the knife to its roots." This image exemplifies the duality between the natural and the human-natural that operates throughout Nietzsche's metaphorical discourses: on the one hand, the soul as a world of natural vegetation; on the other, the possibility of working with the process of growth through the practice of psychical agriculture or horticulture. There is an interplay between natures in this pondering of possible responses to the ambiguous burden that is laid upon us by fate:

> Just as we are the result of earlier generations, we are also the result of their aberrations, passions, and errors, and even their crimes; it is not possible wholly to free oneself from this chain. . . . The best we can do is to combat our inherited and hereditary nature with our knowledge of it and even have a new, disciplined culture *[Zucht]* fight our archaic and innate acquisition, and we implant in ourselves a new habitude, a new instinct, a second nature, so that the first nature withers away . . . —always a dangerous attempt, because it is so difficult to find the borderline in negating the past, and because second natures are mostly weaker than the first ones. (*HL* 3)

Since a part of our inheritance as human beings is baneful, some historical knowledge is necessary for combating it: it is a truism of depth psychology that what remains unconscious is on that account difficult, if not impossible, to guard against. With two (or more) natures contending in the soul, one has recourse to the several practices connoted by the word *Zucht*—an important term in Nietzsche's psychology which refers to the cultivation of plants and breeding of animals, as well as to the training or disciplining of human beings. In these relations one acknowledges the presence of a living other, capable of action as well as reaction, and must take care not to press the discipline so far that it destroys the natural endowment.

A more sophisticated feature of the psyche than nutrition, distinctive of the "animal" soul as discussed by Aristotle, is sexual procreation, which in humans is often accompanied by the passion of erotic love. Just as the vegetal imagery is meant to suggest that there are processes in the psyche that are best engaged through the practice of husbandry, so there are affairs that are best understood under the metaphorics of *erōs*. (The only things Socrates comes close to admitting expertise in are things erotic.)[49] In the opening section of the essay on history, in the context of the horizon that every being must draw around itself in order to survive, Nietzsche adduces the example of a man "seized and transported by a great passion, for a woman or for a great idea," and remarks "how different the world has become for him!" The perspective of passion is above all narrow and strait, blind to all else, and so unjust—just as all life is.

> It is the most unjust condition in the world: narrow, ungrateful to what is past, blind to dangers and deaf to admonitions, a small vortex of life in a dead sea of night and forgetting. And yet this condition— unhistorical, antihistorical through and through—is the womb not only of the unjust but of every just deed too. . . . The one who takes action . . . forgets most things so as to do one thing. . . . [He] loves his deed infinitely more than it deserves to be loved; and the finest deeds take place in such an overabundance *[Überschwang]* of love.[50]

The good action is action infused with *erōs,* when things are seen with the penetrating power of love, even if the deeper vision is at the expense of the broader. (This is not to deny that some of the worst deeds may be done in the grip of passion: Nietzsche will write later of the fatal weight of "the stupidity of the passions" [*TI* 5.1].)

The problem with the modern attitude toward history is precisely that it lacks passion, having lost touch with the vital drives. The modern historian "has annihilated and lost his instinct, and, having lost faith in the 'divine animal,' he can no longer let go the reins when his reason falters and his way leads through deserts."[51] The diminution of passion in the interests of "objectivity" emasculates the scholar, leading to sterility in the discipline and a lack of creativity.

> Or can it be that a race of eunuchs is necessary as guardians of the great historical world-harem? Pure objectivity certainly suits such creatures beautifully. It almost seems as if the task were to stand guard over history to make sure that nothing comes out of her except more history—but certainly no real events! . . . For the eunuch one woman is like the next, just a woman, woman in herself, the eternally unapproachable. . . . And since the eternal feminine will never draw you upward, you draw it down to you and, being neuters yourselves, you take history also to be neuter.[52]

Behind the allusion to the closing lines of Goethe's *Faust* concerning the power of "the eternal feminine" to draw us ever upward are echoes of Plato's ideas about the role of *erōs* in the practice of philosophy. According to Diotima's speech in the *Symposium,* it is *erōs* that drives the philosopher higher and higher in the ascent toward the ultimate union with absolute beauty.

In pointing up their lack of creativity by calling the objective scholars eunuchs and neuters, Nietzsche specifically denies them the title of "hermaphrodites"—perhaps because he himself is beginning to see psychical hermaphroditism as an ideal.[53] The parallel with Plato becomes even clearer when Nietzsche returns to the theme of love:

> It is only in love, only when shaded by the illusion produced by love, that the human being can create. . . . When someone is compelled no longer to love unconditionally, the roots of his strength are cut off: he must wither away. . . . Only when history, transformed into a work of art, can endure becoming a pure artistic construct, will it be able to preserve instincts—and perhaps even arouse them.[54]

Nietzsche had begun the essay on history by quoting Goethe's saying, "I hate everything that merely instructs me without augmenting or directly invigorating my activities." He takes this as his motto in his discussion of history, which is worthwhile only insofar as it enhances life in the present. Hence the emphasis on approaching the appropriate past with passion, so that from an abundance of love something can be created, and the historical past, as well as one's own past and present existence, can be re-formed into a work of art.

Mastering Multiplicities

> *I accept the clangor and jangle of contrary tendencies. . . . The middle region of our being is the temperate zone.*
>
> Emerson, "Experience"

The writing of the third and fourth *Untimely Meditations* appears to have fulfilled an important psychological need on Nietzsche's part. With these essays the desire to rebel against his mentors, which he was unable to express openly (deprecating Schopenhauer in front of Wagner would be tantamount to slighting the Master himself), began to find an outlet in his writings, which were on one level becoming a form of depth-psychological therapy. On sending a copy of the Schopenhauer essay to Malwida von Meysenbug, Nietzsche wrote in the accompanying letter:

How shall I feel when I have finally put outside of me all the negative and rebellious things that are in me? . . . Just imagine a series of fifty works, all of them—just like the four so far—*forced* out of my inner experience into the light of day.[55]

And while working on the Wagner essay, still with a longer series in mind, he makes a telling remark about its function when he talks about devoting the next five years to finishing the series "in order thereby to cleanse the soul as much as possible of all polemical-passionate clutter."[56] (The products of this kind of catharsis are often unimpressive, artistically speaking, but the last two "untimely ones" are happy exceptions.)

The idea that great human beings are representative of "possibilities of life," potentialities resident within the individual who comes under their influence, is prominent in Emerson. "We need not fear excessive influence," he wrote in "Uses of Great Men," the prelude to *Representative Men:* "A more generous trust is permitted. Serve the great." Emerson encourages an identification with the great figures of the past—Plato, Swedenborg, Montaigne, Shakespeare, Napoleon, Goethe (all except Swedenborg great for Nietzsche, too)—for the purpose of awakening inchoate aspects of our own souls. One can (in Nietzsche's terms) "become what one is" by (in Emerson's) "becoming another": "Be the limb of their body, the breath of their mouth. Compromise thy egotism. . . . Be another: not thyself, but a Platonist; not a soul, but a Christian; not a naturalist, but a Cartesian; not a poet, but a Shakesperian." As long as one eludes the anxiety of influence, in writing of great predecessors one will be writing also of oneself.

Nietzsche may not have become explicitly aware of the autobiographical character of the last two *Untimely Meditations* until later, when, looking back from the culmination of his writing career in *Ecce Homo,* he said of them:

I should not like to deny that basically they speak only of me. The essay "Wagner in Bayreuth" is a vision of my future; by contrast, in "Schopenhauer as Educator" it is my own innermost history, my *becoming,* that is inscribed. Above all my *promise!* . . . It is basically not "Schopenhauer as Educator" who speaks here but his *opposite,* "Nietzsche as Educator."[57]

At the end of the previous chapter he had said of the essay on Wagner:

In all psychologically decisive places I alone am discussed—one can simply substitute my name or the word "Zarathustra" wherever the word Wagner appears in the text. The whole image of the *dithyrambic* artist is the image of the *preexistent* poet of Zarathustra. . . . Even psychologically all decisive traits of my own nature are projected

into Wagner's—the close proximity of the brightest and the most cal-
amitous forces, the will to power as no human being has ever possessed it.[58]

These passages have been taken by followers of Schopenhauer and Wagner
to be exercises in retrospective rationalization on Nietzsche's part, attempts
to negate the significance these figures had for his early development, before he repudiated their influence. But such construals demand that one ignore Nietzsche's open declarations of his admiration for (at least certain
aspects of) Schopenhauer and Wagner throughout his career. They also
overlook his enduring concern with the personal elements in ideas, as well
as his later insights into the phenomenon of psychological projection. While
he may not have been conscious of it at the time, Nietzsche is surely right
to say later that his views of his two mentors were deeply conditioned by
projections onto them of traits latent in his own psyche.

Just as he had earlier characterized the philologist as a synthesizer of
disparate drives, so Nietzsche now painted portraits of the artist as a young
philosopher and of the thinker as a revolutionary artist. In projecting these
ideal images of the two father figures who had had the most profound recent
influence on him, Nietzsche gained insight into the psychology of the
thinker and the artist per se, in part because he was seeing his own psyche
projected as he strove to bring together these divergent traits.

The difficulty of the Wagner essay was compounded by the fact that
since beginning it, in 1874, Nietzsche had been formulating a number of
trenchant criticisms of the Master, which he entered in his notebooks of the
period. After finishing a first draft of the essay, he decided not to publish it
after all, so strong was his ambivalence toward its subject becoming. It was
only later, on the encouragement of his new friend, the young composer
Heinrich Köselitz (later known as Peter Gast), that he decided he could
incorporate at least some of the criticisms in such a way that Wagner would
not be offended and he himself could live with his conscience. The idea was
to present Wagner's shortcomings as elements of his character that he had
overcome on his way to becoming a great artist and human being, and to
have the essay published in time to take it to Bayreuth for the world pre-
mière of *The Ring*. The essay was completed and presented in time, but of
course Wagner overlooked the critical parts of it entirely.[59]

Echoes of Emerson resound through passages in *Schopenhauer as Educator,* especially in the tone of the engagement with the topics of history
and fate.[60] The individual is understood as the focus of multiple forces of
fate, which form the basis for the uniqueness of human individuality—at
least when it can be authentic and determine what is its own, proper self, in

contrast to mere outer shell and protective covering. What makes the individual unique is his or her temporal specificity, a sense of "this-one-time":

> Deep down every human being well knows that he is in the world only one time, unique, and that no such strange chance will throw together a second time such a wonderfully many-colored assortment into a unity such as he is: he knows it, but conceals it like a bad conscience. (*SE* 1)

What would wrest one from absorption in the mass of people is precisely the call of (the good) conscience, which exhorts: "Be yourself! You are not all that which you are now doing, believing, desiring." Nietzsche later appeals—in images reminiscent of Socrates—to "those peculiar conditions in which we are suddenly assailed by unpleasant memories" and wonders what these "gnats [are] that will not let us sleep." The past lays claim to us, calling us to our task in vintage existential fashion.

> There are spirits all around us, every moment of our lives wants to say something to us, but we do not want to hear this voice of the spirits [*Geisterstimme*]. We are afraid that when we are alone and all is still, something will be whispered in our ear, and so we hate quiet and deafen ourselves with sociability.[61]

Nietzsche is still emphasizing the *fated* nature of existence, the dimension of a past destined, something spoken *(fatum)* by a voice *(Stimme)* that yet tends to be drowned out by conversation within the conventions of the contemporary world. The young soul trembles when it hears the call of conscience, for "when it thinks of its true liberation it has a premonition of the measure of happiness that has been destined [*bestimmt*] for it for eternities." Indeed, the major stimulus to our taking responsibility for ourselves is

> the inexplicable fact that we live precisely today, when we had infinite time during which to come into existence, that we possess only a brief today during which to show why and to what end we have come into existence precisely now. We are responsible to ourselves for our own existence [*Dasein*]. One has to take a rather bold and dangerous line with it—especially since, in the best as in the worst case, we are bound to lose it.

Nietzsche's abiding concern with the strangely fated and irrevocably finite nature of our existence issues here in a sense of existential responsibility: even though he no longer believes that we owe our being here to God the creator, he does see us as *indebted* for our existence to the convergence of an enormous number of prior forces. The idea of a responsibility to the ancestors—forces of fate in personal form—will become an important element in his later thinking.

The second section of the Schopenhauer essay broaches the problem of psychical multiplicity in the context of pedagogy, beginning by pondering two contemporary "educational maxims":

> One of them demands that the educator recognize early on the particular strength of each of his pupils and then direct all energies and saps and all sunshine toward it, in order to help that one virtue to attain true ripeness and fruitfulness. The other maxim, by contrast, would have the educator cultivate all the energies in the pupil, tending them so as to bring them into a harmonious relationship with each other.[62]

He suggests that the path of harmonious development might be suitable for "weaker natures," none of whose inclinations amounts to much when taken individually. But a "harmonious totality" worth the name—"the sounding together of many voices in one nature"—will be found only in human beings

> in whom everything—knowledge, desire, loving, hating—strives centripetally toward a root force, and where a harmonious system of movements to and fro, up and down, is formed by the compelling domination *[herrschende Übergewalt]* of this living center.

Nietzsche concludes that the two pedagogical maxims are not mutually exclusive, that together they acknowledge that a well-formed human being will have both a center and a periphery. In that case the educating philosopher will "not only discover the central force, but also know how to prevent its acting destructively on the other forces." The task of education would thus be "to reorganize *[umbilden]* the entire human being into a vitally dynamic solar and planetary system and to understand its higher mechanics."[63] The terms in which he frames the problem of multiplicity here are drawn from his own experience—the many voices, the need for a dominant center to avoid flying off in all directions; but they are also influenced by Plato's imagery—the channeling of fluids, the need for harmony, the reigning sun.

Also crucial to the educative process is the cultivation of the kind of fruitfulness that comes from love in the sense of *erōs* or passion. In an extended comparison of the scholar and the genius, Nietzsche writes: "Science behaves toward wisdom as virtuousness is toward holiness: it is cold and dry; it has no love, and knows nothing of deep feelings of dissatisfaction and yearning."[64] Suspicious of the motivation of the scholar, he analyzes the putative "drive for truth" into a number of other drives that he maintains are the true motive forces behind scholarship. Alluding to the myth of the metals in the *Republic,* he claims that "the scholar consists of a complex net-

work of quite different drives and stimuli; he is an altogether impure metal."
In the interests of a "driveless knowledge," he says, "a host of small, very
human drives and subdrives are poured together." But since there is no
ruling passion,

> the scholar is by his very nature *unfruitful* . . . and has a certain natural
> hatred for the fruitful human being. . . . [The scholar] wants to kill
> nature, to understand it by dissecting it, while [the genius] wants to
> augment *[vermehren]* nature through a new and vital nature.

This rather Romantic opposition between the coldly scientific approach
("we murder to dissect") and the passionate procreative engagement with
nature will undergo considerable refinement when Nietzsche adopts a
cooler, more scientific attitude in his next book, *Human, All Too Human*
(1878).

Before going on to consider the last *Untimely Meditation,* let us look
briefly at a passage from the unpublished notebooks, written while
Nietzsche was working on the essay on Wagner, which anticipates the relevant themes in that essay while illuminating Nietzsche's own life situation
at the time in magnificent vegetal imagery.

> There comes for every man an hour in which he asks himself in won-
> derment: "How is one able to live? And yet one does live!"—an hour
> in which he begins to understand that he possesses an inventiveness
> of the same kind as he admires in plants, which climb and wind and
> finally gain some light and a patch of soil and thus create for them-
> selves their share of joy on inhospitable ground. In describing one's
> life, there is always a point at which one is amazed that the plant is
> still able to live at all. . . . There are careers, those of thinkers, where
> the difficulties have grown enormous; and here . . . one must listen
> attentively, for one can discern here certain *possibilities of life,* merely
> to hear about which confers happiness and strength and inundates the
> lives of successors with light.[65]

Nietzsche here evinces an awareness that he possesses a vegetal strength
that runs deeper than his personal abilities, that forces of nature work
through him at the same time as forces of fate work against him; an amazement that in spite of the difficulties engendered by his professional situation
and the relationship with Wagner, he is still able to grow and to show promise of later flourishing. Anticipating a crucial motif in the essay on Wagner,
he goes on, in a distinctly Heraclitean vein:

> The astonishing thing in such careers is that two hostile drives press-
> ing in different directions are forced to proceed as it were under a
> single yoke: the one who wants knowledge must repeatedly leave the

ground on which human beings live in order to venture out into the uncertain, while the drive that wants life must repeatedly seek a more or less secure place on which to stand. . . . The greater the conflict between life and knowledge . . . the fuller and more flourishing the life.[66]

The image of a psychological multiplicity that emerges (in Dionysian fashion) from a duality, from the crossing of two drives is prominent in *Richard Wagner in Bayreuth*. Nietzsche describes the beginning of "the drama of his life" as follows:

His nature appears in a terrible way simplified, torn apart into two drives or spheres. Below there rages the violent current of a vehement will, which strives for the light through every imaginable course, cave, and gorge, and which longs for power . . . a will with an unbridled tyrannical desire.[67]

From above comes the gentle voice of

a spirit full of love, overflowing *[überschwänglich]* with goodness and sweetness, with a hatred of violence and self-destruction and an aversion to seeing anyone in chains. This is what spoke to Wagner. It let itself down on him and consolingly wrapped its wings around him. It showed him the way.

This love overflows out of emotional excess: *Überschwang,* which connotes welling up, and especially the ecstasy of the mystical experience.[68] In the two drives of his nature are flow and counterflow—while even the first flow is strangely *contra naturam,* consisting of a current that somehow defies the force of gravity by flowing *up* toward the light.

The ability to bear the crossing of these two drives in one's own person is the mark of the dithyrambic dramatist, whose art "lets us experience everything that a soul experiences that goes on a journey, participates in other souls and their destiny, and learns to look into the world from out of many eyes" (*WB* 7). This ability to participate in other souls and see with many eyes, which in *The Birth of Tragedy* is ascribed to the dramatist alone (*BT* 8), will later come to be the hallmark of the astute philosopher and a trait to be cultivated by anyone who aspires to psychological understanding. (Such developments further encourage our taking the dramatic artist in the "Bayreuth" essay as Nietzsche as much as Wagner and the artwork referred to there as *Zarathustra* as much as *The Ring.*)

The effect on the audience of this kind of empathetic participation is an "alienation" *(Entfremdung)* from one's everyday self that has much in common with the Dionysiac experience. How is this effect produced? The feeling is engendered by the upward tendency of one of the artist's two drives: to the dithyrambic artist elevated by the spirit of love, "everything that seems quotidian to others, seems uncanny."[69] One is transported to another realm, existentially alienated, no longer at home. There is a "crossing" of sensation, however, "when to the brightness of his shivering exuberance *[Übermut]* a quite different drive associates itself: the yearning from the heights into the depths, the loving desire for the earth, for the happiness of common ground." Inspiration elevates the artist, drawing one up and out; but there is also a drive down toward earth and body, an impulse of love that brings one back to the hearts of things. And in the tension between the two, something new is generated:

> For those are the procreative moments of his art, when he is held in this crossing of feelings, and that uncannily exuberant surprise *[unheimlich-übermütige Befremdung]* and wonder at the world couple with the longing urge to approach the same world as a lover. The looks he then casts on the earth and life are like sunbeams that "draw up water," create mists, spread thunderclouds around.[70]

Of interest here is the juxtaposition of procreative imagery with signs of the artist's participation in the play of natural forces. Natural flows are countered by unnatural, up and down, and are imagined as procreative forces *within* the same individual, a charting of the flows of *erōs*. The crossing is itself crossed gender-wise in the description of Wagner/Nietzsche's nature: before, the violent stream of masculine energy was said to come from below, and the feminine voice of love from above; now, the feminine appears to be below, as "nature seen naked," while the drive that would approach the world "as a lover," casting beams of light and heat onto earth and water, has a more masculine feel to it. But then, again, the two drives are called "brothers."

If in *The Birth of Tragedy* the work of art is generated out of the sexual (and therefore "unnatural") union of the "brothers" Apollo and Dionysus, this is an indication less of homosexual proclivities in the author than of his recognition that—in Jungian terms—psychological work is an *opus contra naturam,* that psychological imagery works at cross-purposes to the natural.[71] Something corresponding to the "monstrous" crossing between brothers recurs in a description of the gradual *rapprochement* between the two basic forces of Wagner/Nietzsche's nature as described in the "Bayreuth" essay:

> From then on, the higher self no longer condescends to pay service to its violent, more earthy brother: it *loves* him and must serve him. . . . The impetuous drive runs its course as before, but on other paths, toward where the higher self is at home; and the latter correspond-

ingly descends to the earth and recognizes its likeness in everything earthy. (*WB* 8)

This passage affords a sharper image of the "crossing" in the previous quotation, and delineates a schema that will be decisive in Nietzsche's later psychological musings: the "X" described by ascending and descending diagonal vectors intersecting within the soul.

Another kind of crossing associated with Dionysus is the crossing of borders—and especially of the border between the human realm and the rest of the natural world. Nietzsche's writing (discussed here in the guise of Wagner's music) will speak with a voice that breaks down such barriers, enacting an Orphic enchantment that gives voice to natural elements.

> Wagner the *musician* . . . has bestowed a language upon everything in nature that up to now has not wanted to speak . . . He plunges into daybreaks, woods, mist, ravines, mountain heights, the dread of night, the light of the moon, and remarks in them a secret desire: they too want to resound. . . . His music is never indefinite *[unbestimmt]*, merely moody *[stimmungshaft]*; everything that speaks through it, human being or nature, has a strictly individualized passion; storm and fire take on in him the compelling power of a personal will. (*WB* 9)

The borders will be breached just as completely, and nature speak in as melodious polyphony, in the natural lyricism of Nietzsche's *Zarathustra* (to which we shall attend in the next chapter).[72]

Nietzsche's praise of the great artist reverts to the theme of unity versus multiplicity, as he wonders at the "powerful *[übermächtig]* symphonic intelligence" that is able to bring such a mass of material into a harmonious whole.[73]

> To subdue unruly, contending masses to simple rhythms, to run one will through a confusing multiplicity of demands and desires. . . . I am amazed at the possibility of calculating the grand course of a multiplicity of passions that run in different directions.

Even though the artist's "tyrannical will" has by now been moderated through its union with the milder drive—at the end of section 9 Nietzsche praises the "severity and evenness of the [artist's] will"—there is a strong suggestion that the chaos can be ordered only by a will that derives its initial strength from intensely tyrannical desire.

What is interesting about these passages, and about the eulogies of Wagner's operas with which the essay ends, is Nietzsche's anticipation of later, depth-psychological readings of the Wagnerian opus, and especially of *Tristan* and *The Ring*.[74] Just as he had earlier imagined the dynamics of his own psyche enacted in Greek tragedy, he now saw the various currents of his inner life personified in the characters of Wagner's operas—and could thus be one of the first to suggest an "intrapsychical" reading of them. Indeed, Nietzsche's understanding of Wagner's character in relation to the characters in his music-dramas appears to have encouraged the development of his conception of the soul as consisting of a multiplicity of persons (the topic of chapters 8 and 9, below).

The figures Nietzsche writes about in the *Untimely Meditations* have many features that the maturing thinker wanted to develop in himself; but the work of writing himself into existence was hard—for he was as yet neither a philosopher nor an artist but a classics professor with a heavy teaching load. The tensions generated by the writing of the Wagner essay began to take their toll on his already weakened health. He was becoming more and more aware of what one would now call the psychosomatic components in his afflictions. In a letter to Malwida von Meysenbug from Steinabad, where he was taking a cure during the summer of 1875, he wrote: "People like us *never suffer only physically,* but everything is deeply intertwined with mental crises, so that I have no idea how I can ever regain my health through medicines and diets alone."[75] Things became so bad that by the end of the year he admitted to Gersdorff that his sending him a book of Indian proverbs came just at the right time:

> The conviction that life is valueless and the illusory nature of all goals often impresses itself upon me so strongly, especially when I am sick in bed, that I need to hear more about it [from Indian sources], but not combined with Judeo-Christian ways of talking. (13 Dec 1875)

Even though this letter is full of Schopenhauerian-Wagnerian talk of nirvana, Nietzsche also contemplates a solution in terms of unity versus multiplicity, in writing of his desire to achieve a state of health in which "the soul has retained only one drive, the will to know, and has otherwise become free of all drives and desires." In the context of the rest of his thinking about this issue, this desire for unity at the expense of multiplicity is as atypical as the talk of nirvana—and signifies the depths of the desperation to which his ill health could drive him. The separation from Schopenhauer and Wagner is not so far along that a bout of illness does not prompt a relapse into their worldview, which in times of better health Nietzsche was coming to see as life-denying in a way that was inimical to him.

He went home to Naumburg for Christmas, only to suffer the most massive attack of illness ever—a near total collapse of the system. While recuperating, he sent this ominous report to Gersdorff:

> I could no longer doubt that I am afflicted with a serious brain disease, and that my stomach and eye troubles stem from this central condi-

tion. My father died at the age of thirty-six from an inflammation of the brain, and it is possible that with me it will go even faster. (18 Jan 1876)

Nietzsche was thirty-one, and this anxiety that he would succumb to the same disease that killed his father would persist until his final collapse in 1889.

The next month, prevented by his illness from reading or writing, he was forced to give up lecturing at the university. Since his poor health had been interfering with his professional life for some time, the authorities at Basel granted him a year's leave with full pay on medical grounds. By July he felt sufficiently improved to be able to go to Bayreuth, and though he experienced moments of rapture at some points in the performances, the circuslike atmosphere of the festival sickened him. The Wagners were too busy with other things to be able to pay much attention to him, and after the first few days it became clear that the cultural renaissance he had devoted so much of his time and thought to helping Wagner achieve had degenerated into a dismal farce. Fearful of a complete breakdown, Nietzsche fled Bayreuth and took refuge in a small village on the edge of the Bavarian Forest. Although grateful for the quiet solitude there, he felt alienated not only from the Wagners and all they stood for, but also from his remaining friends: Franz Overbeck was just about to be married, and Rohde had just announced his engagement. However, he recovered enough to jot down some fragments that were to form the basis of his next book, *Human, All Too Human*.[76]

At this point all the major themes of Nietzsche's psychology have been introduced: what remains now is their development in more detail. From now on Nietzsche will write most of his works in the form of collections of aphorisms. This choice was to some extent motivated by necessity: his failing eyesight made longer periods of writing almost impossible, and so most of his subsequent works had to be composed in fragments scribbled down in between long bouts of walking or being bedridden. But the aphoristic style is also appropriate to a developing philosophy that is resolutely unsystematic and psychologically experimental. The different atmosphere of *Human, All Too Human* marks a significant transition in Nietzsche's oeuvre, and so calls for a change in our mode of approach.

Part Two

Several things are now going on, on several levels and in various complexes or currents of imagery, behind which stand a number of persons, among them major figures of the Western intellectual tradition—all existing simultaneously: moods, conflicting drives, fathers, and a multiplicity of other characters; myths and within myths mythical images; burgeoning branches and luxuriant exfoliations of imagery.

Nietzsche is at a stage in his life where most of its major features are about to change radically. He is ready to terminate his apprenticeship with Wagner, and is on the point of leaving forever the profession he was induced to enter a decade before, abandoning his home of ten years in Basel to embark upon ten years of writing rather than speaking, a decade of wandering from place to place, with no fixed abode. He will now be trying out different parts of Europe to live in, and experimenting with different styles and narratives for the writing that will fulfill his task.

The situation calls for a change in our way of proceeding, to an approach more appropriate to the complex and manifold topic of the soul as Nietzsche presents and represents it. In giving us a *logos* of *psyche,* he eschews proposing a theory that tells us what the soul is, but rather intimates what the soul is *like* by reporting its speech about itself in images. All the major types of psychological images have already been introduced through the texts considered in part 1. To continue chronologically, work by work, looking at "cross-sections" of Nietzsche's progress on each theme in each text, would likely be somewhat bewildering. Instead we shall follow the growth of each branch of imagery separately, beginning with the pivotal *Human, All Too Human,* proceeding through the texts in order, then returning to the beginning to pick up the next strand.

We shall follow successive strains of imagery in the order outlined in the introduction, ascending through layers of increasing complexity: from imagery of the elements, through fields of vegetal and agricultural metaphor and discourses in terms of animal husbandry, to imagery couched in the procreative activities that we human beings share with our animal relations. (The most complex level of psychological discourse, consisting of metaphors of human community, will be treated in part 3.) While Nietzsche holds these "natural" processes to be going on in the soul at all times, whether one is aware of them or not, there is also the possibility of *engaging* these processes consciously and contributing to the outcome by collaborating with their development. An interlude after chapter 4 explores the ways intervention can work naturally occurring elements into works of art. Similar engagements with natural processes of vegetal growth and sexual reproduction are discussed in the subsequent two chapters. As preparation for the discussion of procreation, an interlude before chapter 6 treats (all too) briefly the "question of woman" in Nietzsche's texts.

This thematic procedure will necessitate repeated passes through many of the same texts, in the course of which connections with features considered on previous passes will become apparent. Whatever exhaustion may be caused by this procedure should be more than compensated for by the advantages accruing from seeing the dynamics of the development of each particular branch of imagery—especially since these may be mimetic of organic developments that take place in the soul itself. In the project of charting the reaches of Nietzsche's psychology, the most modest part may be this second. The sheer abundance of imagery to be covered renders impossible a full discussion of its multiple meanings, and the author has often rested content with a taxonomy of the relevant images, leaving the elaboration of their significance to future occasions and other hands.

Plato comes from this point on to play a more important part, for once we have gone beyond the elemental layer of imagery we find ourselves in fields of images familiar from the Platonic dialogues. Nietzsche once declared himself to be in constant dialogue with Socrates—"Socrates stands, I have to admit, so close to me that I am almost always engaged in a struggle with him" (S 3:333)—but much of this conversation seems to be silent, and becomes fully audible only when we listen attentively to the images for the soul that Nietzsche has borrowed from his major precursor.

The following diagram may help the reader locate the expositions that follow within the matrix of Nietzsche's psychological imagery as a whole. Again it must be emphasized that this schema is not Nietzsche's own, but rather a heuristic device for the purposes of a clearer exposition. Nor is it intended to represent a hierarchy of images: the level of persons is not to be regarded as necessarily superior to the elemental level. The imagery does, however, become more complex at higher levels, if only because each level incorporates—and in that sense supersedes—the level below.

The diagram is intended to show how, for Nietzsche, the drives manifest themselves as images on a variety of levels of metaphor. The branching arrows on the right-hand side are meant to indicate that on each level certain drives, imagined as human agents within the psyche, are capable of working on other drives to produce a more complex level of meaning.

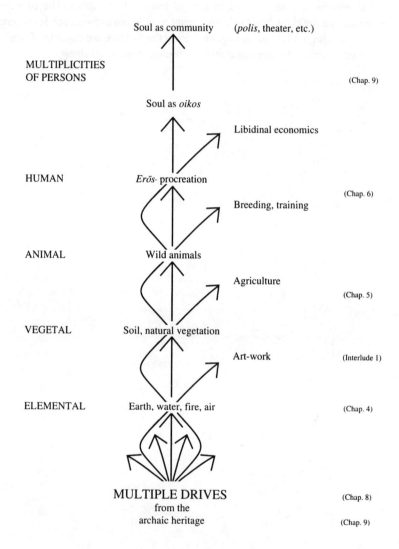

Soul as community   (*polis*, theater, etc.)

MULTIPLICITIES
OF PERSONS   (Chap. 9)

Soul as *oikos*

Libidinal economics

HUMAN   *Erōs*- procreation
                                                    (Chap. 6)
                                   Breeding, training

ANIMAL   Wild animals

                                   Agriculture
                                                    (Chap. 5)

VEGETAL   Soil, natural vegetation

                                   Art-work   (Interlude 1)

ELEMENTAL   Earth, water, fire, air   (Chap. 4)

MULTIPLE DRIVES   (Chap. 8)
from the
archaic heritage   (Chap. 9)

Drives Imagining on Multiple Levels

IV

Land- and Seascapes of the Interior

Why should we not also enjoy an original relation to the universe? . . . Embosomed for a season in nature, whose floods of life stream around and through us, and invite us by the powers they supply, to action proportioned by nature.

Emerson, *Nature*

We have seen Nietzsche entertain in his earliest writings the hypothesis of a continuum of life, or animateness, "beginning with stone" and "progressing to plants, animals, and human beings." This suggests a way of placing his psychological discourses in terms of metaphors drawn from natural phenomena in some kind of rank order. The next three chapters will consider three levels of metaphorics: the elemental layer of geological and meteorological phenomena, the realm of vegetation and cultivation, and the domain of animals and husbandry.

The publication of the first volume of *Human, All Too Human* in 1878 marks the beginning of a new phase of Nietzsche's work. It effects his formal break with Schopenhauer and Wagner, and a turn away from Romanticism toward a distinctly cooler and (in the broad sense of *wissenschaftlich*) scientific view of things.[1] It goes too far to call the book, as some have done, a "positivist" work; but it does differ markedly from Nietzsche's previous writings in the broader range of its subject matter (the whole of culture) and its coolly analytical style.[2] But it is also something of a centaur, and thus a psychologically interesting document insofar as Nietzsche was unable to suppress completely those parts of his personality that had thrived during his youth and later in the encouraging presence of Wagner. Every now and then the calm surface of the text is disrupted by a burst of ecstatic lyricism, which then subsides until sufficient pressure builds for another uprush.[3]

Looking back to when he began work on *Human, All Too Human*, Nietzsche situates the change of style and life in a broader context: "What reached a decision in me at that time was not a break with Wagner: I felt a total aberration of my instinct, of which particular mistakes—whether

121

Wagner or the professorship at Basel—were merely symptoms."⁴ Swayed by the proximity of Wagner toward accepting a university appointment in classics, he had been diverted from what he calls his "task," his *Aufgabe* (in which one hears the "gift"—his task something given him by fate): "How useless and arbitrary my entire existence as a philologist looked in relation to my task."

After his sick leave, much of which he spent in Sorrento in southern Italy, Nietzsche returned to his teaching at Basel. But ill health continued to plague him, and eventually in 1879 he was forced to retire from the university altogether. He was awarded a modest pension, on which he was able to live, with occasional help from friends, for the rest of his life. He dissolved the household in Basel, packed some books and clothes in a trunk, and set off, with no fixed destination. For the next ten years, until his collapse in Turin in 1889, he would wander from place to place—through Switzerland, France, and Italy—in search of a suitable place to live, where the climate would allow him to do the work he had to do. He would travel by train between mountain and sea, from the Swiss Alps to the shores of the Mediterranean, according to the season: moving north to escape the heat of summer and south again in winter.

It was not long after leaving Basel that Nietzsche discovered the upper Engadin and the area of the Swiss Alps near Saint Moritz, to which he would return summer after summer to write. He might well not have survived had he not found that place, plagued as he was by premonitions of death—approaching the age at which his father had died—and by a somatic condition that subjected him regularly to excruciating pain. He drew sustenance from the surrounding landscape of mountains, lakes, and forests, in which he would spend all day on those days when he was not confined to bed by illness. After a severe, intestine struggle, he managed to complete what would become the third part of *Human, All Too Human,* "The Wanderer and His Shadow." He wrote about this work later to his friend Köselitz, to whom he had sent the manuscript for him to make a fair copy: "With the exception of a few lines, the whole thing was thought out *while walking* and sketched in pencil in six small notebooks."⁵ Near the end is an aphorism entitled "Nature as Doppelgänger" in which Nietzsche expresses his deep feelings of kinship with the landscape in which the work was written: "In many places in nature we discover ourselves again, with a pleasant shudder of dread: it is the most beautiful case of the Doppelgänger" (*WS* 338). And after a lyrical description of the natural beauty of the high plateau of the Engadin, he concludes: "How fortunate is the one who can say: 'There is surely much in nature that is larger and more beautiful, but *this* is intimately related and familiar to me, a blood relation, and more indeed than that.'" Nietzsche had lived close to the world of nature since his youth. This later, life-saving experience of the landscape of the Engadin is thus a reinforced ground for the discourses concerning natural phenomena in his psychology.

Exploration of Psychological Space

> *The soul's avowal of its large relations . . . climate, century, re-*
> *mote natures, as well as near, are part of its biography.*
> Emerson, "Beauty"

Both prefaces Nietzsche added to the 1886 edition of *Human, All Too Human* emphasize the psychological dimensions of the book.[6] In the second preface, he writes of "the almost serene and inquisitive coldness of the psychologist who takes a mass of painful things that he has *under* him and *behind* him and diagnoses them retrospectively and, as it were, *impales* them with the point of a needle" (§1). Borrowing language from Paul Rée, he writes in the body of the text that if "that science which inquires into the origin and history of the so-called moral sensations" is to progress, then humanity may not be spared "the cruel sight of the psychological dissecting table with its scalpels and forceps" (*HA* 37). A moving image: Nietzsche, surgically masked, working away at the operating table on the body of modern Western man; but that modern man is none other than he himself, as he performs the operation on his own person. There is a crucial historical dimension to this kind of psychological work, insofar as he believes that the human body incorporates residues of millennia of past experience, some of which can be brought to light by the right kind of examination.

By "psychological observation" Nietzsche does not mean introspection in the sense of observing internal processes of one's psyche.[7] On the contrary, the practice involves a variant of the kind of *ecstasis* discussed in *The Birth of Tragedy*. Here is a comment on the experience of writing *Human, All Too Human:*

> [The author] looks back gratefully—grateful to his wandering, to his hardness and self-alienation, to his looks into the distance and his bird-flights into cold heights. What a good thing that he did not . . . always stay at home "with himself *[bei sich]*"! He was *outside* himself [ausser *sich*], there is no doubt. Only now does he see himself—and what surprises he finds there![8]

When Nietzsche calls his writings from this period his "travel books *[Wanderbücher]*" (*HA* 2, P6), he is referring not only to the conditions under which they were written but also to the fact that they encourage the reader to undertake some psychological wandering to other cultures, climes, and times. He calls the "free spirits" to whom *Human, All Too Human* is addressed "adventurers and circumnavigators of that inner world called 'human being'" (P7). With respect to the kind of exploration he is advocating, the *locus classicus* is in an aphorism entitled "Where One Must Travel To."

> Direct self-observation is not nearly sufficient for us to know ourselves: we need history, for the past flows on within us in a hundred waves; indeed, we ourselves are nothing but that which at every moment we experience of this continual flowing. Even here, when we want to step down into the flow of what appears to be our ownmost and most personal being, the dictum of Heraclitus is valid: one does not step twice into the same river.[9]

Again the theme of the necessity for historical awareness if life is to flourish. Whether we have any sense of history or not, there are multiple layers to our being, through which the past is constantly flowing. Thus self-knowledge is not simply a matter of becoming acquainted with what plays upon the surface of our consciousness here and now. The individual is like a deep well, sunk down through stratum upon stratum of dark earth, the deeper the older, and fed by innumerable underground springs. For the person without history, "that which at every moment we experience of this continual flowing" will be superficial, an awareness of only the topmost levels; familiarity with the past grants access to the deeper currents and lower strata. The dictum of Heraclitus is valid not only because, owing to the flow, the "content" of what is below us is different at every moment, but also because it flows "in a hundred waves," which give rise to a fluctuating interplay among the various layers of flow.

There is another piece of wisdom that Nietzsche claims is "just as powerful and nourishing":

> In order to understand history, one must seek out the living remains of historical epochs; one has to *travel* . . . to other nations—for these are simply older *stages of culture* that have solidified, on which one can take a *stand*—to the so-called savage and semisavage peoples, to where human beings have taken off the garb of Europe or have not yet put it on.

Here is a salutary appreciation of the uncivilized layers of the human psyche, and of the advantages of anthropological and ethnographical research for exploring them. (Many of the insights of Freudian psychoanalysis and Jungian psychology are based on this kind of research.) "But," Nietzsche continues, "there exists a *subtler* art and aim of travel" which does not necessitate actually moving from place to place through literal space.

> It is very probable that the last three centuries are also still living on in all their cultural colorations and reflections *in our very neighborhood:* they just want to be *discovered.* In many families, and in individuals too, the strata *[Schichten]* lie beautifully open to view one on top of the other; in other places, faults in the rock make understanding more difficult.

Historical and psychological understanding will thus involve a kind of geology and archaeology of culture, in which one digs down and explores the sedimented layers of experience in oneself and those around one. Nietzsche is advocating a history *[Geschichte]* that would be an inquiry into strata *[Schichten]* within the individual as well as layers within the culture.

Implicit in this idea is what might be called an *agglomerative* view of the development of the self, as opposed to a *substitutive* view, and one that is just as applicable to phylogenesis, the development of the race or culture, as to ontogenesis, the development of the individual.[10] The substitutive view sees each progressive stage of development as totally replacing the previous stage or stages. In the case of the individual, this would mean that childhood replaces infancy, youth childhood, and so on; until one arrives at the perfectly mature adult who has left all the previous stages behind. With respect to the culture, the "primitive" stage of so-called animism would be replaced by a mode of being in the world in which subject is more clearly differentiated from object; relatively unselfconscious religious culture would give way to scientific enlightenment; and so on—the point again being that the culture that attains the heights of rationally enlightened civilization will have surpassed all vestiges of its primitive beginnings. Simply diagrammed, the development of the individual or the culture over time would look like a series of gradually ascending steps.

By contrast, the agglomerative view sees each subsequent level of development not as substituting for the previous ones but as being *superimposed* on them. Thus the older, more primitive stages of the individual or culture are considered to live on and continue to support and vitalize the layers above. Rather than an image of steps we would imagine a cross-section of a number of layers, or strata, lying one on top of the other—which yields a much deeper conception of the individual or the culture as consisting of all the previous layers simultaneously. Each individual would then be represented not by a point on an elevated plateau, but as a shaft running from the surface vertically down to the lowest stratum.[11] According to a later text, the modern individual would thus be a more profound and complex being than the ancient:

> The past of every form and way of life, of cultures that formerly lay right next to or on top of each other, now, thanks to this mixture, flows into us "modern souls"; our drives now run back everywhere; we ourselves are a kind of chaos. . . . Through our semibarbarism in body and desires we have secret access everywhere, as no noble epoch has ever had, and especially to the labyrinth of unfinished cultures and to every semibarbarism that has ever existed on earth. (*BGE* 224)

The image of the labyrinth adds a third dimension to the cross-sectional picture; but while such labyrinthine complexity of soul offers infinite possibilities for the psychologically adventurous, it also presents considerable problems (see chapter 9, below).

Whereas on the substitutive view the past would affect the separate individual only through things actually present alongside him, on the agglomerative view each person's own beginnings and the beginnings of the culture would be present at all times, although they would for the most part operate unconsciously, having been covered over by subsequent layers of development. As a later note puts it, emphatically: "*In the mental realm there is no annihilation.*"[12] Freud's fondness for archaeological metaphors and his formulations concerning "the immortal wishes of childhood" and the "nonexistence of time" in the unconscious are predicated on something like the agglomerative view, as are Jung's ideas about the extent to which archaic myths continue to play spontaneously through the modern psyche.[13] But ultimately, two-(and even three-)dimensional diagrams such as those just suggested need to be cast aside (like Wittgenstein's ladder), since they are based upon a linear view of time that Nietzsche's idea of eternal recurrence will warp in an annular fashion.[14]

But now the conclusion of Nietzsche's reflections on psychological travel:

> He who, after long practice in this art of travel, has become a hundred-eyed Argos . . . will rediscover the adventurous travels of his ego . . . in Egypt and Greece, Byzantium and Rome, France and Germany . . . in the Renaissance and the Reformation, at home and abroad, indeed in the sea, the forests, in the plants and in the mountains. Thus self-knowledge will become knowledge of everything *[All-Erkenntniss]* with regard to all that is past. (*AOM* 223)

Just as literal travel does, psychological excursions broaden one's perspective, so that one can "see with a hundred eyes." And once the various realms of culture that flow into one's being here now have been explored, one comes upon the realms of nature. To the extent that self-knowledge is called upon to become an omniscience with respect to the past, the psychological task Nietzsche sets for himself—and for us—is formidable indeed.

For Nietzsche, then, there is a vast realm within the human soul corresponding to the world of external nature: an inner space of planets, moons, and galaxies; an "inscape" of land and sea, rocks and waves, sun and winds. This notion of inner space is prefigured in other philosophers— in Saint Augustine especially; and while it is generally foreign to ancient Greek thinking, where the distinction between inner and outer was not well developed, some relevant precursors deserve brief mention. After this we begin with the larger picture, of the universe, and then focus on the basic elements of earth, rock, and stone before moving on to fire and water.

Several of the pre-Socratic thinkers emphasized that, in the words ascribed to Thales, "the whole universe is ensouled" *(to pan empsuchon)*—a view that is obviously unconducive to the development of the distinction between inner and outer. Empedocles, for whom Nietzsche had a special admiration, insisted on "the unity of all life" and was the first to put forward a powerful theory of perception based on the premise that "like can only be perceived by like." Nietzsche discusses these ideas in the courses he gave at Basel on "The Pre-Platonic Philosophers," in which he quotes the famous dictum: "It is with earth that we perceive earth, with water water, with aether the aether, with fire fire, love only with love, and hate only with hate."[15] The idea is that the soul has to have an element already in it somehow, if it is to be able to perceive external things composed of that element.

Plato develops this idea in the *Timaeus* (37a–b), in order to account for the soul's ability to know things within both the intelligible and sensible realms. In the words of Proclus's commentary:

> Since the soul consists of existence, sameness, and difference, in a form intermediate between the indivisible things and the divisible, by means of these she knows both orders of things . . . for all knowing is accomplished by means of likeness between the knower and the known.[16]

Aristotle discusses this idea in *De Anima* (404b), with reference to Empedocles and Plato, but finds serious problems with it. In line with his general inclination to bring Plato's intelligible realm into *this* world, Aristotle claims that while sensation is of particular things outside us, universals are in a sense "in the soul itself" (*De Anima* 417b). A consequence of his well known definition of sense-perception as "receiving the forms *[eidē]* of sensible objects without the matter" is that he endorses the idea of the soul as "the place of forms" *(topos eidōn)*" (424a, 429a).

In the essay on Schopenhauer, Nietzsche likened the educated human being to "a vitally dynamic solar and planetary system"—an apt image, considering that the configuration of the whole is effected by the force of gravity, which Schopenhauer understood as the most basic manifestation of will. It also suggests the way a pattern of will to power can determine the disposition of the developing psyche, imparting an organization to the interaction of the many different elements to prevent them from becoming chaotic and destroying each other. But the most important feature of the image is the dialectic it sets up between inner and outer space, which becomes decisive for Nietzsche's mature psychology.

Prefigurations of an association of inner with outer space are to be found at the beginning of the Platonic tradition, in the myth recounted in the *Timaeus,* a brief discussion of which can introduce a number of psychologically important Nietzschean themes. It helps, in considering the relevant mythemes, to recall that Nietzsche understands myth as "a concentrated image of the world" that "saves all powers of phantasy . . . from indiscriminate wandering" (*BT* 23).

According to the myth of the *Timaeus,* when the divine craftsman sets about creating the cosmos he first creates *soul* to be "mistress and ruler" of the body, which he composes out of the four elements—fire, water, air, and earth.[17] Twice it is said that the soul of the cosmos is set in the center of its body, diffused throughout it, and made to "envelop" it *(perikaluptō)* from outside (*Tim.* 34b, 36e). This image, in which soul has reaches greater than the physical universe, suggests that the inner space of the human soul extends beyond the physical environment. When it comes to the creation of the immortal part of the *human* soul, "the father who engendered [the cosmos]" (37c) composes it from the same ingredients, in the same mixing bowl, and in the same proportions as he had used for the creation of the soul of the universe—even though some impurities had by this time entered in to the mixture (41d). The idea that the human soul is of the very same nature as the soul of the universe naturally supports a conception (espoused by the young Nietzsche) of a continuum of animation stretching from rocks, through plants and animals, to human beings. Before being incarnated in human bodies, the souls are first "sown in the stars" so that they might learn "the nature of the universe" (41e). They are then "sown" in the planets before being entrusted to the created gods, who will join them to the lower parts of the soul before their incarnation in human bodies, which have been composed—like the body of the universe—of the four elements. Such prenatal astral projection would easily account for any cosmic elements or dimensions subsequently discovered within the human psyche.[18]

There follows a magnificent description of what happens when the seed hits the soil, and the orderly "revolutions of the immortal soul" come into contact with "the flowing and ebbing tide of the body" (*Tim.* 43a). Plato accounts for the erratic movements of the neonate in terms of the collision between the circuits of the soul and the "mighty river" formed by the in- and outflow of both nutrition and sensation. The process of nutrition is "a strong tide, ebbing and flowing," while the "affections" *(pathēmata)* of sensation are characterized as influxes of fire, collisions between bodies of earth, flowing waters, and tempestuous winds. The problem is that the "perpetually streaming currents" associated with the body flow counter to "the revolution of the Same," which imparts order to the universe, thereby preventing it from "going on its way and ruling" (43b–d). One can see the infant tottering under the force of this continuous collision, lacking identity, falling short of self-sameness; its soul erratic and irrational insofar as "no one revolution is acting as ruler or guide."[19] A remedy for this condition is hinted at when the good human being is said to "let the revolution of the Same and uniform within him draw into its train all that turmoil of fire and water and air and earth that had later grown about it, and thereby dominate its irrational turbulence by discourse of reason" (42c). The issue of domination, and the image of currents and flows, will figure ever more prominently as the comparison between Plato and Nietzsche is developed.

Plato's solution to the problem of chaos in the inchoate human soul prefigures Nietzsche's likening the psyche of the well educated student to a "solar and planetary system." Timaeus concludes that the best motions to impart to the developing soul are the orderly revolutions of the fixed stars (*Tim.* 43a–44c); these ensure that reason will prevail in the mature psyche and predominate over the turbulence of the lower passions. But for Nietzsche reason alone does not go deep enough: if one goes beyond the parochial confines of the galaxy in which our solar system happens to find itself, the larger picture becomes less clear, the configuration of the greater celestial bodies apparently more chaotic. This image occurs in a text where the scientific spirit of *Human, All Too Human* has matured, and where cool rationality has become tempered by the warmth of imagination: *The Joyful Science* of 1882.

> Those thinkers in whom all stars move in cyclical orbits are not the most profound. Whoever looks into himself as into an enormous world-space and carries milky ways within him, he knows how irregular all milky ways are: they lead right into the chaos and labyrinth of existence. (*JS* 322)

The image of something as large as the Milky Way leading into the labyrinth of existence again disrupts the conventional difference between inner and outer. By going *in* to the world of the human soul, one finds oneself far *out* along the galaxy—yet heading back in, to the chaotic heart of existence.

There are further allusions to themes from the *Timaeus* in *Thus Spoke Zarathustra*. The divine craftsman creates the cosmos by imposing order on chaos; and, as a result of his labors, reason *(nous)* prevails for the most part throughout the universe, with a residual quotient of recalcitrance remaining in the form of the "errant cause" (*Tim.* 48a). Zarathustra proposes an inversion of this view in the course of his attempt to liberate all beings from whatever transcendent principles traditional metaphysics has subjected them to: "A *little* reason, admittedly, a seed of wisdom has been scattered from star to star—this yeast has been mixed into all things: for the sake of folly, wisdom has been mixed into all things!" (*Z* 3.4). And whereas Plato is concerned to impart to the infant soul the rational motions of the fixed stars, Zarathustra admonishes the people in the market square with these words: "I say to you: one must have chaos within to be able to give birth to a dancing star. I say to you: you still have chaos in you" (*Z*, P5). This is not to advocate a complete irrationalism, since the movements of even a dancing star will still be in accord with the music of time. Nietzsche is simply concerned to emphasize that a rationalism that completely suppresses chaos will be sterile.

Some kind of stellar order is invoked in an aphorism entitled "Star Friendship," which has often been taken to refer to the author's aborted relations with Wagner (*JS* 279). Nietzsche likens the friend and himself to two ships that once "rested quietly in one harbor and one sunshine" but are then driven apart by "the all-powerful force of our tasks." The "different seas and suns" in which they end up change them, estranging them from one another. But the author encourages the adoption of a larger, more cosmic perspective: "There is probably a tremendous invisible arc and stellar course, in which our such different paths and goals may be *included* as small stretches of the way—let us elevate ourselves to this idea!" This is a common move in Nietzsche: the invitation to see a current situation with its particular perspective against the background of a more comprehensive context. He does this more often with time than with space, calling attention to the relatively short span of human existence (a few thousand years or so) upon which philosophers tend to base their generalizations about human beings.[20]

There is a significant engagement with the puzzling interplay between inner and outer in Saint Augustine, whose view appears to combine Aristotelian ideas with Neoplatonic theory to produce a conception of the inner space of memory and phantasy—of "the great field" or "spacious palace" of *memoria*—that is a striking precursor of Nietzsche's view.[21] Augustine writes of "the vast cloisters of memory" in which he finds "the sky, the earth, and the sea, ready at [his] summons," wondering how so great a place could yet be somehow inside the soul.[22] The passage deserves to be quoted at some length:

The power of the memory is prodigious, my God. It is a vast, immeasurable sanctuary. Who can plumb its depths? And yet it is a faculty of my soul. Although it is part of my nature, I cannot understand all that I am. This means, then, that the mind is too narrow to contain itself entirely. But where is that part of it which it does not itself contain? Is it somewhere outside itself and not within it? How, then, can it be part of it, if it is not contained in it?

I am lost in wonder when I consider this problem. It bewilders me. Yet men go out and gaze in astonishment at high mountains, the huge waves of the sea, or the stars in their courses. But they pay no attention to themselves. . . . I could not even speak of mountains or waves, rivers or stars, which are things that I have seen, or of the ocean, which I know only on the evidence of others, unless I could see them in my mind's eye, in my memory, and with the same vast spaces between them that would be there if I were looking at them in the world outside myself. When I saw them with the sight of my eyes, I did not draw them bodily into myself. They are not inside me themselves, but only their images.[23]

The cosmos within the human being, situated within the macrocosm of the universe, turns out to contain images that have reaches as vast as those of the outside world.

The interplay between nature and human nature and culture, between the worlds of nature within and outside the human soul, is nowhere more powerfully enacted than in *Thus Spoke Zarathustra*. If Hölderlin's *Hyperion* is a mature *Werther* set in Greece, *Zarathustra* is a hyper-*Hyperion* set in a land- and seascape that stretches from the sun-soaked isles of the Mediterranean to what Byron called the "snowy scalps" of the mountain peaks of Switzerland. The task with which the reader of *Zarathustra* is challenged, and of which Zarathustra strives superhumanly to become master, is that of reintegrating oneself with the human community without thereby losing one's participation in the natural world—and thus to "renaturalize" onself into a "higher, more terrible" nature.

Zarathustra's prologue, and its opening scene in particular, contains the most striking parodic inversions of Platonic imagery. The protagonist rises one morning in his cave on the mountaintop and steps out to address the rising sun as an old familiar.[24] Whereas for Plato the cave (in the *Republic*) is a place of ignorance deep in the bowels of the earth, for Zarathustra it is a place of enlightenment (his ten years of solitude there have yielded an overabundance of wisdom) on a high point of the earth's surface. And whereas the sun is for Plato an image of the absolutely transcendent Good, Nietzsche's sun is so immanent that it depends for its very being on the attention of Zarathustra and his animals: "What would your happiness be," he asks that great star, "if it weren't for those whom you illuminate?" For Plato the real world is a supracelestial realm that is even "above the heavens," whereas the earthly realm so lacks reality that it is relegated to the status of "nonbeing." At least with respect to this metaphysics of transcendence, Heidegger's characterization of Nietzsche's philosophy as "inverted Platonism" hits the mark;[25] and the inversion is nowhere more persistently performed than in the prologue and first several sections of *Zarathustra,* where the locus of value is emphatically asserted to be the earth (and the body) rather than the heavens (and the rational soul). But once we pass the elemental level and reach the vegetal and animal realms, we shall see the similarity of imagery begin to diminish to some extent the opposition between Plato and Nietzsche in other respects.

Earth, Rock, and Stone

> *A man ought to compare advantageously with a river, an oak, or a mountain. He shall not have less the flow, the expansion, and the resistance of these.*
>
> Emerson, "Fate"

In his opening speech to the people in the market place, Zarathustra launches in to his teaching on the *Übermensch* in a way that deemphasizes the connotations of height that one might hear in the "over" of "overman," calling the *Übermensch* "the sense of the earth," and exhorting them above all, and with explicit emphasis, to "*remain faithful to the earth*" (Z, P3). He declares his love for "him who works and invents, so that he builds a house for the *Übermensch* and prepares earth, animal, and plant for him." Under the appropriate conditions, then, the desired attitude may grow naturally out of a reconfiguration of one's relations to the basic phenomena of nature.[26]

Since the Platonic-Christian tradition has always associated the heavens with the divine and the earth with the human, all too human, Nietzsche is concerned to restore to nature and the earth a sense of the divinity with which they were suffused when chthonic gods and spirits held sway. The Dionysian religion Nietzsche advocated in the face of the death of the One God of Christian monotheism is a polytheistic pantheism; and if the whole *(to pan)* is not only ensouled *(empsuchon)* but divinely so—as Thales is also said to have said—there will be gods all over the place, in natural sites as well as in many places within the human soul.[27]

Zarathustra suggests an inversion of the Platonic-Christian worldview in "Before Sunrise," when he praises the purity of the heaven/sky—that "abyss of light"—insofar as it is a "dance-floor for divine accidents . . . [and] a divine table for divine dice and dice players!" (Z 3.4). Nietzsche here counters the skyward orientation of the metaphysical tradition by imagining the heavens as being solid and earthy enough to support fateful fallings of dice and placements of divine feet, and the sky the destination rather than the origin of strokes of divine chance.[28] The image is soon completely subverted, insofar as the table on which the plays of divine chance are made has descended, come down to earth, so that Zarathustra himself may participate in the play.

> If ever I played dice with gods at the divine table of the earth, so that the earth quaked and broke open and thrust up rivers of fire—
>> for the earth is a divine table, which trembles with creative new words and divine dice throws—
>> Oh how should I not lust after eternity and the nuptial ring of rings—the ring of recurrence? (Z 3.16 §3)

Divine forces do not then play through the heavens alone, nor strokes of fate fall only from above: rather, the earth itself, where the becoming of everyday life takes place, is also a locus of divine plays and projections. To experience it as such is to long for union with the eternity that rounds up through the recurrence of every moment. That Zarathustra has himself become a participant in the game of dice alludes to the idea in Nietzsche that the self is itself part of fate.[29]

The immediate effect of divine dice throws on the table is said to be a quaking of the earth—a prime metaphor in Nietzsche for the shocks and shifts that shake one out of the habitual set of perspectives. The ground that hitherto supported one's existence, the set of values on which one took one's stand, begins to break up, leading to the collapse of solid structures of meaning. But while old sources of meaning are closed off, new ones are opened up. As Zarathustra says to his disciples in his speech "On Old and New Tablets":

> Earthquakes bury many wells, and cause much languishing; but they also bring to light inner powers and hidden secrets.
> Earthquakes open up new springs. When old peoples suffer earthquakes new springs gush forth. (Z 3.12 §25)

If these shakings of the basis can be endured, there opens up the possibility of a transformation of the earth itself, an elemental change that transfigures life experience. Just as those ancient alchemists (who realized that with their operations on gross materials they were working with elements of the human psyche) devoted their energies to transforming the base dross of experience into something invaluably radiant, so Zarathustra reveals one of his innermost secrets in saying, with unusual emphasis: *"The heart of the earth is gold"* (Z 2.18). And in his speech "On the Spirit of Gravity" he says, "Whoever teaches human beings to fly, he has moved all boundary stones away; all boundary stones will themselves fly into the air for him, and he will baptize the earth anew—as 'the light one'" (Z 3.11 §2). This passage intimates the possibility of a reorientation of the basic forces of the universe in which what gives things their weight is no longer a single force—gravity—pulling all things uniformly in one direction, but rather a matrix of multiple and dynamic energies. (The image here repeats, in a different medium, as it were, the point made in "Before Sunrise," where all things stand—or dance—as if in their own illumination, before the single source of light has itself become visible.) Under such conditions values are easily invertible and perspectives reversible, and the demarcations ("boundary stones") between categories no longer fixed and immutable. These do not, however, disappear, giving rise to anarchy and indeterminacy; but they "fly into the air" and become light enough to be easily moved around. The alchemical tone to these passages concerning the transformation of earthy matter is reinforced when in Zarathustra's encounter with his archenemy, the spirit of gravity, the latter calls him "you philosophers' stone!"[30]

There is another dimension of meaning to the image of rock or stone in Nietzsche's psychology, having to do with the unalterable nature of the past. In a speech bearing the pointedly religious title "On Redemption," Zarathustra talks about how the creative will of human beings, which is potentially the great liberator, is actually a prisoner. In speaking of its impotence with respect to the past, he says, "That time does not run backward, that is what enrages [the will]; 'That which was'—that is the stone it cannot roll away" (Z 2.20). In a speech on redemption this image has obvious biblical connotations concerning resurrection; but Zarathustra regards this teaching to the effect that "the stone 'It was' is unmovable" as "insanity." That the past may not after all be unalterable is suggested in an earlier chapter, "The Tomb-Song," where Zarathustra first engages the problem of how to redeem his past—or, to use psychological rather than soteriological language— how to come to terms with the failures and disappointments of his youth.

> How did I endure it? How was I able to overcome such wounds and even employ them? How did my soul rise again out of such tombs?
>
> Yes, there is something invulnerable, unburiable in me, something that explodes rock: that is *my will*. Silently it strides unchanged through the years.[31]

There is a way to redeem the past, through a transformation of the will into a configuration of will to power that allows the past itself to be transformed.

But an appreciation of how this can happen requires a fuller picture of will to power.[32]

One of the most powerful images Nietzsche draws from the mineral realm is to be found in *Beyond Good and Evil*. In aphorism 230 he discusses the "strange and wonderful task" of "translating the human being back into nature," in the hope of revealing "the terrifying [and] eternal basic text" of *homo natura*. The next aphorism begins as follows:

> Learning transforms us, it does what all nourishment does that does not merely "preserve"—as the physiologist knows. But in our ground, "deep down" inside, there is something unteachable, some granite of spiritual fate *[Fatum]*, of predetermined decision and answer to predetermined selected questions. In every cardinal problem there speaks an unchangeable "this is I." (*BGE* 231)

The immediate background to this idea of an immutable foundation to the human psyche is provided by Schopenhauer, who argued that the empirical character is unalterable on the grounds that it is the unfolding of an act of the will, which stands outside time altogether.[33] Nietzsche alludes to this idea in the essay on Schopenhauer when he writes that a person's true educators and formative teachers *(Bildner)* "show you the true primal sense and basic material of your being, something absolutely ineducable and unmalleable *[unbildbar]*, but in any case difficult to get to, bound and paralyzed" (*SE* 1).

An illuminating commentary on the "granite of spiritual fate" comes from the Japanese philosopher Nishitani Keiji, who adduces the short essay by Goethe entitled "On Granite" ("Über den Granit").[34] In this gem among his geological writings, Goethe recalls how once he sat on an exposed piece of granite on top of a mountain and reflected upon how the granite extended deep down into the bottom-most stratum of the earth, and had remained the same throughout a long history of changes in the earth's crust.[35] He writes of "the ancient discovery that granite is both the highest and the deepest . . . the solid ground of our earth," and of "the serene tranquility afforded by that solitary, mute nearness of great, soft-voiced nature." In contrast to the fertile valleys, the granite peaks "have never generated anything nor devoured anything living: they exist prior to and superior to all life."

Nietzsche was no doubt familiar with this essay, and his discovery of the majestic peaks of the upper Engadin will have afforded him a special empathy with the grounds of Goethe's reflections on rock. When one thinks of Nietzsche's early musings concerning a continuum of life stretching from stone to human beings, and how this idea manifests itself in the belief (found in many different cultures) that rocks can be "reservoirs" of soul energy, the image of granite—as the absolute antithesis of life—at the ground of the psyche may come as something of a shock. All the more so since it is such a fitting image for the very bottom of the soul, for that in us that we cannot change, a fate of which we are innocently unconscious—and which we become aware of only slowly and with difficulty, if at all. It constitutes the core of our being, which reaches back down through the deepest strata of history. Although the soul is generally thought of as a principle of life, the human soul that is the concern of depth psychology has a special connection with death and that which is farthest from life—a connection mediated beautifully by the image of the granite of fate.[36]

Stone held a special significance for Nietzsche insofar as it was by a magnificent pyramidal rock on the shore of the lake of Silvaplana that he was first struck by the thought of eternal recurrence in the summer of 1881. He relates the story in *Ecce Homo,* where he refers to the thought as "the basic conception" of *Zarathustra* and "the highest formula of affirmation that is attainable."[37] The thought that enables the greatest affirmation of life struck the thinker as he stood by a pyramid of absolutely lifeless matter.

There are other psychologically significant references to the earth in Nietzsche's writings, but since these have to do with earth as *soil (Erdreich, Boden),* as the medium in which vegetal growth takes place, they will be discussed in the next chapter.

Suns and Vital Fires

> *A man is a fagot of thunderbolts. All the elements pour through his system: he is the flood of the flood, and fire of the fire; he feels the antipodes and the pole, as drops of his blood: they are the extension of his personality.*
>
> Emerson, "Beauty"

The primary representative of fire in the soul in Nietzsche's works is the sun, and the classic passages are in *Thus Spoke Zarathustra.* The image also figures earlier, in *The Joyful Science,* as in the aphorism about star-friendship discussed above (*JS* 279). There what estranges the two friends is the divergence urged by their respective tasks, and what changes them is their ending up under disparate suns. The meaning of this figure is made clearer a few pages later, in connection with the theme of "an overall philosophical justification for a way of living and thinking" (*JS* 289). Such a justification is said to work like

> a warm sun that hallows, fructifies, and shines upon [the individual] alone ... bringing all his powers to ripeness and blossoming, and preventing the emergence of the small or large weeds of grief and

moroseness—so that finally one exclaims longingly: but would that many such new suns might yet be created!

Again there are resonances from the essay on Schopenhauer, where the educator was imagined to "direct all energies and saps and sunshine" toward his pupil's primary strength and to "clear away all weeds" that might hinder his growth (*SE* 2, 1).

Just as the pilots of the friend-ships have little control over the winds of their tasks which drive them into diverse climes, so it is impossible to dictate the nature of the sun that provides the illumination for one's *Weltanschauung.* The image suggests that the basic philosophical justification for one's life is not something that can be chosen at will, but is rather something given by fate. Nietzsche's expressed desire that "many new suns be created" is a call for an openness to multiple sources for worldviews as opposed to an insistence that there can be only one. It is not meant to imply that the individual is capable of creating such a source at will.[38]

In Plato the sun stands for that which illuminates and sustains something even more fundamental than a worldview or a life—namely, the universe. The Idea of the Good is, as absolutely transcendent, one and the same for all, whereas Nietzsche is arguing that some existences may be illuminated and sustained by their own particular sources. At the end of a conversation later in *The Joyful Science,* one of the interlocutors (clearly a mask of Nietzsche himself) says: "I am not a seeker. I want to create my own sun for myself" (*JS* 320). It would cut too sharply across the general drift of the image of the sun in Nietzsche to imagine that the desire to create one's own sun could be fully realized: an individual would be capable at most of contributing to the conditions of the creation of his or her own sun.

In *Zarathustra* the image of the sun still stands for the power that sustains a worldview, while in some contexts it is an image of the will as will to power—and occasionally even of Zarathustra himself. At the beginning of the prologue Zarathustra establishes himself together with his eagle and serpent as familiars of the sun in his opening greeting, in which he remarks that the sun has come up to his cave *(Höhle)* every day for the past ten years.[39] The cyclical course of the sun through the text signifies times at which crucial events take place—as in such chapter titles as "Before Sunrise," "At Midday," "The Nightwanderer-Song."[40] Noon, as the time of the sun's zenith and the greatest illumination, is also the point at which the forces of light begin to give way to the forces of darkness; and conversely with midnight, the darkest hour. These times are times of the psyche also: hours of brightest consciousness and of deepest shadow, a procession of moments that enacts the constant cycling between psychological alertness and oblivion. Just as before sunrise the open heaven appears to Zarathustra as an "abyss of light!" (Z 3.4), so after sunset one of the most important episodes of the text takes place, the enigma that presented itself to him in a vision: "Recently I walked gloomily through a corpse-colored dusk. . . . Not only a single sun had set for me" (3.2).

When Zarathustra remarks to the sun its daily ascent to his cave, there is an assonance between *Höhle* (cave) and the German words for "height" *(Höhe)* and "hell" *(Hölle).*[41] This schema is replicated in the second part of the sentence where Zarathustra says "me, my eagle, and my snake": he is accompanied by the animal that is at home in the heights and the animal that dwells in the chthonic realm, beneath the earth. Together they have performed the useful function of accepting the sun's abundance *(Über-fluss)*—with connotations of the literal translations "overflow" and "super-fluity"; but when Zarathustra says that he is now "tired" of his wisdom, "like a bee that has gathered too much honey," he uses the word *überdrüssig* to connote a superfluity that is unpleasant.[42] This not only echoes the sun's *Überfluss* a few words before, but also suggests that he wants to "hand over"—*überreichen*—his surplus wisdom when he finishes by saying, "I need hands that stretch out [to receive it]."

Zarathustra likens himself to the sun by saying that, in order to give away some of his abundance, he will have to "descend to the depths" like the sun when it "sets behind the sea and so brings light to the underworld." The interplay between the upper and lower worlds is continued by his calling the sun "you over-rich star": *überreich* ("over-rich") suggests *Über-Reich,* which would mean "over-realm" in contrast to the under-realm of the *Un-terwelt* ("underworld"). The parallels between Zarathustra and the sun thus form a chain of images linking the richness of solar overflow with the riches of the ruler of the sunless realm, the underworld, domain of Hades the invis-ible.[43] The underworld as the realm of death—a psychological realm that we inhabit every moment of the day and night, rather than an eschatological realm reached only at the end of our days—enriches experience by rounding life out on the far side at every moment.[44] This is the force of the refrain in Zarathustra's famous roundelay: "The world is deep, / And deeper than the day had thought" (Z 3.15, 4.19).

When Zarathustra asks the sun to "bless the cup that wants to overflow" the *überfliessen* (overflowing) sets up a contrast with the verb *untergehen* ("to set" of the sun; "to sink" of a ship; "to decline, go under, perish" of a person, people, or empire) that will play throughout the rest of the text.[45] He goes on to liken himself to the sun itself by saying that he has accumu-lated so much wisdom during his ten years of solitude on the mountaintop that he is a "cup that wants to overflow," that he has to "go down *[unter-gehen]*"—to set like the sun, yet to go down among human beings again, and at the same time descend to the underworld.[46]

One implication of the image of the sun as justifier of a worldview, as presented in *The Joyful Science,* is that the tenor of the life will depend on the strength of the sun that illumines it. The antithesis between north and south as zones of the soul in Nietzsche's works is exemplified in the contrast between temperate and tropical. The abundance of life that is engendered by a tropical climate is often perceived as "evil" from the temperate perspective.

> It is a delight for me to see the wonders that are hatched by a hot sun: tigers and palms and rattlesnakes.
>
> Among human beings, too, hot sun produces a beautiful brood and there are many wonderful things about those who are evil. . . .
>
> For in order that the *Übermensch* not lack his dragon, the overdragon who is worthy of him, a great deal of hot sun must yet glow upon damp primeval forest! . . .
>
> And you wise and knowing ones, you would flee from the burning sun of the wisdom in which the *Übermensch* so pleasurably bathes his nakedness![47]

Any evocations here of images from the paintings of William Blake are appropriate: lines such as these would, after all, inspire major paintings by Max Beckmann and Edvard Munch.[48] What they signify is the importance of a strong and radiant source behind a worldview, so that the life led within it may be lived with maximum vitality. That they do *not* imply a condoning of primitive savagery will become clear when we discuss the problem of the optimal disposition of the drives and passions.

The sun illuminating one's worldview shines with differing strengths at different times in one's life and at different stages on the way of "becoming what one is." A crucial stage on this way is designated by the image of "the great noon," when the human being "stands in the middle of his way between animal and *Übermensch*": "Then the one who goes under will bless himself, so that he may be one who goes over and across; and the sun of his knowledge will stand at noon for him" (Z 1.22 §3). The idea of a sunlike knowledge is central to Nietzsche's conception of how we understand the world and our selves. Unlike the moon, which is an inanimate reflector of cool light, the sun sustains and drives the life of what it illuminates. Nietzsche dismisses the putatively disinterested, "lunar" knowledge at which philosophy has traditionally aimed, in favor of an experience of things that is "solar" and to that extent life-enhancing.[49]

Fire is for Plato a paltry image of the sun: it is what casts the shadows that captivate the benighted dwellers in the dark cave. One might therefore expect the image of fire to have correspondingly greater value in Nietzsche's metaphorics. Most of his references to fire occur in connection with the *passions,* which are imagined, somewhat conventionally, as fiery. This aphorism does, however, shine with a particular brilliance: "Love and hate are not blind, but simply dazzled by the fire they themselves carry with them."[50] Later in the same work Nietzsche writes of our "mixed nature," of our being "now glowing with fire, now chilled by the spirit" (*HA* 637). What saves us from being consumed by the fire of the passions, which tends to make us unjust (remember how love, in particular, was said to narrow our perspective unduly), is the cool detachment provided by the intellect.[51]

A somewhat similar picture is to be found in Plato, for whom the passions come from the lower two parts of the tripartite soul, from what he calls the "spirited" and "appetitive" parts, which are seated in the thorax, or trunk of the human body.[52] The "spirited" part of the soul, associated with the area from the neck down to the diaphragm, is the seat of courage and such fiery emotions as anger. When a man believes himself wronged, his spirit *(thumos)* is said to "boil up" or "seethe" with anger.[53] In the *Timaeus* Plato describes a physiological arrangement that moderates the heat of passion. The gods who create the human body position the spirited part of the soul near the head, seat of the rational soul, "within hearing of the discourse of reason" (*Tim.* 70a). Since the *thumos* is liable to "boil with anger" and the heart to throb and undergo "a swelling of passion by means of fire," the gods place the lungs around the heart in order "to cool [it] and so provide refreshment and ease in the burning" (70b–d). This account does justice to the experience that slow, deep breathing is able to calm violent waves of emotion and cool the fires of passion.[54]

In *Dawn of Morning* the idea of self-combustion, associated again with a split within the self, is given an illuminating new twist. In analyzing the "drive to distinguish oneself," Nietzsche discusses the various ways of impressing other people with one's power, from the method of the barbarian, who inflicts pain on others, to that of the ascetic, who achieves an even more impressive distinction by having others observe him enduring suffering inflicted on *himself.* He writes of

> the triumph of the ascetic over himself, his eye turned inward, which sees the human being split into a sufferer and an observer, and which looks into the outside world only in order to collect, as it were, wood for [burning itself at] its own stake, this last tragedy of the drive for distinction, in which there is only one person who burns himself to charcoal.[55]

Nietzsche was long fascinated by the phenomenon of asceticism, not least because he was for most of his life an accomplished ascetic himself (however cruelly he may have exposed the workings of the "ascetic ideal" in his later writings).[56] His comments on the ascetic are of great psychological interest in the light of his maxim to the effect that morbid states of the soul "show in a magnifying glass certain states that are normal but as normal are difficult to see."[57] In the passage from *Dawn of Morning* the fire in which the ascetic consumes himself comes from the burning desire to hurt others when it is retroflected upon *the self.* We shall later see Nietzsche posit this retroflection of drives (that accompanies the self-splitting characteristic of the ascetic) as a general feature of psychodynamics.

A variant of ascetic self-combustion is to be found in the chapter "On the Way of the Creator" in *Zarathustra,* in which the protagonist advises one of his disciples about the necessity for a certain kind of solitude if one desires to be creative, but also warns him of the dangers involved: "There are feelings that want to kill the one who is solitary; if they do not succeed, then they themselves must die! But are you capable of being a murderer?" (Z 1.17). In order to "become what one is," it is necessary at times to kill off feelings or other psychological factors that may otherwise hold one back. Though in the case of the ascetic the elements to be annihilated may be different, fire may also be a means. At the same time there is an alchemical tone to Zarathustra's injunction: "Solitary one, you are going the way to yourself! . . . You must want to burn yourself up in your own flame: how could you wish to become new unless you have first become ashes!"[58] A later comment to his disciples invokes the necessity for parts of the self to be burned out if one is to have something worth teaching, as well as for passion to be a source of what is taught: "And when someone goes through the fire for the sake of his teaching, what does that prove! It is much more to the point if one's teaching comes out of one's own fire!" (Z 2.4). This image exemplifies Nietzsche's understanding of the philosophical life as "a constant transformation of everything that we are . . . into light and flame" (*JS,* P3). His ideal as an author was to have his life embodied in his work, so that "he himself [would be] nothing more than the grey ashes, while the fire has everywhere been saved and carried forward" (*HA* 208). This idea gives a constructive twist to an observation sometimes made about the end of Nietzsche's career—to the effect that "he burned himself out."

A pre-Promethean form of fire that figures prominently in Nietzsche's autobiographical essays *lightning.* As a youth he had a particular love of electrical storms, and in a note from the time of *Zarathustra* he writes: "I want to vanish in a dark thunderstorm: and for my last moments I want to be human and lightning at the same time."[59] In Zarathustra's Prologue the *Übermensch* is referred to as a bolt of lightning, which signifies both that the condition affords a kind of sudden illumination (a Heraclitean flash in contrast to the steady, more global illumination of the Platonic sun), and also that it is potentially destructive. Toward the end of the book the tension within Zarathustra's wisdom approaches the flash point: "My wisdom has been gathering for a long time like a cloud, it grows quieter and darker. Thus does all wisdom that is to give birth to bolts of lightning some day" (Z 4.13 §7). It is true that Nietzsche was more sensitive to the weather than most people, and his extraordinary susceptibility to electrical charges in the air surely prompted some of the lightning imagery in his work. But the imagery works psychologically irrespective of one's relation to meteorological phenomena. Dark clouds and a heavy atmosphere in the soul are not necessarily signs that one should reach for the antidepressants, but may rather portend that gathering psychical tensions are about to be discharged in flashes of psychological insight or outbursts of creativity.[60]

There comes a point in Zarathustra's development at which he has exercised sufficient violence on himself to warrant being hard on his disciples and the rest of his fellow human beings. Anticipating a time when those he has been addressing will have become barren soil and infertile ground, he says:

> And *soon* they are to stand before me like dry grass and steppe, and truly! tired of themselves—and thirsting more than for water for *fire!*
>
> Oh blessed hour of lightning! Oh mystery before noon! Coursing fires I shall yet make of them and heralds with tongues of flame.[61]

Again images from Blake's paintings and illuminated manuscripts come to mind.

Zarathustra's frequent identification with the wind has a similar import: to get rid of decaying debris that may hinder healthy growth. An enemy of the Christian "preachers of slow death," he is an advocate of *quick* death: "Many too many live and hang far too long on their branches. Would that a storm would come and shake all this lazy and worm-eaten stuff from the tree!" (Z 1.21). Playing on the etymology that links spirit *(Geist, pneuma)* with breath and wind, Zarathustra exhorts the "higher humans" to follow him in emulating storm winds, storm spirits, and laughing storms that dance their way across sea and land, destroying decaying vegetation and clearing the air of clouds of melancholy and gloomy spirits (Z 4.13 §20).

There is also a more benign dimension to the image of wind, where it appears as a natural force which, in spite of some regularities, is inherently variable—and thus calls for flexibility on the part of the human being who would borrow from its power. In the elegant tropes of one of Nietzsche's pithiest apothegms:

> The shortest way is not the straightest one possible, but rather that on which the most favorable winds fill our sails: thus the wisdom of sailors. Not to follow this is to be *obstinate:* firmness of character is here polluted by stupidity. (WS 59)

This is reminiscent of a remark of Socrates in the *Republic* which shows his respect for the autonomy of the *logos* that animates philosophical conversation: "You see," he admits to Adeimantus, "I myself really don't know yet, but wherever the argument, like a wind, tends, thither must we go" (*Rep.* 394d).

Taken purely by itself, rather than as a medium for animal or human flight, air is the least significant of the elements in Nietzsche's psychological imagery. Just as the body needs to breathe in order to survive, so the soul can thrive only in an appropriate medium—but he tends not to call attention to this medium unless it impresses by its movements, as in winds or storms. Since the aerial aspects of Nietzsche's imagination have already been discussed by one of the great explorers of the imaginal, we can simply note his enthusiasm for clear, cool, invigorating air as a precondition of intellectual and psychological creativity.[62] The following passage, which echoes features of the myths of Icarus and the *Phaedrus* as it praises the atmosphere induced by (joyful) science, rounds out the associated themes by bringing together images of air, water, fire, and earth.

> In *this* severe and clear element one has one's full strength: here one can fly! Why should one descend again into those muddy waters, where one has to swim and wade and get one's wings dirty! — No, it is too hard for us to live there. Can we help it if we are born for the air, for the pure air, we rivals of the beam of light, who would love to ride on specks of ethereal dust, like the beam—and not away from the sun but *toward it*! But since we cannot do that, we will do the only thing we can: bring light to the earth, be "the light of the earth"! And for that we have our wings and our speed and severity; to that end we are virile and even terrible, like fire. May those fear us who do not know how to warm and illumine themselves by us![63]

Rivers—from Lake to Sea

> *Passions and sudden transitions reveal the bottom of the ocean within us: what monsters and wonders of the sea come suddenly to light!*
>
> Herder

Of the psychological metaphors Nietzsche draws from the natural realm, the most frequent contain images of *water*. His method is distinguished by the attention he pays to clues from physiology, and he was aware that the greater part of the human body, as of most living things, consists of water:

"With what foreign superiority we treat what is dead, the inorganic, while all the time we are three-fourths water!"[64] In his youth a keen swimmer in lakes and rivers, in his later wanderings Nietzsche always lived near water—whether river, lake, or sea. The experimenter in him would appreciate the change of perspective offered by bodily activity in a different medium from earth and air.[65]

The aquatic images in Nietzsche's texts divide naturally into images of streams and rivers, springs and wells, lakes and oceans. At the most general level, water simply represents life. The ocean is often in Nietzsche's texts an image of the vastness of psychical life, of which we usually see only the constantly moving surface and seldom its deeper reaches. It thus also represents an image of the totality of interpretive forces he calls "will to power," in which individual waves resulting from its ebbs and flows are not self-identical collections of matter but rather ever-changing patternings of energies. A less expansive—though no less general—image is that of the *river*. The ambiguity of the German *Fluss* between "river" and "flux" allows Nietzsche to use "the river of becoming" as a metaphor for existence as a whole. A graphic illustration (from an early work) of how different types of thinker negotiate "the river of becoming" combines the metaphor of the flow with images of rock that connote ground on which to take a stand. The fleet-footed thinker inspired by the "alien, unlogical power [of] phantasy" is compared with a more ponderous philosopher who depends on the calculating power of reason.

> It is like seeing two hikers coming upon a wild mountain stream that is rolling rocks along its course. One of them runs light-footedly across, stepping on one rock after another, even though they then plunge into the depths behind him. The other stands there helpless for a while: he must first build himself some foundations to support his heavy, deliberate steps; sometimes this fails, and then no god helps him across the stream.[66]

Here is a prefiguration of the thinker as dancer, who sees through the illusion of firm ground but avoids plunging into the abyss by cultivating a lightness of foot that is responsive to the rhythms of natural phenomena. One can imagine this image's coming from experiences Nietzsche had while hiking in the mountains and streams in the area around Basel and Luzern—while his eyesight was still good enough to permit agility in negotiating rock-strewn mountain streams. But what helps one cross light-footedly, stepping instinctively and without explicit calculation, is perhaps less the assistance of a god than imagination aided by a kind of somatic memory: the recollection of a natural, inborn ability inherited from the ancestors—and, ultimately, from our animal ancestors—what Nietzsche will

later call our "preschooling" in animality.[67] In contrast to the disembodied
anamnēsis of Plato, this kind of recollection is a memory of *the body,* the
recall of abilities embodied there.[68]

One of Zarathustra's wittiest parables remarks how when there are bridges and railings over the river, nobody believes anyone who says, like Heraclitus, "*Alles ist im Fluss*" ("All is in flux" or "Everything is in the river").[69]
The typical response is to point out that such things as bridges and railings
are *over [über]* the river, so that not everything is *in* it—an allusion to the
Platonic idea that a framework of unchanging forms stands motionless
above the ever-changing flux of the sensible realm. In contemporary terms:
by fabricating fixed structures of concepts and ideas we can manage existence without having to immerse ourselves in the flux of becoming. When
winter comes and the river freezes, one appears to have even more solid
grounds for holding that "fundamentally everything stands still." Zarathustra calls this "a fine winter-doctrine" and "a good thing for an unfruitful
time." But eventually the thawing wind arrives—"A raging bull, a destroyer
who with angry horns breaks up the ice! But ice itself—*breaks bridges!*"
Upon the advent of a teacher with a teaching powerful enough to demolish
all previous structures, there will be no grounds for denying that "everything is, after all, in the flow of becoming."

Given that the body has equivalents to rivers and streams in its veins and
arteries and other channels, it is natural to associate these with the psychological phenomena that are closest to the physical—namely, with flows of
passion and emotion. The association has been common in Western philosophy, despite its relative lack of interest in affective processes. In the *Timaeus*
Plato portrayed the human body as the site of "a strong river" and the "perpetually streaming current" of nutrition and sensation.[70] In modern philosophy, Kant makes a helpful distinction between affect (or emotion) and passion by likening *Affekt* to "water breaking through a dam" and *Leidenschaft*
to "a stream that burrows ever deeper in its bed."[71]

A paradigmatic example of Nietzsche's fluvial imagery is this passage
from *Wagner in Bayreuth,* in which he wonders at the possibility (later actu-
alized by the author of *Zarathustra*) "of calculating the grand arc of a total
passion from a mass of passions flowing off in different directions":

We sense it already at the beginning [of any act in Wagner's dramas],
that we are in the presence of opposing individual currents, but also
of a stream with one powerful direction which holds sway over all of
them. This stream moves uneasily at first, over hidden jagged rocks
. . . [until] at the end the stream plunges down into the depths, in all
its fullness, with a daemonic pleasure in the abyss and seething waters. (*WB* 9)

He later uses the meanderings of a river to characterize the digressions in a thinker's thought, in an aphorism whose ending is remarkable in the light of his concerns with the hardness of the stone in the soul: "[Some thinkers] are rivers with many meanderings and isolated hermitages, . . . then the river flows on again, past rocky cliffs and breaking its way through the hardest stone."[72] Even if currents of psychical energy make no impression on the granite of fate, Nietzsche is certainly aware of the power of persevering thought—at least when sustained by passion—to break through the hardest of obstructions.

The main theme in Nietzsche's discussions of the passions is that although they are dangerously powerful, capable of destruction like a mighty river in flood, they are also tremendous sources of psychical energy that need to be conserved—though contained—if there is to be vitality in the soul. One of the features that attracted him to the Greeks was their recognition of the desirability of domesticating rather than suppressing or extirpating the more destructive drives.

> The Greeks would, as it were, devote festivals to all their passions and evil natural inclinations . . . they took these human, all too human aspects of themselves to be unavoidable and, instead of reviling them, preferred to accord them a sort of right of the second rank by integrating them into the customs of society. . . . Rather than repudiating the natural drive that expresses itself in nasty qualities, they regulate it and restrict it to certain cults and days, after having discovered sufficient precautionary measures to be able to grant those wild waters as harmless an outflow as possible. (*AOM* 220)

The basic assumption behind this view is that the drives and impulses that are customarily called evil are natural forces for which a pagan society can, with some ingenuity, find a relatively innocuous form of outlet. Nietzsche blames Christian morality for denying the naturalness of the passions and carrying out a program of suppression rather than rechanneling. Programs of proscription and suppression are advocated to this day by people who refuse to acknowledge the perpetual ubiquity of the destructive drive and are ignorant of the wisdom of prescriptions such as the ancient Greeks developed.

The primary source of the river metaphor in the philosophical tradition is in the *Republic* of Plato, in a passage where one of the basic principles of the hydrological-economic models developed later by Nietzsche and Freud is presented. In the course of a conversation about the character traits of the "philosophic natures," Socrates says to Glaucon:

> We surely know that when someone's desires incline strongly to some one thing, they are therefore weaker with respect to the rest, like a

stream that has been channeled off in that other direction. . . . So, when in someone they have flowed toward learning and all that's like it, I suppose they would be concerned with the pleasure of the soul itself with respect to itself and would forsake those pleasures that come through the body—if he isn't a counterfeit but a true philosopher. (*Rep.* 485d)

The stream here is an image of Platonic *erōs,* and it is clear that Plato imagines the "rate of flow" of desire in the soul to be more or less constant, even while the directions of this flow may vary. Nietzsche appears in his reflections on flows of psychological energies to take a similar principle of constancy for granted.[73]

But for Nietzsche there is a far vaster historical dimension to the psyche than there was for Plato; since the demands of life are no longer able to check the desire for knowledge of the past, "all boundary posts have been taken out and everything that ever was now rushes in on the human being" (*HL* 4). Because of the variety of different streams feeding into it, he considers the medieval soul to be unusually expansive: "Neither antiquity nor our own age has such extensive breadth of soul: its *spaciousness* was never greater [than in the Middle Ages]" (*WS* 222). When a person in whom so many diverse influences came together was carried away by passion, "the rapid flow of the soul had to be more powerful, the whirlpools more bewildering, and the falls more precipitate than ever before." In this figure we see how the interior landscape, in its manifold heritage, conditions the ways psychical energies move through it.

It is a maxim of depth psychology that when something of one's own is constantly denied it becomes alien, other, and thereby disturbing—if not terrifying. Nietzsche claims that a prolonged lack of self-observation has "allowed the passions to grow into such monsters" that they now frighten us. The task is then "to *deprive* the passions of their terrifying character and thereby to prevent their becoming devastating torrents *[Wildwasser]*" (*WS* 37). This requires that we become familiar with them, investigating their sources and charting the directions of their flows, in order to protect ourselves from their extravagances. It also demands a certain kind of mastery to begin with.

> *What is necessary beforehand.* — A man who is not willing to become master over his wrath, his gall and vengefulness, and his lust, and who tries to become master in anything else, is as stupid as the farmer who lays out his field beside a torrential stream without protecting himself from it. (*WS* 65)

Crucial here is the distinction between mastering passions and getting rid of them altogether, which is at the basis of a criticism of "the insanity of religious moralists" in wanting to extirpate the passions, which appears in a note from 1888:

> This most shortsighted and pernicious way of thinking wants to make the great sources of energy, those wild torrents of the soul that often stream forth so dangerously and overwhelmingly, *dry up* altogether, instead of taking their power into service and *economizing* it. (*WP* 383)

The verb *ökonomisieren* not only suggests that the energy of the passions needs to be retained and channeled within the "grand economy of the soul," but with its roots in the *oikos,* or household, it also connotes the domesticating of their wildness.

Let us postpone consideration of the river images in *Zarathustra,* since they are best read in the context of the imagery in that text of lakes and oceans—which is in turn best approached by considering the sea that appears in *The Joyful Science.*

Nietzsche had never seen a real sea until his sojourn in Sorrento in 1876, which he had reached by taking a ship from Genoa to Naples. After leaving his post at Basel and embarking upon a nomadic existence, he would often spend his winters on the French or Italian Riviera. Two winters in Genoa and sea voyages in the Mediterranean prompted a number of Columbus phantasies in which Nietzsche imagined himself discovering hitherto uncharted territories of the soul.[74]

In *The Joyful Science* a madman famously announces "the death of God" (*JS* 125), which amounts to the collapse of all the absolute values that had sustained the Platonic-Christian tradition up to the advent of European nihilism in the nineteenth century.[75] The psychological impact of this collapse Nietzsche sometimes imagines as an earthquake in which the abyss opens up under one's feet, but also as an embarkation in which one leaves behind the firm ground of the land and commits oneself to a passage over the fluctuating surface of the ocean. Among the consequences of "the greatest recent event—'that God is dead'" is an initial response on the part of philosophers and "free spirits" of expectant elation:

> At long last the horizon is free and open, even though it may not be bright; our ships may at last venture out again, ready for any danger; every daring feat is again permitted for the one who seeks understanding; the sea, *our* sea, lies open again, and perhaps there has never been such an "open sea."[76]

After the death of God there is no going back: "we have destroyed the land behind us . . . there is no 'land' any longer" (*JS* 124). To live according to the spirit of adventure advocated by Nietzsche does not make for a more comfortable or serene life, but it does make the human being who experiments in this way more *fruitful*. In the words of one of his most often quoted admonitions: "Believe me! The secret for harvesting the greatest fruitfulness and enjoyment from life is: *live dangerously!* Build your cities by Mount Vesuvius! Send your ships into uncharted seas!" (*JS* 283).

A number of the aphorisms in the works from the early 1880s, as well as numerous passages in *Zarathustra,* were actually composed on the seashore, as their author walked along the border between the realms of earth and water.[77] Listen to this aphorism from *The Joyful Science:*

> Do I have ears still? Am I all ears and nothing beyond? Here I stand in the midst of the burning surf *[Brandung],* whose white flames are licking at my feet. From all sides I am being howled at, threatened, bombarded by shrill cries, while in the deepest depth the old earth-shaker sings his aria, booming like a bellowing bull. He stamps out such an earth-shaking rhythm that the very hearts of these weather-beaten rocky monsters tremble in their bodies. (*JS* 60)

Owing perhaps to a combination of the author's failing eyesight and poor visibility because of stormy weather, the initial experience of the ocean recounted here is more aural than visual. (In the presence of crashing surf it is almost necessary to close one's eyes in order to appreciate the rich complexity of the sound, since otherwise the spectacular visual effects are likely to dominate.) The phrase "nothing beyond [ears]" suggests that the crashing of the surf has dissolved the experiencer's body into the surrounding elements: in the absence of the seeing observer, the experience of sound in which there is no (outside) there opposed to a here (inside) is one of total participation in the environment.

Our relation to the sea is a fine analogue for the complex relation of the individual soul to the play of will to power that makes up the world. On the one hand, the apparently infinite expanse and abysmal depths of the ocean, together with the endless rhythms of its waves, serve to intensify the sense of our spatiotemporal finitude. On the other hand, prolonged contemplation of the ocean tends to lessen its otherness: we come to feel that the rhythms of its waves are a kind of breathing, or slow heartbeat, the movements of the tides those of the body's internal secretions, and that its motions mirror human emotions, from placid calm through agitated turbulence to the climactic crashing of waves against a rocky shore. On the beach, one can feel both apart from and a part of the totality. The synesthesia of Nietzsche's experience is enhanced by the "boiling" sound of the surf—captured by the German word *Brandung,* which is related to our word "burn." (The term evokes the way the surf seems to seethe and boil, as well as the appearance of licking flames on certain types of beach.) The phrases "white flames" and "burning surf" strikingly annul the usual opposition between fire and water, showing how an aware participant can mediate transformations between the elements.

Assailed by the howling storm, Nietzsche experiences the presence of "the earth-shaker"—*Ennosigaios,* an epithet of the Greek god Poseidon. Poseidon is god of the sea, with whom all seafarers need to cultivate the best of relations if they are to fare well; but he is also a power behind several other phenomena discussed in the present chapter. The origins of the name "Poseidon" and its bearer remain obscure, but the view of Wilamovitz (Nietzsche's early nemesis) to the effect that Poseidon was originally a spirit of fertility dwelling beneath the earth has apparently become widely accepted.[78] As a god of fertility he is associated with the water that comes up from the earth in springs and rivers, often appearing in this context as a horse or a bull; and as an originally subterranean power he is held to be responsible for earthquakes (hence the epithet "earth-shaker").[79] In the heavy surf that makes the shore on which one stands tremble, the two sides of Poseidon's nature come together in constant collision—just as the wind accompaniment to his "aria" issues from interaction between the elements of air and earth. (We see that while Nietzsche may no longer be writing *about* myth, mythical figures and themes continue to inform his work.)

Nietzsche's invocation of Poseidon and his attribution of hearts to the monster-shaped rocks on the shore is not simply a quaint piece of archaic anthropomorphism or post-Romantic personifying. To perceive powers of nature in the personal form of a god is to participate in a vital network of connections among natural phenomena. When Nietzsche experiences rocks as monsters with heart, he is not simply projecting the seat of his own emotions onto lifeless forms of stone: he is appreciating that "stone, plant, and animal" lie on a continuum, that rocks too possess a certain animateness. He was one of the first modern thinkers to appreciate that metaphorical experience—seeing something also *as* something else belonging to a different realm of being—is primary and not derivative of some putative "pure" experience. When Nietzsche hears the song of Poseidon in the boom of the surf, or feels the trembling of the rocks' hearts, he is not projecting his own psyche onto soulless phenomena of nature, but rather experiencing the world at a level where the forces animating human beings and the natural elements coincide.[80]

The image is elaborated in the second part of the aphorism, which begins: "When a man stands in the midst of *his* noise, in the midst of the surf of his own works and projects *[Würfe und Entwürfe]* . . ." The storms of life are always more impressive close to the edge, when we stand at the line dividing two different realms. What falls to us there may be threatening, and we can feel overwhelmed by the welter of our own desires and plans. But if we listen attentively, we may catch a tune beneath the cacophony, detect a rhythm behind the chaos, discern a voice not our own. We may sense the presence when the ground wavers of a spirit of fertility, signifying the advent of something creative; we may find ourselves in the company of a protector and guide for impending intellectual expeditions. "Then suddenly," the aphorism continues, "as if born from nothing, there appears before the gate of this hellish labyrinth, only a few fathoms off—a great sailing ship, gliding silent as a ghost." This image opens into "the question of woman," a complex question to which only relatively slight attention can be given, after the next chapter.

The ocean is a major presence in *Zarathustra,* where the action of the drama moves between Zarathustra's cave on the mountaintop and more than one sea far below. The images through which the idea of the *Übermensch* is first introduced include the ocean as well as "the sense of the earth" and lightning. Zarathustra's first words to the crowd in the marketplace associate the *Übermensch* with overcoming and the oceanic movement of will to power by emphasizing the prefix *über-:*

> *I teach you the Übermensch.* The human being *[Mensch]* is something that has to be overcome *[überwunden].* What have you done to overcome the human?
>
> All beings up to now have created something beyond themselves *[über sich hinaus]:* and you want to be the ebb of this great flood, and would rather go back to the animal than overcome the human? (*Z, P3*)

The condition of the *Übermensch* is to be attained by overcoming the human as it has been so far. To translate *der Übermensch* as "the superman" (or even as "the superhuman") is to miss the primary feature of that condition, which—far from instantiating a higher, new and improved version of the human being—is attained by going *over* in the sense of "across and beyond" modern humanity, through self-overcoming.[81] Zarathustra sees this process as part of a larger movement in human history, and the image of ebb and flood suggests that the energy required for this difficult task is to be drawn (at least in part) from the vaster swell. The identification of the *Übermensch* with the ocean also alludes to the vast perspective that is made possible by the transition to that condition: "Truly, humanity is a filthy river. One must surely be an ocean to be able to take in a filthy river without becoming unclean. Behold, I teach you the *Übermensch:* he is this ocean" (*Z, P3*). The current of human history contains much that is unclean and much that is evil; the magnanimity of the *Übermensch* is such that it can absorb the baser elements of this flow without being corrupted.

The most important aquatic image in *Zarathustra* consists of a lake, fed (one presumes) by springs, which overflows into a river that flows down to the ocean.[82] A prefiguration occurs in a short parable in *The Joyful Science.*

> There is a lake which one day refused to let itself flow off, and built a dam where it had flowed off up to then: and ever since this lake has been rising higher and higher. Perhaps just that kind of renunciation will lend us, too, the strength to bear renunciation itself; perhaps the human being will rise higher and higher, from the point where it no longer *flows out* into a god. (*JS* 285)

The lake is an image of the encapsulated soul, in which the waters of *erōs* are contained, standing for what Freud called "the reservoir of libido." A lake is usually insulated from the greater forces around it, a bounded body of water where calm can reign and reflection take place. Although the waters are constantly being replenished (psychical energy continuously introduced into the system through the process of life), the level of energy remains constant since the libido is continually being projected onto things in the world: objects, animals, other people, and (in the large majority of cases the greatest volume of drain-off) onto God. If that projection can be withdrawn, if the energy flowing toward an external figure can be blocked so that it flows back into the soul, forces will accumulate within that can be channeled toward great ends.

In depth-psychological terms, the lake would represent the minor "I," the ego, while the ocean would be the soul in the broadest sense, opening down into what Jung would call the collective unconscious. The first sentence of *Zarathustra* has the protagonist at thirty leaving his home "and the lake of his home" in order to go into the mountains. Distanced from ego-consciousness and aware of the death of God, Zarathustra has refused to let his libido flow off, and it has accumulated over ten years of solitude. We heard part of this apostrophe to the sun earlier:

> Bless the cup that wants to overflow, that the water may flow from it golden and carry everywhere the reflection of your delight!
> See! This cup wants to become empty, and Zarathustra wants to become human again.

A major motif of the book is Zarathustra's self-emptying, the overflowing soul, a kind of *kenōsis* in which the often agonized protagonist empties himself out into the world—and thereby somehow becomes full. In section 4 of the prologue he recites a litany of his loves, a list of traits that conduce to the condition of the *Übermensch.* Among them are these:

> I love him whose soul squanders itself . . . for he always gives and does not want to preserve himself. . . .

I love him whose soul is overfull, so that he forgets himself, and all things are in him: thus all things become his going under.

A number of word-plays are at work here that intensify the theme of over-flowing and outpouring.[83] We learn something about the source of such munificence when Zarathustra gives his speech on the virtue of being generous, "Von der *schenkenden* Tugend," at the end of part 1. There he describes the noble selfishness of those who strive for generosity.

Insatiably your soul strives for treasures and jewels, for your virtue is insatiable in wanting to give *[verschenken]*.

You force all things to you and into yourselves, so that they may flow back *[zurückströmen]* out of your well as the gifts of your love. . . .

There your body is elevated and resurrected; with its joy it enraptures the spirit so that it becomes a creator *[Schöpfer]*, and a valuer and lover and benefactor of all things.

When your heart flows broad and full like a river, a blessing and a danger to those who live nearby: there is the source *[Ursprung]* of your virtue. (Z 1.22 §1)

Now we can understand how those whom Zarathustra loves for their "over-full" souls come to enjoy such plenitude, and also why this overfullness results in their "forgetting" themselves (Z, P4). The hydrodynamics of Zara-thustrian generosity depend on keeping the boundaries of the self permeable and the channels clear for a continuous influx and outflow.[84]

Corresponding to the way we talk in English of "the wellsprings of cre-ativity," the word Zarathustra uses for creator, *Schöpfer,* enhances the force of the imagery of springs and wells insofar as the verb *schöpfen* means to draw up water. Nietzsche is fond of using the image of the well to suggest the depths of the psyche and the time it takes for experiences to reach the bottom-most levels of the soul: "Experience is a slow process for all deep wells: long must they wait before they know just *what* has fallen into their depths."[85] *Brunnen,* the German for "well," also means "fountain" and a number of Zarathustra's uses of the word suggest this more active meaning. At the beginning of "The Night-Song" he speaks of his soul as "a dancing fountain *[ein springender Brunnen]*," and at the end says that his desire breaks forth from him "like a spring"—*Born:* a poetic word, equivalent to "fount" (Z 2.9).

To consummate the connection between source and sea, let us now allow the full image to run its course. At the beginning of part 2, Zarathustra has gained a new perspective on himself and his relations to the rest of human-ity and the world, as expressed in this lyrical outburst:

My impatient love overflows in rivers, downward, toward rising and
setting. Out of silent mountains and thunderstorms of suffering my
soul rushes into the valleys. . . .

Mouth have I become utterly, and the roaring of a stream out of
high cliffs: downward will I plunge my speech into the valleys.

And may my river of love plunge into pathless places! How should
a river not finally find its way to the sea!

Indeed, a lake is in me, solitary and self-sufficient; but my river of
love tears it away, downward—to the sea! (Z 2.1)

This passage presents a picture of how, thanks to the natural flow of *erōs*,
the sense of the separate, encapsulated self is expanded to a more global
awareness. Since lakes are not made empty by the rivers that flow out of
them, the image does not suggest the annihilation of the contained self, but
rather the realization of its enduring connection to the larger realm of life.
This passage presents, incidentally, the inverse of an image that occurs near
the climax of Diotima's speech in Plato's *Symposium.* Whereas Zarathustra's love brings him down into the vale of the world and to the ocean, Platonic *erōs,* when properly channeled, stimulates the lover's soul to rise out
of the world and ascend through the various levels of beauty to the realm
beyond the heavens. At the highest point the soul of the initiate is granted a
vision of "the vast ocean of beauty" with which it then unites.[86]

Returning to land we find two passages from Augustine which provide appropriate motifs for bringing this chapter to a close: one harks back to the
labyrinths of the soul that we began to follow Nietzsche in exploring, while
the other provides a transition to the next chapter.

What, then, am I, my God? What is my nature? A life that is ever
varying, full of change, and of immense power. The wide plains of
my memory and its innumerable caverns and hollows are full beyond
compute of countless things of all kinds. . . . I can glide from one to
the other. I can probe deep into them and never find the end of them.
This is the power of memory! This is the great force of life living in
man, mortal though he is! (*Confessions,* 10.17)

The corresponding images in Nietzsche are perhaps even farther reaching, insofar as the descent into the depths of the self opens out into a wandering in the labyrinths of history and culture. When in the preface to *Dawn
of Morning* he speaks of himself as "a tunneler, a miner, an underminer"
who "descends into the depths and bores into the foundations *[Grund],*" the
foundations are those of the Western tradition as a whole. The vastness of
this task of exploration, daunting to most, serves as a stimulus to an explorer
of the caliber of Zarathustra: "There are a thousand paths that have never

been explored; a thousand healths and hidden islands of life. Human beings and the human earth are still unexhausted and undiscovered." (Z 1.22 §2). It is not only a question of horizontal wandering and vertical excavation. There is another dimension to the engagement with culture and self-cultivation which demands stamina and patience—the field of psychological agriculture, the domain of husbanding the soul. Augustine knew this well: "O Lord, I am working hard in this field, and the field of my labours is my own self. I have become a problem to myself, like land which a farmer works only with difficulty and at the cost of much sweat." (*Confessions*, 10.16).

But before turning there, some reflections on working on things at a more elemental yet highly cultural level.

Interlude 1: Art-Works against Nature

*Thus is Art, a nature passed through the alembic of man. Thus
in art, does nature work through the will of a man filled with
the beauty of her first works.*

Emerson, "Beauty" *(Nature)*

We have been given so far a picture of the psyche as a cosmos containing a
multitude of things. The plethora of metaphors Nietzsche draws from the
natural world gives the impression that these things are going on in the
soul all the time—earths quaking, suns rising and setting, clouds gathering,
storms brewing over the horizon, waves washing on distant shores—
whether one pays attention to them or not. But it is crucial to Nietzsche's
psychology that one can *engage* these images and work with them, and that
this operation will affect the ways the images unfold.

Emerson characterizes the duality that makes possible this kind of work
in the essay "Fate."

> On one side, elemental order, sandstone and granite, rock-ledges,
> peat-bog, forest, sea and shore; and, on the other, thought, the spirit
> which composes and decomposes nature—here they are, side by side,
> god and devil, mind and matter, king and conspirator, belt and spasm,
> riding peacefully together in the eye and brain of every man.

Nietzsche gives expression to the same idea, but with a heightened tension
between the sides that precludes the "peacefully," in a passage addressed to
those who want to *"abolish suffering."*

> In the human being *creature* and *creator* are united: in the human
> there is material, fragment, abundance *[Überfluss]*, clay, dirt, non-
> sense, chaos; but there is also in the human creator, sculptor, hammer-
> hardness, spectator-divinity, and seventh day—do you understand this
> opposition? And that *your* pity is for the "creature in the human," for
> that which has to be formed, broken, forged, torn, burned, annealed,
> and purified—for that which must necessarily *suffer* and *ought* to
> suffer?[1]

157

Detractors of Nietzsche who are outraged by his lack of interest in reducing suffering generally overlook this passage, which makes clear that "the discipline *[Zucht]* of suffering" that he thinks indispensable for "the enhancement of the human" results from what the detractors call "cruelty" inflicted by the self *on itself.* The work of "self-overcoming" is in a sense an *opus contra naturam,* insofar as it takes the individual's natural endowment and works it into something superior by deploying opposing natural tendencies. This is the meaning of culture for Nietzsche: "a new and improved *physis*" (*HL* 10). He describes the work of self-renewal and self-overcoming in metaphors drawn not only from the arts (making one's life a work of art) but also from "the Art" of alchemy (transforming one's experience through practice of the art)—both of these paradigms of *opera contra naturam.*

The idea that one's life can be made a work of art is to be found in some of the Stoic philosophers and became a prominent ideal in Renaissance culture.[2] Nietzsche's contact with Burckhardt may have set him thinking along these lines, as exemplifed in the theme in *The Birth of Tragedy* concerning the justification of existence "as aesthetic phenomenon," which suggests a consideration of life as artwork. More specifically, there is the idea that in the person of the Dionysian artist nature perfects itself in the work of the life. Thanks to the power of the song and the dance,

> the human being is no longer an artist but has become a work of art: the artistic power of the whole of nature . . . manifests itself here among the spectators of the intoxication. The most noble clay, the most costly marble—the human being—is here kneaded and hewn, and to the chisel blows of the Dionysian artist of worlds there rings out the cry of the Eleusinian Mysteries: "Do you prostrate yourselves, millions? Do you sense your creator, world?" (*BT* 1)

That the case of the artist is intended as a paradigm for human existence in general is confirmed later by a passage already discussed (in chapter 2, above), where Nietzsche denies that we are the true authors of the world of art: "We must rather assume that we are simply images and artistic projections *[Projektionen]* for the true creator and have our highest dignity in our significance as works of art" (*BT* 5). Even when he drops the idea of "the true creator" as a type of Schopenhauerian Will, the idea that our lives are— or can be made—works of art persists. The image of the hammer, in particular, will recur.

The *Untimely Meditation* on history speaks of life as a craft, a *Handwerk,* "that has to be learned constantly from the ground up and relentlessly practiced"—so that one can engage in the work of culture, understood as *"organizing the chaos"* (*HL* 10). The Greeks, those consummate artists of life, organized the chaos by reflecting on "their genuine needs and letting pseudo-needs die off"; they were thus able to become "the most happy en-richers and augmenters of the treasure they inherited." One inherits a nature; by working it artistically, through self-cultivation, one can transform that nature into a more valuable piece of culture.

Nietzsche later comes to think that the case of the professional artist is an especially difficult one, insofar as there is only a limited fund of re-sources on which to draw for both the art of self-cultivation and the creation of actual works of art. In an aphorism entitled "As an Excuse for Many a Fault," he writes:

> The ceaseless desire to create and looking to the outside on the part of the artist prevents him from becoming more beautiful and better as a person, from creating *himself*—unless his ambition is great enough to compel him to show himself as equal to the growing beauty and greatness of his works in his life with other people as well. In any case he has only a certain amount of energy: whatever he uses to work on *himself*, how could this be used for his *work?*—and vice versa. (*AOM* 102)

There is an implied comparison here between Wagner, who poured all his energies (and many of his acquaintances' energies) into his works, and an artist such as Goethe, whom Nietzsche frequently praises for having per-fected himself as well.

An unpublished note from the period emphasizes that self-cultivation is not just a matter of "knowing oneself" but also of *making* oneself (though the first may be necessary for the achievement of the second):

> It is a myth to believe that we will find our authentic self after we have left behind or forgotten one thing or another. . . . *To make ourselves,* to *shape* a form from various elements—that is the task! The task of a sculptor! of a productive human being![3]

The idea of artistic self-cultivation is further elaborated in a passage from *Dawn of Morning* entitled "Deploying One's Weaknesses as an Artist":

> If we are absolutely to have weaknesses and must ultimately acknowl-edge them as laws over us, I wish everyone would at least have suffi-cient artistic power to be able to make his weaknesses the foil of his virtues and through his weaknesses make us crave his virtues: some-thing the great musicians were capable of in special measure. (*DM* 218)

"Test fate!" is the idea behind this; "Explore limitations to the utmost." And when one is satisfied that bedrock has been reached, that there is noth-ing more to be done, that certain traits of one's being are irredeemably paltry, then employ art to enhance the overall appearance. Toward the end of the book, Nietzsche expresses his awe of

> the spectacle of that power *[Kraft]* which genius deploys *not for works* but *on itself as a work*—for its own overcoming, for the purification of its phantasy, for order and selection in the influx of tasks and ideas. The great human being is still, precisely in the greatest thing that demands reverence, invisible like a too distant star.[4]

Here the creative, artistic power of genius is said to attain maximum effect not when directed toward literal works of art but when retroflected upon the self, when the personality of the genius is itself taken as the material to be worked.

Insofar as the soul tends to imagine itself as a place and a structure, it would be possible to work on it as an architect; but such work would be hazardous and would demand a courage that Nietzsche thinks is not accessible to us in the modern age.

> How labyrinthine our souls take themselves to be and our ideas of the soul by contrast with [the ancient Greeks']! If we wanted—and could dare—an architecture appropriate to *our* kind of souls (we are too cowardly for it!)—the labyrinth would have to be our prototype! (*DM* 169)

This kind of work would have to proceed largely in the dark, and would expose the worker to monstrously powerful forces not all human. We shall see later (in chapters 8 and 9, below) that Nietzsche comes to think of the modern soul as naturally labyrinthine, as a result of its complex connections with a multiple heritage.

The theme of the artistic ordering of the psyche comes fully to the fore in the *The Joyful Science*. A gem of an aphorism, entitled "Motivating One's Inadequacies," resumes the theme of orchestrating weaknesses, playing this time on the image of the flow of a stream.

> There is admittedly no ploy by which we can turn a meager virtue into a rich, full-flowing one: what we can do is to nicely reconstrue its inadequacy as a necessity, so that the sight of it no longer pains us and we no longer look reproachfully at fate on its account. This is what the wise gardener does when he directs a paltry flow of water through the arms of a spring-nymph, to provide a motivation for its inadequacy—and who among us would not find himself similarly in need of nymphs! (*JS* 17)

The first thing to do would be to explore the possibility that the paltry flow of a particular virtue or talent results from a blockage or obstruction by some other force. But if no inhibiting factors are found, then rather than expending our energies on blaming fate for providing such a poor endowment in this respect, the idea is to channel one's artistic energies into providing a pleasing context that will conceal the inadequacy. After all, no one would expect a mountain torrent to emerge from the arms of a stone or plaster nymph. The result is that we will be happier with ourselves, and those around us will find their experience aesthetically enhanced.[5]

Nietzsche later in the book connects this theme with a line of thinking about *Schein* that began in *The Birth of Tragedy*. As a counterforce to the honesty that would strive to expose the ultimately distressing truths about human existence, there is "art, as the *good* will to *Schein*." Slightly modifying the key formulation, Nietzsche writes:

> As aesthetic phenomenon existence is still *bearable* for us, and through art we are given the eyes and hands and above all the good conscience to be *able* to make such a phenomenon of ourselves. (*JS* 107)

In *The Birth of Tragedy* the Apollonian drive to *Schein*—the shinings of phantasy and artistic illusion, the veil of beautiful phenomena projected over the Dionysian abyss—was considered indispensable to human survival. Now, with talk of the "good conscience," artistic projection is something to be *celebrated*—and individual existence justified as long as one works it into an aesthetic phenomenon.

A major ground for Freud's great admiration for Nietzsche was the latter's willingness to face up to the seamier side of the soul—in himself as much as in others. And yet this awareness does not lead to a fatalistic resignation. As awareness of the more repugnant aspects of our nature grows, considerations of prudence and aesthetics recommend some reconstruction work to conceal the baser features where appropriate.

> To "give style" to one's character—a great and rare art! This art is practiced by one who surveys everything his nature offers in the way of weaknesses and strengths, and then fits it into an artistic plan until each element appears as artistic and reasonable and even the weaknesses delight the eye. Here a large amount of second nature has been added, there a piece of original nature removed—in both cases as a result of long practice and daily work at it. Here something ugly that could not be removed has been concealed, there it has been reconstrued as sublime. Finally, when the work is finished, it becomes clear that the constraint of the same taste has governed and formed everything large and small.[6]

This is the classic formulation of the positively personal side of Nietzsche's "aestheticism," which is as far from a breezy attitude of *laisser aller* as one could imagine. The task of composing one's existence into an aesthetically satisfying phenomenon demands conscientious work as well as refined judgment. The call for the "constraint of the same taste" is meant to disqualify the sort of careless artistic bricolage that would throw together a bit of this and a piece of that without regard to the overall harmony of the parts. The conclusion of this aphorism presents one of Nietzsche's most penetrating psychological insights, and deserves to be engraved in letters of fire above the thresholds of all homes and institutions.

> For one thing is necessary: that the human being *attain* satisfaction with himself—whether by means of this or that poetic composition or art. . . . Whoever is unhappy with himself is constantly ready to take revenge on that account: we others will be the victims—if only because we will have to endure the ugly sight of the person. For the sight of the ugly engenders nastiness and gloom.[7]

The idea is given further exemplification several aphorisms later under the title "What One Should Learn from Artists," in the course of which the analogy finally shifts from the visual to the literary arts. Having learned a number of techniques from artists, we can become, Nietzsche says, even wiser than they in other respects: "For [with artists] this subtle power of theirs generally ends where art ends and life begins; *we* by contrast want to be poets of our lives, first and foremost in the smallest and most everyday matters" (*JS* 299). As "poets of our lives" we would come, through experimenting with perspectives and contexts, and by playing with aesthetic framings and juxtapositions, to *experience creatively*. It is not necessary to produce literal works of art in order to be this kind of poet, as long as the life itself is worked into an aesthetic whole. Montaigne puts the point succinctly: "To compose our character is our duty. . . . Our great and glorious masterpiece is to live appropriately."[8] This was what Nietzsche found so inspiring about the magnificent human types produced by the Renaissance: the formidable flow of life through them not suppressed or inhibited—but artfully channeled, skilfully worked into a play of creative forces.

The kind of artistic creation Nietzsche is talking about here also takes place on an *inter*personal level and a far grander scale. In the course of a diatribe against the short-sighted superficiality of the modern age in Europe, Nietzsche deplores the tendency for people to become mere "actors" ("where all nature ceases and becomes art") and bemoans the lack of "architects" who would build a real society out of individuals. He calls for a regaining of the broad perspective that would see the present in the context of the great sweep of history and the individual against the background of the development of the race.

Who would still dare to undertake works that would take millennia to be completed? The basic faith is dying out . . . that the human being has value and meaning only insofar as it is *a stone in a vast edifice:* for which it would have to be first and foremost *solid,* a "stone"—and above all not an actor! (*JS* 356)

Stone is perhaps the richest source of metaphors for artistic self-cultivation in Nietzsche's texts, and *Zarathustra* the site of the most striking petrographic images. Here is the protagonist in his speech on psychological creativity, which he calls "the lightening of life":

But my ardent will to create drives me to human beings again and again; just as it drives the hammer to the stone.

Ah, in the stone, my fellow humans, there sleeps an image, the image of my images! Ah, that it must sleep in the hardest and ugliest stone!

Now my hammer rages cruelly against its prison. Bits of stone fly like dust; but what is that to me?

I want to perfect it: for a shadow came to me—the stillest and lightest of all things came to me once!

The beauty of the *Übermensch* came to me as a shadow. (*Z* 2.2)

A prime instance, this, of Nietzsche's "philosophizing with a hammer." The finished statue lies sleeping in the block of stone that confronts the sculptor before he begins his work. (The sculptor in German, *der Bildhauer,* already evokes—as a good Apollonian—the image, *das Bild.*) Zarathustra is driven to be hard on his fellow human beings. Having discerned an adumbration of the human's being overcome, Zarathustra is moved to create, to make something of the human condition. To get rid of what is unnecessary in his subjects—the superfluous matters that weigh them down, hold them back, and get in their way—in order to reveal their potential to find their own ways, is hard; not least because they themselves, after generations of petrification under the pressure of traditional strictures, are hardened. The work demands a violent effort, and its effects will cause pain and suffering. But the good student of the good teacher comes to bless the hammer that hurts.

But how, one might ask, is it right for Zarathustra to be so hard on his fellow human beings? Does this episode not enhance the image of Nietzsche as a brutal and protofascist thinker, one who would condone the perpetration of violence upon people "for their own good"? It ought not to, for Zarathustra has *earned* the right to a heavy hand with the hammer: he has become hard through having gone through his own fire, and having already hammered his own self into shape. His hammer is said to rage against "its" prison: the stone is first and foremost Zarathustra's own nature;

and only after he has hammered himself into shape, liberating his possible self from the block in which it lay concealed, does he turn his creative-destructive energies upon others. This psychological dynamic, in which energies are introverted before being directed outward, is a feature of Nietzsche's psychology not to be overlooked.

Zarathustra has gone through the fire "on the way to [him]self"—as it says in the speech "On the Way of the Creator" (Z 1.17). The way to oneself *is* the way of the creator, a way of transformation through fire that "burns, anneals, and purifies."

> You must want to consume yourself in your own flame: how could you want to become new without first becoming ashes!

The process of creation, and especially of self-creation, includes intermittent destruction and decay; the life of the psyche is a cycle of constant deaths and rebirths, risings and dyings and again arisings.

> Creating—that is the great redemption from suffering and the lightening of life. But that the creator may be, that itself takes suffering and much transformation.
>
> Yes, there must be much bitter dying in your lives, you creators! You are thus the advocates and justifiers of all transience. (Z 2.2)

The work of creation, especially the creation of new life in the soul, involves constant struggle and hard labor. A note from the month when the thought of eternal recurrence first struck reads: "Constant *transformation*—you must pass through many individuals in a short period of time. The means is *constant struggle*."[9] By the time this idea comes up in *Zarathustra*, the conflict-generated suffering has become the pains of labor: "Truly, I have gone my way through a hundred souls and a hundred cradles and pangs of birth. I have already taken many a leave; I know the heartbreaking final hours." In order to have experienced so many rebirths, Zarathustra has to have died many deaths, witnessed many parts of his self perish, through being cauterized or burned out when necessary. Yet most of those who survive such an ordeal would say the gain is worth the pain.

The formative force of the hammer is applicable on a larger scale than that envisaged by Zarathustra when employed in the political realm. When Schiller talked about the transformation of the state (in *On the Aesthetic Education of Man*), he adduced the comparison with the "mechanical artist's setting his hand to the formless block and not hesitating to do it violence" (fourth letter). However, "the situation is quite different with the pedagogic and political artist, who has the human being at the same time as his material and his task." This is a case in which the respect and reponsiveness shown to the material is greater, even if the degree of violence is no less.

For Nietzsche, the violence is certainly no less—at least in the case of the initial creation of political communities as imagined in *Toward the Genealogy of Morals*. The work of the "conqueror race" on the "raw material of people and semi-animals" is undertaken by means of "hammer-blows and artists-violence":

> Their work is an instinctive forming and imposition of forms, and they are the most involuntary and unconscious artists there are . . . they are ruled by that frightening artist-egoism that looks like bronze and knows itself to be justified for all eternity in its "work," as a mother in her child. (*GM* 2.17)

In the next section Nietzsche transfers this operation back to the microcosm of the individual, in order to show the effects of the "*active* bad conscience," in which violence is retroflected upon the self, thereby helping to create what Goethe called "the labyrinth of the breast."

> Here the material on which the formative violence of this power is exercised is precisely the human being itself, its whole animal and ancient self—and *not,* as in the larger and more striking phenomenon, *another* human being or *other* human beings.

Nietzsche reintroduces the imagery of motherhood in going on to characterize this "artists-cruelty, this joy in imposing a form upon oneself as upon a heavy, recalcitrant, suffering material" as "the true womb of ideal and imaginative phenomena" and the generative force behind much of the beauty in the world (*GM* 2.18).

To return to the stone: there is an allusion to a different kind in *Zarathustra,* to the "philosophers' stone" *(Stein der Weisen)* of the alchemical tradition, when in "On the Vision and the Engima" the dwarf representing the spirit of gravity mockingly calls Zarathustra "you stone of wisdom *[Stein der Weisheit].*"[10] There appear to be only four (rather cursory) mentions of alchemy in Nietzsche's published works, from which one can conclude that he had no great acquaintance with the details of the alchemical arts.[11] In *The Joyful Science* he recommends to "preachers of morality" that they refrain from praising what they consider the highest virtues, since thereby "all the gold in them will be turned into lead." Such preachers are "well versed in the reversed art of alchemy, in the devaluing of the most valuable" (*JS* 292). The allusion here to Nietzsche's own "revaluation of all values" suggests that he might be engaged in a reversed art of preaching morals, in a "revaluing of the least valuable"—an impression that is confirmed by several passages in letters from the period shortly after he published *The Joyful Science* (and when he was beginning to work on *Zarathustra*).

Nietzsche mentions the philosophers' stone in a note to Paul Rée in May of 1882; and on Christmas Day that year, in the midst of the foundering of his relationship with Lou Salomé, he writes to Franz Overbeck one of the most tortured letters of his career.

> This last *morsel of life* has been the hardest I have ever chewed, and it is still possible that I might *choke* on it. I have suffered from the humiliating and tormenting memories of this past summer as from insanity. . . . I am straining every last fiber of my self-overcoming. . . .
> Unless I discover the alchemists' trick of turning this filth into *gold,* I am lost. I have here the *perfect* opportunity to show that for me "all experiences are useful, all days holy, and all humans divine"!!!![12]

Interesting that these words of Emerson's (included in the epigraph to *The Joyful Science*) should reoccur to Nietzsche at this time of crisis. In another letter to Overbeck some eight months later, after having written the first two parts of *Zarathustra* in separate bursts of inspiration, Nietzsche writes that his latest thinking aims at "the transformation of experience into *gold* and benefit of the highest order."[13] And in a numbered series of notes from the same period, many of which found their way into the third part of *Zarathustra,* he puts the same point in a more graphic image: "Now just give me the worst throw of your dice, fate. Today I am turning everything into gold."[14]

Nietzsche was going through what probably counts as the worst period of physical and psychical torment of his life: Elisabeth's zealous (and jealousy-inspired) intervention in his foundering relationship with Lou Salomé had led to the first complete rupture with his family; Wagner's death earlier in the year had shaken him more profoundly than he had expected; the complicated souring of the plans for a Platonic *ménage-à-trois* with Lou Salomé and Paul Rée was prompting emotions and actions on his part of which he would never have dreamed himself capable; and though he felt he was now writing his books "in [his] own blood," still hardly anyone was bothering to read them. No wonder, then, that the prospect of a perspective on existence by virtue of which one could transform dirt into gold should have held such strong appeal for him.

He was able to overcome the extreme adversity of this period by writing *Zarathustra,* a text that contains dozens of images that figure importantly in alchemy—and especially in alchemy understood as a symbol system for psychological transformation—such as chaos; the stone, fire, sun, and moon; the dragon, eagle, lion, serpent, and ouroborus; the child; and of course lead and gold. Since his knowledge of alchemy appears to have been slight, it is likely that these images surfaced spontaneously in Nietzsche's psyche as a result of the upheavals he was undergoing during this period.

(The idea of alchemy as a metaphorical discourse of self-transformation is basic to Jungian and archetypal psychology, and Jung discusses some of the imagery in *Zarathustra* with specific reference to alchemy.)[15]

The psychological distress of this phase of his life appears—according to his own reports, at least—to have brought Nietzsche close to the brink of madness. In letters to Overbeck and Köselitz, the two people to whom he was closest (and with whom he had no cause to be overly melodramatic), he relates phantasies of going insane. This passage is typical:

> The curious danger of this summer is—not to mince words—insanity. . . . It could come to something that I have never thought possible in my case: that I should become mentally deranged. . . . [Beset by such] feelings of revenge and *ressentiment* . . . my drives and aims have become totally confused and labyrinthine, so that I no longer know how to find my way out.[16]

Nietzsche had long held that the thinker's life should embody the thought; and now that unforeseen life experiences were preventing him from *living* his philosophy, he felt the threat of mental collapse. Since first being struck by the thought of eternal recurrence (in August 1881) he had been struggling with the problem of how to affirm life in the face of suffering and adversity—of how, in the words of a note from that time, to "live in such a way that we want to live again and to live *thus* for eternity!"[17] Another note a year later couches the thought of recurrence in a distinctly alchemical image, that of the *ouroboros,* the serpent that bites its own tail: "Do not fear the flux of things: this flux flows back into itself: it flees from itself not just twice. All 'it was' again becomes an 'it is.' The past bites all that is to come in the tail."[18] It is significant that one of the earliest mentions of "life as artwork" occurs in this same context, in a note from around the first occurrence of the thought of recurrence: "We want to experience a work of art again and again! One should therefore shape one's life in such a way that one has the same desire [for repeated experience] with respect to its individual parts! This is the main idea!"[19]

The image of the stone reappears in a broader artistic and cultural context in *Beyond Good and Evil,* where "the true philosophers" are declared to be "commanders and legislators" on a grand historical scale: "With a creative hand they grasp for the future, and everything that is and has been thereby becomes a means for them, a tool, a hammer. Their 'knowing' is a *creating* . . ." (*BGE* 211). This idea is best understood together with a contrasting idea presented earlier in the book. At the end of the third section, which deals with religion, the apostate author talks about how useful religions are for the philosopher who is concerned with the disciplined cultivation *(Züchtung)* and education of his fellow human beings.

The selective and cultivating influence (always correspondingly *destructive as it creates and shapes*) that can be exercised with the help of religions is always . . . multiple and different according to the type of human being to be placed under its spell and protection. (*BGE* 61; emphasis added)

The conjunction of the destructive and the creative here is reminiscent of the cruelty of Zarathustra's hammer in working its art. The sculptural image recurs in the next aphorism, where Nietzsche warns of the dangers that ensue when religions insist on being ends in themselves rather than means employed by philosophers. He blames Christianity for causing the degeneration of European man through its "transforming all love of the earthly . . . into hatred of the earth and the earthly" (*BGE* 62). Anyone approaching the results of this degeneration with an opposite desire, "with some kind of divine hammer in his hand," would

cry out with fury, compassion, and horror: "Oh you fools, you presumptuous, pitying fools, what have you done! Was that work for your hands! How you have botched and ruined my most beautiful stone!"

Leaving aside the question of the justness of the accusation, we can take Nietzsche's concluding fulmination against the Christian perpetrators for not being "high or hard enough" to take on the task of "sculpting *man* as artists" as something that would also disqualify a neofascist rationalization of violence from claiming a Nietzschean justification.

There is another side (as always, with Nietzsche) to this concern with cultivating hardness, an aspect of Nietzsche's thought that is all the more important to note since it is to be found in one of his diatribes against "sympathy for others." He claims that it is still an open question whether *helping* other people is always in their best, long-term interest, and offers a remarkably nonviolent alternative:

Or else one could *form* something out of oneself, which the other person could then see with pleasure, something like a beautiful, peaceful, self-enclosed garden, with high walls to protect against storms and the dust of the roads outside, but also a hospitable gate.[20]

A later aphorism in *Dawn of Morning* elaborates the horticultural theme in terms of the natural drives, and provides a transition to the topic of our next chapter:

One can deal with one's drives as a gardener and—though few people know this—cultivate the seeds of anger, pity, curiosity, vanity as fruitfully and productively as a beautiful fruit tree on a trellis . . . [whether] in the French or the English or Dutch or Chinese manner. (*DM* 560)

This is a classic formulation of what Nietzsche elsewhere calls the "subli-mation" of the drives: rather than eradicate the tendencies in the soul that are branded as vices, one can work with them in a wide variety of ways, such that they ultimately become not only aesthetically pleasing but also fruitful. One can always, of course, simply "let nature rule" and allow the plants to grow as they will and "fight it out among themselves"; but while there can be a joy in watching the nature within run wild in this way, such permissiveness does not conduce to creative experience.

This interlude has presented a pattern of imagery that is crucial to Nietzsche's psychology, in which material in the soul is worked by an inner artistic agent in order to make the whole psyche an art-work. In the next two chapters we see the schema in which one part (or parts) of the soul is worked on by another part (or parts) repeated in the realms of the vegetal and the animal, where psychical florae are cultivated and faunae domesti-cated and bred. Other mediums in which lives may be made into works, the political state and the drama of existence, will be discussed in chapter 9, below.

V

Husbanding the Soul: Vegetal Propagation

> *It is a long way from granite to the oyster; farther yet to Plato,*
> *and the preaching of the immortality of the soul.*
>
> Emerson, "Nature"

There are several fields of psychological images on which Nietzsche and Plato stand especially close, ranging from soil and the propagation of plants, through the breeding, rearing, and training of animals, to sexual intercourse and procreation of offspring at the human level. It appears unlikely that either thinker had much in the way of direct experience in any of these fields; it is thus all the more interesting that they should both draw so many images from them in their respective portrayals of the life of the soul.[1] The extent to which Nietzsche's Oedipus-eyes are short-sighted with respect to his inheritance from Laius/Plato in these areas becomes evident if one follows the strands of imagery developed by both thinkers in connection with their conception of the best, philosophical life: imagery concerning *propagation,* the cultivating of plants, and *procreation,* the generating of live offspring.

It is not surprising that these two themes should be associated metaphorically early on, in view of the structural similarities between the processes. The correspondence is caught by the ambiguity of the term "husbanding," insofar as a husband is traditionally both the head of a family who provides a home for his wife and progeny (the "hus-" means "house"), and also one who tills and cultivates—"husbands"—the soil and its products (the "-band" comes from Old Norse *bua,* meaning both to "cultivate" and to "dwell").[2] A primary meaning of the term "husbandry" is "management of a household; domestic economy," and so the term embraces all the features and functions of what Nietzsche calls "the great economy" of the soul. The relevant correspondences are between, on the one hand, finding and preparing suitable soil, sowing of seed, germination and sprouting, and finally flowering and fruition, and on the other hand, finding an appropriate mate, intercourse and insemination, conception and gestation, labor and birth. The structural similarities will suggest themselves more compellingly, of course, if one is unaware of the existence of the female ovum. It is a remarkable fact—indicative of the extent to which phantasy informs (and often clouds) scientific insight—that the existence of the ovum was not confirmed until as late as the nineteenth century.[3]

Ancient Greek ideas may be summed up in an account of reproduction advanced by the god Apollo in the *Eumenides* of Aeschylus:

> The mother is no parent *[tokeus]* of that which is called
> her child, but only the nurse *[trophos]* of the new-planted seed
> that grows. The parent is he who mounts. A stranger *[xenē]* she
> preserves a stranger's seed, if no god interfere.[4]

Here sexual procreation is assimilated to plant propagation through the idea of woman as nurse, the one who provides nourishment (*trophē*) for what has been sown. Plato appears, as we shall see, to have subscribed to a similar view of the close analogies between plant and animal reproduction. Aristotle, reasoning from a more empirical perspective, also held that "the female does not contribute seed to generation . . . but only material for the seed to work upon"—a view that would be regarded as authoritative for over two thousand years.[5] The *matēr* simply provides the *materia,* so to speak, in which the germ gestates.

The close correspondence between propagation and procreation is reflected in the relevant terms in Greek and in many other Western languages.[6] Thus it comes naturally to us to speak of "preparing the ground" before introducing a new idea to a potentially unreceptive audience; of "sowing the seed" of some novel notion in the mind of another; or of letting a thought "germinate" for a while, or a part of the mind "lie fallow." We often expect a meeting of the minds to be "fertile" or "productive," and we speak of the "conception" and "birth" of new ideas. A study of how such metaphors operate in the texts of Nietzsche and Plato will uncover extensive ramifications to them as images revelatory of the workings of the psyche. In Nietzsche's case the vegetal imagery is connected with the metaphor systems concerning the elements discussed in the previous chapter, insofar as the growth of vegetation depends on factors of climate and weather that are beyond the range of human control. This circumstance serves to point up the powerful element of contingency in the process of self-cultivation, a feature that is less prominent in Plato's account of this process.[7]

It is surprising that Plato should employ metaphors drawn from the vegetable or animal realms at all, in view of the way his metaphysics privileges the heavens and the realm of intellect over the earth and the body. Plants grow organically, spontaneously, from within, without guidance from a superior governing agent, nor in accordance with any external pattern. The roots of the plant are necessarily hidden in the dark; if they are pulled up into the light, the plant dies. One would expect such considerations to attract Nietzsche to draw metaphors from the vegetable realm, but to make Plato, by the same token, extremely wary of doing so. Plato's unexpected propensity for agricultural metaphors prompts an examination of what he clearly considers secondary and preparatory, the use of imagery, rather than what he regards as primary and final, the logical progression of the dialectic. Such a focus reveals that the tendency of the imagery pulls at times in a different direction and works counter to the dialectical development.[8]

The implications of the entwining of the imagery of propagation and procreation in Nietzsche and Plato are not immediately apparent; but it may be that—to paraphrase Socrates on justice in the city and the individual—"by considering them side by side, and rubbing them together like sticks, we can make [the topic] burst into flame, and once it's come to light, confirm it for ourselves."[9] While the main aim is a clearer understanding of Nietzsche's psychology, an apt comparison may be bilaterally illuminating.

But before beginning, a piece of biographical context will render more comprehensible the increasing amount of vegetal and agricultural imagery in Nietzsche's texts from *Human, All Too Human* on. In spite of his immediate enthusiasm for the landscape of the Engadin after leaving Basel in 1879, Nietzsche soon found the solitude increasingly hard to tolerate— especially since his illnesses continued to plague him. He entertained plans of returning home to Naumburg and renting a tower and an adjoining compound with trees and vegetable gardens near the old city walls. In a letter to his mother he expresses the wish to sign a six-year lease (!) for the place.

> The growing of *vegetables* corresponds perfectly with my wishes and would be in no way unworthy of a future "sage." You know that I am inclined toward a simple and natural way of life, that I gain ever more strength from it, and that for my health there is no other cure. What I need is real *work,* something that takes time and *effort* without taxing my brain. (21 July 1879)

A letter to Köselitz at the end of September suggests that while the whole place was much larger—and thus more work—than he had expected, he was nevertheless thriving. But after a few weeks he reports to Overbeck that he is having with great regret to abandon his horticultural career, owing to the condition of his eyes and because the constant bending was exacerbating his headaches.[10]

Trees on Stony Ground

> *The greatest delight which the fields and woods minister, is the*
> *suggestion of an occult relation between man and the vegetable.*
> *I am not alone and unacknowledged. They nod to me and I to*
> *them. The waving of the boughs in the storm, is new to me and*
> *old.*
>
> Emerson, "Nature" *(Nature)*

Just as literal vegetation grows from the earth spontaneously, without the help of human intervention, so, for Nietzsche, natural growth from the ground of the soul is a rich source of psychological imagery. The most imposing exemplar of the plant realm, and the one that most resembles the human body (aside from certain roots, such as ginseng), is the tree. In shape trees can resemble the human frame, especially those that emerge from the ground in thrusts more than bursts of life-energy. Trees grow naturally in the wild, where they can be gathered from or felled for human consumption; but they may also be cultivated or "farmed."

The image of the human being as a tree had been popular among German thinkers for several generations before Nietzsche flourished, as an especially anthropomorphic instantiation of the "vegetative soul" in nature. These lines from Herder are exemplary:

> The deeper anyone descends into himself, into the construction and
> source of his noblest thoughts, the more will he cover his eyes and feet
> and say: "What I am, that have I become. Like a tree have I grown: the
> germ was there; but air, earth, and all the elements, which I did not
> myself provide, had to contribute to forming the germ, the fruit, the
> tree."[11]

The tree signifies for Herder the organic unity of all the faculties that participate in the unfolding and flourishing of the human soul, as well as its dependence for this flourishing on external forces beyond human control. With his emphasis on the importance of the inorganic conditions of life and his concern with the elemental aspects of the psyche, Nietzsche is as appreciative as Herder of the many external factors that condition the task of self-cultivation.

We saw earlier that Nietzsche deplores the short-sightedness of a modernity in which individuals have lost the sense of themselves as stones in a greater edifice of culture. Given his concern for the long-range view, another feature of trees especially recommends them as images for the way human beings could be: their enormous life span. A major drawback stemming from the demise of the metaphysical worldview is the loss of the vast perspective that went with it.

> [The modern] individual focuses too narrowly on his own short life span . . . and wants to pluck the fruit himself from the tree he plants, and so no longer likes to plant those trees that demand a century of constant tending and are intended to provide shade for long successions of generations.[12]

This idea provides the background for the distinction Nietzsche makes— crucial for an understanding of his task—between creators and enjoyers: "Every enjoyer thinks that the tree was concerned with the fruit, whereas it was really concerned with the seed."[13]

The title of a later aphorism—"Evil"—suggests that we may have to deal with the tree of the knowledge of good and evil as well as with the tree of life:

> Look at the lives of the best and most fruitful human beings and peoples and ask whether a tree that is to grow proudly up into the heights can do without bad weather and storms: whether misfortune and resistance from outside, whether every kind of hatred, jealousy, stubbornness, mistrust, hardness, avarice, and violence do not belong among the *favorable* conditions without which any great growth, even of virtue, is hardly possible?[14]

This is a central theme in Nietzsche's psychology and a succinct expression of the philosophy guiding his school of hard blows. It is certainly a principle that enables one to be "philosophical" about misfortune: the man's biography is full of junctures at which he looks back at a period of extreme misery and realizes in retrospect that he has in fact benefited from it.

Optimal conditions are nothing absolute but depend upon the kind of vegetation that is to grow. In "Zarathustra's Prologue," the protagonist proclaims his love for "him who works . . . to prepare earth, animal, and plant" for the advent of the *Übermensch* (Z, P4). In his next speech he says: "It is time for human beings to plant the seed of their highest hope. Their soil is still rich enough. But some day this soil will grow poor and tame, and no tall tree will be able to grow from it." (P5). The preparation for the self-transformation that, for Nietzsche, affords the highest fulfillment of human being is suggested in arboricultural imagery; in order to overcome the human in oneself, one has to work—and work through—the ground from which the tree of human life grows.

The tree imagery in *Zarathustra* runs for the most part parallel to the theme of husbandry. The image of fruit on a tree which falls naturally to the ground when ripe is central to Nietzsche's conception of the creative process. Zarathustra is impatient with cases that fail to follow this natural progression, and he calls upon storms to come and test the trees of life and to "shake all that is worm-eaten from [them]."[15] The tree of life thrives on soil that is rich, but also hard. Zarathustra addresses the proponents of "the virtue that makes small" as follows: "Fostering too much, giving way too much: such is your soil! But for a tree to become *great,* for that it must strike hard roots around hard rocks!"[16]

The richest arboreal image in *Zarathustra* occurs in the speech "On the Tree on the Mountain," in which the protagonist, in one of his more gnomic utterances, says to the youth:

> It is the same with the human being as with the tree. The higher they climb into the height and light, the more strongly their roots strive earthward, downward, into the dark, the depths—into evil. (Z 1.8)

This image contains the crux and kernel of Nietzsche's amoral psychology. Most previous psychology, he holds, has been infected by Platonic-Christian moralizing and thus fails to understand that constant striving for the heavenly heights and development of the lighter and brighter aspects of one's being leads to imbalance, to a top-heaviness of the tree of life that can easily result in catastrophe. One can maintain stability by emulating the tall tree, which, the higher it grows, the deeper it extends its root system down into the earth, into the obscure unknown and the morally murky. As trees of the knowledge of good *and* evil we are to cultivate a sense of our dependence on darker elements. If we deny those depths to our being, beneath the surface, dark as the interior of the body is dark, if we shrink from extending ourselves down to take nourishment from deeper soil, we are headed back for a fall.[17] It is appropriate to recall that Dionysus is intimately associated with trees, often being referred to as "the tree god" *(Dendritēs)* and considered to preside over the ripening of fruit.[18]

By the time Nietzsche added a fifth book to *The Joyful Science* (in 1887) the tree of *Zarathustra* has burgeoned, again in a Dionysian vein, into one of his most magnificent vegetal images.

> [We incomprehensible ones] are constantly growing and changing, we shed our old bark, we slough off our skins every spring, we become ever younger, more "futural," taller, stronger, we drive our roots down ever more forcefully into the depths—into evil—while at the same time we embrace the sky ever more lovingly and broadly, imbibing its light ever more thirstily through all our branches and leaves. We grow like trees . . . not in one place but all over, not in one direction, but just as much upward and outward as downward and inward. Our energy drives through trunk, branches, and roots simultaneously;

it is no longer possible for us to do only one particular thing, or even to *be* only one particular thing.[19]

What this elaboration of the human-as-tree image shows most importantly is that Nietzsche seems to have made his peace with the multiplicity of his inner drives—or at least to have learned how to live them. It is the image of an ideal situation, in which growth takes place spontaneously and yet with awareness; but given the contingencies that form the horizon for such growth, one would presume that such a condition is attainable only for short periods of time, before some new factor necessitates again some form of conscious intervention.

A similar image comes up in the preface to *Toward the Genealogy of Morals,* which gives a fine picture of the kind of organization that informs Nietzsche's thinking as a whole: an organic structure that grows from within rather than a systematic structure constructed or imposed from without. Speaking of the development over the previous decade of his ideas concerning "the origin of moral prejudices," he writes:

> We hope that this long interim period has done [the thoughts] some good, that they have become riper, brighter, stronger, more complete. But the fact that I still hold to them today, and that they have themselves held to each other ever more tightly and have grown closer together and even grown together, [suggests] . . . that they have grown from a common root. . . . Our thoughts, our values, our yeses and nos and ifs and buts grow from us [philosophers] with the necessity with which a tree bears its fruits—all related to every other and evidence of one will, one health, one soil, and one sun. (*GM,* P2)

The connection between any two of Nietzsche's ideas may not be immediately apparent: if they are not fruits on the same branch, it may be necessary to go back to the main trunk, or cultivate a feeling for the deeper roots of his thinking as a whole, in order to understand the deeper relations.

The emphasis in this passage—perhaps because of its retrospective nature—is on what Hölderlin called "the organization of nature"; but trees may also be planted and cultivated, and we may flourish more fully with the introduction of "an organization that we would give to ourselves." We learn from a speech Zarathustra makes to his jubilant conscience that he has "planted" a number of thoughts in the form of trees, which he refers to as his "children" (Z 3.3). At this point in the text the imagery of propagation comes together with images of procreation, but this first reading focuses on the former.

> O afternoon of my life! What have I not given that I might have this one thing: this living plantation of my thoughts and this morning light of my highest hope!

Companions the creator once sought and children of *his* hope: and look, it turned out that he could not find them unless he first created them himself. . . .

My children are still verdant in their first spring, standing close to one another and shaken by the same winds, the trees of my garden and my best soil.[20]

In line with Nietzsche's belief that trees grow stronger when exposed to adverse conditions, Zarathustra intends to separate and transplant his saplings so that they may become hardier and more robust.

But some day I will dig them up and place each one by itself, so that it can learn solitude and defiance and caution.

Gnarled and bent and with a supple hardness it shall then stand there by the sea for me, a living lighthouse of indomitable life.

Zarathustra had realized earlier that he would have to create disciples worthy of propagating his ideas, and so he now no longer refers to them as "disciples" but rather as his "children." If it seems unnatural that his children should be trees, we should recall that Zarathustra imagines himself as a fig tree and is seen by others as a pine.[21] His understanding of arboriculture tells him that his tree-children are not yet hardy enough to survive on their own, though he will later expose them to the harshness of the elements that will allow them to become strong. There is an intriguing ambivalence to the final image, in which the phallic thrust of the living lighthouse (*Leuchtturm:* literally, "light-tower") is countered by the prior characterization of the trees as "bent" or "buckled." Perhaps it is meant to convey the internal contradictions that drive life as will to power. The testing by harsh weather will prove whether the tree is "master of a long will": the question is whether the will to power (as creative and interpretive energy) that Zarathustra implants in his disciples will take root in such a way that their own creative interpretations may in turn prevail.[22]

All the reasons that attract Nietzsche to arboreal images would be grounds for Plato's avoiding them, since anything in mental life stemming from a process that unfolds in the dark would be dismissed by Socrates as nugatory—precisely since one would be unable to provide reasons for it. One of the very few arboreal images in Plato is one that stands—or hangs—in striking contrast to Nietzsche's trees: the well known "inverted plant" simile in the *Timaeus*. In a recapitulation of the three kinds of soul in the human being, Plato characterizes the rational soul by way of the following figure:

Heaven has given the most sovereign form of soul to each one as a guiding *daimōn*—that part which dwells in the summit of our body and lifts us from earth towards our celestial affinity, like a plant whose roots are not in earth but in the heavens. It is to the heavens, whence the soul first came to birth, that the divine part attaches the head or root of us and keeps the whole body upright. (*Tim.* 90a)

There is a curious doubling of the image of roots here: if the plant of the human soul has its roots in heaven, one can imagine its final florescence embodying itself in the human cortex. But Timaeus then calls the head the root—as if the plant of the soul were suspended from the heavens, with the appendage of the body dangling beneath. In general the image is meant to represent an aspect of Plato's theory of "devolution," his idea of the degeneration of the soul into matter, which was cultivated so fruitfully by the Neoplatonic tradition. The metaphor is playfully inverted by Zarathustra when he speaks of teaching people "no longer to hide their head in the sand of heavenly things, but to carry it freely, an earth-head that creates a sense for the earth" (Z 1.3). But in view of Nietzsche's fondness for vegetal metaphors, Plato's image of the inverted plant must be anathema: the tree of life *turned upside down!*

While this is the extent of the significant tree imagery in the Platonic dialogues, it is worthwhile to look at the role played by trees and other vegetation in the *setting* of the dialogue with the most resonances with Nietzsche's *Zarathustra:* namely, the *Phaedrus.*[23] Only in the *Phaedrus* do we see Socrates leaving the limits of the city and entering the world of nature. As he and Phaedrus walk along the banks of the Illisus, his young companion points out a "tall plane tree" and suggests that they have their conversation while reposing on the grass in its shade (*Phr.* 229a). The plane tree *(platanos)* is sacred to Dionysus. When they reach the tree Socrates waxes uncharacteristically lyrical about its beauty and the beauty of the other trees nearby, and about the place in general—even though in his next speech he denies that "country places and trees" ever teach him anything, whereas people in the city do.[24] After Phaedrus has read aloud the speech of Lysias on love, he swears by the plane tree that he will force Socrates to present a speech of his own in the presence of that very tree.[25]

There are sufficient resonances between the *Phaedrus* and one episode in particular of *Zarathustra,* "At Midday" (Z 4.10), to suggest that memories of the dialogue came along with the stream of inspiration that engendered that episode (unconscious though Nietzsche may have been of its source). It is shortly before noon when the conversation between Socrates and Phaedrus gets underway, as they recline on the grass in the shade of the plane tree, the warm air vibrating with the song of the cicadas around them. Their conversation is filled with references to Dionysus and dithyrambs, some of them admittedly ironic on Socrates' part.[26] Zarathustra too finds himself a grassy spot beneath a tree on which to repose at the noon hour, though in this case the tree is "crooked and knotty."[27] The presence of Dionysus—granted in the *Phaedrus* by the plane tree—is here mediated by a vine: the tree is "embraced and hidden from itself by the rich love of a vine, from which hung an abundance of yellow grapes." And while much of the conversation between Socrates and Phaedrus turns on the nature of the soul, since Zarathustra is alone, his words are addressed *to* his own soul as his only companion and interlocutor.

Socrates is concerned that the cicadas conversing among themselves should not see the two humans "slumbering around the fountain at noon, like sheep," lulled to sleep by their songs. But if the cicadas see the men conversing, they might lend them the divine gift of song; and so "for many reasons," he says to Phaedrus, "we ought to talk and not sleep in the noontime" (*Phr.* 258e–259d). Zarathustra, in contrast, gladly succumbs to sleep beneath his vine-entwined tree at the noon hour, since this sleep, as it "dances" upon him, leaves his soul awake.[28] He is able to talk in his sleep first with his heart and then with his soul; but at noon he loses interest in talk, and even in song. Stillness is crucial at this moment, and so he quiets his soul with the plea: "Do not sing, grass-wings. . . . Don't even whisper!" Fully awake, Socrates speaks of immortal soul which "when it is perfect and fully winged mounts upward and governs the whole world," whereupon mind—*nous:* "pilot of the soul"—is nourished by the sight of what is eternal, "colorless, formless, and intangible" (*Phr.* 246c, 247c). Somnolent in stillness, Zarathustra speaks of the world's becoming perfect—"golden, round, and ripe"—at a moment in which he drops off into "the well of eternity" *(den Brunnen der Ewigkeit).*[29] Whereas immortal souls in the *Phaedrus* ascend beyond the vault of heaven, where "the revolution carries them round" in festal procession around the outer surface of the spherical heavens, Zarathustra's soul responds, "Still! Did the world not just become perfect? Oh the golden round ball!" While Zarathustra falls into the "well [*Brunnen*, fountain] of eternity," the drop nevertheless seems to be somehow *up,* insofar as he addresses the heaven as "you serene, awesome abyss of midday *[Mittags-Abgrund]*!" and asks when it will "drink [back into itself] this drop of dew that fell on all earthly things . . . this wonderful soul." Zarathustra had earlier addressed his soul as a vine with "crowded brown gold grapes" (Z 3.14): all the spheroid imagery in this section—ripe rings, golden balls, brown grapes, and perfect worlds—alludes to the soul's kinship with the spherical heavens that are the *kosmos* of the *Phaedrus.*

Alongside Dionysus (in the form of the vine, golden wine, and the intoxication invoked at the end), Zarathustra's noontime reverie is pervaded by the presence of Pan—"the old noon sleeps, he moves his mouth: is he not drinking a drop of happiness?"—the deity to whom Socrates addresses the famous prayer that ends the *Phaedrus*.[30]

Preparing Suitable Soil

> *Now we learn what patient periods must round themselves be-*
> *fore the rock is formed, then before the rock is broken, and the*
> *first lichen race has disintegrated the thinnest external plate*
> *into soil, and opened the door for the remote Flora, Fauna,*
> *Ceres, and Pomona, to come in.*
>
> Emerson, "Nature"

Just as hunting and gathering preceded agriculture and animal husbandry, so one may distinguish a more basic level of engagement with the vegetal realm of the psyche. But the psychical analogues of gathering plants are of little interest, and so (aside from some of Nietzsche's tree imagery) the major focus of his vegetal metaphors, and of Plato's too, is on the interaction between natural forces and human activity. But since the general orientation of Platonic metaphysics is toward a realm "above the heavens," plain earth imagery is of minor importance and can be dealt with in an initial brief discussion.

For Plato, the cave of ignorance lies deep "beneath the earth"; much of the rank confusion within the soul of the newborn is caused by collisions with "solid lumps of earth"; one who dies without having purified the soul will end up in the underworld of Hades "lying in the mud."[31] Telling too is the myth at the end of the *Phaedo,* where Socrates says that—rather than living on the surface of the earth—we in fact live in large hollows underground: "For this earth of ours, and the stones and the whole region where we live, are injured and corroded . . . and there is nothing perfect there, but caverns and sand and endless mud and mire" (*Pho.* 110a). However, there are other myths in the dialogues where the earth is acknowledged as a potentially creative matrix. In the myth of the metals in the *Republic,* the inhabitants of the *polis* are to be told that they have been "born of the earth" and are to regard "the land they are in [as] a mother and nurse" (*Rep.* 414e). In the myth of the *Timaeus,* just before human souls are incarnated the divine craftsman "sows them in the earth" (*Tim.* 42d). The idea of humans' being born from the earth is also found in the myth of the *Statesman* (267c–277a). In the golden age of Cronos, human beings were not generated from one another but were rather "earth-born": no procreation, but only spontaneous generation from seed under ground. The epoch of the earth-born ends when every soul has "let fall into the earth as many seeds as had been prescribed for each."[32]

Vegetation will not grow, nor plant life burgeon, without proper soil. As usual, Nietzsche's psychological observations in this metaphorical field pertain not only to the individual but also to the *culture* (an apposite term in this context). As individuals we do not create our own ground; it is something given to us by the culture into which we are born, inherent in the soil that is native to us. For Nietzsche this inherited earth has a vastness that we have hardly begun to explore. As Zarathustra says, in the context of a speech on the dangers of being an heir: "The human being and human earth are still unexhausted and undiscovered" (Z 1.22 §2). In view of the geological dimensions to Nietzsche's earth imagery, one will want to read this statement as encouraging not only a search for new horizons but also an in-depth exploration of the cultural and psychological grounds we inherit from our traditions.

This kind of inheritance involves the receipt of a gift that may be a bane as well as a blessing. We tend to be oblivious not only to the quality of the soil handed down to us, but also to the hazards inherent in working in the fields of the soul. An aphorism entitled "Vegetation of Happiness" begins with the observation: "Close by the woe of the world, and often on its volcanic soil, human beings have laid out their little gardens of happiness . . ." (*HA* 591). The ground can be enriched by the deposits of past eruptions, but then the practice of agriculture in such areas will not be without its dangers. Since many human acquisitions "take centuries [to become] strong and ripe . . . we all have within us hidden gardens and plantations . . . we are all growing volcanoes that approach the hour of their eruption" (*JS* 9). Such considerations provide good grounds for undertaking some kind of psychical and cultural seismology.

Even though we regard many previous manifestations of culture as insalubrious, they may well have enriched rather than impoverished the quality of the soil. There are advantages, for example, to being born into a culture that was permeated in its beginnings by religious thinking.

> Is it not on *this* kind of soil, which you sometimes find so displeasing, the soil of impure thinking, that many of the most magnificent fruits of more ancient cultures have grown up? One must have loved religion and art like a mother and nurse—otherwise one cannot become wise. (*HA* 292)

This last sentence is patently autobiographical. A ground that has absorbed the decomposing remains of dead gods, fallen idols, and moribund ideals can—if formerly imbued with love—prove ultimately fertile.

The psychological implications of these images have to do with the "earthiness" of the psyche, the fertility of the medium, with soul as soil, the ground without which ideas cannot take root within us. The vegetal psyche grows naturally out of this medium; and while Nietzsche appreciates such spontaneous vegetation, he realizes that it does not of itself lead to psychological creativity. The move toward agriculture, toward sowing and reaping in the field of the psyche, begins with preparing the ground.

When he first began writing the aphorisms that eventually made up *Human, All Too Human,* Nietzsche was going to collect them under the title "The Ploughshare." The image finally surfaces in *The Joyful Science,* where he warns that if the soil of a culture is left in the charge of "good people" who cultivate "the old thoughts" for too long (unaware, presumably, of the benefits of composting or crop rotation), the soil will become impoverished. The ground must then be broken up and reworked, and for this it is necessary that "the ploughshare of evil come again and again" (*JS* 4). The preparation of the soil may thus be a violent affair, appearing especially brutal from the perspective of the ground, of the foundation of opinions and convictions on which our psychological life is based.

There is a point in *Zarathustra* where the protagonist as husbandman realizes that seeds he has planted have failed to sprout because the ground was not well prepared. He diagnoses a major part of the problem in a speech "On the Virtuous," concerning people whose senses are "lethargic and somnolent" and into whose souls "the voice of beauty [is unable to] slide" (*Z* 2.5). This voice will get through only to souls that are awake; and so Zarathustra prescribes the following, rather drastic remedy:

> Ah, that is my sorrow: they have lied reward and punishment into the ground of things—and now even into the ground of your souls, you virtuous ones!
>
> But like the boar's snout my words will tear open the ground of your souls; *ploughshare* you shall call me. (*Z* 2.5)

No soul can be open for Zarathustra's new teaching as long as its basis is a congelation of traditional ethical views: his incisive words will wake up the souls of the virtuous as they break up their grounds. And even though reward and punishment are less abhorrent to Socrates than to Zarathustra, the former was nevertheless branded as evil by his accusers, who were acutely aware of the subversive effects of his shaking the firm ground of his interlocutors' unexamined prejudices.

Vegetation does, of course, spring from soil that has not been worked; and what comes up there may surprise us, for we are generally unaware of what is going on beneath the surface. "Out of damp and gloomy days, out of solitude, from loveless words directed to us, *conclusions* grow up like mushrooms: one morning they simply appear, where from we don't know, and they stare at us, gray and morose" (*DM* 382). The mycelium that forms beneath the surface of the soil before the mushroom suddenly appears remains invisible. Nietzsche often expresses amazement (especially in the unpublished notes) at the way ideas suddenly surface, clearly as a result of numerous connections and associations that have been made unconsciously. These processes of the vegetal soul are always ongoing, in everyone; but they can be enhanced, and something made of them, only if one participates actively in the process. Indeed Nietzsche comes to think that failure to do so has deleterious effects of its own, insofar as he concludes this aphorism with the warning: "Woe to the thinker who is not also the gardener but only the soil of what grows in him!"

The drawbacks of a passive stance toward psychical plant life were elegantly remarked by Montaigne, in a passage that also draws the parallel (to be traced in the next chapter) between propagation and procreation:

> Just as we see that fallow land, if rich and fertile, teems with a hundred thousand kinds of wild and useless weeds, and that to set it to work we must subject it and sow it with certain seeds for our service; and as we see that women, all alone, produce mere shapeless masses and lumps of flesh, but that to create a good and natural offspring they must be made fertile with a different kind of seed; so it is with minds. Unless you keep them busy with some definite subject that will bridle and control them, they throw themselves in disorder hither and yon in the vague field of imagination. (*Essays,* 1:8, 20–21)

Nietzsche offers similar grounds for becoming "gardeners of what grows within" in an aphorism entitled "Overcoming the Passions":

> The human being who has overcome the passions has entered into possession of the most fertile ground *[Erdreich]*. . . . To *sow* the seeds of good spiritual works on the soil of the subdued passions is then the next urgent task. . . . [Otherwise] all kinds of weeds and devilish stuff will spring up in the rich soil that has been cleared, and there will soon be more rank confusion there than ever before.[33]

The preparation of psychical ground, whether in ourselves or in others in whom we would see ideas propagated, requires hard work that is not always pleasant—involving, as it does, contact with compost, material in the soul which has decomposed. While Plato appears less inclined to dirty his hands with such work than Nietzsche—indeed their projects are in one sense diametrically opposed: the former's being to purify the psyche of all earthly accretions, the latter's to redeem its somatic aspect for the earth—he nevertheless chooses agricultural imagery to depict one of the soul's highest activities. It would be difficult, however, to imagine Socrates speaking as earthily as Nietzsche does when he refers to the artist as "the womb, soil, sometimes the dung and manure, on and out of which [the work] grows" (*GM* 3.4).

Nietzsche wanted with *Human, All Too Human* to focus on the "small, insignificant things," and in the text itself there is an admonition to do so that is couched in agricultural terms. Those people are commended who "know how to manage their experiences—their insignificant, everyday experiences—so that they become arable soil that bears fruit three times a year" (*HA* 625). The idea is that there is much in our experience that we are inclined to overlook, or dismiss as nugatory, but which is valuable for the task of self-cultivation. To get at it may require some digging, a task that is not always enjoyable, for "[in the depths] there is always much that is unpleasant to see"; and yet a down-to-earth outlook will understand that "all human undertakings . . . if their cause is to flourish, need evil-smelling manure" (*HA* 489–90). The idea is amplified in a wry observation under the title "Sowing and Harvesting One's Shortcomings": "Men like Rousseau understand how to use their weaknesses, deficiencies, and vices as manure for their talents" (*HA* 617). While Nietzsche's remarks on Rousseau are often unduly harsh, this one is surely a compliment: proponent of the noble savage as pioneer in the field of organic self-cultivation.[34] Rather than attempting to eliminate waste products from the soil of the soul (unpleasant for the neighbors, apart from anything else), one can become more fruitful by containing them and cycling them back into the soil to promote new growth. Parallel to Nietzsche's attempts at alchemical transmutation of "filth into gold" would be an agricultural transformation of experience felt to be excremental into manure for further plantings. The most important yield from this kind of practice is an attitude of openness and acceptance that is not usually associated with the name of Nietzsche. As he puts it in an aphorism entitled "Good Arable Land":

> All rejecting and negating betrays a lack of fruitfulness: if we were only good arable land, we would basically let nothing perish unused, and would see in every thing, event, and person welcome manure, rain, or sunshine. (*AOM* 332)

This is by no means to suggest that one take every opportunity to wallow in the mire: one learns in treading the path of life further to avoid the muck wherever possible; but where this is not possible, or the manure is dumped by external circumstances, the utilitarian approach is recommended.

Nietzsche soon comes up with an interesting corollary to this idea, one that vividly expresses the seedlike qualities of ideas, in his prescription for doing away with ideas one regards as pernicious. It is not enough, he suggests, to extract "the worm of illogicality" from the idea; and yet one goes too far if one then throws the entire fruit into the mud of ignominy so that people will be disgusted by it. Because there "in the filth" is precisely where "the kernel will quickly put forth new seeds" and thereby start growing again. The most efficient way to kill the idea is "respectfully to *lay it on ice*" (*WS* 211). A striking synthesis, this, of vegetal and experimental metaphor.

Sowings of Psychical Seed

> *[According to Plato] it was the sight of the beautiful youths of Athens that first set the soul of the philosopher into an erotic turmoil and gave it no peace until the soul sunk the seed of all high things into such beautiful soil.*
>
> Twilight of the Idols

As a natural process, seeding takes the form of squandering—too prodigal an affair for human agriculture, where expenditures must be more carefully husbanded.[35] But with the ground properly prepared, sowing of seed can fruitfully begin. At this stage we find Plato more concerned with seed and Socrates a somewhat more assiduous sower than Nietzsche.

In the account of the dithyrambic artist in the essay on Wagner, Nietzsche wrote (about himself): "Whenever a halfway receptive soul opened itself up to him, he cast his seed into it. . . . Everything gradually became an echo of his thought, and of his inexhaustible striving for a future fruitfulness" (*WB* 10). It is every bit as true of Nietzsche as of Wagner that he strove for future fruitfulness, albeit in a different field. A later aphorism entitled "The Most Inept Educator," the tone of which is perfectly Socratic, gives several examples to show that in different people virtues grow out of different parts of their "soil": a skillful educator will ensure that "the seeds of their virtues" are sown "on that part of the ground of their natures where the topsoil is thickest and richest" (*WS* 70). One would then want to call in the Schopenhauerian educator, who directed "all energies and saps and all sunshine" toward the pupil's special strength in order to help it attain "the right ripeness and fruitfulness" (*SE* 2). But it is from *Zarathustra* that we can glean the best sense of what psychical sowing involves for Nietzsche. Of special interest are the echoes in this text of the association established in the Platonic dialogues between seeding and *speaking*.

In "Zarathustra's Prologue" the protagonist proves to be a poor orator at first, though a good learner. His speeches to the people in the market square fail miserably, and his interactions with them are plagued by mutual incomprehension. After his second speech he realizes that he is not getting through: "They don't understand me, I am not the mouth for these ears." He makes a third, equally fruitless attempt to communicate, by saying: "It is time for human beings to plant the seed of their highest hope. Their soil is still rich enough" (Z, P5). The next few exhortations reinforce his sense of urgency concerning the long-term task he wants the people to undertake (planting trees from seed)—but in vain. He finally resolves to give up trying to speak to them altogether; as one who creates, he has no need of a herd or flock. He speaks instead, Odysseus-like, to his heart:

> Companions the creator seeks, and fellow harvesters: for everything in him stands ripe for the harvest. But he lacks the hundred sickles . . .
>
> Companions the creator seeks, and those who know how to whet their sickles well . . . fellow harvesters and celebrants.[36]

Just as he declared himself at the beginning of the prologue to be "overfull" with wisdom (the perfect antithesis to the ignorant Socrates) and desirous of dispensing by overflowing, now he is ripe for the harvest—strangely, since there has been no mention of prior sowing or planting.[37]

In the first part of the book (the only one of the four parts to bear a title: "Zarathustra's Speeches") the protagonist makes twenty-one speeches in and around the town called the Motley Cow. He is clearly on the way to becoming a more discriminating orator, insofar as he now speaks sometimes to groups (with whom he is sufficiently familiar to call them "my brothers") and sometimes to individuals; and by the end of the first part he has even gathered around him some "disciples."[38] At the beginning of the second part of the book, Zarathustra has retired to the solitude of his cave on top of the mountain. The opening sentence describes him as "waiting like a sower who has scattered his seed."[39] He has sown by having spoken, presumably, having seeded the souls of his audience through the numerous speeches he delivered in the world below. But something is amiss: in the dream that has just awakened him he is approached by a child with a mirror (one of the presents given to the infant Dionysus). The face he sees in the mirror is diabolically distorted, and he interprets this to mean that his teachings are in danger: "Weeds are posing as wheat!"[40] Perhaps the planting has been premature, on ground poorly prepared. Socrates would say that the problem stems from the absence of the father of the speeches, the attentive husbandman who would have cleared away the weeds.

This more or less exhausts the seeding imagery in Nietzsche's texts, where most of the sowing appears to take place *within* the individual soul; in the Platonic dialogues, by contrast, the theme of sowing applies primarily *inter*psychically, between the souls of teacher and student.

Though lacking Zarathustra's love of the earth, Socrates nevertheless appears to know more than a thing or two about agriculture. At the beginning of the *Euthyphro,* he offers his accuser, Meletus, ironic praise for realizing that the root of the *polis*'s problems concerns the corruption of its youth. He likens him to "a good husbandman [*geōrgos;* literally, "earth-worker"] who naturally takes care of the young plants first and afterwards of the rest. And so Meletus, perhaps, is first clearing away us who corrupt the young plants."[41]

Socrates resorts to agricultural imagery again in connection with the psychical midwifery for which he is so famous.[42] In the *Theaetetus,* he tries to convince his eponymous interlocutor that midwives possess in addition to their primary art the supplementary skill of matchmaking, which involves knowing "what sort of woman must be with what sort of man to give birth to the best possible children" (*Theae.* 149d). When Theaetetus appears skeptical, Socrates quickly shifts from husbands to husbandry:

> . . . Reflect. Do you believe that the care and harvesting of the fruits from the earth and the recognition, in turn, of what sort of plant and seed must be cast into what sort of earth are of the same or a different sort?
>
> No, but of the same.
>
> And into woman, my dear, do you believe there's a different art of something of this sort, and a different one of harvesting?
>
> It's unlikely, at any rate.

So unlikely that insofar as Socrates knows good soil when he sees it and takes after his mother the midwife, he will be able, when he comes across a potentially fertile soul in a young man, to judge who would make a good intellectual partner and stimulate in him the maximum abundance and fruitfulness.

There is another passage in the *Theaetetus* where Plato associates the soul with the element of earth, even though very briefly, in connection with the well known "wax block" image.[43] It is worth mentioning for the vivid contrast with Nietzsche. Socrates asks his audience to

> set down for talking's sake a wax block in our souls . . . a gift of Memory, the mother of the Muses . . . and whatever we want to remember . . . we strike off into this, as if we were putting in the seals of signet-rings. And whatever gets impressed, let's say that we remember and know as long as its image is in it. (*Theae.* 191c–d)

Just as some kinds of soil are more suited and receptive to seeding than others—though Socrates does not actually draw the analogy here—so some wax is a better gift of memory than other wax. When a person's block is "deep, extensive, smooth, and kneaded in a measured way," it is able to receive faithfully the imprints of what comes through the senses; whereas those whose wax is "shaggy, rough, and somewhat stony . . . full of either earth or dung mixed in, they obtain casts [imprints] without clarity . . ." (*Theae.* 194c–e). From a Nietzschean perspective there is a strangely apotropaic gesture here in the hygienic concern with the quality of the medium of memory. In the context of recording sense impressions the wax is to play a purely passive role, and is imagined as a sterile medium that may be contaminated by dirt or dung.[44] It would thus have to be insulated from what Plato will later call "the ploughland" of the brain.

The most interesting network of agricultural imagery in Plato is to be found in the last part of the *Phaedrus,* which deals with rhetoric and the differences between spoken dialogue and writing. It is relevant to our present concerns insofar as Socrates understands rhetoric as the art of "guiding souls through speeches" (*Phr.* 261a), the consummate practitioner of which art is the dialectician, who embodies the philosophical life at its highest. It is also a place where the themes of propagation and procreation are intertwined. The guiding of souls through *logoi* is a major concern of Nietzsche's too—as long as one understands *logoi* as words (which could be written) rather than speeches; and nowhere does this concern find more vivid expression than in *Thus Spoke Zarathustra.*[45]

Socrates has Phaedrus agree that a rhetorician must, if he is to make a good speech, know the truth about the topic of his discourse (*Phr.* 259e). He then questions the worth of a rhetorician who "does not know what good and evil are" by asking of such a speaker, "What harvest do you suppose [his] oratory will reap thereafter from the seed he has sown?" (260c–d). Not much of one, naturally, is the reply. Metaphors of husbandry crop up again in the context of the difference between the spoken word and the written, which Socrates couches in images of paternity and procreation (the spoken word as legitimate son and the written word as bastard).[46] He switches suddenly to an agricultural figure:

> Now tell me this. Would a sensible husbandman, who has seeds which he cares for and which he wishes to bear fruit, plant them with serious purpose in the heat of summer in some garden of Adonis, and delight in seeing them appear in beauty in eight days, or would he do that sort of thing, when he did it at all, only in play and for amusement? Would he not, when he was in earnest, follow the rules of husbandry, plant his seeds in fitting ground, and be pleased when those which he had sowed reached their perfection in the eighth month?[47]

"Gardens of Adonis" were planted in window boxes and shallow vessels holding only a thin layer of soil; they thus required minimal preparation in comparison with the work of preparing a real plot of land, and none of the patience needed in cultivating it. They were planted at the height of summer, when the sun's heat would both promote premature growth and quickly destroy it. Immature and without substantial roots, the plants would wither in the heat before being able to bear fruit.

The implications of the image of the sensible practitioner of agriculture as opposed to the frivolous horticulturist are made clear a few speeches later. The good husbandman turns out to stand for the dialectician, one who "selects a suitable soul and in it plants and sows words of understanding . . . words that are not fruitless but yield seed from which new words grow up in other characters, whereby the seed is granted immortality" (*Phr.* 277a). The seeds that the sensible husbandman plants in fitting ground are *logoi* spoken in the presence of receptive hearers. Earlier in the dialogue, Socrates had established an affinity between the art of rhetoric and the art of healing, in accordance with which the rhetorician would prescribe to the soul the *logoi* that are best for it. He thus needs to understand the nature of the souls he is dealing with, especially whether they are "simple or multiform," and must be familiar with the various forms of soul (270b–271d). To the simple soul he will address simple speeches, and to the complex soul "many-colored and harmonious" speeches.[48] And since the dialectician is the rhetorician *par excellence,* he will be most expert in recognizing "fitting ground" for the seeds he has to sow.

The main grounds for Socrates's denigration of writing are that the written word is disseminated indiscriminately (the author has no control over what kinds of soul-soil his seeds land in), and that in the absence of its "father" the written word is unable to defend itself against misinterpretation (*Phr.* 275e). But the contrast between the serious husbandry of the dialectician and the playful gardening of the writer also suggests an important difference between the kinds of preparation necessary for each type of discourse. The writer, who sows words in ink by means of a pen (276c), does so in soil that needs no preparation; whereas the careful speaker is concerned to discern the proper time to sow, as well as the proper place. And just as a plot of land requires a lot more work than a shallow window box, one can assume that the serious husbandman is willing to undertake a prior working of the soil of his hearer's souls in preparation for the sowing.[49]

Just as Socrates claims to possess no wisdom, but to be merely a lover of it, he also claims to "possess no art of speaking," and thus to be a mere "lover" of dialectic as opposed to a deft practitioner (*Phr.* 262d, 266b). As usual, he protests too much, and one will not go far wrong to regard him as the kind of husbandman capable of discerning when the ground of a soul could be made receptive after some working over. As suggested earlier, the cross-questioning Socrates undertakes in order to induce a state of aporia in his interlocutor can be seen as a breaking up of the firm ground of conviction that is the basis of the person's prior worldview—in such a way that the soil of the soul will be receptive to new seeds.[50]

In addition to a good eye for suitable ground, and the ability and willingness to prepare it, the dialectician also needs the virtue of patience (the good husbandman waits until the eighth month to see the results of his sowing). The seeds of new ideas require a period of germination after having been sown, before they will sprout and take root. At this stage a discriminating eye is needed that can tell whether the young shoots that are pushing up through the soil are viable, and worth tending, or else mere weeds that should be eradicated. The keen cultivator's eye will correspond to the midwife's ability, which Socrates claims to share (*Theae.* 150c), to tell whether a particular offspring is worth raising or not.

There is, however, a more fundamental implication to these images and ideas—as they occur in Nietzsche's texts as much as in Plato's—which concerns the apparent insignificance of the first signs of growth in the soil of the soul. Initial shoots and buds are easily overlooked and may be trampled underfoot inadvertently, unless one has cultivated an eye for "the small, insignificant things." These little things—an image from a dream, a minor but uncharacteristic slip or mistake, an apparently inconsequential mood—bear close examination, in case they are the initial signs of something substantial that is beginning to grow in the psyche. Vegetal imagery also prompts one to reflect on whether insignificant things that are apparently unrelated may, if they appear around the same time, turn out to be connected after all—by subterranean linkages akin to the mycelium of mushrooms and the root systems of plants and trees.

If the sower has chosen his ground wisely, the germinated plant will eventually bear fruit, which will in turn "yield seed" to be sown in yet other souls—and so on, in perpetuity. The idea implanted in the soul of the hearer will be further disseminated in the form of speeches he makes to other receptive hearers. Plato talks elsewhere about the kinds of immortality enjoyed by various kinds of beings (a topic that is also close to Nietzsche's heart).[51] At the lowest level is the immortality of the plant species, achieved through self-propagation, followed by that of the animals through procreation, a special case of which is sexual reproduction in humans. The highest stage involves psychical or intellectual generation (as described in most detail by Diotima in the *Symposium*). What is remarkable about this hierarchy is that Plato imagines the highest form of generation, dialectic, on the model of the lower levels of activity.

The text in which Plato gives the process of seeding its most primordial elaboration, in significant connection with the procreative process, is the *Timaeus*. One of the richest dialogues psychologically, the *Timaeus* in its cosmic sweep treats of the world soul as much as the soul of the individual. While the divine craftsman is a maker rather than a creator—insofar as he fashions the world from materials already there—he is nevertheless referred to as "the maker and father of the universe" and also as "the father who engendered it" (*Tim.* 28c, 37c). For the propagation of life, one of this father's first acts is insemination—but as a process couched in the most basic terms of husbandry. In making the divine part of the human soul from the leftovers of the world soul, the cosmic craftsman divides it up into individual souls and then—like a *geōrgos*—sows them: "some in the earth, some in the moon, some in the other instruments of time [the stars]" (42d). The development of the souls is from then on out of his hands, as it were, depending to some extent, presumably, on the nature of the medium in which they have been planted and on local meteorological conditions.[52] Initially, it is the immortal souls themselves that are sown; once the universe has been constructed, subsequent sowing takes place largely within or between souls.

Seeds come up again near the beginning of the third section of the *Timaeus,* where an essential phase in the fitting of the human body around the soul is the forming of the marrow. The "roots" of the mortal creature are said to be "implanted" in the marrow as the medium in which "the bonds of life" join soul to body (*Tim.* 73b). In making the marrow, the craftsman is described as "contriving a mixture of seeds of every sort *[panspermia]* for every mortal kind," and as "implanting" in the marrow the various kinds of soul. He then molds into spherical shape "the ploughland, as it were, for the reception of the divine seed" (73c). This spherical ploughland of marrow is the brain (that most furrowed of organs), and the divine seed implanted in it is semen.[53] The brain, this field full of divine seed and the highest seat of soul, is said to be connected by a cylindrical column of marrow to the genitals—to a part capable of ejaculation of the seed in the man, and to a "ploughland of the womb" in the woman.[54] This would imply—it is not explicitly stated—that there is arable soil at both ends of the female spinal column, providing grounds for generation and immortality, the higher field on the intellectual and the lower on the physical plane.

It is not surprising that propagation and procreation should be so closely connected at the lower end, since earlier in the dialogue Timaeus had associated vegetation with the lowest form of soul in the human being. In order to provide nourishment for the human body,

> [the gods] gave birth to a substance of a kindred nature to the human being's . . . so as to be a living creature of a different sort. These are trees, plants, and seeds, now tamed and schooled by husbandry into domestication, though formerly there were only the wild kinds, which are the older. (*Tim.* 77a)

The substance of plants is "akin" *(syngenē)* to ours (Emerson's "occult relation between man and the vegetable"), otherwise we would be unable to
assimilate it for nourishment. The "living creature" that is vegetation is said
to "partake of the third kind of soul," whose seat in the human body is the
area around the stomach and entrails and the organs of generation.[55]

Combining the agricultural imagery from the *Theaetetus, Phaedrus,* and
Timaeus yields a composite image in which the dialectician sows seeds in
the form of speeches, these speech-seeds (*logoi spermatikoi* in the literal
sense) issuing from the mouth enter through the hearer's ears, and then germinate in the ploughland of the brain. If they take root properly there, they
will themselves grow and bear fruit, scatter seed again through the mouth,
and thereby begin the whole cycle anew. With this picture in mind, let us
turn again to Nietzsche, and in particular to *Zarathustra,* to ask how good a
husbandman/rhetorician the protagonist is by Socratic standards.

Cultivation, Irrigation, Fruition

> *Humans began and grew up from the happiness of plants, and
> grew until they ripened; from then on they have been in cease-
> less ferment, inwardly and outwardly, until now the human race
> lies there in chaos, endlessly disintegrated.*
>
> Hölderlin, *Hyperion*

The cultivation of plants requires more effort, naturally, than the finding of
suitable ground and sowing. There is the subsequent care and nurture of
what has been planted, a sine qua non of which is watering or irrigation,
and then the final fruiting and the harvest. From the *Republic* of Plato to
Schopenhauer as Educator the cultivation of plants has been found an especially apt analogy for the education of children.[56] Socrates gives seminal
expression to his concern for providing the appropriate milieu and nourishment for the developing soul by saying: "Concerning every seed or thing
that grows, whether from the earth or animals . . . we know that the more
vigorous it is, the more deficient it is in its own properties when it doesn't
get the food, climate, or place suitable to it." (*Rep.* 491d). In particular, there
will be no chance of cultivating "the nature of the philosopher" toward the
appropriate virtues "if it isn't sown, planted, and nourished in what's suitable" (492a). The concern is echoed in Montaigne, who holds the education
of children to be the locus of "the greatest and most important difficulty in
human knowledge."

> Just as in agriculture the operations that come before the planting, as
> well as the planting itself, are certain and easy; but as soon as the

plant comes to life, there are various methods and great difficulties in
raising it; so it is with men: little industry is needed to plant them, but
it is quite a different burden we assume from the moment of their
birth, a burden full of care and fear—that of training them and bringing them up. (*Essays*, 1:26, 109)

Though childless himself, Nietzsche was as concerned as his illustrious predecessors with the problems of education, even after giving up teaching,
and he had recourse to similar imagery of cultivation to work those concerns out.

We left Zarathustra in the solitude of his cave. He had been "waiting like
a sower who has scattered his seed," but is shocked by his dream into fear-
ing that the sowing of his teachings has not been a success—that "weeds
pose as wheat" (Z 2.1). The sudden resolution to seek out his "friends" in
the world below transforms him, such that "a new speech" comes to him
(some of which we heard in the last chapter): "Mouth have I become utterly,
and the roaring of a stream out of high cliffs: downward will I plunge my
speech into the valleys. And may my river of love plunge into pathless
places!" We shall soon be able to hear this new speech as a counterpart to
"the stream of *logoi* that flows out of the mouth" in the *Timaeus*. And we
might also construe this flow of speech as a response to the abortive sowing
Zarathustra engaged in earlier. Like seeds falling on unprepared ground, his
speeches fell on uncomprehending ears. To speak with the stream of "a new
speech" may be to irrigate the ground in which the sowed seeds lie, so that
they might germinate and sprout after all. The ideas could be safely lodged
in the more promising heads among his audience, requiring only a little
watering with words of explanation to make them start to grow.

During his second period of solitude pressure has again built up, so that
Zarathustra's speech is now endowed with formidable powers of nature,
animated by the energies of mountain torrents, storm winds, dark clouds,
hail showers, and bolts of lightning. The Byronic language of his speech
builds from power to power and surges through the vegetal realm to the
animal: Zarathustra will ride the chariot of the storm and mount his wildest
steed with the help of his spear. Finally his "wild wisdom" appears in the
form of a lioness, a creature too wild to be contained in seed, animated
analogue of the sowing-in-the-soil-of-souls motif on the level of animal
procreation.

My wild wisdom became pregnant on lonely mountains; on rough
stones she bore her young, her youngest.

Now she runs crazily through the hard desert and seeks and seeks
for soft grass—my old, wild wisdom!

On the soft grass of your hearts, my friends!—on your love she would like to bed her most beloved![57]

One is reminded of the soft grass beneath the plane tree of the *Phaedrus;* but consider the difference between being the recipient of seed sown by a sensible sower and having the young of Zarathustra's lioness bedded on the lawn of one's heart. A piece of biographical background can be found in a passage from a letter to Lou Salomé which synthesizes vegetal and procreative imagery: "I am now seeking people who could be my heirs; I am carrying something around with me that is in no way to be read in my books—and am seeking the most beautiful and fertile soil for it."[58]

Zarathustra's second period of solitude has allowed his thinking to mature and his ideas to ripen, and it looks as if he is on the way to becoming what Nietzsche earlier called an "aristocrat of the spirit." Contemporary scholarship in most fields would benefit immeasurably if its practitioners took to heart this aphorism, entitled "Quiet Fruitfulness":

> The born aristocrats of the spirit are not overly zealous: their creations appear and fall from the tree on a quiet autumn evening, without being precipitately desired, promoted, and pushed aside by something new. The desire to create unremittingly is vulgar and betrays jealousy, envy, and ambition. If one is something, one really doesn't need to do anything—and yet nevertheless does a great deal. There exists above the "productive" human being an even higher species. (*HA* 210)

The penultimate sentence is a beautiful evocation of what the Daoists call *wu wei,* unforced activity that is in harmony with the greater processes of existence. This is not to deny that a great deal of effort has to go into the work of thinking or artistic creation, but only to emphasize that at certain stages a patient "letting be" is called for. Forced creations will look premature and will be indigestible by their recipients.[59]

In his first speech after coming down from the mountain again, Zarathustra addresses his audience as "my friends," which indicates a more sensitive selectivity (and greater familiarity) with respect to his hearers.[60] The opening lines recast his project of disseminating his teaching—or else initiate a parallel project—in exclusively natural images that are, as it were, preagricultural:

> The figs are falling from the trees, they are good and sweet; and as they fall their red skins break open. A north wind am I to ripe figs.
>
> Thus like figs these teachings fall to you, my friends: now drink their juice and their sweet meat! It is autumn around us and clear sky and afternoon.

> See, what fullness is about us! And from the stream of overflowing
> it is beautiful to look out over far seas. (Z 2.2)

The fruits of Zarathustra's mountain meditations—figs: fruits intimately associated with Dionysus, the seeds of which are many and prominent—have
ripened.[61] There is no mention of his having planted these fig trees, and they
appear to have come to fruition naturally and without human intervention.
Unlike Socrates' dialectician who sows seeds with serious intent in suitable
souls, Zarathustra produces teachings that ripen spontaneously and fall to
the ground naturally. Those that fail to fall in a timely fashion he will help
along—but again in the form of a natural phenomenon, the north wind. He
does not pick the fruits himself and distribute them to disciples. The figs
simply lie there, their tender red skins seductively split open, while Zarathustra invites his friends to partake of their juice and sweet meat—to ingest
and incorporate his teachings if they so desire.

In fact this is a fine image for the book *Thus Spoke Zarathustra* itself.
After the death of God and the demise of metaphysics, the philosopher who
has thought "beyond good and evil" cannot stay in the business of com-
mending courses of action or telling his audience what they "ought" to do.
A picture of a life—Zarathustra's—lovingly nourished, comes to fruition
in the author; he simply puts it out, leaving it up to his readers to take or
leave it.

We saw how the torrent of speech from Zarathustra's mouth flowed into
imagery of animal pregnancy: a hint concerning this transformation is given
by his calling his new speech "the stream of his *love*" (Z 2.1). Again we
come across flows of *erōs,* which take us from the natural currents of rivers
and streams (previous chapter) to the motive force behind sexual union
(next chapter). The course leads through the field of watering and irrigation
in the vegetal realm, and so the topic is best dealt with here, though there
will be spillings over backward and forward. The issue for both Plato and
Nietzsche is the extent to which experience is to be infused with *erōs* and
the nature of that permeating desire. The imaginal background to Zarathustra's flow of speech is to be found in the *Timaeus* and *Phaedrus.*

In the course of an account of the creation of the various parts of the human
body, Timaeus speaks of speech as "the stream of *logoi* that flows out of
the mouth, ministering to intelligence, [which] is of all streams the best and
noblest."[62] Since the seat of the intelligence is the ploughland of the brain,
it makes sense that if one implants the seed of a teaching or the germ of an
idea in another intellect, its growth could be nurtured by the introduction of
further speeches amplifying the original implant. A similar image occurs in
the *Sophist,* where the Stranger suggests that thought and speech are the
same. Whereas "the conversation *[dialogos]* that comes to be within the

soul before itself without sound" is thinking *(dianoia),* speech *(logos)* is "the stream that proceeds from the soul through the mouth with noise" *(Soph.* 263e). One is reminded of Socrates' modest protestation to Phaedrus that what little he knows about the topic of love he did not himself make up, but was rather "filled through the ears, like a pitcher, from the wellsprings of another."[63] A far cry, this, from Zarathustra's identification of himself with deep wells, surging fountains, and lakes that overflow in veritable torrents of speech.

One source of watering for the ploughland of the brain, then, is from outside, a flow of sound through the ears. But there would appear to be an internal source of moisture too. In the course of his account of the genesis of the human body, Timaeus relates how the gods construct a complicated hydraulic system for the various kinds of bodily fluids—"a system of conduits, cut like runnels in a garden, so that the body might be, as it were, watered by an incoming stream" *(Tim.* 77c). The ultimate purpose of the system appears to be to keep the sustainer of life, the seed-marrow, well "watered" (82d). If the marrow is *over*watered, however, there will be "disease in the soul":

> When the seed in a man's marrow becomes copious with overflowing moisture like the overabundance of fruitfulness in a tree, he is filled with intense labor pains and with pleasure in his desires and in their offspring; and for the most part of his life he is maddened by these intense pleasures and pains. *(Tim.* 86c)

This overflow of moisture from the substance of the seed-marrow, which is conveyed in an arboreal image and sounds much like the Dionysian affliction from which Zarathustra suffers, is for Plato the ground of sexual incontinence. The solution to this problem is given in terms of the three parts of the soul, and involves training the highest part, lodged in the head, the rational soul that is "the part that is destined to govern" (89d).

The short passage that concludes the *Timaeus* and deals with the differentiation of the sexes and the production of all other living creatures from human beings—the reverse of Darwin—forms a stirring finale in which the themes of ploughland and seed are recapitulated in an image of tree and fruit. The seed-marrow stretching down from the brain issues in the male genital as the embodiment of "an *erōs* of begetting," and in the woman the matrix or womb is described as "a living creature *[zōion]* with a desire for childbearing." In the event that the *erōs* (of the man) and the desire (of the woman) bring the two together, they may "pluck as it were the fruit from the tree, and sow the ploughland of the womb with living creatures."[64] But this is, for Plato, a lower-grade response to and consequence of the original sowing of the ploughland of the brain by the gods, and the plucking of the fruit from the tree a rather crude way of alleviating the "overabundance of fruitfulness" owing to excessive moisture in the seed-marrow.

Although *erōs* is the main topic of the next chapter, it is appropriate at this point to consider the powerful erotic flows and counterflows that come up in the *Phaedrus,* in the course of Socrates' account of erotic *mania (Phr.* 248–56). After a lyrical description of the experience of the soul before its incarnation in a human body, when its wings lifted it up to the realm above the heavens to behold the eternal and unchanging Ideas, true "beauty shining in brilliance," Socrates goes on to talk of two alternative reactions to the sight of beauty in this world.[65] One who has no memory of the preincarnate vision of absolute beauty will be "eager like a four-footed beast to mount and beget children" *(Phr.* 250e). But when one who remembers the supracelestial vision comes across "a godlike face or the look of a body that is a good imitation of ideal beauty," he worships the beautiful boy "as if he were a god." As the lover gazes upon the beloved,

> the effluence of beauty enters him through the eyes, and he is warmed;
> the effluence moistens the germ of the feathers [of the soul] . . . and
> as the nourishment streams upon him, the quills of the feathers swell
> and begin to grow from the roots all over the soul.[66]

There is a contrasting image in *Zarathustra,* when the protagonist feels "wings growing" at the sight of the pathetic nakedness of the "higher humans" (Z 2.21). In this case it is their ugliness that prompts a flight *away* from them, into "far futures" where the *Übermensch* bathes his nakedness in "the burning sun of wisdom." In the *Phaedrus* account, the growing of the feathers gives rise to a strange mixture of pain and pleasure that Socrates likens to the sensation in the gums as new teeth begin to grow in. (The teething image suggests a rebirth of the soul that is reminiscent of Nietzsche's use of the image of the child.)

The ensuing description of the condition of the lover's soul in the alternating presence and absence of the beloved is a veritable orgy of sexual metaphors. When the lover is in the presence of the beloved, he is able to drink in the warm flow of the boy's beauty, and this is balm to the overstimulated soul *(Phr.* 251c). In the absence of the beloved, however, "the mouths of the passages in which the feathers begin to grow become dry and close up," whereupon the swelling quills penetrate painfully the soul's membrane. The soul is said to be "maddened" *(emmanēs*—whence the erotic *mania)* by the consequent mixture of pleasure and pain. But on seeing the beloved again the torment of the lover's soul is relieved by its being "bathed with the waters of yearning" and thereby eased of its "birth pangs."[67] Much of the power of Plato's allegory for falling in philosophic love derives from the riot of polymorphous and bisexual imagery he uses to describe this erotic ferment—most of which takes place *within* the lover's soul.

The vision of the beloved awakens memories in the lover not only of absolute beauty but also of the particular god the lover followed in his preincarnate state. Inspired by the sight of the beloved, the lover then searches within himself to find which god is making him enthusiastic (in the original sense of the word): "If they draw the waters of their inspiration from Zeus, like the Bacchants, they pour it out upon the soul of the beloved and make him, so far as possible, like their god" (*Phr.* 253a). This counterflow to the flow of beauty that enters the lover's eyes suggests a powerful psychological projection: the beloved is himself no more Zeus than is the lover, but a projection of the divine image flows through the lover onto the beloved. That this is not a conscious operation is suggested by the phrase, "like the Bacchants," whose distinguishing feature is to be "outside of themselves."

The subsequent development of the relationship is described in similarly aquatic metaphors.

> When their intimacy is established . . . the current of the stream which Zeus . . . called "the stream of longing" sets in full flood toward the lover. Part of it enters into him, but when his heart is full the rest brims over, and . . . so the stream of beauty returns once more to its source in the beauty of the beloved. It enters in at his eyes, the natural inlet to the soul, where it moistens the passages from which the feathers shoot . . . and in turn the soul of the beloved is filled with love.[68]

In the best case for Plato, where the lovers are able to resist the temptations of the flesh, they will go on to live a life of true happiness that is made possible by the proper power relations within the soul: "self-controlled and orderly, holding in subjection that which engenders evil in the soul, and giving freedom to that which engenders virtue" (*Phr.* 256b). One wonders whether, in comparison with the polymorphous joys of intrapsychical erotism described earlier in the dialogue, physical intercourse might in any case be something of an anticlimax.

All this talk in Plato of flows of fluid and overflowing moisture forms the background for the streams that course through the text of *Zarathustra*. The major difference is that the various flows that pervade that text tend to prevail within the protagonist's psyche, or to flow between his soul and the world, rather than between two souls as in the *Phaedrus*.

Although Zarathustra's watering of the earth was imagined in terms of natural phenomena rather than human practices, he does engage in human-scale watering as well—though in a highly unconventional way. In his first prolonged conversation with his soul, he says to her:

> O my soul, I gave your soil all wisdom to drink, all new wines and immemorially old and strong wines of wisdom.
>
> O my soul, I poured every sun on you and every night and every silence and every yearning: —then you grew up for me like a vine.
>
> O my soul, over-rich and heavy you stand there now, a vine with swelling udders and crowded brown gold grapes:—
>
> crowded and compressed by your happiness, waiting with your overflowing and still ashamed of your waiting.[69]

In exposing his soul to the sun Zarathustra is aligned with the Socratic cultivator, since the sun, as "offspring of the good," provides everything with "generation, growth, and nourishment" (*Rep.* 508b–509b). But it also seems that he is concerned deliberately to induce in his soul a condition corresponding to the somatic condition Timaeus warned against, in which "the seed in a man's marrow becomes copious with overflowing moisture like the overabundance of fruitfulness in a tree." Indeed, he goes even further, and his fondness for Dionysiac extremes assumes a distinctly alchemical aspect as he "waters" the vine of his soul with the fermented essence of its own products. A nice twist, too, on the trick of turning water into wine.[70]

An abundance of loving care has rendered the vine of Zarathustra's soul fully ripe. The plant's flowering or ripening into the fullness of the fruit is often a sign that it is about to die, a death that may be the condition for the scattering of the seeds of new life. For Zarathustra as creator it is not just that everything ripe dies, but rather that "All that is ripe—*wants* to die."[71] Not only that, but the vine as it comes to full fruition is imagined to *long* for the sharpness of the harvester's blade. Zarathustra goes on to sing to his soul:

> In torrential tears pour out all your suffering over your fullness and over all the urge of the vine for the vintager and the vine-knife![72]

The vintager who will come in a boat across the sea of yearning, his "diamond vine-knife" ready in his hand, is of course Dionysus. The "hundred sickles" of Demeter mentioned in the prologue have been melded into the single blade of Dionysus's diamond knife.

The idea of the vine's "suffering fullness" is given an explicitly Dionysian elaboration in the last book of *The Joyful Science,* where Nietzsche distinguishes between the suffering of Romanticism (from impoverishment of life) and of a deeper, more fruitful suffering.

> The one who is richest in fullness of life, the Dionysian god and human, can afford not only the sight of what is terrible and questionable

but even the terrible deed and every luxury of destruction, decomposition, and negation. For such a one what is evil, absurd, and ugly seems as it were permissible, as a consequence of an abundance *[Überschuss]* of procreative and fertilizing energies which is capable of turning any desert into lush farmland. (*JS* 370)

The image of the knife brings to mind the practice of *pruning,* and in view of the range of activities represented in Nietzsche's agricultural imagery it is surprising that he makes so little metaphorical use of this practice. In view of his lifelong preoccupation with mastering the multiplicity of his talents and keeping tendencies toward dilettantism in check, one would have expected images of plants in need of pruning to be more abundant. When a life is pulled in many different directions, and attempts to sustain an outflow of its energies along too many branches at one time, it fails to thrive. Plants in that situation begin to straggle, failing to fill out into abundant bloom. Emerson puts in nicely, in discussing (in the essay "Power") a possible psychical "economy" that would involve

the stopping off decisively our miscellaneous activity, and concentrating our force on one or a few points; as the gardener, by severe pruning, forces the sap of the tree into one or two vigorous limbs, instead of suffering it to spindle into a sheaf of twigs.[73]

What is needed are pruning shears to cut back runners and branches from the main stem to a number that permits their optimal development. (In cases of more luxuriant growth, the image of the machete, unsentimentally wielded, may be more appropriate.) While to the nongardener pruning may look like a brutal and cruel undertaking, when performed by an expert the cutting back will promote fuller and more healthy growth. As a gardener friend once said, "Pruning can be the kindest cut of all."[74] It is interesting that the cut that prunes the plant has a similar effect—through the medium of sap—to the damming of a tributary current of water: flow that is denied an outlet will redirect itself along other channels, increasing the pressure along those outflows. The most significant mention of pruning in Nietzsche occurs in *Twilight of the Idols,* in the course of a deprecation of modernity on account of the undisciplined chaos of its instincts.

A reasonable educational principle would call for the *paralyzation* of at least one of these instinct-systems under an iron pressure, in order to allow another to come into power, gain strength, become master. Today one would first have to make the individual possible by *pruning:* possible means here *whole.* (*TI* 9.41).

The Dionysian image of Zarathustra's soul as an overripe vine also evokes the idea of *fermentation,* a feature of Nietzsche's conception of life that he has in common with Hölderlin—whose Hyperion speaks of "fermenting life's [turning] into the noble vintage of joy" (*Hyp.* 1.2.10). After Zarathustra undergoes his most crucial transformation, in "The Convalescent," his eagle and serpent say to him:

> Did a new insight come to you, a sour and heavy one? You lay there like leavened dough, and your soul rose and swelled over all its rims.[75]

He has at last become "ripe for his fruits." And in his last song, Zarathustra sings:

> All joy wants the eternity of all things, wants honey, wants yeast, wants drunken midnight . . . (Z 4.19 §11)

Life as joy wants yeast because it wants *itself,* itself to be *more,* multiplying immoderately in medium after medium into eternity.

In view of the profusion of images considered in this chapter, a brief summing up may be helpful. The life of the soul manifests on one level as vegetation, as a vegetal realm that reflects as it projects a realm of vegetation in the external world. Awareness of the vegetal phenomena of the soul grants the possibility of interacting with them and enhancing their unfolding. We *are* that growth in any case; but awareness of this enables us to *work* with it. Parallel to the task of self-cultivation is participation in the cultivation of other souls, imagined in terms of education and dissemination of ideas.

As in literal agriculture, the first requirement has to do with acquainting oneself with the nature of the soil and giving it appropriate preparation. After the sowing comes a period of waiting, since it takes time for ideas that have penetrated the ground of the soul to germinate and sprout, and the process cannot be hurried along.[76] The initial growth goes on underground, in the dark, and one must resist the curiosity that would dig the sprouts up and expose them fatally to the light. But then it is important to ascertain what kind of shoots have come up, so that one may provide appropriate care. In tending new growth in another, one may water the plot with refreshing discourses; in the case of seedlings in the field of one's own soul, the irrigation could come through listening to the speeches of others, and perhaps also—*pace* Socrates—through judicious reading.

Subsequent growth will be to a large extent dependent upon external weather conditions over which one has little control; one can only try to strike a balance between protecting the young growth from the violence of the elements and exposing them to it so as to make them hardy and strong. While all of one's budding ideas will need sunlight and moisture in order to grow, there are some plants (the vine in particular) that also require seasonal exposure to frost in order to flourish. This consideration may make it easier to endure long winters of the soul, insofar as one can suppose that during periods of apparent stasis new developments of life are being prepared beneath the surface. While related to the seasons and climate of the outside world, the cycles in the psychical environs will be different; and just as labor in the field of the psyche, though rooted in nature, is also an *opus contra naturam,* its products will differ from the natural. Remember Nietzsche's speaking of "harvesting in ourselves the fruits of *all* seasons."[77]

There is in fact relatively little talk of harvesting in either Plato or Nietzsche, but it is clear that timing would be an important factor in the psychological realm. As one's thoughts finally come to fruition, it would be important to acquire the knack of knowing when to harvest: too early, and the plants or fruits prematurely picked will be small and hard to assimilate; too late, and the crops will wither and the fruits rot, and all the cultivation will have been in vain. The overall impression one gains from the appearance of these themes in the texts is that the joy of the harvest consists mainly in seeing the process of propagation itself continue beyond the scope of one's own labors in the field.

Interlude 2: The Psychical Feminine

> *Within himself, outside himself, Nietzsche dealt with so many women.*
>
> Jacques Derrida, *Spurs*

Before going on to consider husbanding in the sexual sense, it is appropriate to touch upon the vexed "question of woman" in Nietzsche's texts. A full treatment of this complex problem would lead too far afield; but something can be said about Nietzsche's ideas concerning feminine aspects of the psyche within the compass of a brief interlude. The short justification for eschewing a fuller treatment is simply that the psychological ideas discussed in the present study are not gender-specific, and where Nietzsche's insights pertain only to the male psyche they have been ignored.

The other thing most armchair (or bar-stool) philosophers "know" about Nietzsche—aside from the fact that he fathered the philosophy on which National Socialism was based—is that he was one of the world's greatest misogynists. It is true that he came to hate his sister on account of her interference in the Lou Salomé affair, and that his feelings of dependence on his mother were imbued with the ambivalent emotions that generally attend such cases; but otherwise he seems to have enjoyed cordial and often affectionate relationships with a number of intelligent and aristocratic women, several of whom were feminists.[1] When Nietzsche was young, Sophie Ritschl, Cosima Wagner, and Malwida von Meysenbug (all older women) were charmed by his cultured intelligence; while the two people who most often saw him face-to-face during the last few years of his sanity were Resa von Schirnhofer and Meta von Salis (both of whom were younger). It is true, too, that he never married or enjoyed a sustained sexual relationship; and while he did make a proposal or two, there appears to have been some deep-seated inhibition of physical *erōs* in his relationships with women. As we have begun to see already, much of Nietzsche's erotic energy was sublimated into his writing; and if he was in fact aware that he had contracted syphilis as a university student, this knowledge would have intensified his ascetic tendencies and self-imposed moral strictures into a more or less absolute celibacy. While the apparent absence of sexual relationships with women has prompted the surmise that Nietzsche was homosexual, the evidence for this is by no means conclusive—nor would it be of major significance if it were.[2]

The first thing that is called for with respect to the remarks about woman, women, females, and the feminine that occur throughout Nietzsche's writings is a clear distinction between those that refer to *women* (to real, flesh-and-blood *Weiber* or *Frauen*) and those that refer to *woman (das Weib)* or the feminine *(das Weibliche),* and to a variety of figures for such things as wisdom, truth, and life. Many readers have been unnecessarily upset by taking remarks belonging to this latter class to be referring to real women, or by mistaking a comment concerning life or truth for a pronouncement on women in general. But even after separating out the nonliteral and symbolical references, there may appear to be a residue of remarks that are uncharacteristically narrow—even to the point of stupidity. Instead of citing mitigating circumstances concerning Nietzsche's upbringing as the only male in a household of neurotic females, the ambivalent dependence on his mother, the dreadful torment occasioned by Lou Salomé's rejection of him, and his often troubled relations with the nefarious Elisabeth Förster-Nietzsche, let us note that the author himself explicitly acknowledges the stupidity of many of his remarks.

Considering the context of a series of eight aphorisms in *Beyond Good and Evil* purporting to treat "woman-in-herself," one sees that it is introduced by a lapidary paragraph concerning the "unteachable . . . granite of spiritual fate" at the bottom of every soul.[3]

> In every cardinal problem there speaks an unchangeable "this is I"; concerning man and woman for example, a thinker cannot learn better but only learn more thoroughly—only discover ultimately what in him "stands firm" on this topic. . . . Later, one sees in [one's "convictions"] only steps on the way to self-knowledge, signposts to the problem that we *are*—rather, to the great stupidity that we are, to our spiritual fate, to what is *unteachable* "deep down." (*BGE* 231)

In contrast to the optimistic phantasy that we are free to remake ourselves however we wish, Nietzsche is pointing here to a place in the depths of the human soul, circumscribed by fate, that is utterly inaccessible to alteration or improvement. (It is what depth psychologists will later refer to as the impersonal layer of the collective unconscious that determines the archetypal "givens" of psychical life.) And in case the reader should overlook the bearing of this statement on what follows, Nietzsche concludes the aphorism by saying that in view of the courteousness that he has just evinced *toward himself,*

I shall perhaps be more readily allowed to pronounce a few truths concerning "woman-in-herself," on the assumption that it is now understood from the outset how very much these are merely—*my* truths.

Quite apart from the way the talk of "truths" compounds the irony of the "woman-in-herself," it would be difficult to find a stronger qualification of statements as being "personal, all too personal"; but this has still not prevented rabid feminists from leaping on the subsequent aphorisms and denouncing them as evidence for Nietzsche's sexist misogyny.[4] While they contain some admittedly gratuitous elements, these aphorisms are an incisive criticism of the more mindless features of the feminism that was then popular—features sadly reflected in certain areas of the movement in our time.[5]

One of the most intelligent French commentators on Nietzsche has issued repeated warnings against labeling him a misogynist, suggesting that his "famous misogyny" may need to be "rethought and reevaluated from a standpoint that would differentiate it into types."[6] By the same token, two types of feminism that were prevalent in Nietzsche's time need to be distinguished. The first pressed for an across-the-board equality between men and women, and was opposed by Nietzsche on the grounds that just as women are endowed differently from men physically, so are they differently endowed psychically and spiritually. (From Nietzsche's antiegalitarian standpoint it is by no means a denigration of women to deny that they are equal to men. After all, he does not think that *men* are equal to men—or indeed that *anything* is equal to anything else.) The second type of feminism fought against injustice toward women in such a way as to allow the specifically "womanly instincts" and qualities to make their fullest contribution to culture—an enterprise of which Nietzsche in his role as "a true friend of women" (*BGE* 232) by no means disapproved.

The feminists Nietzsche inveighs against espouse a feminism that has been characterized as "the operation by which woman wants to resemble a man, the dogmatic philosopher," with all his belief in absolute truth, objectivity, and so forth, and his clumsily *macho* ways of pursuing them.[7] These are the women who have despised woman far more than men ever have (*BGE* 232), who have brought about a "degeneration" and *"retrogression"* on the part of women which Nietzsche clearly deplores: "Since the French Revolution the influence of woman in Europe has generally *diminished* as rights and demands have increased."[8]

The depth connoted by the image of the granite of stupidity "deep down" may be understood in a different way, though as complementary to the idea of the unteachable rather than incompatible with it. As suggested in the introduction, above, it is reasonable to suppose that as a thinker thinks in greater depth, moving ever farther from the surface layers of the personality shaped by particular life experiences, he or she may come upon "truths" that pertain to human beings in the culture as a whole (and perhaps even beyond that particular culture) rather than merely to the thinker personally. At this level gender differences are irrelevant; and when Nietzsche is thinking and writing at this level, his psychological experiments work irrespective of the gender of the subject—just as the profounder insights of, say, Virginia Woolf are in no way conditioned by her literal gender.[9] (This is not to deny that when Nietzsche is *not* thinking at this depth, his remarks may bear the stamp of the personal, all too personal and be correspondingly less enlightening.)

Nietzsche's psychological insights derive their general validity from his experience of psychological bisexuality: following the Aristophanes of the *Symposium* and anticipating the more thoroughly elaborated ideas of Freud and Jung, he develops a view of the human psyche as inherently androgynous. It is true that his texts contain frequent exhortations to manliness and deprecations of effeminacy, but these are counterbalanced by commendations of receptivity and praise for what are traditionally regarded as feminine virtues.[10] The point is important, and may be sharpened by a brief exemplification.

Some feminist commentators have denigrated Nietzsche's use of imagery of pregnancy, for example, on the grounds that he wants to "have it both ways" by expropriating female capabilities for the aggrandizement of the male. But this is to miss the point completely: there is nothing in Nietzsche's texts to suggest that, psychologically speaking, women cannot and do not have it both ways too. Pregnancy of soul is, as Diotima assured Socrates, something that goes deeper than gender difference; and just as Nietzsche wants to claim that he, and other males, can be psychologically pregnant, so he would by no means wish to deny that women are capable of insemination in the psychological realm. While the penis may be the prerogative of the male (whether or not this excites envy in others), the phallus most certainly is not. Penetrating insight, hard-driving argument, seminal ideas are all independent of differences in gender.

Let us take the risk of emulating Nietzsche's way of treating deep problems as cold baths ("quickly in and quickly out again"—*JS* 381) and hazard a remark on one of his most notorious aphorisms concerning woman, in the hope of alleviating the results of too one-sided a reading. *Beyond Good and Evil* 238 stands at first glance to alienate those for whom not only sexism but also orientalism is distasteful. It begins with a warning:

> To go wrong on the basic problem of "man and woman," to deny here the most abysmal antagonism and the necessity of an eternally hostile

tension . . . is a *typical* sign of shallowness, and a thinker who has shown himself to be shallow on this point—shallow in instinct!—must be regarded as generally suspect.

This is the problem Nietzsche cited earlier (*BGE* 231) as an example of the profoundest "given" in the psyche, concerning which it is impossible to learn but only to discover "how it stands" with one. To "go wrong" on this problem can then only be a matter of not getting deep enough, of getting caught up in superficialities and thus failing to reach the bedrock of fateful stupidity at the bottom of the soul, of failing to get down to "the problem that we *are*." Bear in mind, too, that we are considering passages from a book whose opening sentence famously ventures the supposition that "truth is a woman," and from a series containing the pronouncent that "nothing is more foreign to woman, more repugnant and more hostile, than truth" (*BGE* 232). Such considerations will warn the attentive reader against a literal reading, and perhaps also encourage a more psychological understanding of these passages concerning woman.

In contrast to the superficial thinker who has not plumbed the depths of his soul on this topic, we have the man who has "depth" of intellect and spirit as well as in his desires—who "can think of woman only *orientally*."

He must take woman as a possession *[Besitz]*, as lockable property *[verschliessbares Eigentum]*, as something destined for and finding fulfillment in service—he must depend here on the tremendous reason of Asia, on Asia's instinctual superiority, just as the Greeks did formerly, those best heirs and students of Asia.

If this pronouncement is to be taken only literally, it is difficult to imagine how Meta von Salis and Resa von Schirnhofer were not offended by it (*Beyond Good and Evil* being a text that Nietzsche discussed with them both). A clue to these remarks is provided by a couple of aphorisms in *Human, All Too Human* as well as by the references to Asia. Nietzsche had engaged the theme of spiritual depth in a series of notes written ten years earlier, which roundly condemn modern hyperactivity and its obsession with amassing as many experiences as possible, themes which finally appear in print in an aphorism entitled "Modern Restlessness."[11] The unpublished notes culminate in high praise of the contemplative life (properly understood as a vital form of activity) and an expression of admiration for "the hundredfold-inherited contemplativeness of the Asians."[12] A later note confirms that "oriental" is by no means a derogatory term: in a fragment from 1884 Nietzsche resolves thenceforth "to learn to think *more orientally* about philosophy and knowledge."[13] Insofar as Asia combines within itself tremendous reason with superior instinct, it exemplifies the enormous antagonism between male and female as an image for all primal oppositions. (Nietzsche would have been acquainted with this idea through his readings of Emerson and Schopenhauer, if not more directly.)

Consider further that this talk of woman as "possession" is coming from the mouth of one who would later claim to be "a *psychologist* without equal":

> May I in this context venture the supposition that I *know* women? That belongs to my Dionysian dowry. Who knows? perhaps I am the first psychologist of the eternal feminine. (*EH* 3.5)

Nietzsche's experience of relationships with women (very few of which would appear to have been carnal), while more extensive than is generally supposed, is hardly sufficient to qualify him as such an expert in feminine psychology. But he did become a consummate expert in the form of contemplativeness practiced by Montaigne, in which judgments concerning other persons are to be referred *intra*psychically prior to being applied externally. Montaigne ascribes the technique to Plato—though of course it is also to be found in the Judaeo-Christian tradition (as exemplified by the mote that is so much more easily visible in the eye of the other):

> Let us always have this saying of Plato in our mouths: "If I find a thing unsound, is it not because I myself am unsound? Am I not myself at fault? May not my admonition be turned around against me?" A wise and divine refrain, which scourges the most universal and common error of mankind. . . . A hundred times a day we make fun of ourselves in the person of our neighbor and detest in others the defects that are more clearly in ourselves, and wonder at them with prodigious impudence and heedlessness.[14]

We saw (in the previous Interlude) that Nietzsche encouraged the retroflection of violent energies upon the self, and he follows Montaigne in advocating a similar reflexive technique for judgments. In a passage concerning the difficulties of friendship that is highly reminiscent of the past master, he writes:

> Insofar as we come to know ourselves and to regard our being as a changing sphere of opinions and moods and thereby learn to lower our estimation of ourselves, we bring ourselves into equilibrium with others. It is true that we have good grounds for despising each one of our acquaintances, even the greatest among them; but we have equally good grounds for turning this feeling back upon ourselves.[15]

The idea of the necessity for cultivating contempt as well as love for oneself on the path toward self-knowledge is developed in graphic detail in

Thus Spoke Zarathustra. An exemplary passage is at the end of "On the Way of the Creator":

> Lonely one, you are going the way of the lover: you love yourself and therefore you despise yourself, as only lovers can despise.
>
> The lover wants to create, because he despises! What does he know of love who did not have to despise precisely the thing he loved![16]

Self-love must, for Nietzsche, proceed hand-in-hand with self-knowledge and knowledge of others: a difficult task precisely because "so much within the human being is like an oyster: repulsive and slippery and hard to grasp" (Z 3.11 §2). Armed with these kinds of psychological insights, Nietzsche fought a relentless fight (unremarked by his detractors) against "the most universal and common error of mankind."

These considerations should prompt us, more particularly now, to take Nietzsche's talk of woman psychologically, retroflecting it on the subject rather than referring it to the object. Another clue comes from the mention of his "Dionysian dowry," insofar as Dionysus—by contrast with the unremittingly masculine Apollo—is an androgynous character, whose followers were almost all women. On the more personal plane, Wagner had prided himself on his own psychological bisexuality, and Nietzsche was surely influenced by the Master's emphasis on this as a precondition of artistic creativity.

The task would then be to take woman as a possession (rather than being possessed by her) in the sense of an image or images of the feminine in the male psyche—as with the "mother imago" in Freud and Jung's notion of "anima." And indeed Nietzsche writes that "Every man carries in him an image of woman derived from the mother" (*HA* 380). What could be more one's "own" *(eigen),* more a possession, than this image, which "determines whether, in his dealings with women, [a man] respects them or despises them or is in general indifferent to them"? We should then want to understand *verschliessbares Eigentum* as something of one's own, *propre,* something one wants to hold in, to close off, keep from running off, contained within the vessel of the psyche.[17] The "little women" *(Weiblein)* Nietzsche claims to know so well would then be psychical images, persons in the household of his soul. As such, they would be complexes, amalgams of inner and outer, real and imaginal, images projected both within the vessel of the psyche and also on to figures in the outside world: Franziska, Diotima, Sophie, Isolde, Cosima, Malwida, Carmen, Lou Salomé, Resa, Persephone, Meta, Ariadne.[18] There would also be a continuum here, ranging from the personal to the archetypal—just as *anima* is on one level more personal, an image of the feminine embodied in feminine figures at work and play in the male psyche in general, and at the deepest level "the arche-type of life itself."[19] Toward the more personal end of the spectrum, Nietzsche's talk of the feminine will pertain to female denizens of the male psyche, and so would have to be taken conversely, *mutatis mutandis,* as applicable to the female psyche; but at the deeper level, the talk of woman may refer to the life of the soul irrespective of gender.

A careful consideration of Nietzsche's remarks on women may help the undogmatic reader to shake the unfruitful habit of reading his texts in terms of opposites, whereby one understands the virtues he ascribes to women—such as the genius for dissimulation, vulnerability, wildness, the "cunning litheness of the beast of prey," the naiveté of their egoism—as being "nega-tive." If one can suspend the knee-jerk reaction to such ascriptions and the concomitant impression of Nietzsche as a detractor of women, it might be possible to appreciate his concern to see them rise to levels that are *differ-ent*—and not necessarily inferior—from those on which men are accus-tomed to operate.

VI

Husbanding the Soul: Animal Procreation

> *Who can guess how much firmness the sea-beaten rock has taught the fisherman? how much tranquillity has been reflected to man from the azure sky, . . . how much industry and providence and affection we have caught from the pantomime of brutes?*
>
> Emerson, "Discipline" *(Nature)*

Aside from horses, it is likely that Nietzsche had even less experience with actual animals than with real plants, though the importance of animal images for his psychology is greater. (He did, at least, *read* widely in the biology of his time.) A theme that runs throughout his writings is the continuity between animals and humans—as a natural extension of the continuum from the inorganic to the realm of vegetation. Whereas Plato is concerned to have human beings withdraw their energies from their animal natures and (re)direct them up toward divine capabilities, Nietzsche take delight in bringing us back down to earth and emphasizing our kinship with the animals.[1] Nevertheless, as one moves from the florae of the soul to its faunae, the relations between Plato's and Nietzsche's psychological imagery remain close and complex, and reflection on them instructive.

The essay "Homer's Contest" from 1872 begins with an assertion of the unbreakable continuity between nature and human culture.

> Human beings, in their highest and most noble powers, are nature through and through, and bear within them nature's uncanny double character. Their terrible capacities and those that count as inhuman are perhaps even the fertile soil from which alone all humanity, in its impulses, deeds, and works, is able to grow. Thus the Greeks, the most humane people of antiquity, possess a trait of cruelty and a tiger-like joy in destruction. (*KSA* 1:783)

Since Nietzsche goes on to talk of the way the Greek considered "the release of the full flow of his hatred" as a necessity, and how then "the tiger would leap out, with a look of sensual cruelty flashing from its terrible eye," one can infer that a main feature of the continuity with nature is our continuing kinship with the animals—especially in the realm of the passions.

In *The Birth of Tragedy,* one effect of the Dionysiac experience was to dissolve the boundaries between the human and animal realms completely: under the charm of Dionysus, to whose chariot panthers and tigers are yoked, beasts of prey "approach peacefully" and animals acquire the power of speech (*BT* 1). The part-animal attendants of Dionysus, the satyrs, as they appear in the satyr chorus of the tragedies, are said to be "the primordial image of the human being, and the expression of its highest and strongest impulses" (*BT* 8). In *Schopenhauer as Educator,* Nietzsche prompts reflection on "where the animal stops and where the human being begins," claiming that for the most part we do not "raise our sights beyond the horizon of the animal" and "fail to emerge out of animality" (*SE* 5). Most of human history can be understood as "a continuation of animality," and the genuine task of culture is concerned with the rare exceptions—those types who become truly human—and is *"to promote the generation* [Erzeugung] *of the philosopher, the artist, and the saint in us and outside us, and thereby to work at the perfecting of nature."* If the saint seems an unlikely member of a Nietzschean trinity, one must bear in mind that this character is of a distinctly Dionysian-Schopenhauerian cast, insofar as his "I" has been dissolved in such a way that his "suffering life" is experienced as "the deepest feeling of belonging, sympathy, and unity with all living things." It is important to realize, too, that these truly human types do not represent a *break* with nature but its highest self-realization, since the striving for self-knowledge is something Nietzsche holds to be inherent in all levels of the natural world.

By *Dawn of Morning* he has come to see that certain experiences afford direct access to our history and even our animal past:

> In outbreaks of passion and the phantasizing of the dream and insanity the human being rediscovers his own history and the history of humanity: *animality* with its wild grimaces; his memory now reaches back far enough, whereas his civilized state evolves from a forgetting of such primal experiences.[2]

This idea is then developed, with greater emphasis on animality, in *The Joyful Science.* Nietzsche begins aphorism 54 by saying that this realization *(Erkenntnis)* has transformed drastically his relations to existence as a whole:

> I have *discovered* for myself that ancient humanity and animality, indeed the entire primal age and past of all sentient being continues in me to create, to love, to hate, to infer. —I suddenly awoke in the middle of this dream, but only to the consciousness that I am indeed

dreaming and that I *must* continue to dream if I am not to perish. (*JS* 54)

This constant creating, loving, hating, and inferring he calls a "dream": something always going on, of which we are mostly unaware. And yet something to which we can awaken, realizing that archaic and animal phantasies constantly condition every moment of our experience. It is impossible to shut down the operations of this phantasy activity; but to wake up to them affords a perspective that transforms our experience. This becomes clearer in one of the next aphorisms, addressed "To the Realists," where Nietzsche stresses the impossibility of forgetting "your heritage, your past, your training—your entire humanity and animality!"[3] Our present experience is conditioned by "the passions and loves of former centuries" as they have been incorporated in the human body as the medium of sensation and perception. These passions and loves are then rooted in our animal natures inherited from an archaic past.

We have seen the passions imagined as elemental forces of nature—as mighty winds, raging torrents, burning desire of the desert; they also come through powerfully in images of animals. We can now inquire into the "ecology" of the soul understood as the *logos* of its *oikos,* the way it speaks of its household and the denizens thereof, of its inner ménage and menagerie. Specifically, what kinds of relations obtain between animal forces contained within the household and those that are in the wild, undomesticable? And under what organization of the passions of the soul, imagined as potentially domesticable energies, would we flourish best?

The richest field for this inquiry is *Thus Spoke Zarathustra,* which contains an abundance of faunae unmatched in any other work of Western philosophy. Not since Aristotle's magnificent treatises on animals has such a vast and varied bestiary crawled, soared, swum, trotted, and slithered through the pages of a philosophical text. Over seventy different species are mentioned by name, ranging from domestic animals to wild beasts, from fishes to birds, insects to reptiles. The focus in what follows will be on animal images associated with the passions as well as with animal husbandry.

Stalking the Wild Life

Just as vegetation grows naturally, prior to cultivation by human beings, so animals exist in the wild before being domesticated and subjected to husbandry. But just as humans have always been dependent on vegetation in order to survive, and before agriculture there was gathering, so before the domestication of animals there was *hunting*. In analyzing the "drive for truth" into its component drives, Nietzsche distinguishes

> a certain dialectical tracking- and play-drive *[Spür-und Spieltrieb]*, the hunter's joy in following mischievous fox trails of thought, so that it is not really truth that is sought but the seeking itself, and the main pleasure is in cunning creeping around, encircling, and the artful kill.[4]

Part of the renaissance of psychology as Nietzsche understands it involves pursuing the discipline as a kind of hunt.

> The human soul and its limits, the range of inner human experiences that has been reached so far, the heights, depths, and extents of these experiences, the entire *previous* history of the soul and its as yet unexhausted possibilities—that is the predestined hunting ground for a born psychologist and friend of the "great hunt." (*BGE* 45)

Heraclitus remarked that *phusis,* nature, loves to hide itself; and this is especially true of the *phusis* within the *psuchē:* one cannot count on its denizens to present themselves but must rather rout them out. The psychologist—himself such a rare beast—will occasionally despair in the face of the vastness of his task, confronted by "this great primeval forest."

> And so he wishes he had a few hundred helpers and keen, well trained hounds that he could drive into the history of the human soul in order to round up *his* game. In vain . . . [for] there where the "great hunt" begins, there also begins the great danger—and it is just there that [scholars] lose their keen eye for tracks and nose for scents.

In being on the track *(Spur),* after the trace, Nietzsche is not as much on his own as he makes out: he has an accomplished precursor in the field in the person of Socrates. In the *Republic,* for instance, when Socrates and Glaucon are seeking the nature of justice by way of the related notion of moderation, the former styles certain phrases as being its "tracks" (*Rep.* 430e). And when they believe they have "spied out" the three constitutive virtues of courage, wisdom, and moderation, Socrates says: "So then, Glaucon, we must, like hunters, now station ourselves in a circle around the thicket and pay attention so that justice doesn't slip through somewhere and disappear into obscurity. Clearly it's somewhere hereabouts" (432b).

Just as Nietzsche is always on the hunt for *Erkenntnisse*—insights, flashes of recognition, knowledge and understanding of the world of the soul and its histories—so Plato makes the hunt a leitmotif in his trilogy, *Theaetetus, Sophist,* and *Statesman.* In the *Theaetetus* the hunt is for *epistēmēs,* "knowledges" in the fields of sciences—imagined as wild birds, which we "hunt," capture, and bring up "at home" *(oikoi)* in an aviary within the psuche

(*Theae.* 197c). Having caught and brought into the household of the soul creatures from outside, we then rear and raise, nourish and tend them, these warm little bodies of knowledge, in a domestic setting. But since they are avian creatures, a second hunt is necessary, within the domestic enclosure in which they are to hand (*hupocheirious:* under our thumbs, at our fingertips), whenever we wish to consider or employ particular elements of our understanding. We need to cultivate the ability to "hunt down" a particular bird, grasp it with the hand of the soul, and release it again (back into the cage) when we are finished. Since the birds in the dovecote of the soul are differently disposed—"some are in flocks apart from the rest, some in small groups, and some are alone and fly through all of them in whatever way they happen to"—one is likely on occasion to mis-take a bird, take the wrong one in hand: "while they're all flying about, one misses and seizes another instead of an other."[5]

Nietzsche plays on this aviary image when he laments the way his thoughts lose their vitality when they are set down on paper: "Oh, it is only birds that grew weary of flying and flew astray [that] can now be caught with the hand";[6] and he gives it a piscine turn when he likens the possession of opinions to having fish in a fish pond (*WS* 317). Acquiring opinions would here be a matter of putting out some effort and being blessed with a modicum of luck. The image has in common with the Platonic aviary that the contents of the container are *living beings*—in contrast, Nietzsche suggests, to those people who are content with a "fossil cabinet" and having "convictions" in their heads.

The whole of the *Sophist* is a hunt for the nature of the sophist (*Soph.* 218c), who turns out to be a remarkably elusive quarry insofar as the search moves through the fields of farming, fishing, and fowling before finally running him to ground. At one point the stranger from Elea calls him "amazing and very difficult to be caught sight of, since even now he has very skillfully and elegantly fled into a species that affords no way for a definite tracking" (236d). At the outset the stranger had suggested that since the genus of the sophist is "hard to hunt down, [they] make a practice run of his pursuit" with something easier. He proposed the example of the angler—disingenuously, it turns out, when he and Theaetetus discover a "kinship of the angler with the sophist" insofar as they are both "hunters" (221d). The stranger defines angling as an acquisitive type of "in-liquid-hunting" of animals by means of "upward hooking." The ways of anglers and sophists then diverge, insofar as the former hunt in the sea, rivers, and lakes, using a martial art that is "tyrannical" and "violent," while the latter hunt on the earth for "nurslings" in the "meadows of wealth and youth," using the persuasive art of "conviction-producing." More precisely, sophistics is "a wage-earning art that hunts . . . wealthy and prominent young men." At this point it is the wage-earning, merchandising characteristic of the lowest part of the soul that distinguishes the sophist from the philosopher as embodied by Socrates; but the sophist remains an elusive animal—"the beast is complex and many-colored *[poikilos]*," says the stranger—and the distinction between him and the true dialectician becomes ever more vague as the dialogue proceeds (222a–226a).

In the opening scene of the fourth part of *Zarathustra,* the protagonist is portrayed as an angler, a fisher of men of a certain type. During the years since his last retreat to his cave, his happiness has accumulated within him: "What is happening to me," he says to his eagle and serpent, "is what happens to all fruit that becomes ripe. It is the *honey* in my veins, which makes my blood thicker and also my soul more still" (Z 4.1). His situation has changed, however, from the opening scene of the book, where the overaccumulation of honey-wisdom oppressed him in the absence of hands outstretched to receive it. Perhaps as a result of his experiences with husbandry, he has learned how to "squander" what has been given to him, "a squanderer with a thousand hands."[7] He has at any rate learned how to use the honey of his happiness as *bait.*

> For if the world is like a dark forest of animals and a garden of delight
> for all wild hunters, it strikes me even more as an abysmally rich sea
>   —a sea full of colorful fishes and crabs . . .
> A strange thing is the human world, the human sea: *that* is where I
> now cast my golden fishing rod and say: Open up, you human abyss![8]

Remember Zarathustra's teachings falling like ripe figs and lying there invitingly; this time he extracts honey from his own ripeness to use as bait for his angling. Rather than coming down to ground level, he now stays up in the heights and dangles his happiness as a hook over the abyss. Should any of his fellow humans take the bait, in pulling them up he will raise them in more senses than one:

> *That* is what I am from the ground up and the very beginning: pulling,
> attracting, drawing up, raising—a raiser, rearer, and discipliner
> *[Zieher, Züchter, und Zuchtmeister]* who once said to himself, by no
> means in vain: "Become that which you are!"

The fate of fish caught may be preferable to the rigorous regimen to which Zarathustra's catch will be subjected.

Just as the *Sophist* was a hunt for the nature of that beast, so Plato's *Statesman* is a search for the distinctive nature of the statesman in contrast with the sophist or the philosopher.[9] Early in the conversation the stranger suggests that they might see the statesman under the paradigm of the cattleman, nurturer of the human herd, pointing out that the cowherd is able to combine successfully several different arts:

> The cattleman is himself the nurse of the herd, himself the physician, himself as it were the marriage-broker, and in the case of the lyings-in that occur, the single knower of midwifery. . . . No one else is mightier than he to soothe [his nurslings] and by enchanting gentle them, both with instruments and by the mouth alone he handles best the music of his own herd. (*Stat.* 268a–b)

In view of Socrates' accomplishments as a physician, marriage-broker, and midwife of souls, the statesman may be closer to the philosopher than at first appears. But after a while the analogy fails to hold, and the paradigms of shepherd and cowherd are rejected in favor of the well-known image of the weaver. If we take the *polis* as an image of the soul (as Plato does in the *Republic*), then the statesman will be one who weaves patterns of order into the complex fabric of psychical energies. Since the citizens of the soul are more self-sufficient than sheep or cows, his role will be less like a "herd-nurturer" and more like a coordinator of the activities of his subjects.[10]

Nietzsche's contempt for the herd and its morality is such that neither he nor Zarathustra can see himself as a shepherd of the human flock. Indeed, as early as "Zarathustra's Prologue," when he realizes the futility of addressing his speeches to the people, he announces his intention to become a kind of Antishepherd: "Zarathustra shall not become the shepherd and sheepdog for a herd! To lure many away from the herd—that is what I have come for" (Z, P9). In a similar vein he later reviles the priests as "shepherds [who] still belong to the sheep" (2.4). And yet there is a sense in which he acknowledges the intrapsychical herd, when he characterizes the body as "a flock and a shepherd" (1.4). Significant too is his later identification, in his enigmatic vision, with the young shepherd into whose throat the black snake of nihilism has crawled.[11]

Again it is the prologue that sets the tone, insofar as Zarathustra there makes it clear that to follow the way to the *Übermensch* is by no means to leave the animal behind. In his second attempt to get his teaching across to the people, Zarathustra emphasizes the "across" sense of the *über[Mensch]* by rejecting the idea that the human is on a higher plane than the animal: "The human being is a rope fastened between animal and *Übermensch*—a rope across *[über]* an abyss" (Z, P4). This image, which plays off the presence of the tightrope walker who is about to perform in the marketplace, emphasizes the necessity of maintaining a connection to the animal if one is to make it across the abyss to the condition of the *Übermensch*. It is impossible to go over unless the rope is held in tension; and if one casts off behind and loses the connection back to one's animal past there will be nothing to prevent a plunge into the abyss. Zarathustra goes on to play on the idea of the human being as a going over *(Übergang)* and a going under *(Untergang)*—a drama about to be enacted by the tightrope dancer who, on his way over the abyss, will fall and go under to his death.[12]

In being aware of the livestock within the soul, Zarathustra is also alive to the potential drawbacks from harboring such animals. He warns the "higher men": "In solitude there grows whatever one brings into it, including the beast within. For that reason solitude is for many people inadvisable."[13] Zarathustra's speech is soon echoed by the figure of the Enchanter *(der Zauberer,* the magician), when he talks about fear: "Fear of wild animals—that has been bred into the human being for the longest time, including the animal that he harbors within and fears: Zarathustra calls it 'the beast within'" (Z 4.15). Of the various ways of dealing with the animals of the inner *oikos,* some are more salutary for the psychical economy as a whole than others.

The image of the hunter appears in connection with a class of people, "the sublime ones," whose accommodations with the savage beasts of the soul have not been adequately worked out. Zarathustra's criticizes of one of their number as follows:

> He still has not yet learned laughter, nor beauty. Grimly this hunter came back from the forest of knowledge.
>
> He returned home from the fray with wild animals: but out from his seriousness there looks another wild animal—one not yet overcome!
>
> Like a tiger he stands there still, who wants to spring; but I do not like these tensed-up souls. (Z 2.13)

Socrates the hunter is rarely this grim; the context suggests a Kant or a Hegel, a thinker who has attained (or at least aimed at) the sublime by transcending his animal nature as exemplified in the body. But to be sublime, for Zarathustra, it is not appropriate to kill off the savage beasts of the soul—since there will always be one or more that survive to tyrannize from within. The struggle with psychical faunae can engender unhealthy tensions in the soul, though these may be reduced by moving the body, exercizing the muscles, channeling the energies into vigorous physical activity. Zarathustra recommends a rather brutal regimen for those who would be sublime:

> He should do as the bull does, and his happiness should smell of earth and not of contempt for the earth.
>
> I should like to see him as a white bull, snorting and bellowing as he goes in front of the ploughshare: and his bellowing will be in praise of everything earthly.

Nor is it enough to have subdued the beast within: Zarathustra also demands humor and beauty as signs of the comfortable accommodation that comes from a successful self-overcoming.

> He subdued monsters, he solved riddles: but he still has to redeem his monsters and riddles; he still needs to transform them into heavenly children.
> His knowledge has not yet learned to smile and to be without envy; his streaming passion has not yet become still in beauty.

If monsters are dominated without then being redeemed, their energies will be lost to the domestic economy, and the passions will no longer stream through. To ask that the passions become "still . . . in beauty" is not to suggest that they be stilled; the appropriate image is that of a waterfall: the passions still flow, but are not unnaturally constrained, and are thus able within certain bounds to manifest a freedom that may superficially appear as chaos. The association of passion and beauty suggests that behind this discussion is again the *Symposium,* where the proper channeling of *erōs* is said to lead to absolute beauty. If one substitutes (will to) power for *erōs,* Zarathustra's subsequent characterization of beauty can be read as a play on the central image of the *Symposium:* "When power becomes gracious and descends into the visible: beauty is what I call such a descending."

In the *Timaeus,* with its distinction between the mortal and immortal parts of the soul, the higher part of the mortal soul, the spirited, was associated with the heart, blood, and lungs, whereas the lower part, the appetitive, is the seat of "the tribe of desires," passions that have to do with nutrition and sexual reproduction. The gods are said to have housed or "implanted" the lowest part of the soul in the area around the belly—

> constructing in this region as it were a manger for the body's nourishment. There they tethered it like a beast untamed but necessary to be kept fed along with the rest if a mortal race were ever to exist. Accordingly, they stationed it here with the intent that, always feeding at its stall and dwelling as far as possible from the seat of counsel [the calculating soul] it might cause the least possible tumult and clamor. (*Tim.* 70d–e)

A purely vegetal soul would nourish itself silently, with no disturbance to the rational part; but the appetites of the desiring part of the soul include sexual ones, and the reproductive urge tends to generate commotion. It is remarkable, however, in view of its distance from the rational soul, that the appetitive should be said to have even "some apprehension of reality and truth"—through its being the seat of divination by dreams while the intellect is asleep (71d–e).

There are several similar instances of images of the lowest being associated with the highest. In the *Phaedrus,* for example, when mind as "pilot of the soul" ascends to the realm beyond the heavens it is said to "gaze upon truth and be nourished," and to "behold and feed upon the other eternal verities" (*Phr.* 247d–e). After the descent and return home, the driver of the soul-chariot of the gods "puts up the horses at the manger and feeds them with ambrosia . . . and nectar." The ascent is too arduous for most human souls to achieve, and so they cease striving and "feed on opinion" (248b). Those few than manage the ascent discover on reaching the lofty plain of truth that "the fitting pasturage for the best part of the soul [intellect] is in the meadow there, and [that] the wing on which the soul is raised up is nourished by this." Not only does the "manger" in the human belly—for the nourishment of the "untamed beast" of the lowest part of the soul— appear to have a divine counterpart at which heavenly horses feed, but both these kinds of feeding have counterparts in the supracelestial meadow frequented by the highest part of souls both human and divine.

In a discussion in the *Republic* of the proper environment in which to bring up the guardians (the highest, ruling class in the *polis*), Socrates recommends that it not contain images that are "licentious" or "graceless"— "so that our guardians won't be reared on images of vice, as it were on bad grass, every day cropping and grazing on a great deal little by little from many places, and unawares put together some one big bad thing in their soul" (*Rep.* 401b–c). This grazing image is remarkable in view of the more vivid association of cattle with the *lowest* part of the soul and the condition that arises from its being overfed. People who are dominated by the lower desires become not only greedy but also violent, so that "after the fashion of cattle, always looking down and with their heads bent to earth and table, they feed, fattening themselves and copulating; and for the sake of getting more of these things, they kick and butt with horns and hoofs of iron, killing each other because they are insatiable" (586a–b). The frequency with which the highest operations of the soul are characterized in the dialogues by means of metaphors drawn from its lowest functions suggests that Plato was aware (at some level) that what he explicitly conceives of as an ordered hierarchy may ultimately be a matrix of interdependent elements and processes.

In the course of an inquiry into what disposition of forces within the individual soul would constitute justice, Socrates proposes to Glaucon that they "mold an image of the soul in speech" of "one of those natures such as the Chimaera, Scylla, Cerberus . . . [consisting of] many ideas grown naturally together in one."[14] In view of Nietzsche's penchant for referring to his works and his profession as centaurs, one can suppose a special interest in this image of Plato's. The components of the figure Socrates proposes imagining are three: "a many-colored, many-headed beast that has a ring of heads of tame and savage beasts and can change them and make all of them grow from itself," a lion, and a human being.[15] Insofar as we are to imagine this trio animating each individual, the three components would represent the appetitive, spirited, and calculating parts of the soul respectively.

Socrates further characterizes the many-headed beast as "many-formed," "snake-like," and "mob-like," and as representing "the most godless and polluted part" of our nature (*Rep.* 589e–590b). It is clear from an earlier discussion of the tripartite soul that the appetitive soul is the largest and potentially the strongest of the three parts, with a tendency to tyrannize the rest of the soul and if possible enslave it (442a). Socrates had earlier decried the condition where "the smaller and better part is dominated by the inferior multitude" (431a), and he warns of the dangers of domination by this "bad multiplicity" in other dialogues.[16] The image of the lion does not appear elsewhere in the *Republic,* though there are several canine associations to the spirited part of the soul. The tendency of *thumos* to boil up and seethe was noted earlier; but it is somewhat amenable to reason insofar as it may be "called in by the speech within like a dog by a herdsman" (440d). This image reminds Glaucon of an earlier analogy: "we put the auxiliaries [the class representative of the spirited soul] in our city like dogs obedient to the rulers, who are like the shepherds of a city."[17]

Given this picture, the possible dispositions of forces within the soul range between two extremes. *Injustice* prevails, according to Socrates, when one

> feasts and makes strong the manifold beast and the lion . . . while starving the human being and making him weak so that he can be drawn wherever either of the others leads and doesn't habituate them to one another or make them friends but lets them bite and fight and devour one another. (*Rep.* 588b–589a)

If the bestial parts of the soul are permitted to dominate the human part, there will be nothing to prevent them, savage and untamed as they are, from fighting with one another. Thus Socrates argues that it is actually better for the bestial parts themselves—each can get a fair amount of what it wants— if they are both "ruled by what is divine and prudent" (590d).

The condition of *justice* within the psychical household, in which its various members and the commonwealth as a whole will optimally thrive, is one in which

> the human being within will be most in control . . . and will take charge of the many-headed beast—like a farmer, nourishing and cultivating the tame heads, while hindering the growth of the savage ones—making the lion's nature an ally and, caring for all in common,

making them friends with each other and himself, and so rear them. (*Rep.* 589a–b)

This paradigm of animal husbandry would seem to make good psychological sense, especially if it can realize its aim of having all three parties be friends with each other. When the sensible farmer is in charge, "each part [of the soul] may . . . mind its own business and be just and, in particular, enjoy its own pleasures, the best pleasures, and, to the greatest possible extent, the truest pleasures"[18] A far cry, this, from the extreme asceticism of the Socrates portrayed in the *Phaedo*.

It is important to note—contra some of Nietzsche's criticisms of Plato—the relatively benign tone of Socrates' prescription for internal justice, insofar as its way of dealing with the multiplicity of lower desires, as represented by the many-headed beast, is neither tyrannical nor especially puritanical. The "tame heads" are presumably what Socrates earlier called the "necessary" desires—"those we aren't able to turn aside justly . . . and whose satisfaction benefits us," the desire for adequate food and drink, for example (*Rep.* 558d–559c)—and these are to be nourished and cultivated. The treatment of the savage heads, the "unnecessary" desires, is not overly harsh: their growth is simply to be hindered, presumably by restricting their nourishment. There is no suggestion that the savage heads be lopped off, or brutally subjugated, or harshly punished (as in some of the more ascetic dialogues).[19]

The Socrates of the *Republic* is not, however, entirely consistent on the issue of the lower pleasures and desires. Before introducing the Chimerical figure, and in preparation for a discussion of the tyrannical type of person, he had proposed further consideration of "the kinds and number of the desires":

Of the unnecessary pleasures and desires, there are, in my opinion, some that are hostile to law and that probably come to be in everyone; but, when checked by the laws and the better desires, with the help of argument, in some human beings they are entirely gotten rid of or only a few weak ones are left, while in others stronger and more numerous ones remain. (*Rep.* 571b)

This passage seems to suggest—by the "entirely"—that it is possible after all to starve the savage heads of the beast to death, and also—by the "probably"—that in some people the many-headed beast may have only tame heads to begin with. (Nietzsche would argue for the extreme implausibility of the second possibility and the undesirability of the first.) When Glaucon asks what kinds of unnecessary desires Socrates means, he replies:

Those that wake up in sleep when the rest of the soul—all that belongs to the calculating, tame, and ruling part of it—slumbers, while the beastly and wild part . . . pushing sleep away, seeks to go and satisfy its dispositions. . . . In such a state . . . it doesn't shrink from attempting intercourse, as it supposes, with a mother or with anyone else at all . . . it omits no act of folly or shamelessness.[20]

The disturbing effects of the lowest desires during sleep can be mitigated by following a regimen before retiring in which one "awakens the calculating part [of the soul] and feasts it on fair arguments and considerations," and then also "feeds the desiring part in such a way that it is neither in want nor surfeited—in order that it will rest and not disturb the best part by its joy or its pain" (*Rep.* 571d–e). The conclusion Socrates draws from these considerations appears to contradict his introductory musings on the unnecessary desires: "What we wish to recognize is the following: surely some terrible, savage, and lawless form of desires is in everyone, even in some of us who seem to be ever so measured. And surely this becomes plain in dreams" (572b). This eminently realistic attitude toward the omnipresence of brutal desires can be taken as representative of the Socrates of the *Republic,* insofar as it is confirmed in the Chimerical figure that follows. It is the expression of an ontological assumption basic to a moral psychology that Nietzsche also shares—and which distinguishes Plato and Nietzsche (as well as Freud and Jung) from the more wishful-thinking moralists who like to suppose that human beings are basically good, essentially lacking evil desires. On this view the many-headed beast would have only tame heads to begin with, but external circumstances (such as poor upbringing or a bad environment) could have the effect of turning some of the tame heads savage. There would appear to be no way of adjudicating the validity of such fundamental assumptions—the world divides into people who believe some version of one or the other. But the "inherent goodness of man" view does appear to be more dangerous: in the absence of belief in the fundamentality of brutal drives and desires, one is less inclined to look for ways of dealing with them than if one believes they will always be there and that the problem of how to channel them into nondestructive outlets must be confronted.

Accommodating Animals

Given Nietzsche's general reluctance to view the soul as hierarchically ordered—and least of all as a fixed hierarchy with reason at the top—and his more generous attitude toward the desires and passions, it is not surprising that there is no counterpart in his writings to the Chimerical figure of the *Republic.* One does find images corresponding to the elements of that figure, but their relationships have been displaced in some interesting ways. The image of the many-headed beast immediately suggests Nietzsche's understanding of the multiplicity of *drives* that make up psychical life, especially since he emphasizes their tendency toward tyrannical domination. The many heads connote for Plato the various voracious appetites of the beast, but for Nietzsche they would also suggest the variety of aims and ways of seeing represented by the drives.[21]

An image in *Zarathustra* makes a negative allusion to the many-headed beast when, in his speech "On the Pale Criminal" Zarathustra asks:

> What is this man? A heap of illnesses that reach through the spirit into the world: there they want to find their prey.
>
> What is this man? A ball of wild snakes who are seldom at peace with each other—and so they go forth for themselves and seek prey in the world. (Z 1.6)

Nietzsche would, then, agree with Plato that if the desires are simply left to themselves, with no control imposed, the result will be an unproductive chaos. Most of the other references to snakes in the text are to Zarathustra's familiar companion, and the snake is viewed in general positively, as a representative of chthonic wisdom—"the cleverest animal under the sun," according to Zarathustra.[22] The generally positive picture of the serpent here is in part a response to the portrayal in the Old Testament: for Zarathustra it is appropriate that human beings be invited to taste the fruit of the tree of the knowledge of good and evil—if only so that they learn that it is indeed a matter of taste (and will to power).[23]

A variation of the many-headed beast appears in the first of "Zarathustra's Speeches," which deals with "the three transformations of the spirit" into a camel, then into a lion, and finally into a child (Z 1.1). Insofar as the camel represents the reverent spirit that disciplines itself by dutifully assuming the burden of tradition, one may assume that at this stage the desires have been suppressed by moral constraints. At any rate, some kind of alienation has taken place, since the camel ends up in the barren environs of the desert.[24] When repressed over a prolonged period, the terrifying features of the passions and desires may be assumed by the restraining powers of morality—as exemplified in the image of the great dragon, a third beast, which appears at the transition between the camel and the lion in the desert. The dragon represents the terrible power that has accrued to traditional mores over the centuries—"thousand-year-old values shine on [its] scales"—which the camel is powerless to resist. The monstrous apparition reappears at the conclusion of a discourse on the conventions of evaluation in terms of good and evil in "On the Thousand Goals and One": "Truly, it is a monster the power of this praising and blaming. Tell me, who is going to subdue it, brothers? Tell me, who will throw a yoke over the thousand necks of this beast?" (Z 1.15). These figures that echo Plato's image for the lowest part of the soul pertain to moral evaluation—a function, for Plato, of the highest part—and at the same time to the bestial origins and instinctual grounds of all moralities and the challenge of restraining them when they become monstrous.

Such is the power of what for the camel-spirit is "master and god," the irresistible force of the commanding "Thou shalts" that gleam golden on every one of the dragon's scales, that an animal with the strength of the lion—a beast of prey rather than of burden—is needed to overcome it. And to take for oneself the right to one's own new values, to say "I will" in the face of the shining scales, is from the perspective of the reverent camel a distinctly predatory act. The lions in *Zarathustra* and the *Republic* share the qualities of courage and strength; but whereas for Plato that strength is optimally employed in keeping the many-headed beast in check, the force of the lion in *Zarathustra* is directing toward overcoming the dragon of morality. The lion does, however, play a mediating role in both: in the *Republic* the energies of the lion/auxiliaries are to be employed for the sake of the commonweal, while in *Zarathustra* the strength of the lion serves to clear the ground for the creation of new values, for the nascent creativity symbolized by the child as the third transformation of the spirit.

In the rest of *Zarathustra* the lion plays a positive role with respect to the protagonist, while the other representative of the spirited part of the soul, the dog, is cast in a predominantly poor light.[25] Zarathustra warns one of his listeners about the bad effects of conventional moralities on the passions:

> Eventually all your passions became virtues and all your devils angels.
>
> Once you had wild dogs in your cellar: but in the end they changed into birds and lovely singers.
>
> From your passions you brewed your balsam; you milked your cow, melancholy—and now you drink the sweet milk of her udders.[26]

Here is a picture of the unruly desires tamed and made soft, their brutal strength transmuted into the dull nurturing of the domestic cow. But few people, in Zarathustra's view, are equal to the task of taming the wild drives, and most can control the beast within only at the price of having it turn upon themselves and force them to extreme asceticism: "These are the terrible ones, who carry around inside them the beast of prey and have no choice but lust or self-laceration" (Z 1.9). The inner beast possesses canine cunning and is unusually difficult to overcome:

> These people certainly restrain themselves: but the bitch sensuality looks enviously out of everything they do.

Even into the heights of their virtue and into the cold of the spirit this beast follows them with her restlessness.

And how cleverly the bitch sensuality knows how to beg for a piece of spirit when denied a piece of meat! (*Z* 1.13)

Again the idea is that this kind of self-restraint, while it may prevent the inner beast from acting out, will not make it disappear: sublimation can raise the dog to spiritual heights—but it remains a dog, and an abject creature at that. Most of the dogs that appear in *Zarathustra* represent the lowest drives, and none of them corresponds to the worthy sheepdogs of the *Republic*.[27]

Courage is a prime virtue for Nietzsche as it is for Plato, but in *Zarathustra* it is a courage to look into the abyss of human life—and of one's self—and face up to the bestial and evil elements in it. The traditional hero has the courage to slay the beast, but Zarathustra seeks the "over-hero," the hunter who will bring it back alive to the household of the soul, and domesticate it without taming. Such courage requires a worthy antagonist, and so must be allied with a "human intelligence" that is not put off by the prospect of evil things:

It is a blessing to see the wonders that are hatched by a hot sun: tigers, and palms, and rattlesnakes. . . .

So that the *Übermensch* will not lack his dragon, the over-dragon that is worthy of him, a lot more hot sun still must shine on damp, primeval forest!

Your wild cats will have to have turned into tigers, and your poisonous toads into crocodiles: for the good hunter should have fine game to hunt! (*Z* 2.21)

Against the background of such tropical burgeoning of luxuriant life, the sight of the all too temperate "higher humans" impels Zarathustra to extravagant flights of phantasy: "Then my wings grew, that I might soar into far futures. Into farther futures and more southerly souths than any sculptor *[Bildner]* has ever dreamed of." Another motive for his flight was revealed earlier, when Zarathustra, repulsed by the sight of the rabble gathered around the fountain of life, asked himself: "Was it my nausea that created wings for me and the power to divine the presence of springs? Truly, I have to fly into the highest heights in order to find again the fount of joy" (*Z* 2.6). This is not a Platonic flight that transcends the earth, but rather a flight within the temporal realm from one part of it to a higher part.[28] Zarathustra is not drawn to the ascent by a vision of the Good, as in the *Symposium* or *Phaedrus,* but rather by the prospect of the magnificent evil that flourishes *under* a hot sun. Later on, the sun again fires Zarathustra's longing to rise above the highest and best human exemplars so far, giving rise in him to a "great wing-rushing yearning."[29] Thus inspired, he flies into far futures and hot souths, "quivering, an arrow, through sun-drunken rapture."

These images recall the description of the fourth kind of divine madness discussed in the *Phaedrus,* erotic *mania,* the madness of one who "when he sees beauty on earth, remembering true beauty, feels his wings growing and longs to stretch them for an upward flight, but cannot do so, and, like a bird, gazes upward and neglects the things below" (*Phr.* 249d). It is in the *Phaedrus* that the other famous Platonic image for the tripartite soul occurs, in the figure of the two horses and the charioteer.[30] The image *contra naturam* of the winged horses symbolizes the elevating powers of the lower passions and signifies their indispensability if the soul is to move at all.[31] Although they are of different colors and dispositions, the two steeds are at least animals of the same species—suggesting less of a split (than in the Chimerical figure) and more of a symbiosis between the two kinds of passions in the lower soul. A significant difference between the images in the two dialogues is that in the *Phaedrus* the lowest kind of soul is imagined as a mammal, an animal closer to the human than is the reptilian beast of the *Republic.* In the horses and charioteer image, moreover, the human part communicates with even the dark (inferior) horse by means of language. In the *Republic* and *Timaeus* the lowest part of the soul is so far away from the highest that it is completely incapable of obedience (*ob-audire,* to hearken to), unlike the spirited soul which is imagined as being amenable to reason through speech.

This is a feature of Plato's imagistic treatment of possible dispositions of the passions that is absent in Nietzsche: the idea that while those passions that affect the spirited soul may occasionally become overanimated, get out of hand, and run out of control, one can generally *speak* to them—even in their animal aspects—and elicit with words a response to the dictates of reason. These animals—noble sheepdogs, white horses, powerful lions— are therefore important intermediaries in the chain of command, insofar as they can understand and respond to human speech on the one hand, and keep in check the lower, more unruly denizens of the soul on the other.[32]

Nietzsche's images of horses tend, perhaps owing to equestrian experiences in his youth, to be of horse and rider—suggesting a closer, more intimate relationship between the human and animal parts of the soul than does the image of the charioteer and team.[33] In discussing the way an "aristocratic culture" handles the passions, he likens it to

> either a rider who experiences delight in making a passionate and proud animal walk in the Spanish step . . . or one who feels his horse

shooting along under him, right at the edge where horse and rider might lose their heads, but takes delight precisely in keeping his head. (*DM* 201)

Nietzsche also appears to be more appreciative than Plato of the advantages of harboring beasts within the soul that can help one bear the heavier and more prosaic burdens of life—as evidenced by the image of the camel in *Zarathustra,* and by this later passage from *Beyond Good and Evil:*

> To have and not to have one's affects, one's pro and contra, at will, to condescend to them, for a few hours; to *seat* oneself upon them as upon a horse, often as on a donkey: for one must know how to use their stupidity as well as their fire. (*BGE* 284)

A careful consideration of the equine image of the *Phaedrus* shows that Nietzsche's reading of Socrates/Plato as advocating a "tyranny of reason" over the lower drives is far from fair.[34] It is true that the bloody subdual of the dark horse at the hands of the charioteer may appear to be an act of deliberate domination. But a careful reading of this phase of the image reveals that the subjugation is not a calculated act of cruelty on the part of the charioteer, but an almost incidental effect of a greater force's acting on him. The first time the dark horse persuades the others to approach the loved one, the sight dazzles the driver as if "by lightning" and awakens the memory of absolute beauty—in the face of which he falls back in fear and awe, and is thereby "forced" to jerk the reins back with such force as to bring the horses to their knees (*Phr.* 254b). The second time, he is taken unawares by the surge of power with which the dark horse pulls when inspired by the vision of the beautiful: the sudden acceleration makes him "fall back like a racer from the starting rope." Since the dark horse has taken the bit between his teeth and is straining forward, the sudden restraint has effects that are cruel and bloody. But it is this strangely instinctual "reflex" reaction—rather than deliberation or reflection—on the part of reason guiding the lower powers that is the force behind self-restraint.[35]

Leaving aside the hyperascetic picture of Socrates in dialogues such as the *Phaedo,* and focusing on the images from the *Republic, Phaedrus,* and *Timaeus,* the picture of the passions that emerges is in fact remarkably close to the one found in Nietzsche. Unlike the prescriptions issuing from the ascetic strains in Christianity—the object of Nietzsche's most withering scorn for their attempt to extirpate the bestial passions—Plato's position acknowledges such passions as natural congeners of the higher drives, and as driving forces that help elevate the soul to the heights of truth. The farmer who rears the many-headed beast to be friends with the lion and himself is a far cry from the ascetic hero who would vanquish it completely.

When Nietzsche does diverge from Plato, it is out of a concern with the amount and distribution of energy within the household of the psyche. He cannot endorse the Platonic prescription for "hindering the growth" of the "negative" drives because of the loss of energy this would entail, and the resultant sapping of the creative urge. His desire to retain as many powerful energies as possible within the "great economy" of the soul is well summed up in a note from 1887:

> *Summa: mastery* over the passions, not their weakening or extirpation. The greater the will's power of mastery, the more freedom may be given to the passions.
> The "great human being" is great by virtue of the range of free play of his desires and of the still greater power that is able to take these magnificent monsters into service.[36]

What exercises mastery over the "magnificent monsters" of the passions and takes them into service is the *will*. If this seems overly Platonic and an uncharacteristically conventional opposition for Nietzsche—will *versus* the passions—it must be remembered that he understands the will as being above all "a *complex* of feelings" and "an *affect* of command" (*BGE* 19). This will become an increasingly important question as the comparison with Plato is developed: what is the nature of this will that takes the monsters of the passions into service? *Whose* will is this will? How is the will's function here different from the work of the farmer who domesticates the many-headed beast?

But now it is time to move from talk of animals to a consideration of the distinctively human senses of the word "husband," in order to pursue the inquiry into the themes of procreation and birth on the level of human beings.

Psychical Intercourse

The opening paragraph of *The Birth of Tragedy* compares the interplay between the Apollonian and the Dionysian to intercourse between the sexes, as they stimulate one another to ever "more energetic births" and finally, in coupling, engender the artwork that is Attic tragedy (*BT* 1). One may well wonder at the nature of the parties involved in this relationship, at the constitution of these fraternal art-deities that are capable of coupling and giving birth. In any case, a general precondition for the intercourse that generates offspring, for Nietzsche just as for Plato, is *erōs;* and along with an emphasis on *erōs* in the early work there goes a privileging of artistic creation over objective knowing. An unpublished note from the period reads: "Our salvation lies not in *knowing* but in *creating!* Our greatness lies in the highest sheen, in the most noble ferment."[37]

The theme of love appears several times in the *Untimely Meditations* in connection with the idea of creativity. The beginning of the essay on history discusses the effect on the psyche of "a violent passion, for a woman or for a great thought": such passion is "the womb" of every worthwhile deed, and "the best deeds come to pass in such an abundance *[Überschwang]* of love."[38] Later in the essay Nietzsche reiterates that "it is only in love, only when surrounded by the illusion of love, that the human being creates."[39] This illusion is the "beautiful sheen" produced by the Apollonian drive, and is prefigured in Plato's account of the way beauty inspires desire. The dithyrambic artist in the essay on Wagner/Nietzsche is informed by an "overflowing" *(überschwänglich)* love and "shivering exuberance *[Übermut]*"; driven by a "stream that plunges now into this valley, now into that one, boring its way into the darkest ravines," he is possessed by "the longing urge to approach the world as a lover" (*WB* 2, 7). In casting sunbeamlike looks upon the earth that engender mists and thunderclouds, the artist furthers the fructifying power of the forces of life. In view of the multiple crossings responsible for Wagner/Nietzsche's creativity, the artist's approaching the world as a male lover does not preclude his also playing the part of the female:

> He lives like a fugitive, who strives *[trachtet]* to preserve not himself but a secret; like an unfortunate woman who wants to save the life of the child she carries in her womb rather than her own: he lives like Sieglinde, "for the sake of love."[40]

Parallel to the theme of the artist who fecundates the world and inseminates his audience runs the development of an image that is caught (in English, at least) by the ambiguity of the word "know" (in the epistemological and biblical senses). Knowing and loving are intimately associated in Plato's philosophy, insofar as *erōs* is an integral part of love of wisdom. In terms of Nietzsche's distinction between drives, whereas the Apollonian stance involves distance, a holding back that enables cool and dispassionate reflection, the Dionysian involves an abolition of distance, a dissolution of boundaries, a firing up of the natural passions in the service of a total merging or union with what is to be known. (Remember the Dionysian satyr as an "image of the sexual omnipotence of nature.") An early aphorism entitled "Employing Ebb and Flood" invokes, in an epistemological context, the image of a flow that is the force behind psychical attraction and repulsion: "For the purpose of knowledge one must know how to employ that inner current *[Strömung]* that draws us to a thing, and also that current which after a while pulls us away from the thing" (*HA* 500). These currents run closely parallel to the flows of Platonic *erōs* and Freudian libido. In encouraging a sensitivity to the tides of the psyche, Nietzsche is calling for an eroticizing of experience. This becomes clearer in an aphorism later in the book entitled "Love as a Ploy":

> Whoever really wants to come to *know* something new (whether a person, an event, a book) does well to take up this new thing with all possible love. . . . For by doing this one penetrates the new thing right to its heart, to the point that moves it: and this is just what it means to know it. . . . The [prior] overestimation of it, the temporary suspension of the critical pendulum, was just a ploy to lure out the soul of the thing. (*HA* 621)

This kind of loving, as if between persons, is aligned with the Dionysian drive that would dissolve boundaries so that the knower can unite with the known—even if there is then a subsequent distancing.

In *Zarathustra* an intertwining of the themes of propagation and procreation is first intimated in the speech "On Child and Marriage," where on the human level the two senses of husbanding are connected through the ambiguity of the word *pflanzen,* which means "to plant" and—in the reflexive form—"to reproduce oneself." Zarathustra addresses one of his "brothers" as follows:

> You should cultivate [*bauen:* also, "build"] beyond yourself. . . .
> You should not only propagate but 'superpagate' yourself! [*Nicht nur fort sollst du dich pflanzen, sondern hinauf!*] May the garden of marriage assist you! (*Z* 1.20)

When Zarathustra later speaks explicitly of sexual desire, he again draws on horticultural imagery:

> Voluptuousness . . . the garden-pleasure of the earth, the exuberance [*Überschwang*] of thanks to the now from all future.
> . . . for the lion-willed the great heart-strengthener and the reverently preserved wine of wines. (*Z* 3.10 §2)

Within the context of the garden, the gratitude of potential future generations expresses itself as *Überschwang:* the *Über-* evokes the "over" of "overflowing" together with all the rising of sap and welling of fluids we saw earlier, and the *-schwang* alludes to pregnancy. The image thus recalls how the lioness of Zarathustra's wild wisdom "became pregnant on lonely mountains" (*Z* 2.1).

It is significant for the comparison with Plato that the themes of sexual intercourse, pregnancy, and birth have their source in a speech on creativity which has strong epistemological overtones. While Zarathustra regards creativity as "the great redemption from suffering," the self-transformations it requires bring with them their own kinds of pain.

> Yes, there must be much bitter dying in your lives, you creators! You are thus the advocates and justifiers of all transience.
>
> For the creator himself to be the child that is born anew, he must also want to be the mother who bears and the pangs of the birth-giver.
>
> Truly, through a hundred souls I went my way, and through a hundred cradles and pangs of birth. I have already taken many a farewell; I know the heartbreaking final hours. . . .
>
> In knowing, too, I feel only my will's pleasure in begetting and becoming; and if there is innocence in my knowledge, this is because there is in it the will to procreation *[Wille zur Zeugung]*. (*Z* 2.2)

Important here—though often conveniently overlooked by enthusiasts of spiritual rebirth—is that in order to be "born again" one must first undergo some kind of death. Whereas the dying practiced by the Platonic philosopher (especially as described in the *Phaedo*) is a dying away from the world of the senses in order to be reborn in the intelligible realm of the eternal Ideas, Zarathustra is talking about a recurrent death and rebirth *within this life*. Rather than being lovers of the imperishable principles that inform the universe, Zarathustra's creators are "advocates and justifiers of all transience." Parts of the self are constantly dying off, and new parts being born—accompanied by the pangs that attend literal parturition. The passage through a hundred souls thus refers less to any experience of past lives than to Zarathustra's undergoing deaths and rebirths in this life. And yet the talk of begetting and procreation with respect to knowledge is somewhat puzzling. In what sense does Zarathustra understand knowing as an erotic or sexual activity? An answer to this question is best sought against the background of the correspondence between *erōs* and will to power—which Zarathustra calls "the inexhaustible procreative life-will" (*Z* 2.12)—as fundamental forces that move the soul.

There are adumbrations of Zarathustra's idea that knowing involves a "will to procreate" in the *Untimely Meditations*. In the essay on history, Nietzsche laments the condition of "modern man": "he has lost and destroyed his instinct, and can no longer trust the 'divine animal' and let go the reins when his understanding falters and his way leads through deserts" (*HL* 5). He goes on to associate the result of such a condition—"a race of eunuchs"—with "pure objectivity." The engagement with history on the part of objective scholars who lack the drive of *erōs*—"neuters," he calls them—will be sterile and without issue. This theme is developed in the essay on Schopenhauer, where the scholar is contrasted with the genius:

The scholar is by his very nature *barren* . . . and has a certain natural hatred for the fruitful human being; . . . he wants to kill nature, to understand it by analyzing it, whereas the genius wants to augment nature by means of a new and vital nature. (*SE* 6)

In *Zarathustra* the will to procreate plays an important part in the speech "On Immaculate Perception," where the protagonist addresses the "pure knowers," the "immaculate knowers," whose ideal would be "to love the earth as the moon loves her, and to touch her beauty with the eye alone" (*Z* 2.15). The speech begins with a parable, in which the moon on rising appears to Zarathustra "as if it would give birth to a sun," a phenomenon he dismisses as the false pregnancy of a lascivious monk. The parable is addressed to those whose highest aim is "to look at life without desire" and "with a will that has died." So far it sounds as if the targets of Zarathustra's scorn run from Kant to Schopenhauer, while the further references to the "monk in the moon" and to "contemplativeness" evoke the Christian epistemological tradition. But there are Platonic overtones here too. Insofar as the pure knowers want "to love the earth . . . and touch her beauty only with the eye," their *erōs* would appear to be the desexualized converse of that which inspires the Platonic lover of wisdom, being directed downward rather than up toward the intelligible realm.

The opposite of "looking at life without desire" is perhaps best expressed in a well-known passage in *Toward the Genealogy of Morals,* where Nietzsche writes about the advantages of employing "precisely the *variety* of perspectives and affect-interpretations for the purpose of knowledge" (*GM* 3.12). Arguing against the possibility of an Apollonian objectivity, to be attained by a "perspectiveless seeing" and a suspension of the will and all "active and interpretive forces," he advocates a Dionysian multiplication of perspectives and affects:

The *more* affects we can let speak about a thing, the *more* eyes, and different eyes, we can bring to bear on the same thing, the more complete our "concept" of the thing, our "objectivity" will be. To eliminate the will altogether, to disconnect each and every affect—even supposing we could manage such a feat—wouldn't that mean a *castrating* of the intellect?

Biographers tend to comment on the apparent lack of sexual experience in Nietzsche's life, though few commentators would characterize him as intellectually impotent. This is where his *erós* finds release: not through the literal organs of generation, but through the eroticized intellect in its passion for understanding.[41]

To the "immaculate" knowing advocated by many philosophers, which is purely passive and "wants nothing from things," Zarathustra opposes the procreative power of his creative love of the earth:

> Where is innocence? Where there is the will to procreate. . . .
> Where is beauty? . . . where I must love and go under, so that an image does not remain a mere image.
> Loving and perishing *[Untergehen]*, that has rhymed for eternities.
> The will to love—that is also a will to death. (Z 2.15)

Again there are allusions in the association of the will to procreate with beauty, love, and death to the ascent toward absolute beauty described in the *Symposium,* the driving force of which is *erōs,* whose aim Diotima characterizes as "procreation in something beautiful, through both body and soul."[42] But the conclusion of Zarathustra's speech performs a magnificent erotic inversion of the climax of the discourse Diotima delivers to Socrates. Zarathustra is watching the sun rise over the ocean:

> Innocence and creative desire is all sun-love!
> See how she comes impatiently over the ocean! Don't you feel the thirst and hot breath of her love?
> She wants to suck at the ocean and drink its depths up to herself in the heights: there the ocean's desire rises up in a thousand breasts.
> It wants to be kissed and sucked by the sun's thirst; it wants to become air and height and a footpath of light and light itself!
> Truly, like the sun I love life and all deep seas.[43]

The lover in the *Symposium* mounts the ladder of *erōs* in order to consummate at the top a union with "the vast ocean of the beautiful," lofty sister-image to the sun as offspring of the Good, whereas Zarathustra identifies himself with the sun that would seduce the ocean of life up to its own height. The complexity of the sexual imagery is compounded by the generative sun's being of feminine gender *(die Sonne),* in counterpoint to the ocean of life, which is neuter *(das Meer, das Leben)*—but nevertheless identified throughout the text with a *woman.*

Zarathustra claims that any knowledge gained through pure perceiving—obsessed with eliminating all traces of will and desire in order chastely to receive and, coolly moonlike, to reflect reality—will be sterile and barren: "But this shall be your curse, you immaculate ones, you pure perceivers, that you will never give birth . . . even though you lie wide and pregnant on the horizon!" To the extent that he opposes to this passive-reflective attitude the "innocence and creative desire [of his] solar love," Zarathustra is accusing the pure perceivers of a lack of *erōs*—not a charge that can fairly leveled at Socrates, who sincerely insists that he is not a wise man but rather a "lover." And indeed the image of the pure perceivers lying pregnant but unable to give birth recalls the lover in the *Symposium* who is pregnant in soul but dependent on stimulation from the radiant beauty of the loved one to provoke the onset of labor.[44]

Zarathustra accuses the pure perceivers of wanting to touch the beauty of the earth only with their eyes. It is true that the serious knower in Plato is directed toward a realm "above the heavens" rather than toward the earth; also that Plato was the first to speak of "the eye of the soul," and that his emphasis on optical metaphors for the higher modes of knowing has been determinative for the Western metaphysical tradition.[45] However, the touching that is done with the physical eyes according to Plato's theory of perception is no coolly reflective affair, but rather a fiery production. According to the *Timaeus,* the eyes are themselves "light-bearing" *(phōsphora)* and visual perception is a result of the collision of the "stream of fire," issuing from within the body and "flowing through" the pupils of the eyes, with the external "kindred" fire of daylight surrounding an object—the whole process being understood in terms of touch.[46]

Plato's fascination with vision may blind us to the number and variety of haptic and "cheiric" metaphors he uses in connection with attaining knowledge of the highest things. In a number of dialogues he writes of the soul's "reaching out for," "touching," "grasping," or "laying hold of" truth or being—words that in Greek have sexual connotations.[47] But the most explicit language concerning procreative union with the absolute occurs in the *Republic,* where philosophers are described as being "*lovers* of that which *is* and of truth" (*Rep.* 501d). Socrates's account of their erotic activity is graphic:

> [It] is the nature of the real lover of learning to strive for what *is,* and he . . . goes forward and does not lose the sharpness of his passionate love nor cease from it before he grasps the nature itself of each thing which *is.* . . . And once near it and having consorted and coupled with what really is, having engendered intelligence and truth, he knows and lives truly, is nourished, and so ceases from his labor pains, but not before.[48]

What is most striking here is the shift from masculine sexual metaphors to a radically hermaphroditic complex of imagery.[49] The words Socrates uses here suggest a pointed instrument's not being blunted in the course of a man's begetting offspring upon a woman. And yet the term for "engendering" is suggestive of a switch of gender—confirmed by the subsequent mention of labor pains. Somehow, through attaining its goal, the lover's desire must have been directed back upon him in such a way as to impregnate his own soul. Such a lover of truth is far from the type Zarathustra despises as a "pure knower": indeed, combining as he does the functions of fathering and giving birth, he is as versatile a player in the procreative drama as Nietzsche's protagonist proves to be.

The general enmity for "philosophic natures" in the city discussed by Socrates forces the real lover of learning to leave, and to leave philosophy "abandoned and unconsummated"—and thus open to the reproach that "of those who have intercourse with her, some are worthless and the many worthy of many bad things."[50] ("Supposing" again, with the author of the preface to *Beyond Good and Evil,* "that [philosophy as well as] truth is a woman.") And if such unworthy suitors should take possession of philosophy in this manner, "What sort of things," Socrates inquires with concern, "are such men likely to beget? Aren't they bastard and ordinary . . . [mere] sophisms?"[51]

The corresponding sexual imagery in *Zarathustra* tends to be less explicit—but is more graphic through its lyrical compounding of elemental, vegetal, and animal images:

> That I might someday be ready and ripe in the great noon: ready and ripe like glowing bronze, a cloud pregnant with lightning and a swelling milk-udder:—
> ready for my self and for my most hidden will: a bow burning for its arrow, an arrow burning for its star:—
> a star ready and ripe in its own midday, glowing, pierced through, blissful with annihilating sun-arrows:—
> a sun itself and an inexorable solar will, ready to annihilate in victory! (Z 3.12)

This is the speech in which Zarathustra exhorts his brothers to be "procreators and cultivators and sowers of the future" and to seek out their "children's land." At its climax here, cultivator and breeder come together in the magnificent juxtaposition of ripeness and the milk-udder, amidst an explosion of erotic arrows flying in all directions—while the pregnancy is at the same time extended to the more elemental phenomenon of the cloud.[52]

True Pregnancies and Ultimate Issues

Nietzsche's first eulogy to psychical pregnancy occurs in *Dawn of Morning,* where he writes:

> Is there a more sacred condition than that of pregnancy? . . . Everything is veiled, ominous, one knows nothing of what is going on, one simply waits and tries to be *ready.* . . . —*it* is growing, *it* is coming to light: *we* have no hand in determining either its worth or the hour of its arrival. . . . This is the proper *ideal selfishness:* constantly to care

for and watch over and keep the soul still, so that our fruitfulness may *fulfill itself beautifully.* (*DM* 552)

A prime virtue here, as in the case of husbandry of the soil, is patience. There are major phases in the process over which one has no control, and where interference by the conscious mind would be detrimental. What is necessary is not action but attention, watchful care over the deeper and obscurer developments in the soul.

The first talk of pregnancy in *Zarathustra* comes indirectly out of the protagonist's "impatient love" in "The Child and the Mirror" (*Z* 2.1). The turbulence of the raging torrent *(Strom)* of Zarathustra's vocal love builds—through an onomatopoeic accumulation of initial "sh-" sounds (over thirty different words in two pages)—to a full blown storm *(Sturm)*. The terrifying lightning of the storm connects to the image of Zarathustra's wild wisdom as a lioness:

> My wild wisdom became pregnant on lonely mountains; on rough stones she bore her young, her youngest. . . .
> On the soft grass of your hearts, my friends! —on your love she would like to bed her most beloved.

Whereas the just individual in the *Republic* seeks to make the lion in the soul an ally, so that the part whose aim is wisdom can rear and domesticate both the lion and the "snake-like part" (*Rep.* 589a), Zarathustra's wisdom itself assumes the form of a lioness that he is content to let roam wild, independently of his eagle and serpent, trusting to its instincts—in the faith that anyone who can bear such a fierce imposition on the heart will be the wiser for it. More than the teacher's seeding the soil of his pupils' souls, Zarathustra's disciples are to be prepared for the arrival of wisdom in the form of live young, which they are then expected to nurture with love.

The pregnancies in Nietzsche's texts extend over a far broader range than in Plato's: from the animal realm down to the elemental phenomena of water vapor and fire (Zarathustra himself as "a cloud pregnant with lightning"). Near the end of the book is another allusion to the pregnancy of Zarathustra's wisdom: "My wisdom has been gathering like a cloud for a long time now, it is becoming stiller and darker. Thus does every wisdom that is *some day* to give birth to lightning bolts" (*Z* 4.13 §7). Whereas the Platonic pregnancy issues in "intelligence and truth," in a steady illumination like that of the sun, Zarathustra's produces momentary flashes of insight which may speak in forked tongues loud enough to waken the somnolent soul, but which are so momentary as to require quick attention to apprehend. Such offspring bring a reduction of tension and a fresh clarity to the accumulated atmosphere of the psyche.

The earliest Platonic elaboration of the idea of psychical pregnancy occurs in the *Symposium,* where Diotima characterizes the aim of *erōs* as "birth in the beautiful." To dispel the puzzlement this remark produces, she explains:

> All humans are pregnant, Socrates, both in body and in soul, and on reaching a certain age our nature yearns to engender offspring. . . . Therefore when one who is pregnant approaches the beautiful . . . he becomes so exhilarated as to overflow with bringing forth and begetting . . . and when one is pregnant and teeming ripe he is excited by the beautiful because its possessor can relieve him of his heavy pangs.[53]

What is strange here is that the pregnancy appears to precede the sexual act rather than follow from it; and Beauty, rather than having instigated the intercourse in the first place, is said simply to stimulate labor and to preside over the birth as Eileithyia, the goddess of childbirth.

If a man's soul can be pregnant "from the time of his youth" (*Symp.* 209b), one must assume that insemination takes place at an early age, and that when such a man gets older he looks for someone of sufficient beauty to induce labor and birth. This he does by "taking in hand the other's education," whereby "through contact and intercourse with him, he bears and brings forth that with which he has for so long been pregnant" (209c). This would also be the point at which the insemination (though the text does not actually use the term here) of the younger man's soul takes place, which will develop into full-blown pregnancy as he in turn becomes older.

At the ultimate stage in the long ascent of the soul, the lover finally attains union with Beauty itself, divine and eternal, a union that is the most productive of all (*Symp.* 210d–212a). By contrast with the kind of begetting that confers immortality in time (the generation of literal offspring, or the creation of laws, works of art, and so on), the union with absolute beauty lifts the lover out of time altogether and into eternity. In spite of Nietzsche's different conception of eternity (as the eternal recurrence of the moment within time), he is drawn to similar imagery when Zarathustra sings of his desire in "The Seven Seals" (Z 3.16). Up to this point in the narrative, the protagonist has been torn in his love between two female figures, his life and his wild wisdom; now his wisdom has let him see life under the aspect of a Dionysian eternality, so that in a sense these two figures coalesce in the figure of the feminine eternal. In the first verse of the song Zarathustra sings of himself as being

> ready for the lightning in the dark bosom and for the redeeming flashes of light, pregnant with lightning bolts that say Yes! laugh Yes! for prophetic flashes of lightning:
> —blessed is the one who is thus pregnant . . .

> Oh how should I not lust after eternity and the nuptial ring of
> rings—the ring of recurrence?
> Never yet have I found the woman from whom I wanted children,
> unless it be this woman that I love: for I love you, o eternity! (Z
> 3.16 §1)

Zarathustra resembles the lover-philosopher of the *Republic* in being pointedly pregnant and yet uniting with the eternal Other in such a way as to
engender progeny by it too. One imagines the goal in Plato to be spherical,
the consummate form, whereas in *Zarathustra* eternity is imagined as a
ring, a more complex form composed of circles around an empty center.
And just as the Platonic lover is both pregnant and impregnator, so Zarathustra is both bow and the arrow it longs for, arrow and the star it yearns
to pierce, both star and self-annihilating solar will (Z 3.12 §30).

We learn more about Plato's understanding of psychical pregnancy from
the *Theaetetus*. Having been forced by Socrates early in the dialogue into a
state of acute aporia concerning the nature of knowledge, the eponymous
interlocutor expresses frustration at his inability to put an end to his obses-
sive pondering of the question. Socrates explains to him: "The reason is,
my dear Theaetetus, that you're suffering labor pains on account of your
not being empty but pregnant. . . . And then . . . you've not heard that I am
the son of a midwife . . . and that I practice the same art?"[54] Socrates invites
a comparison between the midwife's function on the physical plane and his
own on the intellectual by saying: "Do reflect, then, about that which in its
entirety characterizes midwives." The real midwife is herself past childbearing age, capable of arousing or alleviating the pains of labor through drugs
and incantations, and able to facilitate or, when necessary, abort the delivery
(*Theae.* 149b–d). It is here that Socrates invokes the sowing and harvesting
metaphor discussed earlier, in alluding to midwives' modestly concealed
skill in acting as go-betweens. The image of the matchmaker occurs in
Nietzsche's texts too, though in this case the bride and groom are thoughts
(themselves *logoi* one could say) rather than real people. Faced with the
prospect of two unconnected judgments in our mind,

> we are intrigued by the idea that a marriage might be arranged here,
> a conclusion drawn, and that if there is some issue from concluding
> this union, the honor might accrue not only to the two maritally joined
> judgments, but also to the arranger of the marriage. (*AOM* 26)

By contrast with the picture in the *Symposium,* where Socrates is portrayed as a fecund speaker whose discourses bear abundant fruit among the
young men of Athens, he is presented in the *Theaetetus* as being *only* a
midwife, and himself "sterile of wisdom."[55] In one of his more forceful
professions of Socratic ignorance, he says: "The god compels me to be mid-

wife, and prevented me from generating. Now I myself am obviously hardly wise at all, and have not had a discovery of this sort as an offspring of my soul."[56] And in case there should be any doubt, he adds that those who have associated with him as students "never learnt anything from me, but they on their own from themselves found and gave birth to many beautiful things."[57] In contrast to Socrates's modesty concerning maternity, Zarathustra claims to play the part not only of the mother in the drama of procreation, but of the child as well: "For the creator himself to be the child that is born anew, he must also want to be the mother who bears and the pangs of the birth-giver."[58]

Nietzsche returns to the topic of pregnancy in *Toward the Genealogy of Morals,* in the course of a discussion of the relation of philosophers to the ascetic ideal. He argues that if philosophers practice such features of the ascetic ideal as "poverty, humility, and chastity," it is not because they regard these as virtues—but they cultivate them "as the most authentic and natural conditions of their *best* existence, of their *most beautiful* fruitfulness" (*GM* 3.8). Their "dominating *Geistigkeit*" (spirituality) is simply "the *dominating* instinct that enforces its demands in the face of all other instincts"—just as in Plato, the philosopher practices chastity because "this kind of spirit apparently has its fruitfulness elsewhere than in [literal] children." The philosopher's withdrawal from contemporary society is prompted by "his 'maternal' instinct, the secret love for that which is growing in him," and he behaves as he does

> because his highest master demands it of him, prudently and inexora-
> bly; and he thus has a sense for only one thing, for which alone he
> gathers and saves up everything—time, energy, love, and interest. . . .
> Thus his dominating instinct wills it, at least during periods of great
> pregnancy. . . . It is precisely his 'maternal' instinct that here disposes
> ruthlessly of all other stores and accumulations of energy, of the vigor
> of animal life, for the sake of the work that is developing.

(The ideas of a highest master and dominating instinct will be explored in chapters 8 and 9, below.) The thinker is the mother, then, and the work the child. In talking of the creation of *Zarathustra* in particular, Nietzsche employed images of ripening fruit and—more often—of conception, preg-nancy, and birth, referring to the work in numerous letters as his "son."[59]

At the end of *Twilight of the Idols,* where Nietzsche presents his under-standing of the Dionysian mysteries, he offers his last paean to pregnancy in a passage (echoing several in *Zarathustra*) that again associates it with creative life in general.

> Every single thing in the acts of procreation, pregnancy, and birth
> awoke the most exalted and solemn feelings [in the Greeks]. In the

teachings of the mysteries *pain* is pronounced holy: the "pangs of the one who gives birth" sanctify pain as a whole. . . . For there to be the pleasures of creating, for the will to live to affirm itself eternally, there *must* also eternally be the "agony of the one who gives birth"— all this is signified by the word Dionysus. (*TI* 10.4)

Here Nietzsche confers upon the image of childbirth its broadest and deepest significance: just as the pain of birth does not prompt woman to deny the value of life, so suffering is not to be taken as grounds for the denigration of existence, but rather for its creative affirmation.

It is noteworthy that in all this talk of pregnancy there is no mention of an impregnator: the father, whether a figure in the world or in the thinker's own psyche, is neither named nor even alluded to. This is true also for the pregnancies mentioned in *Zarathustra:* the "sun-arrows" that "penetrate" the "star ready and ripe in its noon" may come to mind—but they are characterized as "annihilating" rather than inseminating.

A similar silence prevails in the pregnancies associated with Socrates. Since he is like the midwife in being able to tell whether a person is pregnant or not, when he encounters a false pregnancy in a youth who has come for instruction he does him the favor of "giving him in marriage to Prodicus" or to some other sophist (*Theae.* 151b). The implication is presumably that since such young men are devoid of conceptions of their own they need to be impregnated by some disseminator of ideas.[60] Nevertheless, if Socrates has never been a mother and claims to be barren and infertile, one might legitimately ask just what qualifies him for the job of midwife—since he himself has just explained that Artemis debars barren women from becoming midwives on the grounds that "human nature is too weak to grasp an art of whatever it is inexperienced in."[61] In view of the power and importance of Plato's images of pregnancy in both the *Symposium* and *Theaetetus,* it is indeed strange that there should be such silence concerning the causes of this condition. The question of paternity is a natural and legitimate one to ask, given the richness of the pregnancy metaphor; but none of Socrates's interlocutors thinks to raise it, nor does Plato appear to consider it an issue. Perhaps some kind of paternity test may help—or at least a consideration of the nature of the progeny that issue from the various pregnancies we have discussed.

In the *Republic* the philosopher's intercourse with Being produces offspring in the form of intelligence and truth. In speaking of pregnancy of soul in the *Symposium,* Diotima gives as examples of the progeny "thoughtfulness and other virtues," "moderation and justice," as well as laws and poems (*Symp.* 209b–d). In her subsequent account of the ascent to the ultimate mysteries of *erōs,* she twice speaks of the union between the lovers as engendering *logous:* words, discourses, ideas (210b–c). When the lover finally weans himself from attraction to the beauty of particulars and attains the highest stage of direct intercourse with Beauty itself, he is described in terms that again evoke agriculture: he "turns toward the vast ocean of beauty and may by contemplation of this bring forth in all their splendor many fair fruits of discourse and meditation in a plenteous crop of philosophy" (210d). If he is able to complete the ascent to absolute Beauty he will

> engender not illusions but true examples of virtue, since his contact is not with illusion but with truth. And when he has engendered a true virtue and reared it up he is destined to win the friendship of the Divine—and will above all humans be immortal. (*Symp.* 212a)

Immortality is attained not by fathering literal children but by engendering through the union of the soul with Beauty true ways of being, and by being in those ways, in ways that endure by influencing others—and so forth in perpetuity.

In the *Theaetetus,* Socrates claims that the midwife's role is minor in comparison with his own "performance."[62] His most important function, as he sees it, for which there is no counterpart in literal midwifery, is to judge whether the soul has given birth to true and genuinely "fruitful" or "productive" offspring, or else to a "mere image and lie," to infertile "wind-eggs" that are not worth rearing (*Theae.* 150c). The fact that Socrates is no longer producing any offspring of his own—if he ever produced any—lets him be completely impartial when judging the worth of his students' progeny. Indeed a condition of accepting his services as a midwife is that the bearer not be sentimentally attached to what is born; one must be prepared to consent to abortion or infanticide in the case of embryonic ideas deemed not worth nourishing or developing.

The lover/educator of the *Symposium* needs companions to help him bring forth children of his soul; the dialectician of the *Phaedrus* seeks fertile souls in whom to sow his words of understanding, speeches that are also his "sons," so that they might propagate themselves in perpetuity. In *Zarathustra* these two pictures come together, in that the protagonist creates companions by planting seeds that will grow into his children. In his speech "On Involuntary Bliss," Zarathustra announces to his conscience his gratitude for having been granted one thing:

> this living plantation of my thoughts and this morning light of my highest hope!
>
> Companions the creator once sought and children of *his* hope: and look, it turned out that he couldn't find them unless he first created them himself.
>
> And so I am in the middle of my work, going to my children and

returning from them: for the sake of his children Zarathustra must consummate himself. (Z 3.3)

In the *Symposium* and *Theaetetus* the inseminating forces remain obscure; in the *Phaedrus* the seeds are words of intelligence. In *Zarathustra* is it the protagonist's own self-love that appears responsible for his pregnancy; the speech continues:

> For from the ground up one loves only one's child and one's work; and where there is great love towards oneself, there is the true sign of pregnancy: thus I have found it.
>
> My children are still verdant in their first spring, standing close to one another and shaken by the same winds, the trees of my garden and my best soil.

Here we learn that the seeds of Zarathustra's thoughts which he sowed in his best soil have germinated and sprouted and are now young saplings, and that by retroflecting his *erōs* upon his own soul he has become pregnant with his work. These are two aspects of one and the same process: his thoughts and work are sapling-children. It is at this point that he speaks of subjecting his tree-children to the harshest possible exposure at the hands of the elements in order to weed out the weaklings—which would be the counterpart to Socrates' rigorous testing of the quality of offspring he has helped to bring forth. A later reference to the kind of propagation Zarathustra is practicing suggests that it may attain a perpetuity that comes close to the kind of immortality at which Platonic procreation aims. In one of his many speeches to the "higher humans" assembled in his cave, he says to them:

> From your seed there could some day grow for me a genuine son and consummate heir: but that is far off. . . .
>
> This present I beseech from your love, that you speak to me of my children. . . .
>
> —what would I not give to have this one thing: *these* children, *this* living plantation, *these* life-trees of my will and my highest hope! (Z 4.11)

The opening section of the fourth part, "The Honey Sacrifice," draws together the themes of pregnancy and ripeness in the presence of Dionysus. Zarathustra's eagle and serpent ask him whether he is concerned about his happiness. "I have long since ceased striving for happiness," he replies, "I am striving after my work" (Z 4.1). These words are an intimation of his continuing pregnancy, in that the word he uses for "strive"—*trachten*—is related to *trächtig*, meaning "pregnant."[63] "What is happening to me," he explains, "is what happens to all fruits that are ripening. There is *honey* in my veins, which makes my blood thicker and also my soul more still." In the final scene of the book, when the sign of the laughing lion with the flock of doves has come, Zarathustra says, with emphasis: "*My children are near, my children*"—and then falls silent (4.20). In his last speech the vegetal and procreative themes come together:

> My suffering and my pity—what do they matter! Am I then striving for *happiness?* I am striving for my *work!*
> Well then! The lion came, my children are near, Zarathustra ripened, my hour has come:—

Plato and Nietzsche share in common the idea that the children of the soul are at one level *logoi,* discourses or ideas of some kind, and that these are in turn capable of reproducing themselves in other souls. But whereas in Plato the range of offspring is restricted to speeches and the various Socratic "virtues" *(aretai),* Zarathustra's progeny extend through the animal and vegetal realms (in the form of lion cubs and trees) to such elemental entities as lightning bolts and stars. As he said in the prologue: "One must still have chaos inside to give birth to a dancing star" (Z P5).

As at the end of the previous chapter, it may be helpful to recapitulate the rather complex relationships among the various procreational schemata in Plato, together with their correspondences in *Zarathustra.* In the *Phaedrus,* although the primary imagery is agricultural, the dialectician is also imagined as the father of his speeches, and these sons as legitimate or bastard according to whether a marriage of souls has been consummated in the living presence of the speaker to the hearer, or whether the absent father simply writes around promiscuously. The crux is the seminal power of the word. Zarathustra's early failures in the field of verbal sowing seem to prompt a retroflection of his *erōs* onto himself—together with a vicarious propagation, as when he urges his "brothers" to become "procreators and cultivators and sowers of the future."

The philosophic lover in the *Republic* engenders intelligence and truth through erotic union with Being, though he himself is the one who becomes pregnant thereby, and participates in the labor and birth. The approach the lover of the *Symposium* makes to absolute Beauty is complemented by the already pregnant lover's being moved by the beauty beheld in a prospective pupil, pedagogical intercourse with whom induces the birth of edifying discourses. A lover possessed of Zarathustra's procreative will strives to know things—in the Biblical sense—so as to impregnate images and generate full realities. Zarathustra's retroflected *erōs* impregnates him, and the offspring of this self-love are his tree-thoughts, his work, himself reborn as his own child. In the *Theaetetus* the impregnation of young Athenians' souls is relegated to the sophists, while Socrates concentrates on the role of midwife to those who are pregnant on their own, and rules on whether the offspring, once sprung, are worth rearing or not. The lioness that is Zarathustra's wisdom is already pregnant by the time she seeks soft grass in the hearts of his disciples as a lying-in place for her delivery. In contrast to Socrates, Zarathustra assumes full parental responsibility, as both father and mother, and subjects his scions to the harshest conditions in order to separate the weak from the strong.[64]

In view of the abundance of sexual imagery in Plato's accounts of psychological creativity, it has been remarked as strange that he never raises "the question of whether a conception does not need to be brought about by a metaphorical intercourse within the mind," and that he refuses to countenance portraying the interaction of "intuitive inspiration and controlled thinking . . . [by way of] the sexual imagery of marriage or intercourse between masculine and feminine aspects of the self."[65] There is a sense in which Nietzsche's handling of the procreative imagery fills in this "blind spot" in Plato. Comparing Zarathustra with Socrates, what is lost as a result of the former's relative sociopathy—creative intercourse between individuals—is compensated for by the gain in psychological understanding when the intercourse is imagined as taking place within each individual psyche.[66] This difference aside, to the extent that creativity is for both Plato and Nietzsche a matter of metaphorical procreation, biological gender is irrelevant and each individual will play both parts. They both emphasize the androgynous nature of the psychological process—that creation is not an exclusively masculine activity but also requires receptivity, an openness of the soul to being entered from without.

Correspondingly, sickness is by no means always a sign of pathology but may rather indicate pregnancy (*GM* 2.19), and the patience of the husbandman is necessary in bearing the uncomfortable burden of something striving to be born. Plato's prescription is that one put oneself together with a companion in the presence of the beautiful, so as to stimulate labor and enhance fertility. But whereas this is—at least in the earlier stages—an interpsychical affair, Zarathustra advocates in addition a self-love that is far from selfishness, through which psyche is impregnated by *erōs* retroflected. In either case, any sentimental attachment to the offspring of the soul that stems simply from the pain of parturition is to be extirpated. And while there is in Plato a tendency to use images from the lowest grade of propagation to represent the highest level of procreation, in Nietzsche's picture the metaphors extend even farther down, and all processes—elemental, vegetal, animal, and human—are imagined to be going on at many different levels at once.

Part Three

The third and final phase of our inquiry entails a turn—before resuming track of Nietzsche's metaphorics, with respect to forms of human community—a shift to the conceptual, involving an elaboration of *ideas* rather than images for the workings of the soul. It is tempting to see this turn as a move to a deeper level, a position underlying the elemental layer of imagery with which the second part began; though it could also be regarded as a move up to a more general, and so more encompassing, level of discourse. It is in any case a reversion to the origins, which is a major trait of Nietzsche's genealogical method. A feature of this method, remarked by the thinker himself, is that it traces apparent unities back to underlying multiplicities— a reversal, in a sense, of the movement of Platonic dialectic, a change of perspective thanks to which what appears to be a single virtue (for example) turns out to be composed of a confluence of several different drives. Almost all topics in Nietzsche's psychology eventually come down to talk of drives.

We heard a fair amount of talk about the drives in considering the development of psychological themes in Nietzsche's earlier writings. Indeed it makes sense to talk of drives as the prime motive forces in the soul insofar as drives are themselves imaged in and by the soul, spontaneously, as elemental forces such as winds and rivers, plants that need nourishment and can be tended, wild animals that may be raised, tamed, or trained. But in moving to a more abstract discourse in terms of configurations of drives we join a major current of discourse concerning the notion of *Trieb* in the German philosophical tradition. The next chapter accordingly traces some of the major features of thinking about the drives on the part of Nietzsche's predecessors, in order to provide an orientation for understanding the important role played by the drives in his own philosophy.

Chapter 8 proceeds chronologically once again, in order to follow the development of Nietzsche's ideas concerning the drives in the course of his career. It turns out to be impossible to do this without running into talk of multiplicities of persons, a discourse that is deeply implicated with his thinking about drives. And insofar as the drives are understood by Nietzsche to interpret patterns of neural stimulation through the medium of imagination, the inquiry leads naturally to a further discussion of the role of projective phantasy in the constitution of experience.

In the early 1880s Nietzsche comes to realize that there is a strong archaic component to the drives that play through the individual, such that our present experience is unconsciously conditioned by forces from the prehistory of "humanity and animality." Chapter 9 treats some of the transpersonal elements and energies that make up the human personality and deals with one of the primary arenas where these archaic drives manifest themselves as persons: namely, the dream. After approaching the nature of the persons that compose the psyche from another perspective—that of drama, masks, and the theater—we broach the question of the optimal organization of the multiple persons that inhabit the individual soul, and examine the most fully elaborated metaphor for such organization: the psyche as *polis,* as inner community. The last part ends by presenting a picture of what is for Nietzsche the most fruitful way of participating in the composing of the soul.

Nietzsche's prescription for burgeoning psychological health is given its finest formulation in one of his last works, *Twilight of the Idols,* in 1888. A few months later the author of this prescription succumbs to madness. In view of his consistent emphasis on the close connection between the ideas and the life, a short epilogue considers the relationship between the consummation of Nietzsche's thinking about psychology and the tragic outcome of his own psychological development.

VII

Emergence of Imagining Drives

Man lives by pulses; our organic movements are such; and the chemical and ethereal agents are undulatory and alternate; and the mind goes antagonizing on, and never prospers but by fits.
                                        Emerson, "Experience"

The most radical feature of Nietzsche's psychology—generally neglected or not well understood in the secondary literature—is his conception of the psyche as a *multiplicity*, in contrast with the traditional idea of the soul as something unitary. The task of the following two chapters will be to elucidate the nature of this multiplicity and the kinds of organization that might optimally prevail there. In view of the topic's importance, setting it in historical context will enhance our appreciation of Nietzsche's achievement. While the idea of psychical multiplicity was very much in the air during the latter part of the nineteenth century, the unique way in which he developed it has deep implications for the ways we understand ourselves.

Over the course of the changing conceptions in the Western philosophical tradition of the relations between self and world, the idea of the self as something unitary has remained fairly constant. Even when understood as a synthesis of elements, the self is viewed as single: one body, one soul, one spirit per person. But it has not always been that simple. In most cultures, around their beginnings, the sense of self appears not to have been restricted to the single individual, but to have comprised several "souls" or *loci* of awareness. This may reflect an initial polytheism, since a subsequent move to monotheism appears to be accompanied by a unification of the human psyche around a single center of control: the "I," or "ego." Christianity lent impetus here also through its insistence on the unity of the candidate for salvation: souls are judged and (if found good) saved as individuals. The monocentric view of the self in Western thought reaches its most concentrated form in the consolidation of the I into the unitary Cartesian ego. The past two centuries, however, have seen (at least in some quarters) a gradual dissolution of the self into a multiplicity again, a resolution into a plurality of personalities. Behind the *personae,* the center may not have held.

251

It is fashionable in some circles to talk knowingly about the "deconstruction of the subject," as if this were a recent innovation, but in fact the dissolution of the traditional conception of the self has been going on for a while. One of the more playful initiators of this process was Laurence Sterne, whose crazily innovative novel *Tristram Shandy* (1759–67) Nietzsche had first read with enthusiasm at the age of fourteen.[1] In France, the work of Diderot had prompted the consideration of dialogical models of the soul. An indirect attack on the unity of the I takes place with Kierkegaard's fragmentation of his authorship into a crowd of pseudonymous persons in the mid-nineteenth century. Less overtly philosophical and more literary cases are those of Dostoevsky, as the creator of what Mikhail Bakhtin has called "the polyphonic novel," and Stendhal, another multiplier of voices, whose psychological acumen Nietzsche praises as much as Dostoevsky's.[2] With Nietzsche, however, a deeper revisioning begins. In explicitly rejecting the Christian doctrine of "soul-atomism," he quickly adds that "it is by no means necessary to get rid of 'the soul' itself and thereby to renounce one of the most ancient and venerable hypotheses" (*BGE* 12). The "new conceptions and refinements of the soul-hypothesis" that he proposes, such as "mortal soul," "soul as subject-multiplicity," and "soul as social structure of the drives and affects" are anticipated in an idea of the soul that originates with the early Greeks, and specifically in the Homeric epics. Since Nietzsche himself embarked upon his career with a lecture on Homer, that is an appropriate place to start.

A Brief History of Psychical Polycentricity

Anthropological research suggests that conceptions of multiple centers of awareness (sometimes equivalent to "souls") within one individual are widespread in the early stages of many cultures, and the archaic age in Greece is no exception.[3] The earliest occurrences of the ancestor of our word "psyche" are in the Homeric epics. But while in the *Iliad* and *Odyssey* the *psuchē* is spoken of as a life-force, a power that sustains the body, animating and lending it movement, Homer nowhere attributes to it any functions associated with waking consciousness.[4] The most frequent use of the term *psuchē* refers to the soul's departing from the dying human being and fluttering down to the underworld, there to pursue a shadowy existence as an image in the realm of Hades the invisible. What *is*, in Homer, responsible for waking consciousness in the living human being is a plurality of centers of psychic awareness. Some of these, such as *thumos, menos, ētor,* and *kēr,* appear to connote distinct (and often emotional) manifestations of the "life-force"; some, such as *phrēn/phrenes* and *noos,* seem more associated with thought and cognition; while others, like *kradiē* (heart), appear to refer also to an anatomical locus. One of the classic studies suggests a distinction between these centers as intermediate "organs" of experience, corresponding to the eyes as physical mediators of sight, and as "termini" of experience, corresponding to the I which sees by means of the eyes.[5] Insofar as many of these terms can denote termini as well as mediators of psychical experience, these centers appear to be relatively independent of the experiencing ego, possessing a certain spontaneity of their own, and even setting themselves up in opposition to the I. This is especially true of the *thumos* as the mediator of instinctual and affective life: one's *thumos* can desire things, and even "debate" about things within.[6] Its range of autonomy is suggested by a characterization as "a subject that orders, urges, hopes, restrains, flutters with anxiety, rejoices, exalts, forbids, has volition and daring, [and] can be arrogant and intransigent, credulous or incredulous."[7]

In spite of the dominance of the *thumos,* the picture of the Homeric psyche that emerges from the more recent scholarship is of a polycentric field of awareness whose several centers possess varying degrees of autonomy in relation to an I that is not in itself another fixed center, but rather a variable "function" of the totality of centers.[8] And yet this multiplicity is not chaotic, but has an integral structure comparable to that of an "interior society," or to the interrelations between "a community of internal agents."[9] This picture is echoed in Nietzsche's characterization of the mortal soul as a "social structure of the drives and affects" and of the body as "a social structure composed of many souls" (*BGE* 19).

Insofar as the idea of the soul that Plato took over from his predecessors—and transformed—was informed in part by the Homeric view, it is not surprising that the image of an interior society should figure in his thinking. Plato is well known for his idea of the tripartite soul (appetitive, spirited, and calculating), prototype of related triads in subsequent psychology (the closest being Aristotle's distinction between the kind of psyche animating the plant, the animal, and the human being).[10] Psychological disorder, which in the *Republic* is called "injustice," is imagined as a state in which internal factions vie with each other for power—as "a certain faction *[stasis]* among those three [parts], a meddling *[polupragmosunē]*, interference, and rebellion of a part of the soul against the whole."[11] As we shall see in chapter 9, to read the *Republic* for its psychology means taking its principal image seriously, and discerning in its picture of the individual psyche as a *polis* populated by a multitude of persons a finer differentiation than the tripartite schema can provide. It is significant that in those dialogues (such as the *Phaedo*) that present the soul as unitary, and where the human being is understood as a duality of soul and body, the relations between the two components are characterized in terms of ruling and serving. Nature is said to direct the body "to serve and be ruled," and the soul "to rule and be master"; soul, as divine, "is by nature fitted to rule and lead," while body, as mortal, is "to obey and serve" (*Pho.* 80a).

Many of the Neoplatonists adopted the tripartite model of the soul, and during the Italian Renaissance the resurgence of Neoplatonism and the concomitant revitalization of pagan polytheism led to a polycentric view of the psyche congruent with Plato's political picture. The psychical space opened up by Augustine was broadened and deepened in the Neoplatonic tradition, until by the time of the Renaissance it was capable of housing the famous Memory Theater of Giulio Camillo.[12] Most prominent among the persons populating *memoria* and imagination during the Renaissance were figures of Greek and Latin antiquity: Petrarch used to write letters to a range of familiars from Homer to Horace, and Machiavelli—whom one is reluctant to call a mere dreamer—was accustomed to engaging "ancient men" in conversation.[13] Nietzsche was a great admirer of Machiavelli, and especially of his writing style, and so he may have been familiar with the letter Machiavelli wrote to his friend Francesco Vettori, in which he gives an account of the circumstances surrounding his writing of *The Prince*.[14] The preparations for writing his masterpiece consisted not only in a study of ancient history but also in a vital dialogue with historical figures in imagination.

> When evening comes, I return home and enter my study; before I go in I remove my everyday clothes, which are very muddy and soiled, and put on clothes that are fit for a royal court. Being thus properly clad, I enter the ancient courts of the men of old, in which I am received affectionately by them. . . . There I do not hesitate to converse with them, and ask them why they acted as they did; and out of kindness they respond. For hours I experience no boredom, I forget all my troubles and my fear of poverty, and death holds no more terrors for me: I am completely absorbed in them.[15]

With the waning of the Renaissance, imaginal discourse died down as the unitary view of the person came again to dominate philosophical thinking. Greatly reinforced by Descartes's identification of the self with a *res cogitans* that was indivisibly one, views of the psyche as unitary prevailed until around the beginning of the nineteenth century. The first signs that things were beginning to fall apart came from the adjacent fields of literature and the various disciplines and practices that were coalescing as the basis for modern psychology.[16]

An important prototype for the idea of the multiple psyche is the more or less universal phenomenon of *possession,* in which a god, daemon, or spirit of an animal or a deceased human being takes over a part of an individual's person and/or body.[17] In typical manifestations the "host" falls into a trance or hypnoid state during which the spirit is able to speak through her or his vocal apparatus. Toward the end of the eighteenth century, the prevailing religious method for the cure of souls, exorcism, was confronted by a secular therapeutic technique known as Mesmerism, which was transformed in subsequent developments into magnetism, somnambulism, and hypnotism. All these practices had in common that they revealed the activity of unconscious forces in the psyche, of other agents possessing varying degrees of independence from the conscious I.

From the beginning of the nineteenth century cases began to appear with ever greater frequency that would formerly have been taken as demonic possession, but which now came to be seen as cases of split or multiple personality. In split personality a secondary, unconscious personality with its own distinctive character and set of memories—and sometimes even its own language—asserts itself in opposition to the normal I. In the phenomenon of multiple personality several such secondary personalities manifest themselves, often displaying close associations among each other of which the conscious I remains ignorant. Occasional discussions of personal forces in the psyche opposed to the empirical ego are found in the work of German clinicians during the first half of the nineteenth century, but it is not until after the 1870s (when Nietzsche was writing on the topic) that major theoretical works on multiple personality began to appear, in the United States and Great Britain as well as Continental Europe.[18]

One of the most famous cases in the history of magnetism as a cure for possession was that of the "seeress" Friedericke Hauffe, who appeared to communicate with discarnate spirits, and whose conditions were described by the poet-physician Justinus Kerner in his *Die Seherin von Prevorst* (1829). This two-volume study has the distinction of being the first monograph devoted to the "case history" of a single patient. Schopenhauer was among the philosophers fascinated by the seeress of Prevorst (Franz von Baader and Schelling, as well as the theologian David Strauss, are also known to have paid her frequent visits). Schopenhauer wrote a long essay on "spirit seeing," published in *Parerga und Paralipomena* in 1851, which makes several references to the Prevorst case and to other works by Justinus Kerner.[19]

Nietzsche learned of such movements as magnetism and somnambulism during his early teens, through spending summers with his maternal grandparents not far from Naumburg. The grandfather, Pastor David Friedrich Oehler, was a cultured Lutheran minister whose library was as large as his mind was broad. "My favorite occupation," Nietzsche wrote of his holidays at the parsonage in Pobles, "was to be in grandpapa's study, and my greatest pleasure was browsing through all the old books and magazines there."[20] It appears that among the more recent of those books were the works of Justinus Kerner. Jung relates how he was puzzled by the episode in *Zarathustra* about the protagonist's descent to the underworld (Z 2.18) until he realized how congruent it was with a passage from Kerner's *Blätter aus Prevorst* (1831–39), a collection of accounts of spirit possession and other paranormal phenomena. He wrote to Elisabeth Förster-Nietzsche to inquire whether her brother had known Kerner's work, and she confirmed that he had indeed been acquainted with it from his stays at the Oehler's house in Pobles.[21]

When in the next chapter we trace the development of Nietzsche's ideas about the multiplicity of the psyche, we see that they find expression both in terms of *drives (Triebe)* and as images of *persons*. In an aphorism from 1879 Nietzsche assumes the existence of a "drive to imagine and compose persons" that operates constantly on an unconscious level, and an unpublished note from eight years later suggests that the drives are themselves susceptible of appearing as persons as they pass through the medium of the imagination, and are thereby "transformed into demons whom one fights."[22] But first, some background context to Nietzsche's use of the term *"Triebe,"* with an initial focus on the latter part of the eighteenth century.

Herder, Kant, Schiller, Fichte

The idea of *Triebe* as major motive forces in the human psyche came to prominence with the *Sturm und Drang* movement, beginning in the 1770s. The term *Trieb* had been current in the language before that time, but it was not until the aphorisms of Lichtenberg that it began to acquire philosophical significance.[23] Nietzsche greatly admired Lichtenberg's style (WS 109), and was influenced by the content as well as the form of his *Aphorisms*. A representative passage concerning the drives is the following, from Lichtenberg's notebooks of 1768–71:

> It is ludicrous to maintain that one is sometimes not really in the mood for anything: I believe that the moment one feels strong enough to suppress a major drive *[einen Haupttrieb zu unterdrücken]*, the drive to work and act, is the moment one is perhaps best fitted to undertake the strangest and greatest things. It is a kind of mental inertia in which the soul can see much that is unusually small . . . [as if through a microscope].[24]

This could well pass for one of Nietzsche's psychological aphorisms, with its initially counterintuitive tone and its ultimate incisiveness. What is interesting here is the idea that a major drive can be repressed, even if no question is raised concerning the identity of the repressing agent. We shall have occasion to return to Lichtenberg in connection with his remarks on the fictional status of the I and the importance of dreams.

The first major precursor is Herder, who in his essay *Vom Erkennen und Empfindung der menschlichen Seele* argues against "cold, unfeeling doctrines of the soul" that hold thinking to be its essence and "feelings and drives" mere disorderly "additions."[25] The proper activity of the soul consists in more than thinking: "Sensation provides the soul with raw materials, with its catch *[Beute]:* the soul impresses its image on them." But along with this active imposition of its own form, the soul suffers passions, and is buffeted by drives, such that it needs an agent of order: "Reason and virtue . . . are born out of conflict, and reveal themselves as kingly power and order, which can and should become itself the strongest and purest passion" (*EMS* 574). Herder elaborates the political metaphor, going on to write of the way nature has subordinated animal *Reizbarkeit* to "higher processes and rulers," and of paths of sensation that reach all the way up "to the highest princess regent, the thinker" *(zur obersten Regentin der Denkerin)* (595). Even more significant than the feminine gender here is the characterization of the thinking agent as a "regent" rather than a monarch, as a provisional agent rather than a permanent ruler. The true queen would presumably be (soul as) nature, who, because of the impossibility of the regent's being able to grasp "the seed of every sensation," buried the source of stimulation in "the innermost darkness." Again and again Herder refers to this source as an "abyss"—*der Abgrund des Reizes* (596).

The hand of the regent within can be seen, for Herder, in "every vital work of a human soul": "Read the spirit of its author and you will see which senses ruled in him and which were ruled, and the laws according to which he ordered the chaos of his sensations" (*EMS* 632). And if the idea that the thinking part of the soul is the best ruler is fairly conventional, Herder places extraordinary emphasis on the continuity between the ruler and her subjects: "Both [reason and virtue] are born from conflict: reason from conflict among sensations, virtue from conflict among drives. And the stronger the drives, the better and more powerful subjects and servants the princess regent will have in her realm" (637). The ideas of regents, of ordering the internal chaos, of virtues arising from drives, and of the desirability of conserving the strength of the drives—all these will figure in Nietzsche's understanding of *Triebe.*

Herder's interests in poetry and aesthetics led to a concern with the creative drive in general and its imaginative powers in particular. He understands a creative drive *(Bildungstrieb)* to underlie the productive powers of both human beings and the natural world, as a reflection of the divine *Bildungstrieb.* In particular, "the poet imitates this divine formative power; or rather, he works under its influence with understanding and intention."

Herder also sees an important memorial element to the originative power of imagination: "So this wizardess calls forth not only the forms of things buried inside us as they appeared to us once in the past; she also causes forms never seen before to appear; she creates and generates."[26]

The primary source of the idea of the productive imagination in German thought is the work of Johann Nikolaus Tetens, whose major work, *Philosophische Versuche* (Philosophical essays), was published in two volumes in 1777. Tetens distinguishes three levels in what he calls *Vorstellungskraft,* the "power of presentation" understood as the soul's ability to present images internally: *Perceptionsvermögen* (the ability to synthesize the data of sense into images), *Phantasie* or *Einbildungskraft* (the faculty that performs various operations of analysis and synthesis on images from the first level, according to rules of association), and *Dichtungsvermögen* (the ability to create new, poetic images).[27] But while Tetens was influential, and especially on Kant, it is the latter's work that was the richest source for subsequent thinking about the imagination in the German tradition.

Kant's major achievement was to bring together on the one hand the understanding of the operations of the soul as dynamic and organic that came from Leibniz and Spinoza (the latter mediated by F. H. Jacobi) and on the other the more empirical and scientific conceptions from associationist psychology. Kant's many discussions of the imagination throughout his career embrace the full multiplicity of previous theories and issue in a bewildering array of ideas about its operations. His treatments of *Einbildungskraft* concern on the one hand the *reproductive* functions of the imagination, its ability to reproduce and associate the data of sensory experience, and on the other its *productive* powers, imagination in its "transcendental" aspect, in its ability to create schemata in advance of any experience whatsoever. His aim was to elaborate a conception of the imagination as an underlying third power that would be the synthetic root of these two branches.

In the *Critique of Pure Reason,* Kant characterizes the agent of the important operation of "synthesis" (of the manifold of pure intuition) as follows: "Synthesis itself, as we shall soon see, is the mere effect of the imagination, *a blind though indispensable function of the soul,* without which we should have no knowledge whatsoever, but of *which we are seldom even conscious.*"[28] When he writes later that "the imagination has to bring the manifold of intuition into an image," Kant remarks in a footnote that "no psychologist so far has realized that the imagination is a necessary ingredient of perception itself" (A120). Corresponding to the empirical, reproductive imagination, which produces particular images, he goes on to posit the pure, productive (transcendental) imagination, which generates general *schemata,* "through which and in accordance with which images are possible in the first place" (A141/B181). If the schematism is one of the harder

notions to fathom in the first *Critique,* there is comfort in Kant's own characterization of it as "a concealed art in the depths of the human soul, whose
true manipulations we can hardly ever prise from nature and lay open to
our gaze."

While this topic deserves extensive treatment, its relevance can at least
be summed up as follows: Kant thinks that knowledge of the world is possible only on the basis of a deep-level, unconscious imaginative activity that
helps constitute our experience in general.[29] This idea is taken up by Schiller
in *On the Aesthetic Education of Man* (1795) and is elaborated by Fichte
and Schelling, who integrated the idea of creative imagination into a central
role in their respective systems of idealism.[30]

By contrast with the imagination, the idea of *Triebe* is of lesser importance in the Kantian philosophy. It does, however, figure in one of Kant's
last works, *Religion within the Limits of Reason Alone* (1793); and since it
occurs in the context of vegetal imagery and some significant personifications, it is worth a brief consideration here. Kant mentions three drives as
constitutive of the human "predisposition for animality": the drive for self-
preservation, for propagation (sexual drive), and for community (social
drive).[31] Kant denies that vices "stem naturally from this predisposition as
a root," but adds that "all kinds of vices can be grafted onto it." The propensity for evil, which he regards as "something deeply rooted" in human nature, stems from the fact that the human being adopts into the maxim for
conduct not only the moral law but also "motive forces *[Triebfeder]* of his
sensual nature" (6:175; 31). Whether a human being is good or evil is then
a matter of the *order* that obtains between the two kinds of *Triebfeder* within
the maxim that regulates his behavior:

> The distinction between a good man and one who is evil cannot lie in
> the difference between the motive forces which they adopt into their
> maxim, but rather must depend on *subordination: on which of the two*
> *he makes the condition of the other. . . .* One must be subordinated to
> the other as its supreme condition. (6:175–76; 31–32)

The second book of this work concerns "the conflict of the good with
the evil principle for sovereignty *[Herrschaft]* over the human being," and
begins as follows:

> To become morally good it is not enough merely to allow the seed of
> goodness implanted in our species to develop without hindrance;
> there is also present in us an active and opposing cause of evil to be
> combatted. . . . [The Stoics] mistook their enemy, [who is] not to be
> sought in the merely undisciplined natural inclinations . . . [but is
> rather] as it were an invisible foe who screens himself behind reason
> and is therefore all the more dangerous. (6:197; 50).

In a footnote at this point Kant emphasizes the necessity of recognizing the presence of wickedness as "another opponent in the human subject, with whom virtue must join combat," failing which recognition "the rebellion is often stilled, but the rebel himself not conquered and exterminated." It is this emphasis on the evil element in the human will that makes Kant's prescription more sophisticated than those of Plato and the Stoics, to which it is otherwise similar:

> Natural inclinations, *considered in themselves,* are *good,* that is, not a matter of reproach, and it is not only futile to want to extirpate them but to do so would be harmful and blameworthy. Rather, let them be tamed and instead of clashing with one another they can be brought into harmony in a wholeness which is called happiness. (6:198; 51)

Observing that it makes little difference, practically speaking, whether we take the seducer to be within ourselves or outside, Kant writes that it is not surprising that the "the Apostle" (Paul) represents "the *invisible* enemy" as being outside us: "We struggle not with flesh and blood (natural inclinations), but with princes and powers—with evil spirits."[32] He then proceeds to discuss "the personified idea of the good principle" (6:201; 54) and the "struggle of the good and evil principles with each other," again in personified terms:

> Holy Scripture sets forth this intelligible moral relationship in the form of a narrative, in which two principles in the human being, as opposed to one another as is heaven to hell, are represented as persons outside him; who not only pit their strength against each other but also seek to establish their claims *legally* as though before a supreme judge. (6:221; 73).

The rest of Kant's discussion of how to combat the sovereignty of the evil principle is pursued in terms of the persons and princes of light and darkness.

This kind of discourse of *domination* is developed and expanded in the *Sturm und Drang* movement, for which Herder had been the primary spokesman, and which increasingly employs metaphors of political power. Typical here is Schiller's *On the Aesthetic Education of Man,* which has been aptly and elegantly characterized as "a sustained equivoque on political states and states of the human mind."[33] As mentioned earlier, Schiller anticipated with his idea of the sense- and form-drives Nietzsche's conception of the Apollonian and Dionysian as drives in constant interplay. In this text the idea is part of a larger project of maximizing human freedom by forming the forces that comprise the personality into a harmonious totality, in the context of the establishment of a moral political state.

In the fourth letter, Schiller characterizes the task as a bringing of the natural drives of the human being into harmony with the motives *(Triebfeder)* issuing from human reason. (At this point he refers in a footnote to a recently published work by his "friend Fichte," to which we shall shortly turn.) This task has become especially difficult in the modern age, where "[thanks to] the increasingly complex machinery of State . . . the inner unity of human nature was severed too, and a disastrous conflict set its harmonious powers at variance" (sixth letter). The situation in which the intuitive and speculative parts of the soul are set against one another brings to light a tyrannical tendency on their part:

> with this confining of our activity to a single sphere, we have given ourselves a master within, who not infrequently ends by suppressing the rest of our potentialities. While in the one a riotous imagination ravages the hard-won fruits of the intellect, in another the spirit of abstraction stifles the fire at which the heart should have warmed itself and phantasy been kindled.

It is this tendency toward tyrannical domination that made the question of educational strategy—whether to cultivate the strongest talent specially or all talents equally—such a pressing one for Schiller (as well as for Nietzsche).

Those undertaking the task of creating ethical character would do well, Schiller says, to emulate the way of Nature, as a way of mitigating the power of "blind drives":

> The strife of elements in moral man, the conflict of blind drives, has first to be appeased, and crude antagonisms first have ceased within him, before we can take the risk of promoting multiplicity. On the other hand, the independence of his character must first have become secure, and subjection to external forms of despotism have given way to a becoming liberty, before the multiplicity within him can be subjected to any ideal unity. (seventh letter)

While Nietzsche was surely influenced by Schiller's formulation of the problem, and would agree on the importance of working toward a solution of it (we shall see him engage precisely the problem of the *risk* of promoting multiplicity), he will be highly suspicious of any programs proposing to subject "the multiplicity within . . . to any ideal unity."

Schiller's discussion of the drives again associates them with the imagination (and again prefigures Nietzsche's ideas). The saving grace in the dismal political situation of modernity is, for Schiller, art; and both the production and the appreciation of art depend on the driving power of the imagination. Just as the imagination, through its links with memory, has a special relation to the past, it also, through the figure of the poet, presages the future of a culture.

> Even before Truth's triumphant light can penetrate the recesses of the human heart, the poet's imagination *[Dichtungskraft]* will intercept its rays, and the peaks of humanity will be radiant while the dews of night still linger in the valley. (ninth letter)

In his concern to avoid the dryness of the philosophical term *Einbildungskraft,* Schiller tends to use more poetic synonyms—or when he does use the philosophical term, he leavens its meaning by association with the idea of *play.* In describing how the artist effects the synthesis of the possible with the necessary, he writes of his "setting the stamp of [the ideal] upon the play of his imagination." The artist is able to effect this synthesis (just as in Herder) insofar as "the divine formative drive *[Bildungstrieb]*" operates through him.

The highest level of imagination, for Schiller, is manifested in the operations of the "play-drive" *(Spieltrieb),* which arises from the confluence of the two basic drives toward matter and form (fourteenth letter). He again anticipates Nietzsche in understanding the play-drive as underlying not only "the whole edifice of aesthetic art" but also "the more difficult art of living" (fifteenth letter). The kind of play in question is serious as well as joyful, and ordered by rules rather than anarchic. The inclination for play is associated with "joy in *Schein,*" insofar as the play-drive is accompanied by "the aesthetic art-drive." It is in the "world of *Schein*" alone, in "the insubstantial realm of the imagination," that the human being has the freedom to create according to his own laws. But for Schiller, as for Nietzsche, it is not a matter of arbitrary phantasy but of conforming to the "absolute legislation of the imagination" (twenty-sixth letter).

A more extensive treatment of the idea of the drives—and another that ascribes to them imaginative activity—is to be found in Fichte's *Wissenschaftslehre,* and specifically in its earliest incarnation as the *Foundation of the Entire Doctrine of Science* of 1794.[34] In Fichte's idealism, the I *(das Ich)* is understood as an activity (rather than a substance or thing) that "posits" itself as determined by the not-I and also as determining the not-I. The activity of the I consists in an "outward drive" *(Trieb nach aussen)* that would strive to infinity if it were not at some point "checked" and "driven back" *(zurückgetrieben)* by something foreign and alien to it: the "not-I."[35] Insofar as the I feels itself checked in its infinite striving, it posits a corresponding counterstriving, a force *(Kraft)* working against the activity of the I (1:286–87). The activity of the I, then, is a drive, which Fichte defines as "a self-productive striving that is fixed, determinate, and definite," an inner activity that drives toward the outside (287–88). A similar ascription of primacy to a force emerging from the interior—characteristic of the philosophy of Leibniz—is found in another work from the same year, where Fichte writes:

> Drive is the first and foremost in human beings. And impulse demands its object in advance of any kind of knowledge and in advance of the object's existence. It simply demands something, even if what it demands does not exist at all. What can and will make us happy is determined in advance by our drives.[36]

This passage could well serve, as we shall see, as a motto for Nietzsche's understanding of the drives. Fichte then proceeds to characterize the major goal of humanity, which he sees as never attainable but always to be striven for, in terms of power and domination: "The final end of the human being is to subordinate to himself all that is irrational, to master it freely and according to his own laws" (6:299). This ambition is more directly expressed in one of Fichte's best known works, *Die Bestimmung des Menschen* (1800), where the I, at the initial stage of "Doubt," strives after a condition in which it is not determined by any powers other than its own:

> Then shall the power that is determined by my will and subject to its dominion reach into the world of nature. I will be the master of nature, and she shall be my servant; I will have an influence on her according to my power, but she shall have none on me.[37]

While much of Nietzsche's talk of the drives will be couched in similar terms of power and domination, the goal of such absolute mastery of nature is quite foreign to him.

In the *Wissenschaftslehre,* Fichte goes on to argue that a "feeling" in the I signifies a restriction of a drive, that particular feelings will represent particular drives, and that each particular drive determines what is to be posited as its object: "If the drive is determined as Y, for example [say, hunger], then not-Y [no hunger] must necessarily be posited as its object" (1:290). He then adds a parenthesis that again prefigures Nietzsche's understanding:

> But since all these functions of the soul take place according to necessary laws, we do not become conscious of our own action, and are necessarily bound to assume that we have received from without what we have in fact ourselves produced by our own forces, and according to our own laws.

Fichte later reiterates the point by rejecting "the assumption that our acting and willing are dependent on the system of our presentations *[Vorstellungen]*"; rather "our system of presentations depends on our drive and our

will." For Nietzsche, the drives eventually come to be associated—or identified—with will to power.

The autonomy of the drives is discussed in more detail in the third of
Fichte's "Lectures concerning the Scholar's Vocation."

> All drives have their foundation in our nature—but no more than their
> foundation. Every drive has to be *awakened* by experience before we
> can become conscious of it. . . . Experience, however, is not depen-
> dent on us; neither, therefore, is the awakening and the development
> of our own drives at all dependent on us.
>
> The independent not-I, considered as the basis of experience, that
> is, *nature,* is something manifold. . . . Before we can freely resist na-
> ture's influence on us, we must have become conscious of our free-
> dom and able to use it. This state, however, can be attained in no other
> manner except by the awakening and development of our drives—
> something which does not depend on us. (6:313–14)

It would seem from this account that the extent to which an individual is
capable of exercising his or her freedom, and to cease being wholly under
the sway of the drives, is largely a matter of chance—insofar as "the awakening and development of our drives" is not something over which we have
any control. (We shall see Nietzsche ascribe a similar degree of autonomy—initially, at least—to the drives.) Insofar as we appear to have *some*
choice concerning the kinds of experiences we expose ourselves to, we
would to that extent be able to *participate* in—if not fully determine—the
awakening and development of our drives. But Fichte's questioning of the
extent to which experience is really "not dependent on us" is presumably
motivated by a realization (shared by Schopenhauer and Nietzsche) of the
extent to which external circumstances appear to limit the range of our
choice in this matter.

Another text from 1794 begins with the observation that an interest in
truth is based on an internal drive, on one of "our pure drives," the drive for
truth.[38] Based as it is on a drive, such an interest cannot, for Fichte, "be
produced, "though it can be *heightened:* it is an activity that must be stimulated from outside "without any conscious assistance from us" (8:343). The
origin of the freedom that would enable us to "heighten" a drive (and, presumably, to "diminish" another), and thereby act in the moral realm, thus
remains obscure. What first makes it possible for the I to act in a way that
is not determined by a drive, or to choose to heighten one of the pure, as
opposed to the natural, drives?

> This first act of freedom, this breaking loose from the chains of neces-
> sity, is something that occurs without our knowing how. . . . From
> somewhere a spark of fire falls into our soul, where it will perhaps

glow for a long time in hidden darkness. Then it flares up and spreads, until it eventually inflames the entire soul. (8:343)

A passage in *Schopenhauer as Educator* concerning the "drive for justice" as one of the many drives that motivate the scholar employs strikingly similar imagery:

> For if a spark from the fire of justice fall into the soul of a scholar, it can eventually come to glow throughout his life and striving, purifying and consuming them, so that he no longer has any rest and is forever driven out of the tepid or frosty mood in which most scholars do their daily work. (*SE* 6)

The similarity leads one to suspect another instance of what Jung calls cryptomnesia—that Nietzsche at some point read the passage from Fichte, forgot having read it, and then later employed similar imagery without being aware of its source. In any case, we shall see Nietzsche later confront the same enigma concerning the genesis of the freedom of the I, as drive, with respect to other drives.

Fichte then observes that a drive can be "cultivated" *(ausgebildet)* by means of pleasure, going on to ask whether some among the higher drives—and which ones—should be subordinated to others. He hastens to answer that "the aesthetic drive is to be subordinated to the drive for truth, and also to the highest drive of all, the drive for moral goodness" (8:344). The mystery remains, however, concerning not only how one is to gain the freedom to arrange an order of rank among the higher drives (as opposed to the drives' arranging it themselves), but also—more importantly—*who* it is that gains such freedom. Fichte's answer would, of course, be "the I"; but the relations of identity or difference that obtain between the I (itself a drive) and the drives are left unexamined and undetermined.[39]

Fichte concludes the *Wissenschaftslehre* with a lengthy "deduction of the main drives of the I," coming up with a "drive to real activity," a "drive to reflection," a "drive to determine," a "drive toward change in general," and a "drive toward reality."[40] Drives, through being checked, lead to "the action of the I's reflecting on itself," and this gives rise to "the presentational drive" *(Vorstellungstrieb)* which he characterizes as "the primary and highest expression of drive [through which] the I first becomes an intelligence" (1:293–94). But the highest drive of all turns out to be the "drive for harmony," which is equivalent to the "drive for interdetermination" through the I itself, "the drive for absolute *unity* and completeness of the I in itself."[41]

In subsequent elaborations of his theory, Fichte ends up with a fairly conventional distinction between "nature-drives" and "pure drives" that are able, thanks to the consciousness that comes from reflection, to organize the lower drives. The origin of this freedom and the nature of its agent still, however, remain obscure. Nevertheless, his system is important as the first comprehensive philosophy in which the idea of drives plays a fundamental role, and for its emphasis on the drives as powers operating beneath the level of consciousness that profoundly inform our experience. Even though Fichte's concern with the unity of the I, his idea that there is a kind of moral imperative to unify the natural dispersion of the self, is couched in terms that would be too traditional for Nietzsche's taste, it nevertheless constitutes an important precursor of the latter's own project (as we shall come to appreciate after the next two chapters).[42]

Fichte follows and elaborates Kant's ideas about the major role of the transcendental imagination and its schematism in the constitution of experience, thereby also anticipating some of Nietzsche's ideas concerning creative phantasy. In introducing the imagination as that which makes possible the "interplay" between subjective and objective, Fichte makes the quite Nietzschean proposal of initiating "an experiment with the wonderful power of productive imagination in ourselves, without which [experiment] nothing at all in the human mind is capable of explanation."[43] In Fichte's system, it is "through the imagination, which unites what is contradictory" that the opposites of the I and the not-I are joined together (1:218). Later its indispensable role is made even more explicit:

> All reality—*for us* being understood, as it cannot be otherwise understood in a system of transcendental philosophy—is brought forth solely by the imagination. . . . On this activity of the imagination is grounded the possibility of our consciousness, our life, our being for ourselves, that is, our being as I. (1:227)

Again, speaking of "creative imagination," Fichte writes of it as

> something that all human beings are quite certainly endowed with, since without it they would have no presentations at all; though by no means all of them have it at their command, to create therewith in a purposeful manner, or if, in a fortunate hour, the required image should appear before their soul like a flash of lightning, to seize the image, examine it, and to register it inerasably for whatever use they wish. It is this power that determines whether or not we philosophize with spirit. (1:284)

Even if Nietzsche did not read much Fichte, the latter's ideas would have exerted an indirect influence on him early in his career through the mediation of his favorite poet, Hölderlin. By the time Fichte was called to the University of Jena in 1794, he was already a celebrity (at the age of thirty-one). Hölderlin was just one of several luminaries in the audience for the lectures Fichte gave during his first two years at Jena, in which the idea of the drives figured prominently. (Other "Romantics" influenced by Fichte in Jena at this time were Novalis and Friedrich Schlegel—both also alumni of Schulpforta.) Fichte's philosophy made a deep impression on Hölderlin, which is evidenced especially in his *Hyperion,* the complete version of which was published in 1799.

Since Hölderlin was a protégé of Schiller's as well as an admirer of Fichte, it is not surprising that he should understand the drives as basic motive forces of the human being. In a letter to his brother (4 June 1799), Hölderlin writes of "the primordial human drive to idealize, or to elaborate, rework, develop and perfect" what nature has wrought. He sees it as one of the major problems of the modern age that this drive, "which animated the ancestors," is now weakened, and he regards the cultivation of "the art-and shaping-drive" *(der Kunst- und Bildungstrieb)* as a service that we render to nature by means of philosophy (which brings the drive to consciousness), the arts (which provide living images of it), and religion (which shows the drive that the "higher world" is to be found right there, in nature itself). Hölderlin does not, however, follow Fichte in his drive to dominate the not-I of nature, but advocates, in contrast, a reunion with nature on a higher plane (an idea taken up later by Nietzsche). In an early version of *Hyperion,* he writes: "The school of fate and custom had made me, although innocently, unjust and tyrannical against nature. . . . I did not accept the readiness with which nature offers reason her hands, for I wanted to dominate her."[44]

Psychological Ramifications

Among the many philosophers influenced by Fichte was J. F. Herbart, who is perhaps better known as the founder of a school of pedagogy and the creator of a theory of "dynamic associationism" in psychology. While it is unlikely that Nietzsche read Herbart, the latter is important as the inspirer of the "dynamic psychiatry" of the late nineteenth century and as a precursor of Nietzsche's ideas on psychical multiplicity. Nietzsche certainly read *about* Herbart in the course of his intensive study of F. A. Lange's *History of Materialism.* Lange engages in a discussion of Herbart's mathematical psychology, in which he points out the inconsistency of holding, as Herbart does, that the soul is absolutely simple and unitary and also that it consists in a multiplicity of states or ideas.[45]

While Herbart does talk of drives, the more relevant notion is his conception of ideas (*Vorstellungen,* presentations) as *forces,* as dynamic powers within the soul that are capable of banding together and disbanding, rising above and sinking below the "threshold of consciousness," and inhibiting and repressing each other. Although in his *Lehrbuch zur Psychologie* (Manual of psychology) Herbart steadfastly holds to the "unity of the soul," he also speaks of the "characteristic self" of each person as a "complex" *(Complexion)* to which "supplements" are constantly being added and fused in the course of the person's life.[46] He adds in a significant parenthesis:

> If this did not happen, the unity of the person would be lost, which does in fact happen in some kinds of insanity, in which a new I *[ein neues Ich]* is produced from a particular group of ideas that is functioning separately, from which there arises a changing personality when the groups of ideas alternately enter consciousness. (404)

At the same time as he asserts the unity of the person, Herbart also clearly implies the possibility of its duplexity—if only in pathological cases—insofar as a group of ideas constituting a "new I" can set itself up in opposition to the group that forms the original I. His ambivalence is reinforced by a note added to the second edition (1834), and especially by the tension between the emphasized phrase and the double negative that follows it:

> In every human being, the I often generates itself in a variety of idea-groups; and although in the mentally healthy person *no multiple I* arises from this, this multiplicity is nevertheless not insignificant for character-formation generally and morality in particular. (405)

While Herbart's psychology often turns highly abstract and technical—there can be pages at a time almost devoid of words and filled with mathematical formulas representing the complicated dynamics of the psychical system—it also contains a discourse (no doubt deriving from Fichte) that characterizes the relations between groups of ideas in terms of power and domination. A chapter entitled "On the Uncontrolled Play of the Psychical Mechanism" deals with the topic of "self-mastery" *(Selbstbeherrschung)* the possibility of which depends on "the working together of several idea-groups" (419). Purposive behavior depends on

> the power of the *dominant idea-group,* in which the willing of the main intention resides, over the rest of the idea-groups that are subordinated to it in various hierarchies. There is no lack of evidence to show how tyrannically the dominant will can often sacrifice all minor wishes, so that a single prejudice or a single passion can, as it were, devastate and lay waste the entire soul.

Herbart goes on to suggest that "the conditions for self-mastery . . . lie in the relationships between the ruling and the subordinate idea-groups" (421). He speaks of how an unfulfilled desire gathers around it a mass of ideas that turn first into phantasies and then into a kind of thinking. This leads him to the interesting conclusion—one anticipated by Herder and also reached later by Nietzsche—that a passion, thanks to its association with concepts, can be said to have its own understanding, or that a passion can work *as* a kind of understanding and so is not necessarily opposed to reason.[47] Again, Herbart is forced into talking about multiplicities when he would clearly rather not:

> We have spoken here of *more than one* understanding, and so we must if we think of understanding as a *force* or as an *ability*. For the effectiveness, the mental energy, lies nowhere other than in particular idea-groups; and there are many of these and many different kinds of them, *all of which can operate as understanding*. The same is true of the imagination, the memory, and reason—in short of all the so-called faculties of the soul. (422; last emphasis added)

Thus, Herbart concludes, when we speak of *"one* understanding, *one* imagination, and so on," we are employing names of logical classes that do not refer to anything actual. In the face of this multiplicity, Herbart proceeds quickly to a consideration of what he calls "moral self-mastery," and to a Kantian account of the way "moral judgments" are capable, through their connections with "strong groups of thoughts," of overpowering the idea-groups that constitute immoral desires (423–24).

The book finishes with a chapter entitled "Psychological Observations on the Determination of the Human Being," in the course of which Herbart draws the parallel between the well-ordered soul and the well-ordered political state.[48] The happy end is that the best characters will be those in which (Kantian) moral maxims hold greatest sway.

Herbart's ideas play an important role in one of the most remarkable contributions to nineteenth-century psychiatry, a book on the pathology and therapy of psychical illnesses by Wilhelm Griesinger. *Die Pathologie und Therapie der psychischen Krankheiten* is a monumental work published in 1845, when the author was only twenty-eight. Griesinger went on to become the first director of the famous Burghölzli mental hospital in Zürich and also the founder of university psychiatry. Influenced by the philosophy of German Idealism, he synthesized elements from Herbart's dynamic associationism and some ideas from Schopenhauer into one of the first comprehensive psychologies of the ego.[49] While it is unlikely that Nietzsche was familiar with Griesinger's work, several features of it are worth considering as precursors of Nietzsche's ideas—and as a framework for understanding his psychology in the more personal sense.

One of the basic premises of Griesinger's psychology concerns the importance of unconscious psychical activity, which he regards as "much greater and more determinative for individuality than are the relatively few

conscious ideas."[50] Like Herder, though with a more comprehensive understanding of the nervous system available to him, Griesinger stresses the importance of *Reiz,* and emphasizes the phenomenon of *projection,* which is
germane to both perception of the external world and to ideation *(Vorstell-
en)* within the psyche, especially in the process of phantasy (§18). The
drives also play an important role, and Griesinger distinguishes (following
Fichte) between sensual drives—for nourishment and sex—and spiritual
drives—for knowing, collecting, family, love of children (§23). He emphasizes that the foundation of human drives consists not only in feelings but
also in idea-groups *(Vorstellungsmassen),* though these are by their very
nature dark and obscure. Again the motif of struggle is prominent: "in the
desires and drives . . . certain idea-groups (relating to the condition to be
attained) struggle against the circumstances that oppose them," and these
idea-groups seek to affect the motor apparatus in their drive toward external
expression (§24). In cases where the idea-groups that constitute the drives
come to clear consciousness, we talk of "willing."[51]

Griesinger's discussion of the drives leads him naturally to a consideration of the nature and scope of the freedom exercisable by the I. It is not
simply the case that when a drive (or idea-group) attains sufficient strength
it translates itself into activity, since there often comes into play a principle
derived from associationist psychology, according to which a presentation
that becomes sufficiently strong and enduring will call forth an opposite or
contrasting idea.[52] This prevents the drive from attaining discharge: "There
then arises in consciousness a conflict. The entire idea-group that represents
the I is brought into play and makes the final decision by either repressing
or favoring the original idea" (§26). Several conditions must be fulfilled if
the individual is to gain some degree of freedom with respect to the drives:

> He must have a mass of well-ordered ideas that are easily evoked by
> each other, and from which is formed a strong kernel, the I. . . . The
> association among ideas must be unhindered, so that, around the ideas
> that are on the point of becoming will, other, newly arising ideas may
> gather in order to oppose them. One must also have a strong I that is
> capable of tipping the scales, by having its idea-complex strengthen
> one of the parties in the opposing ideas and thereby repress the other.

The picture is reminiscent of Herbart's—with the I understood as a group
of ideas or presentations—except that the idea of the drives is more prominent and there is correspondingly less insistence on the unity of the psyche.
Griesinger goes on to say that freedom depends on the ability of "the idea-
complex of the I" to influence and inform the process of willing, framing
the issue, once again, in terms of mastery:

[Freedom depends on] the domination of the I over current strivings, on the possibility of self-mastery. The more compact and unitary the I, the stronger the character, the more decisively the I can shout its yes or no into the driving forces of the current ideas.

It is interesting that Griesinger calls the process that makes such domination possible *Besonnenheit* ("reflection"; §27)—a favorite term of Herder's.

Griesinger is more open than Herbart was to the possibility of multiple centers of awareness, and he goes farther than any of his predecessors in inquiring into the nature of the I that is the agent of freedom in the soul. He begins with Herbart's idea that the idea-group that constitutes the I can be augmented in the course of an individual's life, but he then qualifies the I as "an abstraction" and introduces an important *personal* element.

The I is an abstraction . . . that in the progression of psychical processes constantly takes in new content. But this assimilation . . . takes place very gradually, and what has not yet been assimilated at first appears in opposition to the I, as a *you* within the individual. Eventually . . . several closed, articulated, and strengthened idea-groups [similar to that constituting the I] are formed; two (and not only two) souls then live in the human breast, and according to whether one or the other of these idea-groups predominates, *all of which can represent the I,* the I is transformed or is split within itself. (§28; emphasis added)

We saw Herbart raise the possibility of a second I, only to reject it; but Griesinger's allusion to the duplexity within the breast of Goethe's Faust introduces the possibility of several I's, and in broaching the possibility of a "you" within the psyche he opens up the way for a *dialogical* understanding of the psyche.[53] He goes on:

Our I is something very different at different times, according to whether age, the various duties in life, experiences, momentary excitations of these or those, or the idea-group representing the I are more highly developed and have pressed into the foreground. We are "another and yet the same." My I as a doctor, my I as a scholar, my sensual I, my moral I, and so on—the complexes of ideas, drives, and vectors of will denoted by these words—can come into conflict with each other, and one of them can at various times repress the others.

Griesinger apparently was writing here from direct, personal experience, as the following passage from an obituary by a younger colleague makes clear:

For in a sense there was not just one personality in [Griesinger]: there were not only two, but ten, and—if you will—a hundred human beings in him. His soul was like a vast building containing countless rooms and chambers.[54]

One last feature of Griesinger's picture is worth mentioning, which has to do with his understanding of moods and affects as falling into two classes, "affirmative" and "negative."

> From the slightest mood *[Stimmung]* to the most raging affect, there are two possibilities: either a condition of furthering and expansion of the I, in which the I has a feeling of well-being and so behaves affirmatively toward the new process in consciousness and seeks to retain it; or a condition of inhibition, repression and depression, in which the idea-complexes of the I are checked and thrown back in their flowing toward striving . . . and where the I thus behaves negatively toward the new ideas. (§32)

It was some twenty years later, shortly before the publication of the second edition of Griesinger's book, that Nietzsche would pen his account of moods as tensions arising from the accommodation of new guests in the boarding house of the soul.

VIII

Dominions of Drives and Persons *(1869–1887)*

With sufficient background sketched in, the present chapter traces the development of Nietzsche's thinking about the drives, giving special attention to the ways it issues in discourses concerning persons. The talk of drives, though apparently more theoretical than imagistic discourse, turns out to be deeply implicated in personal and transpersonal imagery. We have touched on the topic of the drives frequently in the course of the preceding chapters; but since the notion is germane to Nietzsche's psychology, appearing throughout his works from the earliest to the latest, it is worthwhile to consider its development in detail.[1] Such consideration calls for another pass through Nietzsche's works, one that runs parallel to (and in some sense beneath) the development of his imagery traced in earlier chapters.

Tyrannical Drives, Engaging Persons

> *The secret of the world is the tie between person and event. Person makes event, and event person. . . . The soul contains the event that shall befall it . . . Thus events grow on the same stem with persons; are sub-persons.*
>
> Emerson, "Fate"

Not only does Nietzsche's "On Moods" contain the first instance in his work of the political metaphor for the psyche (civil war, oppression of the people by a minority class), but it also has the first mention of the drives: "How often the will sleeps and only the drives and inclinations are awake!"[2] The first public talk of the drives is in the inaugural lecture of 1869, in association with a political metaphor. Nietzsche offers a genealogy of philology as a joining together of "completely heterogeneous scientific and ethico-aesthetic drives . . . under a common name, under a kind of seeming monarchy *[Scheinmonarchie]*" (S 3:157). In view of the description in "On Moods" of the various factions vying for power within the psyche, one

274 Dominions of Drives and Persons

might well ask how well a nominalism, the merely apparent monarchy of the name, will be able to hold these differing drives together. And when he reemphasizes "the diversity—enmity even—of the basic drives that have been put together, though not fused, under the name philology," and observes that their mutual hostility necessitates the application of "force" if they are to be made to "grow together" (S 3:159–61), Nietzsche is articulating a feature of the drives that remains germane throughout his thinking about them.

There also appears in this lecture an idea the immediate source of which was presumably Wagner (it is not found in works after 1870)—that of the "folk-drive" *(Volkstrieb)*. Nietzsche entertains the idea of "a mysterious streaming forth, a profound artistic folk-drive that manifests itself in the individual lyrist as an almost indifferent medium," and of "the Homeric poems as the expression of that mysteriously flowing drive" (S 3:166). Though denying that it helps elucidate the Homeric question, Nietzsche suggests that an important consequence of the discovery of the "folk-soul" *(Volksseele)* was that people came to see "the great mass-instincts, the unconscious folk-drives [as] the bearers and levers of so-called world history" (S 3:167). This adds to the picture of the drives as multiple and mutually antagonistic their being collective and impersonal and capable of operating unconsciously.

In notes from the autumn of 1869, Nietzsche associates the folk-drives of the Greeks with the festivals of Dionysus, contrasting them with the "conscious knowledge" that hampers the development of modern art:

> With the Greeks the origins of drama go back to the incomprehensible expressions of folk-drives: in those orgiastic festivals of Dionysus there reigned such a degree of being-outside-oneself, of *ekstasis,* that people felt and behaved like persons transformed and enchanted.[3]

Here is a prefiguration of the effects of the Dionysian drive as discussed in *The Birth of Tragedy:* the power of the collective drive can efface the empirical personality. Another note from the same year adds a new dimension in saying that *music* is "through and through symbolic of the drives."[4] It is surprising, in view of Nietzsche's love of music, that he leaves this theme undeveloped—though perhaps it comes too close to Schopenhauer's idea that music is the most profound of the arts in being a direct expression of the Will, unmediated by language or images. Each theme in a sonata or symphony, for example, could be imagined as representing a particular drive, with the subsequent development and eventual resolution of tension between themes mirroring ways the drives interact with each other in the human psyche. In a concerto, the solo instrument would stand for the complex of drives that makes up the I, while the orchestra would represent all the other drives. A quartet would narrate the interactions among three or four drives of more or less equal status, with greater numbers of instruments representing greater psychical complexity. (Nietzsche was especially fond of the Beethoven Octet.)

In the essays from the few years before the publication of *The Birth of Tragedy,* Nietzsche introduces twenty or so drives by name, such as the scientific drive, the mythological drive, the political drive, the art-drive, and the seasonal spring-drive that he sees as the engenderer of tragedy.[5] (We saw earlier, in chapter 3, that a major concern during this period was with the problem of keeping "the indiscriminate drive for knowledge" in check, by balancing it with the forces of phantasy.) While the art-drive is associated with Apollo and the Olympian world, the spring-drive is said to manifest itself not only "in the rapturous rush of the Dionysian orgies" but also in the Eleusinian Mysteries.[6] But perhaps the most important comment on the operations of the drives is this: "Our entire drive-life *[Triebleben],* the play of feelings, sensations, affects, acts of will, is known to us—and here I must go against Schopenhauer—even under the most intense self-scrutiny only as representation, and not in its being."[7] The assertion here is that we are not aware of the drives directly, but only mediately, through ideas, images, and concepts. Nine years later Nietzsche will emphasize that "nothing can be more incomplete than one's image of the totality of drives that constitutes one's being" (*DM* 119), going on to talk of how they operate for the most part unconsciously.

One of the "psychological innovations" he ascribes in retrospect to *The Birth of Tragedy* is its picture of the multiple psyche. The Dionysian drive is said to have the effect of nullifying the *principium individuationis* by breaking down the barriers separating the person from the world, so that (according to the paradigm of the Dionysian artist) it is the "I" at the ground of all things that speaks through him. But this dissolution is also a dismemberment—"the authentically Dionysian *suffering*"—of the unitary personality into a multiplicity, as suggested in this striking characterization of the poet (as a paradigm of the psychologically creative human being generally):

> The poet is a poet only insofar as he sees himself surrounded by figures who live and act before him and into whose innermost being he sees. . . . A character is not a composite of particular traits gathered together, but rather a strikingly alive person before his eyes, distinguished from the otherwise similar vision of the painter only by its continuing to live and act. . . . Basically the aesthetic phenomenon is simple: if one is able constantly to be viewing a living play and to live

surrounded by hosts of spirits, one will be a poet; if one feels the drive
to transform oneself and speak out of other bodies and souls, one will
be a dramatist. (*BT* 8)

By virtue of the power of Dionysus one can resolve oneself into a plurality
of persons and play, thanks to the patron deity of masks, a variety of parts
in the drama of life. This picture of life as a play of vital interactions with
"living and acting" persons of the imagination is attested by depth psychology as well as by dramatists and novelists who have chosen to write about
the experience of literary creation.[8] One can imagine Wagner's regaling his
young admirer with vivid accounts of his personal experience while writing
The Ring.

A strange fragment from the unpublished notes from the end of 1872
suggests a relation to an inner voice that is different from that in the note
from a few years earlier that spoke of the "terrifyingly inarticulate and inhu-
man tone" of the voice of the figure behind his chair (S 3:148). The fragment bears the title "Oedipus: Conversations of the Last Philosopher with
Himself."

> I call myself the last philosopher, for I am the last human being. No
> one talks to me but I myself, and my voice comes to me as the voice
> of a dying man. With you, dear voice, with you, the last breath of the
> memory of all human happiness, may I spend just one hour more.
> Through you I deceive my way out of solitude and lie my way into
> multitude and love, for my heart . . . cannot bear the terror of the lone-
> liest loneliness and compels me to talk as if I were two. Do I still hear
> you, my voice? You whisper as you curse?[9]

To the extent that this fragment can be read autobiographically, it represents
from the psychotherapeutic perspective considerable progress over the previous encounter. The voice is now sufficiently articulate to permit an inner
dialogue—even though the use of the words "deceive" and "lie" suggests
that the writer is not fully convinced of the truth of his recent assertion
concerning the reality of the persons, bodies, souls, and spirits with whom
the poet/dramatist converses in the course of his work.

A few years later, in the context of a discussion of "the unconsciousness
of drives" and the "strange condition" in which unpleasant memories spontaneously assert themselves against our will, circumstances that engender
in us "fear of memory and turning within [*Erinnerung und Verinnerlich-
ung*]," there is more talk of voices:

> We are constantly surrounded and approached by spirits; every mo-
> ment of our lives wants to say something to us, but we do not want to
> hear this spirit-voice. We are afraid that when we are alone and silent,

that something will be whispered in our ear, and so we hate silence and deafen ourselves with sociability. (*SE* 5)

Just as the voice that whispered in "the loneliest loneliness" anticipates the voice of the demon who first suggests the possibility of the eternal recurrence (in *JS* 341), and who likewise approaches and whispers in "the loneliest loneliness," so these spirit-voices speak to us in our silent solitude, in a stillness that prefigures the stillness of death (*JS* 278).

After *The Birth of Tragedy* Nietzsche's psychological concerns move toward a genealogy of the "strikingly alive persons" introduced there, while at the same time his sense of the multiplicity of the self comes to be embodied in stylistic analogues and reflected in the different forms his writings begin to assume.

It is a main trait of the genealogical method to take what appears to be a unitary phenomenon and disclose its multiple origins, showing it to be generated by a plurality of drives. In the *Untimely Meditations* the drive for truth is said to be composed of "curiosity, fear of boredom, envy, vanity, the play-drive, drives that have nothing to do with truth" but are conflated with the truth-drive (*HL* 6). Correspondingly, the scholar "consists of a complicated network of very different drives and stimuli, he is an utterly impure metal"—to which alloy is added "a certain dialectical tracking and play-drive"; he is the result of "a pouring together of a host of small, very human drives and drivelets *[Triebchen!]*."[10] Four years later Nietzsche quotes these remarks, marking them *as* quotes but without referring to their origin, and adds that the same is true of the genealogy of "the artist, the philosopher, and the moral genius" (*HA* 252). This is apparently the first instance of self-quotation in Nietzsche's texts, a practice he was to engage in with increasing frequency over the years (usually citing the source), one with many hermeneutic and psychological implications concerning the convoluted textures of life and work.

The dithyrambic dramatist of *Wagner in Bayreuth* is an elaboration of the figure of the poet-dramatist in *The Birth of Tragedy,* and together they add up to Socrates' worst nightmare. Recall the latter's awareness of the seductive power of *mimēsis* and the tendency for imitating to become embodied as habit, and his concern to protect the young and impressionable guardians from its pernicious effects (*Rep.* 395). Nietzsche echoes this concern, in the context of the special problem of the artist in the modern era, when he writes: "Especially the artist in whom the innate power of imitation is particularly strong must fall prey to the feeble many-sidedness of modern life as to a serious childhood illness" (*WB* 2). This kind of remark is an expression of Nietzsche's early concerns with mastering his own inner multiplicity (substituting, as usual, "Nietzsche" for "Wagner" throughout). The essay's characterization of the youthful Wagner as being possessed by "a nervous hastiness in grasping a hundred things, a passionate pleasure in almost pathologically intense moods" is patently a portrait of the author himself as a young man. The condition of a "feeble many-sidedness" prefigures what for Nietzsche was a persistent problem, which one might call—adapting a phrase of Hegel's—"bad multiplicity."[11]

Just as Socrates was wary of the lower desires because of their tendency to dominate tyrannically the other powers of the soul, so Nietzsche (sensitized no doubt by his relationship with Wagner) was well aware of the tyrannical bent of any powerful drive. With reference to the way Wagner's nature was "torn apart into two drives" he writes, with pregnant restraint: "had it been connected with a narrow spirit, a will with such a boundlessly tyrannical desire could have become a fatality" (*WB* 2). And in Wagner's case, the danger stemming from the multiplicity of modern life is compounded by the situation within:

> Each of his drives strove into the immeasurable, and each of his talents—from joy in its own existence—wanted to tear itself away from the others to attain its own satisfaction; the greater their abundance, the greater was the tumult and the greater their hostility when they crossed one another.[12]

This vivid characterization alludes to the need for some kind of coordination among competing drives in order to avoid destructive chaos. At this point in his career (in the mid-1870s) Nietzsche ascribes to his subject a "ruling passion" that was able to "bring his entire nature together," and thereby get rid of all "fumbling, straying, and proliferation of subsidiary shoots" (*WB* 2). Wagner is said to have "remained loyal to his higher self, which demanded of him the total deeds of his many-voiced *[vielstimmig]* being" (*WB* 3). So far, the solution to the problem of inner multiplicity sounds consonant with the Platonic prescription—except that in Nietzsche the nature of this "higher self" remains obscure.

There is a divergence, as one would expect, when it comes to the artist. Nietzsche cites as the crux of Wagner's power his "daemonic *infectiousness*,"[13] which compels participation in his "effusive and overflowing nature" (*WB* 7). Thanks to this Dionysiac infectiousness, Wagner's art "lets us experience everything that a soul experiences that goes on a journey, participating in other souls and their fates, and learning to look into the world through many eyes." Capable in this way of "all species of changes," this kind of artist would clearly not "harmonize with [Plato's] regime," which is free from "double" or "manifold" men (*Rep.* 397d–e). As the archetypal "dithyrambic dramatist," Wagner is able "to think in all the arts at once" and thereby exercise upon the audience "the most uncanny and magnetic enchantment." Such a figure is, as Nietzsche remarks here, the epitome of the "imitative" artist—"who is able by wisdom to become every sort of thing and to imitate all things"—that Plato would have banished from the city (*Rep.* 398a). While for the author of the *Republic* such imitators are liable to "maim the thought of those who hear them" (595b), for Nietzsche the modern community incorporates "bad reason and power" and so the imitative artist can be enlisted in the struggle against these forces (*WB* 7).

Socrates ends his discussion of poets, rhapsodes, and their audience in the *Republic* on an uncharacteristically musical note that nevertheless reinforces the pro-Apollonian, anti-Dionysian tenor of his discourse. He is concerned to determine which musical instruments to allow in the city—an important question in view of the power of music to move the soul and affect its development.

> There'll be no need of many-toned or panharmonic instruments for our songs and melodies [or] . . . instruments that are many-stringed and play many modes. . . . [And] isn't the flute the most many-stringed of all, and aren't the panharmonic instruments themselves imitations of it? (*Rep.* 399c–d)

The use of such instruments would produce too many conflicting moods in the soul of the good citizen. But in thus "choosing Apollo and Apollo's instruments ahead of Marsyas and his instruments" (Marsyas, the hapless satyr whose temerity in challenging Apollo with the instruments of Dionysus was rewarded with a flaying alive), Socrates is also intimating that the city's treatment of polyphonic players would be less than gentle. (One shudders to contemplate Socrates' response to the Dionysian tones of the Wagnerian orchestra.)

The discussion in the *Untimely Meditations* concerning the two drives and the many is transposed in *Human, All Too Human* to an architectural setting:

> A human being makes the best discoveries concerning culture in himself when he finds two heterogeneous powers holding sway there. Supposing someone lives as much for love of the visual arts or of music as he is enraptured by the spirit of science, and he regards it as impossible to resolve this contradiction by annihilating one of the powers and giving the other completely free rein: the only alternative is for him to make himself into a large enough hall of culture that the two powers can dwell in him, even if at different ends of the building, while between them reside conciliatory mediating powers that possess sufficient strength to resolve any conflict that might break out. (*HA* 276)

Here the early metaphor of the boarding house of the soul is amplified by means of an opposition between two primary powers or drives. In the corresponding macrocosm, the task of "great cultural architecture" has been "to compel the contending powers into harmony by an overpowering assembly of the other, less quarrelsome powers, without thereby suppressing them or putting them in chains." Important here is that the conflict between two predominant powers is not resolved by a third party that is superior to them, but by an assembling of lesser forces situated *between* them.

Nietzsche goes on to present the same situation through a different metaphor that reiterates his continuing concern to avoid a fruitless dissipation of energies. The difficulty in sustaining the tension between the two powers stems from a tendency toward tyranny, insofar as "science presses for the absolute dominance of its methods":

> And yet if one does not give in to this pressure, there arises the other danger of a feeble vacillation back and forth between different drives. A metaphor may help to suggest how this difficulty might be resolved: one must remember that the *dance* is not the same as a languid reeling back and forth between different drives. High culture will resemble a daring dance: which is why one needs a great deal of suppleness and strength. (*HA* 278)

This aspiration of Nietzsche's to a high culture stemming from disciplined drives is central to his thinking—though generally overlooked by his detractors. The softer Nietzsche enthusiasts have done him a disservice in this respect, by ignoring the Apollonian discipline he thinks necessary for acquiring the suppleness and strength required for the true dance. Higher culture demands that a variety of drives be cultivated, but there must after all be some measure, some order imposed on them. The spontaneity of the dance is exemplary here, since it is by no means anarchic, but rather accommodates itself to the rhythms of the music. And indeed Nietzsche then moves to a musical metaphor in an aphorism that explains its title, "Why Higher Culture Is Necessarily Misunderstood." Here he declares himself musically a supporter of Marsyas—but of a Marsyas reconciled with Apollo—in advocating the many over the one and the two, bemoaning once again the narrowness of scholars.

> One who has furnished his instrument with only two strings, like the scholars who possess aside from the *drive for knowledge* only an acqured *religious* drive, does not understand people who are able to play on more strings than two. It lies in the nature of higher, *more many-sided* culture that it is always falsely interpreted by the lower. (*HA* 281)

In view of the need for order, it is not surprising that the topic of tyranny should figure prominently in discussions of the drives. People who are possessed by a powerful lust to rule *(Herrschsucht),* and yet are frustrated in finding opportunities for external discharge, "may eventually come to tyrannize certain parts of their own being, segments or stages, as it were, of themselves" *(HA* 137). The paradigm case of such a retroflection of the drive to control is the ascetic, though Nietzsche concludes that *in general* "the human being takes great pleasure in doing himself violence with exaggerated demands and in divinizing the tyrannically demanding agent in his soul." In the appropriate context, however, a certain kind of tyranny can be distinctly productive, as suggested in an aphorism entitled "Genius of Tyranny": "When there is active in the soul an invincible desire for tyrannical self-assertion, and the fire is kept going steadily, even a minor talent (in politicians or artists) will gradually become an irresistible force of nature" *(HA* 530). Nietzsche goes on to apply the political metaphor not only to desires and drives but also to concepts. By contrast with the "tyrants of the spirit" that were revered in third-century Athens or eighteenth-century France, modern heads are ruled by a "democracy of *concepts . . . many together* are master: a *single* concept that wanted to be master is now called an *'idée fixe'" (WS* 230). It is clear that Nietzsche is no more enthusastic about democracy in the state of the mind than in the external realm.

The problem of the one and the many with respect to the development of talents, first broached in agricultural terms in *Schopenhauer as Educator,* is now discussed in terms of a more sinister metaphor:

> For the individual himself the *uniform* development of his powers is surely more useful and productive of happiness; for every talent is a vampire that sucks the blood and strength from the other powers, and an overdriven production can bring the most gifted person close to madness.[14]

As Nietzsche sees it, this problem is more acute in the modern age than it was formerly. An aphorism entitled "Talent" reads:

> In a humanity as highly developed as ours now is, everyone acquires from nature access to many talents. Everyone has *inborn talent,* but in only a few is sufficient toughness, endurance, and energy inborn and instilled, so that the person really becomes a talent, and *becomes* what he *is*—such that it is discharged in works and actions. *(HA* 263)

Again we see how the problem of ordering the multiplicity of drives, with which Nietzsche has been concerned since his early youth, becomes more complex and more acute as he realizes how much it is compounded with the passing of the generations.

In the works that comprise the second volume of *Human, All Too Human* the talk of drives takes a turn toward the personal, as the focus of Nietzsche's philosophical inquiry changes and the circumstances of his life grant him greater solitude.

Thoughts as Personal Presences

As a background against which to sketch out Nietzsche's understanding of ideas as vital, dynamic presences in the psyche, it is helpful to consider Plato's conception of *logoi* as animate beings—a conception that is often ignored, or else dismissed as a quaint figure of speech or crude personification for the sake of dramatic effect. The true nature of *logoi,* as Plato understands them, is best approached in the context of Socrates' inclination, discussed earlier, to view the search for understanding as a kind of hunt, regarding the objects of knowledge as a species whose members are likely to be hard to catch and keep hold of.

The idea of *logoi*—words, speeches, discourses, arguments—as living beings is made most explicit in the *Phaedrus,* in the discussion of rhetoric as the art of making speeches. Socrates gets Phaedrus to agree that "every *logos* must be organized, like a living being *[zōion],* with a body of its own, as it were" (*Phr.* 264c). Plato is concerned to emphasize the vital autonomy of spoken discourse, of the argument—the *Sache,* as Heidegger would say—of interpersonal dialogue. In fact the conversation between Socrates and Phaedrus is still going on only because Socrates earlier seemed "to hear some *logoi* approaching and protesting," whom he invited to join the discussion by saying: "Come here, then, noble creatures, and persuade the fair young Phaedrus . . ." (260e–261a). This conception of the *logos* as a distinct, vital being, some third force in the dialogue, is central to Socrates' whole enterprise.

In the *Theaetetus,* Socrates and his young interlocutor frequently find their conversation harder going than they expected. At one point they are in such perplexity that Socrates sees only a vague possibility of their being able to extricate themselves. "But if we turn out to be perplexed in every way," he says, "then, I suspect, in all humility we'll hand ourselves over to the *logos* to be trampled on like the seasick and be handled in whatever way it wants."[15] Shortly thereafter, as they begin to find a way out, but Theaetetus still has no idea what they should say, Socrates replies, "Doesn't the *logos* really then, my boy, rebuke us beautifully and point out that we do not correctly seek for false opinion prior to knowledge and let knowledge go?" (*Theae.* 200c). Throughout the course of this dialogue (as of many others) there is constant and careful attention to where the argument is leading, and to the possibility of its acting like the famous *daimonion* in counseling against certain approaches or directions of inquiry.

In the *Sophist,* by contrast, Theaetetus and the stranger appear to have gained the upper hand in their dealings with a discourse so obstreperous that it would "have the nerve to lay down that 'that which is not' is": "There is the *logos* [of Parmenides]," says the stranger, "which, if it should be put to a fair degree of torture, would as certain as anything make its own confession" (*Soph.* 237a–b). In the *Statesman,* the hunt for the nature of the beast is carried out in a more cooperative atmosphere, insofar as the stranger says at one point that they should have put the statesman in the class of people who "tend"—grouping him among tenders of herds and flocks—"since the *logos* was indicating that we should have done so" (*Stat.* 275e). This is the advantage of having an interlocutor like Socrates, who has little on his agenda and no theses of his own to propose or theories to propound: he *listens* to what the others are saying—and especially to what the *logos* has to say. He is always on the lookout for some sign or indication from the argument itself, treating it with as much respect (or more) as he does the other living beings with whom he is conversing.

With *Assorted Opinions and Maxims* in 1879, Nietzsche's thinking about the drives, and about thinking itself, takes a dynamic turn to the topic of personality. An aphorism entitled "From the Innermost Experience of the Thinker" begins:

> Nothing is more difficult for the human being than to apprehend a thing impersonally: I mean to see in it just a thing and *not a person.* One may well ask whether it is possible at all for a human being to suspend the clockwork of his drive to imagine and create persons for even a moment. For he deals with *thoughts*—even the most abstract ones—as if they were individuals with whom one has to struggle or make friends, whom one has to tend, care for, and nourish.[16]

Earlier the passions were imagined as animals, as animate beings within the soul that could be nurtured, domesticated, or trained; now through the thinker's innermost experience the psyche is peopled and the soul populated on a higher level by vital conceptions, living thoughts and ideas. A return, in a sense, or reincarnation, of the autonomous *logoi* of Socrates.

If we keep watch on ourselves, Nietzsche suggests, and listen (with the third ear, so to speak) when we discover a new proposition, we find that our relation to it is personal through and through. We may be put off by the thought's "defiant and autocratic" attitude, which might prompt us to adduce "a counterproposition as an enemy," or to weaken him by attaching a "perhaps" or a "probably" to him, so as to "break the personally burdensome tyranny of the unconditional." Or, if the new idea appears retiring and timid, she may elicit from us a "parental, or chivalrous, or compassionate" attitude. And when faced with two apparently independent propositions we may try to arrange a marriage between them, in the hope of seeing some intellectual progeny from the union.

If, however, the new proposition strikes us as being *true,* "one will submit to him and pay him homage as a leader and prince, according him a seat of honor." And yet, if he should later come to appear questionable, we shall have no hesitation—as "tireless king makers of the history of the spirit"—in ejecting him from the throne and setting a rival in his place. One is reminded of the passage in the *Republic* that describes a phase of psychological transformation in which the son of the timocratic type of man turns oligarchic: "He thrusts love of honor and spiritedness headlong out of the throne of his soul, and . . . puts the desiring and money-loving part on the throne, and makes it the great king within himself" (*Rep.* 553b–c). If we entertain the image of person-thoughts, Nietzsche notes, reflecting on our intercourse with ideas in this way, we shall come to doubt the existence of anything like "a drive for knowledge in and for itself." With this picture, he is taking the "association of ideas" of earlier psychology and making it into an internal "sociology of ideas," a politics of the realm of thought.[17]

The question naturally arises here, as Nietzsche acknowledges, why "in this *secret* struggle with thought-persons, in this mostly concealed marriage-brokering of thoughts, state-founding of thoughts, pedagogy of thoughts, and tending of poor and infirm thoughts," human beings should have come to prefer "the true" over the untrue. The answer is that we do so now out of "habit, heredity, and upbringing"—but originally because the true was more "useful and productive of honor" than the untrue.[18] But note that the preference for thoughts considered true has its roots in several fields: in the realms of matchmaking with an eye to progeny, of educating the young and immature (both eminently Socratic concerns), of husbanding and nurturing the strength of the weak—questions of societal relations as well as political issues. Intellectual life is then lived at many levels simultaneously, intrapsychically and interpersonally, in terms of several different discourses at one time.

Especially significant here is the idea that the individual's "I" is not seen as the ruler of the realm of ideas: while there are some ideas over which it can exercise control, there are others to which it is in thrall. We are encouraged to experiment with this picture on the premise

> that we *are afraid of* our own thoughts, conceptions, and words, but
> that we also *honor* ourselves in them, investing them willy nilly with
> the power to reward us, despise us, praise and blame us, and that

we thus deal with them as with free intelligent persons, with independent powers, as equals with equals. (*AOM* 26)

A picture is emerging that is far more complex than the dialogical models of the psyche proposed by thinkers in the tradition from Plato to Herbart and Griesinger.

Nietzsche began this aphorism on "thought-persons" by posing the question of whether it is possible to "shut down the drive to imagine and create persons for even a moment." There is no indication that he thinks such a thing is possible; the person-creating drive would seem to operate as continuously as the drive for nourishment or the erotic drive. Nor is there more than the slightest suggestion that the ideal of "apprehending a thing impersonally" is to be striven for: without love, for Nietzsche, it is impossible to penetrate to the heart of things. Nevertheless, the suspension of the person-creating drive does seem to be, if not desirable, then at least feasible.

In *The Wanderer and His Shadow* Nietzsche draws a picture of philosophers that complements his earliest one, amplifying the notion of the philosophical work as something intensely personal.

> They lack all *impersonal* interest in problems of knowledge: just as they themselves are persons through and through, so all their knowledge and insights grow together again into a person, into a living multiplicity whose individual parts are interdependent and interpenetrating and communally nourished.[19]

It is "the *life*" in "these *personality-infused* structures of knowledge" that can give the magical impression of something complete, just as an organism gets its structural unity from the life that animates it. One is reminded of Socrates' claim that every *logos* must be "organized, like a living being, with a body of its own, as it were, so as not to be headless or footless, but to have a middle and members composed in fitting relation to each other and to the whole" (*Phr.* 264c).

The emphasis on "life" and "personality" may help us better understand Nietzsche's conception of the book as "almost a human being." It is because it is so deeply infused with the personality of its author that the book can "ignite new life, delight, terrify, and engender new works"—the writer having "written in blood" and poured into it "everything in him that was life-engendering, energizing, elevating, and enlightening" (*HA* 208).

The issue of the vitality of thought prompts us to bring to mind what was happening in Nietzsche's personal life (seen from the outside) around this time. Leaves of absence from the professorship at Basel had proved ineffectual in stemming the continuing deterioration of his health. When *Human, All Too Human* was published in May of 1878, the dismay and disappointment of almost all his friends—including even Rohde and Overbeck—was profound and palpable. Although Nietzsche had substituted "the artist" for several references to Wagner before publication, the book sealed the fate of that relationship as far as the Master was concerned. Only two people were encouraging: Jacob Burckhardt, who called it a "sovereign" book, and Paul Rée, several of whose ideas had been incorporated into it. Rée sent Nietzsche an enthusiastic letter of praise immediately after receiving his copy, in which he made the perspicacious comment: "What a human being you are—or rather not one but *a conglomerate of human beings*."[20]

Nietzsche had entertained hopes that the breach with Wagner could be mended, trying to understand his "apostasy" as exclusively intellectual and not personal (difficult, in view of his understanding of the intellectual *as* personal), and hoping that the Master would come to see it that way. But in the summer Wagner published a two-part article in his "house journal," the *Bayreuther Blätter,* which—without actually mentioning Nietzsche by name—decried the new turn in his philosophy. Nietzsche was deeply hurt by what he took to be Wagner's small-mindedness. At Easter in 1879, when *Assorted Opinions and Maxims* was published, he received the news—salt on the open wound—that only 120 copies of *Human, All Too Human* had been sold in the year since its publication. This forced upon him the harsh realization that he was pouring all his energies, ruining his health in the process, into writing books that virtually nobody was reading.

Nietzsche's illnesses had forced him to withdraw from human contact as much as he could, retreating for solitary cures at spas whenever his professional obligations would permit. Within the previous year he had broken with his old friend Gersdorff, and a young friend, Albert Brenner, had died. He had been relieved of some of his teaching duties because of his failing health, and finally in May of 1879 he tendered his resignation to the University. He was awarded a retirement pension for six years, which was subsequently extended.

Nietzsche left Basel—his home of ten years—toward the end of the month, and by the end of June he found himself for the first time in the upper Engadin, in Saint Moritz, where he wrote *The Wanderer and His Shadow.* It may be difficult to imagine how uplifting the first experience of ascending to that magnificent mountain landscape must have been. The train line to Saint Moritz (altitude 1775 meters) had only recently been opened and was one of the first lines to take advantage of the newly perfected technique of dynamiting tunnels. The feat of engineering is as remarkable as the views from the train are spectacular: bridges span abysmally deep ravines eroded by foaming torrents, while cloud-crowned peaks capped with snow rise to over four thousand meters on either side. Five years earlier, Nietzsche had written of "climbing as high into the pure, icy

Alpine air as ever a thinker had climbed" (*SE* 5); but at that time he had inhaled that air only from the pages of Byron's poetry. From now on he would breathe it through his own nostrils often enough for it to infuse the pages of his subsequent works: "Whoever can breathe the air of my writings knows that it is an air of the heights, a *strong* air" (*EH*, P3).

Two things are striking about the letters Nietzsche wrote after leaving the security of his position and home in Basel: the stern commands to his few close addressees not to let anyone know his whereabouts, so that he could maintain his solitude; and his expressions of blissful relief at having at last found his *"own"* landscape. In sending his address to his sister, he adds: "Please keep my whereabouts a secret from everyone. Otherwise I must immediately leave this place that pleases me so much and, so far, really *does me good.* I cannot bear a visit from *anyone.*"[21] To Overbeck he wrote the same day: "I have now taken possession of the Engadin and am in *my own* element—quite wonderful! I am closely *related* to *this* part of nature! Now I feel some relief. . . . Keep my whereabouts *secret* from everyone." And to his mother a week later: "What endears this place to me are the woods, the lakes, the best hiking paths—as they have to be for someone who is almost blind as I am—and the most refreshing air, the best in Europe."[22]

The visual beauty of the Engadin is so spectacular that it is easy to forget that Nietzsche was barely able to see it. But the man was ever prone to synesthesia, and the richness of that world along other sensory dimensions—the sound of waves lapping the shores of lakes, the rushing of mountain torrents, the wind through the pines and firs, cowbells on the lower pastures, and birdsong on the higher alps; the springy softness of paths thick with fragrant pine needles; the manifold scents of the vivifying air—would have offset any sense of loss from failing eyesight. He could at least see well enough to "hear" the music of the landscapes he lived in. He would later write eloquently of the way the hills around Portofino "come down to the sea with such an even rhythm . . . there where the Gulf of Genoa ends its song" (*JS* 281), but the music of the landscape of the Engadin is even more beautiful. The multiple contours of the mountains around Sils-Maria play an "endless melody"—though more like Haydn than Wagner—descending down to the surface of a lake and then rising again on the other side in sequences of elegant contrapuntal accents.

Above all one can imagine how lack of intercourse with real people over the next ten years—Nietzsche's customary environments were a small room in a modest pension and the landscapes through which he would hike daylong (when not confined to his room by illness)—would allow the persons of the psyche to present themselves all the more clearly. An unpublished note from late 1880 reads:

> Strange! I am dominated at every moment by the thought that my history is not only a personal one, that I am doing something for many people when I live like this and work on and write about myself this way. It is always as if I were a multiplicity, which I address in intimate, serious, and comforting terms.[23]

And to judge from the following passage from a letter to Gersdorff of three years later, no place seems to have been more conducive to intimate communication with this multiplicity than the area around Sils-Maria.

> My dear old friend, I am now in the upper Engadin again, for the *third* time, and again I feel that here and nowhere else is my true home and breeding ground. Oh, how much still lies hidden within me and wants to become word and form! It cannot possibly be sufficiently still and high and lonely around me, so that I can hear my innermost voices![24]

Though solitary, Nietzsche was not alone; the wanderer with his shadows.

When, later still, in the spring of 1886 Nietzsche writes a retrospective preface for the first volume of *Human, All Too Human: A Book for Free Spirits,* he speaks of the solitude surrounding the conception and execution of the work and of the consequent necessity of *inventing* the "free spirits" for whom the book was written. "At that time I needed them for company . . . as brave companions and familiar spirits with whom one chats and laughs . . . as compensation for the friends I lacked" (*HA,* P2). These spirits were already beginning to play their parts in Nietzsche's texts, a notable debut being that of "the Shadow" in the dramatic vignettes that frame *The Wanderer and His Shadow.* The Shadow initiates the dialogue, and the Wanderer responds in surprise—"It is almost as if I heard myself speaking, though in an even weaker voice than mine"—and is at first incredulous that his shadow could actually be addressing him: "I hear it, but can't believe it." The Shadow is reluctant to let the Wanderer transcribe their conversation, but relents when he realizes that "everyone will see in it only [the Wanderer's] views: no one will think of the Shadow." An unpublished note from the period speaks of the desirablity of having the drives become more personable toward each other:

> All our drives must first become more anxious and mistrustful, then gradually acquire more reason and honesty, becoming more clear-sighted and thereby increasingly losing the *grounds for mistrust* of each other. In this way a greater, more fundamental joyfulness can arise.[25]

By *Dawn of Morning* the drives have become so personable that Nietzsche takes it as a point of honor for people who live alone to engage them seriously as interlocutors:

To those who are solitary—If we do not respect the honor of other persons in our conversations with ourselves just as much as we do in public, we are not decent human beings. (*DM* 569)

Short dialogues appear with increasing frequency in Nietzsche's next books—often between interlocutors designated simply as "A" and "B"—until in *Zarathustra* the entire work takes the form of a dramatic narrative. Not only does Nietzsche's alter ego, the eponymous protagonist, engage in dialogue with a variety of other characters (and animals), all of them figures of the author's imagination, but he also converses with a number of "inner" figures of his own imagination: Zarathustra almost outdoes Odysseus in conversing not only with his soul, but also with such a variety of interlocutors as his heart, his shadow, his conscience, his happiness, Life, his fate, his loneliness, his stillest hour, his wild wisdom—all as personal presences.

The Fabric(ation) of Experience

> *Dream delivers us to dream, and there is no end to illusion. . . .*
> *As we pass through [successions of moods], they prove to be*
> *many-colored lenses which paint the world in their own hue,*
> *and each shows only what lies in its focus . . . We animate what*
> *we can, and we see only what we animate.*
> Emerson, "Experience"

With *Dawn of Morning* (1881) the discourse concerning psychological persons dips again into the realm of impulse and instinct—and takes an unprecedented new turn.[26] Careful consideration of a series of aphorisms in the second book of that text reveals a remarkable revisioning of the I in terms of drives. The epigraph from Emerson here is meant to suggest a reversion to Nietzsche's early ideas about moods, and that moods may well be manifestations of drives.[27]

Aphorism 105 bears the title "Seeming Egoism" *(Schein-Egoismus)* and again puts into question the ontological status of the ego. (Nietzsche here uses the word *ego* instead of his customary *Ich.*) For all their apparent egoism, most people

> do nothing for their ego but only for the phantom of their ego that has been formed in the heads of those around them and communicated back to them—as a result of which everybody lives in a mist of impersonal, semipersonal opinions and arbitrary and, as it were, poetical evaluations, each one always in the head of the other, and that head in turn in other heads: a wonderful world of phantasms, that yet manages to appear so sober![28]

The ego is seen here as being constituted by others rather than by the self, as a "sheen-ego," a self-image composed of projections from those around us—and so reflecting on, in a phantastic hall of mirrors. "What a world of phantoms we live in! Topsy-turvy and void—yet a world that is *full* and *above all* dreamed!" (*DM* 118). The fiction generated by the opinions of others is hard to dismiss because there is generally a lack of force from within, "all because no individual in this crowd is able to oppose the general, pale fiction with an effectual ego, accessible to and established by himself, with which to annihilate the fictional one" (*DM* 105).

The standing of the ego, here resolved into a kind of phantom appearance projected by others, is further weakened in aphorism 109. The title, "Self-Mastery and Moderation and Their Ultimate Motive," invokes two virtues extolled in Plato's *Republic: enkrateia* and *sōphrosunē*.[29]

I find no more than six different ways of combating the violence of a drive.

[1] One can avoiding opportunities for the gratification *[Befried-igung]* of the drive . . . [thereby] weakening it and making it dry up and wither away.

[2] One can impose on oneself strict regularity in gratifying it . . . so that by restraining its ebb and flood within strict time periods one gains intervals during which it no longer disturbs one. . . .

[3] One can deliberately give oneself over to wild and unconstrained gratification of a drive, in order to reap disgust for it and so gain power over it: assuming that one does not do as the rider who rides his horse to death and breaks his own neck in the process. . . .

[4] There is an intellectual ploy whereby one connects gratification of any kind so firmly with some very painful thought, so that with practice the very thought of gratification is always immediately experienced as very painful. . . . [At this point Nietzsche inserts some parenthetical examples concerning Christ, Lord Byron, and Napoleon, remarking on how if one escapes from the tyranny of a particular drive one can experience "joy in tyrannizing the drive and making it gnash its teeth, as it were."]

[5] One effects a dislocation of one's energies by imposing on oneself some kind of difficult and strenuous work, or by deliberately submitting to a new attraction and pleasure and thereby leading one's thoughts and plays of physical energy on to other paths. It comes to the same thing if one favors a different drive for a while, gives it ample opportunity for gratification and thus makes it squander the energy that would otherwise have been at the disposal of the drive

that through its vehemence has grown burdensome. Some will also know how to keep in check the particular drive that would like to play master by giving all the other drives they know a temporary encouragement and festival, and having them consume all the food the tyrant wants for himself alone. Finally,

    [6] Whoever can . . . weaken and depress the *entire* somatic and psychical organization will also naturally succeed in weakening a particular violent drive along with it . . . as the ascetic does.[30]

Socrates would clearly endorse the practice of methods 1, 2, and 5. The image of making the drive "dry up and wither away" echoes his complaint against imitative poetry that "it fosters and waters [the lower desires] when they ought to be dried up."[31] In the *Phaedo* Socrates observes that people who are self-restrained out of "self-indulgence" rather than from wisdom "fear that they may be deprived of certain pleasures which they desire, and so they refrain from some because they are under the sway of others. . . . They conquer pleasures because they are conquered by other pleasures."[32] Having all the other drives "consume all the food the tyrant wants for himself alone" is equivalent to the farmer's "nourishing and cultivating the tame heads [of the many-headed beast] while hindering the growth of the savage ones" (*Rep.* 589b). This would be an especially effective strategy against "the tyrant *erōs*" which, as "leader of the idle desires insists on all available resources being distributed to them."[33] The horse and rider image evokes the team of horses in the *Phaedrus,* while the "ebb and flood" and "leading one's thoughts and plays of physical energy on to other paths" are reminiscent of the flow of *erōs* in the *Republic.*

    In view of the weakening of the ego effected a few aphorisms earlier, its dissolution into projected appearances, a pertinent question concerning the various strategies for dealing with obstreperous drives is this: Just *who is* this "one" who avoids opportunities, imposes strict regularity, gives itself over, associates gratification, effects dislocations, and can weaken and depress the entire system? An answer comes at the end of the aphorism.

That one *wants* to combat the violence of a drive at all is not within our power, neither the choice of method nor whether that method will succeed. Rather, in this whole process our intellect is clearly just the blind tool of *another drive* that is a *rival* of the one that is torturing us by its violence: whether it be the drive for peace and quiet, or fear of disgrace and other evil consequences, or love. So while "we" think we are complaining about the violence of a drive, it is basically one drive *that is complaining about another;* that is: the perception of suffering from this kind of *violence* presupposes that there is another drive that is just as violent or even more violent, and that there is going to be a *struggle* in which our intellect is going to have to take sides *[Partei nehmen]*.

Whereas in the optimal scenario for Plato the calculating part has control from above of the rest of the soul, Nietzsche is claiming that subjugation of an importunate drive is effected only by another drive, such as the drive for peace and quiet, that is using the intellect as a tool. (Shades of Schopenhauer here, who repeatedly characterizes the intellect as a tool of "blind will.") This is a major move in decentering the psyche, in decentralizing the powers of the soul and dismantling their hierarchy, whereby the intellect, whose hegemony had rarely been questioned by the tradition, is demoted to the status of a tool. The traditional "top-down" hierarchy of faculties is reconfigured as a field of drives of varying intensities battling it out among themselves. And yet the last sentence of the aphorism seems to impede the radical step taken by what goes before, insofar as the idea that the intellect has to (or even can) take sides in the impending struggle appears to contradict its being characterized as a "blind tool."

An indication of the radical direction of Nietzsche's thinking about this issue is provided by an unpublished note from the period, which better explains what is going on when "I" think that "I" am complaining about or prevailing over the vehemence of a drive.

> The I is not the attitude of one being to several (drives, thoughts, etc.) but the ego is *a plurality of personlike forces,* of which now this one now that one stands in the foreground as ego and regards the others as a subject regards an influential and determining external world. . . . *Within ourselves* we can also be egoistic or altruistic, hard-hearted, magnanimous, just, lenient, insincere, can cause pain or give pleasure: as the drives are in conflict, the feeling of the I is always strongest where the preponderance *[Übergewicht]* is.[34]

This passage suggests that the I is not something stable that is independent from the drives, but that any preponderant drive (or group of drives) may "stand in the foreground as ego" and complain, or prevail, as "I."

The next two aphorisms in *Dawn of Morning* concern the issue of *suffering.* Nietzsche suggests that "The Striving for Distinction *[Auszeichnung]*" (the title of aphorism 113) be understood as the demonstration of our domination—however subtle and indirect—of those next to us, as "the *impress*" we make on other souls. At the top of the "long ladder" of cruelty is the ascetic, whose drive to distinction is discharged in the feeling of power that comes from triumph over himself effected by making *himself* suffer, "burning himself to charcoal."[35] Nietzsche then assimilates to the ascetic the person who suffers from illness, physically tortured by it. Distanced forcibly from the comfort of everyday life, the sufferer counters the physical pain by taking it as psychical pain that is self-inflicted—crying out to himself:

> "Be for once your own accuser and hangman, and take for once your suffering as punishment imposed by you on yourself! Enjoy your superiority as judge; better yet: enjoy being arbitrary, your tyrannical willfulness!" (*DM* 114)

A remarkable ploy this: an emulation of the ascetic, where a part of the soul arrogates to itself the power of illness to torture—by understanding itself as "inflicting the bitterest suffering" on another part of the soul. This strategy would be what enabled Nietzsche himself to go on living in the face of the torment caused by his illnesses (and sheds new light on claims concerning a psychosomatic component to his ill health). In psychopolitical terms, it is a case of setting up a "countertyrant" against the tyranny of physical suffering:

> Our pride towers up as never before: it is an incomparable stimulus for it—in opposition to a tyrant such as pain is, and against all its insinuations to us that we should bear witness against life—precisely to *advocate life* in the face of this tyrant.[36]

The next aphorism bears the title "The So-called 'I'," and begins by remarking the inadequacy of language for fathoming "inner processes and drives" (*DM* 115). Nietzsche claims that "anger, hatred, love, compassion, desire, knowledge, joy, pain—are all names for *extreme* states," and that we are completely unaware of the more moderate processes that continuously "weave the web of our character and fate."

> *We are none of us that* which we appear to be from the states for which alone we have consciousness and words . . . we misread ourselves in this apparently most clear script of our selves. And yet *this opinion of ourselves . . .* the so-called "I," continues to collaborate on our character and fate.

Here is a counterpart to the "sheen-ego" described earlier, projected by the opinions of others, which evolves as a misreading of the text of the inner psyche—and yet nonetheless plays just as important a part in our development.

All these themes culminate in aphorism 119, entitled "Experiencing and Fabricating" *(Erleben und Erdichten),* and one of the longest and richest in the book. The title is meant to imply that experience is largely a matter of poetic composition, that we make the bulk of it up as we go along. Nietzsche begins by suggesting that the project of "knowing oneself" may be constrained by quite narrow limits.

However far we may drive our self-knowledge, nothing can be more incomplete than the image of the totality of *drives* that constitute our being. We can scarcely even name the cruder ones: their number and strength, their ebb and flood, their play and counterplay, and above all the laws of their *nourishment* remain quite unknown to us. Their nourishment is thus a matter of chance: our daily experiences throw a piece of prey now to this drive, now to that one, which they seize greedily, but the entire coming and going of these events does not stand in any rational relation to the nutritional requirements of the drives as a whole, with the result that some of them are starved and waste away, while others are overfed. Every moment of our lives sees some polyp-arms of our being grow and others wither, all according to the nourishment that the moment provides or fails to provide.

Images from several levels—elemental, vegetal, and animal—coalesce in this description of the sustenance and development of the drives. The most striking feature of the situation, adumbrated by several of the preceding aphorisms, is that the activity of the drives generally goes on unbeknownst to us, below the threshold of consciousness: we remain for the most part blissfully oblivious to "the laws of their nourishment." But if the sustenance of the drives is so dependent on chance, one wonders how more than a fortunate few can survive. Nietzsche addresses this question after a further description of the way each drive tests every experience in order to see whether it contains anything it can use for its own purposes. If it continues to find nothing in the way of nourishment, it will "wither away like a plant without rain." But the situation is not as desperate as it may seem:

Perhaps this cruelty of chance would strike us more vividly if all drives took it as seriously as *hunger,* which does not rest content with *dreamed food.* Most drives, however, especially the so-called moral ones, *are content with precisely that*—as long as my supposition is allowed that the significance and worth of our dreams is to *compensate* to some extent for the fortuitous absence of "nourishment" during the day.[37]

It is hard to imagine a more just arrangement: if we are constitutionally unaware of the constant play of drives that underlies our consciousness, it seems only fitting that the majority of them should not require us to arrange for their *actual* sustenance. In ascribing to phantasy and dream a major role in the overall economy of the soul, Nietzsche stands in a line of German thinkers that runs through Lichtenberg and Novalis—issuing later in Freud's idea that the dream is the fulfillment of an unconscious wish, and in Jung's understanding of dreams as compensatory for shortcomings and lacunae in consciousness. He goes on to elaborate on the phenomenon of dreaming:

> These fabrications *[Erdichtungen]*, which afford free play and discharge to our drives . . . are interpretations of nervous stimulation during sleep, *very free,* very arbitrary interpretations of the motions of the blood and intestines, the pressure of the arm and the blankets, and the sounds from the bell tower, of weathercocks, night revelers, and so on. That this text, which in general remains very similar from night to night, should be commented on in such different ways, that poetic reason should today and yesterday *imagine* such different *causes* for the same nerve stimuli—is because the prompter [*Souffleur*—as in the theater] of this poetic reason is today different from what it was yesterday, a different *drive* wanted to satisfy itself, to be active, to exercise itself, to refresh or discharge itself, just that particular drive was in flood, while yesterday it was a different one.[38]

Nietzsche gave a similar interpretation of the phenomenon of the dream in an earlier aphorism entitled "Logic of the Dream" (*HA* 13). There he talks in terms of the "seeking and positing of causes for the excitement of sensations" rather than of drives, but the schema is the same and the agent for the production is similarly said to be phantasy. He delineates the operational parallels between dream and phantasy ("the gate and portico of the dream") by invoking the waking condition in which, when the eyes are closed, the colors and shapes we see tend to coalesce into definite shapes.

> Now the understanding, in concert with phantasy, immediately works this in itself formless play of colors into definite figures, shapes, landscapes, lively groups. . . . The mind asks where these impressions and colors come from, and supposes the causes are these figures and shapes. . . . Here, then, phantasy continuously presents images [to the mind], depending on the visual impressions of the day for their production, and dream-phantasy operates in just the same way. (*HA* 13)

In fact the parallels between dream and phantasy go back to Nietzsche's first book, in which Apollo, patron of the dream, "also rules over the beautiful *Schein* of the inner phantasy-world" (*BT* 1).

The important development in *Dawn of Morning* lies in the explanation of the immense variation in the fabricated dream narratives, which have as their basis more or less the same, rather restricted range of stimulation (proprioceptive stimuli from the sleeping body, sounds in and outside the bedroom, and so on). The difference derives from the fact that the interpretation of stimuli and the phantasizing of causes are *performed by different drives* in differing conditions of need, depending on how much or little nourishment they have been receiving from daytime experiences. But the most important move made by the new account is the extension of the parallels between dream and phantasy into the realm of waking experience.

> Waking life does not have the same *freedom* of interpretation that dreaming does, it is less poetic and unrestrained—but do I have to make explicit that when we are awake our drives do nothing other than interpret nerve-impulses and posit their "causes" according to their own needs? that there is no *essential* difference between waking and dreaming? . . . that all our so-called consciousness is a more or less phantastic commentary on an unknown, perhaps unknowable, but felt text? (*DM* 119)

While this last part is often quoted in the secondary literature, it is not clear that the import of the whole has been fully appreciated. Nietzsche is suggesting that our waking experience is based in a deep-level, ongoing phantasy activity, constantly conditioned by projections from a play of drives of which we are generally unconscious. (Remember Kant's characterization of the transcendental imagination as "a blind though indispensable function of the soul, without which we should have no knowledge whatsoever, but of which we are seldom even conscious.")

The idea is that the much greater amount of stimulation provided by waking experience correspondingly restricts the phantastic interpretations that the drives may project. In terms of the *texture* of what Nietzsche calls the "text" of stimuli: when one is asleep, the text is sparse, providing relatively few strands for phantasy to weave the fabric of experience around, and thus a lot more space to "fill in," whereas the waking state sets up a denser texture of stimulation, establishing more of a pattern in advance, which restricts the free play of phantasy in projecting its images. One can also understand the primary text of experience as a pattern of impulses inscribed upon the nervous system. At this level there is no consciousness, no things, no images. Then—in the language of "On Truth and Lie"—"a nerve stimulus is transferred into an image: first metaphor . . . [in a] complete overleaping of one sphere into a quite different and new sphere."[39] Already in the earlier essay Nietzsche had talked of "the drive to imagine metaphors" as "the fundamental human drive"; of "a mass of images flowing forth in fiery fluidity from the primordial faculty of human phantasy"; and of the "*aesthetic* relation" between the spheres of subject and object, as "a freely fabricating and freely inventing middle-sphere."[40] Images can appear, and from them concepts be derived, and from there a world of things—only when the phantastic operation of the metaphorical drive comes into play.

Nietzsche goes on in *Dawn of Morning* to give an exquisite example illustrating the part played by the drives in constituting our experience.

Take some trivial experience. Suppose we notice one day in the marketplace that someone is laughing at us as we go by. Depending on which drive is at its height in us at the time, the event will have this or that significance for us—and it will be a quite different event depending on the type of person we are. One person will absorb it like a drop of rain, another will shake it off as he would an insect, one will try to pick a fight over it, one will check his clothes to see whether they are any cause for laughter, one will be prompted to ponder the nature of the laughable as such, another will be happy to have contributed inadvertently to the sum total of happiness and sunshine in the world—and in each case a particular drive will have attained gratification from the event, whether it be annoyance, or combativeness, or deliberation, or benevolence. The drive seized the occurrence as its prey. And why precisely that drive? Because it was thirsty and hungry and on the lookout. (*DM* 119)

Quite apart from the possibility—frequent in such cases, and chastening to violent reactors—that the laughter was in fact occasioned by someone just behind us and not by anything to do with us at all.

The effect of this example, and the ideas it exemplifies, is to shake the belief in an objective world (which is not to resolve everything into mere subjectivity). It is not just that "what actually happened" is a function of the perspectives of the various participants; a great deal depends on which among the variety of perspectives *within* each participant is brought to bear upon the situation.[41] Nietzsche rounds this rich aphorism out with a series of pregnant questions:

What then are our experiences? Much *more* that which we put into them than that which lies within them? Or is it really that in themselves there is nothing to them? To experience is to fabricate?

It is not that there is *nothing* to them, for Nietzsche, even though he is arguing that to experience is to fabricate. But there is less freedom for this fabrication in the day-world, and this is what makes it the world it seems to be. There is *something* going on: some resistance to our projections; important senses in which the world "pushes back," as it were (compare the recalcitrance of Fichte's "not-I"); aspects that refuse to be reinterpreted or reconfigured as anything but *there*. This is not to deny that we can drift woefully astray in our projections, alienating ourselves from the world by withdrawing into a realm of solipsistic phantasies; but it is to say that we have much more freedom, and can play a much more important role in composing the narrative of our experience, than we are accustomed to think.

To the question of why there appears to be a "real world" out there, or of why there seems to be such a degree of harmony among various individuals' projections, Nietzsche would offer several responses. At one level, *language*—with its propensity to generalize—irons out many of the differences, and this eventually conduces to a "laziness" (and consequent haziness) in our very perceptions of the world.[42] We come to see very much what we have been taught, with the aid of a common language, to see. *Memory* also plays an important role, insofar as similar sequences of projections that are found to "work," to be successful or pleasurable, are recollected and tried again more frequently. At an even deeper level—and Nietzsche's reluctance to talk about myth after the break with Wagner prevents him saying much about this—memory operates over wide spans of generations, so that archetypal patterns are laid down in the productive imagination, leading to collective structures of phantastic projection. Some of these mythical patterns will be cultural, while others may be more universal— deriving from whatever physiological structures are common to all members of the species.

Two aphorisms from the last book of *Dawn of Morning* reintroduce the personal into the interplay between inner and outer that is set up by the operations of the drives. In opposition to the narrow ideal of scientific method as impersonal, "Researchers and Experimenters" recapitulates the idea (from *AOM* 26) that one deals with thoughts as with personal individuals and sets it in the context of what could be called a "personal experimentalism."

> There are no scientific methods that alone lead to knowledge! We must deal with things experimentally, now angry with them and now kind to them, being just, passionate, and cold toward them in succession. One person addresses things as a policeman, another as a father confessor, a third as an inquisitive wanderer. Something can be wrested from them now through sympathy, now through force; one person progresses to insight through reverence for their secrets, another through indiscretion and roguishness in explaining their mysteries. (*DM* 432)

Though it is not explicitly stated here, the clear implication (in the context of Nietzsche's treatment of the broader topic) is that we can deal with things in a variety of ways thanks to the variety of persons—the policeman, father confessor, reverent initiate, and so on—within each one of us.

Nietzsche's experimental method depends on the deployment of a range of perspectives deriving from the multiplicity of persons within each person. Just as the drive for knowledge is not simple but complex, so a single-minded inquiry will reveal only one aspect of the issue (perpetuating what Blake derided as "single vision and Newton's sleep"). Since Bacon proposed torturing nature in order to extort her secrets, and Kant proposed putting nature on the witness stand and using cross-examination to make her talk, the prevailing scientific-philosophical attitude has leaned toward domination.[43] For Nietzsche, such an approach will on rare occasions be appropriate, but there are many other methods that will be effective in other situations; and a flexibility that allows for a wide range of approaches will be the most enlightening. It is a matter of letting a variety of drives and persons interpret. To do this requires a prior awareness of precisely their variety, which might be induced by the kinds of questions Nietzsche poses under the title "Do You Even Know What You Will?"

> Have you ever noticed *what kind of* will holds sway behind your seeing? . . . Do you think that today, when you are frozen and dry like a clear winter's morning and there is nothing weighing upon your heart, that somehow your eyes have improved? Or aren't warmth and enthusiasm necessary for doing *justice* to a thing of thought *[Gedankending]*?—*and that is precisely what seeing is!* As if you *could* deal with things of thought differently from the way you deal with people! (*DM* 539)

Here again is the idea that thoughts are personal powers to which (whom) it is impossible to do justice as long as one tries to deal with them impersonally, while the rest of the aphorism reemphasizes that it is equally impossible to subtract the contribution of our imaginations from any of our dealings with things. This implies less the impossibility of suspending the operations of the "person-creating drive" than the inherently personal nature of drives—all of which are in principle capable of manifesting themselves as persons.

Unpublished Notes from 1881

There is a sequence of around fifty pages in an unpublished notebook from 1881 that contains a string of gemlike observations that illuminate the topics we have just been dealing with, such as the relations among the drives, the I, projective phantasy, and persons. The sequence also leads up—not entirely coincidentally—to the first entry, dated "early August 1881 in Sils-Maria," concerning Nietzsche's central thought of the eternal recurrence of the same.[44] (This excursus will be of most interest for readers concerned with seeing Nietzsche's modes of thought, with its vacillations to and fro on crucial topics, during one of the most productive phases of his career. Readers of German may simply want to consult the original texts of the notes, while those less interested in Nietzsche's mode of working may prefer to proceed directly to the next section.)

At the outset, an agricultural metaphor that suggests that harvesting may after all be an *inter*psychical as well as an intrapsychical process:

> We must not let our life slip through our hands, thanks to some "goal"—but rather harvest from ourselves the fruits of *all* seasons. We strive after others, and everything outside us, as after nourishment. Often it is fruits that have ripened just for our year. Must one always have only the egoism of the robber or thief? Why not that of the gardener? Joy in the tending of others, as in the care of a garden! (*KSA* 9:11[2])

Then, in a paragraph that appears to undermine the idea of egoism altogether, Nietzsche adopts a rather Schopenhauerian-Buddhist stance toward the individual ego, in an atypical sequence of emphasized exclamations.

> We are buds on a single tree—what do we know about what can become of us from the interests of the tree! . . . *Stop feeling oneself as this phantastic ego!* Learn gradually *to jettison the supposed individual!* Discover the errors of the ego! Realize that *egoism is an error!* But not to be understood as the opposite of altruism! That would be love of *other supposed* individuals! No! *Get beyond* "me" and "you"! *Experience cosmically!* (*KSA* 9:11[7])

This remarkable outpouring of cosmic feeling, reminiscent of passages from Nietzsche's earlier, "Romantic" period, may have been occasioned by the recurrence of an access of mystical experience—perhaps prompted by immersion in the landscape around Sils-Maria.

A paragraph beginning with a commendation of "wanting to know things as they are" and a condemnation of "egoistic seeing" goes on:

> What is needed is *practice* in seeing with *other* eyes: practice in seeing apart from human relations, and thus seeing *objectively* [sachlich]! To cure this enormous delusion of human beings! (*KSA* 9:11[10])

This ideal, of suspending anthropomorphic projections onto things in the attempt to see them "objectively"—*sachlich* is hard to translate: the idea is to let the thing, the *Sache,* the topic itself dictate how it is to be approached—will soon come into tension with the ideal of *maximizing* the personal element, or multiplying the personal perspectives in order to attain the fullest understanding of things.

After a note suggesting that "fabrication" *(Erdichtung)* on the part of "phantasy" might be responsible for constituting the larger part of our experience (a prefiguration of *DM* 119), Nietzsche writes:

Understanding is an astonishingly rapid projective phantasizing and drawing of conclusions. . . . When conversing with people I frequently have their facial expressions much more clearly before my eyes than my eyes are actually able to perceive: it is a fiction added to what they are saying, the interpretation in gestures of their face. . . . the greatest part of the perceptual image is not sense impression but *a product of phantasy.* (*KSA* 9:11[13])

There is another allusion to conversing with an other five years later, as the conclusion of an aphorism (*BGE* 192) that portrays the dual aspect of the contribution of phantasy to the constitution of experience. On the one hand, the admixture of imagining drive or affect in all perception generally leads to a sloppy kind of phantasizing that is conditioned primarily by laziness.

It is more comfortable for the eye to respond in a given case by regenerating an image that has been generated frequently in the past, rather than ascertaining what is divergent and new in the impression. . . . Even the "simplest" sensory processes are *dominated* by affects such as fear, love, and hate, including the passive affects of laziness.

Looking at a tree, for example, it is too much effort to attend to the unique and almost infinite richness of the experience: "It is so much easier to phantasize an approximation of a tree. Even in the strangest experiences we do the same thing: we make up the greater part of the experience."[45] This indicates an ancient human propensity for falsifying—though Nietzsche suggests that it can be put more tactfully by saying: "One is much more an artist than one knows." The realization of the element of artistic creativity in experience opens up the possibility of a rigorous kind of phantasizing that is conditioned by careful attentiveness—by a discipline that can be practiced only when one becomes aware of one's part in the process. It is at this point that Nietzsche repeats the example of a conversation in which the image of his interlocutor's face appears in greater detail than his physical eyes are capable of rendering: "And so the fineness of the play of [the person's facial] muscles and the look of the eyes *must* have been imaginatively contributed by me." The contribution of the experimentally artistic experiencer may have a subtlety of which the person's perceptual apparatus alone would be incapable.[46]

The original note from 1881 continues by drawing attention to the temporal dimensions of the constitution of experience:

Phantasy is to be substituted in place of the "unconscious": it is less a case of unconscious reasoning than of *projected possibilities* [hingeworfene Möglichkeiten] given by phantasy. Our "external world" is a *phantasy-product,* in the construction of which earlier phantasies are employed again as accustomed, habitual activities.

Here the deep-level phantasy activity that conditions all experience is extended back into the past: earlier phantasies are incorporated in present imagining, and forward into the future: phantasy constantly "projects possibilities."[47] The idea is developed in terms reminiscent of Kant's notion of the productive, transcendental imagination:

> Range of the *poetic* power: we cannot do anything without projecting in advance a *free image* of it *[ein freies Bild davon zu entwerfen].* . . . This image is very general, a schema. . . . An *ideal image* precedes our entire development, a product of phantasy: the true development is unknown to us. We *must* make this image. . . . Science is incapable of creating these images, though it is a major source of *nourishment* for this drive. (*KSA* 9:11[18])

There is an echo here of the "drive to create metaphors" discussed in the essay "On Truth and Lie." It is possible that memories of having read (about) Kant on the transcendental imagination are also playing a part here—while at the same time the language anticipates Heidegger's notion of the projection of world in understanding (and especially his account of the schematism in *Kant and the Problem of Metaphysics*).

A note that announces the task of describing "the history of the *sense of the I*" contains the following suggestions:

> Perhaps it will end with our recognizing instead of the I the relationships and enmities among things, thus *multiplicities* and their laws: with our *seeking to free* ourselves from the *error* of the I. . . . Transform the sense of the I! Weaken the personal tendency! Accustom the eye to the actuality of things! *For the time being* look away *from persons as much as possible!* (*KSA* 9:11[21])

Given Nietzsche's emphasis up to this point on the unavoidability of the personal approach, the admonition to "look away from persons as much as possible" is remarkable—unless "for the time being" is meant to suggest that the dropping of the personal perspective is merely a provisional expedient. A *nota bene* appended to this note emphasizes the benefits that accrue from "bracketing" the personal:

> *Letting* things (and not persons) *possess* us, and as great a range as possible of *true* things! What will *grow* from this is yet to be seen: we are *fertile soil* for things. *Images of existence* [Bilder des Daseins] must grow from us: and we should be in the way that this fruitfulness compels us to be. . . . Images of existence are *the most important thing* there has ever been—they rule over humanity.

The hyperbole of this last statement is especially striking. The idea of letting things possess us in such a way that images of existence grow from us as from fertile soil is worthy of some of Rilke's greatest poetry (though it is unlikely that Rilke read these notes), while these images of existence anticipate the archetypes *(Urbilder)* as understood by depth psychology.

But there now comes a remarkable volte-face on the topic of the personal versus the impersonal:

> The task: to *see* things *as they are! The means:* to be able to see with a hundred eyes, from *many* persons! It was a mistake to emphasize the impersonal and to characterize seeing with the eye of one's neighbor as moral. To see from [the viewpoint of] *many* neighbors and with purely personal eyes—that is the right thing. The "impersonal" is merely the personal *weakened,* something feeble: it can admittedly be useful every now and then, where there is a need for dispelling the clouding of passion from one's vision. (*KSA* 9:11[65])

This formulation, with its forceful repudiation of impersonality, would seem to carry the day—especially since its thesis is reinforced in a published text some six years later (*GM* 2.12). But one of the motives behind this vacillation is interesting in itself, and also because it may hint at impersonal withdrawal as a *stage* on the way toward "seeing things as they are."

The motive has to do with death and the realm of the dead, and is first sounded in terms reminiscent of Buddhist renunciation.

> To procure the advantages of one who is dead—nobody bothers about us, neither for nor against. To think oneself away out of humanity, to unlearn desires of all kinds: and to employ the entire abundance of one's powers in *looking.* To be the *invisible onlooker!* (*KSA* 9:11[35])

Another passage that would seem to derive from a less than ordinary experience of being-in-the-world. And if the chronological ordering of the notes is reliable, Nietzsche pursues the theme of the realm of the dead even after giving up his hopes for impersonality.

> Fundamentally false evaluation of the *dead* world on the part of the *sentient* world. Because we *are* [the latter] and *belong* to it! . . . The "dead" world! eternally in motion and without erring, force against force! . . . It is a *festival* to go from this world across *[überzugehen]* into the "dead world." . . . Let us see through this comedy [of sentient being] and thereby *enjoy* it! Let us *not* think of the return to the inanimate as a regression! We become quite *true,* we perfect ourselves. *Death* has to be reinterpreted! We thereby *reconcile* ourselves with what is actual, with the dead world.[48]

This note seems to have provided a basis for aphorism 278 of *The Joyful Science,* "The Thought of Death," and is quite consonant with remarks elsewhere in Nietzsche's writings concerning the underworld and the realm of Hades, the invisible.[49]

The idea of crossing over to the realm of the inanimate finds its way into the published works through the image of stone, as we have seen, and at this time in the brief and limpid aphorism entitled "How One Ought to Turn to Stone": "Slowly, slowly, to become hard like a precious stone—and finally to lie there, still and to the joy of eternity" (*DM* 541). This is the inanimate counterpart to the "book become almost human," and has to do with the hardness that is necessary for one's creation to leave its mark on history.[50]

In a note that begins by questioning whether it is even possible, let alone desirable, for the "will" to be silent in the practice of science, Nietzsche continues:

> In fact *all our drives* are active [in science], but as it were in a particular political order and accommodation with each other, so that their result is not any kind of phantasm: one drive stimulates another, each one phantasizes and wants to push through *its* kind of error: but each of these errors immediately becomes in turn the handle for another drive. . . . One puts out so many images that eventually one of them *works:* it is like shooting from a large number of guns at one piece of game; a great dice-play, often not in one person but in many, playing itself out over generations. . . . It is a hunt. The more individuals one has in oneself, the greater the prospect will be of one's discovering a truth—then the struggle is *within* him. (*KSA* 9:11[119])

A number of now familiar images appear together in this note, the most important feature of which is the emphasis on the efficacy of having some sort of political order obtain among the drives. This notion recurs in a note that remarks the difference in development between social and individual drives, and brings talk of inner multiplicity to a directly personal level.

> The free human being is a [political] state and a society of individuals. . . . People who live alone, as long as they do not go under, develop themselves into societies, a number of work areas are developed, and correspondingly a great struggle of drives for nourishment, space, and time. Self-regulation is not something attained immediately. In fact the human is on the whole a being that necessarily goes under because it has not yet attained it. (*KSA* 9:11[130])

Nietzsche himself had ten years during which to experience himself as a society of individuals; the question will arise later of whether he eventually went under from a lack of self-regulation.

At any rate, when at the beginning of August 1881 Nietzsche was struck by the thought of eternal recurrence, the first note that he committed to paper, with the famous inscription "6000 feet above the sea and much higher above all human things," resumes talk of the drives. The first part consists of a sketch of five headings under the title "The Recurrence of the Same," while the rest is a commentary on the fourth heading: "The innocent one. The individual as experiment."

> Our striving after seriousness consists in understanding everything as becoming, denying ourselves as individuals, looking into the world through as *many* eyes as possible, *living* in drives and activities *in order to* make ourselves eyes for that, giving oneself over to life *from time to time* so that one can later rest one's eyes on it: *entertaining* the drives as the foundation of all knowing, while being aware of where they oppose knowledge—in short, *to wait* and see to what extent *knowledge* and *truth* can be incorporated. (*KSA* 9:11[141])

Note that this ultimate incorporation is to take place through the medium of the drives, through our "entertaining" them—*unterhalten:* literally, *holding* ourselves *between* and among them, while understanding our selves as plays of drives that persist through the generations.

Drives Archaically Imagining

> *The feat of the imagination is in showing the convertibility of every thing into every other thing. Facts which had never before left their stark common sense, suddenly figure as Eleusinian mysteries.*
>
> Emerson, "Beauty"

Published the year after *Dawn of Morning,* in 1882, *The Joyful Science* effects a revolutionary transition in the discourse concerning the drives by opening up an *archaic* dimension to it. In an aphorism entitled "Consciousness of *Schein*" (*JS* 54), Nietzsche announces a personal discovery that has utterly transformed his experience of himself and the world. Three aphorisms earlier he had reemphasized the experimental nature of his thinking: "I admire any piece of skepticism to which I can reply, 'Let's try it!' But I have no interest in any thing or question that does not admit of experiment" (*JS* 51). The aphorisms that follow are thus to be taken as invitations to experiment rather than propositions in a theory of human nature.

I have *discovered* for myself that ancient humanity and animality, indeed the entire primal age and past of all sentient being continues in me to create *[fortdichtet]*, to love, to hate, to infer.[51]

Though not made explicit here, it is clear from the larger context that ancient humanity and animality operate in us through the medium of *drives,* the force of the past flowing in Dionysian drives through the body and Apollonian appearances shining forth from it as well-formed figures in phantastic projections. Three aphorisms later, Nietzsche addresses "the realists"— those "sober human beings who feel [themselves] forearmed against passion and phantasizing and would dearly like to make [their] emptiness a matter of pride and ornamentation"—on the topic of the contribution to experience of the phantasizing drives.

> You still carry around the valuations of things originating in the passions and loves of former centuries! Your sobriety still embodies a secret and indestructible drunkenness! Your love of "reality" for example—oh that is a primordial "love" indeed! In every feeling, in every sense impression there is a piece of [this] ancient love: and some phantasy, some prejudice, some piece of unreason, some ignorance, some fear, and heaven knows what else has worked on and woven at it. That mountain there! That cloud! What is "real" about it? Just take the phantasm and the entire human *contribution* away from it, you sober ones! Yes, if only you *could!* If only you could forget your heritage, your past, your training—your entire humanity and animality! (*JS* 57)

The shining of Apollo, however serene, gains its power from the intoxicated rush of Dionysus; each individual phantasm welling up, impelled, from a deep, transpersonal source. The experiment Nietzsche would have his readers undertake involves supposing that the drives that constitute our present experience have their roots in the archaic past: not only in our personal prehistory, but in the past of the human race—and on back beyond the animal past behind that. The deep-level phantasy activity that contributes to every moment of experience has an archaic, mythical dimension to it. Even if one could "forget [this] heritage," the archaic phantasizing would still not cease. As Sallustius said, profoundly, of a myth—though meaning *myth* as such: *"This never happened—but is always going on."* The point is important enough to merit hazarding an extratextual example or two in order to drive it home.

A woman is walking in the mountains, wandering through woods, along calm lakes. The mountains appear as gentle monsters, noble animals, creatures with strangely furrowed hides glowing green and gray in the warm sun, breathing thanks to the expectant waters. The phenomena of nature mirror themselves, naturally; not just mountains in lakes, but animals reflected in mountains. They are there, really, those formidable creatures, monstrous forms—shadowed forth from ancient memories of beasts more actual, images emerging from the archaic recesses of the soul. "That mountain there!" The mythic infusion is an integral condition of present reality, no merely subjective contribution.

A man is sitting by the sea, contemplating the later rays of the setting sun. The ocean lies spread out before him, a slumbering monster with gently rippling skin. Reflected in these wrinkles are movements of the air far above patterned in water vapor. As the wind blows, a vast array of clouds approaches, slowly floating, from the far horizon. Gigantic masks, figures of gods, daemonic visages appear in gradual majesty; animals too—lizards, angelfish, louring lions, and leaping steeds—all suspended in a lofty procession of animation. "That cloud! What is 'real' about it?" This man is no anthropomorphizer: it is not that he projects his personal fears and desires onto clouds that are "really" there, apart from the animal realm. But through his presence the clouds body forth their interfusion with archaic creatures.

But what if one does "remember" one's heritage: is Nietzsche not suggesting that it is impossible to subtract "the entire human contribution" from our experience in any case? Consider what he says after imparting his discovery of the continued operations through him of "ancient humanity and animality":

> I suddenly awoke in the middle of this dream, but only to the consciousness that I am indeed dreaming and that I *must* continue to dream, if I am not to perish, as the somnambulist must dream on, in order not to fall. (*JS* 54)

We cannot help being dreamers, mediums for the shining projections of myth, by day as at night, somnambulistic sites for the influx of the distant past. But we can awake within the dream, and become aware of the dispositions of the dynamic forces that compose the worlds of our experience. Through understanding the living reality of *Schein,* Nietzsche comes to feel

> that here there is sheen and will o' the wisp and a dance of spirits,
> that in the company of all these dreamers even I, who "recognize,"
> am dancing my dance, that the one who recognizes it is a means for
> the prolongation of the earthly dance and thereby one of the masters
> of ceremonies *[Festordner]* of existence.

Awareness of the dream, then, allows us to participate more fully in the festival of becoming, to play in what Freud will later call "the symphony of life," as part of "the mighty and primordial melody of the drives."[52]

Since *Thus Spoke Zarathustra,* being a dramatic narrative, is farther from theoretical discourse than any other of Nietzsche's works, it is not surprising that it should contain few mentions of the drives.[53] With the publication of *Beyond Good and Evil* (1886), however, the discourse of drives reaches its highest pitch and unfolds its profoundest implications. The first section of the book, "On the Prejudices of the Philosophers," is especially rich in psychological insights.

We saw earlier that Nietzsche understands all philosophies as "involuntary and unwitting memoirs" of their authors, seeing them as expressions of "basic human drives" (*BGE* 6). Let us recall some other remarks from that aphorism, which will now appear in a somewhat different light.

> Each one of [the basic human drives] would all too gladly present *itself* as the ultimate purpose of existence and the legitimate *master* of all the other drives. For every drive is domineering, and as *such* it tries to philosophize. . . . *Who the philosopher is* [depends on] the order of rank in which the innermost drives of his nature are disposed to each other.

The tendency of the drives toward tyrannical domination is reinforced when Nietzsche characterizes philosophy itself as a drive—and as *will to power:* "Philosophy always creates the world in its own image, it cannot do otherwise; *philosophy is this tyrannical drive itself, the most spiritual will to power,* to 'creation of the world,' to the *causa prima.*"[54] Philosophy is "the most spiritual will to power" because it exemplifies at the highest level the *interpretive* function of the drives—and from this point on, when Nietzsche speaks of will to power, he will emphasize that it is fundamentally interpretation.[55]

This point deserves to be stressed, in view of the widespread misunderstandings of this central Nietzschean idea. Physical power is crude by comparison with will to power: the deployment of one's energies toward exercizing brute force over others (imprisoning or banishing them, torturing and killing them) is a relatively short-lived undertaking, a local phenomenon the effects of which rarely endure beyond one's own death (or the collapse of a regime one has founded). To offer a convincing interpretation of the world, by contrast, to have others see things in a different way, is to exercize a much more subtle and enduring form of power—and one with the potential to reach far beyond one's geographical or historical situation. As Emerson remarks in "The American Scholar": "Not he is great who can alter matter, but he who can alter my state of mind." A similar consideration is the ground for Nietzsche's (albeit ambivalent) admiration for both Socrates and Jesus: lacking physical power they nevertheless exerted tremendous influence through their respective interpretations of existence. While their enemies are for the most part forgotten, both these figures are alive and at work millennia after their physical deaths.

The purpose of this lengthy engagement with the idea of drives will now be clear: insofar as they imaginally interpret the world (as presented in nerve stimuli), the drives are manifestations of will to power. We are now in a position to see why Nietzsche understands the person as a mask and focal point for ancient currents of will to power, and psychology as "morphology and *doctrine of the development of will to power*."[56]

The *"new* psychologist" will work from a new understanding of the psyche, which turns out to be a refinement of an old idea of the soul. Stimulated by his reading of Lange (and, through him, of Boscovich), Nietzsche had been arguing for some time against what he called "materialistic atomism," the idea that the world ultimately consists of some kind of "matter" understood as "solid stuff."[57] He now extends his criticism to an even more basic manifestation of the tendency, which he ascribes to the Christian tradition under the name *soul-atomism,* the view that "takes the soul as something indestructible, eternal, indivisible, as a monad, as an *atomon*." He proposes that we abandon this notion and substitute "such new conceptions and refinements of the soul-hypothesis . . . as 'mortal soul,' 'soul as subject-multiplicity,' and 'soul as social structure of the drives and affects'" (*BGE* 12).

One reason for the persistence of the idea of the unitary soul has to do with the human tendency to be "seduced by words."[58] The subject-predicate structure of the sentence "I think" misleads us into supposing that, if there is thinking going on, there must be some agent (designated by the sign "I") that is doing the thinking (*BGE* 16). One of Lichtenberg's later aphorisms reads as follows:

> We should say *it thinks,* just as we say *it lightens [es blitzt].* To say *cogito* is already to say too much as soon as we translate it *I think.* To assume, to postulate the *I* is a practical requirement.[59]

Following Lichtenberg, Nietzsche also anticipates the Freudian idea of the "it" (*das Es;* the "id"):

> A thought comes when "it" wants, and not when "I" will it. . . . It thinks: but that this "it" is precisely the famous old "I" is, to put it mildly, merely an assumption, an assertion, and above all not any kind of "immediate certainty."[60]

The important further implication is that in being pushed aside by the It the I is no longer one, alone, home only to itself. It is, rather, many; and not the monolithic entity it would appear to be. The linguistic sign in English that stands for the first-person singular, that singularly capital figure and up-standing pillar of phallic assertion that is the "I" (more imposing, interestingly, unemphasized than as "*I*"), tends to reinforce the illusion of unity more strongly than do the corresponding signs in other European languages *(ich, je, io, ego).**

An unpublished note from the summer of 1885, when Nietzsche was writing *Beyond Good and Evil,* explicates the connections between the autonomy of the "I think" and the dissolution of the I into a multiplicity of persons, in a rich amplification of the idea of "thought-persons" that was first proposed in *Human, All Too Human.*

> A thought is, in the figure in which it comes, a multivocal sign that requires interpretation ... before it finally becomes univocal. It comes up in me—where from? how? I simply don't know. It comes, independently of my will, usually surrounded and obscured by a mass of feelings, desires, aversions, and also other thoughts. . . . One pulls him out of this mass, cleans him off, sets him on his feet, and then sees how he stands and how he walks—all of this in an astonishing *presto* and yet without any sense of hurry. Just *who* does all this—I have no idea, and I am surely more a spectator than originator of this process.[61]

The question of just who does do all this will become gradually more pressing. Nietzsche's train of thought about thoughts then takes a juridical turn:

> One then presides over him [the thought] as in court, and asks: "What does he mean? What must he mean? Is he right or wrong?"—and one calls on the assistance of other thoughts, and undertakes comparisons. Thinking thus shows itself to be a kind of practicing and enacting of justice, in which there is a judge, an opposing party, and even an examination of witnesses, on which I am permitted to listen in some-

---

*It may be noted here, in the sole footnote of the book, that no use has been made of the first person singular pronoun (aside from in the acknowledgments). The pronoun appears in a number of quotations, of course, and there is frequent talk of the "I"—but the I has not spoken itself. (It has been mentioned but not used.) If this is modesty on the part of the present author, it is by no means merely false: what is important here are Nietzsche's ideas, rather than Parkes's. This circumstance discounts timidity and fear of being contradicted as possible motives, insofar as the main aim is to impart Nietzsche's psychology. There is admittedly an element of reaction against the frequent abuse, through overuse, of the first person singular in current academic prose, whether owing to carelessness about style or unseemly egoism (or both). But the main grounds for avoiding the use of "I" are psychological and philosophical—since the whole point of Nietzsche's psychology is to put the I in question, to prompt the question "Who?" at its every appearance, to hear the polyphony behind the apparent univocality of the first person singular. (In this context the use, in reggae songs, of the magnificent locution "I and I," so beloved of Rastafarians, is well worth pondering.)

what—though only a little, since it seems that most of it escapes
me. . . . That a multiplicity of persons appears to participate in all
thinking is by no means easy to observe, since we are basically trained
in thinking *not* to think about thinking.

When the nineteen-year-old Nietzsche used to "eavesdrop on [his] own
thoughts and feelings" he would hear "the hum and buzzing of wild parties"; now, twenty years later, at least some of the parties are more sober,
contending with one another in courts of law. And there are, of course, many
other kinds of proceeding than legal taking place among the "multiplicity
of persons" that constitutes the soul.[62] The note ends by invoking the theme
of the plethora of unconscious physiological processes that underlies our
"overall condition," the signs and symptoms of which we are constantly
interpreting. But beneath the level of our impersonal and abstract interpretations there is a vital community of persons, to which we remain—through
our undeveloped powers of observation—for the most part oblivious.

Nietzsche proceeds in *Beyond Good and Evil* to a discussion of the *will,*
in which he argues first—against Schopenhauer—that will is above all
"something complex, something that is a unity only as a word" (*BGE* 19).
He insists that willing consists of a *plurality* of feelings, including a feeling
of a state *away from which* and a state *toward which,* of the "from" and
"toward" themselves (attraction and repulsion: Freud's *Lust* and *Unlust*),
and an accompanying feeling in the muscles that "begins its play" as soon
as we "will." Second: in every act of willing there is some kind of thinking,
"a commanding thought." Thoughts can command only insofar as they are
persons; at a certain level we deal with them personally and they personally
with us.[63] And third: will is an *affect,* comprising the affects of commanding
and obeying.

A person who *wills*—commands something in him that he thinks
obeys. But now consider the most wonderful thing about will: . . .
insofar as we are in any given case the commanding *and* the obeying
parties, and as obeyers know the feelings of constraint, compulsion,
pressure, resistance, and movement that generally begin immediately
upon the act of willing; and insofar as, on the other hand, we are
accustomed to disregard this duality and conceal it from ourselves
by means of the synthetic concept "I," a whole series of erroneous
conclusions and consequently of false evaluations of the will itself
has become attached to the act of willing.

The unitary notion of the "I" fools us into thinking that the first person
singularly wills, whereas in any act of willing—whether successful or
not—there is at least a second person involved. Nietzsche characterizes the
executive instruments that help carry out a command of will as "under-

wills" or "under-souls," inserting the significant parenthesis: "for our body is simply a social structure of many souls." In terms of the schema elaborated in *Dawn of Morning,* one drive issues commands while other drives obey—or else rebel. In cases where a drive with which one does not identify as "I"—some "it" within—prevails, it may be overcome by another drive (or coalition of drives) which will, when successful, identify itself as "I." But as with the earlier model, where it is drives "all the way down" (as William James would say) and "all the way up," in the present picture it is "souls" and "wills" all the way—rather than a case of wills acting upon nerves or muscles. Nietzsche sums up these points in a political image, by saying that what happens in a successful case of willing is "what happens in every well-constructed and happy commonwealth, that the ruling class identifies itself with the successes of the commonwealth as a whole."[64]

In view of the similarity between this view and the Homeric picture of the individual as an "interior society" or a "community of internal agents," it is interesting that in the next aphorism Nietzsche talks of philosophy as itself something "driven" into a definite order by archaic forces. The thinking of philosophers is thus "far less a matter of discovering than of recognizing, recollecting, a return home to a distant and ancient household of the entire soul, out of which their concepts originally grew. Philosophizing is thus a kind of atavism of the first rank" (*BGE* 20). Thus the strange "family resemblance" of all Indo-European philosophizing is explained by the proximity of the linguistic households in which they developed.[65] The idea that language conditions thought (weaker than linguistic *determinism*), that thinking is "unconsciously guided by similar grammatical functions," leads Nietzsche to the following pregnant supposition:

> Philosophers in the domain of the Ural-Altaic languages (in which the concept of the subject is most poorly developed) will most probably look "into the world" differently and be found on different paths from Indo-Germans or Muslims.

This surmise appears to be valid—at least in the case of one member of the Ural-Altaic family in which sophisticated philosophies have developed: namely, Japanese. The concept of the subject is so "poorly developed" in Japanese that the grammatical subject is rarely used.[66] Descartes would have found it impossible to develop his idea of the *cogito* in Japanese, insofar as the equivalent of the Japanese "I think" is simply "There is thinking going on"—its being left to the context to decide who is doing the thinking. It is thus not surprising that the Buddhist idea that the I is a fiction should have found fertile soil in Japan.[67] Taken out of context, Nietzsche's remarks concerning "the spell of particular grammatical functions" might be misunderstood as some kind of "competitive philology," as implying that a strong sense of the subject makes for more powerful thinking.[68] But since they occur in the course of a series of attacks on the reality of the I, the interesting implication is that a weak concept of the subject would likely conduce to some quite robust philosophizing.[69]

In case the idea that the vital drives of human beings are inherently tyrannical should seem to rest on an unnaturally pessimistic view of human nature, Nietzsche sets it in the context of an understanding of natural life in the widest sense. He claims that the natural-scientific idea of "nature's conformity to law" is merely one interpretation rather than a reflection of reality, and furthermore an interpretation that issues from "the democratic instincts of the modern soul," which would have the slogan "Everywhere equality before the law" apply to the natural as well as the human realm (*BGE* 22). He offers an alternative interpretation in terms of "the tyranically inconsiderate and relentless enforcement of claims of power," imagining an interpreter "who would portray the universality and unconditionality in all 'will to power' so vividly that almost any word, and even the word 'tyranny,' would ultimately appear unusable or as a weakening and attenuating metaphor—as too human." Nietzsche anticipates the response that *this* is only another interpretation (one far less "politically correct" now, of course, than when he proposed it), and his riposte is "so much the better." The radically inegalitarian metaphor of tyranny is again proposed experimentally—as an interpretation that will enrich and enhance one's experience rather than impoverish it.

The aphorism that concludes the first section of *Beyond Good and Evil* begins with an announcement of Nietzsche's program as a depth psychologist.

All psychology so far has got hung up on moral prejudices and fears: it has not dared to descend into the depths. To understand psychology, as I do, as morphology and *doctrine of the development of will to power*—nobody's ideas have even come close to this. (*BGE* 23)

Several decades before Freud (whose ideas likewise come too close for comfort to a number of moral prejudices and fears), Nietzsche cites "unconscious resistances in the heart of the researcher" as the major block on the road to psychological insight. The "strong and hearty conscience" is repulsed by "a teaching to the effect that the 'good' and 'bad' drives mutually condition each other"—and even more so by "a teaching of the derivability of all good drives from bad ones." The prospect is capable of occasioning nausea in all but the most robust researchers.

Suppose, however, that someone takes the affects of hatred, envy, covetousness, and lust to rule as life-conditioning affects, as things that basically and essentially must be present in the overall economy of life, and so must be enhanced if life is to be enhanced—such a person will suffer from such an orientation of his judgment as from sea-sickness.

This is by no means to say that negative drives and affects are simply to be given free reign, but rather to suggest that moral qualms impoverish the overall economy of life by demanding that such "unsalutary" forces be excluded from it or extirpated.

The section ends with a prophetic pronouncement, addressed to those souls courageous enough to venture into the "new realm of dangerous insights" opened up by these ethically suspect considerations, and which anticipates the resurgence of psychology in the form of the depth psychology of the twentieth century.

> Never yet did a *deeper* world of insight open itself up to audacious adventurers and travelers; and the psychologist who makes this kind of "sacrifice"—*not* a sacrifice of the intellect: quite the contrary!—will at least be entitled to demand in return that psychology be recognized again as queen of the sciences, for whose service and preparation the other sciences exist. For psychology is once again the way to the fundamental problems.

Psychology leads to the fundamental problems because the psychologist is always inclined to ask of any science or theory or worldview: From what perspective are things being seen that they appear this way? Which moral prejudices are conditioning these phenomena? What psychological needs on the part of the inquirer are being satisfied by the advocacy of conclusions such as these—or by the refusal to countenance considerations such as those? This drive for depth is by no means anti-intellectual: psychological inquiry in the Nietzschean mode is severe and penetrating, demanding rather a sacrifice of the *heart* in the sense that the inquirer must be prepared to give up all comforting sentimentality concerning the human condition.

Several aphorisms from the second section of *Beyond Good and Evil* prepare the reader for the explicit association of the drives with will to power, a move that is central to Nietzsche's psychology and to his thinking as a whole. The psychological dialectic between inside and outside that we have seen discussed in terms of projection and imagination and on the assumption of a community of persons within the soul now takes an interesting turn in an aphorism that arises from the tension in Nietzsche's own person between the drive for solitude and the drive for community. The rare human being will naturally want to be able to retreat from the crowd into a "citadel" of solitude (*BGE* 26). And yet one who craves insight into the human condition will be driven by an opposite drive into contact with human beings who are "the rule" rather than the exception, as he is. A person of refined taste will on occasion be sickened by intercourse with his coarser fellows; and yet one who persists in remaining "proudly in his citadel" is clearly "not made, not predetermined for knowledge."

> If he were, he would one day have to say to himself, "The devil take my good taste! The rule is more interesting than the exception—than me, the exception!" and he would go *down* [hinab], and above all "inside" *[hinein]*. . . . But if he is lucky . . . he will come across real shortcuts and alleviators of his task . . . [through acknowledging] the animal, commonness, and "the rule" *in himself.* (*BGE* 26; latter emphasis added)

There is a parallel here to the move made by Zarathustra when he leaves the solitude of his cave on the mountaintop and goes down to the world below in order to "become human" again—especially insofar as his encounters with the "stinking rabble" there generally occasion nausea. Since Nietzsche saw *Beyond Good and Evil* as a more conventional presentation of the ideas in *Zarathustra,* this passage concerning the inquirer's going down and *in* should prompt us to read Zarathustra's problems with coming to terms with the rabble as his difficulty in accepting—and affirming—the stinking rabble in his own soul.

To go down and in for the sake of insight is to embark upon a task that is mythic in its dangers. One who would be "independent" in Nietzsche's sense must have courage:

> He enters a labyrinth, and multiplies a thousandfold the dangers that life in itself brings with it—of which not the least is that nobody can see how and where he loses his way, becomes solitary, and is torn to pieces by some cave-minotaur of conscience. (*BGE* 29)

Presumably the chances of being subjected to such a Dionysian dismemberment are lessened if one is in touch with an Ariadne figure who could help lead one back out and up.

Here, now, is an account of the major experiment Nietzsche proposes we undertake with the idea of drives as will to power (note the hypothetical tone with which it opens):

> Supposing nothing else were "given" as real except our world of desires and passions, that we could get down or up to no other "reality" than the reality of our drives—for thinking is simply a relationship of these drives to each other: is it not permitted to make the experiment and ask whether this "given" is not *sufficient* for understanding on this kind of basis the so-called mechanistic (or "material") world? I mean . . . as something of the same level of reality as our affect itself—as a more primitive form of the world of affects, in which

everything still lies contained in powerful unity, prior to ramifying and developing itself in the organic process, as a kind of drive-life? (*BGE* 36)

If we are going to understand will as causally effective, Nietzsche goes on, we should wield Occam's razor and try positing nothing more than will, try understanding the world on the hypothesis that it is wills all the way down. As with the body understood as a structure of wills, "'Will' can naturally have an effect only on 'will'—and not on 'matter' (not on 'nerves,' for example)." In stressing the homogeneity of these agents, Nietzsche is following Herder (perhaps unwittingly), who in his essay on the soul has this to say about the power relations obtaining between soul and body:

> But if the soul is force *[Kraft]* . . . and if the body in its various parts animated by stimulation and sensation is also only force, a realm of invisible, inner, only less bright forces . . . is it a contradiction that soul should work on an entire realm of darker stimuli, sensations, and bodily forces? These are of the same nature as the soul, just very different orders and grades. . . . The knowing soul reigns over a realm of lower but just as invisible inner beings as she herself is. She reigns, as Leibniz would say, over a world of slumbering, dreaming, half-waking monads. (*EMS* 624)

Indeed Nietzsche's idea of will to power can be seen as a culmination of monistic tendencies in the tradition from Leibniz and Spinoza through the German Romantic thinkers as epitomized by Herder. The aphorism ends in a grand finale of experimentalism.

> Supposing, finally, that we were to succeed in explaining our entire drive-life as the development and ramification of one basic form of will—namely, of will to power . . . supposing one could find in this the solution to the problem of procreation and nourishment—it is *one* problem—one would then have the right to determine *all* effective force univocally as: *will to power.* The world seen from within, the world determined and defined in its "intelligible character"—would be precisely "will to power" and nothing besides.[70]

From this we can draw a picture of the human being, body and soul, as a microcosmic configuration of drives (will to power) situated within the macrocosm of the world as an encompassing matrix of will to power (drives)—bearing in mind that this interplay between inner and outer extends temporally across many generations. The task of ordering the plays of drives within the individual thus involves understanding them within that larger matrix, in the context of the greater field of interpretive will to power that is the world. If all existence is interpreting, then all phenomena are expressing in their being: *This* is what it means to be, or become. Emphatically, the basic elements assert themselves. Where vegetation prevails is the claim: *This* process is what sun and earth, water and air, really are. Trees, magnificent exemplars, speak most powerfully of the realm of plants. Animals supervene, intimating *This* is what the elements and vegetation are, as they incorporate. And humans, presenting themselves as the supreme embodiment of mineral, vegetal, and animal, represent the grandest interpretation of all.

The discussion of drives can be rounded out with a consideration of the phenomenon of their *retroflection,* which sheds light on the connections between the projection of persons and the medium of the imagination. In his concern with the origin of master and slave moralities, Nietzsche comes upon a case of retroflection of the drives that parallels the ascetic practice discussed earlier. He supposes a decisive type of retroflection takes place in every society, after the point at which peace with neighboring societies is first established. As long as a community has external enemies, it encourages in its stronger members the development of drives that issue in physically powerful actions.

> Certain strong and dangerous drives, such as the joy in undertaking things, foolhardiness, vengefulness, craftiness, rapacity, and the lust to rule, which had so far not only been honored as beneficial to the community—albeit under different names from those chosen here— but also had to be cultivated and disciplined into great strength . . . are now experienced as doubly dangerous, since the channels for their discharge are no longer there, and they are gradually branded as immoral and exposed to slander. (*BGE* 201)

It is not only a matter of physical power, since Nietzsche goes on to number among the "highest and strongest drives" that come to threaten the community such things as "lofty and independent spirituality, the will to stand alone, and even great reason"; but the phenomenon of retroflection of the drives is most easily understood in the context of the more overtly physical instincts—as in the later discussion in *Toward the Genealogy of Morals.* In his inquiry into the origin of what he calls "bad conscience" Nietzsche writes of it as

> the serious illness that human beings must succumb to under the pressure of that most fundamental of changes they have ever undergone— when they finally found themselves enclosed within the sphere of society and peace. . . . All of a sudden, for these half-animals that were well adapted to wilderness, war, prowling, adventure, all their instincts were devalued and "suspended." . . . For this new and un-

known world they no longer had their old guides, their regulating, unconscious, and infallible drives. (*GM* 2.16)

Now comes the crucial turn (another that anticipates a major element of psychoanalytic theory):

> All instincts that do not discharge themselves toward the outside *turn inward*—this is what I call the *internalization* of the human being: thus it was that the human being first developed what later came to be called the "soul." This entire inner world, originally as thin as if it were stretched between two membranes, extended and expanded and acquired depth, breadth, and height in proportion as outward discharge was *inhibited.*

The interiority of the soul developed then from the retroflection of drives that were originally directed outward. This idea is amplified in a note from the *Nachlass* of the same year (1887):

> Inwardness arises when powerful drives that have been denied outward discharge by the establishment of peace and society try to make themselves harmless by *turning inward in concert with the imagination.* The need for enmity, cruelty, revenge, violence turns back and "retreats"; covetousness and domination become a desire for knowledge; the power of dissimulation and lying is reflected in the artist; *the drives are transformed into demons* with whom one fights, and so on.[71]

This last point is the crux: as drives are retroflected they are transformed through the medium of phantasy into persons—and in the case of so-called "negative" drives into "demons," autonomous powers capable of standing in opposition to the I. By this time one might suppose that Nietzsche's earlier hypothesis of a "person-creating/imagining" drive can be dropped—or else expanded to cover the entire field—insofar as *any* drive would now seem capable at some level of appearing as a person.

IX

Archaic Casts and Psychical Regimes

> *In different hours, a man represents each of several of his ances-*
> *tors, as if there were seven or eight of us rolled up in each man's*
> *skin—seven or eight ancestors at least—and they constitute the*
> *variety of notes for that new piece of music which his life is.*
>
> Emerson, "Fate"

In previous chapters we saw how the drives can manifest themselves in images of natural phenomena—as raging torrents, burgeoning plants, ferocious animals, and so on; but it became clear from the last chapter that they also have a primary propensity to present themselves, through the medium of the imagination, as persons. The two principal drives discussed in Nietzsche's early work are named after the divine persons of Apollo and Dionysus. The Dionysian drive dissolves the individual into a multiplicity by prompting entry into "other natures," impelling the individual to identify with other persons—and, by extension, with humanity and nature as a whole. The Apollonian drive projects a sheen of phantasy over the abyss of sensation, resolving neural impulses into shining figures of the imagination—whether Olympian gods and goddesses or persons more closely associated with the dreamer's own biography. While in his earlier thinking Nietzsche ascribed our inability to deal with the world impersonally to the constant operation of a "person-creating drive," he later appears (after some vacillation on the issue of the personal) to understand all drives as being naturally self-personifying—at least up until the last year of his writing.

Not only does a drive project a world from one of numerous personal perspectives within the psyche, but the drives also tend thereby to project a play of persons. It is instructive to inquire into the patterns that inform this play. And just as the drives derive from the archaic past, so the associated persons will have genealogies extending back beyond the individual's birth. A major medium through which such persons appear is the phenomenon of the dream. Insofar as Nietzsche entertains the idea of drama as a model for life and the actor as a paradigm for the human agent, one may expect to find theatrical images playing a part in ordering the multiplicity of the soul. But there is another source of relevant imagery to be found in ancient Greek thought, which Nietzsche draws on and elaborates more fully: namely, Plato's idea of the psyche as *polis,* as political community. While some commentators remark parallels between Nietzsche and Plato in passing, most have overlooked the insights to be gained from a careful comparison on the topic of the political organization of the inner community.[1]

Before embarking on the final phase of our inquiry, a more general remark concerning the implications of this theme is in order. Although the topic of the multiple self has important ramifications in a number of fields of philosophical inquiry, it has been generally ignored.[2] Many problems in philosophy and their putative solutions rest upon an unquestioned conception of the unity of the self. Whether we understand ourselves as some kind of simple unity or as a complex multiplicity of persons or agents is less a theoretical question than an existential issue with far reaching psychological and ethical implications. If there are multiple knowers and agents in each person, the complexities of epistemological problems and questions of moral responsibility are intriguingly compounded.

In reengaging the (im)personal aspect of the drives in the final two sections of the chapter, we resume our examination of the images Nietzsche employs to characterize the operations of the psyche, at the most complex level of images of human community. It is at this last level that the problem of ordering the multiplicity of the soul is at its most pressing—and so may be most fruitfully examined.

Patterns Personal and Impersonal

> *If I have described life as a flux of moods, I must now add, that there is that in us which changes not, and which ranks all sensations and states of mind. . . . The question ever is, not, what you have done or forborne, but, at whose command you have done or forborne it.*
>
> Emerson, "Experience"

The idea of psychical multiplicity is naturally inhibited by belief in a single self—a belief that tends to be shaken, however, by experience of the world as constant flux. Indeed Nietzsche, like the Buddhists, sees the belief in the substantiality of the self, as well as in the substantiality of things other than the self, as a kind of defence against the insecurity engendered by a constantly changing world. The experience of the I as something unstable and in flux undermines faith in its unity, and the realization of a multiplicity in turn raises the question of how to organize the elements and events within.

One finds this issue treated with limpid clarity by Montaigne, with his notion of the "undulating I"—though he himself became such a remarkably well ordered individual that signs of his struggle to impose order on his inner multiplicity are hard to discern. The beginning of the essay "On Repentance," which happens to mention most of the major themes of the present chapter, establishes the close connection between the flux of the world and the undulating self.

> The world is but a perennial movement. All things in it are in constant motion. . . . Stability itself is nothing but a more languid motion. I cannot keep my subject [myself] still. It goes along befuddled and staggering, with a natural drunkenness. . . . I do not portray being: I portray passing . . . whether I am different myself, or whether I take hold of my subjects in different circumstances and aspects.[3]

Nevertheless, in observing himself Montaigne is able to discern a pattern to the flux, which he talks about in the context of differentiating inner from outer, private from public standards.

> Those of us especially who live a private life that is on display only to ourselves must have a pattern established within us by which to test our actions, and, according to this pattern, now pat ourselves on the back, now punish ourselves. I have my own laws and court to judge me, and I address myself to them more than anywhere else.[4]

The difficulty of being morally autonomous, in the literal sense of providing one's own moral laws, is emphasized also through the metaphor of the image of actors and the theater.

> It is a rare life that remains well ordered in private. Any man can play his part in the side show and represent a worthy man on the boards; but to be disciplined within, in his own bosom, where all is permissible, where all is concealed—that's the point. (*Essays,* 3:2, 613)

The difference between seeming and being, between the mask and whatever is behind it, outward show and inner drama, will concern us later in the chapter.

For Montaigne, as for Nietzsche, there must be an ordering agency within the soul if one is to live well, and in this context he proposes the image of an "inner court"—an image we saw the latter use in connection with thinking in general rather than only moral judgment. Montaigne goes on to say more about this "ruling pattern": "There is no one who, if he listens to himself, does not discover in himself a pattern all his own, a ruling pattern, which struggles against education and against the tempest of the passions that oppose it" (3:2, 615). Like the law Zarathustra imposes upon himself, this ruling pattern is unique to the individual. Montaigne was a major precursor in the art so highly prized by Nietzsche of "listening with the third ear," and this passage shows that the ruling pattern is something *discovered*—something naturally "given," and like Nietzsche's "granite of fate" in being resistant to education—even though the inclination to listen for it or the will to follow it may not be. In expressing gratitude that his own passions are in general not so strong as to make it difficult to follow his ruling pattern, Montaigne amplifies the political metaphor (along Platonic lines):

> I customarily do wholeheartedly whatever I do, and go my way all in one piece. I scarcely make a motion that is hidden and out of sight of my reason, and that is not guided by the consent of nearly all parts of me, without division, without internal sedition. (*Essays,* 3:2, 618)

The important division, for Montaigne, is that between inner and outer, private and public—a distinction that is more complicated in Nietzsche, as is also that between reason and other motive forces in the psyche. (We shall consider the political metaphor for these internal relations in the last section of this chapter.)

Montaigne inquires elsewhere, in the frame of the courtroom metaphor, into the relations between the will and a multiplicity of other forces—in a way that suggests that in his younger days he was not so immune to "internal sedition" after all. In "On the Power of the Imagination" he sketches a picture of the body that anticipates Nietzsche's idea of it as "a social structure of many souls," in a passage that sets out from a humorous reflection on the capricious behavior of the male organ.

> People are right to notice the unruly liberty of this member, obtruding so importunately when we have no use for it, and failing so importunately when we have the most use for it, and struggling for mastery so imperiously with our will, refusing with so much pride and obstinacy our solicitations, both mental and manual. (*Essays,* 1:21, 72)

Montaigne then moves to exonerate the penis from charges of insubordination, on the grounds that they have been trumped up by other organs of the body who are equally importunate in their own ways.

> For I ask you to think whether there is a single one of the parts of our body that does not often refuse its function to our will and exercise it against our will. They each have passions of their own which rouse them and put them to sleep without our leave.

Playing the part of the defense attorney, he pleads for leniency toward his client, citing numerous instances of willful behavior on the part of the facial muscles, heart, lungs, pulse, hair, skin, hand, tongue, stomach, bladder, and intestines—all of which are represented as what Nietzsche calls "under-wills."

Insofar as much of Nietzsche's talk of psychical multiplicity is in terms of persons within the individual, one wants to ask who these persons really are—what it means to speak of them as *persons,* where they come from, and how it is that they are now there.

For Nietzsche the soul is naturally the site of multiple figures of the imagination, particular images, all perspectives personal. Persons as images are not concepts or ideas, nor abstractions of any kind: one's anger is not a person, nor one's hunger, nor one's intellect. An image-person has a visage, a particular face, and moreover a *voice,* so that one can be addressed by it and so engage in dialogue. The old crone from last night's dream is a person, even though the dreamer has never encountered her in real life, as is the image of a writer one admires but has never met except in phantasy. Bizet's Carmen is a person, fictional in nature, while Ariadne is a mythical person. A deceased father is a person, as an image that lives on in memory and dream, while a mother still living is a person in two senses: as a psychical image, with whom one engages in dialogue in imagination, and also as a person in her own right, leading an independent existence. The problem is that Nietzsche (like every man) cannot perceive his mother directly, without the mediation of the image of her that lives in his psyche. The way he experiences his actual, flesh-and-blood mother is conditioned by his inner image of her, which is in turn informed by experience of the real woman. And yet the core, as it were, of this image is older and impersonal—a figure of woman formed long before the individual's birth. The same is true of any person with whom one has dealings in the real world: "We do the same when awake as in the dream: we first invent and create the person we are dealing with—and immediately forget that we have done so" (*BGE* 138). The oscillation between inner and outer continues.[5]

Let us go back for a moment to Nietzsche's ideas about the ways the past, where these persons seem to come from originally, enters into our present existence. In the essay on history he remarks on the tendency to dismiss the past, because of its burdensome nature, as mere appearance— as something not fully real.

> The human being braces himself against the great and ever greater weight of the past: this presses him down or bends him sideways, weighing down his steps as an invisible and dark burden which he would like to deprecate as mere appearance *[Schein]*. (*HL* 1)

What is past is not all foreign: part of recent history is our own personal history, the past that we ourselves have experienced directly and thereby incorporated. The task of assimilation, made possible by the individual's "plastic power," and comprising pasts both personal and impersonal, is thus almost boundless:

> For the most powerful and tremendous nature there would be no limit to the historical sense . . . it would draw to itself and take in the entire past, its own and the most foreign, and as it were transform it into blood.[6]

But the absorption of the past is also a source of conflict, a conflict similar to that described in "On Moods" between incoming experiences and older residents of the household of the soul. In the essay on history, Nietzsche presents a comparable "image of the mental processes taking place in the soul of the modern human being":

> Historical knowledge streams in unceasingly from inexhaustible wells, things strange and incoherent press in on us . . . and our nature strives to receive and arrange and honor these strange guests, but they are themselves in conflict with each other, and it seems necessary to constrain and master them if we are not ourselves to perish in the struggle. Habituation to such a disorderly, stormy, and conflict-ridden household gradually becomes second nature, though this second nature is unquestionably much weaker, more restless, and altogether unhealthier than the first. (*HL* 4)

The power of mastery sufficient to keep the guests from the past in order and the discernment necessary to maintain the balance between admitting the flow of the past and experiencing life in the present are a rare combination—which is why Nietzsche emphasizes that history can be borne *"only by strong personalities"* (*HL* 5). But even for ordinary mortals, the attainment of this kind of balance is an integral feature of a rich psychological life.

But let us first look "closer to home," in the personal prehistory of the individual, for the source of at least some of the voices that participate in a person's internal dialogue. An aphorism near the beginning of *The Wanderer and His Shadow* bears the title "Content of the Conscience."

> The content of our conscience is everything that was regularly *demanded* of us without reason during our childhood, by persons whom we respected or feared. . . . The faith in authorities is the source of conscience: it is thus not the voice of God in the human breast, but rather the voice of some other human beings in the human being. (*WS* 52)

Insofar as we encounter in the course of growing up a number of "persons whom we respect or fear," a variety of "authorities" (parents, teachers, dominant peers), one would expect the conscience to speak with many voices. This idea strongly prefigures Freud's ideas about the origins of conscience, which he imagines is constituted by the introjection of images of the parents above all.[7] And indeed it may be helpful to take a brief look in this context at a relevant strain in psychoanalytical thinking about how the ego is formed.

Having no direct experience of fatherhood, except in relation to his books, Nietzsche has little to say about children; but if one looks to the psychoanalytical literature on the developmental formation of personality, one finds accounts couched in imagery that emphasizes the multiplicity of the psyche and is consonant with Nietzsche's ideas. The neonate is imagined to have no conception of the distinction between inner and outer, self and not-self. The boundary between self and world is constructed by a laborious process of introjection and projection, analogous to the physical activities of swallowing and disgorging, in which one takes in what one likes and spits out what is distasteful. The developing I clings to this mechanism of the primitive "oral" phase, insofar as identification with "role models" continues to take place by means of introjection, by incorporating the other person into the psyche. The most striking instance of this phenomenon occurs at the beginning of the formation of the "over-I" *(Über-Ich),* when the child introjects the parents (or parent-substitutes) in order to help resolve the Oedipus complex. Depth psychology in general sees the I not as something given, but rather as a *construct* (both Freud and Jung speak of the *Ich-Komplex*), something put together by the psyche in order to cope with the external world. The implication of these developmental accounts, which are based on a vast amount of experience of child analysis, is again that the self is in large part composed of others, that each person is in fact many persons.[8]

An unpublished note (from the year *The Wanderer and His Shadow* appeared) shows that Nietzsche anticipated the psychoanalytical idea of introjection, though without using that exact term for the process. Especially significant is the mention of drives in this context:

> Our relation to ourselves! . . . We retroflect all good and bad drives upon ourselves . . . we never treat ourselves as an individual but as a duality and multiplicity; we practice all social relations (friendship, revenge, envy) on ourselves . . . *we are always among a multiplicity.* We have split ourselves up and continue to do so. . . . We have transposed "society" into ourselves, in miniature, and to retreat into oneself is thus no kind of flight from society, but an often painful dreaming-on *[Fortträumen]* and interpreting of our experiences on the schema of earlier experiences. We take into ourselves not only God but all beings that we recognize, even without the names: we are

the cosmos, *insofar as we have conceived or dreamed it.* Olives and stones have become a part of us: the stock exchange and the newspaper as well.[9]

The whole of society—olives, stones, and all: this is an important sense in which "the soul is all things" for Nietzsche. (And the presence in there of the stock exchange and even the newspaper certainly explains the nausea that afflicts characters like Zarathustra.)

If all beings that we recognize are potential denizens of the soul, no wonder self-knowledge is such a long and laborious task. A slightly later aphorism begins by emphasizing the difficulty of "observing oneself" and living up to the maxim "Know yourself!" and goes on to encourage closer inquiry into "the voice of conscience":

> Your judgment "this is right" has a prehistory in your drives, inclinations, aversions, experiences, and lack of experience: you must ask "*how* did [this conscience] arise?" and then "*what* is really driving me to listen to it?" (*JS* 335)

Just as he had earlier advocated dealing with thoughts and ideas in a wide variety of personal modes, Nietzsche now recommends a corresponding range of attitudes to adopt toward the voices of conscience.

> You can listen to its command like a good soldier who hears his officer's command. Or like a woman who loves the one who commands. Or like a flatterer and coward who is afraid of the commander. Or like someone stupid who obeys because no objection occurs to him. In short, you can listen to your conscience in a hundred ways.[10]

If we are to learn to listen in a hundred ways, would we not be hearing through as many pairs of ears? And might the commands we hear not issue from at least as many mouths?

For Freud the *Über-Ich* is formed by the superimposition, as it were, of the parental imago upon an original image or template *(Urbild, arche-type)*, a prior pattern of the punishing parent that is inherited from generations of ancestors.[11] Jung adopts a similar schema, with his idea of archetypes, images of persons—the mother, the old wise woman, the eternal youth—that are, paradoxically, the *im*personal basis of the individual's personality. (Impersonal in the sense of collective images that antedate the individual's existence.) One finds in Nietzsche a similar archaic dimension to the persons that make up the society within each psyche. An aphorism entitled "From the Mother" anticipates Freud's idea of the "parental imago" as well as Jung's notion of "anima":

Every man carries in him an image of woman derived from the mother: it is this image that determines whether he will revere women or disparage them or else be generally indifferent toward them.[12]

Later depth psychology makes explicit what is only implied here: namely, that the image of the personal mother is itself informed by aeons of experience of "woman." It is clear from a later aphorism (couched in more assertive and less experimental terms than is characteristic of Nietzsche's psychological pronouncements) that the "image of woman" (strictly speaking: the physiological propensity to produce it) would be something inherited through many generations:

One cannot erase from a person's soul what his ancestors most liked to do and did most constantly. . . . It is absolutely impossible that a person should *not* have the qualities and preferences of his parents and ancestors in his body. (*BGE* 264)

Let us now examine one of the major grounds for this supposition of archaic inheritance and the idea that so much is "in the blood": namely, the phenomenon of the dream.

Dreams and Archaic Inheritance

I knew an ingenious honest man who complained to me that all his dreams were servile, and, that, though he was a gentleman by day, he was a drudge, a miser, and a footman, by night. Civil war in our atoms, mutiny of the sub-daemons *not yet subdued.*

Emerson[13]

Recall first the major role played by the dream in *The Birth of Tragedy,* where Apollo, just as he presided over "the beautiful sheen of the inner world of phantasy," was also the patron of "the beautiful sheen of the dream worlds, in the generation of which every human being is fully an artist" (*BT* 1). Insofar as one is an artist in this respect, one's creation is totally spontaneous, with no deliberate participation on the part of the conscious self. This is the beauty of the dream: that it naturally offers a picture of the psyche as a play of drives appearing spontaneously as persons. Nietzsche emphasizes the general inaccessibility of the drives to explicit awareness: with the business of conscious deliberation inhibited during sleep, the drives are able to manifest themselves more clearly. The difficulty is of course to see their play—or rather to bring to consciousness and retain in memory the drama in which one has played a part while asleep.

When attuned to one's dreams and practiced in the art of recording them, it is possible to retrieve several lengthy dreams per night; and if attention is paid to them over the long run, the amount of experience of the dream worlds that can accumulate over the years is considerable.[14] Given this potential bulk (especially relative to what we remember from waking life), and in view of the artistically "beautiful sheen" of such experience, the mainstream of Western philosophy has evinced a distinct lack of interest in the phenomenon of the dream. While several thinkers of Romanticism were exceptions in this respect, one of the immediate inspirations for Nietzsche's reflections on the dream surely came from the aphorisms of Lichtenberg.

With remarkable prescience, Lichtenberg emphasizes repeatedly the continuities and commonalities between waking and dreaming experience.

> Again I commend dreams: we live and experience just as well in the dream as when awake and *are* the former just as much as the latter. One of the distinctions of human beings is that they dream *and also know it*. We have hardly made appropriate use of this phenomenon. The dream is a life that, together with the rest of our lives, constitutes what we call human life. Dreams merge gradually into our waking state, and it is impossible to say where a person's waking experience actually begins.[15]

Nietzsche is following Lichtenberg when he assimilates the operations involved in phantasy and in the dream (as discussed in the previous chapter), as is evidenced by this aphorism from *Beyond Good and Evil* (which follows the passage discussed earlier concerning our propensity to "phantasize approximations" of things):

> "Whatever happened in the light goes on in the dark": but also the other way round. What we experience in dreams, provided we experience it often, ultimately belongs as much to the total economy of our souls as anything "actually" experienced. . . . And even in the most serene moments of our waking spirit we are led a little by the habits of our dreams. (*BGE* 193)

It was earlier, in *Human, All Too Human,* that Nietzsche had opened up an archaic dimension to the phenomenon of dreaming. In his initial talk of "dream-thinking" and its similarity to so-called primitive modes of thought, his reconstruction of the experience of "the savage" is condescendingly hard-scientific (uncharacteristically so—and surely a function of his recent repudiation of the ideas of Wagner and Schopenhauer). Nevertheless, the basic idea is psychologically profound and experientially enriching. In an aphorism entitled "Dream and Culture," he writes:

> [In the dream] our memory . . . is taken back to a condition of imperfection such as may have been normal for everyone by day and in

waking during the primeval ages of humanity. . . . We all resemble in
our dreams the savage . . . in the bad inferences of which we are guilty
in the dream. . . . The perfect clarity of all dream-images, which presupposes unconditional belief in their reality, reminds us again of conditions of earlier humanity, in which hallucination was extraordinarily
common and moreover seized whole communities and entire peoples
at one time. Thus, in sleep and in dream we recapitulate the entire
curriculum of earlier humanity. (*HA* 12)

The next aphorism explains what is meant by "bad inferences." Nietzsche
details the manifold processes and events that impinge upon the organism—
from within as well as from outside—during sleep, and suggests that the
mind is thereby prompted to search for grounds for this manifold stimulation: "the dream is the *seeking and imagining of causes* for the feelings thus
aroused" (*HA* 13). That this process is equivalent to the drives' interpreting
nerve stimuli is confirmed by subsequent talk of the role of "aroused phantasy." Above all the process is, at its depths, an extremely conservative one.

In my opinion, just as nowadays people still infer in the dream, so
human beings used to infer *in waking too* for thousands of years. . . .
In the dream *this primordial piece of humanity continues to operate
in us,* for it is the basis on which higher reason developed and continues to develop in every human being. The dream takes us back to
remote conditions of human culture and gives us a means of understanding them better. Dream-thinking is so easy for us now because
we have been so well drilled over vast stretches of human development in precisely this form of phantastic and easy explanation in
terms of the first thing that strikes us. To this extent the dream is a
form of recreation for the brain, which during the day has to satisfy
the more stringent demands on thinking that are imposed by higher
culture. (*HA* 13; second emphasis added)

Freud quotes part (and paraphrases part) of this passage with the highest
approval in *The Interpretation of Dreams* (chap. 7c), and he continued for
some time to entertain the idea of an "archaic inheritance" that manifests
itself in the dream.

Nietzsche's ideas on the dream were influenced to some extent by his
acquaintance with ancient Greek attitudes toward dream experience—and
indeed, his overall position is well summed up by the following elegant
characterization by a classical scholar of the attitudes of the Greeks.

Man shares with a few other of the higher mammals the curious privilege of citizenship in two worlds. He enjoys in daily alternation two
distinct kinds of experience . . . each of which has its own logic and

its own limitations; and he has no obvious reason for thinking one of them more significant than the other. If the waking world has certain advantages of solidity and continuity, its social opportunities are terribly restricted. In it we meet, as a rule, only the neighbors, whereas the dream world offers the chance of intercourse however fugitive, with our distant friends, our dead, and our gods.[16]

Both the Homeric idea that dreams come to us from the underworld of Hades and its more shamanistic counterpart, according to which the soul travels in dreams *to* the underworld, inform much of Nietzsche's thinking about dream and phantasy. It is more than a poetic conceit, then, when he entitles the last aphorism of *Assorted Opinions and Maxims* "Descent into Hades."[17]

> I too have been in the underworld, like Odysseus, and shall be there even more; and I have not only sacrificed rams to be able to talk to some of the dead, but have not spared my own blood as well. Four pairs have not refused themselves to me: Epicurus and Montaigne, Goethe and Spinoza, Plato and Rousseau, Pascal and Schopenhauer. I have had to engage these figures in the course of my long, solitary wanderings. . . . Whatever I say, resolve, and think through for myself and others, I look to these eight and see their eyes likewise fixed on me. (*AOM* 408)

Just as the shadowy images Odysseus encountered in the underworld were unable to speak until they had been given blood to drink, so the archaic images in the depths of the soul do not fully become persons, capable of conversing, until they have been animated by having psychical energy devoted to them. Several similar passages make it clear that during the self-imposed solitude of Nietzsche's last productive decade he was not alone—but rather enjoyed conversation, Machiavelli-style, with shades from the tradition in the underworld of dream and phantasy. Such activity conduces, through its direct relations with the dead, to a more lively conception of history as well as a deeper experience of life.

An aphorism entitled "Happiness of the Historian" begins with a piece of direct speech contrasting the world of the one who lives historically with that of the metaphysician. Nietzsche then appends the comment:

> This is what someone said to himself in the course of a walk in the morning sun: someone for whom in history not only the spirit but also the heart is constantly transforming itself anew, and who, by contrast with the metaphysician, is happy to harbor within him not "an immortal soul" but rather *many mortal souls*. (*AOM* 17)

On one level Nietzsche is referring here to the way the drives that constitute the psyche arise and perish, come together and diverge, in perpetual fluctuation, producing as they do so the variety of persons thanks to which we may become "researchers and experimenters."[18] On another level is the underworld, ultimate home of mortal souls—but imagined as a psychological realm in the present and past, beneath every event, rather than an eschatological realm in the future.

Shades encountered in Hades are unable to communicate until given blood to drink, until after an infusion of vitalizing fluid. There is another sense in which the shades of the past reach us through blood, one suggested by Nietzsche's saying that the past can be transformed into blood by the "plastic power" of the human psyche.[19] Our personal past does not need to be transformed into blood, since it is in a sense already precipitated there. But one of the major developments in Nietzsche's thinking between the *Untimely Meditations* and *The Joyful Science* consists in the increasing realization of how much more of the "foreign" past comes to us through "the blood." In an aphorism entitled "Ultimate Lesson of History," another voice conversant with historical inquiry and cognizant of the burden of the past says:

> "The spirit of that [bygone] age would bear down upon you with the weight of a hundred atmospheres: what is good and beautiful in it you would not be able to enjoy, while you would be incapable of digesting what is bad in it." . . . And yet is everyone not able to withstand it in his own age? Yes, but only because the spirit of his age does not only lie *upon* him, but is also *within* him. (*AOM* 382)

We are able to withstand the enormous "external" pressure of the past (as manifested in the history of culture and institutions) because it is equalized, as it were, by the flow of the past into the contemporary psyche from within, by the past that we inherit "in the blood." A major contributor to the spirit of the age will then be the flow that was characterized in *The Joyful Science* as the continuous operation within us of "the entire primal age and past of all sentient being" (*JS* 54).

The notion has a distinctly Lamarckian tone to it, and indeed Nietzsche mentions Lamarck in *The Joyful Science* (99) as well as in some of the later notes. His espousal of the idea of the inheritance of acquired characteristics has prompted some commentators to dismiss the "archaism" in his thinking on the grounds that Lamarck's theories have been discredited. But quite apart from the fact that Lamarckian ideas have recently been regaining some credibility, these dismissals miss the point of Nietzsche's concern with the topic. His belief in the inheritance of acquired characteristics stems from a salutary refusal to separate soul from body, or spirit from matter; but the important thing is to take remarks about things being "in the blood" in the experimental spirit in which they were meant. The point of Nietzsche's announcement of his discovery that "ancient humanity and animality" continue to operate through him in the present is to invite the reader to understand his or her present experience in this way—to behave and reflect *as if* every moment of experience were being informed by archaic forces.

Such experimentation carries with it, if assiduously practiced, a heavy responsibility that increases as one realizes the extent to which one is the *heir* of a tradition. Nevertheless, if sufficient strength of spirit has been cultivated and the burden shouldered in the right way, the results can be liberating rather than merely oppressive.

> Anyone who knows how to experience the history of humanity as *his own history* . . . [if he could] endure this immense amount of grief of all kinds . . . as a person with a horizon of millennia in front of and behind him, as the heir of all the nobility of all previous spirit and an heir with a sense of obligation . . . if one could take all of this upon one's soul . . . this would have to result in a happiness that up till now no human being has known. (*JS* 337)

The importance for Nietzsche of "obligation" and "responsibility" toward the past is worth emphasizing, since he is so often understood to have had a merely nihilistic attitude toward tradition. The transformation of the spirit into a camel, as described in Zarathustra's first speech ("On the Three Transformations"), constitutes a crucial stage of development, in which the individual gains strength through assuming the burden of the traditional values of the culture. The next stage, in which the lion overcomes the great dragon with an overwhelming "No" to tradition is just as crucial: there has to be a complete break, so that the individual can realize its freedom. But the third stage ultimately involves a *reappropriation* of the appropriate elements of the tradition that has been rejected.[20] The child of the third transformation signifies innocence and a new beginning, but it is only a beginning (it figures, after all, in the very first of Zarathustra's many speeches). The creativity symbolized by the child does not issue in a creation *ex nihilo,* but rather in a reconstruction or reconstrual of selected elements from the tradition into something uniquely original.[21] The Dionysian child in Heraclitus plays on the eternal shore, destroying and reconstructing using the same materials.

The assumption of responsibility (not to mention the maintenance of psychical order) is a more difficult undertaking in the modern age, since the inherent multiplicity of drives is compounded by what is inherited from previous generations.

> Human beings from an age of disintegration in which races are thrown together indiscriminately have the inheritance of multiple origins in their bodies, that is, opposite . . . drives and value standards

that fight amongst themselves and seldom give each other peace. (*BGE* 200)

Such human beings will tend to be weaker than normal, and to long for "the war that they themselves are" to come to an end: they will suffer from a case of "bad multiplicity." But there is also a brighter side to this phenomenon.

> But if the conflict and war in such natures works as *additional* incentives and stimuli to life, and if true mastery and refinement in waging war with themselves—self-mastery and self-outwitting—has been inherited and bred along with these powerful and irreconcilable drives . . . then enigmatic human beings will arise that are destined for victory and seduction.[22]

There is a larger element of risk for modern individuals to open up to the full flow of the past, but the rewards are correspondingly greater. In this context, then, one should read the "far" in the following passage as referring to temporal as well as spatial reach, as a measure of an individual's capacity for responsive assimilation of present and past ages.

> A philosopher . . . would be compelled to find the greatness of man . . . precisely in his comprehensiveness and multifacetedness, in his wholeness in multiplicity: he would even determine worth and rank by how much and how many kinds of things a person could carry and take upon himself, by how *far* he could extend his responsibility. (*BGE* 212)

Nietzsche again sounds the theme of multiplicity and the special dangers it poses in the modern age, and especially in Europe, owing to the vast complexity of its inheritance. The need for the "plastic power" discussed in the essay on history becomes more pressing than ever:

> The past of every form and mode of life, of cultures which earlier lay right next to or on top of each other, now streams . . . into us 'modern souls,' our instincts now run back everywhere, we are ourselves a kind of chaos. . . . Through our semibarbarism in body and desires we have secret access in all directions, such as no noble age has possessed, above all access to the labyrinth of unfinished cultures and to every semi-barbarism that has ever existed on earth. (*BGE* 224)

While such a situation may provide opportunities for great creativity, the vast array of possibilities may simply overwhelm and bewilder. The potential for greatness in the modern age is tremendous—though it is precisely the tremendous instinctual confusion informing (or deforming) the age that enervates it, making it the most decadent of times and thereby diminishing the possibility of a human being's achieving greatness.[23]

But before engaging the problem of how greatness might be achieved through mastering the instinctual chaos and ordering the persons in the inner community, let us approach the question of the nature of these persons from another direction. Taking as a cue the roots of our word "person" in the Latin *persona,* let us see if we can gain insight into the persons inhabiting the Nietzschean psyche by way of the image—crucial to his psychology in general—of the *mask,* which is in turn set in the context of the metaphors of world as theater and life as drama.

Plays of Masks

> *If you could look with [the cat's] eyes, you might see her surrounded with hundreds of figures performing complex dramas, with tragic and comic issues, long conversations, many characters, many ups and downs of fate.*
>
> Emerson, "Experience"

Like many children, Nietzsche had been a keen amateur playwright and director of dramas in the home and at the homes of his friends. His enthusiasm for the theater persisted and was finally afforded sophisticated opportunities for satisfaction—in the role of audience rather than producer—during his student years in Bonn and Leipzig. Leipzig in particular was a city of culture with a variety of talented musicians, actors, and opera singers in residence and passing through, and the young student's major indulgence was frequent visits to concerts and the theater.[24] Nietzsche enjoyed infatuations with a number of famous singers and actresses, mooning over their photographs and dedicating songs to them. In a letter of 1866 to the actress Hedwig Raabe (not known to have been actually sent), the twenty-one-year-old student writes modestly of the "few songs" he is presenting to her: "My first wish is that the insignificant dedication of these insignificant songs does not signify the wrong thing to you. Nothing is farther from my intentions than to wish by this dedication to draw attention to my own person."[25] He is writing out of gratitude to her for bringing to life the characters she has played.

> Basically it is your roles that I and surely everyone admire. Along with the sweetness and pain with which my own childhood appears before my soul as something lost but yet formerly present, I think of your original figures, always true to life and good-hearted. Even if on the path of my life to come I am to encounter these figures only seldom—and just a short while ago I no longer believed they were real—my belief in them is now firmly rooted once more. This I owe

to you alone, and thus I hope you will not take the liberty of this letter amiss.

This radiant feminine figure, "the blonde angel," whom Nietzsche was too shy to meet in person though she lived not far away with relatives of his, and with whom he was—according to Elisabeth—"totally in love," was a medium for parts of his own personality, psychical figures that he would indeed encounter again in the course of his life. Famous though Fräulein Raabe was—perhaps *because* of her celebrity—Nietzsche had no desire to meet her: what fascinated was the *personae* of the drama, the figures played by the actress who, in person and out of character, would be bound to disappoint.

When he returned to Leipzig in 1868 after a brief period of military service (cut short by injuries sustained through a slip while mounting his horse), Nietzsche embarked upon the most socially extraverted period of his life, characterized by frequent attendance at opera and theater—even though he was also working hard at his philology studies. Through a friend, he had found lodgings in the house of a Professor Biedermann, editor of the *Deutsche Allgemeine,* Leipzig's foremost newspaper. He participated in the rich social and cultural life in the Biedermann home, which was (in spite of the name) a cosmopolitan gathering place for a variety of artistes and denizens of the beau monde. There he came to know personally an actress with whom he and Rohde had been infatuated two years earlier, the ravishingly sentimental Susanne Klemm. While he speaks of seeing her home after evenings chez Biedermann as "a pleasant duty," personal acquaintance (often an attenuator of projections) apparently led to the cooling of his former ardor.[26] Through his connections with the newspaper, Nietzsche was able to attend numerous concerts and plays in a semiofficial capacity, and his expertise in music brought him the offer of the position of opera critic. In spite of his growing enthusiasm for opera— it was at this time that he was first overwhelmed by performances of the overtures to *Tristan* and *Die Meistersinger*—he declined, no doubt out of respect for the formidable writing commitments for his degree in philology.

It was in November of 1868 that Nietzsche was first introduced to Wagner, whose love for and understanding of the theater—not to mention the extreme theatricality of his personal life—made an enormous impression on the younger man. His interest in Attic tragedy in particular was fueled by contact with the Master, whose enthusiasm for Schopenhauer had opened up the possibility of seeing (and living) life as drama and of entertaining a tragic view of life. For Schopenhauer, theater was a major metaphor for the activity of the will, which "portrays itself in a million figures of endless diversity and so performs the most colorful and baroque play without beginning or end, and which hides itself so thoroughly behind all these masks that it fails to recognize itself and thus often treats itself harshly."[27] But whereas for Schopenhauer the cosmic play of manifold phenomena masks an underlying unity, for Nietzsche, as we shall see, the variety of masks masks—if anything—another multiplicity.

Looking back at *The Birth of Tragedy* some sixteen years after its publication, Nietzsche found it to be "full of psychological innovations and artists' secrets"; and while the former consist in looking at "art in the perspective of life," the latter invite us to look at life in the perspective of drama.[28] There is a central figure in *The Birth*, a major presence that never appears again in any of his subsequent works—at least not under this name: "the mysterious primordial One" (*BT* 1). The language here is distinctly Schopenhauer-Wagnerian. Insofar as the Apollonian and the Dionysian, as "art-drives of nature," also play through the human being, the primordial One assumes a quasi personal aspect: the Dionysian artist who has lost his individuality in song and dance is said to become in turn an art-work in the hands of "the Dionysian artist of worlds." Nietzsche suggests in retrospect that the One is the god Dionysus, through whom an aesthetic meaning for the world can be created in the wake of the death of the metaphysical God of the Platonic-Christian tradition.

> In fact the whole book knows only an artistic meaning as a deeper meaning behind all occurring—a "god," if you will, but certainly only a completely reckless and immoral artist-god, who wants to experience in building as in destroying . . . his own pleasure and autarchy, and who in creating worlds redeems himself from the *distress* of fullness and *overfullness,* from the *suffering* of the conflicting forces compressed within him.[29]

The human counterpart to this figure would be the person of the lyric poet, who, as a precursor of the Attic tragedian and prototype of the human being in general, is a mask of the primordial One. When the lyrist says (or sings) "I," the word actually issues from a deeper source: "The 'I' of the lyrist resounds out of the abyss of Being *[Abgrund des Seins]*."[30] Whereas the epic poet (and the plastic artist, who is related to him) is able to contemplate his images as something separate from his self, the lyric poet is one with his—as projections from the primordial One.[31] The self of the lyrist is then itself an artistic composition of images projected from a deeper self, and his identity as an "I" dependent on the primordial One, who is the only true "I-ness." The person of the lyrist is, as it were, a mask of a deeper personality, something that both conceals and reveals the real "I" behind or beneath it.

Nietzsche goes on to argue that a work that is merely subjective is no work of art and a subject in the sense of the egoistic individual can be no artist.

> Insofar as the subject is an artist, it has already been released from its individual will and become as it were a medium, through which the one truly existing subject celebrates its redemption in *Schein*. . . . We are simply images and artistic projections for the true creator and have our highest dignity in our significance as works of art.

The drama of life, then, is "the comedy of art" created by the primordial One (also known as the World-Genius, the True Subject, the Genuine Creator—all Dionysian personfications of Schopenhauerian Will) for its own eternal entertainment, of which it is simultaneously "creator and spectator." The dignity of the lyric genius—and by extension, though to a lesser extent, of the rest of us—lies in his ability to merge with the primordial world-artist in the act of artistic creation, and thereby become at once "poet, actor, and spectator."

Nietzsche characterized the members of the Dionysian chorus as consummate artists because of their ability to induce the audience to participate in their projecting a vision of gods and spirits onto the scene behind them (*BT* 8). The chorus is helped in this project by the dramatic effect of the *mask*—a phenomenon associated in different ways with both Dionysus and Apollo—which presents to the audience the figure of the hero or god being portrayed and thereby helps induce the collective projection of a superhuman image.[32] A similar phenomenon occurs in interactions between persons outside the theater, in the everyday world. Naturally masking, a person puts up a front, a screen that in certain situations invites the projection of an image of divine power. It is in fact precisely there, where strong emotions and passions hold sway, that the personal is infused with a transpersonal power, that thanks to the mask the personal relationship is enhanced by a superhuman presence. Just as Nietzsche's remarks about tragedy are to be taken to refer to the larger human drama as well, so his talk about masks and projections are susceptible of psychological generalization.

After *The Birth of Tragedy* the themes of masks and masking begin to play a more central role in Nietzsche's work, both in his looking at life through metaphors of the mask and other aspects of the dramatic arts, and also in his literary styles of masking his meanings with layers of irony, parody, and other tropes. They are also central to his life: at the personal level, he often felt that use of masks was an absolute necessity if he was to continue to live.[33] But before pursuing this theme further, it will help to reflect on some features of the literal mask.[34]

The literal mask is first and foremost a surface, mediating between outside and inside. *Larvatus prodeo:* masked I go forth and present myself *as* such-and-such a person. But as it reveals, the mask also conceals: while a literal mask protects the most vulnerable part of the body (the death mask and surgical mask being special and interesting cases), its figurative counterpart conceals that aspect of our exterior which most betrays the inner life. The skin of the face is itself a medium of revelation: through facial expressions—the blush, the twitch, the sudden pallor—we may look shocked, guilty, or shamefaced. Hence the attraction of a mask, behind which the eyes ("windows of the soul") can see without being easily looked into. Yet these functions of the mask depend on its not being whole: there must be gaps in it, for without holes for the eyes and mouth it cannot be seen and spoken through. A theatrical mask allows selective expression—through dynamics of speech and gestures of the head—of the wearer's feelings, intentions, and desires.

The customary opposition between the mask and the individual him- or herself suggests that masks front or confront some thing called the self, something that maintains its personal identity behind and beneath the procession of different *personae* one adopts in the course of a day or a life. There is the impression, reflecting on the experience of masking one's feelings or speaking from behind a mask, that how one appears or what one says is other than what one is or believes, that one's "true" self has remained veiled. And that if one would, one could choose to abandon the deception, drop the pretense, face up to reality, and simply be oneself, one self, one's real self. But what would such a self be like? Would it be like—or even be—anything? Or is there perhaps nothing behind the masks, a void beneath the surface, an abyss of emptiness—that might yet turn out, after all, to be some kind of source?

When Nietzsche's interest shifts to the metaphorical mask, he tends at first to see psychological masking as something inauthentic. In the *Untimely Meditation* on history the mask is a mere front set up to conceal the "weakened personality" characteristic of the modern human being (*HL 5*). Since we have lost the innocent insight of the child and our instincts have been extinguished by a surfeit of history, "no one any longer dares to show his person, but masks himself as a cultured man, a scholar, a poet, a politician." Such a weak personality, lacking an inner drive by which to orient itself, timidly consults history in order to learn how to react: "He thus gradually becomes an actor and plays a role—indeed many roles usually, which is why he plays each one so badly and flatly." Here masks are understood as a compensation for a lack of life-force flowing through the individual, a failure of the instincts to guide the person's life.

In *Schopenhauer as Educator*, Nietzsche elaborates the theme of the man who is "totally exterior surface with no kernel, a tattered, daubed, puffed up bag of clothes" (*SE* 1). Out of laziness and fear we cover our individuality with veils that conform to conventional appearances.

> But how can we find ourselves again? How can the human being know itself? It is a thing dark and veiled; and if the hare has seven skins, the human can slough off seventy times seven and still not be able to say, "Now that is what you really are, that is no longer outer shell."

Nietzsche is not so much condemning surface appearances as bemoaning the fact that human beings are so reluctant to engage in the difficult work of penetrating these layers of masks for the sake of self-understanding. He goes on to talk of how people "reach passionately for the fantastic events portrayed in the theater of politics, or else themselves proudly parade about in a hundred masks . . . industriously mindful of their common comedy and not at all of themselves" (*SE* 4). Here the metaphor of the theatrical play illuminates an inauthentic way of being, in which one simply plays a role and loses oneself in it—remaining empty of the life force.

In *Human, All Too Human,* however, Nietzsche intimates a realization that the difference between authentic being and masked seeming may not be so great after all. In an aphorism entitled "How Seeming *[Schein]* Becomes Being *[Sein]*," he writes about how the person easily becomes the role that is at first only played.

> The actor is ultimately unable, even in the deepest pain, to cease thinking of the impression his person and the whole scenic effect is making, at the funeral of his child for example: he will weep over his own pain and its expressions as his own spectator. The hypocrite who always plays the same role ends up no longer being a hypocrite. . . . When someone fervently wants for a very long time to *seem* something, it will eventually be difficult for that person to *be* anything else. The profession of almost everyone, even of the artist, begins with hypocrisy, with an imitating from outside and a mimicking of what works effectively. One who always wears the mask of friendly expressions must eventually gain power over benevolent moods, without which the expression of friendliness cannot be effected—and finally these moods gain power over him, and he *is* benevolent.[35]

To the extent that the player becomes the role and the face the mask, the difference between authentic and inauthentic would seem to dissolve. Does it make sense to say that the true self is left behind, behind the mask, when the person has become the *persona* and the individual has identified with the role? In the presence of Dionysus, god of the mask, the self itself becomes problematic.

The duplex being of Dionysus governs the various dualities of the mask as bidirectional mediator between self and other, inside and outside. In addition to being a distinguished progenitor of ancient Greek drama, Dionysus is a power that annuls personal identity through his roles as god of wine and intoxication, of madness and the dance.[36] The mask, like its patron deity, effaces individuation. It is in principle usable by anyone, insofar as a young boy can play the part of an old man with the help of a good mask and appropriate posture. A mask that transforms your appearance radically you can pass to me, and it will alter mine in a quite different way; and yet it will annul our respective individualities equally. The production of a plurality of effects by one and the same mask bears testimony to the remarkable multiplying power of masking as a manifestation of Dionysus—*polueidēs* and *polumorphos*—god of many forms.

The roles played by masks in the process of deception are complex and multifarious. Just as the literal mask may function to disguise or else protect the wearer's face, so a person may engage in metaphorical masking for the purpose of self-protection or deception. The use of a mask as disguise does not necessarily intend to deceive, even though it conceals the face; and indeed the beauty of masks as disguise lies in their duplex function of presenting and withholding, revealing and concealing, at the same time. The opaque surface may in this sense serve as a sign for what lies behind it.

The mask is duplex in another sense, in that it may be turned toward the outside or within. We may deceive ourselves either by masking aspects of the external world that we are unwilling to acknowledge ("putting a good face on things"), or else by internal masking, whereby we conceal from ourselves parts of our selves we would rather not face. At the same time, we seldom present ourselves to the outer world fully, but mostly through the medium of masks that conceal some part or parts of our person. Again, this kind of masking is not necessarily deceptive for the sake of self-interest, as the example of "putting up a good front" shows. Its external effect may in turn affect what lies within, insofar as the choice of a particular mask signifies a part of the person and may eventually bring out a side of the personality that would otherwise remain hidden. This possibility becomes important as Nietzsche begins to reflect more on the multiplicity of the personality.

The idea of masking parts of ourselves from ourselves is expressed in an especially pithy aphorism from *Dawn of Morning* which alludes to the way the sense of self is formed by the opinions of others as well as to the theme of making oneself a work of art: "We are like shop windows in which we ourselves are constantly arranging, concealing, or illuminating our supposed qualities, which others ascribe to us—all in order to deceive *our-*

selves" (*DM* 385). Life as drama is, for Nietzsche, a special case of life as artwork—and can be realized simply by looking in the right way, using what he calls "the third eye."

> What! You still need the theater! Are you still so young? Be clever and look for tragedy and comedy where it is better played! Where things are more interesting and interested! It is not that easy, admittedly, to remain a spectator in such cases—but learn to be one! And then in almost all difficult and painful situations that befall you will have an escape hatch to joy and a refuge, even when your passions assail you. Open your theater-eye, the great third eye that looks into the world through the other two! (*DM* 509)

The injunction to learn to be a spectator is less an encouragement to detachment than an invitation to double vision and bipresence: to open the theater-eye is to supplement the perspective of the actor with that of the spectator rather than to substitute the latter for the former.

By now Nietzsche has become reconciled to masking as a basic trait of life. In *The Joyful Science,* he writes of "the pleasure in masks, the good conscience of everything masked" as something inherent in the beginnings of Western culture, as "the bath and recreation of the ancient spirit" (*JS* 77). Past masters of the mask are, of course, actors:

> Only artists, and especially those of the theater, have given men eyes and ears to see and hear with some pleasure what each man himself is . . . only they have taught us . . . the art of putting ourselves "into a scene" for ourselves. (*JS* 78)

Nietzsche appears to be more charitable toward the histrionic art because he is now beginning to understand falseness as the manifestation of a fundamental human drive to falsify and simplify the world for the sake of control (*JS* 110–12). This is a form of the archaic phantasy that conditions all our experience. Not to take responsibility for participating in the constitution of the world, actively to forget that the ancestors and we ourselves have been making most of it up as we go along, to take facts as simply given and to play our parts with undiluted seriousness, is to be cowardly, naive, and comical. It is not the phantasizing *per se* that he objects to—it belongs to our nature—but our pretending that we had no part in it, playing the role of the dispassionate spectator viewing with the innocent "I."

Nietzsche writes enthusiastically of the possibility of participating in the workings of archaic phantasy with reflective awareness, playing them out fully, living the myth further, dreaming the dream onward. As a counterpart to the masking of aspects of the self involved in "giving style to one's character" (discussed earlier), we can "learn from artists" how to mask aspects of the rest of the world through a variety of aesthetic strategies, and thereby become "poets of our own lives."[37] Nietzsche clearly wants to retain from the *Untimely Meditations* the view that most people are simply self-deceiving in their refusal to face up to the grim facts of life. But there is another kind of masking that could be called, on account of its self-awareness, "authentic." Indeed, at its most authentic, this play of masking reaches the level of poetry, where the actor becomes the author. Nietzsche argues that "the higher human beings" who are capable of "seeing and hearing thoughtfully" are no longer simply "*spectators* and *listeners* before the great play of sights and sounds that is life," nor are they simply "*actors* in this drama": they are actually "the true poets and continuous creators of life"—by virtue of their creating, as artistic philosophers, "the whole eternally growing world of valuations, colors, weights, perspectives, scales, affirmations and negations," making of this world a *Dichtung,* a poetic play and literary work (*JS* 301). Not that they compose this poem *ex nihilo* or arbitrarily make it up—any more than a literal poet creates out of nothing or anarchically. As with the rest of us, their phantasy constitutes in concert with other projections a common reality.

Just as the image of the mask in Nietzsche is ambiguous, his remarks in the last book of *The Joyful Science* on actors and role-playing remain somewhat ambivalent.[38] On the one hand, European society forces people into a particular role, determined largely by their occupation; one becomes identified with the role, which then constricts development of character along other dimensions: "Almost all Europeans confuse themselves with their role . . . they forget . . . how many other roles they *could have played*" (*JS* 356). The mask is seen here as something constricting, something that inhibits—as the literal mask does—the range of expression of the fully human being. The pressures of life can form the face into a mask, which then *becomes* the person so well that the self fuses with, comes to be, its mask. It is possible, however, to go to the other extreme—Nietzsche gives "the Americans today" as an example (one just as valid *today*)—of assuming that a person can play absolutely any part whatsoever. This leads to one's becoming a total actor and forgetting altogether that one is playing roles.

Nietzsche also pursues the analogy between masks and clothing: "It seems that we Europeans absolutely cannot do without that masquerade which one calls clothes" (*JS* 352). While clothes conceal, they also share the expressive function of masks insofar as they present aspects of our selves and project the appropriate "image." (Again the effect is bidirectional: much of the impression a well-tailored three-piece suit makes on the viewer comes from the effect it has on the wearer, from the way it draws her out—and into the part.) As for concealment, Nietzsche claims that it is not even "the wild beast of prey" in us that we wish to cover up, but rather "the shameful sight of the tame animal" that morality has made us become. (One thinks, for example, of the modern leather jacket.)

While Nietzsche is now able to recommend histrionics in the nonpejorative sense, he remains deeply ambivalent about "the problem of the actor," which arises precisely from the histrionic art. He puts it here in quite Dionysian terms that are applicable to life in general:

> Falseness with a good conscience; the pleasure in dissimulation bursting forth as a power that pushes aside the so-called "character," flooding and sometimes extinguishing it; the inner demand for a role and mask, to enter the mode of *seeming* [Schein]; an abundance of all kinds of adaptability that can no longer be satisfied in the service of the most immediate and narrow utility. All this is perhaps true not *only* of the actor?[39]

The talk of *Schein* recalls the theme of the Apollonian from *The Birth of Tragedy*. There Nietzsche had speculated that the ancient Greeks were forced, in order to be able to live at all, to mask the terror of the Dionysian abyss by projecting a veil of "beautiful sheen" over it (*BT* 1–2). Since the Apollonian is, like the Dionysian, an "art-drive of nature," the projection of a world of images in dream or fantasy is not simply an avoidance strategy on the part of a people who finds the real world a vale of tears, nor an arbitrary piece of self-indulgent whimsy on the part of an individual wishing to escape the constraints of reality: it is rather, Nietzsche claims, a process inherent in the nature of things and informing the structure of all life.[40] The process of masking is thus of considerable ontological significance, insofar as it is not something contingently practiced by human beings but is rather woven into the very fabric of existence. Thus, when Nietzsche wonders whether "all this is perhaps true not *only* of the actor," he is suggesting that it *is* true not only of artists but of the actor and artist in himself and every person. "Falseness with a good conscience" is possible because falseness is impossible to avoid: but a good conscience can be enjoyed as long as one faces up to that upon which one is putting a better face, as long as one becomes conscious of playing a part.

Nietzsche's understanding of the necessity and desirability of masks finds its consummate expression in *Beyond Good and Evil*, which is his first major exercise in literary masking—aside from *Zarathustra*—and a masterpiece of esoteric writing.[41] Early on the author announces, self-referentially, that "everything that is profound loves masks" (*BGE* 40). A note from the period points up the pathos behind this utterance, remarking the necessity—for some—of "taking refuge" in happiness:

> We sit ourselves down on the street where life rolls by in a drunken procession of masks . . . doesn't it seem as if we know something that

makes us *afraid?* With which we don't want to be alone. A knowledge of something that makes us tremble, whose whispering makes us pale? This stubborn aversion from mournful dramas . . . this arbitrary Epicureanism of the heart, which worships the mask as its ultimate deity and savior . . . It seems as if we know ourselves to be all too fragile, perhaps shattered already and unhealable; it seems as if we fear the hand of life, and that it must shatter us, and we take refuge in life's sheen. . . . We are serious, we know the abyss: *that's* why we are defensive with respect to everything serious.[42]

Numerous themes come together here, from the necessity for a veil of Apollonian *Schein* to mask the abyss, to the idea that all life is a play, drama, intoxicating and devastating tragedy—and that the sense of theater must be maintained if one is not to go under.

The aphorism from *Beyond Good and Evil* emphasizes again the extent to which the mask, the surface of one who is profound, is formed also by external forces, projections from outside. Everyone who knows his depths well enough will want a mask—

and supposing he does not want it, he would still some day realize that there is nevertheless a mask of himself there—and that that is good. Every profound spirit needs a mask: moreover, around every profound spirit a mask is continually growing, thanks to the constantly false, namely *shallow* interpretation of every word, every step, every sign of life he gives.

In fact one need not even be so profound to have experienced incongruous reactions from other people based on their projections of inappropriate features onto one's expression. The drive to dissimulate recurs in this text, in the form of

that not unproblematic readiness of the spirit to deceive other spirits and to dissimulate before them, that constant pressure and compulsion of a creative, image-forming, changeable force: in this the spirit enjoys the multiplicity and craftiness of its masks, and also enjoys the feeling of security in this—it is precisely through its protean arts that it is best defended and concealed! (*BGE* 230)

Again this creative force is understood as a natural drive, and as such is neither to be lauded nor deplored: our responsibility is to be aware of how it works through us, and our prerogative to let it play. But the "creative, image-forming, changeable force" mentioned here is always in tension with another drive of "the spirit."

Counter to this will to sheen *[Wille zum Schein],* to simplification, to the mask and cloak, to the surface in short—since every surface is a cloak—there works that sublime inclination of the one who would know, who takes and *wants* to take things profoundly, multiply, thoroughly: as a kind of cruelty of the intellectual conscience and taste.

This passage makes clear Nietzsche's view that there is in the human spirit a fundamental tension generated by the opposing drives to mask and to unmask. Nietzsche the genealogist, the great unmasker, is at the same time a past master of masking and a consummate respecter of veils.[43] The mask is behind one of the last questions of the book, in which the author asks "whether behind every one of [the philosopher's] caves there is not, must not be, another deeper cave . . . an abyss behind every ground, beneath every 'grounding'"—prompting the further question: "behind every mask, another mask?" Perhaps there is no firm face as foundation for the makeup, no substantial self. Or is Nietzsche not to be trusted in this matter, with these confessions of a mask? He ends the aphorism after all with the enigmatic caution: "Every philosophy also *conceals* a philosophy; every opinion is also a hiding-place; every word also a mask" (*BGE* 289).

If we remember that the Dionysian personality plays many roles, and if we bring all Nietzsche's talk about the human spirit's "multiplicity of masks" together with his idea of the multiplicity of persons within the soul, the conclusion follows that we can play a plurality of parts in the course of a day or a life, donning and doffing a variety of *personae,* thanks precisely to the plurality of persons within each one of us. If one entertains Shakespeare's image of all the world as a stage, then all the men and women may not be merely players. And if one man in his time plays many parts, his acts may succeed one another more rapidly than the seven ages enumerated by Jaques might suggest. The idea of life as drama, and the world as theater, becomes more profound as one realizes that more than one drama is being played out in each person by more than one player. And in view of the archaic nature of the drives behind these persons, it is reasonable to conclude further that the plays enacted by these characters will not be only contemporary, but will rather be informed (like the Attic tragedies that inspired Nietzsche's early work) by ancient myths and mythemes. While the details of the stories we act out, as well as the characters in them, will appear new, the basic plots and figures are not. And yet because of his concern to distance himself from the Schopenhauerian-Wagnerian enthusiasm for myth, Nietzsche declines to elaborate further.

Schopenhauer suggested that if the drama of life has a plan, "then *fate* is the director"; transposed to the inner realm of multiple actors, this image suggests what one might call "the soul as theater company." But again Nietzsche's ambivalence about the figure of the actor, as evidenced by his ultimate characterization of Wagner as the bad actor par excellence, may have prevented him from developing this idea.[44]

Ordering the Psyche Polytic

> *Faust complained that he had two souls in his breast. I have a*
> *whole squabbling crowd. It goes on as in a republic.*
>
> Bismarck

As Nietzsche's conception of the psyche as a polycentric field of persons developed, he became more engaged by the question framed by Plato concerning the ways in which this inner population might be ordered politically, or the optimal disposition of the forces that hold sway in the intrapersonal community.[45] Although he never actually mentions Plato in his remarks concerning the political organization of the psyche, it is illuminating to look at his ideas in the light of the analogy elaborated in the *Republic,* and enlightening to try to discern as clearly as possible just where and how they diverge from Plato's. Both thinkers agree on the value of likening the multiplicity of the soul to the community of the *polis,* and that various kinds of intrapsychical political organization are possible. The interesting question, with which we shall begin, is this: Which does each regard as the optimal regime, and for what reasons?

To read the *Republic* for its psychology means taking its principal image seriously, its picture of the individual psyche as a city populated by a multitude of persons. In book 2 Socrates is challenged by his interlocutors to show "what profit justice in itself is to the man who possesses it, and what harm injustice does" (*Rep.* 367d). Because of the difficulty in discerning precisely what justice consists in, Socrates proposes the analogy between the individual and the city, on the grounds that justice will be more easily visible in the larger entity.

> Perhaps there would be more justice in the bigger and it would be easier to observe closely. If you want, first we'll investigate what justice is like in the cities. Then, we'll also go on to consider it in individuals. . . . If we should watch a city come into being in speech [we might] also see its justice coming into being, and its injustice. (*Rep.* 368e–369a)

Proceeding to let "a city come into being in speech," Socrates elaborates an image of the ideal *polis* which he extends through to the last two books of the dialogue, by which time the more important city is the inner city, and his frequent talk of "the regime inside the man" and "the regime within" has become perfectly natural.

Socrates suggests that the most just regime for a city is one in which each citizen "is brought to that which naturally suits him—one man, one job—so that each man, practicing his own, which is one, will not become many but one; and thus, you see, the whole city will naturally grow to be one and not many" (*Rep.* 423d). Injustice in the city obtains when members of the three classes of citizens meddle in the business of citizens of other classes, and justice when proper ordering prevails:

> Meddling among the classes, of which there are three, and exchange with one another is the greatest harm for the city . . . [whereas] the money-making, auxiliary, and guardian classes doing what's appropriate, each of them minding its own business in a city, would be justice and would make the city just. (*Rep.* 434c)

Socrates then proposes applying what they have learned about justice in the city to the case of the individual. Applying the division of citizens into three classes to the individual yields the three forms of the soul: the appetitive, spirited, and calculating. Justice in the soul is then characterized as the condition in which "each of the three parts minds its own business," and where the calculating part rules over the other two, since "it possesses within it the knowledge of that which is beneficial for each part and for the whole composed of the community of these three parts" (441e, 442c). The just man

> doesn't let each part in him mind other people's business or the three classes in the soul meddle with each other, but really sets his own house [*ta oikeia*] in good order and rules himself; he arranges himself, becomes his own friend, and harmonizes the three parts, exactly like three notes in a harmonic scale, lowest, highest, and middle. And if there are some other parts in between, he binds them together and becomes entirely one from many, moderate and harmonized. (*Rep.* 443d)

This passage brings images of ruling and domestic economy together with a musical metaphor that suggests the kind of unity to be fashioned from multiplicity. The supposition that there might be more parts "in between" the three suggests that if we take the analogy between the city and the individual seriously, the tripartite division into classes of citizens would be only a first step. The image Socrates elaborates is susceptible of finer differentiation—ultimately into a much larger plurality of practitioners, a population (in principle) of thousands.[46] His final summation of justice in the soul is expressed simply in terms of power relations: "To produce justice is to establish the parts of the soul in a relation of mastering, and being mastered by, one another that is according to nature" (444d).

In view of the isomorphism between *polis* and psyche, Socrates suggests that there are "likely to be as many types of soul as there are types of regimes possessing distinct forms," and that the regime corresponding to the rule of the calculating part over the other two will be "kingship" if there is one ruler and "aristocracy" if there are several (*Rep.* 445c–d). He is about to go on to speak of four other types of regime corresponding to bad and unjust arrangements within the individual soul when the others interrupt and force him to say more about the nature of community in the best external regime.

It is not until book 8 that Socrates resumes his characterization of the four remaining types of regime and the corresponding personality types, a consideration of which will allow the discussants to decide which regime is the happiest and best (*Rep.* 544a). After reminding his listeners of his claim that the best man is like an aristocracy, Socrates describes a progressive degeneration of the individual through four further types of inner regime corresponding to timocracy, oligarchy, democracy, and tyranny. Nietzsche would for the most part concur in rejecting these degenerate regimes. The prospect of an inner timocracy, with the entire psyche driven by the spirited part and under the domination of the faction that loves victory and honor, would no doubt appeal to the "warrior spirit" in Nietzsche, but he would deplore the concomitant diminution of the passion for knowledge and understanding.

Similarly an inner oligarchy, in which the appetitive part of the soul dominates and love of money and physical pleasure prevails, would be no more appealing to Nietzsche than to Socrates. The only redeeming feature of the oligarchic arrangement, for Socrates, is that miserly acquisitiveness "enslaves" all desires other than the "necessary" ones; but since such a person must "forcibly hold down the bad desires," he would be divided against himself and there would be "faction within" him (*Rep.* 554a–d). Although such a man might be "more graceful than many," "the true virtue of the single-minded and harmonized soul would escape far from him." Nietzsche would be less concerned with single-mindedness, and does not see self-division as necessarily a bad thing—though he would have nothing but contempt for the motive force at work in this case.

The image of Nietzsche as a revolutionary often leads people to imagine that politically he would favor democracy, and would thus be a democrat psychopolitically too. It is thus worth showing why he is in fact as against democracy intrapsychically as he is in real politics. One can begin with the grounds for Socrates' low estimation of democracy as a regime under which "the city is full of freedom and free speech . . . and license to do whatever one wants" (*Rep.* 557b). This freedom and license give rise to a variegated multiplicity, the attractions of which Socrates depicts with a brush more heavily soaked in irony than usual.

[Democracy] is probably the fairest of the regimes. Just like a many-colored cloak decorated in all hues, this regime, decorated with all dispositions, would also look fairest, and many perhaps, like boys and women looking at many-colored things, would judge this to be the fairest regime.[47]

Because of the multiplicity of regimes in microcosm democracy contains, it is "a convenient place to look for a regime." Indeed anyone in the business of organizing a city is advised to visit a democracy and simply choose—as in "a bazaar" or general store—whatever type of regime he desires. Democracy is said to be "a sweet regime, without rulers and many-colored, dispensing a certain equality to equals and unequals alike."[48] Nietzsche could hardly have put the problem more pointedly himself: it is the assumption of equality that renders democracy ridiculous in his eyes from the start. Like Plato, Nietzsche sees that people are by no means equal and similarly believes in the benefits of *orders of rank,* of gradations from noble to base.

According to Socrates' genealogy of the democratic type of man, one party of desires within a young soul oligarchically organized is fed and reinforced by "desires of a kindred and like form from without" (*Rep.* 559e). Alliances are then formed to strengthen the oligarchic party within, so that "faction and counterfaction arise in him and he does battle with himself." But again the base desires grow and multiply in secret, and finally rise up and "take the acroplis of the young man's soul, perceiving it empty of fair studies and practices and true speeches, and it's these that are the best watchmen and guardians in the thought of men whom the gods love."[49] If the young man can eventually bring about some sort of accommodation between the oligarchic party within him and the successful invaders, he will end up with a democratic regime.

He then lives his life in accord with a certain equality of pleasures he has established. To whichever one happens along, as though it were chosen by the lot, he hands over the rule within himself until it is satisfied; and then again to another, dishonoring none but fostering them all on the basis of equality. . . . And there is neither order nor necessity in his life. . . . This man is all various and full of the greatest number of dispositions. . . . Many men and women would admire his life because it contains the most patterns of regimes and characters.[50]

Nietzsche might appear on the surface to find the idea of an intrapsychical democracy somewhat more appealing than the external kind—at least insofar as it involves a rotation through a multiplicity of desires dominating and styles of governing. What pulls him away from Socrates on this issue is, as usual, the ancient tension between the one and the many. Whereas the ideal for Socrates is an arrangement in which "each man, practicing his own, which is one, will become not many but one" (*Rep.* 423d), for Nietzsche, the advocate of "many-stringed culture," one can "become what one is" precisely through acknowledging one's multiplicity and employing the energies generated by the conflicts within it. "Love of *one* is a barbarism," reads one of his briefest aphorisms, "for it is practiced at the expense of all others" (*BGE* 67). And one would find a person's "greatness," if one were a philosopher, "precisely in his embracing comprehensiveness and multiplicity" (*BGE* 212). The great number and variety of characters and regimes embodied by the democratic type could, with proper organization, conduce to a fluidity of leadership of which Nietzsche would surely approve.

Nevertheless, he would be as dismissive as Socrates of a life that lacked "order and necessity," and perhaps even more concerned that a *Rangordnung* be acknowledged—within as well as among individuals. Even if the rulers change from time to time, at least there must be rulers who exercise power; for Nietzsche the democratic type of soul is too undiscriminating, slack, and anarchic to be productive. His later paradigm for such a soul is Wagner, whom he would regard as vacillating between the democratic and tyrannical types. He often speaks as if Wagner failed to organize his "multiplicity, abundance, and arbitrariness"—unless by resorting to tyranny—and was thus the typical *decadent,* whose style consists in "anarchy of atoms, disgregation of the will, 'freedom of the individual' morally speaking— expanded into a political theory: '*equal* rights for all'" (*CW* 11, 7). Had it not been for the fact that "the tyrant within him, his actor's genius, compelled him," Wagner's lack of self-discipline would have prevented him from achieving anything worth while.

Indeed the great danger of the democratic regime, for Socrates, is precisely its tendency to degenerate into tyranny, which he regards as the worst possible regime, internally as well as externally. What democratic types tout as "complete freedom" becomes in the son of a democratic man "complete hostility to law," and this leaves him open to the blandishments of "dread enchanters and tyrant-makers" (*Rep.* 572d–e). These bad influences "contrive to implant some love *[erōs]* in him—a great winged drone—to be the leader of the idle desires that insist on all available resources being distributed to them." *Erōs* would thus be the archetypal drive in Nietzsche's sense, the drive of drives. In the preceding three regimes there is—despite the domination by one particular faction—some degree of balance, insofar as each of the three parts of the soul retains some measure of representation. The tyrannical regime is the worst kind because, in the person "in whom the tyrant love dwells and pilots all the elements of the soul," *erōs* "lives like a tyrant . . . in all anarchy and lawlessness; and, being a monarch, will lead the man whom it controls, as though he were a city, to every kind of daring . . ." (*Rep.* 573d, 575a). This situation can lead to the complete subjugation of the calculating and spirited parts of the soul, leaving the desiring part to dominate absolutely—a condition shown in Socrates' famous depiction of the tyrannical type to be the unhappiest of all.

Nietzsche had direct experience of the tyrannical personality in his relationship with Wagner, and was himself no stranger to the dangers of intrapsychical tyranny.[51] While he would by no means endorse the absolute tyranny condemned by Socrates, he does see psychical tyranny as a *sometimes* necessary evil—and, for certain creative types, as a welcome evil to be cultivated for the enhancement of humanity as a whole. This is a crucial point, and one overlooked by readers who imagine Nietzsche's ideal to consist in undisciplined, Dionysian letting-it-all-flow-out. We noted earlier his appreciation of the way a tyrannical drive, precisely by virtue of its monopolizing all the available energies, can accumulate tremendous power, which can be directed toward effecting great things. And so, for Nietzsche, a form of tyranny in which one's task *(Aufgabe)* in life, as constituted by a particular complex of drives, holds ruthless sway over the other members of the psychical community may be a most productive arrangement—though by no means a comfortable one (for either the person tyrannized or those around him). He characterizes the *Aufgabe,* "that hidden and imperious something," as "the tyrant in us [that] wreaks terrible retribution for every attempt we make to avoid or elude it."[52]

In the light of the importance of this theme in Nietzsche, his extended criticism of Socrates in *Twilight of the Idols* is somewhat overdone. Given Nietzsche's almost fanatical concern with self-mastery for most of his life, which translated into frequent commendations of that virtue in his philosophical writings, a regime in which the highest part of the soul rules the lower parts could not be entirely inimical to him. In "The Problem of Socrates" he writes concerning the situation in fifth-century Athens that "everywhere the instincts were in anarchy," and that Socrates' response was to say: "The drives want to play the tyrant; one must devise a *countertyrant* who is stronger." Socrates is said to have attained "self-mastery" by setting up reason as such a "countertyrant." This position—of "rationality at any cost" and "*having* to fight the instincts"—Nietzsche brands as *décadence.*[53] The overemphasis on tyranny gives an unfair picture of Socrates's prescription for justice within the soul, which calls simply for "[a feeding of] the desiring part [of the soul] in such a way that it is neither in want nor surfeited," allowing it (as long as it "minds its own business") to "enjoy its own pleasures [as] the best pleasures" *(Rep.* 571e, 586e)—where the qualification "the best" is presumably intended to rule out the lower part's pleasure in tyrannical domination. Recall, too, the solution Socrates proposed in terms of the Chimerical image of the tripartite soul, in which the human being within is to take charge of the many-headed beast—like a farmer, nourishing and cultivating the tame heads, while hindering the growth of the savage ones—making the lion's nature an ally and, caring for all in common, making them friends with each other and himself, and so rear them.[54]

The regime to which the lowest part of the soul is to be subjected here is by no means cruel or tyrannical—especially in comparison with the radical Christian prescriptions for treating unruly passions which Nietzsche inveighs against in *Twilight of the Idols*.[55] We shall see soon that the problem lies in the perpetual domination of the passions by reason as something self-identical and of an entirely different nature from the drives.

From a Nietzschean point of view, however, there is an anomaly in the Platonic account of the progressive degeneration of the inner regime from a monarchy of the intellect to the type dominated "from below" by the tyrant *erōs*. Socrates speaks throughout as if there exists an overseeing agent somehow external to the tripartite psyche—at least until the degeneration reaches its nadir in the tyrannical personality type. The just human being "harmonizes the three parts . . . and becomes entirely one from many"; the timocratic type "turns over the rule in himself to the spirited part"; the oligarchic character "thrusts spiritedness out of the throne and makes the desiring part the great king within himself"; while the democratic personality "hands over the rule in himself to whichever [pleasure] happens along."[56] But *who*—Nietzsche would want to ask—harmonizes, turns over the rule, ejects and installs, suppresses and fosters, awakens and soothes? It is incomprehensible that the "calculating part" should choose to hand over the rule to any of the other parts; nor can this apparently independent director consist in the unity of all the parts, since in the cases in question the parts, being unharmonized, fail to constitute a unity. It will help if we keep this question in mind—and be sure to apply it to Nietzsche, too—as we proceed.

We saw in the last chapter that political discourse assumed unprecedented importance in Nietzsche's psychology with the publication of *Beyond Good and Evil,* where he elaborated a hypothesis of the soul as "social structure of the drives and affects" and of the will as manifold relations of commanding and obeying within a community of agents or parties. A number of unpublished notes he made during the writing of this book provide a more detailed picture of the inner regime. But before looking at these, we need to consider briefly how Nietzsche understands the *intellect* at this point in his career.

In *Dawn of Morning,* at the end of the aphorism that introduced the idea of an interplay of drives without any separate ruler different in kind, there was an equivocation concerning the role of the intellect. It was said to be merely "the blind tool of *another drive*" and yet there was also talk of "a *struggle* in which our intellect [would have] to take sides" (*DM* 109). This issue is soon resolved, in *The Joyful Science,* where Nietzsche characterizes *intelligere* as "only *a certain disposition* [Verhalten] *of the drives toward each other.*"[57] The intellect, then, is not something separate from or other than the drives, but rather a certain *configuration* of them (within the larger matrix of will to power).

It is a radical move to dispense in this way with the positing of an independent director, to negate the idea of the intellect as something separate and of a different nature from—and thus capable of ruling over—the various drives. If this seems counterintuitive phenomenologically, insofar as we generally have the impression of being able to struggle with the various drives because "I" enjoy the status of an autonomous overseer, we must bear in mind that, according to Nietzsche, every drive has its own perspective: "It is our needs that *interpret the world:* our drives and their for and against. Every drive is a kind of lust to rule, every drive has its perspective, which it would like to impose upon all the other drives as a norm."[58] Thus the changing identity of the ruler apparent is concealed by the mask of the first person singular: the realization dawns that a variety of inner parties may, according to the situation, be voicing the word "I." An earlier note reads: "The multiplicity of persons (masks) in one 'I.'"[59]

Just as the soul is to be understood as "social structure of the drives and affects," so the body, which is for Nietzsche distinct but not different from the soul, is to be understood as "a social structure of many souls" (*BGE* 19). In a note from 1885 he recommends taking the body and physiology as a model, since by so doing

> we gain the right idea of the nature of our subject-unity, namely as regents at the head of a community . . . also of the dependence of these regents on those who are ruled and conditions of order of rank and division of labor as what makes possible both the individual and the whole. Just as living unities are constantly arising and perishing and there is no "eternity" to the subject. . . . The definite *ignorance* in which the regent is kept concerning the particular activities and even disturbances within the community belongs to the very conditions under which government is possible. . . . The most important thing, however, is that we understand the ruler and his subjects *[Untertanen]* as being of *the same nature*—all feeling, willing, thinking. . . . To inquire of the subject *[Subjekt]* directly concerning the nature of the subject is risky because it could well be useful, and important for its activity, for the subject to misinterpret itself. For that reason we ask the body . . . [in order to] see whether the subordinates themselves might not deal with us directly.[60]

It is significant that the rulers are described as *regents*—figures merely standing in for others—rather than as monarchs, since this helps dispel the idea of a permanent, self-identical governing agent.[61] There is some ambiguity here concerning whether there is only one regent at a time or more than one. Given the idea of living unities constantly arising and perishing and the connaturality of rulers and ruled, one may assume that at times there might be a single regent and at other times a regency comprising several members.

Another note from 1885 confirms the idea that the intellect is a tool and emphasizes the multiple nature of the regency:

It all depends on the proper characterization of the unity that comprises thinking, willing, feeling and all the affects: clearly the intellect is only a *tool,* but in whose hands? In the hands of the affects certainly: and these are a multiplicity behind which it is not necessary to posit a unity: it suffices to conceive the multiplicity as a regency.[62]

The "proper characterization of the unity" of our mental and psychical life would then be as a multiplicity that is configured in such a way that a group of drives or affects holds at least temporary hegemony over the whole. The idea of a governing group rather than individual is emphasized in another note from the same year:

The assumption of the *unitary subject* is perhaps unnecessary; perhaps it is just as permissible to assume a plurality of subjects whose interplay and struggle are the ground of our thinking and our consciousness in general? A kind of *aristocracy* of "cells" in which the power to rule resides? Certainly of equals who are accustomed to ruling and know how to command?
My hypotheses:
the subject as multiplicity
the constant transitoriness and ephemerality of the subject, "mortal soul"[63]

The notion of a ruling aristocracy is familiar from the *Republic;* but the difference is that these rulers are to be understood not as representatives of reason, constituents of the "calculating part" of the psyche, or as enduring self-identical agents, but rather as offices or positions capable of being held by a succession of different figures.

One last note from the end of 1885 sketches a program for the drives and affects that Nietzsche will advocate until the end of his career, and which again acknowledges their archaic dimension.

Overcoming the affects? No, not if that means their weakening and annihilation. *But to take them into service:* which may involve tyrannizing them for a long time (not even as an individual, but as a community, a race, etc.). Eventually one gives them back their freedom with confidence: they love us like good servants and ultimately go where our best inclines.[64]

Here we see that the tyranny that organizes the chaos of the affects is not quite the work of a lifetime: though it is a protracted task, in the ideal case the tyranny is "eventually" relaxed in such a way that one can enjoy spontaneous existence; but it is in a sense the work of a series of lifetimes, insofar as it can take many generations before the requisite organization is attained.[65]

Good Nietzscheans will want to ask at this point: *Who*, or which agency, tyrannizes the affects and takes them into service? and, if the tyrannized affects are to be given back their freedom, *to whom* are they then to act as "good servants"? To answer "I" and "to me" is now uninformative, in view of the dissolution of the I into a multiplicity; the answer is presumably: to an affect or drive, or group of affects or drives, acting as a regency, or as a group of aristocratic affects provisionally in power. Nietzsche also refers to the power that dominates affects or passions as "the will," which would sound strangely conventional—will versus the passions—had the will not been resolved into a multiplicity, as above all "a *complex* of feelings" and "an *affect* of command" (*BGE* 19). A note from 1887 reads:

> *Summa: mastery* over the passions, *not* their weakening or extirpation! The greater the will's power of mastery, the more freedom may be given to the passions. The "great human being" is great by virtue of the range of free play of his desires and of the still greater power that is able to take these magnificent monsters into service.[66]

The will that "masters" the passions turns out then, somewhat paradoxically, to be constituted by them. This is made clear in a note from the following year, under the heading "Role of Consciousness," where Nietzsche denies that consciousness plays any part in directing the "subterranean" interplay of somatic operations. The "higher authority *[Instanz]*" is "a kind of directing committee in which the various *dominant desires* make their voices and power effective."[67] Here it is made explicit that the directing agency is, as it were, a committee constituted by the desires that dominate at the time.

Now it is possible to lay out the grounds for the differences between Nietzsche and Plato as far as internal politics are concerned. Given that under the optimal Platonic regime the ruling reason attempts to "befriend" the lower drives and direct the necessary nourishment to all but the most antisocial of them, Nietzsche's dissatisfaction with this arrangement appears to have two grounds. The first concerns the drawbacks of what might be called—to paraphrase one of his own wittier coinages—a "monotono-cracy" of single-minded reason. In Plato the coordination of the desires takes place under the direction of a reason that is always self-identical, re-maining the same over the course of the individual's development. In view of Nietzsche's contrasting emphasis on "becoming" over "being"—whether in the inner or the outer realms—he could hardly advocate a single drive's remaining in charge indefinitely. The notes just considered suggest a model in which a succession of drives, each of which would in principle be capable of "philosophizing," cycle through the highest office in accordance with the experiential context and the individual's stage of development.[68] It would be a question of an aristocracy rather than a monarchy, of dissolving the philosopher-king into a governing body of several thinkers, splintering the hegemony of the intellect into a matrix of relationships among the various affects, drives, and passions. Such an arrangement would be dictated by the idea that the intellect is nothing other than *"a certain relationship of the drives to each other,"* which is recapitulated in a late note (1887–88): "The misunderstanding of passion and *reason,* as if the latter were an entity in itself and not rather a condition of relationships among various passions and desires; and as if every passion did not have its quantum of reason."[69] On this view reason would not be seen as a permanent ruler, nor as an indepen-dent director at the head; there would be no need for any leader separate from the led.

While Nietzsche is by no means an irrationalist, he follows Herder in relativizing reason by integrating it with the other powers of the soul, and thus cannot endorse the Platonic identification of reason as the royal road to virtue and happiness. For Plato, "one must imitate Socrates and institute a perpetual *daylight* in opposition to the dark desires—the daylight of rea-son. One must be clever, clear, bright at any cost: every giving in to the instincts, to the unconscious, leads *downward*."[70] The problem with such a regime, for Nietzsche, is that the balance of power in the psyche is too one-sided, overly top-heavy, for a fruitful and creative existence. It depends, of course, on just what one wants to become. For a life that is calm and serene (if rather boring), he would surely endorse the soul well harmonized under the rule of single-minded reason, a paradigm of Apollonian order. But for a richer life he would hold it necessary to celebrate a greater pressure of population in the psyche, to allow a more Dionysiac disposition of forces, one capable of sustaining changing rulers and the tensions of tyranny, as well as chronic *polemos* among parties in the *polis* within. In this case the vicious and violent drives whose growth Socrates wants to hinder would be—though restrained and trained—*retained* as indispensable sources of energy.[71]

And with this we arrive at the second, related source of Nietzsche's dissatisfaction with the Platonic ideal, which is a more general concern with the amount and distribution of energy within the psyche, with what since Freud has been called "libidinal economics." Nietzsche is reluctant to endorse the Platonic prescription for "starving the savage heads of the beast" (hindering the growth of negative drives) because of the loss of energy this would entail, and the resultant sapping of the creative urge. He is concerned rather to retain as many powerful energies as possible within the "great economy" of the soul. In view of the power that has traditionally been ascribed to the "many-headed beast" of the lower drives, and of the savagery of the beasts of prey that prowl through the Nietzschean psyche, how does one pull off the difficult trick of *training* without *taming,* of harnessing the power of the "magnificent monsters" of the passions without damaging or being savaged by them?

Several chapters in *Twilight of the Idols* help answer this question by filling out the pattern sketched in the note from 1885: "Eventually one gives them back their freedom with confidence: they love us like good servants and ultimately go where our best inclines." What emerges from the later text is a picture of a two-phase relationship with the drives. The initial state is characterized by "the inability to resist a stimulus," and the response that constitutes the first phase is a "preschooling in spirituality." This preparatory education involves "*not* reacting immediately to a stimulus, but gaining control over the restraining, repressing instincts."[72] This first phase is the same as in the Platonic-Socratic program, but is for Nietzsche simply a preliminary strategy for the sake of an eventually greater freedom. An earlier aphorism entitled "Self-control" makes it clear that this virtue is merely a means and by no means an end in itself. A person all of whose energies are directed toward self-control is no dancer, but rather "stands there with a gesture that wards off, armed against himself":

> Of course he can thereby be *great!* But how intolerable he has now become for others, how difficult for himself, how impoverished and cut off from the most beautiful chance occurrences of the soul! And from all further *instruction!* For one must be able to lose oneself from time to time, if one wants to learn something from things other than ourselves.[73]

Nietzsche goes on to explain that he understands *Geist,* or spirit, as "the great self-mastery"; but he then concludes—and this is the crux—"One must have need of spirit in order to attain spirit; one loses it when one no longer needs it" (*TI* 9.14). The will's "power of mastery" becomes such that it is now safe to "give back to the drives their freedom," in the confidence that they will now "go where our best inclines." By the end of this second phase, in which "the entire affective system is stimulated and intensified," one is able to act with total spontaneity—strangely but knowingly "unable *not* to react"—moved now by the mysterious power of Dionysus (*TI* 9.10).

One can fully channel the power of the "negative" drives only when one has the courage to relax the harsh discipline to which they have long been subjected, allowing their massive energies to flow again through the "great economy" of the soul. This is a dangerous undertaking which conduces to a kind of freedom of which only the greater human beings are capable.

> One would have to look for the highest type of free human being there where the greatest resistance is constantly being overcome: five steps away from tyranny, right at the threshold of the danger of servitude. This is psychologically true, if one understands the "tyrants" here as terrible and relentless instincts, which demand a maximum of authority and discipline to counter them. (*TI* 9.38)

The source of this "authority and discipline" will not be the ego or reason or something other than the drives, but rather simply another instinct or drive, or group of drives. This organization of forces verges on tyranny in two directions: it issues from the relaxation of protracted tyranny on the part of ordering drives, and it is thus always in danger of relapsing into tyranny at the hands of previously subdued forces that have regained sufficient strength to cause chaos again. Nietzsche presents a paradigm of the highest type of human being in the person of Goethe: "What he wanted was *totality* ... he disciplined himself into a totality, he *created* himself" (*TI* 9.49). Goethe's greatness lies in his ability to live his ideal:

> Goethe conceived of a strong, highly cultured human being, adept in a range of physical skills *[Leiblichkeiten]*, self-controlled and with reverence for himself, who can dare to grant himself the full range and richness of naturalness, and who is strong enough for this freedom.

This courage to "grant [one]self the full range of richness and naturalness" is the key to burgeoning psychological health for Nietzsche. At some point in the practice of self-discipline it is possible to relax control of the "magnificent monsters" that are the drives, affects, and passions, and trust them to move us spontaneously in the appropriate ways. The aphorism concludes with the affirmation that belief that such an ideal is livable is belief in *Dionysus*—but this would be a Dionysian life that is no longer in opposition to Apollonian existence but has superseded it by incorporating and going beyond it.

It is difficult, ultimately, to express the organization of this kind of great soul in political terms. In the initial stages it may be that a monarch (that one could call reason, intellect, or will, and which calls itself "I") is established, who severely disciplines the unruly elements in the psyche. But in a soul disposed to creative activity, a particular combination of drives—one's "task"—will take over, in the persons of "an aristocracy of regents," who would continue to rule with iron hands. According to one's stage of development and the external situation, the composition of this regency would change over time, with new drives joining and old ones leaving or being dismissed. After a period of this kind of regime—a sort of "serial tyranny by committee"—the originally unruly drives may have undergone sufficient discipline for the iron rule to be lifted. The ideal state would be one in which as much power as possible is ultimately returned to the greatest variety of energetic drives, affects, and passions, in the expectation that all parties will spontaneously organize themselves to the optimal benefit of the "psychopolis" as a whole.[74] The will that would then hold gentle sway over the monstrously powerful drives no longer operates only through the conscious ego, but rather works and plays as "will to power"—a configuration of the interpretive energies that constitute *life* in the widest sense.

We recall, however, that Nietzsche eventually proposes that not only all life but all force whatsoever—the world as a whole—be considered as a play of will to power. Looking back over the topics through which we have ranged and the levels of discourse with which we have dealt, it appears that for Nietzsche the answer to the question of what the soul is like is that ultimately it is like everything: galaxies, solar systems, minerals from rocks to metals, bodies of water, dances of fire and wind. The soil of the soul supports plant life, which in turn nourishes the faunae of the psyche. Not only natural worlds but the worlds of human community move and have their being within as well as without. As Aristotle said, the soul is in a way all things, and so the boundaries between inner and outer are dissolved. This was a major theme in *Zarathustra*—as announced in the protagonist's prologue:

> I love him whose soul is overfull, so that he forgets himself, and all things are in him: thus all things become his going under. (Z, P4)

If all things are in the soul, there is no longer any outside; which means the perishing of the separate self. And yet the ideal is no static condition, but rather one of overflow, downpour, and uprush—flows of *erōs* in Dionysian *Rausch*, a constant arising and abating of drives. Zarathustra praises above all

> the most comprehensive soul, that can run and wander and roam farthest within itself . . .
>   the soul that loves itself the most, in which all things have their streaming and counter-streaming, their ebb and flood.[75]

He addresses his own soul, who is "waiting for overflow," as follows:

> O my soul, there is nowhere a soul that would be more loving and embracing and comprehensive than you! Where would future and past be closer together than in you? (Z 3.14)

Recall all the images of overflow, *Überfluss,* that pervade the text of *Zarathustra.* When one looks into the source of such abundance, it appears to be the world itself. Zarathustra says to those who, like he himself, are striving after the virtue of effusive generosity:

> You force all things to yourselves and into yourselves, that they may flow back out of your spring as gifts of your love.[76]

A suggestion here of systole and diastole in the flows of *erōs.* The influx also comes from the past, as we saw, driving in from afar with natural efflux. Living life to the full would then be a matter of *flowing* or streaming rather than simply going with the flow that flows through all things.

This, then, is the sense in which *Thus Spoke Zarathustra* is a play of images constituting a consummate picture of the most comprehensive soul, of psyche in totality. It is possible, and enlightening, to read the entire text as a complex image of a single soul—Zarathustra's—and to understand as the major theme the Dionysiac dissolution of the unitary I through multiple overflowings into a plurality of persons, in the context of a plethora of natural phenomena. The first indication that all the characters in the book are aspects of Zarathustra's personality is that the second of the twenty-two speeches in part one, which is entitled "Zarathustra's Speeches," is actually delivered by a "wise man" who is clearly an alter ego for the protagonist (Z 1.2). Beginning with the soothsayer in part 2 (2.19), and culminating in the host of "higher humans" in part four, a variety of "alter" types takes the stage. The most telling event is Zarathustra's inviting all these characters into his cave on the mountain-top, that sacrosanct haven of solitude, toward the end of the book.[77] This invitation and reconciliation is equivalent to the process described by depth psychology in which the I faces and attempts to come to terms with all the parts of the psyche that have been subject to repression or projection onto others. The final ending of *Zarathustra* is enigmatic, insofar as the higher humans fail to assimilate the protagonist's teachings and remain resistant to change, forcing Zarathustra to the realization that they are not the companions he needs after all.

The life that is lived comprehensively as will to power, having gone through Apollonian discipline and beyond the realm of spirit, will range through all the domains of Dionysus through channeling a maximal influx from the life of the past so as to generate the most fecund future. Nietzsche exemplifies this kind of life in the figure of the *Übermensch.* Insofar as this figure is "the sense of the earth" one remains—even at the peak of high culture—the soil of the soul, the streaming rain that showers upon it, the sun that shines on the sap that drives vegetation up from the earth, as well as the storms that test and strengthen that striving growth. We still "grow as plants," as Herder said.

The *oikos* of Dionysus embraces the sap of plants and the powers of animals as well as humans. In Dionysus is the wisdom of the serpent, the pride of the panther, lion, and eagle. To aspire to the condition of the *Übermensch* is not to abandon one's animal nature but to train and thereby sublimate it. Just as Dionysus appears as a variety of animals, so the life of the *Übermensch* incorporates and exemplifes the animal in its modes of perceiving and acting—but an animal that has been bred and disciplined and so infused with human spirit that its spontaneity is now *super*natural. Zarathustra's speech on the transformations of the spirit into camel, lion, and child is not meant to imply that the animal realm is transcended: when one no longer needs spirit one leaves it behind and enters the realm of the Dionysian, where vegetal and animal functions are quickened by their having passed through the human spirit.

To return, finally, to *Twilight of the Idols:* the spontaneity that comes from granting oneself the full range of naturalness is rooted in an adroitness of the well trained body *(Leib)*—in what Nietzsche calls, with reference to Goethe, skillful *Leiblichkeiten.* "The proper place of culture," he insists, "is the body" (*TI* 9.47). It is a matter of attuning the flows of energy that comprise the body with the flows of energies that comprise the macrocosm so as to attain the state of *strömen*—the streaming that goes beyond "going with the flow" to *flowing* with the flows. This requires the strength and suppleness we have seen Nietzsche assert as preconditions of the genuinely Dionysian *dance.*[78]

It is not only the flows of the macrocosm, the forces of nature, that are dangerous in their massive power, but also—because of the archaic dimension—the flows within the individual body. Nietzsche emphasizes the dangers when he explicates his "concept of genius" (*TI* 9.44), characterizing great men and great ages as "explosive materials in which an enormous amount of force has been accumulated." The great human being, the genius, is a "squanderer" of the enormous influx that is the source of greatness:

> He flows out *[strömt aus]*, he overflows *[strömt über]*, he consumes himself and does not spare himself—fatally, disastrously, involuntarily, as a river that bursts its banks does so involuntarily.

A major source of the danger is then this: that even when the individual possesses in great measure the plastic power that would assimilate the past, there is at the stage where control has been relaxed and one is daring to be natural no guarantee that the delicate balance can be maintained. One's openness to the drives that flow in from the archaic (and more recent) past has to correspond to the capacity to assimilate—yet without the help of an independent regulatory agency. If such an agency is retained, in the form of a separate unitary I, the consequent restriction of flow will inhibit the attainment of greatness. But if the inflow greatly exceeds the capacity, there is the danger that the entire system will explode.[79]

In talking about the dangers of greatness, several months before his own system became unable to sustain the pressures on it, Nietzsche is clearly talking about himself. In his last productive year—working at fever pitch he authored six books in 1888, four of them major—Nietzsche overflowed, consumed himself, and did not spare himself in striving to accomplish his task. The river broke its banks as he wrote himself over the edge of the abyss; the final explosion was fatal and disastrous, as the great health collapsed in upon itself. But what concerns the student of Nietzsche is not the *imitatio magistri,* the emulation of the actual man's existence, but the ways the life portrayed in his writings—"life passed through the fire of thought"—vivifies the existence of the reader by opening it up to broader and deeper possibilities of experience. Nietzsche's psychological ideas thus have a value for the rest of us that is independent of the tragic fate of his own person.

Next to the note in which Nietzsche claimed to have "the *most comprehensive* soul" of any European who had ever lived is another, one that ends with the most poignant of questions.

> There is a false saying: "How can someone who can't save himself save others?" Supposing I have the key to your chains, why should your lock and my lock be the same?[80]

Epilogue: A Dangerous Life

The intellect of man is forced to choose
Perfection of the life, or of the work,
And if it take the second must refuse
A heavenly mansion, raging in the dark.

                                                    Yeats

Much has been left open by the preceding chapters, in good faith; but something needs to be said in response to the questions raised at the very end. If Nietzsche's reflections on psychology culminate in a picture of "the great health"—souls burgeoning on many levels with various parts in the psyche shaping, forming, commanding, exercising protracted discipline on other parts until ultimately control is relaxed so as to allow spontaneous activity from awareness of a full range of perspectives—how then are we to understand the proponent's prompt collapse into madness, especially given his emphasis on connections between the ideas and the life? Is Nietzsche's teaching on the soul inherently dangerous, are the reaches of his psychology fraught with peril, and is the emphasis on the experimental and experiential detrimental to his readers' mental health? Or can his ideas be celebrated as salutary in spite of the hazards that may attend some of them?

These questions are best approached through a complement to the political model of psychological health that found its ultimate depiction in *Twilight of the Idols*. We saw how the soul in Nietzsche also seems to call for expression through ideas about life as a play enacted in the theater of the psyche, and that his disillusion with Wagner's theatricality may have disinclined him from pursuing these ideas. Taking a lead from the way that subsequent depth psychology employs imagery of drama, one can extrapolate from his metaphors concerning masks, roles, and psychical actors in order to reconstruct a picture of psychological order that is consonant with the rest of Nietzsche's thinking. These considerations may put us in a better position to ponder, if only provisionally, the meanings of his madness.

Improvising Roles

The idea of multiple personality came increasingly to prominence in the course of the nineteenth century, and we saw earlier (chapter 7) how dialogical models of the soul were developed by theorists such as Herbart and Griesinger. During the final decade of Nietzsche's literary output the phenomenon had begun to be investigated through scientific experiment, especially in France. Studies of hysterical illness and the phenomena of hypnotic trance and psychical automatism by such researchers as Charcot, Bernheim, and Janet were appearing to provide empirical confirmation of the idea that several different consciousnesses can coexist in one person.[1] These findings were taken seriously by an American thinker in the lineage of Emerson: William James. In the *Principles of Psychology* (first published in 1890, the year after Nietzsche stopped writing), James writes as follows:

> It must be admitted that *in certain persons,* at least, *the total possible consciousness may be split into parts which coexist but mutually ignore each other,* and share the objects of knowledge between them.[2]

The French psychologists considered dissociation of consciousness to be a pathological condition, occurring only when there is a general mental lability to begin with. James's view was in contrast more open:

> How far this splitting up of the mind into separate consciousnesses may exist in each one of us is a problem. . . . All these facts, taken together, form unquestionably the beginning of an inquiry which is destined to throw a new light into the very abysses of our nature. (1:210–11)

In a later chapter of the book, entitled "The Consciousness of Self," James offers a formulation of the problem of multiple selves that is as graphic as it is pragmatic.

> Properly speaking, *a man has as many social selves as there are* [groups of] *individuals who recognize him* and carry an image of him in their mind. . . . He generally shows a different side of himself to each of these different groups. . . . We do not show ourselves to our children as to our club-companions, to our customers as to the laborers we employ, to our own masters and employers as to our intimate friends. From this there results what practically is a division of the man into several selves; and this may be a discordant splitting, as where one is afraid to let one set of his acquaintances know him as he is elsewhere; or it may be a perfectly harmonious division of labor, as where one tender to his children is stern to the soldiers or prisoners under his command. (1:294)

These reflections on the variety of social selves within each individual are quite consonant with Nietzsche's ideas about masks and the drives and persons that don and doff them. Multiplicity typically generates problems of order, which James goes on to address in a section bearing the rather Nietzschean title "Rivalry and Conflict of the Different Selves."

> Not that I would not, if I could, be both handsome and fat and well dressed, and a great athlete, and make a million a year, be a wit, a *bon-vivant,* and a lady-killer, as well as a philosopher; a philanthropist, statesman, warrior, and African explorer, as well as a "tone-poet" and saint. (1:309)

The dilemma (or polylemma) is nicely expressed, and James proposes a resolution of the problem in characteristically concrete terms:

> But the thing is simply impossible. The millionaire's work would run counter to the saint's; the *bon-vivant* and the philanthropist would trip each other up; the philosopher and the lady-killer could not well keep house in the same tenement of clay. Such different characters may conceivably at the outset of life be alike *possible* to a man. But to make any one of them actual, the rest must more or less be suppressed. So the seeker of his truest, strongest, deepest self must review the list carefully, and pick out the one on which to stake his salvation. All other selves thereupon become unreal.

While this method surely makes for intrapsychical order, there would be the danger, from the point of view of the later Nietzsche, of a "monotonocracy" of the ego. Things would be calm and well ordered, but the selection of a *single* self "on which to stake one's salvation" would result in a soul too lacking in internal conflicts to achieve greatness—or even an above-average level of creativity. Psychodomestic strife, however, brings with it dangers of its own: lethargy and dilettantism on the one hand, and psychical anarchy on the other. But before attempting to resolve this issue, let us look at the more radical solution that is to be found in depth psychology.

An inquiry such as the one anticipated by James as "destined to throw a new light into the very abysses of our nature" was in fact begun in Europe just a few years later by Freud, in his investigations into hysteria. In an essay from 1893 entitled "A Case of Hypnotic Healing," Freud shows how in hysteria "painful opposing ideas" (representations of drives that have been repressed as incompatible with the person's self-image) assume an autonomous existence through being dissociated from normal I-consciousness.[3] The remarkable capacity of these opposing ideas to take over the body by creating symptoms with respect to which conscious willpower is impotent induces Freud to characterize them as "counter-wills." He goes on to speak of how the power of the counter-will gives hysteria a "daemonic quality," and says of the opposing ideas that "they are stored up, and continue an unsuspected existence in a kind of shadow-realm, until they emerge as ghosts and take control of the body" (*SEF* 1:126–27).

Freud elaborates the notion of dissociation two years later in *Studies on Hysteria,* a text in which metaphorical imagery gives way to more scientific terminology. There he writes: "In hysteria there are groups of ideas that have arisen in hypnoid states . . . which are associable amongst themselves, and which represent a more or less highly organized second consciousness, a '*condition seconde*'" (*SEF* 2:15). A later account of the phenomenon, in the essay "Repression" from 1915, subsumes it under one of Freud's early theories of the drives, though traces of the earlier tendency toward personifying persist. There Freud observes that repression

> does not prevent the representation of the drive from persisting in the unconscious, organizing itself further, forming derivatives of itself and making connections. . . . [It rather] develops in a more unchecked and luxuriant manner . . . [and] proliferates, so to speak, in the dark. (*SEF* 14:149).

In the dim underworld of the soul, far removed from the light of consciousness, these groups of ideas link themselves up with other elements that have been repressed or have fallen below the threshold of awareness, such as dream images, phantasies, and latent memories. As more and more of these elements coalesce, something like a separate personality begins to form. Although Freud does not go on to develop the idea of "second consciousnesses" explicitly—presumably for fear of appearing unscientific—his picture of the psyche, with its various "systems," "agencies," and "forces," remains multiple and polycentric. Both Freud and Jung see the ego as one agency among several, and as a *construct,* something put together by the psyche in order to cope with the external world. Where Nietzsche talked of "the synthetic concept of the I," they both speak of the *Ich-Komplex,* of the I as something twined together from various strands.

Jung was initially almost as concerned as Freud to have his psychology accepted as a scientific discipline, but was prepared—perhaps as a result of his early studies of psychic phenomena—to take the idea of "second consciousnesses" more seriously than his predecessor.[4] In developing his theory of the "feeling-toned complexes" (Jung introduced the term "complex" into our psychological vocabulary), he characterizes them as "part-souls," "splinter psyches," and "fragmentary personalities" (8:202–4). He is more radical than Freud in regarding the complexes as autonomous agents in the soul that are naturally and spontaneously personifed, and less tentative than James in insisting that the complexes are "not entirely morbid by nature but are *characteristic expressions of the psyche* . . . among the normal phenomena of life," and that it belongs to their nature to be personified as figures that are truly "spontaneous agents" (6:209–18). The spontaneity of these figures manifests itself most clearly in the phenomenon of the dream, but also through what Jung calls "active imagination":

> [The] personification of the complexes is not in itself necessarily a pathological condition. In dreams, for instance, our complexes often appear in a personified form. And one can train oneself [in active imagination] to such an extent that they become visible or audible also in a waking condition. (18:150)

He is fond of describing the technique of active imagination through the metaphor of the theatrical play:

> You choose a dream, or some other fantasy-image, and concentrate on it. . . . A chain of fantasy-images develops and gradually takes on a dramatic character. At first it consists of projected figures, and these images are observed like scenes in the theater. . . . [The imaginer] will notice that as the actors appear one by one and the plot thickens . . . he is being addressed by the unconscious, and that *it* causes these fantasy-images to appear before him. He therefore feels compelled . . . to take part in the play. (14:706)

What is crucial for Jung here is that one understand and experience the I as just one actor on a par with the others: to distance oneself by observing the play in a detached manner, or to attempt to produce and direct it, fails to effect any worthwhile development. Such moves gratify the ego's desire to remain in control, and so effect no shift in the balance of power in the psyche.

When Freud advocates coming to terms with the autonomous elements of the unconscious, the purpose is relatively conservative: to give the I freedom to reassert its hegemony over the other psychical agencies and its control over access to the musculature. The goal of a Jungian analysis can be more radical: to move the "center of gravity" of the psyche away from the I in the direction of the unconscious, thereby diminishing the I's control and shifting the balance of power toward the autonomous complexes and the archetypal figures of the collective unconscious. But Jung is clearly ambivalent about this ex-centric move away from unity toward multiplicity: sometimes his position is radically polycentric and in harmony with Greek polytheism; but at other times, when he insists on the unity of the concentered "Self," he seems to remain under the sway of Christian monotheism. A therapeutic motive is also operative here, in that there may be a need for a unitary I to hold the other personalities in check so as to prevent psychosis.

In dealing with the complexes, especially those with a strong archetypal core, Jung emphasizes the importance of the I's relating itself to them rather than identifying with them.[5] From the Jungian perspective the "normal" ego-centered person, the artist, the case of multiple personality, and the psychotic would lie on a continuum. In the "normal" human being the I is able to control the complexes through moderate repression, while in the case of the artist the membrane, as it were, between ego-consciousness and the complexes is imagined to be more permeable.[6] Persons in whom a strong ego fails to develop are prone to the condition of multiple personality; and if defensiveness on the part of the ego leads to massive repressions, these may give rise to an accumulation of energy in the unconscious powerful enough to prompt an insurrection on the part of the repressed and an overthrow of the ego—a psychotic break. The question becomes how to avoid a tedious monarchy of the ego without lapsing into chaos and psychosis.

Let us attempt a synopsis of the ideas we have been considering by recasting the problem in terms of actors and roles. Most people would agree with William James that in the course of a day one plays a variety of roles, donning a different mask or *persona* according to the situation. A man may, for instance, play the part of father, administrator, house-husband, teacher, and lover between the times of rising and retiring. But when "the seeker of his truest, strongest, deepest self . . . picks out the one [character] on which to stake his salvation," is it really the case that "all other selves thereupon become unreal"? It may seem natural to say that there is one person—"I"— who plays these many parts, but Nietzsche would want to press the question "*Who is it that speaks* through the various masks?" Is it really the same one, some one, single person, the unitary I, who plays these different parts? Or does a variety of roles not rather require a plurality of persons as well as *personae* to play them? Is the one I seeing and speaking through many masks—or is the ego rather obscuring the issue, homophonizing or monotonizing a variety of voices from the deeper soul?[7]

It is simply counterproductive to ask the heroic ego to play all the parts that are demanded of an individual in the course of a lifetime. Not only would this be a hyper-Herculean labor, in which the constant changing of masks would quickly exhaust even the most indefatigable actor, but the one-man (or -woman) show would be as boring as it would be inefficient. One might propose that the I acknowledge the presence of other actors, but that it nevertheless stay firmly ensconced in the role of director. But the question arises: Why bother with the expense (in terms of psychical energy) of a director at all? A powerful motive here is fear that there would be chaos, debilitating lethargy, or else complete anarchy in the absence of a single I in control—fear that one would suffer the fate that befell Nietzsche himself.

The Western tradition has been grounded for so long in a monarchy of the I and a tyranny of univocal reason that we cannot believe that there could be psychical spontaneity without anarchy, polyphony without discord, or pluralism without psychosis.[8]

The chaos of psychosis would appear to erupt because the unconscious figures of the psyche are dissociated from the I and from each other. But if the separating membrane can be made gradually more permeable, allowing interaction and communication among all members of the cast, there is no reason why there should not be what James called "a perfectly harmonious division of labor" in responding to the demands of life—which would obviate "the necessity of standing by one of the empirical selves and relinquishing the rest." Borrowing the schema drawn from Nietzsche's talk of psychopolitical regimes, one could propose that the internal actors start out their careers as members of a conventional theater company under the direction of a firm-handed director. As the individual becomes more autonomous, it is more helpful to imagine a company moving toward improvisational theater, with scripts or prompts constantly coming in from outside and the most accomplished players rotating through the directorship. With the passing of time the actors would practice their art with discipline, get to know each other's style, and broaden the repertoire; and there would finally come a point at which there was no need for a director, and the company could become fully improvisational. At every juncture the actor(s) most suitable to play the part or respond to the prompt would do so, without having to be directed by an independent agent.

This picture turns out to be applicable to Nietzsche's ideas about drives and persons, and in particular to the part of *Dawn of Morning* 119 that we deferred discussion of in chapter 8. There he gave the example of noticing that someone in the marketplace was laughing at us, claiming that the occurrence would have different meanings for us depending on which drive was lying in wait to interpret it. He elaborates with a further example:

> The other morning at eleven o'clock a man suddenly collapsed right in front of me, as if struck by lightning; all the women in the vicinity screamed out loud; I myself got him to his feet and waited until he had recovered his speech. During the whole event not a muscle of my face moved nor any feeling stirred, whether of horror or pity, but I did what reason required and went calmly on my way. Now suppose that I had been told the previous day that tomorrow at eleven o'clock someone near me would collapse in this fashion: I would have suffered all kinds of anticipatory torment, would have spent a sleepless night, and at the crucial moment would perhaps have done just the

same thing as the man instead of helping him. For in the meantime all kinds of drives would have *had time* to imagine the experience and comment on it.

We all know the experience of carrying out internal conversations in anticipation of some important event where we are not sure how to behave: this is a case of listening to the voices of the drives as they "imagine and comment." While certain situations might call for the kind of deliberation in which various drives have their say, this can often be an uneconomical way to proceed, involving as it does an unnecessary dissipation of psychical energy. The ideal would be to react—and act—the way Nietzsche did at the man's sudden collapse. To say that he "did what reason required" is not to suggest that something called the rational drive predominated, since reason is nothing more than a certain "disposition of the drives toward each other." His ability to do spontaneously what reason required depended on his drives' happening to be so disposed toward each other that, at the crucial moment, the appropriate drive (or group of drives) was able to interpret the situation and gain immediate access to the musculature in order to discharge itself.

Another, extratextual example may help to amplify this important point. A young woman, mild-mannered and soft-spoken, has been having trouble with her car. She has taken it to the repair shop repeatedly, at great inconvenience, but the problems have still not been rectified. After a while she realizes that the problems lie more with the inefficiency of the mechanics than anything else. Her upbringing has taught her that it is unladylike to yell and scream, and she feels intimidated by the gruff manager from whom she has been politely demanding satisfaction. In the face of continuing frustration, her resolve builds and she issues over the phone a polite but firm ultimatum. The night before she is to go and pick up the car, having been assured that this time everything will finally be in order, with no excuses, she has a vivid dream. In the dream she is in a parking lot and a terrifying three-hundred-pound hulk with muscles of steel and the face of a grizzly bear is picking up men in overalls and throwing them against a brick wall. The alarm interrupts the dream at crack of dawn, and—more than a little shaken by its violence—she takes a bus to the repair shop. The manager greets her with yet another facile excuse for the car's still not being ready. An unprecedented surge of energy courses through her frame: veins stand out on her forehead and knuckles turn white as she grips the edge of the counter. A voice unrecognizable as her own blasts the grin from the face of the manager as he retreats into the repair bay. Within thirty minutes she is driving the car away, the problems finally fixed at no extra charge.

As in Nietzsche's example, if she had been told the day before that she would have to play the part of the hulking brute, myriad drives would have argued about it, keeping her awake, and the performance would have failed. If more time had intervened between her having the dream and turning up at the repair shop, and the I had sternly resolved to direct the brute onto the stage, there would have been room for all kinds of stage fright and forgetting of lines. But the hypnoid state in which she arrived at the scene had the effect of impairing normal ego-functions, and the brute was able to take the stage and roar his lines without impediment. A creature of such size and strength had presumably been growing there for years, completely unbeknownst to the lady of the demure demeanor.

In terms of theatrical discourse, once the players have become familiar with the repertoire and each other, why not simply let the appropriate character come forward and play his or her part according to the occasion? For an academic lecture, let the "old wise man" give it; if an innocent eye needs to be brought to the problem, let the child take a look; where nurturing is called for, the mother may at first be able to respond more effectively than others; if it comes to the ultimate things, send in the savior; and in the face of bureaucratic obstructions, if the flexible circumventer cannot dance her way around, it may be necessary after all to send in the hulking brute from the previous night's dream. At all events, the thing to do is to "deal with things experimentally" (*DM* 432), being open to the perspectives of many persons at once. It is not a case of abolishing the much-maligned ego altogether: behind the mask of the I is usually the archetypal figure of the hero, whose muscular power and head-on approach is quite appropriate in certain situations.[9] There is no need to dismiss the "heroic ego" from the troupe; he is simply to be prevented from directing all the time or constantly upstaging the other characters.

Notes on the Edge

The conditioning circumstances of Nietzsche's mental collapse consist in a complex network of forces operating on several different levels. Organic factors surely played an important part; sheer mental exhaustion, accompanied by a strong feeling that he had harvested to the full the fruits of his labors, may have rendered him simply too weak to go on; the solitude to which he had committed himself apparently proved ultimately unbearable. There is after all something heroic about the way Nietzsche renounced in clear self-consciousness the human contacts that he knew would have sustained him, in order to devote himself to the task of writing the works he knew he had to write. What deepens the tragic dimension of this self-sacrifice is the way the pressures of prolonged solitude appear eventually to have shaken his faith in those among his psychological ideas that could have been, under more fortunate circumstances, his salvation.

Encroaching euphoria engendered a feeling of perfectly ripened achievement at the end of Nietzsche's career—above all in that most autumnal of works, *Ecce Homo*. In writing *Zarathustra* he had "given humankind the greatest gift it has ever been given . . . a book with a voice reaching over millennia, not only the highest book there is . . . but also the most profound," and he had subsequently published another masterpiece *(Beyond Good and Evil)* re-presenting the same basic ideas in a more accessible form.[10] He had made plans for a vast, synoptic work to be called *The Will to Power: Attempt at a Revaluation of All Values,* but eventually abandoned it. He then planned a more concise, but not much less ambitious book under the title *Revaluation of All Values;* but in the early days of 1889 he gave up this project too, and prepared *The Antichrist(ian)* for publication in its stead.[11] In completing *Twilight of the Idols*—a masterpiece of incisive concision—Nietzsche produced as perfect a summation of his mature thought as could be imagined.[12] The interleaf page of *Ecce Homo,* in which he rounds out his life by recounting it to himself (and the rest of us) gives a strong sense that everything that needed to be done has been done, that posthumously the seeds will quicken and propagate themselves in perpetuity.

> On this perfect day, when everything is ripening and not only the grape turns brown, a ray of sun fell on my life: I looked back, I looked forward, and never did I see so many good things at one time. Not in vain did I bury my forty-fourth year today, *rightfully* bury it—whatever of life was in it has been saved, is immortal. [Three books]—all gifts of this year, in fact of its last quarter! *How could I not be grateful to my entire life?*[13]

Nietzsche is fully aware that the time for his achievement to be appreciated has not yet come, but is confident—as a true disciple of Dionysus—that he will at least, eventually, be "born posthumously" *(EH* 3.1).

But this kind of regeneration cannot take place without corresponding processes of decay; and Nietzsche assiduously tracks the movements of his soul that betoken decadence, remarking them relentlessly, issuing warning signs to himself along the way. The preface to *Ecce Homo* opens with the author's announcing himself in an odd duplexity as *der und der*—"he and he," "this person and that person"—and as "a disciple of the philosopher Dionysus" *(EH,* P1–2). The main body of the book opens with his declaring himself, as a descendant of his deceased father, a *decadent,* already dead; while as his mother, the woman who granted him life, he lives on. His father died at thirty-six (he refrains from mentioning) of brain disease. As the son, he writes, he had to endure excruciating cranial pain, debilitating migraines, while engaged in the thinking necessary for his work; and yet another part of him (*der*, presumably) came alive, rose to the occasion and bore him through the physical torment. It is as if he could feel a degenerative brain disease gradually sapping his vitality, to the point where the image of succumbing to his father's fate became a reality, while at the same time other forces buoyed him up in waves of euphoria.

The nature of Nietzsche's illnesses and the etiology of his final collapse into insanity are questions that have exercised the talents of doctors, medical historians, psychiatrists, and lay writers for a hundred years. Under the circumstances certainty is no doubt unattainable; but a recent study, which surveys a vast range of the literature with unprecedented thoroughness, concludes that the original diagnosis of progressive paralysis (apparently occasioned by a syphilitic infection) is the most probable explanation—even though the complexity of his symptoms suggests an interplay between organic and psychical factors.[14]

One of the most remarkable features of Nietzsche's final illness is that after the initial collapse there were brief periods, especially during the ensuing year, in which his behavior seemed more or less normal. Indeed his mastery of improvisation on the piano lasted for well over a year, suggesting that the musical faculties escaped the ravages of the encroaching encephalitis for longer than the rational and verbal.[15] But the most striking testimony comes from what were apparently independent impressions on the parts of his friends Overbeck and Köselitz. The latter wrote to Overbeck after visiting Nietzsche at the asylum in Jena just over a year after his collapse:

> The question of whether one would be doing Nietzsche a favor if one reawakened him to life must be left aside. . . . I have seen Nietzsche in certain conditions where it seemed to me—a terrible thought!— that he was *faking* madness, as if he were glad that it had ended *thus*. It is highly probable that he could write his philosophy of Dionysus only as a madman—it is admittedly not yet written, although he thinks he has sketched it out at least.[16]

Overbeck, who probably knew Nietzsche better than anyone did, had a similar impression on more than one occasion. He characterizes his judgment concerning Nietzsche's insanity as follows:

> It came every now and then to vacillate, in that I could not help having the horrifying thought, at least momentarily—though this happened during several of the periods in which I witnessed Nietzsche's mental illness—that his madness was simulated. An impression that is fully explicable only on the basis of the experience I had in general of Nietzsche's self-maskings.[17]

Since these two men were Nietzsche's closest friends, such testimony needs to be taken more seriously than it has been. And if one thinks—*pace* Kösel-itz—that the "philosophy of Dionysus" had not only been written (in *Ecce Homo* and the *Dionysus Dithyrambs*), but also published (as *Zarathustra, Beyond Good and Evil,* and *Twilight of the Idols*), then the terrible suspicion that Nietzsche remained the great dissimulator to the end and was indeed faking insanity may ultimately be warranted. It is even possible, in accordance with his own views about the way the actor can become the role, that what started out as dissimulation eventually became the real thing.

Nietzsche wrote several times in eloquent praise of "free death," of ending one's life when it has proved to be no longer productive: in his own case, his courage may have failed at the crucial moment, and the collapse then deprived him of the resolve that would have obviated the grotesque horror of the final decade. At any rate, the tone of many letters and notes from Nietzsche's last productive year suggests that even if his task was not one hundred percent completed, he had nevertheless had enough. He had been writing masterpieces in his own blood for fifteen years, and hardly anybody seemed to care—much less to understand. And even though he was confident (on good days) that he would eventually be not only read but understood, he was simply unable—like the archetypal Samuel Beckett character—to go on.

Some understanding of Nietzsche's eventual collapse may be gained from a consideration of a phenomenon that figures importantly in his psychological ideas—and that would play a major role in subsequent depth psychology—namely, *projection.* Freudians like to say that in any love relationship there are at least four players: the couple, the man's mother, and the woman's father. On Nietzsche's view of the multiple psyche, with a cast of many characters on the side of each person constantly projected onto the other, the situation is infinitely more complex. The woman's projections of her father onto the man will constellate a "charge" around the father-drive in him, eliciting further counterprojections, and vice versa, and so forth—producing multiple generations in a complex social matrix. What ensues is a multifaceted interplay of mirrors, with drives and persons being projected and reflected and refracted off other drives and persons *ad infinitum.* Because of the unusual vehemence of Nietzsche's energies and the consequent force of many of his personal projections, it is understandable that his attempts during his nomadic years to stay in immediate personal contact with his friends should have foundered. "It is just too difficult for me to be with other people," is a common refrain from his letters. Having some sense of the dangers of solitude for someone like himself, it was hard for him to give up trying to conduct close relationships in person, and the repeated failures set up an unstable oscillation between solitude and personal contact. His closest friends were well aware of the dangers of the means he had felt forced to adopt in order to fulfill his task and write what needed to be written. Overbeck warned him when he left his home in Basel and ended up in the mountains of the Engadin: "I can only keep repeating my urgent advice to you *not* to commit yourself to any plan that would condemn you to continued solitude."[18]

The complexity of contemporary personal relationships is further compounded by the archaic dimension of the drives that animate them. The potential inflow to the human soul is tremendous: drives thousands of years old, bringing in their wake archaic persons (often wearing the masks of contemporaries), flood in at every moment. Under normal circumstances much of the flow of this *erōs* is projected onto things and persons in the external world; primordial phantasies lend a sheen to the natural world about us and animate our relations with friends and acquaintances. The presence of other persons in our environs elicits and absorbs a certain amount of psychical energy, and images from our own psyches are constantly projected onto the persons we deal with in our actual lives: "We do just the same when awake as we do in dreams: we first invent and make up the person we are dealing with—and then immediately forget it."[19] But after leaving Basel, Nietzsche lived alone for the next decade, habitually spending—health permitting—most of his waking hours walking in natural landscapes. And even though his relations with the residents of Nice, Sils-Maria, and the places in Italy he wintered in were invariably cordial, they were only occasional and superficial. So while the natural environs responded comfortably to the projections of many drives, absorbing their flow in appropriate measure, Nietzsche's world provided no conduit for the *person*-drives, no screens for the projections of human figures.[20] The serene landscape around Sils-Maria (far less populated then than now) would have repelled the powerful personal energies emanating from this soul so open to influx. In such solitude, with no outlet for the constant inflow, the accumulated energies reverberate from the screens of phantasy and sheen of the dream, and with time the pressure becomes dangerous.

Some of the notes written after two years of solitude suggest an ambivalence on Nietzsche's part concerning his condition. At the beginning of 1881 he appears to appreciate only the positive aspect of the withdrawing (or redirecting) of projections that solitude makes possible:

> Advantage of solitude: we discharge our total nature—even its bad moods— *toward our primary objective* and not onto other things and people. Thus we live it *through!*[21]

As long as that primary objective is viable and still absorbs one's imaginative energies, the drives are well channeled into creative activity; but should the objective be fulfilled, those energies will rebound from the walls of solitude onto the subject, throwing the multiplicity of the soul into supercharged disorder. Another couple of notes from the same period suggest that Nietzsche was after all aware of the tendency of the inner regime to become radically disordered when the energies of the drives are contained within the circuits of the individual body. Recall his writing: "We retroflect all good and bad drives upon ourselves ... we have transposed 'society' into ourselves, in miniature, and to retreat into oneself is thus no kind of flight from society." A qualifying remark in a subsequent note intimates a sense of the danger: "The free human being is a political state and society of individuals. ... People who live alone, *as long as they do not go under,* develop themselves into societies."[22] In the absence of an internal order to contain the energies there is the danger of destructive fragmentation. Nietzsche saw this with disconcerting clarity at the end: "*To suffer* from solitude is also an objection—I have always suffered only from 'multitude'" (*EH* 2.10)—meaning the multitude of persons within the solitary individual.

In a letter to Köselitz written from Sils-Maria in August 1881 (which opens with the first intimation of the thought of eternal recurrence—though not by name), Nietzsche broaches the topic of a possible explosion of the entire psychical system:

> Ah, my friend, together with this the premonition crosses my mind that I am really living an extremely dangerous life, for I belong to those machines that can *explode!* The intensity of my feelings makes me shudder and laugh.[23]

These feelings were feelings of joy and jubilation at having been struck by "the most affirmative" of all possible thoughts. But this was before the dreadful foundering of the affair with Lou Salomé, an event that hurt Nietzsche more deeply than any hurt he had suffered previously—especially since it also destroyed his friendship with Paul Rée and poisoned his relations with his sister and mother. His letters of the period—during which he was also struggling to come to terms with a welter of emotions occasioned by the news of Wagner's death—express the intensest feelings of melancholy and despair.[24] The self-imposed solitude of the ensuing years would only intensify such moods.

It is a fascinating and sobering exercise to read the series of invocations of explosion that lead up to the end.[25] Finally, in *Ecce Homo,* just before the catastrophe, talk of explosives recurs: Nietzsche conceives the philosopher as "a terrifying explosive that puts everything in danger," and says of himself: "I am no man, I am dynamite."[26]

For the last time, schematically: Nietzsche's prescription for psychological creativity reads as follows—open up to the maximum number and force of conflicting drives; let them be mastered by a single, dominant drive, or group of drives; to avoid monotony, subject the multiplicity to protracted discipline at the hands of a series of ruling passions; then, when the discipline has been fully embodied, control can be relaxed, one can dare to be natural, and the multiplicity will spontaneously order itself. In his own case, however, with the increasing intensity of the drives flowing through his soul in the later years of solitude, order became ever harder to maintain, and one can see him reverting to a less radical intellectual position in the attempt to avoid chaos.

We followed earlier some remarkable vacillation in the notes of 1880, when Nietzsche was coming to the most radical formulation of the idea of the psyche as a multiplicity of personal presences. While he came down on the side of a population of persons comprising an interior society, the vacillation resumes a year or two later—as exemplified in an aphorism concerning "the most ancient religiosity." This kind of religiosity operates on the assumption that whenever anything happens there is "a personal, willing being working in the background."

> For enormously long periods of time human beings believed only in persons (and not in matter, forces, things, and so forth) . . . [which is] a piece of atavism with the most ancient origins. . . . Schopenhauer, with his assumption that everything that exists is something that wills, enthroned a primordial mythology. (*JS* 127)

The pejorative tone here is strange in view of the number of occasions, both before and after the writing of this aphorism, on which Nietzsche espouses with enthusiasm the view of the psyche as a personal multiplicity—a "mythology" that implies a corresponding extrapsychical world of persons. Equally odd is the deprecatory flavor of the label "atavism," insofar as Nietzsche will soon characterize the thinking of philosophers as "a discovery, a recognition, a recollection, a return home to a distant and primordial household of the soul as a whole . . . an atavism of the highest rank" (*BGE* 20). Recall that his entire view of cultural and individual psychological development is predicated upon the idea that atavism is operative constantly, that primitive stages of development persist rather than being surpassed.

In the six years following the publication of *The Joyful Science* Nietzsche's sense of the value of conceiving of the psyche as a multiplicity of persons does not seem to have wavered, his major concern being—as we saw—with the problem of how that multiplicity is best ordered. Toward the end, however, this sense does begin to waver. The idea that greatness is achieved through harnessing the most powerful drives and passions possible is still prominent—but the slight change of wording in a repetition of a key note betokens a subtle change.[27]

> Mastery over the passions, *not* their weakening or extirpation! The greater the will's power of mastery, the more freedom may be given to the passions. The great human being is great by virtue of the range of free play of his desires: *but he is strong enough to make these monsters [Untiere] into his own pets [Haustiere].*[28]

The conclusion here is tamer than in the version penned a year earlier—"and by virtue of the even greater power that can take these magnificent monsters into service"[29]—suggesting domestication at the hands of a dominant individual rather than a transfer of power to life-forces issuing from beyond the individual.

Now, in place of the former celebration of intense multiplicity, there is an emphasis on what used to be only a preliminary phase: the domination under a *single* drive or passion. A note from 1888 that reemphasizes morbidity as a component of the great health—"We *need* the abnormal; we give life a tremendous *choc* through great illnesses"—urges the distinction between

> 1) the *dominating passion,* which even brings with it the supreme form of health whatsoever [and]
> 2) the conflict among passions, duplicity, triplicity, multiplicity of "souls in one breast": very unhealthy, inner ruin, falling apart, betraying and intensifying inner division and anarchy.[30]

Here the advantages of multiplicity—on the model of "many mortal souls"—which Nietzsche had stressed for so many years are forgotten, and "bad multiplicity" alone comes to the fore. Along with this shift is a reversion to the deprecation of personifying that we saw in the earlier discussion of "ancient religiosity":

> In the same way that the uneducated person still now believes that anger is the cause when he is angry, the mind when he thinks, and the soul when he feels, and just as even now a mass of psychological entities are unthinkingly posited as putative causes, so the human being at a much more naive stage explains the same phenomena with the help of psychological personal-entities. He would explain states that appear to him strange, enchanting, overwhelming as obsession

and being under the power of a person. . . . The naive *homo religiosus* resolves himself into *several persons*.[31]

In most of his prior thinking about the personality, resolution of the self into several persons had been the norm, and not the prerogative—or naive shortcoming—of the *homo religiosus*.

One of Nietzsche's last engagements with the idea of personal multiplicity occurs in the context of several aphorisms on the "psychology of the artist" that celebrate his overflowing and fructifying Dionysian power. In speaking of the way "the entire affect-system" is overcharged so that it discharges "its powers of portraying, imitating, transfiguring, transforming, every kind of mimicry and play-acting all at once," Nietzsche emphasizes "the lightness of the metamorphosis, the inability *not* to react"—and remarks in the same breath the similarity to "certain kinds of hysterics, who also enter into *any* role at any prompting" (*TI* 9.10). The difference is that the driving forces that course through the Dionysian personality have been ordered as a result of protracted discipline: the assumption of one among many possible roles is thus appropriate to the situation and not arbitrary as in the case of the hysteric.[32] The "Dionysian human being"—Nietzsche has expanded the subject from the artist narrowly understood—is capable of activity that is perfectly attuned to the circumstances:

> He possesses the instincts of understanding and intuiting in the highest degree, as well as the highest degree of the art of communication. He enters into every skin, into every affect: he transforms himself constantly. . . . The actor, the mime, the dancer, the musician, and the lyrist are in their instincts fundamentally related and essentially one. (*TI* 9.10–11)

Echoes here, on a higher, more refined plane, of the Dionysian artist praised in the early works in the persons of Wagner-Zarathustra-Nietzsche (*WB* 7–9), only now more comprehensively integrated in the manner of Goethe.

But when Nietzsche returns to this theme shortly thereafter, a shadow has fallen on this figure. The very last mention of multiple persons in the unpublished notes characterizes the "modern" artist—read "Wagner"—as embodying only the "bad" version of personal multiplicity.

> The *modern* artist, in his physiology closely related to the hysteric, is also distinguished as a character by this pathology. . . . The absurd irritability of his system, which makes crises out of all experiences and brings "the dramatic" into the smallest fortuities of life, makes him utterly unpredictable. He is no longer a person, at best a rendez-vous of persons, among whom now this one and now that one shoots out with shameless assurance. Precisely for this reason

> he is great as an actor: all those poor will-less people whom doctors
> study so closely astonish one with their virtuosity in mimicry, trans-
> figuration, and ability to enter into almost any character that may
> be *demanded.*[33]

Here the "problem of the actor" casts its shadow on our ability to have
many persons play many parts, obscuring the disciplined spontaneity and
perfected naturalness of a Goethe. The good Dionysian, as we just saw,
would be a well integrated company or society of persons (rather than a
mere "rendez-vous"), among whom the appropriate one would act in harmony with the situation and with an assurance that would be far from
"shameless." There are signs that Nietzsche is losing faith in the Goethean
figure who emerged from the culmination of his psychological thinking in
Twilight of the Idols.

But what, one might ask, about Nietzsche's ultimate concern (in that
same work) with the great psychological error of positing agents—the will,
the spirit, the I—behind all activities, "doers" in everything that happens?[34]
Does the idea of multiple persons not retain the doer, or at least resolve the
human agent into a multiplicity of doers—falling short of the ideal, where
there would simply be multiple doings without doers, activity without
actors? Nietzsche surely did understand things this way at times—the psyche as a field of forces devoid of agency: simply a play of drives in spontaneous creative interaction with the more cosmic play. But the issue again is
not whether these persons of the psyche are ultimately real or unreal, or
more or less real than the drives; it is rather a question of which understand-
ings most enhance our lives. There is no doubt that Nietzsche experienced
himself at times as a "normal," conscious ego in a world inhabited by other
egos and things; at times as a multitude of persons in the midst of a vast
historical pageant and festival of life; and at times (of maximum exaltation
and deepest contemplation) as a subplay of forces within the matrix of the
greater, cosmic play. No one of these experiences, or self-understandings,
negates or invalidates the others: they are perfectly complementary. The
important question is: Which is the more fruitful way of understanding ourselves at this particular juncture in our lives and in the specific historical
context?

From the perspective of depth psychology, Nietzsche's picture of the
soul as a play of multiple persons is just the right picture, and one that
might have lessened the chance of explosion had he been supported by
actual personal contacts to sustain it. But under the circumstances—
lacking a companion of the caliber of Lou Salomé, and in the absence
of a depth psychologist who could have affirmed the viability of personal
multiplicity and advised against retreat to an apparently safer intellectual

standpoint that would repudiate it—the thing was simply impossible, and the man could not go on.

At the end, then, going over the edge, he writes as Dionysus to Cosima Wagner, his favorite anima figure and soul-image, addressing her as "Princess Ariadne, my beloved":

> Among the Indians I was the Buddha and in Greece Dionysus; Alexander and Caesar are my incarnations, and likewise the poet of Shakespeare, Lord Bacon. Finally I was Voltaire and Napoleon, perhaps also Richard Wagner. . . . But this time I come as the conquering Dionysus, who will make the earth a festival. . . . I also hung on the cross . . . (3 January 1889)

The next day, this four-line letter to the Danish critic Georg Brandes, which haunts the soul of every Theseus to have penetrated Nietzsche's labyrinth:

> To my friend Georg,
>   After you discovered me, it was not such a feat to find me: the difficulty now is to lose me . . .
>
> The Crucified[35]

And finally, after a flurry of letters and cards signed "Dionysos" or "The Crucified," the last letter, dated 6 January 1889, to Jacob Burckhardt, containing the ultimately unsettling and unforgettable line:

> What is unpleasant and jeopardizes my modesty is that, fundamentally, I am every name in history.

And so are we all, potentially; and the greatest danger attending one who would become great is the collapse of the boundaries that prevent cataclysmic identification with all those names. The task for the rest of us would be to select those names in history in whose company we are to become what we are. For more secure natures who are not such candidates for greatness, it may be possible nonetheless to be fruitfully multiple without following Nietzsche over the edge of the Dionysian abyss: possible to compose the manifold soul, channeling its ebbs and flows and sustaining its cycles of creation and destruction, without suffering in our persons the irrevocable dismemberment of Zagreus.

Notes

Introduction

1. The first book to take Nietzsche's psychological ideas seriously was Ludwig Klages, *Die psychologischen Errungenschaften Nietzsches* (Nietzsche's psychological achievements) (Leipzig, 1926). While this work contains some valid insights, the reading of the texts is generally so skewed by Klages's idiosyncratic irrationalism that many of the important ideas fail to come through. Walter Kaufmann's *Nietzsche: Philosopher, Psychologist, Antichrist* (Princeton, 1950), which remains the classic study in English in spite of its several biases, pays much-needed attention to Nietzsche's psychology; but through neglecting the idea of the drives *(Triebe),* Kaufmann misses altogether Nietzsche's radical conception of the multiple soul— which is what makes his psychology so revolutionary.

In a subsequent study, Kaufmann remarks on how extraordinary it is that Nietzsche's psychology should have been ignored for twenty-five years after his death, that Klages's book should also have been ignored, and that his own previous work emphasizing the importance of Nietzsche's psychology should itself have elicited no research or commentary on that topic in the course of a further thirty years *(Discovering the Mind,* vol. 2, *Nietzsche, Heidegger, and Buber* [New York, 1980], 66). Kaufmann suggests that the reason for this neglect is "resistance," defensiveness on the part of readers (and nonreaders) whose pride is threatened by Nietzsche's disclosures of the irrational bases of our awareness and behavior. The same year this second study of Kaufmann's appeared, a judicious comparison of Nietzsche and Freud was published in France: Paul-Laurent Assoun, *Freud et Nietzsche* (Paris, 1980). A more general study that is also worth consulting is Louis Corman, *Nietzsche: Psychologue des profondeurs* (Paris, 1982).

Three other books that purport to engage the topic of Nietzsche's psychology are: Gerhard Wehr, *Friedrich Nietzsche: Der "Seelen-Errater" als Wegbereiter der Tiefenpsychologie* (The "diviner of souls" as a precursor of depth psychology) (Freiburg, 1982); Liliane Frey-Rohn, *Jenseits der Werte seiner Zeit: Friedrich Nietzsche im Spiegel seiner Werke* (Zürich, 1984), published in English as *Friedrich Nietzsche: A Psychological Approach to his Life and Work* (Einsiedeln, 1988); and Jacob Golomb, *Nietzsche's Enticing Psychology of Power* (Ames, Iowa, 1987). All are reasonably competent treatments but rather unexciting. Golomb's study (which one imagines reads better in the original language) is the philosophically most sophisticated, but it presents an overly safe and sanitized version of Nietzsche haloed by an excess of sweetness and light.

A book whose title might appear to promise interesting things—Leslie Paul Thiele, *Friedrich Nietzsche and the Politics of the Soul* (Princeton, 1990)—disappoints by its superficiality. The subtitle, *A Study of Heroic Individualism,* suggests to the reader familiar with Nietzsche's philosophy that the approach is lamentably one-sided. For a more reflective and exciting treatment of some of Nietzsche's psychological ideas, based on a careful reading of texts in context, see Henry Staten, *Nietzsche's Voice* (Ithaca, N.Y., 1990).

An excellent recent introduction to Nietzsche's thought, and one that is sensitive to the biographical context as well as Nietzsche's psychology and artistry, is Volker Gerhardt, *Friedrich Nietzsche* (Munich, 1992). Gerhardt notes early in his study (p. 21) the remarkable fact that Nietzsche was the first thinker to use the expression *Sinn des Lebens* ("meaning of life"), in an unpublished note from 1875 (*KSA* 8:3[63]).

2. It is easy to underestimate the enormous popularity of Byron throughout Europe. He not only was unusually popular for a poet, but was also admired by almost all the best European writers of the time. For an informative account of Nietzsche's engagement with Byron, see David S. Thatcher, "Nietzsche and Byron," *Nietzsche-Studien* 3 (1974): 130–51. Evidence of Emerson's renown in Europe as well as America is the fact that Nietzsche was able to read a German translation of *The Conduct of Life* in 1862, only two years after the original text was first published.

3. For a different and illuminating approach to situating Nietzsche within the Western literary tradition (and contemporary literary theory), see Bernd Magnus, Stanley Stewart, and Jean-Pierre Mileur, *Nietzsche's Case: Philosophy as/and Literature* (New York and London, 1993).

4. Montaigne, as cited in Virginia Woolf, "Montaigne," in *The Common Reader* (first series). Woolf opens her essay by remarking the extreme difficulty of writing about oneself: "This talking of oneself, following one's own vagaries, giving the whole map, weight, colour, and circumference of the soul in its confusion, its variety, its imperfection—this art belonged to one man only: to Montaigne."

5. Introduction to *Montaigne's Essays and Selected Writings,* bilingual edition, trans. and ed. Donald M. Frame (New York, 1963), v. The sentence from Emerson that follows is from "Montaigne, or, the Skeptic" in *Representative Men.* It is interesting to note that both Montaigne's *Essais* and Emerson's *Essays* are published in German as *Versuche.*

6. *On the Use and Disadvantage of History for Life,* Foreword; *Dawn of Morning* 432, 501. As well as proposing a variety of *Experimente,* Nietzsche uses the terms *Versuch* (experiment, test, attempt) and *versucherisch* (tempting) in connection with his methods.

7. The "Western" here is somewhat problematic, insofar as there appears to be some degree of influence from Indian—and especially Buddhist—sources on the development of Nietzsche's thinking. There are, in any case, remarkable parallels between certain thrusts in his philosophy and currents of (East) Asian thought such as Buddhism, Confucianism, Daoism, and Zen, and the extent of Nietzsche's influence on Chinese and Japanese thought in the twentieth century has been vast. On

these themes, see Graham Parkes, ed., *Nietzsche and Asian Thought* (Chicago, 1991), and "Nietzsche and East Asian Thinking: Influences, Impacts, and Resonances," in Kathleen Higgins and Bernd Magnus, eds., *The Cambridge Companion to Nietzsche* (forthcoming).

8. *Beyond Good and Evil* 39; *Ecce Homo* 2.3. For a comprehensive account of the decisive influence exercised on the development of Nietzsche's ideas by French thinkers and writers, see W. D. Williams, *Nietzsche and the French* (Oxford, 1952). Williams argues (pp. 9, 91f.) that although Nietzsche received Stendhal's *Promenades dans Rome* as a present from his sister in 1871, it was not until 1880 that he "discovered" him and began reading him in earnest.

9. *Human, All Too Human* 37. The Hollingdale translation—based perhaps on an earlier edition—has "moral" instead of "psychological" dissecting table.

10. Nietzsche himself, in a note on the back cover of the first edition of *The Joyful Science,* orders these works in a group, saying that their "common goal is to establish a new image and ideal of the free spirit."

11. The best study of *Zarathustra* in English—and perhaps in any language—is Laurence Lampert, *Nietzsche's Teaching: An Interpretation of* Thus Spoke Zarathustra (New Haven and London, 1986). But since Lampert's treatment of part 4 of *Zarathustra* is relatively slight, an important supplement is Gary Shapiro, *Nietzschean Narratives* (Bloomington and Indianapolis, 1989), especially chapter 4.

12. In a letter to Georg Brandes of 19 February 1888, Nietzsche wrote from his pension in Nice: "On my next trip to Germany I plan to engage the *psychological* problem of Kierkegaard" (emphasis added). The parallels between Kierkegaard's psychology and Nietzsche's are as striking as they are numerous, and deserve thorough investigation. The subtitle of Kierkegaard's *Repetition* (1843), for instance, is *Et Forsøg i den experimenterende Psychologi* (A venture *[Versuch]* in experimenting psychology). For an account of Kierkegaard's understanding of psychology as "experimental" in the sense (closely related to Nietzsche's) of "imaginatively constructing," see the editors' notes on this subtitle in Søren Kierkegaard, *Fear and Trembling / Repetition,* ed. and trans. Howard V. Hong and Edna H. Hong (Princeton, 1983), 357–62.

13. Plato, *Phaedrus* 246a. The Odysseus and Oedipus imagery that follows is Nietzsche's own, from *BGE* 230. The Socrates quotations are from *Republic* 488a, *Gorgias* 493d, and *Rep.* 588b.

14. Plato's most sustained image, the allegory of the cave in the *Republic,* begins with Socrates's introductory suggestion that he and his listeners "make an image *[apeikason]* of our nature . . . likening it to a condition of the following kind" (*Rep.* 514a). But when Glaucon later asks about the power of dialectic, Socrates replies that if they could follow the path of dialectic to the end they "would no longer be seeing an image, but rather the truth itself" (*Rep.* 533a).

15. *KSA* 7:19[107]; English translation of this note in Daniel Breazeale, ed. and trans., *Philosophy and Truth: Nietzsche's Notebooks from the Early 1870s* (Atlantic Highlands, 1979), 17. References to this translation, which has sometime been slightly modified, will be abbreviated as *PT* followed by the page number.

16. Fragment 45 (Diels-Kranz) of Heraclitus reads: "You will not encounter the limits of the soul, whatever path you go down; such is the depth of its being."

Nietzsche had the greatest admiration for Heraclitus, as evidenced especially by the chapter on him in "Die Philosophie im tragischen Zeitalter der Griechen," (*KSA* 1:799–872). This text is available in a recently reprinted—though, unfortunately, not improved—translation by Marianne Cowan: *Philosophy in the Tragic Age of the Greeks* (Washington, 1987). Through an interest in his fragments on the part of both Freud and Jung, the ideas of Heraclitus have exercised a considerable influence on depth psychology (see the references to him in James Hillman, *Re-Visioning Psychology* [New York, 1975]).

17. Preface to *Beyond Good and Evil*. In the retrospective preface to *Dawn of Morning* from the same year, Nietzsche writes that thinkers with "the conscience of artists" are "heirs" of a tradition of millennia (§4).

18. See especially *Beyond Good and Evil* 23, 36, 44; to be discussed below, chapter 8.

19. For a fine discussion of the important part played by "the foreign" in Nietzsche's thought, see Eberhard Scheiffele, "Questioning One's 'Own' from the Perspective of the Foreign," in *Nietzsche and Asian Thought,* 31–50.

20. *Dawn of Morning,* Preface, 1. This is a remarkable characterization, in view of the fact that Nietzsche was not to discover Dostoevsky—in the form of his *Notes from Underground* in a French translation—until the next year. He writes of his discovery of Dostoevsky in a letter to Franz Overbeck of 23 February 1887: "The instinctual feeling of relatedness spoke to me immediately, my delight was extraordinary." He goes on to characterize *Notes from Underground* as "a stroke of genius in psychology" and to complain, with uncharacteristic crankiness, that "the whole of European psychology suffers from the *superficialities* of the Greeks." An interesting discussion of *Notes from Underground* in a Nietzschean context can be found in Nishitani Keiji, *The Self-Overcoming of Nihilism,* trans. Graham Parkes with Setsuko Aihara (Albany, 1990), especially 139–56.

21. The quote is taken from Emerson's essay "History"; see the discussion of Emerson by Walter Kaufmann in the introduction to his translation of *The Gay Science,* 7–13. Emerson was eminently concerned with "the process . . . of transmuting life into truth," the "strange process by which experience is converted into thought." Though in his discussion in "The American Scholar" (from which these expressions are taken) Emerson does not explicitly mention illness, he does refer to "drudgery, calamity, exasperation, want" as "instructers in eloquence and wisdom" and "the raw material out of which the intellect moulds her splendid products."

22. *KSA* 13:14[65] = *WP* 47; 1888. Freud's second book, *The Psychopathology of Everyday Life* of 1901, is predicated upon the idea that an exploration of the points at which things go wrong (the so-called *Fehlleistungen:* slips of the tongue or pen, forgettings, omissions, and other "mischievements") yields valuable insights into the "normal" functioning of the psyche. ("Mischievement" is Walter Kaufmann's happy coinage to translate Freud's *Fehlleistung,* instead of the barbaric "parapraxis" of the *Standard Edition*.) Jung was led to his theory of the feeling-toned complexes (to be discussed briefly in the epilogue, below) through his careful examination of subjects' delayed or otherwise abnormal responses in his word-association experiments of 1905, by focusing on points at which "the experiment fails, when people make mistakes" (*Collected Works of C. G. Jung* [Princeton,

1970–77], vol. 18, para. 99; see also the earlier accounts of these experiments in volume 2). There is an interesting phenomenological analogue in Heidegger's focus on "breakdowns" in the smooth operation of equipment *(Zeug)*, which grants insight into the otherwise inaccessible phenomenon of "world" in *Being and Time* (§16).

23. *Human, All Too Human* 208. In a similar vein, Montaigne likens his book to his child: "To this child, such as it is, what I give I give purely and irrevocably, as one gives to the children of one's body. The little good I have done for it is no longer at my disposal. It may know a good many things that I no longer know and hold from me what I have not retained and what, just like a stranger, I should have to borrow from it if I came to need it. If I am wiser than it, it is richer than I" *(The Complete Essays of Montaigne,* trans. Donald M. Frame [Stanford, 1958], 2:9:293). Subsequent references to Montaigne's *Essais* will be to this translation, by way of the book, chapter, and page numbers.

24. In the context of remarking the precariousness of the noble soul's existence by comparison with that of the lower soul (because of the complex multiplicity of the conditions of the former's life), Nietzsche notes: "In a lizard a lost finger is replaced again; not so in the human being" *(BGE* 276).

25. *Human, All Too Human* 208. Compare this passage from Emerson's journals (to which Nietzsche did not apparently have access): "Plato and the great intellects have no biography. As a good chimney burns up all its own smoke, so a good philosopher consumes all his own events in his extraordinary intellectual performances." See *The Journals and Miscellaneous Notebooks of Ralph Waldo Emerson,* ed. William H. Gilman *et al.* (Cambridge, Mass., 1960–), 9:266 (referred to from now on simply as "*Journals*" followed by the volume and page numbers). Another pertinent passage from the journals reads: "The old writers such as Montaigne, Milton, Browne, when they had put down their thoughts, jumped into their book bodily themselves, so that we have all that is left of them in our shelves; there is not a pinch of dust besides" (10:350). An excellent biographical study of Emerson, rich in apt quotations from the journals, is Joel Porte, *Representative Man: Ralph Waldo Emerson in His Time* (New York, 1979).

26. *Ecce Homo.* See, on the topic of this "exergue," Jacques Derrida, *Otobiographies: L'enseignement de Nietzsche et la politique du nom propre* (Paris, 1984), 53; English translation by Avital Ronell in *The Ear of the Other* (New York, 1985), 11. Noting that the preface to this book entitled *Ecce Homo* bears the signature "Friedrich Nietzsche," and that the work ends on an opposition between two names: "Dionysus versus the Crucified," Derrida remarks that this "should suffice to pluralize in a singular fashion the proper name [Friedrich Nietzsche] and the homonymic mask." Indeed it does suffice and should make us reflect on the question of to whom or what the name "Friedrich Nietzsche" refers. Derrida points out that the last words of the exergue signify the peculiarly "auto-biographical" nature of this late text: it is not only a writing of a life by the liver himself, but the writing is also *for* himself, addressed primarily to himself.

27. A fascinating in-depth reading of *Ecce Homo* is Sarah Kofman, *Explosion I: De l'"Ecce Homo" de Nietzsche* (Paris, 1992).

28. One can be skeptical of this claim and still agree that many of the published texts *are* masks of one kind or another; see below, chapter 9. The figure of Heidegger

will be notably absent from the study that follows: while his interpretations of Nietzsche are formidable in power as well as bulk, they generally ignore the psychological dimensions of his thinking. For an excellent account of the Nietzsche-Heidegger relation, in the context of the contemporary debate between hermeneutics and deconstruction, see Ernst Behler, *Derrida-Nietzsche, Nietzsche-Derrida* (Munich, 1988); English translation by Steven Taubeneck: *Confrontations: Derrida, Heidegger, Nietzsche* (Stanford, 1991).

29. For the distinction between lumpers and splitters, see Bernd Magnus, "Nietzsche's Philosophy in 1888: *The Will to Power* and the *Übermensch*," *The Journal of the History of Philosophy* 24, no. 1 (1986): 79–98.

30. For this approach, see Robert C. Solomon and Kathleen M. Higgins, eds., *Reading Nietzsche* (New York, 1988).

31. Anthony Quinton in a review in *The Times* of Bryan Magee's *The Philosophy of Schopenhauer* (Oxford and New York, 1983). Familiarity with Schopenhauer is a *sine qua non* for a full appreciation of Nietzsche's psychology, and Magee's book provides an excellent introduction for the uninitiated reader. (Chapters 7, 8, and 9 are especially relevant to Schopenhauer's psychology.)

32. Letter to Carl Fuchs, 29 July 1888.

33. Aristotle, *De Anima* 431b, where he begins a summary of what he has said about the soul by saying: "*eipōmen palin hoti hē psuchē ta onta pōs esti panta.*"

34. Even though the present study attempts to remedy the general neglect of the topic of the drives in the secondary literature, the treatment is by no means complete. While the major discussions in the works Nietzsche prepared for publication have been addressed, there are literally thousands of mentions of drives in the unpublished notes, many of which are interesting and only some of which have been discussed. The crucial question of the relations between the various (groups of) drives and the "I" has only begun to be engaged; but the hope is that this inchoate treament will stimulate further discussion of this key topic.

35. "Phantasy" and its cognates are spelled throughout with "ph" rather than "f" in order to signal their derivation from a Greek root meaning "appear," or "come to light," in a sense that does *not* imply an inferior ontological status—and because Nietzsche accords a certain kind of phantasy a major role in constituting our experience. See, especially, "Dionysian and Apollonian Drives" (chap. 2), "Flows of Phantasy" (chap. 3), and "The Fabric(ation) of Experience" (chap. 8), below.

36. For a comprehensive philosophical study of the self which engages the Christian understanding of the soul in considerable depth and detail, see Charles Taylor, *Sources of the Self* (Cambridge, Mass., 1989).

37. For an insightful treatment in a Nietzschean context of two importantly subversive proponents of the Christian notion of the soul, Bacon and Descartes, see Laurence Lampert, *Nietzsche and Modern Times: A Study of Bacon, Descartes, and Nietzsche* (New Haven and London, 1993).

38. The fact that Freud's major concern is with the soul and the psychical rather is obscured by the standard English translations of his works, which have him talking about the "mind" and the "mental." For an eloquent account of what has been lost in most translations, see Bruno Bettelheim, *Freud and Man's Soul* (New York,

1982). In general Freud's magnificent prose has been poorly served by the renditions in the canonical English version, *The Standard Edition of the Complete Psychological Works of Sigmund Freud*. Freud's German was, like Nietzsche's, refreshingly *un*jargonated, though one would hardly know it from the English translations, which insist on substituting Greek- and Latin-based neologisms for the straightforward terms Freud used for his key ideas. For Freud's *Ich* we are given "ego" instead of "I"; *das Es* becomes "the id" rather than "the it"; and for *Besetzung* ("charge") we get the barbaric "cathexis." To translate Freud's terminology more straightforwardly also points up how much he borrowed from Nietzsche—especially in such instances as his use of "I," "it," and "drive" *(Trieb)*. Translations of quotations from Freud's works will therefore be my own from the original German.

I. Seeds in Psychical Soil

1. Unless otherwise specified, biographical information is taken from the three-volume work by Curt Paul Janz, *Friedrich Nietzsche Biographie* (Munich and Vienna, 1978). The currently most accessible biography in English is Ronald Hayman's *Nietzsche: A Critical Life* (New York, 1980), which draws heavily from Janz's work. Also recommended is R. J. Hollingdale, *Nietzsche: The Man and His Work* (Baton Rouge, 1965).

2. *Friedrich Nietzsche: Sämtliche Briefe (Kritische Studienausgabe),* vol. 1. All subsequent excerpts from the letters are translations based on this edition.

3. Karl Schlechta, ed., *Friedrich Nietzsche: Werke in drei Bänden* (Munich, 1956), 3:9. Subsequent references to this edition will be abbreviated in the body of the text as "S" followed by the volume and page numbers.

4. Schlechta, 3:18. Nietzsche would soon come across a similar sentiment in Emerson: "Yet nature soothes and sympathizes. In the green solitude [the youth] finds a dearer home than with men" ("Love").

5. Paul Deussen, *Erinnerung an Friedrich Nietzsche* (Leipzig, 1901), 16.

6. Cited in Elisabeth Förster-Nietzsche, *Der junge Nietzsche* (Leipzig, 1912), 27.

7. Preserved in the *Nachlass* from 1854 to 1858 (when Nietzsche went to Schulpforta) are some eighty poems totalling twenty-five hundred lines, two short plays, and several dramatic fragments. These are discussed in great detail in Hermann Josef Schmidt, *Nietzsche Absconditus: oder Spurenlesen bei Nietzsche* (Berlin-Aschaffenburg, 1991), parts 1/2, 173–417.

8. Johann Wolfgang Goethe, *Die Leiden des jungen Werther*, letter of 18 August 1771. We shall see later how important images of ripening fruits and roaring mountain torrents become for Nietzsche's psychology; also Werther's praise of extraordinary individuals as "intoxicated and crazed," which prefigures Nietzsche's idea of the Dionysian. For a comprehensive account of Nietzsche's relation to (especially German) Romanticism, see Adrian Del Caro, *Nietzsche contra Nietzsche: Creativity and the Anti-Romantic* (Baton Rouge and London, 1989).

9. Goethe, *Werther,* letter of 17 May 1771.

10. Goethe, *Werther,* letter of 21 June 1771.

11. See Thatcher, "Nietzsche and Byron," 130–31, 151.

12. Nietzsche, "Über die dramatischen Dichtungen Byrons," in *Friedrich Nietzsches Werke. Historisch-Kritische Ausgabe,* ed. Hans Joachim Mette (Munich, 1934), 1:9 (hereafter abbreviated "*HKA*").

13. From Thomas Medwin, *Conversations of Lord Byron* (London, 1824), 80; cited by Thatcher in "Nietzsche and Byron," 135.

14. In his essay on Montaigne, Emerson relates Leigh Hunt's comment to the effect that "Montaigne was the only great writer of past times whom [Byron] read with avowed satisfaction." Though it is doubtful whether Byron's taste in previous literature was quite so narrow, it was by no means parochial.

15. George Gordon, Lord Byron, *Childe Harold's Pilgrimage,* 3.72.

16. *Childe Harold's Pilgrimage,* 3.72. Quoted in Arthur Schopenhauer, *Die Welt als Wille und Vorstellung* 1:51; English translation (often modified when cited below) by E. F. J. Payne: *The World as Will and Representation* (New York, 1966). This work will be referred to by the abbreviation "*WWR*" followed by the volume and section number.

17. Schlechta, 3:46. Compare Goethe's Werther: "Just as nature inclines toward autumn, it becomes autumn in me and around me. My leaves are turning yellow, and the leaves of the neighboring trees have already fallen" (letter of 4 September 1772).

18. See *Dawn of Morning* 119. The example of bands around the ankles appearing in a dream as snakes first appears in *HA* 13. The interaction between phantasy and dream, which is alluded to in *The Birth of Tragedy,* will be discussed in chapters 2 and 8, below.

19. Schlechta, 3:95–98; English translation in *Selected Letters of Friedrich Nietzsche,* ed. and trans. Christopher Middleton (Chicago, 1969), 4–6.

20. *Ecce Homo,* "Z" 1: "One can perhaps consider the whole of *Zarathustra* as music." Some of the imagistic parallels between *Hyperion* and *Zarathustra* will be noted below, in chapters 4 and 5.

21. In the *Untimely Meditation* on David Strauss, Nietzsche quotes Friedrich Vischer's referring to Hyperion as "the Werther of Greece" (*DS* 2).

22. Friedrich Hölderlin, *Hyperion,* in *Hölderlin: Werke und Briefe* (2 vols.), ed. Friedrich Beissner and Jochen Schmidt (Frankfurt, 1969), 1:301; English translation (frequently modified in the quotations that follow) by Willard R. Trask (New York, 1959), 27. The text is divided into two parts, each consisting of two books, which consist of a series of letters. Subsequent references to *Hyperion* will be abbreviated as "*Hyp.*" and followed by the part, book, and letter numbers—thus (for the above citation): 1.1.4.

23. To judge from the books in his personal library, Nietzsche was by 1862 acquainted (in German translation) with both the first and the second series of Emerson's *Essays* (first published in 1841 and 1844), as well as with the essays comprising *The Conduct of Life* (1860). Though two studies of Emerson's influence on Nietzsche appeared over thirty years ago—Eduard Baumgarten, *Das Vorbild Emersons im Werk und Leben Nietzsches* (Heidelberg, 1957), and Stanley Hubbard, *Nietzsche und Emerson* (Basel, 1958)—the interesting connections between the two have only recently begun to be appreciated. In an essay that conveys a fine sense of the high seriousness of Emerson's thought, Stanley Cavell discusses the influence of Emer-

son's "moral perfectionism" on Nietzsche: see the second part of "Aversive Thinking," in his *Conditions Handsome and Unhandsome* (La Salle, Ill., 1990). The most comprehensive comparison is to be found in George J. Stack, *Nietzsche and Emerson: An Elective Affinity* (Athens, Ohio, 1992).

24. "Fatum und Geschichte" and "Willensfreiheit und Fatum," in *HKA* 2:54–69. Each of Nietzsche's presentations contains one explicit mention of Emerson, both in connection with quotations from "Fate" (though the specific source is not cited). Emerson's idea that the soul somehow contains its own fate, and that what appears to befall it from outside is thus already a part of it, is one that stayed with Nietzsche—though in gradually modified form—throughout his career. For a meticulous tracing of the ideas in Nietzsche's two presentations to passages in Emerson, see chapter 1 of Hubbard's *Nietzsche und Emerson*.

25. Certain strains in German (idealist) philosophy had exerted some influence on Emerson; see René Wellek, *Confrontations: Studies in the Intellectual and Literary Relations between Germany, England, and the United States during the Nineteenth Century* (Princeton, 1965).

26. Again we are indebted to Stanley Cavell, for showing the philosophical power and subtlety of Thoreau's writings. See, especially, *Senses of Walden* (New York, 1972; expanded edition: San Francisco, 1981).

27. Letter to Carl von Gersdorff (also an Emerson enthusiast), 24 September 1874.

28. See section 3 of the translator's introduction to Walter Kaufmann's translation of *The Gay Science* (New York, 1974), as well as the notes on the *Essays* from the autumn of 1881 in *KSA* 9:13[1–22].

29. *KSA* 9:12[68]; letter to Franz Overbeck, 24 December 1883.

30. Letter to Overbeck, 22 December 1884. Though the Emerson essay was written around 1867, it was not published until after his death, in the *Atlantic Monthly* for October 1883.

31. *Beyond Good and Evil* 36; the idea of will to power as a universal (interpretive) force will be discussed in chapter 8 below. The idea of a continuum of force or energy runs through most of Emerson's musings on nature, as well as through much German *Naturphilosophie* (being especially prominent in the work of Schelling) culminating in Schopenhauer's theory of the Will.

32. *KSA* 11:38[12] = *WP* 1067; 1885.

33. "Willensfreiheit und Fatum," *HKA* 68. The reference to the Hindu conception of fate is a quotation (though not marked as such) from Emerson's essay "Fate."

34. References to the "unconscious mind" are common throughout Emerson's writings, while the following sentence from "Fate" clearly had an impact on Nietzsche's psyche that reverberated all the way through to *Ecce Homo*: "How shall a man escape from his ancestors, or draw off from his veins the black drop which he drew from his mother's or father's life?"

35. See Janz, 1:35–80. A superb performance by John Bell Young of fourteen piano pieces composed by Nietzsche during the early 1860s (plus three from the 1870s) is available on compact disc: *Piano Music of Friedrich Nietzsche* (Providence: Newport Classic, 1992). A second outstanding disc, *The Music of Friedrich*

Nietzsche (Providence, 1993), contains sixteen of Nietzsche's songs (sung by John Aler, tenor, with John Bell Young, piano), most of which were composed between 1861 and 1864.

36. See Janz, 1:94–96. Janz, who is probably the world's foremost expert on Nietzsche's music, notes that the 1862 symphonic poem is "his first large-scale musical composition, and one that he truly finished" (95). John Bell Young performs the work on *Piano Music of Friedrich Nietzsche*. Nietzsche's observations on the symphonic poem, as well as the "programme" he wrote for the piece (after the music had been written), can be found in Schlechta, 3:102–5.

37. Letter to Franziska Nietzsche, 27 April 1863.

38. Letter to Franziska Nietzsche, 2 May 1863.

39. Schlechta, 3:113. My translation of "Über Stimmungen" is to be found in the *Journal of Nietzsche Studies* 2 (1991): 5–10.

40. *The Republic of Plato,* trans. Allan Bloom (New York and London, 1968), 443c–d. All subsequent references to the *Republic* will be to this superb translation. Freud employs the metaphor of the house in a similar context when, at the end of the eighteenth lecture of his *General Introduction to Psychoanalysis* (1916), he talks of the "I" as being "not even master in its own house" (*SEF* 16:285). The following year he expands on this theme in the short essay "A Difficulty in the Path of Psychoanalysis" in terms quite similar to Nietzsche's in "On Moods": "[In certain neuroses] the I feels uneasy; it comes up against limits to its own power in its own house, the soul. Thoughts emerge suddenly without one's knowing where they come from, nor can one do anything to drive them away. These alien guests seem to be more powerful than those which are at the I's command. . . . *The I is not master in its own house*" (*SEF* 17:141–43).

41. It is not clear when Nietzsche first read the *Republic*. In the spring semester of 1864 at Pforta, he had a class with August Steinhart, in which they read (in the original Greek) Plato's *Phaedo*. See Johann Figl, "Nietzsche's Early Encounters with Asian Thought," in *Nietzsche and Asian Thought,* 54. Figl also notes (p. 61) that Nietzsche studied Plato's *Symposium* in August 1864. Nietzsche was to discuss the *Republic* regularly in the lecture courses he gave at Basel from 1871 to 1876, "Einleitung in das Studium der platonischen Dialoge" (Introduction to the study of the Platonic dialogues): *Nietzsche's Werke,* ed. Otto Crusius and Wilhelm Nestle (Leipzig, 1913), vol. 19 ("Philologica" III), 235–304. In §30 Nietzsche discusses Plato's idea of justice as an accommodation between the three parts of the soul, with explicit mention of the idea of *oikeiopragia* (minding one's own business) in the *Republic*.

42. The "guests" of the soul are discussed in a historical light in the second *Untimely Meditation,* "On the Use and Disadvantage of History for Life," §4.

43. The idea of the economy of the soul is of major importance in Emerson's later works, where it is applied to husbandry, sexuality, and writing (see the chapter entitled "Economizing" in Joel Porte's *Representative Man*). The *locus classicus* is the penultimate paragraph of the essay "Wealth": "The merchant's economy is a coarse symbol of the soul's economy. . . . Well, the man must be capitalist. Will he spend his income, or will he invest? His body and every organ is under the same law. His body is a jar, in which the liquor of life is stored. Will he spend for pleasure?

The way to ruin is short and facile. Will he not spend, but hoard for power? It passes through the sacred fermentations, by that law of Nature whereby everything climbs to higher platforms, and bodily vigor becomes mental and moral vigor."

For Nietzsche, as we shall see later, the body is rather a vessel *through* which the energies of life *flow.* There is an anticipation here of Freud's ideas about the economics of libidinal energy. After Nietzsche, corresponding notions of economy are developed by Georges Bataille, and then by Jacques Derrida (see his "From Restricted to General Economy: A Hegelianism without Reserve," in *Writing and Difference,* trans. Alan Bass [Chicago, 1978]). For an excellent treatment of Nietzsche in terms of "libidinal economics," see Henry Staten, *Nietzsche's Voice* (Ithaca, 1990). In his essay "The Poet" Emerson writes of the "*dream*-power" of the poet as that "by virtue of which a man is the conductor of the whole river of electricity." See the apt adaptation of this image to the Nietzschean body as a "capacitor" in Daniel W. Conway, *Nietzsche's Dangerous Game: Philosophy in the Twilight of the Idols* (Cambridge, forthcoming), chapter 1.

44. For a good discussion of Emerson and Nietzsche on the idea of economy, see Gary Shapiro, "On Presents and Presence," in *Alcyone: Nietzsche on Gifts, Noise, and Women* (Albany, 1991).

45. See the brief discussion in "A Brief History of Psychical Polycentricity," in chapter 7, below.

46. See the numerous references in Bloom's index to *The Republic of Plato* under "faction" *[stasis].* The correspondence between the macrocosm of the *polis* and the microcosm of the *psuchē* is the topic of "Ordering the Psyche Polytic," in chapter 9, below.

47. Schlechta, 3:114. Compare Hölderlin's Hyperion who, in bemoaning the poor quality of contemporary educators, says: "Good Lord! The owl would chase the young eagles from the nest and show them the way to the sun!" (*Hyp.* 1.1.7).

48. Schlechta, 3:115. The notion of the moment *(Augenblick)* becomes crucial in Nietzsche's mature thought, where the constellation of the self and the world is held to be at every moment different and unique.

49. The bell that had tolled for his father's funeral made a lasting impression on Nietzsche—as evidenced by its important role in *Zarathustra* twenty years later. At the beginning of that work Zarathustra asks the crowd gathered in the marketplace: "Where is the lightning to lick you with its tongue? . . .

"See, I teach you the *Übermensch:* he is this lightning . . . a bolt of lightning from the dark cloud of the human" (*Z,* P3).

50. Toward the end of *Zarathustra,* in the section entitled "At Noon" (where the connection is made between the eternal recurrence and the "moment"), Zarathustra has just fallen asleep beneath a vine-entwined tree and asks his soul: "You really want to sing, don't you, my soul? You are lying in the grass. . . .

"Precisely the least, the softest, lightest, a lizard's rustling, a breath, a flash, a momentary blink of the eye *[Augen-Blick]*—a *little* makes the way of the *best* happiness. Be still!" (*Z* 4.10).

51. Letter to Elisabeth, 11 June 1865. This letter is included (as are several of the letters referred to below) in Middleton's *Selected Letters of Friedrich Nietzsche.*

52. Letter to Paul Deussen, 4 April 1867.

53. Not long after his discovery of Schopenhauer, Nietzsche came across another book that was to have a profound influence on his thinking, F. A. Lange's magnum opus on the history of materialism: *Geschichte des Materialismus und Kritik seiner Bedeutung in der Gegenwart* (Iserlohn, 1866). Nietzsche first mentions his enthusiasm for the book in a letter to Gersdorff from the end of August 1866. For a comprehensive account of Lange's influence on Nietzsche, see George J. Stack, *Lange and Nietzsche* (Berlin and New York, 1983).

54. Schopenhauer, *The World as Will and Representation,* 1:21; see also 1:22 and 23.

55. See Richard Blunck, *Friedrich Nietzsche: Kindheit und Jugend* (Munich and Basel, 1953), 160–61. Blunck, whose unfinished work is the acknowledged basis for much of Janz's treatment of Nietzsche's childhood and youth, describes Nietzsche's social life in Leipzig as follows: "At hardly any other period of his life did he let all currents and events of the day—political and artistic—affect him so much, nor was as sociable and mobile in such a large circle of people" (p. 160).

56. A recent detailed account of Nietzsche's early development is Carl Pletsch, *Young Nietzsche: Becoming a Genius* (New York, 1991). However, Pletsch's focus on what he sees as Nietzsche's single-minded pursuit of genius tends to blind him to his subject's prolonged grappling with the problems engendered by the *multiplicity* of his talents.

57. Freud imagines that the *Über-Ich* is constituted by the introjection of the "parental imagos" (and especially of the father image in the case of a boy), which then merge with an archaic image of the punishing parent that is inherited from generations of ancestors (see *The Ego and the Id,* sect. 3, "The Ego and the Super-Ego"). One advantage of the translation "over-I" in the context of conscience is the overtone of "eye," which conveys the idea of an ever-watchful presence.

58. For a good account of Nietzsche's musical tastes as a young man, see Frederick R. Love, *Young Nietzsche and the Wagnerian Experience* (Chapel Hill, 1963), 7ff. In an autobiographical essay from 1858, Nietzsche had written: "I developed [through my love of church music] an inextinguishable hatred of all modern music and everything that wasn't classical" (S 3:27). The hatred turned out to be extinguishable after all, which suggests that the vehemence of this attitude may have served a certain apotropaic function.

59. Letter to Rohde, 9 November 1868.

60. Letter to Rohde, 16 January 1869. Almost two years earlier Nietzsche had expressed to Paul Deussen (in the letter mentioned above) his fears of being prematurely trapped in a constricting profession: "My desire is to be able to earn a few hundred thalers a month in a manner that is not overly time-consuming, so that I can preserve some freedom in my existence for a few years. I would very much like, for example, to go to Paris at the beginning of next year and spend a year working in the libraries there. . . . Do you really want to jump into an academic position with both feet as soon as possible? I have quite the opposite desire: to remain free from such external bonds for as long as possible" (4 April 1867). Many of Nietzsche's letters to his friends during 1867 and 1868 mention the "year in Paris"; see, especially, the letters to Gersdorff (6 April 1867), Rohde (3 April 1868, 3 May 1868), and Deussen (2 June 1868).

61. "Thinking wants to be learned as dancing wants to be learned, *as* a kind of dancing. . . . do I still have to tell you that one must also be able to dance with the *pen*—that one must learn to *write?*" (*TI* 8.7).

62. This is the title he cites in a letter to Elisabeth of 29 May 1869.

63. Schlechta, 3:157. The unusual "multifragmented" would seem to say more about the speaker than his subject!

64. Letter to Rohde, 2 February 1868. An unpublished note from this period reads: "A chain of events or endeavors in which one looks for coincidences of external fate or a baroque capriciousness later turns out to be a path along which the sure hand of instinct had been feeling its way" (Schlechta, 3:148–49).

65. An excellent source of firsthand accounts of Nietzsche's character and personality is Sander L. Gilman, ed., *Begegnungen mit Nietzsche* (Bonn, 1985), a relatively small selection of which is available in English translation in the same editor's *Conversations with Nietzsche: A Life in the Words of His Contemporaries* (New York and Oxford, 1987).

66. Letter to Gustav Krug, 4 August 1869.

67. Letter to Rohde, end of January 1870. For a fine discussion of the complexities of Nietzsche's relationships with Wagner and Cosima, see René Girard, "Strategies of Madness—Nietzsche, Wagner, and Dostoevski," in *"To double business bound": Essays on Literature, Mimesis, and Anthropology* (Baltimore, 1978), 61–83.

68. Old and venerable though the institution was—the University of Basel had been in continuous operation since 1460—the student population was small, numbering around 160 (!) during Nietzsche's time there.

69. Letter to Gersdorff, 6 April 1867.

70. Letter to Rohde, mid-February 1870. For an ingenious reading of *The Birth of Tragedy* as "centauric literature," see Peter Sloterdijk's *Der Denker auf der Bühne,* translated as *Thinker on Stage: Nietzsche's Materialism* (Minneapolis, 1989), especially chapter 1.

71. See Nietzsche's letters from 28 August to 20 October 1870. In the last of these he writes to his friend Gersdorff: "The atmosphere of those experiences enveloped me like a gloomy fog; for some time afterwards I could hear the cries of pain that seemed as if they would never end."

II. *The Melodic Centaur*

1. "Das griechische Musikdrama," "Socrates und die Tragödie," "Das dionysische Weltanschauung"; *KSA* 1:515–77. Also relevant is "Einleitung zu den Vorlesungen über Sophocles Oedipus rex," in Friedrich Nietzsche, *Werke* (Leipzig, 1912), 17:291–325.

2. Letter to Rohde, 4 February 1872. This passage is quoted in M. S. Silk and J. P. Stern, *Nietzsche on Tragedy* (Cambridge, 1981), 61, accompanied by a note in which the authors say that "this remark has been unwarrantably taken to imply that . . . the 'task,' in fact, was an embarrassment to [Nietzsche]." While Silk and Stern are right to be suspicious of Elisabeth Förster-Nietzsche's account of the genesis of *The Birth of Tragedy,* which strives to minimize the influence of Wagner's ideas on her brother's thinking during this period, they tend to underestimate the extent to

which Nietzsche was distancing himself from Wagner's ideas by the time he wrote the final version. For a judicious account of this distancing (not mentioned in Silk and Stern's bibliography), see T. Moody Campbell. "Nietzsche-Wagner, to January, 1872," *PMLA* 56 (1941): 544–77.

3. "Das griechische Musikdrama," *KSA* 1:516; 1870.

4. The magnetic somnambulist is the modern equivalent of that other type of woman who "gives information about things of which she has no conception when awake"—namely, the priestess of the oracle of Apollo.

5. The nationalistic tone of this pronouncement is quite uncharacteristic of Nietzsche and is clearly colored by Wagner's ideas about the renaissance of German art. It must be borne in mind that Nietzsche's favorite opera at this time was *Die Meistersinger von Nürnberg,* a masterpiece that is arguably disfigured by the ultra-nationalistic twist at the end. All goes splendidly for the first four hours—indeed until minutes before the final curtain, when the listener unfamiliar with the work (and the composer's ideology) is subjected to a rude shock when Hans Sachs's hymn of praise to the mastersingers suddenly turns crudely nationalistic. The great Art becomes "holy German art," and the listener is enjoined to beware of things *welsch*—Welsh, French, Italian, or simply "foreign" influences that may be planted "in German soil" and thereby contaminate pure German *Kunst.*

6. *KSA* 7:1[2]; 1869.

7. A letter to Gersdorff (2 March 1873) begins with the words: "My dear friend, the drumming in Basel for the three days of Fastnacht is so terrible that I have fled here to Gersau on the Vierwaldstättersee." Another mention of the festival occurs in a letter to his mother two years later (12 March 1875): "During Fastnacht I was in Luzern, in order to escape the noise of the drums in Basel, and there I found deep snow and magnificent quiet; it was like a great pause in the midst of loud music, in that one could *hear* the quiet." A significant feature of the phenomenon that is Dionysus is the alternation between loud noise and deathly quiet. For an account of Nietzsche's interest in the phenomenon of the festival and its importance in his relationship with Wagner, see Peter Bergmann, *Nietzsche, "the Last Antipolitical German"* (Bloomington, 1987), especially chapters 3 and 4.

8. *KSA* 1:518. This pernicious fragmentation is discussed in *The Birth of Tragedy* under the image of dismemberment; see next section.

9. *KSA* 1:521; 1870.

10. Nietzsche apparently received equally important encouragement and inspiration from Ritschl's wife Sophie and from Cosima von Bülow. His jocular reference to Frau Ritschl, who was fifty at the time, in a letter to Rohde (6 August 1868) as "my intimate 'lady-friend'" is typical of his frequent positive remarks about her in his letters. Sophie Ritschl was for him not merely a good mother-figure but also a muse of sorts (as Cosima was to become); in the same letter he writes, "I have been composing again: feminine influences." These women are the first in a series of what Jung would call "anima figures" for Nietzsche, many of whom had—like Malwida von Meysenbug, whom he would meet in 1872—distinctly maternal natures. For further discussion of the image of the feminine in Nietzsche, see Interlude 2, "The Psychical Feminine," below.

11. Nietzsche's account of the meeting is preserved in the long letter to Rohde of 9 November 1868.

12. Nietzsche's later references to Wagner as a musician-become-"actor" and his art as "a form of hystericism" bear testimony to the composer's extraordinary capacity for ecstatic projection of himself into another person (*CW* 7). Nietzsche refers in this section to some notes in *The Will to Power*, where (without mentioning Wagner by name) he compares "the *modern* artist" to the hysteric (*WP* 813 = *KSA* 13:16[89]). For a brief discussion of this note, see the epilogue, below.

13. Letter to Rohde, 28 February 1869.

14. Letter to Franziska and Elisabeth Nietzsche (his mother and sister), 20 April 1869.

15. As Frederick Love has noted, Nietzsche's extravagant praise of the opera, and especially the second act, "was in large degree the product of a fertile imagination working with scores and a piano under the suggestive influence of the composer himself" (*Young Nietzsche*, 65). For an excellent account of Nietzsche's engagement with Wagner's music and ideas, see Roger Hollinrake, *Nietzsche, Wagner, and the Philosophy of Pessimism* (London, 1982), which also contains a helpful "calendar" of their relationship between November 1868 and February 1883. Nietzsche had been introduced to Hans von Bülow's piano-vocal score of *Tristan* in 1861 (by Gustav Krug), and Hollinrake's account shows that in the early 1870s Nietzsche would often play music from *Tristan* with Wagner and Cosima and other members of their circle.

16. *KSA* 7:12[1]. While Nietzsche's strangely idiosyncratic interpretation of Euripides (and of the *Bacchae* in particular) has been much discussed and criticized, Martha Nussbaum has recently offered an eloquent defence of his interpretation of the Dionysian and of Greek tragedy in general. See her introduction to *The Bacchae of Euripides*, trans. C. K. Williams (New York, 1990), as well as her article "The Transfigurations of Intoxication: Nietzsche, Schopenhauer, and Dionysus," in *Arion* 1:2 (1991): 75–111.

17. *KSA* 1:526.

18. See Friedrich Schiller, *On the Aesthetic Education of Man: In a Series of Letters*, letters 12, 14, 15. Nietzsche talks about a *Spieltrieb* in the *Untimely Meditations* (*HL* 6, *SE* 6) and *The Joyful Science* (*JS* 110). It is difficult to follow the development of Nietzsche's ideas about the drives by way of Kaufmann's translations, since he renders *Trieb* sometimes as "tendency" (as in the first section of *The Birth of Tragedy*), sometimes as "impulse" (as in *The Gay Science*), and sometimes as "drive" (as in *Beyond Good and Evil*). Even though Nietzsche sometimes uses *Trieb* and *Instinkt* interchangeably, it is best to translate *Trieb* as "drive" in order to retain the dynamic connotation of the term, which is in contrast to the more passive or reactive *Instinkt*. Nietzsche had already referred to the Apollonian and Dionysian as "the two basic drives" in a note from 1871 (*KSA* 7:7[124]).

Some thirty years after *The Birth of Tragedy*, Freud would formulate the first of several theories concerning the drives—though again it is impossible to tell this from the English translations, which have him developing theories of the "instincts"—in which he tended to emphasize the sexual components of the drives.

While "instinct" is sometimes appropriate as a translation of *Trieb,* its connotations are again too passive/reactive to render the active urgency suggested by the German equivalent of "drive." (There will be little talk in what follows of the active/reactive distinction, made famous by Gilles Deleuze, since Nietzsche very rarely employs those terms to characterize the drives.) For a detailed comparison of the ideas of *Trieb* (in French, *pulsion*) in Nietzsche and Freud, see Paul-Laurent Assoun, *Freud et Nietzsche* (Paris, 1980), 83–150.

19. To support his claim that Dionysus "has something feminine in his nature," Walter F. Otto cites such epithets as *ho gunnis* ("the womanly one"), *thēlumorphos* ("womanly stranger"), and *arsenothēlus* ("man-womanish"); *Dionysus: Myth and Cult,* trans. Robert B. Palmer (Bloomington and London, 1965), 175–76. Kerényi cites the same epithets and adds: "The surname Dyalos, 'the Hybrid,' must certainly refer to a hermaphroditic being, and together with other names of the sort must be derived from hushed-up tales of the god's bisexuality" (Carl Kerényi, *The Gods of the Greeks* [New York, 1960], 273).

20. *Myth, Religion, and Mother Right: Selected Writings of J. J. Bachofen,* trans. Ralph Manheim (Princeton, 1967), 158, 201. Bachofen also writes of "the intimate union which the two powers [of Apollo and Dionysus] concluded in Delphi" and of "the encounter between the Greek and the Oriental world": "We see the two great antitheses locked in struggle, but finally reconciled in some measure by the Dionysian cult" (pp. 116–17).

21. *The Birth of Tragedy* 2. It is interesting to note that Schopenhauer uses the term *Kunsttriebe* (though one would hardly know it from Payne's translation as "mechanical skill") to refer to the art-drives by which animals build nests, spin webs, and so on. See *WWR* 1:23, 2:27.

22. A fair amount of material from earlier drafts of the present chapter has been omitted in the light of the appearance of John Sallis, *Crossings: Nietzsche and the Space of Tragedy* (Chicago, 1991). In the chapter on Dionysus, Sallis gives a sophisticated account of the significance of the theme of doubling in deconstructing the identity of Dionysus, though his treatment is less concerned with psychology than with the history of metaphysics.

23. Schopenhauer, *The World as Will and Representation,* 1:63. Although Schopenhauer does not use the term here, these phenomena are paradigms of what one calls "the uncanny" *(das Unheimliche).* Think in this context of Freud's famous essay of that title, which was published in 1919 (*SEF* 17:217–52), and also of Heidegger's use of the term *unheimlich* in talking about the experience of *Angst* (*Sein und Zeit* §§40, 68b). In both cases, the disconcerting phenomenon brings with it a premonition of death.

24. Nietzsche goes on to reemphasize the double nature of Dionysus as the dismembered god—as "a cruel, barbarized demon and a mild, gentle ruler." John Sallis (*Crossings,* 49) cites a perfect expression of the double nature of Dionysus from the *Bacchae* of Euripides: "Dionysus, son of Zeus, consummate god, / most terrible *[deinotatos],* and yet most gentle, to mankind" (lines 860–61).

25. Sallis offers a succinct summing up of the bearing these themes have on the identity of Dionysus: "Whether it is a matter of the duality of dismemberment and reunion or of the duality of dismemberment and consumption, both sides of the

duality bespeak a disruption of the limits that would delimit the individual, either effacing those limits by way of a reunion or consumption that would reunite the individual to what otherwise would be determinately other; or else canceling by dismemberment the limits that otherwise would enclose the individual, tearing the individual to pieces" (*Crossings,* 50). Another excellent discussion of the *Bacchae* is Jean-Pierre Vernant's "The Masked Dionysus of Euripides' *Bacchae*," in Jean-Pierre Vernant and Pierre Vidal-Naquet, *Myth and Tragedy in Ancient Greece,* trans. Janet Lloyd (New York, 1988).

26. *The Birth of Tragedy* 1. The German *Schein,* as Nietzsche uses it in this text, covers a broad range of meanings: from shining, through appearance, to semblance and illusion. It is one of the more impossible terms to translate, though "sheen" seems a fair equivalent (the entry in *The Concise Oxford Dictionary* reads: "splendour, radiance, brightness; gloss etc. on surface") insofar as it connotes both the shining and the surface associated with the Apollonian. See Sallis's illuminating discussion in *Crossings,* 25–33. What Sallis does not mention is that Nietzsche's use of *Schein* is indebted to Schiller's discussion of the notion in the twenty-sixth letter of *On the Aesthetic Education of Man,* where he equates "the world of *Schein*" with "the insubstantial realm of the imagination." In the final paragraph of the last letter in the series, Schiller actually uses the expression "*schönen Schein.*"

27. *The Birth of Tragedy* 1. A good source for the Romantic understanding of the dream is Albert Béguin, *L'âme romantique et le rêve* (Paris, 1939), a text nicely applied depth-psychologically by James Hillman in *The Dream and the Underworld* (New York, 1979).

28. See below, chapter 9. It has taken the work of depth psychologists such as Freud and Jung to convince us just how important a part the dream plays in the overall functioning of the psyche. In *The Interpretation of Dreams,* the book Freud considered his masterpiece and which was published the year of Nietzsche's death, he argues at length that in a dream there is nothing fortuitous or superfluous. See especially the book's opening sentence, in which the author announces a procedure through which "every dream turns out to be a meaningful psychical [image-] construction *[ein sinnvolles psychisches Gebilde]*."

29. The connection is made by Aristotle (*De Anima,* 429a): "As sight is the most highly developed sense, the name *phantasia* has been formed from *phaos,* because it is not possible to see without light" (Aristotle, *On the Soul; Parva Naturalia; On Breath,* trans. W. S. Hett [Cambridge, Mass., and London, 1936]).

30. *The Birth of Tragedy* 3. A similarly sobering assessment of the human condition may be found in the first chorus of the *Antigone* of Sophocles; see Heidegger's interpretation in *Introduction to Metaphysics,* which takes the chorus's characterization of the human being as *to deinotaton* as highlighting the irreducibly strange and *unheimlich* nature of human existence. Martin Heidegger, *Einführung in die Metaphysik* (Tübingen, 1953), 112–26; *An Introduction to Metaphysics,* trans. Ralph Manheim (New Haven and London, 1959), 146–65.

31. *The Birth of Tragedy* 5, 24. Kaufmann's translation, "It is only as *an* aesthetic phenomenon" (emphasis added), is misleading insofar as it suggests that existence and the world are one phenomenon among others, thereby missing the Kantian-Schopenhauerian connotations of the phrase.

32. These ideas of Nietzsche's on phantasy and the dream form an important link in the chain of thinking that stretches from the German mystical and Romantic traditions, through Freud, and to the theories formulated by Jung concerning archetypal phantasy and the "collective unconscious." They will be discussed in detail in part three, below.

33. *The Birth of Tragedy* 4. A comparable judgment with respect to the Greeks is to be found at the beginning of the chapter on dreams in E. R. Dodds, *The Greeks and the Irrational* (Berkeley, 1951), 102. Nietzsche remarks that "in spite of all the dream literature and numerous dream anecdotes of the Greeks, we can speak of their *dreams* only conjecturally" (*BT* 2). Working on the basis of more evidence than was available to Nietzsche, Dodds offers a fascinating reconstruction of the Greeks' dream experience that is largely consonant with Nietzsche's conjectures.

34. In a discussion of the Will as "thing-in-itself," Schopenhauer writes: "This one being portrays itself in a million forms of endless variety and thereby performs the most baroque and colorful play without beginning or end" (*WWR* 2:25).

35. The term *Projektion* is the same term that both Freud and Jung will employ in developing their depth-psychological ideas of projection: see the discussion of projection in chapter 8, below.

36. *The Birth of Tragedy* 5. By translating this as "from the depth of his being," Kaufmann obscures two important points. First, Nietzsche's use of the term "abyss," though consonant with Schopenhauer's reiterated characterization of the will as "abysmal" *(abgründig),* avoids a metaphysical positing of Being as some sort of ground *(Grund).* Second, the whole point of Nietzsche's discussion is to emphasize the radically *impersonal* nature of the lyrist's voice: it does not issue from *his* being at all, but rather from a source that is abysmally *other.*

37. Letter to Burckhardt, 6 January 1889. See the epilogue, below, for further discussion of this issue.

38. Plato, *Ion* 534a, trans. Allan Bloom, in Thomas Pangle, ed., *The Roots of Political Philosophy* (Ithaca and London, 1987), 356–70.

39. *Republic* 393a. See the fine discussion of mimesis in Plato in Eric Havelock, *Preface to Plato* (Cambridge, Mass., 1963), chapter 2. Another elegant engagement with Plato's attitudes toward poetry is Iris Murdoch, *The Fire and the Sun: Why Plato Banished the Artists* (Oxford and New York, 1977).

40. *Republic* 395d. The rhapsode of Socrates' subsequent description sounds like the Robin Williams of the Athenian streets: he is not only able to impersonate other people but can also imitate "horses neighing, bulls lowing, the roaring of rivers, the crashing of the sea," as well as "axles and pulleys, the voices of trumpets, flutes, and all the instruments, and even the sound of dogs, sheep, and birds" (*Rep.* 396b–397a). The greatest early modern representative of this type is the eponymous protagonist of *Rameau's Nephew* by Diderot.

41. *Republic* 397e. Nietzsche actually quotes the continuation of this argument of Socrates (398a) in the essay on Wagner written a couple of years later. There he says that "we others, who live in a different polity, long for and demand that the magician come to us, even though we may fear him" (*WB* 7).

42. *Nachklang einer Sylvesternacht,* together with *Monodie à Deux* (1873) and

Hymnus an die Freundschaft (1874), can be heard on John Bell Young's *Piano Music of Friedrich Nietzsche.*

43. Letter to Rohde, 23 November 1871; see also the letter to Gersdorff of 18 November 1871.

44. *The Birth of Tragedy,* "Attempt at a Self-Criticism," §3. Peter Sloterdijk remarks pertinently: "[Nietzsche's] encounter with Wagner loosened the tongue of the man of letters: the musician began to perform through the instrument of philology" (*Thinker on Stage,* 8). Sloterdijk's first chapter is especially perceptive on this issue.

45. See below, chapter 9, for a more detailed discussion of masks and projection.

46. See Havelock, *Preface to Plato,* especially part 1.

47. *Republic* 607c, 608a. Although he mentions the Dionysian only in passing and Nietzsche not at all, Havelock's discussion of the power of imitative recitation or drama is quite consonant with the account of the Dionysian in *The Birth of Tragedy.* A passage from the conclusion of the chapter entitled "The Psychology of the Poetic Performance" describes the rhapsode—in terms Nietzsche reserves for tragedy—as one who "recited effectively only as he re-enacted the doings and sayings of heroes and made them his own . . . making himself 'resemble' them in endless succession. He sank his personality in his performance. His audience in turn would remember only as they . . . submitted to his spell. As they did this they engaged also in a re-enactment of the tradition with lips, larynx, and limbs, and with the whole apparatus of their unconscious nervous system" (p. 160). Also of interest is Havelock's characterization of the Socratic dialectic as "a weapon for arousing the consciousness from its dream language and stimulating it to think abstractly" (p. 209).

48. Nietzsche begins this sentence with a very strange remark: "When, in making a forceful attempt to fix our gaze upon the sun, we turn away dazzled . . ." Depending on how frequently he engaged in such forceful attempts, Nietzsche's eye troubles could be attributable to a more mundane cause than is generally supposed.

49. We shall return to the connection between hypnotism and the Dionysian in the epilogue, where hysteria will also be seen to belong to this complex of themes.

50. For a brief characterization of Nietzsche's stance against nationalism, see Graham Parkes, "Wanderers in the Shadow of Nihilism: Nietzsche's 'Good Europeans,'" *History of European Ideas* 16, nos. 4–6 (1993): 585–90.

51. "Über Wahrheit und Lüge im aussermoralischen Sinne," *KSA* 1:887; English translation, *PT* 88–89.

52. *KSA* 1:887–88; *PT* 89.

53. Böcklin lived in Basel from 1866 until he moved to Munich in the autumn of 1871, and thus overlapped Nietzsche's stay there by two years. There is no evidence that the two men ever met, though Nietzsche was familiar with Böcklin's work. The original draft of a passage that found its way into *Human, All Too Human* (*HA* 217) cites Böcklin as one of the painters who has "made the eye more intellectual" and "whose artistic understanding has conquered the ugly side of the world" (*KSA* 14:137). A note from 1881, in which Nietzsche is praising Swiss artists over German, claims that Germany has not produced "a *path-breaking* painter of the stature of Böcklin" (*KSA* 9:11[249]).

III. *Struggles for Multiple Vision*

1. Letter from Liszt to Nietzsche, 29 February 1872.
2. Letters to Franziska Nietzsche and to Rohde, 24 and 28 January 1872.
3. Letter to Rohde, 28 January 1872.
4. Letter to Rohde, 4 February 1872.
5. Cited in Janz, 1:470.
6. For a good account of the controversy, see chapter 5 of Silk and Stern, *Nietzsche on Tragedy*. The relevant primary sources (reviews by Rohde, Wilamowitz's *Zukunftsphilologie!*, Wagner's open letter to Nietzsche, Rohde's response to Wilamowitz, and Wilamowitz's reply to Rohde) are collected in Karlfried Gründer's *Der Streit um Nietzsches "Geburt der Tragödie"* (Hildesheim, 1969).
7. Letter to Gersdorff, 1 May 1872.
8. Letters to Rohde, 7 July and 25 July 1872; letter to Hans von Bülow, 20 July 1872.
9. Letter from von Bülow to Nietzsche, 24 July 1872. A version (for piano four hands) of this piece is available on the compact disc by John Bell Young et al., *The Music of Friedrich Nietzsche*. Listening to it with an unbiased ear, one is inclined to agree with Tali Makell's judgment (expressed in the essay in the accompanying booklet, "The Aesthetic Nietzsche: Philosophy from the Spirit of Music") that there was a considerable personal element in von Bülow's criticisms. On the other hand, Frederick Love has remarked on the extent to which the *Manfred-Meditation* borrows techniques and figures from Wagner, adding that "the tonal anarchy that reigns here must not, in all fairness, be imputed to Wagner, although his example did little to counteract Nietzsche's tendency in this direction" (*Young Nietzsche*, 72). Eckhard Heftrich is surely right in suggesting that the shock from learning von Bülow's reaction is what made Nietzsche eventually decide against attending yet another performance of *Tristan* a few weeks later (Eckhard Heftrich, "Nietzsches 'Tristan,'" *Nietzsche-Studien* 14 [1985]: 22–34).
10. Letter to von Bülow, 29 October 1872. An earlier draft of the letter contains, among several psychologically revealing passages, the following comment about moods: "The only thing I know about my music is that *it allows me to master moods* that, if unstilled, would perhaps become harmful" (emphasis added).
11. Nietzsche begins a letter to Wagner (8 November 1872) with this news: "There is something that very much upsets me at the moment: our winter semester has begun and I don't have a single student! Our classics students have stayed away! . . . The fact is easy to explain—I have suddenly acquired such a bad reputation in my field that even our small University suffers from it!"
12. *KSA* 1:641–752.
13. Lecture 3; *KSA* 1:699–700.
14. See chapters 5 and 6, below. A large part of the discipline to which Nietzsche thinks students should be subjected is discipline in their "mother tongue"—a theme discussed by Derrida (in relation, naturally, to the listening ear) in *Otobiographies*, 77–80; *The Ear of the Other*, 21–22.
15. *Twilight of the Idols* 9.48. See also *Beyond Good and Evil* 230, where Nietzsche contemplates the "strange and crazy task" of renaturalizing the human

by recognizing again "the terrible basic text *[der schreckliche Grundtext]* of *homo natura*" (Kaufmann's translation omits the "terrible").

16. *KSA* 1:744–45.

17. Thought-provoking as his handling of the topic is, Derrida may overemphasize the possible connections between Nietzsche's call for a *Führer* in education and culture and the *Führer* of the National Socialist movement fifty years later (*Otobiographies,* 90–94; *The Ear of the Other,* 27–29).

18. *Bändigung des Erkenntnistriebes—KSA* 7:19[72]; *PT* 22. Subsequent notes cited in this paragraph can be found in *KSA* 7:19[11–51] or *PT* 5–18.

19. The indiscriminate drive for knowledge burgeons especially in the sciences-become-technological (or "information") age: witness millions of students whiling away their time exploring the databases of the internet.

20. *KSA* 7:19[257]; *PT* 53.

21. Breazeale notes that Nietzsche was influenced by the work of his elder contemporary C. F. Zöllner, one of the founders of astrophysics, who argued that sensation extends throughout all of matter (*PT* 36, 118). The notes referred to in this paragraph are to be found in *KSA* 7:19[149–65] or *PT* 35–38.

22. *KSA* 7:19[76]; *PT* 23. The notes referred to in the next two paragraphs are to be found in *KSA* 7:19[77–79] or *PT* 23–24.

23. For a comprehensive account of the development in Europe of the idea of creative phantasy, see James Engell, *The Creative Imagination: Enlightenment to Romanticism* (Cambridge, Mass., 1981).

24. *KSA* 7:19[79]; *PT* 64 (see Breazeale's note on the Chladni acoustical figures).

25. For a brief account of Herder's ideas, see Isaiah Berlin, *Vico and Herder: Two Studies in the History of Ideas* (New York, 1976). The first chapter of Charles Taylor's *Hegel* (Cambridge, 1975) gives a good characterization of Herder as a precursor of German Romanticism and Idealism. Herder's ideas are discussed at greater length in chapter 7, below.

26. Nietzsche was clearly put off by Herder's adherence to Christianity: in the only substantial discussion of him (in *The Wanderer and His Shadow*) he refers to him as an "ambitious priest." But one wonders whether the closeness of some of Herder's major ideas to Nietzsche's own may have prompted this distancing. Certainly some of his rich characterization of Herder is applicable to the characterizer himself: "But he possessed in the highest degree a sense for the weather and for scent; he saw and picked the first fruits of the season sooner than anyone else . . . his spirit between light and dark, old and young, was like a hunter on the lookout everywhere there were transitions, subsidences, tremors, signs of inner springs and growth" (*WS* 118).

27. See *Ecce Homo* 1.3, where Nietzsche writes that the brother of his paternal grandmother, Erdmuthe Krause, was a professor of theology who was called to Weimar as Herder's successor. He mentions this connection in several letters from 1887 and 1888: to Franz Overbeck (4 and 17 July 1887), Heinrich Köselitz (18 July 1887), and his mother (12 August 1887), as well as in the *vita* he sent to Georg Brandes (10 April 1888).

28. Johann Gottfried Herder, *Werke,* ed. Wolfgang Pross (Munich and Vienna,

1987), 2:543–723. Subsequent references to this text will be made by the abbreviation *"EMS"* followed by the page number of this second volume.

29. Herder, *EMS* 556–57 and section 1 generally (1774).

30. *KSA* 1:877; *PT* 80. This dark basis of consciousness anticipates in many respects the unconscious of depth psychology.

31. Herder, *EMS* 601 (1775). See Nietzsche's characterization of the drives in *Dawn of Morning* 119, and the discussion of this aphorism in chapter 8, below.

32. *KSA* 1:879; *PT* 82–83.

33. "The real mystery concerns the surface on which nervous activity sketches forms in pleasure and pain; sensation at the same time projects *forms,* which then in turn generate new sensations" (*KSA* 7:19[84]; *PT* 26).

34. *KSA* 7:19[82]; *PT* 25–26. The idea of an "all-preserving *[alles aufbewahrende]* memory" (discussed in *KSA* 7:19[147]; *PT* 40) that records traces of everything registered by the senses is another one adopted and developed by Freud and Jung.

35. An excellent discussion of these metaphors—and of Nietzsche's metaphors in general—is Sarah Kofman, *Nietzsche et la métaphore* (Paris, 1972), an excerpt from which is available in English translation in Laurence A. Rickels, ed., *Looking after Nietzsche* (Albany, 1990), 89–112.

36. "Die Philosophie im tragischen Zeitalter der Griechen" (*KSA* 1:799–872); *Philosophy in the Tragic Age of the Greeks,* hereafter abbreviated as *PG.*

37. *KSA* 1:814; *PG* 40.

38. *KSA* 1:817; *PG* 44. The word translated by "collected" and "restraint" is *Besonnenheit; besonnen* not only signifies the prudence that comes from reflection, but can also mean "shone on by sun" ("besunned")—which sets up an interesting tension with the cool of the *Wiederschein. Besonnen* also suggests the sunlike eye of Apollo, which can look so coldly distant.

39. *KSA* 1:801; *PG* 23.

40. *KSA* 1:815; *PG* 41–42. For the importance of "personifying" in depth psychology, see chapter 8, below.

41. *KSA* 7:29[205]; *PT* 109. The idea of the philosopher Nietzsche's life as literary artwork is examined at erudite length in Alexander Nehamas, *Nietzsche: Life as Literature* (Cambridge, Mass., 1985). See Interlude 1, below, for a discussion of the topic of making one's life a work of art in other artistic media.

42. It is difficult for us, in the context of contemporary intellectual life, to appreciate the import of such a deprivation (which nowadays would have to include typing at the word processor and watching television or films).

43. Letter to Gersdorff, 2 March 1873.

44. Letter to Wagner, 18 April 1873. In the following paragraph, Nietzsche modestly suggests that Wagner may perhaps think better of him when he sees the essay on Strauss that he is currently working on.

45. For a fine discussion of this essay, see chapter 11 of Laurence Lampert's *Nietzsche and Modern Times,* "Philosophy and the Deadly Truths."

46. Nutritive imagery runs through the first several sections of the second *Meditation.* Under the decadent aspect of the antiquarian approach to history, the person may "sink so low that he is finally content with any kind of food, and gobbles up

even the dust of bibliographical minutiae" (*HL* 3). An age's need for history is "evoked by hunger"; modern man can end up "dragging around a huge mass of indigestible stones of wisdom"; the sensibility of modern culture "lies within, like a snake who has swallowed rabbits whole," thereby creating fears that such a culture might "perish of indigestion" (*HL* 4). In showing how dangerous for life is "an oversatiation of history," Nietzsche talks of the way the war is hardly over before it is put on to the printed page and "set before the jaded palates of those hungry for history as the latest stimulant" (*HL* 5).

47. *On the Use and Disadvantage of History for Life* 11. The theme of nourishment also figures in the essay on Schopenhauer, where the educator is characterized as above all a *liberator* and culture as liberation—"clearing away all weeds, rubble, and vermin that would encroach on the delicate buds of the plants, an outpouring of light and warmth, a loving downpour of nocturnal rain" (*SE* 1). The educator as mediator of culture is imagined as a gardener and natural protector of his pupils as plants. One of the educational maxims discussed in the essay recommends that the educator direct "all energies and saps and all sunshine" toward the pupil's special strength in order to help that one virtue attain "the right ripeness and fruitfulness" (*SE* 2).

48. Henry Staten is good on this theme: see *Nietzsche's Voice,* especially chapter 7, "The Exploding Hero."

49. In the *Lysis* Socrates makes an uncharacteristic confession of knowledge: "there is one gift that I have somehow from heaven—to be able to recognize quickly a lover or a beloved" (204c). See also the numerous references to *ta erōtika* in the *Symposium* (for example, 198d, 201d, 207a–c, 209e).

50. *On the Use and Disadvantage of History for Life* 1. Compare Emerson in the essay "Art": "Love and all the passions concentrate all existence around a single form. It is the habit of certain minds to give an all-excluding fulness to the object, the thought, the word, they alight upon, and to make that for the time the deputy of the world."

51. *On the Use and Disadvantage of History for Life* 5. The images of animal and deserts echoes Meister Eckhart, a passage from whom Nietzsche quotes in the Schopenhauer essay: "The beast that carries you to perfection the fastest is suffering" (*SE* 4).

52. *On the Use and Disadvantage of History for Life* 5. This is the source of an important strain in Nietzsche's thinking about the roles of passion and objectivity in the practice of history or philosophy, which we shall see him later generalize into a view of the place of passion in life-experience as a whole.

53. See the further discussion of *erōs* and intrapsychical sexual relations in chapter 6, below.

54. *On the Use and Disadvantage of History for Life* 7. For Plato, creativity is possible only by virtue of *erōs.* According to the *Symposium,* "illusion" is produced by love only at the lower levels (of physical, heterosexual love), while the creativity of the artist issues from a lower grade of *erōs* than the pure desire of the philosopher. More on this topic, in detail, in chapter 6 below. Nietzsche taught classes on Plato at Basel every year until 1874, when the essays on history and on Schopenhauer were published. 1870: the *Phaedo;* 1871: "The Dialogues of Plato" and the *Phaedo;*

1872: the *Protagoras;* 1873: "Plato's Life and Works" and the *Phaedo;* 1874: the *Gorgias.* In 1876 he devoted one of his classes to "Plato's Life and Works" and another to reading the *Apology, Phaedo,* and *Symposium.* (See Karl Schlechta, *Nietzsche-Chronik: Daten zu Leben und Werk* [Munich and Vienna, 1975] under the appropriate years.)

Wilhelm Dilthey was developing similar ideas about the role of creative imagination in historical scholarship around the same time, though Nietzsche's inspiration surely came from seeing his colleague Jacob Burckhardt at work.

55. Letter to Malwida von Meysenbug, 25 October 1874.

56. Letter to von Bülow, 2 January 1875.

57. *Ecce Homo,* "The Untimely Ones" 3.

58. *Ecce Homo,* "The Birth of Tragedy" 4.

59. On receiving his copy of the essay, Wagner wrote to Nietzsche: "Friend! Your book is tremendous! But where did you get your experience of me from?" (cited in Janz, 1:714). Apparently Wagner's question was rhetorical and asked quite naively. A good overview of the genesis of the Wagner essay is provided in the introduction by Gary Brown to the translation in *Unmodern Observations,* ed. William Arrowsmith (New Haven and London, 1990), 229–52.

60. Recall that Nietzsche's first composition after his encounter with Emerson, "Fatum und Geschichte," dealt with these two topics. Stanley Cavell notes a number of passages in the essay on Schopenhauer that have clear affinities with passages in Emerson, in "Aversive Thinking," 49ff.

61. *Schopenhauer as Educator* 5. Compare this observation of Emerson's, from the essay "Nominalist and Realist": "All persons, all things which we have known, are here present, and many more than we see; the world is full." The talk of whispering in solitude anticipates the first published mention of the thought of eternal recurrence (*JS* 341), where in one's "loneliest loneliness" a demon proposes the possibility of eternal recurrence. Prior to the next presentation of the thought, in *Zarathustra,* the "spirit *[Geist]* of gravity" whispers in Zarathustra's ear, "dripping drops of lead into [his] ear" (Z 3.2 §1). Nietzsche's talk of the "good conscience" (and the vintage existentialist exhortation in this essay in general) anticipates Heidegger's discussion of the voice of conscience *(Stimme des Gewissens)* that calls one to authenticity in *Being and Time* (§§54–60).

62. *Schopenhauer as Educator* 2. In the sixth letter of *On the Aesthetic Education of Man,* Schiller argues that the one-sided cultivation of a particular power at the expense of the equal development of all of them has a deleterious effect on the individual, even though it may be beneficial for the human race as a whole: "Only by concentrating the whole energy of our spirit on a single focus, and gathering together our entire being into a single power, are we able as it were to lend wings to that particular power and lead it artificially far beyond the bounds that nature appears to have set for it." But while the world may benefit from this arrangement, the individual suffers: "The exertion of individual talents produces extraordinary human beings, but only their even tempering produces happy and complete human beings."

63. The image of the solar or planetary system appears again in an aphorism in which a person's changed opinions are said to "illuminate particular aspects of the

constellation of the personality that up to now, under a different configuration of opinions, had remained dark and unrecognizable" (*AOM* 58).

64. *Schopenhauer as Educator* 6. While Nietzsche's attitude toward *Wissenschaft* ("science" in the broadest sense, sometimes "scholarship") will become much more charitable in his next few works, at this point he is still under the sway of Schopenhauer and Wagner.

65. *KSA* 8:6[48]; *PT* 143 (summer 1875). Pletsch discusses this passage in *Young Nietzsche,* 181–82. The thinkers Nietzsche has in mind here as exemplars are the pre-Socratic philosophers.

66. The rest of the passage draws from an essay by Lichtenberg on Captain Cook, and is full of imagery of adventurers circumnavigating the globe and exploring "the most dangerous realms of life," exemplified in particular by Cook's spending three months "working his way along a chain of cliffs, plumb-line in hand."

67. *Richard Wagner in Bayreuth* 2. In the next section Nietzsche remarks on the "hostility" that results from a "crossing *[Kreuzung]* of drives." John Sallis discusses one of the later *Kreuzungen* in this text in *Crossings,* 141–42.

68. Nietzsche had already used the prefix *über* in *The Birth of Tragedy* to refer to the Dionysiac experience as something supernatural *(Übernatürliches),* and it will occur more and more often in connection with the *overflowing* that is characteristic of the soul of the Dionysian artist and thinker—culminating in the initial account of the *Übermensch* in the prologue to *Zarathustra* (see next chapter).

69. In this opposition of *alltäglich* (quotidian) and *unheimlich* (uncanny) there is a remarkable anticipation of Heidegger's account of the experience of *Angst* in *Being and Time* (§40), where anxiety in the face of *das Nichts* pulls one out of the "everyday" way of being and makes everything seem *unheimlich.* Earlier in the essay on Wagner, Nietzsche writes of "the terrible anxiety *[Beängstigung]* that death and time occasion in the individual" (*WB* 4). In section 7 he describes the reaction of the audience to the dithyrambic *Gesamtkunstwerk* as follows: "[The work] will overpower as with the most uncanny and magnetic magic *[der unheimlichste, anziehendste Zauber].* . . . In an ecstasy . . . we no longer understand ourselves, no longer recognize the most familiar things; we lack all standard of measure, everything regulated and fixed begins to move. . . . We hear with every mighty step the hero takes the dull echo of death, and in its closeness *[Nähe]* we sense the highest stimulus to life."

70. *Richard Wagner in Bayreuth* 7. The imagery of this passage anticipates the tropes of "On Immaculate Conception" in part 2 of *Zarathustra.* Roger Hollinrake has remarked on the similarity, and notes that Wagner himself had spoken earlier of "the yearning from the heights for the depths" (*Nietzsche, Wagner, and the philosophy of pessimism,* 91–92).

71. See Hillman, *Re-Visioning Psychology,* chapter 2, especially "An Excursion on the Naturalistic Fallacy" (82–86). John Sallis refers to the opposition between Apollo and Dionysus as "monstrous," *Crossings,* 14–21.

72. In *Ecce Homo* Nietzsche notes that in section 9 of *Wagner in Bayreuth,* "the *style* of *Zarathustra* is described with incisive certainty and anticipated" (*EH,* "The Birth of Tragedy" 4).

73. Nietzsche later had second thoughts about the validity of this claim (at least

as applied to Wagner). Later, perhaps more perceptively, he praises Wagner for his brilliant deployment of *small* things, and faults him on the overall construction of the whole. In *The Case of Wagner* (§7) he discusses the composer's "incapacity for organic form": "Wagner is admirable and gracious only in the invention of what is smallest, in elaboration of detail . . . our greatest *miniaturist* in music, who can compress into the smallest space an infinity of meaning and sweetness."

74. Bryan Magee's excellent short study, *Aspects of Wagner* (Oxford and New York, 1988) highlights some of the anticipations of Freud, while M. Owen Lee's *Wagner's Ring: Turning the Sky Round* (New York and London, 1990) alludes to Jungian readings of *The Ring*.

75. Letter to von Meysenbug, 11 August 1875.

76. In the retrospect in *Ecce Homo,* Nietzsche calls *Human, All Too Human* "the monument to a crisis," with which he "broke free of what in my nature *did not belong to me*" (*EH,* "Human, All Too Human" 1). The beginnings of the book, he says, "belong in the weeks of the first Bayreuth Festival; one of its preconditions is a profound alienation *[Fremdheit]* from everything around me there" (§2). At the end of the second section he refers to the work's psychological content: "In a place called Klingenbrunn, hidden deep in the woods of the Bohemian Forest, I . . . wrote a sentence in my notebook every now and then under the title 'The Ploughshare,' nothing but *hard* psychological observations that may perhaps still be found again in *Human, All Too Human.*"

IV. *Land- and Seascapes of the Interior*

1. In the preface to the second volume of *Human, All Too Human,* added in 1886, Nietzsche speaks of it as "a continuation and redoubling of a spiritual-intellectual cure, of the *antiromantic* self-therapy that my still healthy instinct . . . had itself invented and prescribed for me" (§2). He goes on to talk of the way Wagner, "who had seemed to be all-conquering, but was actually a decaying, despairing Romantic [with his last work, *Parsifal*], suddenly sank down, helpless and shattered, before the Christian cross" (§3). With the publication of *Human, All Too Human* Nietzsche crossed his former mentor in more ways than one: apparently the copy he sent to Wagner crossed in the mail with a score of *Parsifal* the composer had sent to him. In *Ecce Homo* Nietzsche asks of "this crossing of the two books": "Did it not sound as if two *swords* crossed one another?" (*EH,* "HA" 5).

2. The often insightful study by Lou Andreas-Salomé, *Friedrich Nietzsche in seinen Werken* (Vienna, 1894), tends to overstate the positivist traits of the work, just as it exaggerates Nietzsche's "religious drive." English translation by Siegfried Mandel: Lou Salomé, *Nietzsche* (Redding Ridge, Conn., 1988).

3. See, especially, *HA* 292, 638; *AOM* 408; *WS* 308.

4. *Ecce Homo,* "Human, All Too Human" 3.

5. Letter to Heinrich Köselitz, 5 October 1879.

6. In the second edition Nietzsche put the three hitherto separated parts together, with "Assorted Opinions and Maxims" (1879) and "The Wanderer and His Shadow" (1880) making up "volume two."

7. Nietzsche retained this dim view of introspection to the end. In *Twilight of*

the Idols he will write: "The psychologist must look away from *himself* in order to see at all" (*TI* 1.35). Also relevant are notes from the same period under the headings "The Psychologist" and "The Psychology of the Psychologist" (*KSA* 13:14[27,28] = *WP* 426).

8. *Human, All Too Human,* Preface, §5. By translating it "*beside* himself," Hollingdale fails to capture the ecstatic force of the emphasized "*ausser* sich."

9. *Assorted Opinions and Maxims* 223; see also *HA* 616 and *WS* 188.

10. These terms are borrowed from E. R. Dodds, who uses them in a somewhat different context; see *The Greeks and the Irrational,* 179. Nietzsche's espousal of an "agglomerative" view anticipates the adoption of similar assumptions on the parts of both Freud and Jung.

11. As we shall see later in the chapter, Nietzsche is fond of using the well as a metaphor for the individual soul.

12. *KSA* 12:7[53]; 1886–87. The first part of this note is a striking anticipation of one of the most basic tenets of Freudian psychodynamics: "Representations *[Vorstellungen]* and perceptions are not engaged in a struggle for existence but for domination: a representation that is overcome is not *annihilated,* but only *repressed* [zurückgedrängt] or *subordinated.*"

13. In the first chapter of *Civilization and its Discontents* (1930), Freud gives especially clear expression to an idea he has worked with for a long time, concerning "the survival of what is original alongside what has come from it later." He elaborates: "In the psychical domain *[Auf seelischem Gebiet]* the preservation of the primitive alongside what has been transformed out of it is so common as to render superfluous the citing of examples." And again: "In the life of the soul *[im Seelenleben]* nothing that has been formed can perish [and] everything remains preserved somehow."

14. There is no space to elaborate this idea here; but one could hint at how it would go by adducing Heidegger's distinction between a kind of past that passes away *[das Vergangene]* and one that endures *[das Gewesene],* as well as his conception of a self that is open to all three "horizons" of time at once (*Being and Time,* §65). See also the characterization of "presencing" *(Anwesenheit)* in *Zur Sache des Denkens* (Tübingen, 1969), 13; and also *Holzwege* (Frankfurt, 1972), 244, 295.

15. Empedocles, fragment 109D (Diels-Kranz); Nietzsche, "Die vorplatonischen Philosophen," *Werke* 19:190, 196.

16. Proclus, *Commentary on the Timaeus of Plato,* 2:298; cited by Cornford in *Plato's Cosmology* (London, 1937), 94.

17. Plato, *Timaeus* 34c, 32c. Unless otherwise noted, translations of Plato's dialogues are those in the bilingual edition of the Loeb Classical Library (Cambridge, Mass., and London). In the case of the *Timaeus,* however, the renderings by F. M. Cornford in his *Plato's Cosmology* have been favored, though modified on occasion in the light of the Loeb edition translated by R. G. Bury.

18. This section of the *Timaeus* inspired these lines of Emerson's (with which Nietzsche was familiar): "I am present at the sowing of the seed of the world. With a geometry of sunbeams, the soul lays the foundation of nature" ("Intellect").

19. *Timaeus* 44a. The infant is for Plato generally representative of the lowest,

appetitive part of the soul, whereas in *Zarathustra* the child is the image of the self reborn and of an advanced transformation of the spirit (*Z* 1.1, "On the Three Transformations").

20. The most eloquent criticism of the "lack of historical sense" in philosophers is in *Human, All Too Human* 2.

21. Augustine, *Confessions,* trans. R. S. Pine-Coffin (Harmondsworth, 1961), book 10, chapter 8. An interesting discussion of Augustine's *memoria* in the context of classical mnemotechnics is to be found in Frances Yates, *The Art of Memory* (Chicago and London, 1966), at the end of chapter 2, "The Art of Memory in Greece: Memory and the Soul." For a superb phenomenological study of memory from perspectives consonant with Nietzsche's and those of depth psychology, see Edward S. Casey, *Remembering: A Phenomenological Study* (Bloomington and Indianapolis, 1987); and, from a rather different perspective, David Farrell Krell, *Of Memory, Reminiscence, and Writing: On the Verge* (Bloomington and Indianapolis, 1990).

22. This was the passage that Petrarch happened to light upon at the peak of Mont Ventoux, and which inspired his motto, "Nothing is wonderful but the soul" and his essay "The Ascent of Mont Ventoux," which in turn deeply informed the Renaissance idea of the soul (see Hillman, *Re-Visioning Psychology,* 195–97).

23. In the case of the precepts of the "liberal sciences," however, these endure in the memory "apart from the rest" as if "in a more inward place," and as themselves rather than in the form of images (*Confessions,* 10.9). Augustine's resolution of his puzzlement as to how things that clearly did not enter through the senses can yet be "in" him echoes the account of *anamnēsis* in Plato's *Meno:* "They must have been in my heart even before I learned them, though not present to my memory. Then whereabouts were they? . . . It must have been that they were already in my memory hidden away in its deeper recesses, in so remote a part of it that I might not have been able to think of them at all, if some other person had not brought them to the fore by teaching me about them" (10.10). This hint that something akin to the Neoplatonic archetypes of *nous* is to be found in the human soul prepares us for an archaic—if not exactly archetypal—dimension to the labyrinths of the soul as imagined by Nietzsche.

24. A fascinating account of the solar imagery in Nietzsche (and in *Zarathustra* especially) is to be found in Bernard Pautrat, *Versions du soleil: Figures et système de Nietzsche* (Paris, 1971), which offers subtle readings of Nietzsche's texts often in the light of Hegel and along Derridean lines.

25. John Sallis has helpfully highlighted Heidegger's use of the term *Herausdrehung,* "twisting free," in the context of Nietzsche's overturning of Platonism (Crossings, 2). See the section entitled "Nietzsches Umdrehung des Platonismus" in Heidegger, *Nietzsche* 1:231–42. Heidegger often appears overly concerned to portray Nietzsche's thought as simply an inversion of Platonism, and thus as caught in traditional metaphysics. To emphasize that Nietzsche *"twisted* free" from Platonism is to suggest that the inversion is simply a first move, to be followed by a twist or torque onto another plane of discourse entirely. This would be more in accord with Derrida's reading of Nietzsche.

26. A note from 1881 reads: "The inorganic *conditions* us through and through:

water, air, earth, geology, electricity, and so forth. We are plants under such conditions" (*KSA* 9:11[210]).

27. For some illuminating depth-psychological perspectives on polytheism, see the discussions in James Hillman, *Re-Visioning Psychology* and the essay "Psychology: Monotheistic or Polytheistic," reprinted as an appendix to David L. Miller, *The New Polytheism: Rebirth of the Gods and Goddesses* (Dallas, 1981). This pioneering work by Miller offers a fine overview of the field with frequent and appropriate invocations of Nietzsche's ideas. Nietzsche's concern with polytheism is established from the start with *The Birth of Tragedy,* but the most succinct account of the psychological relevance of polytheism is in *The Joyful Science* 143. The Japanese philosopher Nishitani Keiji is especially sensitive to hints in Nietzsche's texts concerning the nature of his Dionysian polytheism: see the references in *The Self-Overcoming of Nihilism,* and especially the section in chapter 4 entitled "The Self-Overcoming of Nihilism" (pp. 62–68).

28. Gilles Deleuze offers an interesting discussion of the dice throw in *Nietzsche and Philosophy,* trans. Hugh Tomlinson (New York, 1983), 25–38. An earlier occurrence of the dice throw which sheds some light on its roles in *Zarathustra* is in *Dawn of Morning* 130.

29. For an illuminating treatment of this Emersonian idea of the self's identity with fate, see Nishitani, *The Self-Overcoming of Nihilism,* chapter 4.

30. *Zarathustra* 3.2 §1, "On the Vision and the Enigma." More of the imagery concerning stone in *Zarathustra*—and especially its alchemical aspects—will be discussed in the Interlude following this chapter.

31. *Zarathustra* 2.11. The "divine moments" whose passing Zarathustra mourns in this chapter surely originated in the idyllic times Nietzsche spent with the Wagners at Tribschen, "On the Blissful Isles" as the title of the second chapter of part 2 has it. Roger Hollinrake points out that the question, "How did I endure it?" ("*Wie ertrug ich's nur?*") is borrowed from *Tristan und Isolde,* act 2, scene 2 (*Nietzsche, Wagner, and the philosophy of pessimism,* 79).

32. For a fine discussion (consonant for the most part with Nietzsche's ideas, though without invoking them) of the creative and freely recreative functions of memory, see Edward Casey, *Remembering,* especially part 4.

33. Schopenhauer, *The World as Will and Representation* 1:55; see also his *Essay on the Freedom of the Will,* chapter 3.

34. Nishitani Keiji, *The Self-Overcoming of Nihilism,* 91–92.

35. It is interesting to note that Zarathustra, who is above all a dancer who has cultivated lightness of foot in the face of the ever-present abyss *(Abgrund),* later speaks of a similar experience. Having decided to try luring people up to his height rather than descending to their level, he says: "With both feet I stand securely on this ground—on an eternal ground, on hard primeval rock *[Urgestein],* on this highest and hardest of all primeval mountains" (Z 4.1).

36. An aphorism from *Dawn of Morning* entitled "How One Ought to Turn to Stone" reads: "Slowly, slowly, to become hard like a precious stone—and finally to lie there, still and to the joy of eternity" (*DM* 541). There is a brief discussion of this aphorism in the context of Nietzsche's concerns with death and the inanimate realm in the section "Unpublished Notes from 1881" in chapter 8, below. For an

412 Notes to Pages 136–38

account (Nietzschean *malgré lui*) of the role of death in life as understood by archetypal psychology, see Hillman, *Re-Visioning Psychology,* especially part 4, "Dehumanizing or Soul-making."

37. *Ecce Homo, "Z"* 4. In the first major presentation of the idea of eternal recurrence in "On the Vision and the Enigma," the dwarf who is the spirit of gravity "squats on a rock" near the gateway of "the Moment" (*Z* 2.2, §2); part 4 opens with Zarathustra's "sitting on a rock in front of his cave, looking out in silence . . . over the ocean and out over winding abysses" (4.1).

38. Compare Hölderlin's Hyperion, who in an agitated mood says to himself: "It is as if you wanted to create another sun and new dependents for it, as well as an earth and a moon" (*Hyp.* 1.1.8).

39. *Thus Spoke Zarathustra,* Prologue, §1. The mood of intimacy is enhanced by Zarathustra's calling the sun by the familiar second-person pronoun *du* rather than the formal *Sie.*

40. *Zarathustra* 3.4, 4.10, 4.19. One of the most lyrical aphorisms in *The Wanderer and His Shadow* (*WS* 308) bears the title "At Midday" and anticipates several themes in the similarly titled chapter of *Zarathustra* (4.10). Compare Emerson: "Not the sun or the summer alone, but every hour and season yields its tribute of delight; for every hour and change corresponds to and authorizes a different state of the mind, from breathless noon to grimmest midnight ("Nature").

41. Zarathustra often speaks of bringing things or people "up to [his] height"; there is a play on the assonance between *Höhe* and *Hölle* between lines 27 and 30 of the third page of "On Those Who Pity" (*Z* 2.3), and in "On Great Events" the fire-hound that Zarathustra encounters on his descent to the underworld, addressing it as "friend hellishnoise *[Höllenlärm],*" ends up crawling back into his cave *(Höhle)* (*Z* 2.18).

42. The first part of the image echoes Socrates's ascription of the power of vision to the "overflow from the sun's treasury" at *Rep.* 508b. Socrates there refers to the eye as "the most sunlike of the organs"; Zarathustra in his opening speech addresses the sun as "you tranquil eye" *(du ruhiges Auge).* The apian aspect of the image resonates with Plato's image of the poets as bees gathering honey from the gardens of the Muses (*Ion* 534a–b). Honey is one of the many fluids of which Dionysos is the god, including sap, milk, semen, blood, and wine (see, for example, Plutarch, *De Iside et Osiride* 35.)

43. One of the epithets of Hades as ruler of the underworld is *Plouton,* "the wealth-giving"; see Carl Kerényi, *The Gods of the Greeks* (New York, 1960), 231.

44. James Hillman adduces Renaissance perspectives on death and the underworld in *Re-Visioning Psychology,* chapter 4, especially in the sections entitled "Renaissance Pathologizing" and "Hades, Persephone, and a Psychology of Death." The sense of the underworld as a place we inhabit throughout life is beautifully captured by Rilke (perhaps influenced by Nietzsche in this respect) in passages from his letters from Muzot: "Like the moon, so life surely has a side that is constantly turned away from us, and which is not life's opposite, but its completion to perfection, to plenitude, to the truly whole and full sphere and globe of *Being.* . . . Death is the *side of life* that is turned away from us, unillumined by us: we must try to achieve the greatest awareness of our Dasein, which is *at home in both inseparable realms,*

inexhaustibly nourished from both" (letters of 6 January 1923 and 13 November 1925, in Rainer Maria Rilke, *Briefe* [Frankfurt, 1950], 806–7, 896). Heidegger discusses these passages in his essay "Wozu Dichter?" and observes that "Death and the realm of the dead belong to the totality of beings as its other side" (*Holzwege*, 124).

45. For an insightful comparison of the figures of Zarathustra, Socrates, the sun, and "going down" in *Zarathustra* and Plato's *Republic,* see Daniel W. Conway, "Solving the Problem of Socrates: Nietzsche's *Zarathustra* as Political Irony," *Political Theory* 16, no. 2 (1988):257–80, especially 261–67. There are also allusions here to the overflowing that is a primary image in Neoplatonism; aspects of Nietzsche's parody of this tradition in Zarathustra's prologue are discussed in Robert Gooding-Williams, *Nietzsche's Pursuit of Modernism* (forthcoming), chapter 3. *Zarathustra* is also replete with imagery (much of it parodic, naturally) from the Christian tradition; the allusions have been well documented by Kathleen Higgins in her *Nietzsche's "Zarathustra"* (Philadelphia, 1987).

The kind of Dionysian overflow embodied by Zarathustra is to be found in Emerson, who writes (in "The Method of Nature") of "that redundancy of excess of life which in conscious beings we call *ecstasy,*" and of the possibility of our being "vessels filled with the divine overflowings."

46. In expressing the desire to descend to the depths just as the sun does when it goes down behind the ocean, Zarathustra alludes to the solar hero of several mythologies who courses across the heavens in a chariot during the day and goes down into the ocean at sunset, in order to make the subterranean "night-sea journey" back to the orient, whence he will be reborn at dawn the next morning. Zarathustra's similarity to the dying and rising heroes of mythology is emphasized in a later passage where he again likens himself to the sun:

"For I want to go to human beings one more time: I want to go under *[untergehen] among* [unter] them; dying I want to give them my richest gift!

"I learned that from the sun, when it goes down, the over-rich one" (*Z* 3.12 §3).

47. *Zarathustra* 2.21. A discussion of temperate versus tropical as "zones of culture" is to be found in *Human, All Too Human* 236.

48. Specifically Beckmann's *Young Men by the Sea* (1905) and Munch's *Men Bathing* (1907–8). For a discussion of Nietzsche's influence on Beckmann, see Ernst-Gerhard Güse, *Das Frühwerk Max Beckmanns: Zur Thematik seiner Bilder aus den Jahren 1904–1914* (Frankfurt and Bern, 1977), and Dietrich Schubert, *Max Beckmann: Auferstehung und Erscheinung der Toten* (Worms, 1985). One thinks too of Munch's *The Sun* (on the wall of the Oslo University Aula), and of several suns by Van Gogh.

49. See *Zarathustra* 3.15, "On Immaculate Perception"; to be discussed in chapter 6, below.

50. *Human, All Too Human* 566. The image recalls the plight of the dweller in Plato's cave who "is released and suddenly compelled to stand up, to turn his neck around, to walk and look up toward the light"—and is thus "dazzled" by the light of the fire (*Rep.* 515c).

51. There is a constant vacillation on this issue in the development of Nietzsche's thought. During his "Schopenhauer-Wagner" period, he deprecated conscious reflection in favor of Dionysian creativity; in *Human, All Too Human* the

cool, scientific spirit predominates; in *Zarathustra* the creative heat of solar understanding has more or less eclipsed reflective lunar knowing; and by the time of *Twilight of the Idols* there is finally an accommodation between detached spirit and Dionysian soul (*TI* 9.10, 9.14, 9.49), see chapter 9, below.

52. There will be a discussion of Plato's imagery for the tripartite soul in chapter 6, below. For now it is important to note that when Plato talks of the "spirited" element in the soul *(to thumoeides)*, "spirit" is to be understood as the animating energy of a warrior when we say that he has "fighting spirit"—or of an animal like a horse when we say it is "spirited." "Spirit" *(Geist)* as used by Nietzsche usually has the connotation of "intellect" or means "spirit" in the religious or cultural sense—and would thus correspond more to the highest, rational or calculative part of the soul *(to logistikon)* in Plato.

53. *Republic* 440c. One of Socrates's fanciful etymologies in the *Cratylus* supposes that the word *thumos* comes "from the seething *[thuses]* and boiling of the soul" (419d).

54. For a comprehensive discussion of the background to these ideas, see R. B. Onians, *The Origins of European Thought* (Cambridge, 1951), especially 93–122. This book contains an abundance of material relevant to the themes of the next two chapters of the present work; see, especially, the chapters in part 2 entitled *"Psychē"* and "The Stuff of Life."

55. *Dawn of Morning* 113. Nietzsche has in mind here Indian asceticism in particular, where *tapas,* the word for ascetic practices, also has connotations of fire and burning. For more on this, see Michel Hulin, "Nietzsche and the Suffering of the Indian Ascetic," in *Nietzsche and Asian Thought,* 64–75.

56. The following aphorism, *DM* 114, which develops the theme of enduring suffering, is clearly autobiographical—and as such illuminates Nietzsche's peculiar brand of "life-affirming" asceticism.

57. *KSA* 13:14[65] = *WP* 47; 1888—discussed in the Introduction, above.

58. *Zarathustra* 1.17. Compare Hyperion: "Now I had become calm. There was no longer anything that drove me from my bed at midnight. Now I no longer seared myself in my own flame" (*Hyp.* 1.1.9).

59. See the letter to Gersdorff of 7 April 1866, where Nietzsche gives a Schopenhauerian account of his exaltation in a thunderstorm; the note from the *Zarathustra* period is cited in Janz, I, 98. Emerson was fond of the image of lightning: "But the lightning which explodes and fashions planets, maker of planets and suns, is in him" ("Fate").

60. After his experience as a medical orderly in the Franco-Prussian War, Nietzsche apparently kept a formidable array of drugs on hand, which he used to alleviate the more debilitating symptoms of his various ailments. (It seems as if his use of chloral hydrate against insomnia may have been excessive.) Nevertheless, a consideration of the persistent severity of some of his attacks make one doubt whether he would have been able to survive at all without some recourse to medication.

61. *Zarathustra* 3.5, §3. Compare this exclamation from the mouth of Hyperion's friend Alabanda: "Oh may someone light the torch for me *[zünde mir einer die Fackel an],* so that I may burn the weeds from the field! May someone prepare the

mine for me *[die Mine bereite mir einer]* with which I can blow the dull clods from the face of the earth!" (*Hyp.* 1.1.7). This construction using the imperative form of the verb with the dative of the first person singular pronoun ("do such-and-such *for me!*") is a ubiquitous feature of Zarathustra's rhetoric; many of the seven-hundred-odd occurrences of *mir* in the text are parts of this construction.

62. See Gaston Bachelard, "Nietzsche and the Ascensional Psyche," in *Air and Dreams,* trans. Edith R. Farrell and C. Frederick Farrell (Dallas, 1988). The author of several fine works on the imagination, Bachelard is stragely dismissive of the earth, water, and fire imagery in Nietzsche's texts. The term "imaginal" is borrowed from Henri Corbin, who used its French equivalent in his writings on the imagination—as a term that refers to the realm of the imagination without the ontological denigration implied by the word "imaginary," which almost always implies the precedent "merely."

Nietzsche never tires of praising the air of the upper Engadin, and indeed the air there is unique in its bracing fragrance. His confidence that he has managed to incorporate this kind of air into his texts is evident from this remark in the preface to *Ecce Homo:* "Whoever knows how to breathe the air of my writings knows that it is an air of the heights, a *strong* air. One must be made for it, or else there is no small danger of catching cold there" (§3).

63. *The Joyful Science* 293. Had Zarathustra had a muse like Hyperion's Diotima, she might well have exhorted him in these terms to go down from his cave: "You must descend, like a beam of light, like refreshing rain into the land of mortality; you must illuminate like Apollo, shake and animate like Jupiter, or else you are not worthy of your heaven" (*Hyp.* 1.2.19).

64. *KSA* 9:11[207]; 1881.

65. On the whole, Nietzsche seems to have found the ocean above all to have a salutary effect on his being. This comment, in a letter to Overbeck from Rapallo on the Italian coast near Genoa, is typical: "The proximity of the sea offers a relief for my head—and that is not to be underestimated since, as you may imagine, I now again have a great deal of physical suffering" (31 December 1882).

For an extended engagement with Nietzsche, and with the character of Zarathustra especially, in the context of aquatic imagery, see Luce Irigaray's opalescent—if occasionally opaque—*Amante marine: de Friedrich Nietzsche* (Paris, 1980); English translation by Gillian C. Gill, *Marine Lover of Friedrich Nietzsche* (New York, 1991). This is a work of great lyrical beauty and psychological insight, though it appears on occasion to be strangely blind to the natural imagery in Nietzsche's texts. Since many different voices in Irigaray's text—and especially in the section entitled "Speaking of Immemorial Waters"—address a variety of aspects of "Friedrich Nietzsche," a critique of her treatment is difficult. But while she is right to remark that none of Zarathustra's companions is a sea creature (*Marine Lover,* 13), it overstates the case to say that "it is always hot, dry, and hard in [his] world." It is admittedly surprising, in view of Nietzsche's love of swimming, that the activity does not figure in the metaphorics of *Zarathustra;* but this does not detract from the importance of the water imagery in this text—or in Nietzsche's texts as a whole. The back cover copy of *Marine Lover* advertises "a pre-Socratic investigation of the elements"; but it is difficult, in view of the material discussed in the present (and the following) chapter, to make sense of the suggestion that Nietzsche/Zarathustra is unable "to embrace [himself] with the other in all those elements [earth, water, air, and sun]" and has "forgotten the love your god [Dionysus] had for plants" (p. 57).

66. "Die Philosophie im tragischen Zeitalter der Griechen," §3 (*KSA* 1:814; *PG* 40).

67. *The Joyful Science* 57; see the discussion of this topic in "Drives Archaically Imagining" in chapter 8, below.

68. Compare this note from 1880: "There is no specific organ of 'memory': all nerves, in the leg, for example, remember earlier experiences" (*KSA* 9:2[68]).

69. *Zarathustra* 3.12 §8; see also the reference to "the river of becoming" in Z 2.12.

70. *Timaeus* 43a–d. Conceiving sensation as a kind of movement, Plato associated the word for it, *aisthēsis,* with the verb *aissō,* "to rush."

71. Kant, *Anthropologie in pragmatischer Hinsicht,* §74.

72. *Dawn of Morning* 530. Nietzsche goes on to speak of the thinker as "living in the great stream of thought and feeling," remarking that "even our dreams at night follow this stream" (*DM* 572).

73. The stream of imagery that has its source in the image of the flow of *erōs* in Plato's *Republic* flows on through Nietzsche to Freud, who elaborates the former's hints about economizing the power of the passions into a "hydroeconomics" of the libido. Employing imagery that is complementary to that of the *Republic,* Freud gives the following description of what happens when normal discharge of the sexual drive is rendered impossible: "the libido behaves like a stream whose main bed has become blocked: it proceeds to fill up collateral channels that had perhaps up to this point been empty" (*Three Essays on the Theory of Sexuality,* lecture 1, §6; *SEF* 7:170). In a well known characterization of "the great reservoir of libido," he writes: "The ego is a great reservoir from which the libido that is destined for objects flows out and into which it flows back from those objects" (*SEF* 17:139). Gerasimos Santos remarks the affinity between the passage from the *Republic* and Freud's hydraulic model in *Plato and Freud: Two Theories of Love* (Oxford, 1988), 77; chapters 2 and 3 of this comprehensive work are devoted to the theories of *erōs* in the *Symposium* and *Phaedrus.*

74. See *Dawn of Morning* 575, and the poem "Toward New Seas" in the *Songs of Prince Vogelfrei* which he added to the second edition of *The Joyful Science.* The Columbus theme figures prominently in this latter text, especially in aphorisms 124, 283, 289, 291, 343, and 377.

75. An interesting treatment of the phenomenon of nihilism is Nishitani's *The Self-Overcoming of Nihilism,* much of which deals with Nietzsche. Nishitani has the advantage of some hermeneutic distance from the phenomenon, standing as he does in a quite alien philosophical tradition.

76. *The Joyful Science* 343. See, on this and related themes, Karsten Harries, "The Philosopher at Sea," in Michael Allen Gillespie and Tracy B. Strong, eds., *Nietzsche's New Seas: Explorations in Philosophy, Aesthetics, and Politics* (Chicago, 1988), 21–44. Harries's reading is discussed by Magnus et al. in *Nietzsche's Case,* 181–85.

77. In *Ecce Homo* Nietzsche compares *Dawn of Morning* to "a sea animal sun-

ning itself among rocks": "Ultimately, it was I myself that was this sea animal: almost every sentence in the book was thought, *tracked down* among that jumble of rocks near Genoa where I was alone and still had secrets with the sea" (*EH,* "DM" 1).

78. See W. K. C. Guthrie, *The Greeks and Their Gods* (Boston, 1950), 94–99. Wilamovitz argues that the name "Poseidon" comes from *posis Das,* meaning "husband of Earth," and that the god was originally associated with springs and rivers before becoming god of the sea.

79. Poseidon's presence can be felt throughout much of *Zarathustra,* not only during the episodes at sea, but also as a bull, earthquakes, springs, and so on—as, for example, when Zarathustra says: "Earthquakes open up new springs" (Z 3.12 §25).

80. This point becomes clearer in *The Joyful Science* 310, "Will and Wave," which contains another vivid portrait of the sea-shore and extends the analogy between the ocean and life as will to power.

81. "Overman" is surely preferable to "superman" as a translation of *Übermensch,* though it fails to capture the gender neutrality of the German *Mensch,* which means simply "human being." The neologism "overhuman" would be best, if it were not so inelegant; but it may be preferable to leave the term untranslated. What Zarathustra means by self-overcoming is spelled out in the chapter bearing that title (2.12).

82. In a letter to Rohde, Nietzsche complains of how miserable his solitude is, but goes on to remark: "But on the whole I am astonished at *how many* springs a person can get flowing in him" (24 March 1881).

83. Zarathustra loves him whose soul is liable to squander *(verschwenden)* itself—a verb that also has positive connotations of giving away and distributing: "I want to give away *(verschenken)* and distribute"—so that he always gives *(schenkt).* He also loves him who is liable to forget *(vergessen)* himself—a verb that evokes the similar-sounding *vergiessen,* which means "to spill." His going under would thus be a kind of out- and down-pouring.

84. The images of this passage (and in much of *Zarathustra*) echo not only the "flow" imagery of Neoplatonism but also the talk of flowing that runs through the sermons of Meister Eckhart. The primary theme there is that the creatures of God's creation flow out of Him (in the Father's speaking the Son) and thereafter long to flow back into their divine source. In attempting to characterize the abyss of Godhead *(Gottheit),* Eckhart speaks of it as "the ground, the soil, the stream, the source of Godhead" (Josef Quint, ed., *Deutsche Predigten und Traktate,* sermon 26). He speaks also of God's great "joy in giving, insofar as he wants the soul to widen itself, so that it can receive *much* and He can give *much* to the soul" (sermon 36). In *Zarathustra,* life as will to power would take the place of God in Eckhart—as suggested by Eckhart's own remark that "life lives from out of its own ground and wells up out of its own *[aus seinem Eigenen]*" (sermon 6).

85. *Zarathustra* 1.12; see also the end of Z 1.19, where Zarathustra likens the hermit to "a deep well"; 3.4 and 4.10, where he speaks of "the well of eternity"; also 2. 8.

86. *Symposium* 210d–212a. Another important form taken by Nietzsche's

aquatic imagery is the stream that issues from the mouth in the form of speech—and especially in the case (like Zarathustra's) of an outpouring of love. But discussion of this topic is best reserved for the next chapter, which treats the theme of the working of earth in the craft of agriculture and the image of watering the soil of the brain with words.

Interlude 1

1. *Beyond Good and Evil* 225. In Plato's *Republic,* potential candidates for guardians of the city will be brought "when they are young . . . to terrors and then cast in turn into pleasures, testing them far more than gold in fire" (*Rep.* 413d). In the myth of the metals, the basis for the "noble lie," the subterranean fashioning of the gold, silver, or iron and bronze that is mixed into the souls of those about to be born is undertaken not by the humans themselves but by "the god" (*Rep.* 415a). Nietzsche alludes to the myth of the metals in *HL* 10.

2. For an illuminating treatment of the idea and practice in England, see Stephen Greenblatt, *Renaissance Self-Fashioning: From More to Shakespeare* (Chicago, 1980).

3. *KSA* 9:7[213]; 1880. In a letter to Lou Salomé, Nietzsche writes of how he is finely honing the last draft of *The Joyful Science:* "The sculptor calls this last re-working *ad unguem* [down to the finger- and toe-nails]" (28 June 1882).

4. *Dawn of Morning* 548. Nietzsche's German here is at first glance ambiguous, but is disambiguated by the phrases after the dash. Hollingdale translates "that strength which employs genius *not for works* . . ."; but if *Kraft* were the subject rather than the object of this clause, a few words later would read "*das heisst auf* ihre eigene Bändigung": "*its* own overcoming" *(seine eigene Bändigung)* has to refer to *das Genie.*

5. This idea is applicable to a wide range of psychical traits—and even to physical ones. Think of the difference between a man who slavishly follows the latest sartorial fashions, without regard to how the styles look on his particular frame, and one who realistically assesses the appearance of his several parts, and judiciously selects clothes that will compensate for shortcomings.

6. *The Joyful Science* 290. This theme is given an elegant crustacean turn in a passage from *Zarathustra:*

"And verily! Much that is one's *own* is also hard to bear. And much that is inside the human is like an oyster, nauseating and slippery and hard to grasp—"so that a noble shell with noble decoration must plead for it. But one must also learn this art: to *have* a shell and beautiful sheen *[schönen Schein]* and clever blindness!" (*Z* 3.11 §2, "On the Spirit of Gravity").

7. In *Ecce Homo* Nietzsche describes briefly the marks by which one tells that a person has "turned out well": such a person "pleases the senses [and] is carved from wood that is hard, delicate, and fragrant" (*EH* 1.2).

8. Montaigne, "Of Experience" (*Essays,* 3:13, 850–51).

9. *KSA* 9:11[197]; 1881.

10. *Zarathustra* 3.2, §1. There is a prefiguration of the alchemical theme in Schiller's *On the Aesthetic Education of Man,* where he writes: "Like the chemist,

the philosopher finds combination only through dissolution, and the work of spontaneous Nature only through the torture of Art" (first letter).

11. See *DM* 103; *JS* 292, 300; *BGE* 32. For an enumeration and brief discussion
of Nietzsche's references to things alchemical, see the second half of Richard Per-
kins, "Analogistic Strategies in *Zarathustra*," in David Goicoechea, ed., *The Great
Year of Zarathustra (1881–1981)* (Lanham, Md., and New York, 1983), 317–38.

12. Letter to Overbeck, 25 December 1882. The original of the passage from
Emerson's "History" Nietzsche quotes here is: "To the poet, to the philosopher, to
the saint, all things are friendly and sacred, all events profitable, all days holy, all
men divine." It is unlikely that Nietzsche was familiar with this comment by Emerson about Schiller, which elegantly brings together a number of images that are
central to his psychology: "His productions . . . were the fermentations by which his
mind was working itself clear, they were the experiments by which he got his skill
and the fruit, the bright pure gold of all was—Schiller himself" (*Journals,* 4:55).

13. Letter to Overbeck, 14 August 1883. Almost exactly a year later, in bemoaning his loneliness after breaking off relations with his family, Nietzsche uses
similar transformative imagery: "It belongs to my task to master even this and to
continue by 'transforming into gold' all pieces of fate for the sake of my *task*" (18
August 1884).

14. *KSA* 10:5[1] #130. The same idea is to be found in notes at *KSA* 10:4[76]
and 10:7[155] (also from 1883).

15. See the references to alchemy in *Nietzsche's* Zarathustra: *Notes of the Semi-
nar given in 1934–1939 by C. G. Jung,* ed. James L. Jarrett (Princeton, 1988). Jung's
major expositions of alchemy as a psychological discipline are to be found in *Alchemical Studies* (Princeton, 1967), *Psychology and Alchemy* (Princeton, 1968), and
Mysterium Coniunctionis (Princeton, 1970). See also Hillman's essays, "Silver and
the White Earth" (in two parts), *Spring 1980:*21–48 and *Spring 1981:*21–66; "Alchemical Blue and the *Unio Mentalis*," *Sulfur* 1 (1981): 33–50; and Salt: A Chapter
in Alchemical Psychology," in J. Stroud and G. Thomas, eds., *Images of the
Untouched* (Dallas, 1981), 111–37.

16. Letter to Köselitz, 26 August 1883. In the same month: "You can't imagine
how this madness rages in me day and night" (to Overbeck, 14 August); "as long as
I am not sick (or half insane, which also happens)" (to Köselitz, 16 August); "this
conflict in me [between feelings of revenge and my philosophy, which renounces
all vengeance] is bringing me step by step to *insanity*—I feel this in the most terrifying way" (to Overbeck, 26 August).

17. *KSA* 9:11[161]; autumn 1881.

18. *KSA* 10:4[85]; 1882–83.

19. *KSA* 9:11[165]; 1881.

20. *Dawn of Morning* 174. The unpublished note that is the prototype of this
aphorism begins: "We have the ability to cultivate our temperament as a garden. To
plant experiences in it, and to uproot others . . ." (*KSA* 9:7[211]; 1880). A later note,
in which Nietzsche imagines his works as a garden, a place through which people
might idly stroll and break off bits and pieces of the plants to take home as souve-
nirs, has a much more defensive tone to it (*KSA* 11:38[22]; 1885).

V. *Husbanding the Soul: Vegetal Propagation*

1. At one point in his career Nietzsche fully intended to devote a few years of his life to *gardening,* but the project proved impracticable (see the end of this introductory section, below). If literal farming was of little interest to Plato, there is at least one recorded instance of his writings having affected a farmer. Themistius describes the response on the part of a Corinthian farmer to the *Gorgias* as follows: "He left forthwith his fields and vines, and committing his soul to Plato sowed and raised his teacher's doctrines for crops." Cited in the translator's introduction to the *Gorgias* in Plato, *Lysis, Symposium, Gorgias,* trans. W. R. M. Lamb (Cambridge, Mass., 1925), 250.

2. Heidegger devotes one of his later essays to showing how deeply cultivating *(Bauen)* and dwelling *(Wohnen)* belong together, invoking the Old High German word *buan,* meaning "to dwell." See "Bauen, Wohnen, Denken" in Martin Heidegger, *Vorträge und Aufsätze* (Pfullingen, 1954); English translation in David F. Krell, ed., *Martin Heidegger: Basic Writings* (New York, 1977).

3. The female ovum was discovered by Karl Ernst von Baer in 1827; see James Hillman, *The Myth of Analysis* (Evanston, 1972), 223. Hillman provides a fascinating account of the phantastic conceptions and (mostly) misconceptions of sexual reproduction that have been entertained in the West, with special reference to the problem of female "seed" (see, especially, part 3, "On Psychological Femininity").

4. Aeschylus, *The Eumenides,* lines 658–61, in David Grene and Richmond Lattimore, eds., *Greek Tragedies,* vol. 3 (Chicago, 1960). Since *xenos* can mean "host" as well as "guest" or "stranger," the last sentence also implies that the woman is "host" to the stranger implant. Bachofen quotes this speech of Apollo in support of his claim that the god is "the advocate of father right" (*Myth, Religion, and Mother Right,* 159).

5. Aristotle, *On the Generation of Animals,* 727–29.

6. The Greek *aroura*—whence, presumably, our word "arable," via the Latin *arare,* "to plough"—means "ploughland" and forms a border between the fields of propagation and procreation. *Aroura* is used metaphorically to refer to a woman in her capacity to receive seed and bear fruit (see Plato, *Laws* 839a). At *Cratylus* 406b, Socrates uses the related noun *arotos,* whose literal meaning is "ploughing" or "husbandry," to refer to sexual intercourse. The verb *aroō,* literally "to plough" or "to sow," also means both "to beget" and "to conceive" and, in the passive, "to be begotten." *Arotēr,* literally a "plougher" or "husbandman," also means "father" or "begetter"; *arosimos,* meaning "arable," can also mean "fit for engendering children." Similar ambiguities attach to such terms as the Greek *spermia,* and the verb *trephō* (which corresponds to the *trophos* in the quote from Aeschylus), which means "to tend" and "make grow" of plants as well as "to nourish" and "to nurse."

7. This kind of contingency is a major theme in Martha Nussbaum's magnificent study, *The fragility of goodness: Luck and ethics in Greek tragedy and philosophy* (Cambridge and New York, 1986). Part of one of the epigraphs to this book, from Pindar, reads: "But human excellence / grows like a vine tree / fed by the green dew . . ."

8. The inspiration for this kind of focus comes from the exemplary reading of

Plato in the 1968 essay by Jacques Derrida, "La pharmacie de Platon." Just as for Derrida the notion of *pharmakon* is "caught in a chain of significations" that is not congruent with the systematic intentions of the author named Plato, so one can trace corresponding branches of agricultural imagery that often grow at cross-purposes to the conscious direction of the dialectic. See Jacques Derrida, *La dissémination* (Paris, 1972), 69–198, 108; English translation: "Plato's Pharmacy," in *Dissemination,* trans. Barbara Johnson (Chicago, 1981), 61–171, 95.

9. Plato, *Republic* 435a. The same image of rubbing two strands of ideas together in order to produce an illuminating spark or flame appears in the Seventh Letter (344b).

10. Letter to Overbeck, 24 October 1879. For an inventory of the large number of trees, bushes, and vegetable beds for which he was responsible, see the letter to Köselitz of 30 September 1879.

11. Herder, *Vom Erkennen und Empfinden* (1778), 692. Hölderlin's Hyperion makes a similar point: "We want to grow upward and spread wide our branches and twigs, but soil and weather are what bring us what we will be; and if the lightning falls upon your crown and splits you, poor tree! down to the roots—what part do you have in that?" (*Hyp.* 1.1.7).

See the erudite study by M. H. Abrams, *The Mirror and the Lamp* (Oxford, 1953), especially the section entitled "German Theories of Vegetable Genius" in chapter 7, "The Psychology of Literary Invention: Unconscious Genius and Organic Growth." Heidegger, following Johann Peter Hebel, indulges in similar plant and soil imagery in the "Memorial Address" section of *Gelassenheit* (Pfullingen, 1959), 11–14; English translation in *Discourse on Thinking,* trans. John M. Anderson and E. Hans Freund (New York, 1966), 45–48.

12. *Human, All Too Human* 22. The image is amplified in a later aphorism entitled "Reason and the Tree of Humanity," where Nietzsche writes of "the great task" as follows: "humanity shall one day become a tree that overshadows the whole earth, with millions of blossoms that will become fruits together, and the earth itself shall be prepared for the nourishment of this tree" (*WS* 189).

13. *Assorted Opinions and Maxims* 406; a remark made from the perspective of the artist as tree. With real plants, if their fruits are allowed to ripen naturally, they fall to the ground and there spill their seeds, which may then be ingested by animals and transported elsewhere before dropping to the ground and germinating. While it may look as if insects or animals are preying on the plants, from another perspective the plants, by offering up their fruit to be devoured, are using the animals for their own purpose of self-propagation.

14. *The Joyful Science* 19. Emerson concludes his essay "Compensation" with awed praise of the "deep remedial force" of "calamity," in a magnificent image blending the arboreal and horticultural: "And the man or woman who would have remained a sunny garden flower, with no room for its roots and too much sunshine for its head, by the falling of the walls and the neglect of the gardener, is made the banian of the forest, yielding shade and fruit to wide neighbourhoods of men."

15. *Zarathustra* 1.21. Compare Hölderlin's Hyperion: "The withered, decaying tree may no longer stand where it stands, for it steals the light and air from the young life that is ripening for a new world" (*Hyp.* 1.1.7).

16. *Zarathustra* 3.5, §3. One of the most striking features of the landscape around Sils-Maria is the way the trees—pines and firs mostly—persist up to the tree line, where they have to strike their roots around rocks and boulders in order to stand their ground.

17. The tree is a central image, with similar import, in the Daoism of Zhuangzi (Chuang Tzu): a number of the episodes in *Zarathustra* concerning broad-branched and high-vaulted as well as knotty and crooked trees (Z 3.10 §1 and 4.10, for instance) could well have come from the *Zhuangzi*. For a comparison of the natural imagery in these texts, see Graham Parkes, "Human/Nature in Nietzsche and Taoism," in Roger Ames and Baird Callicott, eds., *Environmental Philosophy: The Nature of Nature in Asian Traditions of Thought* (Albany, 1989), 79–98, and "The Wandering Dance: *Chuang-tzu* and *Zarathustra*," *Philosophy East and West* 29 (1983):235–50.

18. See Otto, *Dionysus,* 157. Kerényi writes of Dionysus's manifesting "the bisexuality that is characteristic of most trees and constitutes their natural completeness" (*The Gods of the Greeks,* 273).

19. *The Joyful Science* 371. The passage is reminiscent of the beginning of Hölderlin's *Fragment von Hyperion* (1794): "There are two ideals of our existence: a condition of the highest simplicity, in which our needs are mutually harmonious among themselves and with our powers, and with everything with which we are connected, *simply by virtue of the organization of nature* and without our having anything to do with it; and a condition of the highest culture, where the same thing would happen with infinitely multiplied and amplified needs and powers, *by virtue of an organization that we would give to ourselves*" (Hölderlin, *Werke und Briefe,* 1:439–40).

20. One is reminded of the apostrophe to "holy nature" at the climax of the first book of *Hyperion:* "You are the same inside me and outside. It cannot be so difficult to unite what is outside me with the divine in me. If the bee succeeds in its small realm, why should I not plant and cultivate what is necessary? And if the Arab merchant was able to sow his Koran and have a people of scholars grow up like an endless forest, then should the field not thrive where the old wisdom returns to new and vital youth?" (*Hyp.* 1.2.19).

21. See *Zarathustra* 2.2 (the fig imagery will be discussed later in this chapter) and 4.11. An earlier aphorism ("The Patient Ones") that clearly comes from Nietzsche's experience of the Engadin reads: "The pine seems to listen, the fir to be waiting; and both without impatience: they do not think of the small human being beneath them, who is consumed by impatience and curiosity" (WS 176).

22. The connection between the image of the tree and Zarathustra's will as will to power is made closer in *Zarathustra* 4.11.

23. Three treatments of the *Phaedrus* are highly recommended: Ronna Burger, *Plato's* Phaedrus: *A Defense of a Philosophic Art of Writing* (University, Al., 1980); G. R. F. Ferrari, *Listening to the Cicadas: A Study of Plato's* Phaedrus (Cambridge, 1987); and Charles L. Griswold, Jr., *Self-Knowledge in Plato's* Phaedrus (New Haven and London, 1986).

24. Plato, *Phaedrus* 230b–d. As one who claims immunity to the charms of

the natural world, Socrates admits that it is only through employing the "charm" *(pharmakon)* of "speeches in books" (Phaedrus is carrying with him a book containing a speech by Lysias) that his companion has managed to lure him out of the city. The word for "speech" here, and in subsequent discussion of Plato, is *logos,* which comes from *legein,* "to say." The word has a great many other meanings, such as "word," "account," "narrative," "formula," "argument," "principle," and so on; but it will usually be translated "speech" in what follows.

25. *Phaedrus* 236e. Near the end of the dialogue Socrates speaks of a tree that is associated in a different way with speeches, when he mentions *logoi* uttered by the sacred oak tree at Dodona, which were considered to be the first prophetic utterances (275b).

26. For example, *Phaedrus* 228b, 234d, 238d, 241e, 253a.

27. The image of grass occurs in *The Wanderer and His Shadow* in an aphorism entitled "Being able to be small" which employs natural imagery in order to extol the benefits of flexibility of perspective: "One must still even now be as close to flowers, grasses, and butterflies as a child is, who is not much bigger than these. . . . Whoever wants to partake of *all* good things must also know how to be small at times" (*WS* 51).

28. Zarathustra actually uses a rhetorical term here, insofar as he says to his heart that sleep "persuades" *(überredet)* him.

29. "Did the world not just become perfect? Round and ripe *[reif]*? Oh the golden round ring *[des goldenen runden Reifs]*—where is it flying to? . . . Still!" (Z 4.10). In the noun *Reif,* which means "ring" or "hoop," there is an assonance to the word for ripe *(reif);* but it also means "hoar frost" and thus also anticipates Zarathustra's calling his soul a "drop of dew" at the end of his speech to the heavens. Right after this "Still!" Zarathustra falls asleep and has to waken himself by saying "Up!"—echoing his exhortation to his "abysmal thought" (of eternal recurrence) to awaken: "Up, abysmal thought *[abgründlicher Gedanke]* . . . you sleepy worm *[Wurm]*!" (Z 3.13). There is an echo here also of the first scene of act 2 of *Siegfried,* where the Wanderer (Wotan) wakens Fafner the dragon by saying "*Erwache, Wurm!*" and Alberich warns him that Siegfried is greedy for "the golden ring" *(den goldnen Reif).* The episode in which Zarathustra exhorts his abysmal thought—"primal grandmother," he calls it—to awaken is, as Roger Hollinrake has pointed out, a replay of the first scene of act 3 of *Siegfried* where Wotan awakens Erda—"eternal woman," he calls her—by calling "Up! Up!"

30. Although Pan is not invoked by name in "At Midday," he is present in the prototype of this lyrical passage in *The Wanderer and His Shadow:* "On a hidden woodland meadow [one] sees the great Pan sleeping; all the things of nature have fallen asleep with him, an expression of eternity on their faces" (*WS* 308).

31. *Republic* 514a, *Timaeus* 43c, *Phaedo* 69c. At *Republic* 363d "the unholy and unjust" are said to suffer the fate of being buried "in mud in Hades."

32. Seth Benardete, *Plato's Statesman* (Chicago, 1984), 272e. This is part 3 of Benardete's translation of the trilogy, under the title *The Being of the Beautiful;* subsequent references to the *Theaetetus, Sophist,* and *Statesman* will be to this translation. In his commentary on this last passage from the *Statesman,* Benardete suggests

that "it would not be misleading to call such [seed-producing] souls, after Aristotle, vegetative" (p. 100): in *De Anima* (413b) Aristotle speaks of plants' participating in the "nutritive" soul *(to threptikon)*.

33. *The Wanderer and His Shadow* 53. This passage recalls the idea discussed earlier of "implanting in ourselves a new habitude, a new instinct, a second nature" *(HL* 3).

34. For a comprehensive treatment of Nietzsche's relation to Rousseau, see Keith Ansell-Pearson, *Nietzsche contra Rousseau* (Cambridge, 1991).

35. Nietzsche discusses the prodigal squandering of nature—"in the realm of culture as much as in planting and sowing"—in section 7 of *Schopenhauer as Educator.* (It is also a topic of discussion in Emerson's essay "Nature.") For the later Nietzsche squandering will play an important role in "post-agricultural" creativity: see chapter 9, below.

36. *Zarathustra,* Prologue, §9. The plants to be harvested change from grains to grapes in the course of the story—but thus still remain within a complex of imagery ruled by Demeter and Dionysus. See Onians, *The Origins of European Thought,* 113, where the metaphor of men as corn is linked to the Eleusinian Mystery cults. Onians also discusses the assimilation of human beings to other "children of Mother Earth," as well as myths of men as "sown ones" *(spartoi)* and autochthonous (referring to the passages from the *Statesman* mentioned earlier).

37. In this respect Zarathustra resembles the lover in the *Symposium* (209) who is pregnant in soul without there having been mention of any kind of psychical intercourse. This image will be discussed in the next chapter.

38. One of the most important features of *Zarathustra* is the way the relations between Zarathustra and his disciples develop in the course of the narrative, especially since these developments have a bearing on the changing relations of the book's author to his audience. The topic is discussed with intelligent sensitivity in Laurence Lampert's *Nietzsche's Teaching.*

39. *Zarathustra* 2.1. Zarathustra is said to wait like a *Säemann,* which sounds like a *Seemann,* a seaman—a homophony that evokes the seafaring Odysseus, to whom the protagonist is several times likened. There is a corresponding wordplay between Zarathustra's being a *Schaffender* (creator) and a *Schiffender* (sailor): just before claiming to be the "heir and soil" of the "sights and apparitions of [his] youth" he refers to himself as *dem einsam Schiffenden* (the lonesome sailor). It may be stretching the point to remark that the "-*sam*" of *einsam* echoes the "*Sam-*" of the *Samen* (seed) that Zarathustra has sown, since the nautical figure seems to stem from a different branch of imagery; but the assonance between *Säemann* and *Seemann* (which resembles *Samen* with the vowels transposed) is reinforced later by the only recurrence of the word *Säemann*—in a context that tightens the connections between sowing, seafaring, and procreation. "Oh my brothers," says Zarathustra, "you shall become procreators and cultivators *[Zeuger und Züchter]* for me, and sowers *[Säemänner]* of the future. . . . It is your *children's-land* you shall love: this love shall be your new nobility—the undiscovered, in the farthest ocean!" (*Z* 3.12 §12). And when he reiterates the exhortation to ship out onto high seas in search of their children's-land, Zarathustra calls his hearers "You old seaman's hearts *[Seemanns-Herzen]*" (§28). We shall consider in the next chapter further plays on the ambi-

guity of the verb *züchten,* which means "to breed" or "rear" animals as well as "to cultivate" plants.

40. Upon interpreting his dream Zarathustra leaps up "like a seer *[Seher],*" which in German sounds exactly like a "sower" *(Säer)* would.

41. Plato, *Euthyphro* 2d–3a. Remember Nietzsche's good teacher who "clears away all weeds, rubble, and vermin that would encroach on the delicate buds of the plants" *(SE* 1).

42. The connection between agriculture and midwifery is made, and the priority between its elements established, in a funeral speech by a woman named Aspasia, as recounted by Socrates in the *Menexenus.* In speaking of the idea of land as mother, she says: "It is not the land [*gē,* earth] that imitates the woman in the matter of conception and birth, but the woman the land" (238a).

43. *Theaetetus* 191c–e. There is an anticipation of the theme of earth earlier in the dialogue when Socrates adduces the rather odd example of mud ("earth kneaded with liquid") as an object of knowledge (147a–c).

44. Quite a contrast with Nietzsche's interest in "psychological manure." For a discussion of Nietzsche's view of the sterility of imagining the medium of memory (and of perception) as passive, see the next chapter on the topic of "immaculate perception."

45. For a detailed discussion of the enigmatic relation between speaking and writing in *Zarathustra,* see Graham Parkes, "The Dance from Mouth to Hand: Speaking Zarathustra's Write Foot ForeWord," in Clayton Koelb, ed., *Nietzsche as Postmodernist* (Albany, 1990), 127–44.

46. *Phaedrus* 275e–276a. Compare *Laws* 841d, where the generation of legitimate offspring is contrasted with the activity of those who "sow unhallowed, bastard sperm in concubines or go against nature and sow sterile seed in males." The discussion of speaking and writing in the final episode of the *Phaedrus* (274b–end) has been treated in depth by Derrida in "Plato's Pharmacy." The theme of speeches as live offspring will be treated in the next chapter.

47. *Phaedrus* 276b. This passage is framed by a contrast expressed in sexual terms, and will be discussed in the next chapter. This section of the *Phaedrus* is set in an illuminating context of themes in ancient Greek myth and ritual by Marcel Detienne in *The Gardens of Adonis,* trans. Janet Lloyd (Atlantic Highlands, 1977), chapter 5, "The Seeds of Adonis."

48. *Phaedrus* 277c. The word translated here by both "complex" and "many-colored" is *poikilos,* which also means "cunning"; we will encounter it later (in chapter 9) as applied to the democratic regime and personality type. The name of the town in *Zarathustra,* the Motley Cow, may well be an allusion to Plato's fondness for this term.

49. It is interesting that Plato nowhere seems to consider the possibility that the book as "garden of Adonis" could serve as an intermediate matrix for the seeds of speech: the seed always lies in the ground as if dead, after all, before germinating. The problem would then be how to get the seeds into the soul through the eyes in the act of reading, rather than having them enter in the flow of speech through the ears. Part of the requisite image later became current in European letters, insofar as "ploughshare" was a common metaphor for "stylus," so that one could sow words

with the pen in the medium of the "furrowed" page. For a discussion of this field of imagery, see Ernst Robert Curtius, *European Literature and the Latin Middle Ages,* trans. Willard R. Trask (Princeton, 1973), chap. 16, "The Book as Symbol."

50. The state of aporia suffered by Euthyphro is typical: toward the end of the dialogue that bears his name he has lost any firm ground on which to take a stand— as evidenced by his complaint to Socrates that the *logoi* they propose keep moving about and refuse to stand still (*Euth.* 11b–d).

51. In the *Symposium* Diotima explains to Socrates that all mortal beings are able to "partake of immortality" at various levels through reproducing themselves, in such a way that "everything naturally values its own offshoot" (208b). In the *Phaedo,* at the beginning of the argument for the immortality of the soul based on the reciprocal generation of opposites from opposites, Socrates urges Cebes to consider the question not with regard to human beings only, "but with regard to all animals and plants . . . to all things which may be said to have birth *[genesis]"* (70d).

52. For a sophisticated discussion of the notion of *chōra* (the "third genus" between the intelligible and the sensible, the "receptacle" of becoming) in the *Timaeus,* and one that touches on many of the topics of this and the next chapter, see Jacques Derrida, "Chōra," in *Poikilia: Études offertes à Jean-Pierre Vernant* (Paris, 1987), 265–96.

53. This is explicitly stated at *Timaeus* 91b. As Cornford has pointed out, "[The seed] is divine as being part of the marrow which contains the immortal part of the soul, and also as being the vehicle and means of the immortality of the species" (*Plato's Cosmology,* 295).

54. *Timaeus* 91b–d. For a comprehensive account of the connections between seed and generation and immortality in the Greek tradition, see Onians, *The Origins of European Thought,* 108–22. The idea of a conduit between brain and genitals figures also in Indian tantric and Chinese alchemical practices, in which the male seed is retained and redirected up the spinal column to the brain.

55. *Timaeus* 77b; compare the vegetative soul in Aristotle's *De Anima.*

56. In the Aristotelian school agriculture was described as the art of "educating" (*paideuein*) plants (cited by Detienne in *The Gardens of Adonis,* 12).

57. There is a subtle play within the last dozen lines of this speech on the word *Rasen,* meaning "grass" or "lawn." Just before the appearance of the lioness, Zarathustra speaks of his "raging" (the verb *rasen*) like a storm over the heads of his enemies. Worried in case his friends will be frightened by his wild wisdom, he wishes that his "lioness wisdom could learn to roar tenderly." So that when he speaks of his lioness's searching for soft grass, he says *"sie sucht nach sanftem Rasen"*— which could also be understood as meaning that she is "seeking soft raging" (learning to roar tenderly).

58. Letter to Lou Salomé, 26 June 1882.

59. The idea that "thought ripens into truth" through a certain kind of activity is an important one in Emerson, who emphasizes the impossibility of adequate reflection on our recent actions: "The new deed is yet a part of life—remains for a time immersed in our unconscious life. In some contemplative hour, it detaches itself from the life like a ripe fruit, to become a thought of the mind" ("The American Scholar").

60. "On the Blessed Isles" (Z 2.2). This is also the first speech (and section) in the book whose title does not begin with the formal *Von* ("On . . ." or "Of . . ."): the German is "Auf den glückseligen Inseln."

61. While Dionysus presides over the moisture and sap of plants in general, there are two other trees with which he is as closely associated: the cypress and the pine. Shortly after invoking the fig tree, Zarathustra says, "I am indeed a forest and a night of dark trees: but whoever is not afraid of my darkness will find rose-bushes among my cypresses" (Z 2.10). And near the end of the book the protagonist is compared to a pine tree (4.11). Although Zarathustra earlier invited strangers and poor people "to pluck for themselves the fruit from [his] tree" (2.3), his stillest hour admonishes him nevertheless: "Oh Zarathustra, your fruit is ripe, but you are not ripe for your fruit!" (2.22).

62. *Timaeus* 75e. Earlier in the dialogue Timaeus characterizes sound in general as "the stroke inflicted by air on the brain and blood through the ears and passed on to the soul" (67b). There is a prototype of the image of the "flow of a conversation" in the *Theaetetus*, where Socrates warns of the danger of admitting too many "by-products" to their talk by saying: "Now let's stand apart and withdraw from these things . . . for if we don't, always more will keep on flowing in and choke up the speech with which we began" (177b–c). In the *Statesman*, the stranger speaks at one point of the way "the present *logos* flooded in on [them]" (302c).

63. *Phaedrus* 235d. Compare *Theaetetus* 206d, where Socrates characterizes speech as "that which makes one's own thought evident through sounds with words and phrases, just as if it were into a mirror or water one was striking off one's opinion into the stream through one's mouth."

64. *Timaeus* 91b–d. At *Laws* 837c the lover on the physical plane is said to "hunger after the bloom [of the loved one's body] as it were that of a ripening peach, [urging] himself on to take his fill of it."

65. Socrates' talk of the way beauty "shines in brilliance" (*Phr.* 250b, 250d) is evocative of Nietzsche's accounts of "the beautiful shining" of the Apollonian in *The Birth of Tragedy*.

66. *Phaedrus* 251b. In an informative discussion of the ancient Greek notion of *aiōn*, Onians (200–209) cites Aristotle as saying that the region around the eyes is the part of the head that is "most abundant in seed *[spermatikōtatos]*" (*De Generatione Animalium*, 747a). A superb account of this section of the *Phaedrus* is to be found in chapter 6 of Ferrari's *Listening to the Cicadas*. Ferrari notes that the word used for the "stump" of the feathers at 251b6, *kaulos,* is used in the medical literature to mean "penis," and he also relates the "moistened lips" of this passage to the image of the embodied soul as an oyster in its shell at 250c. One is reminded of a pronouncement of Zarathustra's that echoes the theme of self-knowledge in the *Phaedrus:* "And much within the human being is like an oyster: repulsive and slippery and hard to grasp" (Z 3.11 §2). Ferrari pertinently notes the similarities and differences between Plato's account and Freud's ideas about sexual pleasure as outlined in the *Three Essays on the Theory of Sexuality.* The idea that the pain-cum-pleasure of sexual excitement is a manifestation of eros's seeking growth, striving to be more, has obvious parallels with Nietzsche's idea of will to power.

67. *Phaedrus* 251e. The soul was said to be similarly "maddened" in the more

physiologically oriented account (just discussed) in the *Timaeus,* in which the "over-flowing moisture" of the seed-marrow causes intense "labor pains" *(ōdinas) (Tim.* 86c). At this point in the *Phaedrus* Socrates indulges parenthetically in a fanciful etymology, by which he derives the term for "yearning" *(himeros)* from words mean-ing "rushing stream of particles." Compare the passage from the *Cratylus* (419e–420a) where he derives *himeros* from "the stream *[rhous]* which most draws the soul, because it flows with a rush *[hiemenos],*" and *erōs* from the fact that "it flows in from without, and this flowing . . . is introduced through the eyes."

68. *Phaedrus* 255c–d. For an illuminating discussion of the hydro-vegetal imag-ery in this section, see Anne Lebeck, "The Central Myth of Plato's *Phaedrus,*" *Greek, Roman, and Byzantine Studies* 13 (1972):267–90.

69. *Zarathustra* 3.14. The strangely powerful juxtaposition of images of cultiva-tion with mammalian images of motherhood occurs earlier in the text (3.2 §30), and will be discussed in the next chapter.

70. In a passage in the *Journals* that deals with the cultivating of vegetation, Emerson writes of his wanting to be "a good husband" and waste "no globule of sap," and that the good husband "waters his trees with wine" (*Journals* 10:82).

71. *Zarathustra* 4.19 §9 (emphasis added). This theme with respect to Zarathus-tra is an extension of Montaigne's magnificent image concerning the accumulation of wisdom: "To really learned men has happened what happens to ears of wheat: they rise high and lofty, heads erect and proud, as long as they are empty; but when they are full and swollen with grain in their ripeness, they begin to grow humble and lower their horns" (*Essays,* 2:12, 370).

72. *Zarathustra* 3.14. There is an echo of this image in the fourth part, in the song "Among Daughters of the Desert" where the singer likens himself to a luscious brown date "lusting after the ice-cold, snow-white, sharp incisors" of a young maiden (Z 4.16). This later image is remarkable for its combination of elements of oral eroticism—and for the apparent absence of castration anxiety on the part of the singer.

73. Joel Porte has remarked (*Representative Man,* 246) the tension in Emerson's soul—sympathetically echoed in Nietzsche's—between careful management of the impulses and prodigal release, citing these juxtaposed passages from the *Journals:* "Shall a man . . . in his garden cut down the spindling shoots of his pear tree or pinch off the redundant buds of his grapevine to give robustness to the stock, & not learn the value of rejection in his own spiritual economy?"; and, in a Zarathustrian vein: "The fountains of life must be stirred & sent bounding throughout our system, or else we ebb so soon into the Stygian pool of Necessity to drink of its infatuating bowl, & seal our doom" (10:112).

74. It would be equally fruitful to reflect on the implications of the practice of *grafting* when applied to the psychical realm. Neither Plato nor Nietzsche appears to employ the imagery of psychical grafting, though the idea does figure in the work of Derrida. (See, for example, the note on *greffe* in "Plato's Pharmacy" [*Dissemina-tion,* 151].) At the next level of complexity would be the surgical cut, to which Nietzsche alludes in a letter to Overbeck: "I now understand the suffering I have undergone as in some sense a necessity: I have excised from my soul three of four

wishes for happiness of a personal nature that were persisting, and I am now more free that I was before" (6 March 1883).

75. *Zarathustra* 3.13, §2. Compare Goethe's Werther, who laments at one point: "The yeast that used to set my life in motion is no longer there" (20 January 1772).

76. In the life cycle of the plant, death is a crucial stage: "That which thou sowest is not quickened except it die" (1 Corinthians 15). The seed is the point at which the opposites of life and death touch: for many a plant, to produce the seeds of new life is itself to die.

77. *KSA* 9, 11[2]; 1881. In this same note Nietzsche mentions the joy that comes from tending others as if they were gardens.

Interlude 2

1. See the accounts by Lou Andreas-Salomé, Emily Fynn, Malwida von Meysenbug, Ida von Miaskowski, Ida Overbeck (née Rothpelz), Meta von Salis-Marschlins, Resa von Schirnhofer, Isabella von Ungern-Sternberg (née von der Pahlen), and Helen Zimmern in Gilman's *Begegnungen mit Nietzsche.*

2. The monumental tome by Joachim Köhler, *Zarathustras Geheimnis* (Nördlingen, 1989), tries to make the case that Nietzsche was homosexual and a pederast. While Köhler has done a great deal of work and brought forward some interesting features of Nietzsche's biography, the "evidence" for his subject's homosexuality does not consist of any revelatory new materials but rather in a distinctly quirky reading of selected passages in *Zarathustra.*

3. *Beyond Good and Evil* 232–39. "*Weib an sich*" is an ironic allusion to Kant's "thing in itself," which Nietzsche regards as an absurd phantasm. This would lead one to expect a higher degree than usual of irony in the remarks on women that follow.

4. Some feminist commentators have expressed concern about Nietzsche's "gender-specific writing" and especially his use of "male pronouns" to refer to the ideal of the free spirit. It is true that, as a child of his time (for once), Nietzsche first thinks of the good philosopher as male; but obviously if he is writing about *der freie Geist* the pronouns he uses will—out of grammatic necessity—be masculine. In fact there is relatively little "gender-specific" language in Nietzsche's writings, though this fact tends to be obscured by the translations of both Kaufmann and Hollingdale, who insist on rendering *Mensch* mostly as "man" rather than "human being." Even Nietzsche's term *Übermensch* is gender-neutral, though the neologism "overhuman" in unlikely to gain wide currency. But at least we have been spared—so far—a book in translation with the title *Manly, All Too Manly.*

5. Any feminist critique of Nietzsche has to take account of the remarkable enthusiasm for his ideas on the part of a number of prominent figures in the women's movement in Germany around the turn of the century. For a discussion of the variety of attitudes toward Nietzsche on the part of the German feminists, see R. Hinton Thomas, *Nietzsche in German Politics and Society 1890–1918* (La Salle, 1986).

6. Sarah Kofman, "Baubō: Theological Perversion and Fetishism," in Michael Allen Gillespie and Tracy B. Strong, eds., *Nietzsche's New Seas* (Chicago and London, 1988), 177, 180, 193, 198.

7. Jacques Derrida, *Spurs: Nietzsche's Styles,* trans. Barbara Harlow (Chicago and London, 1979), 64–65. For some illuminating commentary on this text, and on the topic of woman in Nietzsche in general, see David Farrell Krell, *Postponements: Woman, Sensuality, and Death in Nietzsche* (Bloomington, 1986).

8. *Beyond Good and Evil* 239. Kofman draws from her discussion of this issue the important conclusion that Nietzsche "distinguishes different types of women, just as he distinguishes different types of men. From a genealogical point of view, an affirmative woman is closer to an affirmative man than a degenerate woman. And some women are more affirmative than some men" (*Nietzsche's New Seas,* 193).

9. For a discussion from a Nietzschean perspective of a number of philosophical themes in one of Woolf's novels, see Graham Parkes, "Imagining Reality in *To the Lighthouse,*" *Philosophy and Literature* 6, no. 1 (1982):33–44.

10. For a psychoanalytically informed account of Nietzsche's defensiveness with respect to the feminine, and in particular his strange dissociation of the feminine from the Dionysian, see Staten's *Nietzsche's Voice,* especially chapter 6. An extended meditation on the broader theme of Nietzsche's (dis)relation to the feminine is the second section of Luce Irigaray's *Marine Lover of Friedrich Nietzsche,* entitled "Veiled Lips." For a more recent, and eminently sensible treatment of the topic, see Lampert's *Nietzsche and Modern Times,* 368–87.

11. *KSA* 8:17[41]-[57]; *Human, All Too Human* 285.

12. *KSA* 8:17[55]; 1876.

13. *KSA* 11:26[317].

14. Montaigne, *Essays* 3:8, 709. Another past master of this retroflective technique is Confucius; for a brief discussion of Confucian (and other East Asian) themes in Nietzsche, see "Nietzsche and East Asian Thought: Influences, Impacts, and Resonances." Failure to appreciate Nietzsche's use of this technique has led to countless misinterpretations of his philosophy, an egregious recent example being Ofelia Schutte's *Beyond Nihilism: Nietzsche without Masks* (Chicago, 1984)—the subtitle alone suggesting an author totally insensitive to Nietzsche's styles. The issues addressed by this book are important, but the method—set up a number of straw Nietzsches from the unpublished *Nachlass* and have at them with a series of ideological (Marxist-feminist) axes—vitiates the greater part of the project.

15. *Human, All Too Human* 376. This reflexive technique is exemplified again by *HA* 587.

16. *Zarathustra* 1.17. Later, in conversing with his soul, Zarathustra exclaims: "O my soul, I taught you the contempt that does not come like the gnawing of worms, the great and loving contempt, which loves most where it most despises" (Z 3.14).

17. The verb *verschliessen* has connotations of stopping or bottling up: hermetically sealed is *hermetisch verschlossen.*

18. The best work on the notion of *anima,* which includes a coherent presentation of Jung's ideas on the topic, is James Hillman, *Anima: an Anatomy of a Personified Notion* (Dallas, 1985). This composite text would be a helpful handbook for any thorough investigation of the feminine in Nietzsche. Another good account from a Jungian perspective is Gareth Hill, *Masculine and Feminine: The Natural Flow of*

Opposites in the Psyche (Boston, 1992). On the figure of Ariadne, see the first chapter of Krell's *Postponements.*

19. These are Jung's words. See Hillman, *Anima,* chapter 4: "Anima and the Feminine." The figure of "Life" in *Zarathustra* (2.10 and 3.15) is a beautiful embodiment of anima as archetype of life; see also Lampert's discussion of the relevant chapters, "The Dancing Song" and "The Other Dancing Song," in *Nietzsche's Teaching.*

VI. *Husbanding the Soul: Animal Procreation*

1. Nietzsche is concerned to put in question the very idea of a hierarchy from plants to animals to humans to spirits to gods. As for many cultures with theriomorphic divinities, for the early Greeks the gods often assumed the form of animals as well as of plants. The opposition between Plato and Nietzsche on this issue, as on many others, reflects the duality of Apollo and Dionysus: whereas Plato tends to share with Apollo a certain distance from the animal world, Nietzsche stays close to Dionysus, who is not only the god of vegetation and sap, but is also referred to as "many-formed" *(polueidēs)* because he can appear as a lion, bull, boar, panther, lynx, snake, ass, or goat.

Much of Nietzsche's thinking about animals moves along lines laid down by Montaigne: see, especially, the section "Man is no better than the animals" in the "Apology for Raymond Sebond," *Essays,* 2:12, 330–58. Near the beginning of this section Montaigne invokes Plato's "picture of the golden age under Saturn," during which "the man of that time had communication with the beasts, inquiring of them and learning from them" (p. 331). The reference is to the *Statesman* 271d–272d.

2. *Dawn of Morning* 312. A note from 1880 reads: "In the human passions the animal awakens again; human beings are aware of nothing more interesting than this regression to the realm of the unpredictable. It is as if they become all too bored with reason" (*KSA* 9:3[12]).

3. *The Joyful Science* 57. These two aphorisms from *JS* will be discussed at greater length in chapter 8, below.

4. *Schopenhauer as Educator* 6. This "dialectical tracking-and play-drive" first appears in notes from a few years earlier (*KSA* 7:29[15]).

5. Plato, *Theaetetus* 197e, 199b.

6. *Beyond Good and Evil* 296. This magnificent finale also likens the author's thoughts to plants that were formerly "full of thorns and secret spices" but are now on the point of being "withered and lacking in fragrance," while at the same time the whole aphorism is addressed to his thoughts in the second person. For a discussion of the idea of thoughts as personal presences, see chapter 8, below. There is an earlier play on Plato's bird-catching image in *JS* 298.

7. This is a sign of Zarathustra's having become more *natural,* in that Nietzsche is frequently impressed by the extreme prodigality of nature and calls her a "bad economist" (*SE* 7). In this he follows Goethe, who in opposition to a natural scientist who had maintained that nature works "highly economically" characterized nature as "prodigal and even squandering" (Eckermann, *Conversations with Goethe,* 7 October 1828).

8. *Zarathustra* 4. 1. The image is the reverse of the opening image of "The Dance Song," where Zarathustra looks into the eyes of the woman Life and feels himself sinking into the abyss. On pulling him out with "a golden fishing rod" she says to him that "all fish" speak of abysses when it is simply a matter of their encountering something *they* are unable to fathom (Z 2.10). There is also an echo here of Zarathustra's earlier exhortation to his "most abysmal thought" (eternal recurrence), which he calls "sleepy worm," to come *up* out of his depths (3.13). The view of the world as an ocean contrasts sharply with the image of Glaucus in the *Republic,* where the soul is imagined as being deformed by its immersion in the sea of physicality: some of the parts of the fisherman's body have been "thoroughly maimed by the waves at the same time as other things have grown on him—shells, seaweed, and rocks—so that he resembles any beast rather than what he was by nature" (*Rep.* 611d).

9. At the outset of the dialogue the stranger encourages Young Socrates to proceed "as if [they] were trackers," and later evinces the impression that "now [they]'re latching on to a kind of trail that leads to where [they]'re going" (*Statesman* 263b, 290d; also 285d).

10. The idea of psyche as *polis* will be elaborated in detail in chapter nine, below.

11. *Zarathustra* 3.2 §2 and 3.13 §2.

12. The customary translation of *Seiltänzer* as "tightrope walker," while idiomatic, misses the *dancer* in the German word—and thereby the connection between the unfortunate high-wire artist and Zarathustra as a dancer on the way to the *Übermensch.*

13. *Zarathustra* 4.13 §13. He speaks here of *das innere Vieh,* which could mean more specifically inner "livestock" or "cattle."

14. *Republic* 588b–c. The "grown naturally together *[sumpephukuiai]*" is important insofar as it suggests a unity to the three parts, in contrast to the duality between the immortal and mortal kinds of soul implied in other dialogues. Allan Bloom notes: "The Chimaera was a lion in front, a dragon behind, and a she-goat in the middle. Scylla had a woman's face and breasts, six dogs' heads, a dragon's tale, and snakes for hair" (*The Republic of Plato,* p. 470). In the *Iliad* (6.181) the Chimaera is described as "lion-fronted and snake behind, a goat in the middle." Nietzsche claims that Plato "took the whole Socrates from the streets" in order to vary him like a tune "into all his own masks and multiplicities," with the result that the Platonic Socrates is "Plato in front and Plato behind and Chimaera in the middle" (*BGE* 190).

15. *Republic* 588c–d. Socrates compares himself in the *Phaedrus* to Typhon (father of the Chimaera), wondering whether he is perhaps even "more complicated" *(poluplokoteron)* than that monster (*Phr.* 230a). Typhon is part human, part beast, and winged (or "feathered") all over, and is said to have "a hundred dragons' heads projecting from his hands . . . with huge coils of vipers," as well as "the hundred heads of a snake growing from his shoulders, and the many tongues of a dragon" (Griswold, *Self-Knowledge in Plato's* Phaedrus, 39–40). There is also a distinctly Dionysian aspect to Socrates' Chimaera: in the *Bacchae* of Euripides the chorus

sings at one point to Dionysus, "Appear as a bull, or as a many-headed dragon, or as a lion breathing fire!" (line 1017).

16. See, for example, *Phaedrus* 238a–b, where Socrates speaks of rule by the principle within us that desires pleasures as "excess" *(hubris),* which has "many names, for it has many members and many forms," and warns in particular of its tendency toward tyranny. (Socrates is actually reporting here a speech purported to be by some "non-lover," but it clearly represents the ascetic side of Socrates himself.)

17. The earlier comparison of the auxiliaries, the military class, to sheepdogs is at *Republic* 416a. Socrates says that the spirited soul is "by nature an auxiliary to the calculating part," and cites as an example of reason's prevailing over the misguided passion of spirit, the reproach Odysseus addresses to his heart in restraining the force of his anger: "And as a bitch . . . growls and rages to fight, so Odysseus' heart was growling inside him as he looked on these wicked actions" *(Odyssey* 20.13–18; Lattimore translation). Socrates later says that when one lets the spirited part of the soul be subjected to the appetitive part, this is equivalent to "habituating it to be an ape instead of a lion" *(Rep.* 590b). There is an echo of this image at the beginning of the song "Among Daughters of the Desert" in the fourth part of *Zarathustra,* where the singer describes himself as "Worthy of a lion, / or of a moral ape" (Z 4.16 §2).

18. *Republic* 586e. The qualification "the best" pleasures is presumably intended to rule out the pleasure taken by the appetitive part of the soul in tyrannical domination of the two higher parts.

19. See, for example, *Phaedo* 94d, where Socrates speaks of "tyrannizing" the desires and passions, and "inflicting harsh and painful punishments."

20. *Republic* 571c–d. This extraordinary passage anticipates psychoanalytical discussions of the nature of dreams in general and Oedipal desires in particular— as Freud himself noted in *The Interpretation of Dreams,* chapters 1(f) and 7(f)—as well being congruent with Nietzsche's understanding of desires in relation to dreams.

21. On the drives' tendency toward tyranny, see especially *Beyond Good and Evil* 6, 9, 158. In *Dawn of Morning* 422, Nietzsche speaks of a person's "fifty drives"; Paul-Laurent Assoun lists sixty (in his *Freud et Nietzsche* [Paris, 1980], 90); but a list compiled during the writing of the present manuscript contains well over a hundred different drives (designated either by compounds—as in "art-drive"— or by preposition and noun constructions—as in "drive for distinction") in Nietzsche's texts.

22. *Zarathustra,* Prologue, §10; compare also "the serpent of knowledge" around the handle of Zarathustra's staff (Z 1.22 §1). There is an allusion in Zarathustra's speech "On the Bite of the Adder" (1.19) to the passage in the *Symposium* where Alcibiades claims to have been "stung" by Socrates' "philosophical speeches, which adhere more fiercely than any adder when once they lay hold of a young and not ungifted soul" *(Symp.* 218a). Nietzsche wrote a short essay in his youth on the speech of Alcibiades.

23. *Zarathustra* 1.15. The image of the serpent, several of the occurrences of

which appear "negative" (the black snake of nihilism, for example, in "On the Vision and the Enigma"), is a good paradigm for the way the images in *Zarathustra* work in general. Their use is carefully crafted so as to frustrate the reader's tendency to class a particular image as good or bad, positive or negative: all the major images are made multivocal, many-valued, in such a way as to preclude the question of whether Nietzsche is "for" or "against" what the image stands for.

24. In the only recurrence of the image of the camel, Zarathustra says that the life of the camellike spirit seems like a desert because "he loads himself up with too many *alien* heavy words and values" (Z 3.11 §2).

25. The lion embodies the strength that Zarathustra will need to summon the most abysmal thought of eternal recurrence, though for a long time he still lacks "the lion's voice for commanding" (Z 2.22, 3.3). The sign that Zarathustra's hour has come will be "a laughing lion with a flock of doves" (3.12, 4.11). In the last section of the book, "The Sign," the laughing lion does indeed come with the flock of doves, and he and Zarathustra seem the best of friends.

26. *Zarathustra* 1. 5. The image of milk and udders appears earlier, in a passage from *Human, All Too Human* which describes the hardness of the life dedicated to the pursuit of understanding: "No honey is sweeter than the honey of knowledge, and the clouds of grief that hang over you will yet have to serve you as udders, from which you will draw milk for your refreshment" (*HA* 292).

27. There is an unpublished note in which Nietzsche compares the passions to wild dogs that must be kept in check, but the image is almost the inverse of that in the *Republic* insofar as "the wildest dog" represents "the will to truth"—which has to be tempered by such forces as the will to uncertainty and the "will to *foolishness*" (*KSA* 11:38[20]; 1885).

28. The background to this flight to the fount of joy may be Mount Helicon in Greece, where there was said to be a fountain sacred to the Muses, which was created by the winged horse Pegasus stamping his hoof on the earth.

29. *Zarathustra* 3.12 §2. The "-rushing" here is *brausend,* which connotes an effervescent flowing-over, and is a term that occurred in the early essay "On Moods": while eavesdropping on his own thoughts and feelings, Nietzsche would hear "the hum and buzzing *[Brausen]* of wild parties, as if there were a rushing *[Rauschen]* through the air as when a thought or an eagle flies to the sun."

30. *Phaedrus* 246a–256d. The triadic figures are connected by their mythical background, insofar as it was with the help of the winged horse Pegasus that Bellerophon destroyed the Chimaera, offspring of Typhon.

31. Martha Nussbaum offers a fine exposition of the change in Plato's attitudes towards the passions between the *Republic* and *Phaedrus* in *The fragility of goodness,* chapters 5–7. She concludes that by the time of the *Phaedrus* Plato is prepared to concede that the "non-intellectual" elements of the soul are "necessary sources of motivational energy," which have "an important guiding role to play in our aspiration towards understanding," and that "the passions . . . are intrinsically valuable components of the best human life" (pp. 214–19). This reading brings out the consonance of the later Plato with Nietzsche on this issue.

32. Just as the spirited part of the soul can be "called in by speech like a dog by a herdsman," so the white horse of the *Phaedrus* "needs no whip, but is guided

only by the word of command and by reason *[logoi]"* (253d)—in contrast to the dark horse of desire, who is deaf and headstrong. Similarly, in the *Timaeus* the spirit "hearkens and is obedient to reason," whereas the "tribe of desires" pays no attention (70a).

33. Until the unfortunate riding accident he sustained in March of 1868 during a period of military service, Nietzsche had been an enthusiastic and accomplished horseman. See the letters to Rohde of 3 November 1867, and to Gersdorff of 1 December 1867 and 16 February 1868. Apparently he was considered the best rider among the thirty recruits in his unit (letter to Rohde of 1–3 February 1868). For more on horses (and other animals and divinities) in Nietzsche's texts, see David L. Miller, "Nietzsche's Horse and Other Tracings of the Gods," in Thomas Harrison, ed., *Nietzsche in Italy* (Saratoga, 1988), 159–70. This collection, while somewhat uneven in quality, contains some excellent essays.

34. See, especially, *Twilight of the Idols* 2, "The Problem of Socrates."

35. Presumably the checking of beauty-inspired passion need not be so mortifying: if one is inclined forward towards the awesome power of the beautiful in advance, so as to be able to go with the sudden start of racing passion, the driving forces can start up without taking the driver aback.

36. *KSA* 12:9[139] = *WP* 933.

37. *KSA* 7:19[125]; 1872. It will not be long before Nietzsche is *equating* (genuine) knowing with creating; see the discussion later in this section.

38. *On the Use and Disadvantage of History for Life* 1. The theme of pregnancy is amplified by the *-schwang* of *Überschwang*, which is cognate with *schwanger*, meaning "pregnant."

39. *On the Use and Disadvantage of History for Life* 7. In the essay on Schopenhauer, Nietzsche writes: "it is in love alone that the soul attains not only a clear, analytic and contemptuous view of itself, but also the desire to look beyond itself and to seek with all its energies a higher self that is still concealed somewhere" (*SE* 6).

40. *Richard Wagner in Bayreuth* 10. The verb *trachten* compounds the force of the pregnancy image through its relation to *trächtig*, meaning "pregnant." This feminine image is obviously more applicable to Nietzsche himself than to the aggressive machismo of Wagner (however much the latter may have prided himself on his psychical androgyny).

41. Relevant to this idea is Freud's discussion of the erotic associations of the "drive to know" *(Wisstrieb),* or the "drive to explore" *(Forschertrieb),* in *Three Essays on the Theory of Sexuality,* where he writes: "Its activity corresponds on the one hand to a sublimated manner of obtaining mastery, while on the other hand it makes use of the energy of scopophilia. Its relations to sexual life, however, are of particular importance." (essay 2, sect. 5). In *Dawn of Morning* Nietzsche refers to the drive for knowledge as "the new passion" and likens us moderns to "unhappy lovers" in this respect, since the uncontrolled drive to know may lead to destruction (*DM* 429). It is in this context that he first mentions the kinship of "love and death" that appears in the next quotation from *Zarathustra.*

42. *Symposium* 206b; *tokos en toi kaloi.* Though the verb from which *tokos* comes, *tiktō,* means "to engender" and is used equally of men and women, the noun

pertains primarily to women and means "childbirth." (It also means "offspring" when used of men or animals, and, by extension, the "interest" generated by capital in finance.) Note that this important speech of Socrates' is primarily indirect reporting of the hieratic instruction of the mysterious Diotima, herald of the eternal feminine. One imagines his coming away from that encounter pregnant with more than a few good ideas.

43. *Zarathustra* 2.15. The indispensability of love in its solar aspect is celebrated in *Hyperion:* "Man is a sun, all-seeing, all-illuminating, when he loves; and when love is lacking, he is a dark house in which only a smoking lantern burns" (*Hyp.* 1.2.18).

44. *Symposium* 206d–e; to be discussed in the next section.

45. See the sections "The Ellipsis of the Sun" and "The Flowers of Rhetoric" in Derrida's "White Mythology," in *Margins of Philosophy,* trans. Alan Bass (Chicago, 1982).

46. *Timaeus* 45b–46c. As with the overflowing of "the effluence of beauty" through the eyes in the *Phaedrus,* this theory of vision appears crude when taken literally, but is rich when regarded in the context of psychological *projection.*

47. In the *Phaedo* Socrates speaks of the soul's "grasping *[haptetai]* the truth," "reaching out for *[haptomenē oregētai]* the reality" (65b–c), and of the philosopher's using "pure reason" to "try to search out *[epicheiroi thēreuein]* the essence of things" (66a)—the literal meaning of *epicheireō* ("to try, attempt") being "put one's hand *[cheir]* to," and *thēra* meaning "hunt" (65b–66a). Amidst all the talk about "beholding with the eye of the soul" in the *Phaedo,* there is a great deal of touching and grasping with the hands too. In the *Symposium,* as the lover at the end of his ascent begins to discern absolute Beauty, he is "almost able to lay hold of the final secret," and, when he succeeds, to "contact" *(ephaptomenoi)* truth (211b, 212a). There is also talk of "laying hold of truth" in the *Timaeus* (90c).

48. *Republic* 490 a–b. The sexual connotations of the word for "grasping" the essential nature of things, *haptomai,* are made clear at *Laws* 840c, where the term means "to have intercourse with" a woman. The *gennēsas,* which most translators render "having begotten" means just as much "having given birth to"—a more fitting reading if, with the *Theaetetus* and *Symposium* in mind, we understand that the lover's *psuchē,* which is feminine, is the bearer. This reading suggests itself especially since the word for labor pains, *ōdis* (as well as the related verb, *ōdinō,* which occurs often in Plato), though it is also used metaphorically to refer to travail and anguish, is used literally only of women.

49. An excellent discussion of this and related themes is Gregory Vlastos, "The Individual as an Object of Love in Plato," in his *Platonic Studies* (Princeton, 1973).

50. *Republic* 495c. Compare the converse image, later in the text, where imitation *(mimēsis),* "an ordinary thing having intercourse with what is ordinary," is said to "produce ordinary offspring" (603b).

51. *Republic* 496a. For Socrates there will no perfection in city, regime, or individual unless, among other things, "a true erotic passion for philosophy flows from some divine inspiration into the sons of those who hold power or the office of king, or into the fathers themselves" (*Rep.* 499b–c).

52. The cloud pregnant with lightning had been accumulating since the pro-

logue, where Zarathustra referred to himself as "a herald of the lightning [of the *Übermensch*] and a heavy drop from the cloud" (*Z*, P4). The heaviness *(Schwere)* of the cloud—dark, heavy clouds lour often over the landscape of this text—betokens its being pregnant *(schwanger)* with rain, which fertilizes the earth from which the *Übermensch* may grow. (The original meaning of schwanger was "heavy with child," the word deriving from *schwer,* meaning "heavy.")

53. *Symposium* 206c–e. The use here of the verb *kuō,* "to conceive" or "be pregnant," must be somewhat metaphorical if we are to attach any sense to the talk of men's being pregnant "in body" as well as in soul; nevertheless, the weight of the imagery is predominantly feminine, even though it becomes clear that Diotima is speaking primarily of men. Presumably we are to think of a situation such as the one described in the *Timaeus* (86c) where the seed-marrow begins to overflow—or like Zarathustra's feeling "overfull with [his] wisdom, like a bee who has gathered too much honey." The verb *pelazō* ("approach") also means "to approach [a woman] in marriage"; and *spargaō* ("teeming ripe") means "to be ripe, swell, be full of milk." "The beautiful" *(to kalon)* refers at this point to beauty embodied and en-souled in a particular person; but whenever Diotima speaks of "the beautiful," from her first definition of *erōs* as bringing forth on it, she is always also referring to absolute beauty as the ultimate goal.

54. *Theaetetus* 148e–149a. Nietzsche, too, appreciates the maieutic benefits of dialogue: "One person seeks a midwife for his thoughts, while another seeks some-one he can help: in this way a good conversation comes about" (*BGE* 136).

55. An elegant treatment of the implications of these differences is Myles Burn-yeat, "Socratic Midwifery, Platonic Inspiration," *Bulletin of the Institute for Classi-cal Studies* 24 (1977):7–16.

56. *Theaetetus* 150c–d. The "god" here refers primarily to Artemis as patroness of midwives, although the masculine gender of the noun may also connote her younger brother, Apollo, who is Socrates's customary tutelary deity (see note 19 in Burnyeat's "Socratic Midwifery"). The word for discovery, *heurēma,* can also mean "foundling child."

57. *Theaetetus* 150d. Socrates later asks Theodorus not to think of him as "a sack of speeches," insisting that in dialogue with another "not one of the speeches comes out of me but always from whoever is conversing with me" (*Theae.* 161b).

58. *Zarathustra* 2. 2. See also *Beyond Good and Evil* 248, where Nietzsche talks about the two types of genius, the one who begets and the one who gives birth, and about the interaction between the two—both as individuals and races.

59. In a letter to Malwida von Meysenbug on the first day of 1883, Nietzsche hopes that he will be able to offer her "a fruit from [his] garden" that will be to her taste; he uses the same image in a letter accompanying a copy of the first part of the book sent to Gottfried Keller four months later (1 May 1883). Nietzsche had first intimated his awareness of being pregnant with *Zarathustra* in a letter to Hans von Bülow at the beginning of December 1882, where he writes of thinking "something new": "It seems to me that the condition of *pregnancy* is the only thing that keeps tying us back to life." After the "birth" of the first part, he frequently refers to the work as his "son": see the letters to Köselitz and Elisabeth (27 April 1883), Marie Baumgartner (28 May), Overbeck (9 July), Ida Overbeck (mid-July), Heinrich von

Stein (22 May 1884), Malwida von Meysenbug (early June), and Overbeck again (12 July). In another letter to Köselitz, Nietzsche writes of the sudden "conception of the second part of *Zarathustra*—and after the conception the birth: all with the greatest vehemence" (13 July 1883). Gary Shapiro offers a brief discussion of Nietzsche's pregnancies in the third chapter of *Alcyone*.

60. Socrates' relentless insistence that his students strive for self-knowledge, find their own way, and thus give birth to conceptions of their own prefigures Zarathustra's repeated emphasis to his "brothers" that they themselves discover "the way to [themselves]":"'That is *my* way now: where is yours?' thus I answered those who asked me about 'the way.' *The* way—there is no such thing!" (*Z* 3.11 §2).

61. *Theaetetus* 149c. The word Socrates uses for "grasp" here, *labein,* is also used of a woman's "conceiving."

62. *Theaetetus* 150a. While the primary meaning of the word *drama* is "action," there is a suggestive play on words here when Socrates speaks of *tou emou dramatos.*

63. The noun *Tracht,* from *tragen,* "to carry," means "load" and is used to refer to the gathering of honey by bees as well as to the carrying of the "fruit of the body" *(Leibesfrucht)* by a pregnant woman.

64. In assuming full parental responsibility, Nietzsche follows Montaigne, who writes: "What we engender by the soul, the children of our mind, of our heart and our ability, . . . are more our own. We are father and mother both in this generation" *(Essays,* 2:8, 291).

65. Burnyeat, "Socratic Midwifery," 13. Burnyeat refers in this context to Marion Milner's excellent study, *On not being able to paint* (London, 1957). There have been several treatments of the theme in the subsequent psychoanalytical literature; but the most fully elaborated studies are by Jung, in his work on the *hieros gamos* and the "syzygy" between animus and anima, the masculine and feminine aspects of the psyche. (See also "The Anima in the Syzygy" in Hillman's *Anima,* 167–83.) It is probable that some of Jung's ideas on this topic were in fact influenced by his repeated readings of and giving seminars on Nietzsche's *Zarathustra.*

66. Stanley Corngold has pointed out that Nietzsche's idea of the soul's desire for itself, its "blessed selfishness" *(selige Selbstsucht; Z* 3.10), is a playful allusion to the title of a lyric in Goethe's *Westöstlicher Divan,* "Selige Sehnsucht" (Blessed longing), in which the lover experiences a kind of death through orgasm, and then "becomes himself through the other, his lover, his candleflame and his grave." Corngold adds the following comment: "Nietzsche's emulation of this poem is remarkable in substituting for the medium of this resurrection not another human being but another mode of self" ("The Question of the Self in Nietzsche during the Axial Period [1882–1888]," in Daniel T. O'Hara, ed., *Why Nietzsche Now?* [Bloomington, 1985], 55–98, 73).

VII. *Emergence of Imagining Drives*

1. See Nietzsche's letter to his family of 25 September 1859. He expresses his enthusiasm for Sterne (and also for Diderot) in an aphorism entitled "The most liberated writer" (*AOM* 113). Ian Watt, in the introduction to his edition, *The Life and Opinions of Tristram Shandy, Gentleman* (Boston, 1965), says the following

about "the strong dramatic element" in Sterne's technique: "Sterne's basic role as author is largely conceived as that of an expert dramatic monologuist specializing in multiple impersonation. It was characteristic of Sterne to praise the Père Clement, a famous Parisian preacher, in these terms: 'His pulpit . . . is a stage, and the variety of his tones would make you imagine there were no less than five or six actors on it together'" (p. xxviii).

2. "Dostoevsky, like Goethe's Prometheus, creates not voiceless slaves (as does Zeus), but *free* people, capable of standing *alongside* their creator, capable of not agreeing with him and even of rebelling against him" (Mikhail Bakhtin, *Problems of Dostoevsky's Poetics,* ed. and trans. Caryl Emerson [Minneapolis, 1984], 6) My thanks to Stuart Hampshire for pointing out the importance of polyphony in Stendhal (private communication).

3. Most scholars agree that the classic study, first published in 1894, is that by Nietzsche's friend Erwin Rohde: *Psyche: The Cult of Souls and Belief in Immortality among the Greeks,* trans. W. B. Hillis (London, 1925). For a good discussion of and references to the relevant anthropological studies, see Jan Bremmer, *The Early Greek Concept of the Soul* (Princeton, 1983), which concludes that the Greeks understood the soul as multiple through the end of the archaic age.

4. See Onians, *The Origins of European Thought,* 93–96.

5. Joachim Böhme, *Die Seele und das Ich im Homerischen Epos (Leipzig and Berlin, 1929).*

6. Deliberations in Homer are often depicted as conversations between a man and his *thumos:* "And troubled, he spoke then to his own great-hearted *thumos*" is a common Homeric formula. One is reminded of Zarathustra's frequent conversations with such interlocutors as his heart, his soul, his wisdom, and his life.

7. Norman Austin, *Archery at the Dark of the Moon: Poetic Problems in Homer's Odyssey* (Berkeley and London, 1975), 107.

8. See, in addition to Böhme: Onians, *The Origins of European Thought;* E. R. Dodds, *The Greeks and the Irrational;* Bruno Snell, *The Discovery of the Mind,* trans. T. G. Rosenmeyer (Cambridge, Mass., 1953); and Hermann Fränkel, *Dichtung und Philosophie des frühen Griechentums* (Munich, 1962). A more recent study, David B. Claus, *Toward the Soul: An Inquiry into the Meaning of* psuchē *before Plato* (New Haven and London, 1981), questions "the widespread interpretation of human life in Homer as a field, so to speak, on which a variety of physical and mental organs compete with one another" (p. 7). Claus's philological study is rigorous and thorough, and points up the questionable assumption made by much of the literature that the meanings of words always evolve from the concrete to the abstract. Nevertheless, his conclusions—which take many uses of Homeric psychological vocabulary to be "personifications" of "thoughts" or "life-energies"—do not seem to be incompatible with what he calls "the 'organic' model" proposed by his predecessors. His main source of discomfort with the "organic" model is that it "implies a largely disunified conception of personality" (p. 14), which would not necessarily, in the light of the present study, be a failing—unless there were no sense of the possibility of organizing the disunity. The study by Norman Austin, which suggests a "social" organization to the Homeric psyche, is not included in Claus's bibliography.

A work that appeared too late to be given the recognition it deserves here is Bernard Williams, *Shame and Necessity* (Berkeley and Oxford, 1993), which the author says has "relations [with Nietzsche] that are very close and necessarily ambiguous" (p. 9). In a chapter entitled "Centres of Agency" Williams adduces many fine arguments against the position pioneered by Bruno Snell, showing that Homeric agents are not as totally different from modern ones are Snell would have us believe. But since Williams cites without demurral the part of Austin's book mentioned above, and goes on to discuss what he calls "the internalized other" in ancient Greek moral psychology, his position may not be incompatible with the one sketched here.

9. Austin, *Archery at the Dark of the Moon,* 111.

10. Aristotle, *De Anima* 414b. In dialogues in which Plato seems to lean toward the idea of a unitary soul ("uniform and indissoluble," as at *Phaedo* 80b), it is as if the whole soul were identified with the highest, immortal part of the soul under the tripartite schema.

11. Plato, *Republic* 444b. The roots of the term *polupragmosunē* would have it mean "doing many things"—which relates to the theme of multiple talents discussed earlier. It is interesting that during his first serious confrontation with the problem of psychical multiplicity in his own person, Nietzsche uses the Greek word twice in letters to his friends (letters of 16 January 1869, to Rohde, and 11 April 1869, to Gersdorff). Remember the passage from "On Moods": "Moods come from internal struggles. . . . Here a civil war between two enemy camps, there an oppression of the people by a particular class, a small minority."

12. On Camillo's memory theater and Giordano Bruno's art of memory, see Frances Yates, *The Art of Memory,* chapters 6–14.

13. See Hillman, *Re-Visioning Psychology,* 193–205; also the first chapter of this book, entitled "Personifying or Imagining Things," which develops the idea of personifying in contradistinction to the notions of animism and anthropomorphism.

14. In *Beyond Good and Evil* Nietzsche praises above all the *tempo* of Machiavelli, "who in his *Principe* lets us breathe the dry, fine air of Florence and cannot help presenting the most serious matters in a boisterous *allegrissimo*" (*BGE* 28).

15. Machiavelli, letter to Francesco Vettori, 10 December 1513; reproduced in Machiavelli, *The Prince,* ed. Quentin Skinner and Russell Price (Cambridge, 1988), 93. See also Hillman's commentary on this letter in *Re-Visioning Psychology,* 199. Part of this same passage is quoted with nostalgia by Allan Bloom in the introduction to another text that laments—though from a somewhat different perspective from that of depth psychology—the impoverishment of the modern soul (*The Closing of the American Mind* [New York, 1987], 35).

16. The best history is the monumental study by Henri Ellenberger, *The Discovery of the Unconscious: The History and Evolution of Dynamic Psychiatry* (New York, 1970).

17. The term "daemon" is a translation of the Greek *daimōn,* which referred to a spirit or a demigod that was morally neutral, as it were. (Think of the *daimonion* of Socrates, or of *Erōs* as a "great *daimōn*" in the *Symposium.*) It was only with the advent of Christian monotheism, and the concomitant belief in a unitary soul, that the *daimōnes* were demonized into "demons."

18. The pioneer in the field is the German clinician Johann Christian Reil, re-

garded by many as the father of rational psychotherapy, whose *Rhapsodien über die Anwendung der psychischen Cur-Methoden auf Geisteszerrüttungen* appeared in 1803. Another path-breaking work is Wilhelm Griesinger, *Pathologie und Therapie der psychischen Krankheiten* (1845). The term "polypsychism" appears to have been coined by the French magnetist J. P. Durand (de Gros), in his *Polyzoïsme* (1868), whose work was developed philosophically by Edmond Colsenet in his *Études sur la vie inconsciente* (1880).

19. Schopenhauer, "Essay on Spirit Seeing and Everything Connected Therewith," *Parerga and Paralipomena,* vol. 1. See also the numerous references to magnetism and somnambulism in *The World as Will and Representation,* as well as Ellenberger, *The Discovery of the Unconscious,* 81.

20. "Aus meinem Leben"; Schlechta, 3:32.

21. C. G. Jung, "On the Psychology of so-called Occult Phenomena" (1902) and "Cryptomnesia" (1905) in *Collected Works,* 1:82–84 and 101–5. Jung characterizes Nietzsche's apparent "plagiarism" as a case of "cryptomnesia," suggesting that he had read the description of the descent to the underworld in the *Blätter aus Prevorst* in his early teens, and that the unconscious memory of the passage had been caught up in the outpouring of inspiration (almost thirty years later) that constituted *Thus Spoke Zarathustra.* The heading of the page on which the original passage appears is: "An Extract of Awe-Inspiring Import from the Log of the Ship *Sphinx* in the Year 1686, in the Mediterranean."

22. *Assorted Opinions and Maxims* 26; *KSA* 12:8[4] = *WP* 376. The posthumous note amplifies a passage in *Toward the Genealogy of Morals* (2.16); both will be discussed in the next chapter.

23. The term seems to have been more commonly used in compounds, such as *Triebfeder* (mainspring, driving force, motive) and *Kunsttrieb* (the constructive instinct of animals).

24. Georg Christoph Lichtenberg, *Gedankenbücher,* ed. Franz Mautner (Heidelberg, 1967), 27; *Aphorisms,* trans. R. J. Hollingdale (London and New York, 1990), 34.

25. Herder, *Vom Erkennen und Empfinden der menschlichen Seele,* 585 (1775).

26. Herder, *Adrastea* (1801); cited in Engell, *The Creative Imagination,* 219.

27. J. N. Tetens, *Philosophische Versuche über die menschliche Natur und ihre Entwicklung* (Philosophical essays on human nature and its development) (Leipzig, 1776–77), vol. 1, "Erster Versuch: Über die Natur der Vorstellungen." Engell notes that Tetens was influenced in this context by the work of the Scottish philosopher Alexander Gerard, whose *Essay on Genius* was being well received in Germany at the time, and that Tetens's *Dichtungsvermögen* corresponds to Coleridge's "secondary imagination," for which it was an important source (*The Creative Imagination,* 121–22).

28. Immanuel Kant, *Critique of Pure Reason,* A78/B103 (emphasis added).

29. Two sophisticated discussions of the transcendental imagination in Kant's first *Critique* are Martin Heidegger, *Kant and the Problem of Metaphysics,* §§26–33, and John Sallis, *Spacings—of Reason and Imagination in Texts of Kant, Fichte, Hegel* (Chicago, 1987), 73–81. Sallis shows how crucial is the role of imagination in the thought of Kant and German Idealism—as well as the extent to which imagi-

nation is occluded by reason in the primary texts. He alludes to Nietzsche only in the exergue to the book; the present work is intended to show that in Nietzsche the imagination continues to be central, though the theme is less occluded—if one knows where to look.

30. For a good overview of these developments, see Engell, *The Creative Imagination,* chapters 16 and 20.

31. Kant, *Die Religion innerhalb der Grenzen der blossen Vernunft,* in *Immanuel Kants Werke,* ed. Ernst Cassirer (Berlin, 1923), 6:165; *Religion within the Limits of Reason Alone,* trans. Theodore M. Greene and Hoyt H. Hudson (La Salle, 1934), 22. The translation will be modified somewhat, rendering *Trieb* as "drive" rather than "impulse," for example.

32. Kant, *Religion,* 6:199–200; 52. As the translators note, the quotation is inaccurate; the original passage reads: "For we wrestle not against flesh and blood, but against principalities, against powers, against the rulers of the darkness of this world, against spiritual wickedness in high places" (Ephesians 6:12).

33. M. H. Abrams, *Natural Supernaturalism: Tradition and Revolution in Romantic Literature* (New York, 1971), 357. The section entitled "The Politics of Vision: Mastery, Servitude, and Freedom" in chapter 6 of this book provides an excellent discussion of the metaphors of political power in Romantic treatments of the soul and its relations to the natural world.

34. J. G. Fichte, *Grundlage der gesammten Wissenschaftslehre; The Science of Knowledge,* ed. and trans. Peter Heath and John Lachs (New York, 1970). The English translation of the title overemphasizes the epistemological aspect of Fichte's transcendental idealism: Fichte understands philosophy as science, as *Wissenschaft,* and the *Wissenschaftslehre* as the "teaching on science," a philosophy as the foundational science of sciences. References to this text will modify the translation somewhat, rendering *das Ich,* for instance, as "the I" rather than "the self." Nietzsche clearly had some acquaintance with Fichte's work—if primarily through his reading of Schopenhauer. Though Fichte was a distinguished alumnus of Schulpforta, and the best known philosopher produced by that school, Nietzsche never discusses any of his ideas, and the few mentions he makes of him are disparaging. For a good account of the relationship, see Oswaldo Market, "Fichte und Nietzsche," *Perspectiven der Philosophie* 7 (1981):119–31.

35. Fichte, *Grundlage der gesammten Wissenschaftslehre,* in *Fichtes Werke,* ed. I. H. Fichte (Berlin, 1971), 1:272; see also 1:227–28. Subsequent references will be to the volume and page number of this (the standard) edition, the pagination of which is given in the margins of *The Science of Knowledge.*

36. Fichte, "Lectures concerning the Scholar's Vocation": English translation in *Fichte: Early Philosophical Writings,* trans. and ed. Daniel Breazeale (Ithaca and London, 1988), 151. This translation also furnishes the pagination of the standard edition in the margins (though the passage just quoted is taken from a note to the Danish edition). Compare also a later statement in the *Wissenschaftslehre:* "Nothing that is in the I is there without a drive" (1:326).

37. Fichte, 2:192–93; *The Vocation of Man,* trans. Roderick Chisholm (Indianapolis, 1956), 28.

38. Fichte, 8:342; "On Stimulating and Increasing the Pure Interest in Truth," *Early Philosophical Writings,* 223.

39. A few years later, in the *System der Sittenlehre* (System of the doctrine of morals) of 1798, Fichte elaborates his philosophy of the drives into a system of characteristic complexity—but along fairly conventional (Platonic-Kantian) lines. In his continuing concern with freedom as a condition for moral action, he distinguishes between the realm of nature, in which I am subject to drive-produced *feeling* over which I have no control, and the realm of freedom, in which I engage in *thinking* and *acting* (4:107–8). Again it is the activity of *reflection* that gives us consciousness and thus the ability to exert control over the lower drives (4:131, 179).

40. *Trieb nach realer Tätigkeit* (1:289), *Reflexionstrieb* (1:291), *Trieb des Bestimmens* (1:307), *Trieb nach Wechsel überhaupt,* and *Trieb nach Realität* (1:320). Another drive posited by Fichte during this period (in the "Lectures concerning the Scholar's Vocation") is the "social drive," which he calls "fundamental" and which consists of the "drive to communicate" and the "drive to receive" (6:306, 315).

41. Fichte, 1:326. The drive to harmony is characterized more fully in the second of the "Lectures" as "the drive . . . toward the harmony of all external things with [the I's] own necessary concepts of them. . . . All of the concepts found within the I should have an expression or counterpart in the not-I. This is the specific character of the human drive" (6:304).

42. For a fine discussion of Fichte's ideas on the unification of the self in the Jena *Wissenschaftslehre,* see Daniel Breazeale, "Philosophy and the Divided Self: On the Existential and Scientific Tasks of the Jena *Wissenschaftslehre,*" *Fichte-Studien* (forthcoming).

43. Fichte, *Grundlage der gesammten Wissenschaftslehre,* 1:208. Compare also: "Imagination is a faculty that hovers *[schwebt]* in the middle between determination *[Bestimmung]* and nondetermination, between finite and infinite. . . . This hovering is characteristic of imagination in its product; in its hovering, so to speak, and through it the imagination produces its product" (1:217).

44. Hölderlin, cited in Abrams, *Natural Supernaturalism,* 361. Abrams cites a similar passage, from the preface to the 1795 version of *Hyperion,* in which Hölderlin bemoans the fact that "we have fallen out with nature, and what was once one . . . is now in conflict with itself, and each side alternates between mastery and servitude."

45. F. A. Lange, *The History of Materialism,* trans. E. C. Thomas (New York and London, 1925), book 3, section 3, chapter 3, "Scientific Psychology."

46. Johann Friedrich Herbart, *Lehrbuch zur Psychologie* (1816), in *Sämtliche Werke* (Aalen, 1964; reprint of the Langensalza edition of 1891), 4:374, 404 (hereafter referred to simply by the page number of this fourth volume).

47. Herbart, 422. Compare this note of Nietzsche's from 1888: "The misunderstanding of passion and *reason [Vernunft],* as if the latter were something in itself and not rather a relationship among various passions and desires; and as if every passion did not have its quantum of reason" *KSA* 13:11[310] = *WP* 387.

48. "*Determination* of the Human Being" renders "*Die* Bestimmung *des Menschen."* *Bestimmung* is a term that is notoriously difficult to translate—meaning

"fixing, regulation, identification, definition, destiny"—and in this context refers to the way one "determines" or "understands" one's existence, especially in the moral sphere. *Die Bestimmung des Menschen* is the title of one of Fichte's best known works *(The Vocation of Man).*

49. A good appraisal of Griesinger's importance in the history of psychiatry is Roland Kuhn, "Griesingers Auffassung der psychischen Krankheiten und seine Bedeutung für die weitere Entwicklung der Psychiatrie," *Bibliotheca psychiatrica et neurologica,* C (1957):41–67.

50. Wilhelm Griesinger, *Die Pathologie und Therapie der psychischen Krankheiten* (Amsterdam, 1964; reprint of the Stuttgart edition of 1867), §16; English translation: *Mental Pathology and Therapeutics,* trans. C. Lockhart Robinson and James Rutherford (New York and London, 1965: facsimile of the English edition of 1867). In view of the unreliability of the English translation, quotations from Griesinger will be translated from the German original and references given simply by section number.

51. Griesinger, §25; the author makes a reference here to Schopenhauer's book *On the Will in Nature.*

52. Griesinger, §19. This idea stems ultimately from Heraclitus, and is later brought to prominence again in Jung's notion of *enantiodromia,* the tendency for psychological extremes to transform into their opposites. *Les extrêmes se touchent.*

53. The existential psychiatrist Ludwig Binswanger later wrote of Griesinger that, with this idea of the intrapsychical "you," he "established the genuinely dialogical character of psychical conflict" more firmly than Freud (cited in Kuhn, "Griesingers Auffassung," 57).

54. C. A. Wunderlich, cited in Kuhn, "Griesingers Auffassung," note 39.

VIII. *Dominions of Drives and Persons*

1. An exception to the general rule of ignoring the Nietzsche's ideas about the drives is Pierre Klossowski: see, especially, the discussions of *(im)pulsions* and *forces pulsionelles* in the second chapter of his *Nietzsche et le cercle vicieux* (Paris, 1978). Richard Schacht does devote a section, in his comprehensive treatment in *Nietzsche* (London and Boston, 1983), to "the theory of affects" (pp. 317–26), but he fails to follow through on the radically *multiplistic* implications of this "theory" (see pp. 367–71, where the unity of what is to control the affects is not questioned). Even the psychologically informed reading by Karl Jaspers, in his *Nietzsche: Einführung in das Verständnis seiner Philosophierens* (Berlin and Leipzig, 1936), offers only a brief treatment of the drives. For a recent account that takes the idea seriously, see John Richardson, *Nietzsche: A Systematic View* (forthcoming), chapter 1.

2. Schlechta, 3:114. Actually there are two earlier mentions of a singular drive: in "Mein Lebenslauf (I)" (1861), Nietzsche writes of "the drive for the good that is hereditary in the human being" [!] (S 3:89); and in the "Fatum und Geschichte" (1862), he speaks of "the eternal drive to produce *[Productionstrieb]*" (*HKA,* 2:57).

3. *KSA* 7:1[1].

4. *KSA* 7:1[49]. This note prefigures aphorism 106 of *Beyond Good and Evil:* "In music the passions are able to enjoy themselves."

5. *KSA* 7:3[60], 3[64], 7[121], 16[13]; 1:521.

6. *KSA* 1:560; 7:7[122].

7. *KSA* 7:12[1]; 1871.

8. Already in the early 1860s, for example, Baudelaire had written in the prose poem "Les Foules": "The poet enjoys this incomparable privilege, that he can at will be himself and another. Like those wandering souls in search of a body, he enters, whenever he chooses, into everyone's character."

9. *KSA* 7:19[131]; *PT* 87 (1872–73).

10. *Schopenhauer as Educator* 6. The "impure metal" is an allusion to the myth of the metals in book three of the *Republic,* in which each class of the *polis* is imagined to have been forged from one particular metal. Much of this section of *SE* is drawn from notes from the previous year (see, especially, *KSA* 7:29[13]).

11. This serves as a reminder that the phenomenon of multiplicity, like several of Nietzsche's central ideas, cannot be taken as simply "a good thing": it can issue, depending on the circumstances and on how it is handled, more easily in degeneracy than in fulfillment.

12. *Richard Wagner in Bayreuth* 3. John Sallis discusses one of the later *Kreuzungen* in this text in *Crossings,* 141–42.

13. "*Dämonische* Übertragbarkeit." Hollingdale translates this as "demonic *transmissibility,*" but "infectiousness" catches the allusion to Plato's description of the mimetic artist, which Nietzsche mentions a few pages later. It also portends the later question (already latent in the ambivalent ambiguities of the praise in *Wagner in Bayreuth*) in the preface to *The Case of Wagner* (§5): "Is Wagner a human being at all? Is he not rather a sickness? He makes sick everything he touches—*he has made music sick.*"

14. *Human, All Too Human* 260. Emerson expresses a strikingly similar idea in his *Journals:* "Talent sucks the substance of the man . . . the accumulation of one point has drained the trunk. Blessed are those who have no talent!" (11:226).

15. Plato, *Theaetetus* 191a. One is reminded of "the great seasickness" of which Zarathustra warns, when, after the death of God has annihilated all firm ground to stand on, one leaves the land and embarks upon the sea of the unknown (*Z* 3.12 §28).

16. *Assorted Opinions and Maxims* 26. In speaking here of an "*Uhrwerk [des] personenbildenden, personendichtenden Triebes,*" Nietzsche is stressing the temporal relentlessness of the operation of the person-creating drive. Jungian psychology takes the pervasiveness of the personal element very seriously; see chapter 1 of Hillman's *Re-Visioning Psychology,* and especially the section entitled "The Soul of Words."

17. It is not that it "gets personal" at academic colloquia and seminars or "becomes political" in university departments: intrapersonal politics are there from the beginning; intellectual disagreement is from the ground up an affair involving personalities—and many more than are dreamed of in most philosophies.

18. In *Dawn of Morning* 507, Nietzsche inveighs against "the tyranny of the true," advocating the necessity of parties for the truth to *struggle* against, and of untruth for us to find occasional recreation in—without which both the truth and we ourselves would become "boring, and lacking in force and taste."

19. *The Wanderer and His Shadow* 171. Compare *AOM* 19, where Nietzsche

denies that the thinker can provide "*the* picture of life," on the grounds that even the greatest thinker can do no more than produce pictures and images *from one* life—namely, his own.

20. Letter from Paul Rée, 10 May 1878; emphasis added.

21. Letter to Elisabeth, 23 June 1879. Similar demands for secrecy are made to Elisabeth again the next day, and to Köselitz the day after that.

22. Letter to Franziska Nietzsche, beginning of July 1879.

23. *KSA* 9:7[105].

24. Letter to Gersdorff, end of June 1883.

25. *KSA* 9:6[274]; 1880.

26. Some passages concerning the drives in the second volume of *Human, All Too Human* are significant insofar as they extend the range of the idea away from the instinctual end of the spectrum: there is "the drive for clarity and purity of thought, for moderation and restraint of feeling" (*AOM* 196), as well as drives for freedom (*AOM* 211) and for domination, victory, and eminence (*WS* 31, 226).

27. It is interesting that in Jungian psychology one is encouraged to focus on moods, in the expectation that in or behind the mood there will be an image—and often the image of a person. Nietzschean psychology would say that in or behind that person would be a drive.

28. *Dawn of Morning* 105. An unpublished note from the period amplifies this theme: "What *others* teach us, want from us, have us fear or pursue, is the original material of our spirit: alien judgments about things. And those are what gives us our *image of our selves*. . . . Our own judgment is only a *propagation* of combined alien judgments! Our own drives appear to us through the interpretations of others" (*KSA* 9:6[70]; 1880).

29. New paragraphs, numbered in brackets, have been inserted in the translation of the following long passage for the sake of clarity.

30. A later aphorism that understands the criminal as suffering from "the burden of *a tyrannical drive*" mentions three ways of solving the problem: "extirpation, transformation, or sublimation *[Sublimirung]* of the drive" (*DM* 202).

31. *Republic* 606d; compare *Rep.* 550a, where the father of the timocratic type of person is said to "water the calculating part of his soul and cause it to grow." For Nietzsche, the imposition of a strict regime on powerful drives is something practiced at the level of the culture as well as the individual: "Wherever *powerful drives* and habits rule, lawgivers are concerned to insert intercalary days on which such drives are put in chains and learn to hunger again. . . . Entire generations and ages appear as such interpolated times of constraint and fasting, during which a drive learns to stoop and submit, but also to *purify* and sharpen itself" (*BGE* 189).

32. *Phaedo* 68e–69a. Compare this proposition of Spinoza's (which may well have influenced Nietzsche): "An emotion can only be controlled or destroyed by another emotion contrary thereto, and with more power for controlling emotion" (*Ethics,* part 4, prop. 7).

33. *Republic* 572e. A similar, physiological strategy with respect to the problem of "the very great power of the so-called 'disorderly Aphrodite'" is offered at *Laws* 841a: "The strength of the pleasures should, as much as possible, be deprived of

gymnastic exercise by using other exercises to turn its flow and growth elsewhere in the body."

34. *KSA* 9:6[70]; 1880 (first emphasis added). Another part of this note echoes the theme of thoughts as persons and adumbrates the idea of a "you" and an "it" and an entire society within the psyche: "Instinctively we make the *predominant* quantity momentarily into the *whole* ego and place all weaker drives perspectively *farther* away and make of them an *entire you* or 'it.' We treat ourselves as a plurality and carry into these 'social relations' all the social customs that we practice with respect to people, animals, places, and things. We conceal ourselves, make ourselves anxious, form groups and parties, conduct legal trials, attack, torture, and glorify ourselves."

35. See the discussion of this aphorism in "Suns and Vital Fires," chapter 4, above.

36. Nietzsche will later characterize Socrates' position in similar terms: "The drives want to play the tyrant; one must devise a *countertyrant* who is stronger" (*TI* 2.9).

37. Remember Plato's vivid description at the beginning of book 9 of the *Republic* of how, when the "tame" part of the soul slumbers, the "wild and beastly part" awakens and seeks to "satisfy its dispositions" in dreams.

38. That great friend and reader of Plato, Stanley Rosen, is less than generous in his treatment of the topic of *die dichtende Vernunft* in this passage: see his "Poetic Reason in Nietzsche," in *The Ancients and the Moderns: Rethinking Modernity* (New Haven and London, 1989), 209–34. He appears not to appreciate (in his discussion on pp. 228–29) that it is the drives themselves that comprise this poetic reason and imaginatively interpret, as will to power, the text of nerve stimuli.

39. "On Truth and Lie in the Extramoral Sense," *KSA* 1:879; *PT* 82.

40. "On Truth and Lie in the Extramoral Sense," *KSA* 1:883–88; *PT* 86–88.

41. It is not until later that Nietzsche comes to connect explicitly drives and perspectives: see, for example, *KSA* 11:26[119] = *WP* 259, 1884; *KSA* 12:7[60] = *WP* 481, 1886/87. The point will be elaborated in the next section.

42. See, for example, *JS* 111 and *BGE* 192; the latter aphorism will be discussed briefly in the next section of this chapter.

43. Kant, *Critique of Pure Reason,* B xiii.

44. *KSA* 9:11[1]–[141], "Spring-Autumn 1881." All subsequent references in this section are to this volume and section (9:11) of the *Nachlass.*

45. There is a nice anticipation of modern phenomenology here, insofar as Nietzsche's example suggests a "bracketing" of experience, a "checking" of ontological positing that enables us to attend to the richness of the phenomena just as they are given. Nietzsche's point is that we are unable to see what we are presented with when in the presence of a tree because the experience is obscured in advance by the projection of a rough image representing the "label" or concept "tree."

46. The prototype for this aphorism is a note from 1880 that reads: "I see a tree and take it for a child. In a conversation I see the person's features quite clearly, but I imagine them in this sharpness" (*KSA* 9:6[402]).

Nietzsche's point here can be "experimentally" verified by people with poor vision: spend some time without corrective lenses, and you will find that after a while things become clearer—and especially the expressions on people's faces. It is obvious that when less (detail) is "given" as visual input, the contribution of phantasy projection becomes correspondingly greater. As someone once said about the psychedelic experience without eyeglasses: "If you're going to hallucinate, you might as well hallucinate *in focus.*"

47. This idea is a striking anticipation of Heidegger's notion of *Dasein* as "thrown projection," in which the understanding constantly opens up a world by the (prereflective, unconscious) projection of possibilities (*Being and Time,* §§29–32).

48. *KSA* 9:11[70]. The image of the festival appears in another passage from the same notebook: "To be redeemed from life and to become dead nature again can be experienced as a *festival*—by the one who wants to die. To love nature! Again to revere what is dead! The dead is not the opposite but rather the womb, the rule, with more sense than the exception" (11[125]).

49. This note also prefigures to some extent Heidegger's existential conception of death, as well as Rilke's (especially as they are presented in Heidegger's essay "What Are Poets For?").

50. This is an important aspect of what Nietzsche means by "philosophizing with a hammer," an image that is connected—through its associations with inscribing stone tablets and printing with type—with the idea of philosophical writing. He chose to reprint a section from *Zarathustra* (3.12, §29, "On Old and New Tablets") at the very end of *Twilight of the Idols* under the title "The Hammer Speaks," in which the following lines occur:

"For all creators are hard. And what bliss it must be for you, to impress your hand on millennia as on wax—

"Bliss, to write upon the will of millennia as on bronze—harder than bronze, more noble than bronze. Only the most noble is totally hard."

For a more detailed discussion of this theme, see Graham Parkes, "The Dance from Mouth to Hand: Speaking Zarathustra's Write Foot ForeWord."

51. *The Joyful Science* 54. Compare this passage from the previous year: "In outbreaks of passion and in the phantasizing of the dream and insanity, the human being rediscovers his own prehistory and that of humanity as a whole: *animality* with its wild grimaces. One's memory for once reaches sufficiently far back, while one's civilized state develops out of the forgetting of these primal experiences" (*DM* 312).

52. Freud, "On the History of the Psychoanalytic Movement," *SEF* 14:62.

53. There are only four occurrences of the term *Trieb* in *Zarathustra:* in 1.8, 1.22, 2.7, and 2.12 (fewer than in any other of his works).

54. *Beyond Good and Evil* 9, emphasis added. See also *BGE* 158: "To our strongest drive, the tyrant in us, not only our reason submits, but also our conscience." (The first note of this idea dates from 1882; see *KSA* 10:3[1] #176.) Nietzsche had referred earlier to philosophy as "the highest struggle *[Ringen]* for the tyrannical domination of the spirit" (*DM* 547).

55. An unpublished note from the period begins, "The will to power *interprets,*" and ends with the emphasized claim: "In truth *interpretation is itself a means of becoming master of something*" (*KSA* 12:2[148] = *WP* 643). An adjacent note, in

which Nietzsche pronounces his formula "Life is will to power" and characterizes moral evaluation as interpretation, ends with the important question and answer: "*Who interprets?* Our affects" (*KSA* 12:2[190]).

56. *Beyond Good and Evil* 23. A note from 1885 reads: "To grasp the 'person' as *deception:* actually *heredity* is a major objection, insofar as a multitude of formative forces from much earlier periods make for its survival: in truth they struggle within the person and are ruled and subdued—a will to power runs through persons, which has need of a *diminution* of perspectives, of 'egoism,' as *a temporary condition of existence*" (*KSA* 11:35[68]).

57. See, for example, *Human, All Too Human* 19. For a discussion of the ramifications of this idea in Nietzsche's philosophy as a whole, see Stack, *Nietzsche and Lange,* chapter 9: "A Force-Point World." Nietzsche will have first come across reference to Boscovich in this bleakly graphic passage from Emerson's essay "Experience": "Was it Boscovich who found out that bodies never come into contact? Well, souls never touch their objects. An unnavigable sea washes with silent waves between us and the things we aim at and converse with."

58. "One really ought to free oneself finally from the seduction of words!" (*BGE* 16). This idea, understood as "unconscious domination and guidance by similar grammatical functions" (*BGE* 20), anticipates Wittgenstein's frequent warnings against being "seduced by grammar."

59. Lichtenberg, *Aphorisms,* 176 (from notebook K, 1793–96).

60. *Beyond Good and Evil* 17; also aphorism 34. Freud claims to have borrowed the idea of *das Es* from the psychologist Georg Groddeck, though indirectly from Nietzsche. In a footnote in section 2 of *The Ego and the Id* he writes: "Groddeck himself no doubt followed the example of Nietzsche, who habitually used this grammatical term for whatever in our nature is impersonal and, so to speak, necessitated by nature."

61. *KSA* 11:38[1]; see also 26[92]. The image of putting the thought "on his feet" echoes Socrates' talk of coming through an inquiry "with the argument still on its feet" (*Rep.* 534c).

62. The note continues in a vein reminiscent of the "thought persons" of *AOM* 26: "The origin of the thought remains hidden . . . insofar as it is precisely *this one* that comes and not another, that he comes with just this degree of clarity and brightness, whether sure of himself and imperious, or weak and needing support, in any case always exciting and inquiring—for every thought has a stimulating effect on consciousness—all this is an expression of our overall condition in signs" (*KSA* 11:38[1]).

63. In a preliminary version of this aphorism Nietzsche writes: "In every act of willing a thought commands" (*KSA* 11:38[8]).

64. Nietzsche may well have been influenced in developing this notion of the body as "a social structure of many souls" by Montaigne: see the discussion of a relevant passage from "On the Power of the Imagination" at the beginning of the next chapter.

65. *Familien-Ähnlichkeit*—another anticipation of an important idea in Wittgenstein.

66. The Japanese language places so much emphasis on the predicate that one

of the distinctive features of modern Japanese philosophy is its development of a "logic of the predicate"—a prominent theme in the influential works of Nishida Kitarō of the 1920s and 1930s.

67. For a general discussion of some distinctive features of Japanese philosophy, see Graham Parkes, "Ways of Japanese Thinking," in Robert Solomon and Kathleen Higgins, eds., *From Africa to Zen: An Introduction to World Philosophy* (Savage, Md., 1992), 25–53.

68. For a discussion of this issue, see Graham Parkes, "From Nationalism to Nomadism: Wondering about the Languages of Philosophy," in Eliot Deutsch, ed., *Culture and Modernity: East and West* (Honolulu, 1991), 455–467.

69. Nietzsche apparently knew next to nothing about Japanese philosophy, though he was acquainted with early versions of the "no-self" *(anātman)* idea in Hinayana Buddhism; see Freny Mistry, *Nietzsche and Buddhism* (Berlin and New York, 1981), especially chapter 2, "The Analysis of Personality and Universe." For more on this topic, see Graham Parkes, "Nietzsche and East Asian Thinking."

70. *Beyond Good and Evil* 36. With its clarity of expression and richness in implications this is surely the *locus classicus* for what Nietzsche means by "will to power"—and yet it is often neglected by commentators in favor of the unpublished note that was placed as the last in the collection *The Will to Power* (*WP* 1067 = *KSA* 11:38[12]). The note comes from the summer of 1885, and so is clearly the prototype for *BGE* 36. While more poetic than the latter, the note fails to make clear the ground for Nietzsche's ultimate identification of "you" (readers) with will to power—namely that will to power manifests itself in *drives*. The brief dialogue that follows immediately after (*BGE* 37) forms an exquisite supplement to the major aphorism.

71. *KSA* 12:8[4] = *WP* 376; emphasis added. Five years later, in an essay from 1893 entitled "A Case of Hypnotic Healing," Freud would write of the "daemonic quality" attaching to hysteria as a result of the repression of unacceptable drives (*SEF* 1:126).

IX. *Archaic Plays and Psychical Regimes*

1. Most Anglophone Nietzsche scholars are agreed that Nietzsche studies in English took a definite turn for the better with the publication in 1950 of Walter Kaufmann's landmark study *Nietzsche: Philosopher, Psychologist, Antichrist* (Princeton, 1950). As well as dispelling some of the more pernicious myths surrounding Nietzsche's ideas, this work called much-needed attention to the importance of his psychology—even though this side of his thinking was to fall once again into neglect. The major shortcoming of Kaufmann's reading of the psychology is that it fails to appreciate the radicality of Nietzsche's revisioning of the soul as *multiple*. This is most evident in his treatment of Nietzsche's views on the traditional relationship between reason and the passions, which is worth examining briefly because it still enjoys widespread acceptance.

Kaufmann places appropriate emphasis on Nietzsche's admiration for the Greeks' success in "organizing the chaos" of their drives and impulses (p. 227). He is referring to a passage in *On the Use and Disadvantage of History for Life,* from which he cites only the phrase "organize the chaos"; but the rest of the passage in which that phrase occurs is worth quoting: "The Greeks gradually learned *to orga-nize the chaos,* by reflecting in accordance with the Delphic injunction upon them-selves, that is, upon their genuine needs and letting merely apparent needs die off" (*HL* 10). Nietzsche reformulates this as a general maxim, which once again attempts to resolve the problem of the one and the many—at least by reducing the many: "Every one of us must organize the chaos in him by reflecting on his genuine needs."

Kaufmann then, however, goes on to argue that, for Nietzsche, "Reason is the 'highest' manifestation of the will to power, in the distinct sense that through ratio-nality it can realize its object most fully" (p. 230). This sounds just like Plato and his view that reason is the highest manifestation of *erōs,* that it is "proper for the calculating part to rule, since it is wise and has forethought about all of the soul" (*Rep.* 441e). Kaufmann concludes that "the truly rational man need not go to war against his impulses. If his reason is strong enough, he will naturally control his passions. . . . instead of extirpating [his impulses] he masters and employs them" (p. 234). Again this sounds like Plato: the rational farmer keeping the many-headed beast in check. It would be strange if the thinker who once described his thought as "inverted Platonism" turned out to be as staunch an advocate of reason as the divine Plato. Kaufmann fails to question the identity of the agent of control by asking *who* exactly it is that "masters and employs" the impulses, or—which amounts to the same thing—by inquiring into the nature of the reason that is strong enough to do this mastering.

In a more recent discussion, Alexander Nehamas brings Plato and Nietzsche to-gether on the topic of the political metaphor, if only briefly: "[Nietzsche's] shocking and obscure breakdown of what we have assumed to be the essential unity of the human individual may be . . . one of [his] great contributions to our understanding of the self as well as to our own self-understanding. . . . The political metaphor for the self, which, despite Nietzsche's reputation, is at least more egalitarian than Plato's, can now set us . . . in the right direction for understanding the phrase [how one becomes what one is]" (*Nietzsche: Life as Literature,* 177). While Nehamas is right about the importance of the political metaphor for the self, it is doubtful whether in Nietzsche's hands it is "more egalitarian than Plato's": Nietzsche's insis-tence upon an "order of rank" seems quite Platonic. And though chapter 6 of this book, entitled "How One Becomes What One Is," contains a careful treatment of the issue of the multiple psyche and its organization, there is relatively little elabora-tion in political terms (pp. 182–83).

2. In recent studies in philosophy of mind and philosophical psychology the question of the multiplicity of the self tends to be raised only to be dropped without much consideration. In a discussion of Freud, Donald Davidson warily broaches the issue of a personal multiplicity: "In attempting to explain such phenomena [as wish-ful thinking, acting contrary to one's own best judgment, self-deception, etc.] Freud-ians have made the following claims: *First,* the mind contains a number of semi-independent structures . . . characterized by mental attributes like thoughts, desires, and memories. *Second,* parts of the mind are in important respects like people . . . in having beliefs, wants and other psychological traits" ("Paradoxes of Irrationality," in Richard Wollheim and James Hopkins, eds., *Philosophical Essays on Freud* [Cambridge, 1982], 290). Davidson does not, however, appear to find this idea

philosophically interesting or helpful, since he declines to pursue it further—except to remark, in evaluating the plausibility of considering various parts of the mind as independent agents, that "there does not seem to be anything that demands a metaphor" (p. 304).

In a closer engagement with Freud, Richard Rorty takes the idea more seriously: "Freud populated inner space . . . with analogues of persons—internally coherent clusters of belief and desire. . . . To take Freud's suggestion seriously is to wish to become acquainted with these unfamiliar persons . . . [and] initiates a task that can plausibly be described as a moral obligation. . . . By turning the Platonic parts of the soul into conversational partners for one another, Freud . . . let us see alternative narratives and vocabularies as instruments for change, rather than as candidates for a correct depiction of how things are in themselves" ("Freud and Moral Reflection," in Joseph H. Smith and William Kerrigan, eds., *Pragmatism's Freud* [Baltimore, 1986], 5–9.). Rorty goes on to praise Freud for undermining the Platonic opposition between reason and the passions as different "species" (human and animal); but the credit for this surely belongs to Nietzsche (if not to Herder).

While it is Freud's notion of the multiple psyche that has caught the attention of some contemporary philosophers, the idea that we consist of many "persons" has been developed in more radical depth by Jung (especially in his theory of the "feeling-toned complexes"). Some more recent writers in the tradition of depth psychology have developed the idea with greater philosophical sophistication: see, in addition to Hillman's *Re-Visioning Psychology,* Norman O. Brown, *Love's Body* (New York, 1966), and James Ogilvy, *Many Dimensional Man: Decentralizing Self, Society, and the Sacred* (New York, 1977). For an account of Jung's ideas on this topic, see Graham Parkes, "A Cast of Many: Nietzsche and Depth-Psychological Pluralism," *Man and World* 22, no. 4 (1989):453–70.

3. Montaigne, *Essays,* 3:2, 610–11. See also 2:12, 455: "Finally, there is no existence that is constant, either of our being or that of objects. And we, and our judgment, and all mortal things go on flowing and rolling unceasingly."

4. Montaigne, *Essays,* 3:2, 613. One is reminded here of Zarathustra's magnificently pointed question and exclamation, which convey the extremely strict character of Nietzsche's existential (im)moral code:

"Can you yourself give yourself your own evil and good and hang your will above yourself as a law? Can you be your own judge and avenger of your own law?

"Terrible it is to be alone with the judge and avenger of one's own law. Thus a star is thrown out into barren space and the icy breath of solitude" (Z 1.17).

It is deliberately perverse of Nietzsche/Zarathustra to use the word "law" in this context, since it is clear that the law one gives oneself—unlike the laws of a state, which apply universally—is to apply *only* to oneself, with no expectation that it should be applicable to any other.

5. While he wants to insist upon a more unified picture of the self than that presented here, Stanley Corngold recognizes the importance of "social metaphors for the self" in Nietzsche's psychology. From a rather different perspective he writes: "The Other is actively 'inside' the self before the self has encountered other persons, in which matrix it discovers itself" ("The Question of the Self in Nietzsche during the Axial Period," 81).

6. *On the Use and Disadvantage of History for Life* 1. At the beginning of *Human, All Too Human* Nietzsche claims that the "hereditary failing of philosophers" consists in "lack of historical sense" (*HA* 2), in their making grandiose pronouncements concerning the "being of man" on the basis of limited experience of human *becoming*. While nowadays this failing consists (in part) in believing that philosophy begins with Bertrand Russell and G. E. Moore, in those days it meant believing that it began with Plato or the pre-Socratics. But for Nietzsche even the latter belief betrays a hopeless shortsightedness and narrowness of perspective, which render ridiculous any attempts to pontificate on the nature of human being within such a limited time frame: "Everything *essential* about human development took place in primeval times, long before the four thousand years with which we are imperfectly acquainted; during this recent period humanity probably has not changed all that much. . . . Thus *historical philosophizing* is necessary from now on, and along with it the virtue of modesty." Such philosophizing would be based on experiential attempts to imagine ourselves back along the continuum that stretches from the present to the primeval beginnings of the race. While such phantastic excursions can be made deliberately—and we have seen Nietzsche act as a travel guide in this respect, psychopomp to the historical dimensions of the soul (*AOM* 223)—they also take place spontaneously, as we shall see shortly, in our dreams.

7. Compare the following passage from Freud, in which the term "I-ideal" is more or less synonymous with "over-I" *(Über-Ich):* "The I-ideal . . . [contains] as a substitute for a longing for the father, the germ from which all religions have evolved. . . . As a child grows up, the role of father is carried on by teachers and others in authority; their injunctions and prohibitions remain powerful in the I-ideal and continue, in the form of conscience, to exercise moral censorship" (*The Ego and the Id,* sect. 3).

8. In addition to Freud's writings on the subject (in particular, *The Ego and the Id*), see the work of Melanie Klein, especially *The Psychoanalysis of the Child* (New York, 1932), and also the chapter entitled "Boundary" in Norman O. Brown, *Love's Body.*

A somewhat similar understanding, though pertaining to the entire course of a person's development rather than just to childhood, can be found in the idea of the *social self* developed by George Herbert Mead. In the words of a contemporary follower of Mead's: "Human beings . . . characteristically, in all societies, *build* each other's minds. . . . Each of us 'takes in' other selves to build a self" (Wayne C. Booth, *Modern Dogma and the Rhetoric of Assent* [Notre Dame, 1974], 110). In a section entitled "The Self as a Field of Selves," Booth writes: "What a puny thing, what an unimaginably subhuman thing one's precious self would be if one had not been . . . made through other selves in social institutions from birth—literally constituted of other selves who are in turn unthinkable except in matrices of human converse" (p. 132).

9. *KSA* 9:6[80]; 1880.

10. A passage concerning conscience in Sterne's *Tristram Shandy* invokes the metaphor of a courtroom filled with contending figures: "—Could no such thing as favour and affection enter this sacred COURT:—Did WIT disdain to take a bribe in it;—or was it asham'd to shew its face as an advocate for an unwarrantable enjoy-

ment.—Or, lastly, were we assured, that INTEREST stood always unconcern'd whilst the cause was hearing,—and that passion never got into the judgment-seat, and pronounc'd sentence in the stead of reason, which is supposed always to preside and determine upon the case" (2:17).

11. The idea—so crucial in Nietzsche—that the individual is the fruit of countless previous generations comes from Emerson: "An individual man is a fruit which it cost all the foregoing ages to form and ripen. The history of the genesis or the old mythology repeats itself in the experience of every child" ("The Method of Nature").

12. *Human, All Too Human* 380. Compare *HA* 385: "Usually a mother loves *herself* in her son more than the son himself."

13. The epigraph is from Emerson, *Journals,* October 1848 (emphasis added). Thanks to George Stack for adducing this remarkable passage.

14. Nietzsche appears to have kept in close touch with the dream world over long periods of his life. He recounts a number of childhood dreams as being of great importance to him, and often mentions dreams in his letters. The best indication of his sense of the importance of dreams in psychological development is the crucial role they play in the inner drama of *Zarathustra.*

15. Lichtenberg, *Aphorisms,* 94 (see also pp. 95, 120, 122–23, 169); *Gedankenbücher,* 128 (see also pp. 123, 125, 167, 170–71). Schopenhauer also emphasized the close relationship between waking and dream experience: "Life and dreams are leaves of one and the same book" (*WWR* 1:5).

16. E. R. Dodds, *The Greeks and the Irrational,* 102.

17. The best depth-psychological treatment of the parallels between the underworld descent and dreaming is James Hillman, *The Dream and the Underworld.*

18. *Dawn of Morning* 432. In a later aphorism, entitled "Mortal Souls," Nietzsche makes the explicit connection between the idea of multiple souls and experimentation, proclaiming that with the demise of the idea of the immortal soul, "We may now experiment with ourselves!" (*DM* 501).

19. See *The Advantage and Disadvantage of History for Life* 1, and the discussion in chapter 3, above. Earlier in *Assorted Opinions and Maxims* there is a striking passage about how to "animate" *(beseelen)* artworks from antiquity with one's own soul: "[Such works] can live on only by our giving them our souls: only *our* blood can bring them to speak to *us*" (*AOM* 126).

20. For more on this reappropriation see Graham Parkes, "Nietzsche and Nishitani on the Self-Overcoming of Nihilism," *International Studies in Philosophy* 25, no. 2 (1993): 51–60.

21. Nietzsche remarks on how the heirs of a tradition often salvage the "building materials" from superseded systems and recombine them in new ways (*AOM* 201).

22. *Beyond Good and Evil* 200. Nietzsche offers as examples of such types Alcibiades, Caesar, Frederick II, and Leonardo da Vinci.

23. For a fine treatment of the theme of decadence in Nietzsche's post-*Zarathustra* writings, see Daniel Conway, *Nietzsche's Dangerous Game: Philosophy in the Twilight of the Idols.*

24. See Nietzsche's letters to his mother and sister of February 1865.

25. Letter (draft) to Hedwig Raabe, June 1866.

26. See Janz, 1:212–14, and Nietzsche's letters to Deussen and Rohde of late October 1868.

27. *The World as Will and Representation* 2:25. In a discussion of determinism later in the chapter, Schopenhauer writes: "The world becomes a play of puppets pulled by wires (motives), without our being able to tell for whose enjoyment. If the play has a plan, then *fate* is the director; if not, then blind necessity."

28. *The Birth of Tragedy,* "Attempt at a Self-Criticism," §2.

29. *The Birth of Tragedy,* "Attempt at a Self-Criticism," §5. It is clear, especially from the mention of autarchy, that the figure of Dionysus is here emblematic of the great human being who is capable of sustaining the tensions produced by powerfully conflicting drives.

30. *The Birth of Tragedy* 5. Kaufmann mistranslates this last part as "from the depth of his being," but Nietzsche's whole point is to deny that the "I" issues from the lyrist's being and to emphasize its transpersonal origin.

31. See the passage from *The Birth of Tragedy* 5, characterizing the lyrist in contrast to the epic poet, in chapter 2 above.

32. For a fine account of the mask of Greek tragedy, see John Jones, *On Aristotle and Greek Tragedy* (London, 1962), especially the chapter entitled "Human Beings." While Jones makes only one, rather slighting reference to Nietzsche, what he says about the mask seems quite consonant with Nietzsche's later ideas on the topic. For instance: "By the erosive flow of action the individual features are carved out, no potent shaping spirit lodges aboriginally behind the face; and thus the Aristotelian stage-figure receives his distinctive qualities" (p. 38). "At the living heart of the tradition the actor is the mask and the mask is an artifact-face with nothing to offer but itself. It has—more important, it is known to have—no inside. Its being is exhausted in its features" (p. 45).

33. See, for example, the letters to Rohde of late February 1870 and to Overbeck of 10 February 1883, where Nietzsche bemoans the fact that he is forced by circumstances to lead a life that is masked and veiled.

34. The origins of our word "mask" are—appropriately—veiled in obscurity; several dictionary entries report: "derivation disputed." A relatively young word (not appearing in French and English until the sixteenth century) it is presumed to come from the Latin *massa* meaning "paste"—whence "mascara"—and *masca* meaning "demon," or "sorcerer." (With the face apparently transformed and transfixed by a mask, the gestures of the rest of the body become enormously expressive—which contributes to the demonically dynamic aspects of the mask.) The word's Greek and Latin equivalents connect immediately with the idea of the person. The Greek *prosōpon* means "front," "facade," or "face"; whence "mask," "character" (in a drama), and "person"—in the original, legal sense. The image is optical, *prosōpon* meaning "at the eyes": as front or facade, that which the eyes meet; as mask that too, but also something held at or around the eyes. In Latin the image takes an acoustical turn, insofar as the components of the word *persona,* meaning "mask," "character," "person," mean literally "through sound." For a more general discussion, see "Features of the Mask in Ancient Greece," in Vernant and Vidal-Naquet, *Myth and Tragedy in Ancient Greece.*

35. *Human, All Too Human* 51. See also the next aphorism, in which the process

by which seeming becomes being is further elucidated: deception is more effective if one pretends to believe in it oneself; and eventually through repeated professions and expressions of belief it becomes incorporated, such that one actually comes to have faith and belief in one's own deception—which thereby ceases to *be* a deception.

36. In the context of a discussion of the *Bacchae* of Euripides, Martha Nussbaum writes: "If Dionysus, god of intoxication and sexual energy, is (in Schopenhauer's terms) will, he is also a playwright, a stage director, a most subtle and versatile actor" ("The Transfiguration of Intoxication: Nietzsche, Schopenhauer, and Dionysus," 92).

37. *The Joyful Science* 299. The aphorism on "giving style to one's character" (*JS* 290) was discussed in Interlude 1, above.

38. Chronological sequence would demand a consideration of *Thus Spoke Zarathustra* at this point, since book 5 of *The Joyful Science* was added later, in 1886. The justification for forgoing this is that the text contains hardly any explicit mention of masks—though the figure of Zarathustra is naturally a mask for the book's author (as, one could argue, are all the other characters in the book).

39. *The Joyful Science* 361. This Dionysiac experience has its mythical and ritual background in the god's close associations with masks; see W. F. Otto, *Dionysus: Myth and Cult*, especially the chapter entitled "The Symbol of the Mask."

40. A note from 1888 reads: "In the inorganic world, dissimulation *[Verstellung]* appears to be lacking; in the organic, cunning begins; plants are already masters in that" (*KSA* 12:10[159]).

41. The theme of esoteric writing is first sounded at *BGE* 30; see, on this topic, Lampert, *Nietzsche and Modern Times,* especially 306–10. See also the discussion of Nietzsche's self-maskings in terms of irony in Ernst Behler, *Irony and the Discourse of Modernity* (Seattle and London, 1990), chapter 3, "Irony in the Ancient and the Modern World."

42. *KSA* 12:3[33]; 1885–86.

43. See, on respect for veils, *The Joyful Science,* Preface, §4.

44. For an eloquent phenomenological treatment of the theater metaphor, see Bruce Wilshire, *Role Playing and Identity: The Limits of Theatre as Metaphor* (Bloomington, 1982), especially part 3.

45. Nietzsche may have been familiar with the (perhaps apocryphal) quote from Bismarck that stands as the epigraph to this section; compare this passage from *Beyond Good and Evil:* "The German soul is above all manifold . . . A German who would dare to say 'Two souls, alas, dwell in my breast' would badly miss the truth or, more precisely, would fall short of the truth by a good many souls" (*BGE* 44).

46. Apart from the classes of the philosopher-guardians, the auxiliaries, and the money-makers, the following kinds of practitioners are mentioned in the text: courtesans, poets, rhapsodes, actors, dancers, teachers, governesses, beauticians, barbers, relish makers, carpenters, potters, smiths, dyers, sailors, farmers, shoemakers, house builders, harpists, equestrians, judges, doctors, chefs, grammarians, wet nurses, shepherds, cowherds, swineherds, and weavers. It is an undertaking to which we rarely rise, to imagine our selves as keenly and precisely as to discern such a variety of types working away within.

47. *Republic* 557c. Nietzsche's attitude toward democracy is expressed in similar imagery concerning events in the town called "The Motley Cow" in *Thus Spoke Zarathustra*.

48. *Republic* 558c. Socrates is similarly ironical in his later characterization of the imitative artist, that master of multiplicity, as "a charming chap" (602a).

49. *Republic* 560b. There is an echo of this image in an aphorism from *Human, All Too Human* entitled "Self-observation," which deals with the problem of getting through one's own psychical defenses: "The human being is very well defended against himself, against being spied on and besieged by himself, so that he usually perceives no more of himself than his outer fortifications. The real fortress is inaccessible to him, invisible even, unless friends and enemies turn traitor and lead him in by a secret route" (*HA* 491).

50. *Republic* 561b–e. This passage is reminiscent of (and may have been the inspiration for) Kierkegaard's magnificent account of "The Rotation Method" of satisfying desires in the first volume of *Either/Or.*

51. In considering the six ways of keeping a tyrannical drive in check, Nietzsche spoke of the benefits that may accrue from "the habit and desire to tyrannize [a] drive and make it gnash its teeth" (*DM* 109).

52. *Human, All Too Human* 2, Preface, §4 (1886). Nietzsche chose to reproduce this passage at the very end of his writing career, in *Nietzsche contra Wagner.* Many of Nietzsche's illnesses can be seen in this light as the work of his *Aufgabe*.

53. *Twilight of the Idols* 2.9–11. By 1888 Nietzsche appears to be using the term "instincts" more often than "drives," though with much the same meaning. Dan Conway argues that in the later works the term *Instinkt* comes to assume the connotation of an outward manifestation of the inherently unobservable *Trieb;* see *Nietzsche's Dangerous Game,* chapter 2. True to his own injunctions concerning the retroflective turn, Nietzsche eventually admits to being a decadent himself—as well as the opposite (*EH* 1.2).

54. *Republic* 589b. The "tame heads" are presumably what Socrates has been calling the "necessary" desires (558d–559d), and these are to be nourished; the treatment of the savage heads ("unnecessary" desires) is not overly harsh: their growth is simply to be discouraged.

55. "The Church combats passion with excision in every sense: its practice, its 'cure' is *castration.* It never asks: 'How does one spiritualize, beautify, divinize a desire?'—it has at all times laid the emphasis of its discipline on extirpation" (*TI* 5.1).

56. *Republic* 443d, 550b, 553c, 561b.

57. *The Joyful Science* 333. Compare *BGE* 36, where "thinking" is said to be "merely a disposition of the drives toward each other." On this topic, see the insightful (and quasi Nietzschean) discussion in A. C. Graham, *Reason and Spontaneity* (London, 1985).

58. *KSA* 12:7[60] = *WP* 481, 1886–87; see also *KSA* 11:26[119] = *WP* 259, 1884.

59. *KSA* 11:26[73]; 1884.

60. *KSA* 11:40[21] = *WP* 492, 1885. Socrates extends the political metaphor to

the body at *Republic* 556e when he characterizes "the sickly body" as "divided by factions within itself." Aristotle applies the political metaphor to the workings of the body in a similar spirit: "We should consider the organization of an animal to resemble that of a city well governed by laws. For once order is established in a city, there is no need of a separate monarch to preside over every activity; each man does his own work as assigned. . . . In animals . . . each part is naturally disposed to do its own task. There is, then, no need of soul in each part: it is in some governing origin of the body, and other parts live because they are naturally attached, and do their tasks because of nature" (*De Motu Animalium*, 703a–b; trans. Martha Nussbaum, in *Aristotle's De motu animalium* [Princeton, 1978]).

In the chapter added to the expanded edition of *Friedrich Nietzsche and the Politics of Transfiguration* (Berkeley and London, 1988), Tracy Strong emphasizes that much of Nietzsche's later writings "is occupied with a critique of the idea of a unitary self" and argues that his perspectivism asserts "that 'I' am a number of different ways of knowing and that there is no such entity as a permanent or privileged self" (pp. 298, 308). Though he mentions Nietzsche's image of the subject as a "regent at the head of a commonality" (p. 300), Strong does not pursue the theme of the political ordering of the "multitudes" that such a subject would contain—perhaps because he pays little attention to the multiplicity of drives and persons that Nietzsche imagines the individual to consist in.

61. As suggested earlier (chapter 7), the image of the regent may come from Herder. The talk of "living unities continuously arising and perishing" as opposed to an "eternal subject" is strikingly reminiscent of the Buddhist idea of *anātman* ("no-self")—Nietzsche's acquaintance with which may even have influenced this particular formulation. See, again, Mistry, *Nietzsche and Buddhism,* chapter 2. One might note that Freud compares the position of the *Ich* to that of a "constitutional monarch" (*The Ego and the Id,* sect. 5).

62. *KSA* 11:40[38].

63. *KSA* 11:40[42] = *WP* 490, 1885. This note makes clear the connection between the ideas of psychical multiplicity and mortal souls as presented in *AOM* 17 and *DM* 501.

64. *KSA* 12:1[122] = *WP* 384, 1885–86. This note exemplifies Nietzsche's penchant for speaking phylogenetically at the same time as of the individual. In the race, or culture, the kind of tyranny he is talking about has been best perfected by followers of the ascetic ideal.

65. The true philosopher, for Nietzsche, who can be expected to be consummately disciplined in this respect, is similarly a product of a long preparation: one has a "right" to philosophy "only thanks to one's heritage, the ancestors, the 'blood.' . . . Many generations must have worked for the preparation of the philosopher" (*BGE* 213).

66. *KSA* 12:9[139] = *WP* 933.

67. "Eine Art leitendes Comité, wo die verschiedenen *Hauptbegierden* ihre Stimme und Macht geltend machen" (*KSA* 13:11[145] = *WP* 524). In translating this passage "a kind of directing committee *on* which the various chief desires make their votes and power felt" (my emphasis), Kaufmann and Hollingdale miss the point of the passage by making it sound as if the various dominant desires are differ-

ent from the committee. Freud follows Nietzsche in using the term *Instanz* in a similar way (in the *Standard Edition* translated as "agency").

68. "All [the basic drives] have at some time practiced philosophy . . . every drive strives for domination: and *as such* it tries to philosophize" (*BGE* 6).

69. *KSA* 13:11[310] = *WP* 387. This idea illuminates Zarathustra's characterization of the body as "a great reason, a plurality with one sense" (*Z* 1.4, "On the Despisers of the Body"). Compare these lines from Herder: "Knowing without *willing* is nothing! a false, incomplete knowing. . . . *No passion is divorced from knowledge:* they can and should all work on it" (*EMS* 617).

70. *Twilight of the Idols* 2.10. One is reminded of the refrain in *Thus Spoke Zarathustra:* "The world is deep, / and deeper than the day has thought." This evaluation of Socrates is far from that expressed in the aphorism from 1880 entitled "Socrates," in which his most distinctive feature is said to be "participation in every kind of temperament" (*WS* 86).

71. Later in *Twilight* he speaks of the value of the "enemy within": "One is *fruitful* only at the cost of being rich in contradictions" (*TI* 5.3).

72. *Twilight of the Idols* 8. 6. From the Socratic perspective, the extreme self-tyranny Nietzsche advocates for this stage might well be said to lack *moderation.* The Nietzschean response would presumably be that the motto "Moderation in all things" applies to moderation itself—and that *im*moderation is sometimes necessary, lest moderation be taken to an extreme.

73. *The Joyful Science* 305. A related and equally rich piece of psychological insight is to be found in an earlier aphorism entitled "Transplantation": "If one has employed the spirit *[Geist]* to attain mastery over the excessiveness of the affects, this often yields the tiresome result of transferring the excessiveness to the spirit and of now indulging excessively in thinking and wanting to know" (*AOM* 275).

74. A political analogy comes to mind here from ancient Chinese political thought. For Confucius, the power *(de)* of the sage-ruler is such that all he has to do is visibly occupy the throne, and the populace will spontaneously respond to the "emanations" of his power by doing what is best for the society as a whole (see, for example, *Analects* 2/1, 12/19, and 15/5). This idea was developed by the Daoists into a more "anarchic" ideal in which the ruler rules by virtue of *wu wei,* by "inaction," or spontaneous activity that does not interfere with the natural flow of things. On this analogy, coercion by a ruling agent is unnecessary: it is sufficient to have an I that *appears* to be in control. For a fine account of the relevant strains in classical Chinese philosophy, see A. C. Graham, *Disputers of the Tao* (La Salle, 1989), especially section 3.

The schema developed by Nietzsche—(1) natural anarchy, (2) disciplined self-tyranny, and (3) enlightened spontaneity—is remarkably parallel to the schema on which many East Asian modes of self-cultivation (self-dissolution and self-emptying) operate, especially those that involve practice of the arts both fine and martial. (See Graham Parkes, "Ways of Japanese Thinking," and especially the section entitled "The Way of the Sword.")

75. *Zarathustra* 3.12 §19. An unpublished note from the period reads: "I have the *most comprehensive* soul of all Europeans who are living or have ever lived" (*KSA* 10:4[2]).

76. *Zarathustra* 1.22, §1. An earlier, more detailed formulation of this idea, in the context of human greatness, occurs in an aphorism entitled "Grades of traveller": "There are some human beings of the greatest power who take everything they see and, after it has been lived through and embodied *[erlebt und eingelebt],* must eventually necessarily live it out *[herausleben]* of themselves again, in actions and works" (*AOM* 227).

77. Film can be a marvelous medium for portraying the multiple psyche, and one of the great masters in this respect is Fellini. Two magnificent cinematic equivalents of Zarathustra's inviting the higher men into his cave occur toward the ends of *8½,* where Guido directs the other characters (appropriately clothed in the white of redemption) to come down the stairs of the spaceship and join him in the circus ring, and of *Juliet of the Spirits,* where Giulietta announces her reconciliation with the other characters through the refrain *Amore per tutti* ("love for all").

78. There is a striking parallel with Daoist practice, where the ideal is to harmonize the configurations of energies (*Qi/ch'i;* Jpn. *ki*) animating the human body with the greater flow-patterns of the universe. Two sports that Nietzsche did not have the occasion to try are fine paradigms of this notion of streaming or flowing: skiing and surfing. Expertise in both is achieved by aligning oneself appropriately with the greatest physical force, *gravity* (a fundamental manifestation of "will" for Schopenhauer), in intimate association with the element of *water.* In the highest accomplishments of surfing, as of skiing, there is no conscious "I" directing: rather the "undersouls" of the feet, and of the muscles and sinews of the legs, waist, shoulders, and arms, work harmoniously together in a minutely orchestrated play.

79. Emerson's conception of the noble soul is more prudent: "The true nobility has floodgates,—an equal inlet and outgo" (*Journals,* 10:69).

80. *KSA* 10:4[4]; November 1882–February 1883.

Epilogue

1. Again, the best single source is Ellenberger's *The Discovery of the Unconscious;* see, especially, chapters 4 and 5.

2. William James, *The Principles of Psychology* (New York, 1890), 1:206.

3. See Freud's essay from 1893, "A Case of Hypnotic Healing" (*SEF* 1:115–28, 126).

4. Jung wrote his doctoral dissertation in 1900 on the topic of "The Psychology and Pathology of So-called Occult Phenomena," in *The Collected Works of C. G. Jung,* vol. 1; subsequent references will be made simply to the volume and page number. For a more detailed discussion of Jung's development of the idea of psychical multiplicity, see Parkes, "A Cast of Many."

5. This echoes Nietzsche's distinction between the Apollonian epic poet who in contemplating his images "is protected by the mirror of *Schein* from becoming one with and being fused together with [them]," and the Dionysian lyric poet who *is* the images whereby "he sees through to the ground of things" (*BT* 5).

6. Recall the poet in *The Birth of Tragedy* who "sees himself surrounded by figures who live and act before him" and who is able "constantly to be viewing a living play and to live surrounded by hosts of spirits" (*BT* 8).

7. James Hillman, in elaborating Jung's ideas about the personified complexes,

writes: "We sense these other persons and call them 'roles' . . . but can there be roles without persons to play them?" (*Re-Visioning Psychology,* 32). Much of Hillman's work prompts us in a Nietzschean fashion to ponder the relationship between the imagination's play of images and the drama of life, and the connections between the persons of the imagination and the *personae* through which we play the roles called for by living in society.

8. See Hillman, *Re-Visioning Psychology,* 24–51 and chapter 2, "Pathologizing or Falling Apart"; also Norman O. Brown, *Love's Body,* especially the chapters entitled "Unity," "Head," and "Nothing."

9. Hillman develops the distinction between the "heroic" and "imaginal" egos in *Re-Visioning Psychology.*

10. *Ecce Homo,* Preface, §4. In a letter to Burckhardt Nietzsche writes that *Beyond Good and Evil* "says the same things as *Zarathustra,* but in a very different way" (22 September 1886).

11. A good account of these various plans and abandonings can be found in chapter 14 of Hollingdale's *Nietzsche: The Man and His Philosophy.*

12. In a letter to Carl Fuchs dated 11 December 1888, Nietzsche writes: "I cannot tell you *what* all has been done: *Everything is finished* [Alles ist fertig]."

13. There is a similar "looking forward" in a note from the period: "I look forward as over a smooth plane: not a wish, no wishing whatsoever, no making of plans, no wanting anything other than it is" (*KSA* 13:16[44]).

14. Pia Daniela Volz, *Nietzsche im Labyrinth seiner Krankheit: Eine medizinisch-biographische Untersuchung* (Würzburg, 1990), especially 298–305. This encyclopedic work, distinguished from others in the field by its unprejudiced approach, is indispensable for an understanding of Nietzsche's illnesses. The original diagnosis of progressive paralysis was made on his being admitted to the Basel psychiatric clinic in January of 1889.

15. In a letter to Overbeck of 26 February 1891, just after visiting Nietzsche at his home in Naumburg, Köselitz writes: "Last year I heard him playing the piano and was astonished at the logic and intensity of his improvising; this year that was all gone. He has lost his feel for rhythm; everything is wrong and confused!" (cited in Janz, 3:139).

16. Heinrich Köselitz, letter to Franz Overbeck of 20 February 1890; cited in Janz, 3:108.

17. Carl Albrecht Bernoulli, *Franz Overbeck und Friedrich Nietzsche: Eine Freundschaft* (Jena, 1908), 2:215. See also Janz, 3:110–12.

18. Letter from Franz Overbeck, 27 August 1879. Had it not been for Nietzsche's solid epistolary relationships with Overbeck and Köselitz, and his salutary friendships with Resa Von Schirnhofer and Meta Von Salis, which flourished because their periods of in-person contact were strictly intermittent, it is doubtful whether he would have maintained his sanity for as long as he did.

19. *Beyond Good and Evil* 138. Nietzsche had first penned this aphorism, in a slightly longer form, in 1882 (*KSA* 10:3[1] #24). See also *DM* 532, for an insightful description of mutual projections between male and female partners.

20. It was in the Engadin that Nietzsche had experienced the landscape as his own *Doppelgänger,* as a familiar to which he was related by blood (*WS* 338).

21. *KSA* 9:8[90].

22. *KSA* 9:6[80]; autumn 1880, and 9:11[130]; 1881 (emphasis added).

23. Letter to Heinrich Köselitz, 14 August 1881.

24. See the letters—especially those to Overbeck and Köselitz—of February, March, and April 1883.

25. In addition to those passages already mentioned, see *KSA* 12:9[137]: "the *great* human beings . . . [are] dangerous, chance occurrences, exceptions, storms. . . . The basic instinct of civilized society is not only to detonate the explosive harmlessly but wherever possible to *prevent* its appearance"; *KSA* 13:14[170] = *WP* 811: "[the artist's] ability to speak of himself by a hundred linguistic means . . . an *explosive* condition"; *Ecce Homo,* "UM" 3: "the philosopher [is] a terrible explosive that endangers everything."

26. *Ecce Homo,* "UM" 3; 4.1. In a letter to Köselitz of 9 December 1888, Nietzsche writes of *Ecce Homo* itself as "the highest superlative of *dynamite*."

27. For example: "Greatness of character does not consist in not having affects—on the contrary one has them in the most terrifying degree—but in keeping them in harness" (*KSA* 13:11[353] = *WP* 928). And more broadly speaking: "The greater and more terrible the passions are that an age, or a people, or an individual can allow itself, knowing how to employ them as a means, the higher its level of culture" (*KSA* 13:16[5]; also 12:9[138]).

28. *KSA* 13:16[7]; 1888 (emphasis added).

29. *KSA* 12:9[139] = *WP* 933; 1887 (discussed at the end of the previous chapter).

30. *KSA* 13:14[157] = *WP* 778. Compare two other notes from the period: *KSA* 13:14[219], and *KSA* 13:11[48] = *WP* 963: "The great passion, the ground and power of [a great spirit's] being, more enlightened and despotic than he himself is, takes his entire intellect into its service. . . . All weakness of will comes from the circumstance where no passion, no categorical imperative [!] is in command."

31. *KSA* 13:14[124]. Part of the next note reads: "Religion is born from *doubt* concerning the unity of the person, an *altération* of the personality." See also *KSA* 13:14[151].

32. The aphorism begins with a reference to the "oppositional concept of the Apollonian and the Dionysian, "both understood as kinds of intoxication *[Rausch]*"; this suggests that the Dionysian is now informed by the Apollonian order characteristic of the beautiful sheen of the dream. The end of the previous aphorism cited Raphael as the epitome of the intoxicated artist.

33. *KSA* 13:16[89] = *WP* 813; summer 1888.

34. *Twilight of the Idols* 6. 3. In an earlier formulation: "'The doer' is merely a fiction added to the deed" (*GM* 1.13).

35. Letter to Georg Brandes, 4 January 1889 (ellipsis in original).

Selected Bibliography

Aristotle. *On the Soul; Parva Naturalia; On Breath,* trans. W. S. Hett. Cambridge, Mass., 1936.

Behler, Ernst. *Confrontations: Derrida, Heidegger, Nietzsche,* trans. Stephen Taubeneck. Stanford, 1991.

Benardete, Seth. *The Being of the Beautiful: Plato's "Theaetetus," "Sophist," and "Statesman."* Chicago, 1984.

Bergmann, Peter. *Nietzsche, "the Last Antipolitical German."* Bloomington, 1987.

Bernoulli, C. A. *Franz Overbeck und Friedrich Nietzsche: Eine Freundschaft,* 2 vols. Jena, 1908.

Brown, Norman O. *Love's Body.* New York, 1966.

Byron [George Gordon, Lord]. *Selected Works,* ed. Edward E. Bostetter. New York, 1951.

Cavell, Stanley. *Conditions Handsome and Unhandsome: The Constitution of Emersonian Perfectionism.* Chicago, 1990.

Cornford, F. M. *Plato's Cosmology.* London, 1937.

Dannhauser, Werner. *Nietzsche's View of Socrates.* Ithaca, 1974.

Deleuze, Gilles. *Nietzsche and Philosophy,* trans. Hugh Tomlinson. New York, 1983.

Derrida, Jacques. *Spurs: Nietzsche's Styles,* trans. Barbara Harlow. Chicago, 1979.

———. *The Ear of the Other,* trans. Avital Ronell. New York, 1985.

———. "Chôra." Pp. 265–96 in *Poikilia: Études offertes à Jean-Pierre Vernant,* Paris, 1987.

———. "Plato's Pharmacy," in *Dissemination,* trans. Barbara Johnson. Chicago, 1981.

Dodds, E. R. *The Greeks and the Irrational.* Berkeley, 1951.

Eckermann, Johann Peter. *Gespräche mit Goethe* (1835), ed. Fritz Bergemann. Frankfurt, 1987.

Ellenberger, Henri. *The Discovery of the Unconscious: The History and Evolution of Dynamic Psychiatry.* New York, 1970.

Emerson, Ralph Waldo. *Essays and Lectures.* New York, 1983.

———. *The Journals and Miscellaneous Notebooks of Ralph Waldo Emerson,* ed. William H. Gilman *et al.* Cambridge, Mass., 1960–.

Engell, James. *The Creative Imagination: Enlightenment to Romanticism.* Cambridge, Mass., 1981.

Ferrari, G. R. F. *Listening to the Cicadas: A Study of Plato's* Phaedrus. Cambridge, 1987.

Fichte, J. G. *Grundlage der gesammten Wissenschaftslehre.* Vol. 1 in *Fichtes Werke,* ed. I. H. Fichte. Berlin, 1971.

———. *Early Philosophical Writings,* ed. and trans. Daniel Breazeale. Ithaca, 1988.

———. *The Science of Knowledge,* ed. and trans. Peter Heath and John Lachs. New York, 1970.

Freud, Sigmund. *Gesammelte Werke.* London, 1940–52.

———. *The Standard Edition of the Complete Psychological Works of Sigmund Freud.* London, 1953–64.

Gerhardt, Volker. *Friedrich Nietzsche.* Munich, 1992.

Gilman, Sander L., ed. *Begegnungen mit Nietzsche.* Bonn, 1985.

———. *Conversations with Nietzsche: A Life in the Words of His Contemporaries.* New York and Oxford, 1987.

Goethe, J. G. *Die Leiden des jungen Werther* (1774). Frankfurt, 1973.

Griesinger, Wilhelm. *Die Pathologie und Therapie der psychischen Krankheiten.* Amsterdam, 1964 (reprint of the Stuttgart edition of 1867).

Havelock, Eric. *Preface to Plato.* Cambridge, Mass., 1963.

Heidegger, Martin. *Kant und das Problem der Metaphysik.* Frankfurt, 1973.

———. *Nietzsche.* 2 vols. Pfullingen, 1961.

Herder, Johann Gottfried. *Vom Erkennen und Empfinden der menschlichen Seele* (1774–78). In *Werke,* ed. Wolfgang Pross. 2 vols. Munich and Vienna, 1987.

Hillman, James. *The Myth of Analysis.* Evanston, 1972.

———. *Re-Visioning Psychology.* New York, 1975.

———. *The Dream and the Underworld.* New York, 1979.

———. *Anima: an Anatomy of a Personified Notion.* Dallas, 1985.

Hölderlin, Friedrich. *Hyperion* (1797–99). In *Hölderlin: Werke und Briefe,* ed. Friedrich Beissner and Jochen Schmidt. 2 vols. Frankfurt, 1969.

Hollingdale, R. J. *Nietzsche: The Man and His Philosophy.* Baton Rouge, 1965.

Hollinrake, Roger. *Nietzsche, Wagner, and the Philosophy of Pessimism.* London, 1982.

Janz, Curt Paul. *Friedrich Nietzsche Biographie.* 3 vols. Munich and Vienna, 1978.

Jung, Carl Gustav. *Collected Works of C. G. Jung.* Princeton, 1970–77.

Kant, Immanuel. *Kritik der reinen Vernunft,* ed. Raymund Schmidt. Hamburg, 1956.

———. *Die Religion innerhalb der Grenzen der blossen Vernunft.* Vol. 6 in *Immanuel Kants Werke,* ed. Ernst Cassirer. Berlin, 1923.

Kaufmann, Walter. *Nietzsche: Philosopher, Psychologist, Antichrist.* Princeton, 1950.

Klages, Ludwig. *Die psychologischen Errungenschaften Nietzsches.* Leipzig, 1926.

Kofman, Sarah. *Nietzsche et la métaphore.* Paris, 1972.

Krell, David Farrell. *Postponements: Woman, Sensuality, and Death in Nietzsche.* Bloomington, 1986.

Lampert, Laurence. *Nietzsche's Teaching: An Interpretation of* Thus Spoke Zarathustra. New Haven and London, 1986.

————. *Nietzsche and Modern Times: A Study of Bacon, Descartes, and Nietzsche.* New Haven and London, 1993.

Lichtenberg, Georg Christoph. *Gedankenbücher,* ed. Franz Mautner. Heidelberg, 1967.

————. *Aphorisms,* trans. R. J. Hollingdale. London, 1990.

Love, Frederick R. *Young Nietzsche and the Wagnerian Experience.* Chapel Hill, 1963.

Magnus, Bernd, Stanley Stewart, and Jean-Pierre Mileur, *Nietzsche's Case: Philosophy as/and Literature.* New York and London, 1993.

Montaigne, Michel de. *The Complete Essays of Montaigne,* trans. Donald M. Frame. Stanford, 1958.

Nehamas, Alexander. *Nietzsche: Life as Literature.* Cambridge, Mass., 1985.

Nietzsche, Friedrich. *Sämtliche Briefe: Kritische Studienausgabe,* ed. Giorgio Colli and Mazzino Montinari. 8 vols. Munich 1986.

————. *Sämtliche Werke: Kritische Studienausgabe,* ed. Giorgio Colli and Mazzino Montinari. 15 vols. Munich 1980.

————. *Werke,* ed. Otto Crusius and Wilhelm Nestle. Leipzig, 1913.

————. *Werke: Historisch-Kritische Ausgabe,* ed. Hans Joachim Mette. Munich, 1934.

————. *Werke in drei Bänden,* ed. Karl Schlechta. Munich, 1956.

————. "On Moods," trans. Graham Parkes. *Journal of Nietzsche Studies* 2 (1991): 5–10.

Nishitani, Keiji. *The Self-Overcoming of Nihilism,* trans. Graham Parkes with Setsuko Aihara. Albany, 1990.

Nussbaum, Martha. *The fragility of goodness: Luck and ethics in Greek tragedy and philosophy.* Cambridge and New York, 1986.

————. "The Transfigurations of Intoxication: Nietzsche, Schopenhauer, and Dionysus." *Arion* 1/2 (1991): 75–111.

Onians, R. B. *The Origins of European Thought.* Cambridge, 1951.

Otto, Walter F. *Dionysus: Myth and Cult,* trans. Robert Palmer. Bloomington, 1965.

Parkes, Graham, ed. *Nietzsche and Asian Thought.* Chicago, 1991.

————. "A Cast of Many: Nietzsche and Depth-Psychological Pluralism." *Man and World* 22/4 (1989): 453–70.

————. "Human/Nature in Nietzsche and Taoism." Pp. 79–98 in Roger Ames and Baird Callicott, eds., *Environmental Philosophy: The Nature of Nature in Asian Traditions of Thought.* Albany, 1989.

————. "The Dance from Mouth to Hand: Speaking Zarathustra's Write Foot Fore-Word." Pp. 127–44 in *Nietzsche as Postmodernist,* ed. Clayton Koelb. Albany, 1990.

————. "From Nationalism to Nomadism: Wondering about the Languages of Philosophy." Pp. 455–67 in *Culture and Modernity: East and West,* ed. Eliot Deutsch. Honolulu, 1991.

————. "Ways of Japanese Thinking." Pp. 25–53 in *From Africa to Zen: An Introduction to World Philosophy,* ed. Robert Solomon and Kathleen Higgins. Savage, Md., 1992.

————. "Nietzsche and Nishitani on the Self-Overcoming of Nihilism." *International Studies in Philosophy* 25/2 (1993): 51–60.

————. "Nietzsche and East Asian Thinking: Influences, Impacts, and Resonances." Forthcoming in *The Cambridge Companion to Nietzsche,* ed. Kathleen Higgins and Bernd Magnus. Cambridge.

Plato. *Ion,* trans. Allan Bloom. Pp. 356–70 in *The Roots of Political Philosophy,* ed. Thomas Pangle. Ithaca, 1987.

————. *The Republic of Plato,* trans. Allan Bloom. New York, 1968.

————. *Euthyphro, Apology, Crito, Phaedo, Phaedrus,* trans. H. N. Fowler. Cambridge, Mass., 1921.

————. *Laws,* trans. R. G. Bury. 2 vols. Cambridge, Mass., 1926.

————. *Lysis, Symposium, Gorgias,* trans. W. R. M. Lamb. Cambridge, Mass., 1925.

————. *Res publica [Republic].* Vol. 4 in *Platonis opera,* ed. John Burnet. Oxford, 1902.

————. *Timaeus, Critias, Clitopho, Menenexus, Epistulae,* trans. R. G. Bury. Cambridge, Mass., 1929.

Porte, Joel. *Representative Man: Ralph Waldo Emerson in His Time.* New York, 1979.

Sallis, John. *Crossings: Nietzsche and the Space of Tragedy.* Chicago, 1991.

Schopenhauer, Arthur. *Die Welt als Wille und Vorstellung.* 2 vols. Stuttgart and Frankfurt, 1960.

————. *The World as Will and Representation,* trans. E. F. J. Payne. New York, 1966.

Schiller, Friedrich. *On the Aesthetic Education of Man: In a Series of Letters* (1795), ed. and trans, Elizabeth M. Wilkinson and L. A. Willoughby. Oxford, 1967.

Shapiro, Gary. *Nietzschean Narratives.* Bloomington and Indianapolis, 1989.

Sloterdijk, Peter. *Thinker on Stage: Nietzsche's Materialism,* trans. Jamie Owen Daniel. Minneapolis, 1989.

Stack, George J. *Nietzsche and Emerson: An Elective Affinity.* Athens, Ohio, 1992.

Staten, Henry. *Nietzsche's Voice.* Ithaca, 1990.

Volz, Pia Daniela. *Nietzsche im Labyrinth seiner Krankheit: Eine medizinisch-biographische Untersuchung.* Würzburg, 1990.

Williams, W. D. *Nietzsche and the French.* Oxford, 1952.

Index of Passages in Nietzsche's Published Works

Subentries (in bold) are to aphorism, part and section number, or other appropriate subdivision. See note on page xiv for a detailed explanation of citations to Nietzsche's works.

Name Index

Abrams, M. H., 420, 442, 443
Aeschylus, 57, 79, 172, 420; *Eumenides,*
  172, 420
Apollo, 65–71, 279, 396, 398, 404, 407,
  431; and masculinity, 172, 211, 420; and
  realms of dream and phantasy, 275, 295,
  306, 319, 327, 337
Ariadne, 211, 315, 323, 381, 430
Aristotle, 17, 103, 105, 127, 172, 359, 420,
  427, 455, 458; *De Anima,* 17, 127, 388,
  399, 423, 426, 440
Assoun, Paul-Laurent, 383, 398, 433
Augustine, 127, 130, 254; *Confessions,* 20,
  154, 155, 410
Austin, Norman, 439, 440

Bachelard, Gaston, 415
Bachofen, J. J., 57, 66, 398, 420
Bakhtin, Mikhail, 252, 439
Bataille, Georges, 393
Beckmann, Max, 139, 413
Beethoven, Ludwig van, 52, 275
Behler, Ernst, 388, 456
Benardete, Seth, 423
Bismarck, Otto von, 346, 456
Blake, William, 139, 298
Bloom, Allan, 392, 400, 432, 440
Böcklin, Arnold, 83, 401
Booth, Wayne C., 453
Breazeale, Daniel, 385, 403, 442, 443
Bremmer, Jan, 439
Brown, Norman O., 406, 452, 453, 461
Bülow, Cosima von (later Cosima Wagner),
  4, 56, 61, 77, 88, 205, 211, 381, 395, 396,
  397

Bülow, Hans von, 57, 63, 84, 86–87, 397,
  402, 406, 437
Burckhardt, Jacob, 21, 57, 75, 84, 158, 286,
  381, 400, 406, 461
Burger, Ronna, 422
Burnyeat, Myles, 437, 438
Byron, George Gordon, Lord, 3, 21, 24, 28,
  29, 30, 31, 32, 33, 88, 131, 290, 384, 389,
  390

Carmen (Bizet), 211, 323
Casey, Edward S., 410, 411
Claus, David, 439
Columbus, Christopher, 148, 416
Confucius, 430, 459
Conway, Daniel W., 393, 413, 455, 457
Corman, Louis, 383
Cornford, F. M., 409, 426
Corngold, Stanley, 438, 452
Curtius, E. R., 426

Davidson, Donald, 451, 452
Derrida, Jacques, 205, 387, 388, 393, 402,
  403, 420, 425, 426, 428, 429
Descartes, René, 20, 97, 312, 388
Detienne, Marcel, 425, 426
Diderot, Denis, 4, 252, 400, 438
Dionysus, 47, 62, 65, 66, 75, 113, 114, 214,
  245, 306, 319, 336, 358, 360–61; and the
  feminine, 66, 211, 243; god of many
  forms, 76, 340, 358; god of masks, 276,
  337, 340; as an infant, 68, 70, 187; in
  Greek tragedy, 78–79; and vegetation, 47,
  176, 179, 180, 196, 200
Diotima (Hölderlin) 34, 35, 415

471

Subject Index

somnambulism, 62, 81, 255, 256, 307, 396, 441

spirit, 9, 34, 36, 45, 140, 153, 195, 209, 242, 330, 331, 344, 361; as camel, 227, 332; evil, 255–56, 260; of fertility, 150–51; as *Geist,* 20, 69, 109, 142, 242, 357; German, 100; of gravity, 134, 165; and the multiple psyche, 251, 254, 255, 344, 345; of the past, 332, 341; in relation to soul and body, 12, 19–20, 331; and self-overcoming, 46, 228, 357; three transformations of, 226–27, 361; spirit-voices, 109, 112, 276, 277; and wind, 142. *See also* free spirits; *thumos*

squandering, 186, 218, 290, 417, 424, 431

stimulation *(Reiz),* 94–96, 270, 316; abyss of, 257; nervous, 94, 96, 250, 257, 295; during sleep, 33, 295–96, 329; and *Trieb,* 95

sublimation, 169, 228, 361, 446

suffering, 67, 72, 154, 167, 291, 336; and childbirth, 164–65, 241, 243; creativity as redemption from, 164, 233–34; desirability of, 35, 157; Dionysian, 69, 200, 214, 275; and overcoming, 158, 163; and pity, 157, 246; physical, 292–93; and need for *Schein,* 73. *See also* asceticism.

super-ego. *See* over-I

theater 120, 250, 321, 341, 367; theater-eye, 341; and masks, 337, 363; soul as theater company, 345, 369; and will, 335; world as, 334, 344–45. *See also* Greeks, and tragedy

thumos (spirited part of the soul), 140, 221, 223, 227, 229, 252–53, 347–48, 351–52, 414, 439

tyranny, 261, 267, 313, 348, 350, 356, 433, 459; of affects, 354–55; by beasts of the soul, 220, 223–24, 278, 351–52; and counter-tyrant, 293, 351, 447; danger of, 280, 350–51; of the drives, 226, 278, 281, 290–91, 308, 313, 351; and the ideal regime, 356, 358–59; productivity of, 281, 351; of reason, 230, 369; and strength of will, 112, 114. See also *erōs*

Übermensch (overman), 30, 139, 152, 163, 198, 228, 360, 361; as lightning, 141, 393; as ocean, 151; and overcoming, 139, 151, 219, 417; preparation for, 175; as "sense of the earth," 132, 151, 361; on translation of the term, 417, 429. *See also* dance

unconscious, 47, 75, 104, 184, 269, 312, 356, 366; and the archaic, 126, 150; and artists, 165; collective, 152, 206, 367, 400; and creativity, 61–62; and dream, 70–71, 294; and imagination, 259; and the multiple psyche, 255–56, 274, 311, 369; and *Volk,* 89, 274. *See also* drives; fate

underworld, 138, 181, 252, 256, 304, 330, 331, 366

voices 52, 110, 151, 276, 277, 368; of drives, 355, 370; and multiplicity, 110, 278, 288, 323–24; and attunement *(Stimmung),* 42–43, 52, 109. *See also* conscience; *daimonion;* spirit

Volk, 83, 88, 89

war, 45, 58, 86, 100, 273, 317, 327, 333

weather, 32, 48, 142, 149, 172, 175, 178, 202, 403, 420

will to power, 108, 128, 134, 137, 226, 264, 417, 427, 448, 449, 450, 451; as play of interpretive forces, 39, 144, 178, 308–9, 316–17, 359; life/world as, 38–39, 45, 50, 149, 234, 316, 359–60; philosophy as (the most spiritual), 308; as primary topic of psychology, 6, 309, 313; as self-overcoming, 46, 151. *See also ēros;* drives, and will

wisdom, 84, 95, 130, 200, 279; Socratic, 80, 190, 241; stone of, 165; of unconscious thought, 56; wild, 194, 233, 239–40, 289, 426; Zarathustra's, 131, 138–39, 142, 187, 198, 218. *See also* love

Zen, 384, 450